FEMINISTS THEORIZE THE POLITICAL

FEMINISTS THEORIZE THE POLITICAL ▶ ▶ ▶

edited by Judith Butler and Joan W. Scott

Routledge • New York • London

Published in 1992 by

Routledge
An imprint of Routledge, Chapman and Hall, Inc.
29 West 35th Street
New York, NY 10001

Published in Great Britain by

Routledge
11 New Fetter Lane
London EC4P 4EE

Library of Congress Cataloging-in-Publication Data

Feminists theorize the political / edited by Judith Butler and Joan W.
Scott.
   p. cm.
  Includes index.
  ISBN 0-415-90273-8 (HB). — ISBN 0-415-90274-6 (PB)
  1. Feminist theory. 2. Feminist theory—Political aspects.
3. Structuralism. 4. Postmodernism—Social aspects. I. Butler,
Judith P. II. Scott, Joan Wallach.
HQ1190.F48   1992   91-20772
305.42'01—dc20   CIP

British Library Cataloguing in Publication Data also available

To the memory of Linda Singer

Contents

Acknowledgments

We would like to express our appreciation to Meg Gilbert who, once again, worked valiantly to help prepare the manuscript; her patience, intelligence, and wit were indispensable in untold ways. We thank as well Marsha Tucker of the Institute for Advanced Study Historical Studies and Social Science Library for helping enormously with the research. Maureen MacGrogan at Routledge has been crucial to the entire process of putting together this work; her acuity, sense of humor, and confidence in the project have been essential.

An earlier version of Ana Maria Alonso's "'Progress' as Disorder and Dishonor: Discourses of *Serrano* Resistance," appeared in *Critique of Anthropology,* Vol. 8, No. 1, 1988, and is reprinted with permission of Sage Publications Ltd.

An earlier version of Judith Butler's "Contingent Foundations: Feminism and the Question of 'Postmodernism'" appeared in *Praxis International,* Vol. 11, No. 2, July 1991, pp. 150–165.

Mae Gwendolyn Henderson, "Speaking in Tongues: Dialogics, Dialectics, and the Black Woman Writer's Literary Tradition," was first published in *Changing Our Own Words,* edited by Cheryl A. Wall (New Brunswick: Rutgers University Press, 1991).

Zakia Pathak and Rajeswari Sunder Rajan, "Shabano," appeared in *Signs,* Vol. 14, No. 3, Spring 1989, pp. 558–582, and is reprinted with permission of the University of Chicago Press.

A longer version of Joan W. Scott's "Experience" essay appeared as "The Evidence of Experience," *Critical Inquiry.* Summer 1991, reprinted with permission of the University of Chicago Press.

Introduction

"Theory" is a highly contested term within feminist discourse. The number of questions raised about it indicates the importance of the debate: what qualifies as "theory"? Who is the author of "theory"? Is it singular? Is it defined in opposition to something which is atheoretical, pretheoretical, or posttheoretical? What are the political implications of using "theory" for feminist analysis, considering that some of what appears under the sign of "theory" has marked masculinist and Eurocentric roots? Is "theory" distinct from politics? Is "theory" an insidious form of politics? Can any politics be derived from "theory," or is "theory" itself a form of political nihilism?

The aim of this book is not to *settle* these questions, but to generate new and productive directions for them. The theory under question is not a monolithic entity. Insofar as the theoretical impetus of poststructuralism constitutes one site of a certain crisis in feminism, it might be said that this anthology explores the benefits to feminism of that crisis. This is not to suggest that poststructuralism is a theory that all of the contributors to this volume accept (indeed it is unclear whether, in the light of poststructuralism, theories constitute positions to be affirmed or denied). Rather, "post-structuralism" indicates a field of critical practices that cannot be totalized and that, therefore, interrogate the formative and exclusionary power of dis-course in the construction of sexual difference.

This interrogation does not take for granted the meanings of any terms or analytic categories, including its own. Rather, it asks how specific deployments of discourse for specific political purposes determine the very notions used. The point is not to apply ready-made concepts to feminist concerns, but to resignify or appropriate them for specific ends. In this volume the value of poststructuralist theories is confirmed or contested in particular contexts. These theories are useful to the extent that they generate analyses, critiques, and political interventions, and open up a political imaginary for feminism that points the way beyond some of the impasses by which it has been constrained.

If the reader consults this anthology to discover what "poststructuralism" is, she will be frustrated and, perhaps, disconcerted. Poststructuralism is not, strictly speaking, *a position,* but rather a critical interrogation of the exclusionary operations by which "positions" are established. In this sense, a feminist poststructuralism does not designate a position from which one operates, a point of view or standpoint which might be usefully compared with other "positions" within the theoretical field. This is, of course, the conventional grammar of theoretical debate: "I am an _____, and I believe _____." And surely there are strategic occasions when precisely that kind of grammar is important to invoke. But the questions raised in this volume concern the *orchestration* of that kind of position taking, not simply within academic discourse, but within feminist political discourse. What are the political operations that constrain and constitute the *field* within which positions emerge? What *exclusions* effectively constitute and naturalize that field? Through what means are women positioned within law, history, political debates on abortion and rape, contexts of racism, colonization, and postcoloniality? Who qualifies as a "subject" of history, a "claimant" before the law, a "citizen"? Indeed, what qualifies as "reality," "experience" and "agency," "the unified self," the "materiality of bodies," the domain of "ethics" and, indeed, of "politics"? Through what differential and exclusionary means are such "foundational" notions constituted? And how does a radical contestation of these "foundations" expose the silent violence of these concepts as they have operated not merely to marginalize certain groups, but to erase and exclude them from the notion of "community" altogether, indeed, to establish exclusion as the very precondition and possibility for "community"?

To perform a feminist deconstruction of some of the primary terms of political discourse is in no sense to censor their usage, negate them, or to announce their anachronicity. On the contrary, this kind of analysis *requires* that these terms be reused and rethought, exposed as strategic instruments and effects, and subjected to a critical reinscription and redeployment.

As a call to this kind of feminist analysis and political intervention, we formulated the following questions for the contributors to this volume.

1. There appears to be a belief that without an ontologically grounded feminist subject there can be no politics. Here, politics is understood as a representational discourse that presumes a fixed or ready-made subject, usually conceived through the category of "women." As a result, analysis of the political construction and regulation of this category is summarily foreclosed. What are the political consequences of such foreclosure? And what political possibilities does a critique of identity categories make possible?

2. What are the points of convergence between a) poststructuralist criticisms of identity and b) recent theory by women of color that critically exposes the unified or coherent subject as a prerogative of white theory?

How do we theorize the split or multiple "subject" of feminism? What is the critical potential released in the serious heteroglossic play of dominant and marginalized discourses?

3. The emphasis of poststructuralist positions on language or signifying practices is often taken to be an emphasis on written documents, particular utterances, or other empirically restrictive "examples" of language. How are language, signification, and discourse *misread,* and what are the political consequences of this misreading? Similarly, the claim of discursive indeterminacy is understood to be the end of politics and political commitment, rather than a site of possible political articulations. How can this be clarified for feminist purposes?

4. To what extent do words like "poststructuralism" and "postmodernism" become terms which become the site for all sorts of fears about the diffusion of power and the loss of cognitive "mastery"? To what extent do the terms used to defend the universal subject encode fears about those cultural minorities excluded in and by the construction of that subject; to what extent is the outcry against the "postmodern" a defense of culturally privileged epistemic positions that leave unexamined the excluded domains of homosexuality, race, and class? How are poststructuralism and postmodernism distinct, and what are the political reasons for their conflation?

5. What is the significance of the poststructuralist critique of binary logic for the theorization of the subaltern? Where are the critical intersections between postcolonialism and poststructuralism that reveal the critique of Western logic as part of the critical decentering of colonial hegemony? What contradictions does Eurocentric theory face in trying to expose the constitutive logic of colonial oppression?

6. What are the political implications of prevalent epistemological paradigms within contemporary feminist theory (i.e., standpoint epistemologies, "situated knowledges," and identity politics)? How can "color," "ethnicity," "gender," and "class" be read as more than attributes that must be added to a subject in order to complete its description? To what extent does the theorization of the subject and its epistemic postures through the categories of race, postcolonialism, gender, class compel a full critique of identity politics and/or the situated or encumbered subject?

7. What is the relationship between binary thinking within feminist theories and frameworks for understanding global politics in which, for example, a homogenized "Third World" is constructed and deployed that effectively augments the strategies of colonization? If Irigaray is right that "the subject is always already masculine," is it not also true that "the subject is always already white"? How do universal theories of "patriarchy" or phallogocentrism need to be rethought in order to avoid the consequences of a white-feminist epistemological/cultural imperialism?

8. Many feminist theorists point out that some poststructuralist analy-

sis, whether conceived as postmodernism, Lacanian psychoanalysis, deconstruction, and/or discourse analysis, totalizes "culture" and thus obscures
"society." What are the problems created by this opposition between "culture" and "society"? What kinds of poststructuralist refigurations of "the
material" are possible? How do we take account of the criticism that claims
that poststructuralism minimizes the difference between "institutional" and
"discursive" oppression?

9. Some feminists have argued that poststructuralism forbids recourse
to a "real body" or a "real sex" and that such recourse is necessary to articulate moral and political opposition to violence, rape, and other forms of
oppression. The line goes something like "rape is real, it's not a text.' By
problematizing the political construction and deployment of "the real," do
feminist arguments informed by poststructuralism end up in positions of moral
relativism and political complicity? What have been the responses to this
question? What kinds of feminist retheorizations of violence and coercion
are possible?

10. What are the critical questions to be addressed to different sorts of
feminist appropriations of poststructuralism, such as those that redeploy
Foucault or Derrida, those that use poststructuralist psychoanalytic frameworks, French feminist theorists (Irigaray, Kristeva, Wittig), and so forth?

11. What limits do disciplinary frameworks pose for feminists working
with poststructuralist theories? What possibilities exist for a feminist rewriting of, say, history or legal argument in poststructuralist terms?

12. Another repeated criticism of poststructuralist thinking is that women
are "just now" beginning to become subjects in their own right and that
poststructuralism deprives women of the right to be included in a humanist
universality. What are the political consequences for feminism of embracing
the subject? What kinds of racial and class privileges remain intact when
the humanist subject remains unchallenged?

13. What kind of political and moral accountability is possible within
a feminist position that works without a notion of a universal subject or
stable self? How can this be answered through a poststructuralist resignification of "agency"? What happens to "experience" when the subject is deconstructed and agency redescribed? If feminist politics can no longer seek
recourse to an unproblematized women's "experience," what happens to the
political goal of elaborating a set of positions in which women can recognize
themselves? If self-recognition is no longer a viable goal (a psychoanalytic
argument regarding the inevitability of misrecognition seems relevant here),
then how are we to rethink the purposes of feminist politics?

14. What is the political status of the split or phantasmatic subject as
theorized within psychoanalytic discourse informed by Lacan? What kind of

refiguration of the political emerges from the psychoanalytic critique of the subject?

15. Critics of poststructuralism often make paradoxical claims: on the one hand, "discourse" and "cultural construction" are said to render the "real" artificial and contingent; on the other hand, discourse is said to "determine" reality unilaterally. What political possibilities are opened up by showing the discursive mobilization of "the real"? How does the play of dissonant discourses within culturally marginalized sites of resistance condition and promote critical interventions? How does this work in discursive practices that are fragmented by power differentials constructed through colonial hegemony, racism, and gender and class oppression?

We sent these questions out as a provocation and challenge, and we assumed at the outset that what would emerge could not be anticipated in advance. As the headings of sections and the titles of papers suggest, this volume represents an effort to call into question and politicize the presuppositions of some feminist discourse; it is a rethinking that reworks disciplinary boundaries along the way. We end up offering a set of essays that will not settle the questions of "theory," but that will instead appreciate the unsettling power—and politics—of theory.

I

Contesting Grounds

1

Contingent Foundations: Feminism and the Question of "Postmodernism"

Judith Butler

The question of postmodernism is surely a question, for is there, after all, something called postmodernism? Is it an historical characterization, a certain kind of theoretical position, and what does it mean for a term that has described a certain aesthetic practice now to apply to social theory and to feminist social and political theory in particular? Who are these post-modernists? Is this a name that one takes on for oneself, or is it more often a name that one is called if and when one offers a critique of the subject, a discursive analysis, or questions the integrity or coherence of totalizing social descriptions?

I know the term from the way it is used, and it usually appears on my horizon embedded in the following critical formulations: "if discourse is all there is . . . ," or "if everything is a text . . . ," or "if the subject is dead . . . ," of "if real bodies do not exist . . . ." The sentence begins as a warning against an impending nihilism, for if the conjured content of these series of conditional clauses proves to be true, then, and there is always a then, some set of dangerous consequences will surely follow. So 'postmodernism' appears to be articulated in the form of a fearful conditional or sometimes in the form of paternalistic disdain toward that which is youthful and irrational. Against this postmodernism, there is an effort to shore up the primary premises, to establish in advance that any theory of politics requires a subject, needs from the start to presume its subject, the referentiality of language, the integrity of the institutional descriptions it provides. For politics is unthinkable without a foundation, without these premises. But do

3

these claims seek to secure a contingent formation of politics that requires that these notions remain unproblematized features of its own definition? Is it the case that all politics, and feminist politics in particular, is unthinkable without these prized premises? Or is it rather that a specific version of politics is shown in its contingency once those premises are problematically thematized?

To claim that politics requires a stable subject is to claim that there can be no *political* opposition to that claim. Indeed, that claim implies that a critique of the subject cannot be a politically informed critique but, rather, an act which puts into jeopardy politics as such. To require the subject means to foreclose the domain of the political, and that foreclosure, installed analytically as an essential feature of the political, enforces the boundaries of the domain of the political in such a way that that enforcement is protected from political scrutiny. The act which unilaterally establishes the domain of the political functions, then, as an authoritarian ruse by which political contest over the status of the subject is summarily silenced.[1]

To refuse to assume, that is, to require a notion of the subject from the start is not the same as negating or dispensing with such a notion altogether; on the contrary, it is to ask after the process of its construction and the political meaning and consequentiality of taking the subject as a requirement or presupposition of theory. But have we arrived yet at a notion of postmodernism?

A number of positions are ascribed to postmodernism, as if it were the kind of thing that could be the bearer of a set of positions: discourse is all there is, as if discourse were some kind of monistic stuff out of which all things are composed; the subject is dead, I can never say "I" again; there is no reality, only representations. These characterizations are variously imputed to postmodernism or poststructuralism, which are conflated with each other and sometimes conflated with deconstruction, and sometimes understood as an indiscriminate assemblage of French feminism, deconstruction, Lacanian psychoanalysis, Foucaultian analysis, Rorty's conversationalism and cultural studies. On this side of the Atlantic and in recent discourse, the terms "postmodernism" or "poststructuralism" settle the differences among those positions in a single stroke, providing a substantive, a noun, that includes those positions as so many of its modalities or permutations. It may come as a surprise to some purveyors of the Continental scene to learn that Lacanian psychoanalysis in France positions itself officially against poststructuralism, that Kristeva denounces postmodernism,[2] that Foucaultians rarely relate to Derrideans, that Cixous and Irigaray are fundamentally opposed, and that the only tenuous connection between French feminism and deconstruction exists between Cixous and Derrida, although a certain affinity in textual practices is to be found between Derrida and Irigaray. Biddy Martin is also right to point out that almost all of French feminism adheres to a notion of high modernism and the avant-garde, which throws some question on whether these theories or writings can be grouped simply under the category of postmodernism.

I propose that the question of postmodernism be read not merely as the question that postmodernism poses for feminism, but as the question, what is postmodernism? What kind of existence does it have? Jean-François Lyotard champions the term, but he cannot be made into the example of what all the rest of the purported postmodernists are doing.[3] Lyotard's work is, for instance, seriously at odds with that of Derrida, who does not affirm the notion of "the postmodern," and with others for whom Lyotard is made to stand. Is he paradigmatic? Do all these theories have the same structure (a comforting notion to the critic who would dispense with them all at once)? Is the effort to colonize and domesticate these theories under the sign of the same, to group them synthetically and masterfully under a single rubric, a simple refusal to grant the specificity of these positions, an excuse not to read, and not to read closely? For if Lyotard uses the term, and if he can be conveniently grouped with a set of writers, and if some problematic quotation can be found in his work, then can that quotation serve as an "example" of postmodernism, symptomatic of the whole?

But if I understand part of the project of postmodernism, it is to call into question the ways in which such "examples" and "paradigms" serve to subordinate and erase that which they seek to explain. For the "whole," the field of postmodernism in its supposed breadth, is effectively "produced" by the example which is made to stand as a symptom and exemplar of the whole; in effect, if in the example of Lyotard we think we have a representation of postmodernism, we have then forced a substitution of the example for the entire field, effecting a violent reduction of the field to the one piece of text the critic is willing to read, a piece which, conveniently, uses the term "postmodern."

In a sense, this gesture of conceptual mastery that groups together a set of positions under the postmodern, that makes the postmodern into an epoch or a synthetic whole, and that claims that the part can stand for this artificially constructed whole, enacts a certain self-congratulatory ruse of power. It is paradoxical, at best, that the act of conceptual mastery that effects this dismissive grouping of positions under the postmodern wants to ward off the peril of political authoritarianism. For the assumption is that some piece of the text is representational, that it stands for the phenomenon, and that the structure of "these" positions can be properly and economically discerned in the structure of the one. What authorizes such an assumption from the start? From the start we must believe that theories offer themselves in bundles or in organized totalities, and that historically a set of theories which are structurally similar emerge as the articulation of an historically specific condition of human reflection. This Hegelian trope, which continues through

Adorno, assumes from the start that these theories can be substituted for one another because they variously symptomatize a common structural preoccupation. And yet, that presumption can no longer be made, for the Hegelian presumption that a synthesis is available from the start is precisely what has come under contest in various ways by some of the positions happily unified under the sign of postmodernism. One might argue that if, and to the extent that, the postmodern functions as such a unifying sign, then it is a decidedly "modern" sign, which is why there is some question whether one can debate for or against this postmodernism. To install the term as that which can be only affirmed or negated is to force it to occupy one position within a binary, and so to affirm a logic of noncontradiction over and against some more generative scheme.

Perhaps the reason for this unification of positions is occasioned by the very unruliness of the field, by the way in which the differences among these positions cannot be rendered symptomatic, exemplary, or representative of each other and of some common structure called postmodernism. If postmodernism as a term has some force or meaning within social theory, or feminist social theory in particular, perhaps it can be found in the critical exercise that seeks to show how theory, how philosophy, is always implicated in power, and perhaps that is precisely what is symptomatically at work in the effort to domesticate and refuse a set of powerful criticisms under the rubric of postmodernism. That the philosophical apparatus in its various conceptual refinements is always engaged in exercising power is not a new insight, but then again the postmodern ought not to be confused with the new; after all, the pursuit of the "new" is the preoccupation of high modernism; if anything, the postmodern casts doubt upon the possibility of a "new" that is not in some way already implicated in the "old."

But the point articulated forcefully by some recent critics of normative political philosophy is that the recourse to a position—hypothetical, counterfactual, or imaginary—that places itself beyond the play of power, and which seeks to establish the metapolitical basis for a negotiation of power relations, is perhaps the most insidious ruse of power. That this position beyond power lays claim to its legitimacy through recourse to a prior and implicitly universal agreement does not in any way circumvent the charge, for what rationalist project will designate in advance what counts as agreement? What form of insidious cultural imperialism here legislates itself under the sign of the universal?[4]

I don't know about the term "postmodern," but if there is a point, and a fine point, to what I perhaps better understand as poststructuralism, it is that power pervades the very conceptual apparatus that seeks to negotiate its terms, including the subject position of the critic; and further, that this implication of the terms of criticism in the field of power is *not* the advent of a nihilistic relativism incapable of furnishing norms, but, rather, the very precondition of a politically engaged critique. To establish a set of norms that are beyond power or force is itself a powerful and forceful conceptual practice that sublimates, disguises and extends its own power play through recourse to tropes of normative universality. And the point is not to do away with foundations, or even to champion a position that goes under the name of antifoundationalism. Both of those positions belong together as different versions of foundationalism and the skeptical problematic it engenders. Rather, the task is to interrogate what the theoretical move that establishes foundations *authorizes*, and what precisely it excludes or forecloses.

It seems that theory posits foundations incessantly, and forms implicit metaphysical commitments as a matter of course, even when it seeks to guard against it; foundations function as the unquestioned and the unquestionable within any theory. And yet, are these "foundations," that is, those premises that function as authorizing grounds, are they themselves not constituted through exclusions which, taken into account, expose the foundational premise as a contingent and contestable presumption. Even when we claim that there is some implied universal basis for a given foundation, that implication and that universality simply constitute a new dimension of unquestionability.

How is it that we might ground a theory or politics in a speech situation or subject position which is "universal," when the very category of the universal has only begun to be exposed for its own highly ethnocentric biases? How many "universalities" are there[5] and to what extent is cultural conflict understandable as the clashing of a set of presumed and intransigent "universalities," a conflict which cannot be negotiated through recourse to a culturally imperialist notion of the "universal" or, rather, which will only be solved through such recourse at the cost of violence? We have, I think, witnessed the conceptual and material violence of this practice in the United States's war against Iraq, in which the Arab "other" is understood to be radically "outside" the universal structures of reason and democracy and, hence, calls to be brought forcibly within. Significantly, the US had to abrogate the democratic principles of political sovereignty and free speech, among others, to effect this forcible return of Iraq to the "democratic" fold, and this violent move reveals, among other things, that such notions of universality are installed through the abrogation of the very universal principles to be implemented. Within the political context of contemporary postcoloniality more generally, it is perhaps especially urgent to underscore the very category of the "universal" as a site of insistent contest and resignification.[6] Given the contested character of the term, to assume from the start a procedural or substantive notion of the universal is of necessity to impose a culturally hegemonic notion on the social field. To herald that notion then as the philosophical instrument that will negotiate between conflicts of power is precisely to safeguard and reproduce a position of hegemonic power by installing it in the metapolitical site of ultimate normativity.

It may at first seem that I am simply calling for a more concrete and internally diverse "universality," a more synthetic and inclusive notion of the universal, and in that way committed to the very foundational notion that I seek to undermine. But my task is, I think, significantly different from that which would articulate a comprehensive universality. In the first place, such a totalizing notion could only be achieved at the cost of producing new and further exclusions. The term "universality" would have to be left permanently open, permanently contested, permanently contingent, in order not to foreclose in advance future claims for inclusion. Indeed, from my position and from any historically constrained perspective, any totalizing concept of the universal will shut down rather than authorize the unanticipated and unanticipatable claims that will be made under the sign of "the universal." In this sense, I am not doing away with the category, but trying to relieve the category of its foundationalist weight in order to render it as a site of permanent political contest.

A social theory committed to democratic contestation within a postcolonial horizon needs to find a way to bring into question the foundations it is compelled to lay down. It is this movement of interrogating that ruse of authority that seeks to close itself off from contest that is, in my view, at the heart of any radical political project. Inasmuch as poststructuralism offers a mode of critique that effects this contestation of the foundationalist move, it can be used as a part of such a radical agenda. Note that I have said, "it can be used": I think there are no necessary political consequences for such a theory, but only a possible political deployment.

If one of the points associated with postmodernism is that the epistemological point of departure in philosophy is inadequate, then it ought not to be a question of subjects who claim to know and theorize under the sign of the postmodern pitted against other subjects who claim to know and theorize under the sign of the modern. Indeed, it is that very way of framing debate that is being contested by the suggestion that the position articulated by the subject is always in some way constituted by what must be displaced for that position to take hold, and that the subject who theorizes is constituted as a "theorizing subject" by a set of exclusionary and selective procedures. For, indeed, who is it that gets constituted as the feminist theorist whose framing of the debate will get publicity? Is it not always the case that power operates in advance, in the very procedures that establish who will be the subject who speaks in the name of feminism, and to whom? And is it not also clear that a process of subjection is presupposed in the subjectivating process that produces before you one speaking subject of feminist debate? What speaks when "I" speak to you? What are the institutional histories of subjection and subjectivation that "position" me here now? If there is something called "Butler's position," is this one that I devise, publish, and defend, that belongs to me as a kind of academic property? Or is there a grammar of the subject that merely encourages us to position me as the proprietor of those theories?

Indeed, how is it that a position becomes a position, for clearly not every utterance qualifies as such. It is clearly a matter of a certain authorizing power, and that clearly does not emanate from the position itself. My position is mine to the extent that "I"—and I do not shirk from the pronoun—replay and resignify the theoretical positions that have constituted me, working the possibilities of their convergence, and trying to take account of the possibilities that they systematically exclude. But it is clearly not the case that "I" preside over the positions that have constituted me, shuffling through them instrumentally, casting some aside, incorporating others, although some of my activity may take that form. The "I" who would select between them is always already constituted by them. The "I" is the transfer point of that replay, but it is simply not a strong enough claim to say that the "I" is situated; the "I," this "I," is *constituted* by these positions, and these "positions" are not merely theoretical products, but fully embedded organizing principles of material practices and institutional arrangements, those matrices of power and discourse that produce me as a viable "subject." Indeed, this "I" would not be a thinking, speaking "I" if it were not for the very positions that I oppose, for those positions, the ones that claim that the subject must be given in advance, that discourse is an instrument or reflection of that subject, are already part of what constitutes me.

No subject is its own point of departure; and the fantasy that it is one can only disavow its constitutive relations by recasting them as the domain of a countervailing externality. Indeed, one might consider Luce Irigaray's claim that the subject, understood as a fantasy of autogenesis, is always already masculine. Psychoanalytically, that version of the subject is constituted through a kind of disavowal or through the primary repression of its dependency on the maternal. And to become a *subject* on this model is surely not a feminist goal.

The critique of the subject is not a negation or repudiation of the subject, but, rather, a way of interrogating its construction as a pregiven or foundationalist premise. At the outset of the war against Iraq, we almost all saw strategists who placed before us maps of the Middle East, objects of analysis and targets of instrumental military action. Retired and active generals were called up by the networks to stand in for the generals on the field whose intentions would be invariably realized in the destruction of various Iraqi military bases. The various affirmations of the early success of these operations were delivered with great enthusiasm, and it seemed that this hitting of the goal, this apparently seamless realization of intention through an instrumental action without much resistance or hindrance was the occasion, not merely to destroy Iraqi military installations, but also to champion a masculinized Western subject whose will immediately translates into a deed, whose utterance or order materializes in an action which would destroy the very possibility of a reverse strike, and whose obliterating power at once confirms the impenetrable contours of its own subjecthood.

It is perhaps interesting to remember at this juncture that Foucault linked the displacement of the intentional subject with modern power relations that he himself associated with war.[7] What he meant, I think, is that subjects who institute actions are themselves instituted effects of prior actions, and that the horizon in which we act is there as a constitutive possibility of our very capacity to act, not merely or exclusively as an exterior field or theater of operations. But perhaps more significantly, the actions instituted via that subject are part of a chain of actions that can no longer be understood as unilinear in direction or predictable in their outcomes. And yet, the instrumental military subject appears at first to utter words that materialize directly into destructive deeds. And throughout the war, it was as if the masculine Western subject preempted the divine power to translate words into deeds; the newscasters were almost all full of giddy happiness as they demonstrated, watched, vicariously enacted, the exactitude of destructiveness. As the war began, the words one would hear on television were "euphoria," and one newscaster remarked that US weapons were instruments of "terrible beauty" (CBS) and celebrates prematurely and phantasmatically its own capacity to act instrumentally in the world to obliterate its opposition and to control the consequences of that obliteration. But the consequentiality of this act cannot be foreseen by the instrumental actor who currently celebrates the effectivity of its own intentions. What Foucault suggested was that this subject is itself the effect of a genealogy which is erased at the moment that the subject takes itself as the single origin of its action, and that the effects of an action always supersede the stated intention or purpose of the act. Indeed, the effects of the instrumental action always have the power to proliferate beyond the subject's control, indeed, to challenge the rational transparency of that subject's intentionality, and so to subvert the very definition of the subject itself. I suggest that we have been in the midst of a celebration on the part of the United States government and some of its allies of the phantasmatic subject, the one who determines its world unilaterally, and which is in some measure typified by the looming heads of retired generals framed against the map of the Middle East, where the speaking head of this subject is shown to be the same size, or larger, than the area it seeks to dominate. This is, in a sense, the graphics of the imperialist subject, a visual allegory of the action itself.

But here you think that I have made a distinction between the action itself and something like a representation, but I want to make a stronger point. You will perhaps have noticed that Colin Powell, the General of the

Joint Chiefs of Staff invoked what is, I think, a new military convention of calling the sending of missiles "the delivery of an ordnance." The phrase is significant, I think; it figures an act of violence as an act of law (the military term "ordnance" is linked etymologically to the juridical "ordinance"), and so wraps the destruction in the appearance of orderliness; but in addition, it figures the missile as a kind of command, an order to obey, and is thus itself figured as a certain act of speech which not only delivers a message—get out of Kuwait—but effectively enforces that message through the threat of death and through death itself. Of course, this is a message that can never be received, for it kills its addressee, and so it is not an ordnance at all, but the failure of all ordinances, the refusal of a communication. And for those who remain to read the message, they will not read what is sometimes quite literally written on the missile.

Throughout the war, we witnessed and participated in the conflation of the television screen and the lens of the bomber pilot. In this sense, the visual record of this war is not a *reflection* on the war, but the enactment of its phantasmatic structure, indeed, part of the very means by which it is socially constituted and maintained as a war. The so-called "smart bomb" records its target as it moves in to destroy it—a bomb with a camera attached in front, a kind of optical phallus; it relays that film back to a command control and that film is refilmed on television, effectively constituting the television screen and its viewer as the extended apparatus of the bomb itself. In this sense, by viewing we are bombing, identified with both bomber and bomb, flying through space, transported from the North American continent to Iraq, and yet securely wedged in the couch in one's own living room. The smart bomb screen is, of course, destroyed in the moment that it enacts its destruction, which is to say that this is a recording of a thoroughly destructive act which can never record that destructiveness, indeed, which effects the phantasmatic distinction between the hit and its consequences. Thus as viewers, we veritably enact the allegory of military triumph: we retain our visual distance and our bodily safety through the disembodied enactment of the kill that produces no blood and in which we retain our radical impermeability. In this sense, we are in relation to this site of destruction absolutely proximate, absolutely essential, and absolutely distant, a figure for imperial power which takes the aerial, global view, the disembodied killer who can never be killed, the sniper as a figure for imperialist military power. The television screen thus redoubles the aerial view, securing a fantasy of transcendence, of a disembodied instrument of destruction which is infinitely protected from a reverse-strike through the guarantee of electronic distance.

This aerial view never comes close to seeing the *effects* of its destruction, and as a close-up to the site becomes increasingly possible, the screen conveniently destroys itself. And so although it was made to seem that this was a humane bombing, one which took buildings and military installations as its targets, this was, on the contrary, the effect of a frame which excluded from view the systematic destruction of a population, what Foucault calls the modern dream of states.[8] Or perhaps we ought to state it otherwise: precisely through excluding its targets from view under the rubric of proving the capacity to target precisely, this is a frame that effectively performs the annihilation that it systematically derealizes.

The demigod of a U.S. military subject which euphorically enacted the fantasy that it can achieve its aims with ease fails to understand that its actions have produced effects that will far exceed its phantasmatic purview; it thinks that its goals were achieved in a matter of weeks, and that its action was completed. But the action continues to act after the intentional subject has announced its completion. The effects of its actions have already inaugurated violence in places and in ways that it not only could not foresee but will be unable ultimately to contain, effects which will produce a massive and violent contestation of the Western subject's phantasmatic self-construction.

If I can, then, I'll try to return to the subject at hand. In a sense, the subject is constituted through an exclusion and differentiation, perhaps a repression, that is subsequently concealed, covered over, by the effect of autonomy. In this sense, autonomy is the logical consequence of a disavowed dependency, which is to say that the autonomous subject can maintain the illusion of its autonomy insofar as it covers over the break out of which it is constituted. This dependency and this break are already social relations, ones which precede and condition the formation of the subject. As a result, this is not a relation in which the subject finds itself, as one of the relations that forms its situation. The subject is constructed through acts of differentiation that distinguish the subject from its constitutive outside, a domain of abjected alterity conventionally associated with the feminine, but clearly not exclusively. Precisely in this recent war we saw "the Arab" figured as the abjected other as well as a site of homophobic fantasy made clear in the abundance of bad jokes grounded in the linguistic sliding from Saddam to Sodom.

There is no ontologically intact reflexivity to the subject which is then placed within a cultural context; that cultural context, as it were, is already there as the disarticulated process of that subject's production, one that is concealed by the frame that would situate a ready-made subject in an external web of cultural relations.

We may be tempted to think that to assume the subject in advance is necessary in order to safeguard the *agency* of the subject. But to claim that the subject is constituted is not to claim that it is determined; on the contrary, the constituted character of the subject is the very precondition of its agency. For what is it that enables a purposive and significant reconfiguration of cultural and political relations, if not a relation that can be turned against itself, reworked, resisted? Do we need to assume theoretically from the start a subject with agency *before* we can articulate the terms of a significant social and political task of transformation, resistance, radical democratization? If we do not offer in advance the theoretical guarantee of that agent, are we doomed to give up transformation and meaningful political practice? My suggestion is that agency belongs to a way of thinking about persons as instrumental actors who confront an external political field. But if we agree that politics and power exist already at the level at which the subject and its agency are articulated and made possible, then agency can be *presumed* only at the cost of refusing to inquire into its construction. Consider that "agency" has no formal existence or, if it does, it has no bearing on the question at hand. In a sense, the epistemological model that offers us a pregiven subject or agent is one that refuses to acknowledge that *agency is always and only a political prerogative*. As such, it seems crucial to question the conditions of its possibility, not to take it for granted as an a priori guarantee. We need instead to ask, what possibilities of mobilization are produced on the basis of existing configurations of discourse and power? Where are the possibilities of reworking that very matrix of power by which we are constituted, of reconstituting the legacy of that constitution, and of working against each other those processes of regulation that can destabilize existing power regimes? For if the subject is constituted by power, that power does not cease at the moment the subject is constituted, for that subject is never fully constituted, but is subjected and produced time and again. That subject is neither a ground nor a product, but the permanent possibility of a certain resignifying process, one which gets detoured and stalled through other mechanisms of power, but which is power's own possibility of being reworked. It is not enough to say that the subject is invariably engaged in a political field; that phenomenological phrasing misses the point that the subject is an accomplishment regulated and produced in advance. And is as such fully political; indeed, perhaps *most* political at the point in which it is claimed to be prior to politics itself. To perform this kind of Foucaultian critique of the subject is not to do away with the subject or pronounce its death, but merely to claim that certain versions of the subject are politically insidious.

For the subject to be a pregiven point of departure for politics is to defer the question of the political construction and regulation of the subject itself; for it is important to remember that subjects are constituted through exclusion, that is, through the creation of a domain of deauthorized subjects, presubjects, figures of abjection, populations erased from view. This becomes clear, for instance, within the law when certain qualifications must first be met in order to be, quite literally, a claimant in sex discrimination or rape cases. Here it becomes quite urgent to ask, who qualifies as a "who," what systematic structures of disempowerment make it impossible for certain injured parties to invoke the "I" effectively within a court of law? Or less overtly, in a social theory like Albert Memmi's *The Colonizer and the Colonized,* an otherwise compelling call for radical enfranchisement, the category of women falls into neither category, the oppressor or the oppressed.[9] How do we theorize the exclusion of women from the category of the oppressed? Here the construction of subject-positions works to exclude women from the description of oppression, and this constitutes a different kind of oppression, one that is effected by the very *erasure* that grounds the articulation of the emancipatory subject. As Joan Scott makes clear in *Gender and the Politics of History,* once it is understood that subjects are formed through exclusionary operations, it becomes politically necessary to trace the operations of that construction and erasure.[10]

The above sketches in part a Foucaultian reinscription of the subject, an effort to resignify the subject as a site of resignification. As a result, it is not a "bidding farewell" to the subject per se, but, rather, a call to rework that notion outside the terms of an epistemological given. But perhaps Foucault is not really postmodern; after all, his is an analytics of *modern* power. There is, of course, talk about the death of the subject, but *which* subject is that? And what is the status of the utterance that announces its passing? What speaks now that the subject is dead? That there is a speaking seems clear, for how else could the utterance be heard? So clearly, the death of that subject is not the end of agency, of speech, or of political debate. There is the refrain that, just now, when women are beginning to assume the place of subjects, postmodern positions come along to announce that the subject is dead (there is a difference between positions of poststructuralism which claim that the subject *never* existed, and postmodern positions which claim that the subject *once* had integrity, but no longer does). Some see this as a conspiracy against women and other disenfranchised groups who are now only beginning to speak on their own behalf. But what precisely is meant by this, and how do we account for the very strong criticisms of the subject as an instrument of Western imperialist hegemony theorized by Gloria Anzaldua,[11] Gayatri Spivak[12] and various theorists of postcoloniality? Surely there is a caution offered here, that in the very struggle toward enfranchisement and democratization, we might adopt the very models of domination by which we were oppressed, not realizing that one way that domination works is through the regulation and production of subjects. Through what exclusions has the feminist subject been constructed, and how do those excluded domains return to haunt the "integrity" and "unity" of the feminist "we"? And how is it that the very category, the subject, the "we," that is supposed to be presumed for the purpose of solidarity, produces the very factionalization it is supposed to quell? Do women want to become subjects on the model which requires and produces an anterior region of abjection, or must feminism become a process which is self-critical about the processes that produce and destabilize identity categories? To take the construction of the subject as a political problematic is not the same as doing away with the subject; to deconstruct the subject is not to negate or throw away the concept; on the contrary, deconstruction implies only that we suspend all commitments to that to which the term, "the subject," refers, and that we consider the linguistic functions it serves in the consolidation and concealment of authority. To deconstruct is not to negate or to dismiss, but to call into question and, perhaps most importantly, to open up a term, like the subject, to a reusage or redeployment that previously has not been authorized.

Within feminism, it seems as if there is some political necessity to speak as and for *women*, and I would not contest that necessity. Surely, that is the way in which representational politics operates, and in this country, lobbying efforts are virtually impossible without recourse to identity politics. So we agree that demonstrations and legislative efforts and radical movements need to make claims in the name of women.

But this necessity needs to be reconciled with another. The minute that the category of women is invoked as *describing* the constituency for which feminism speaks, an internal debate invariably begins over what the descriptive content of that term will be. There are those who claim that there is an ontological specificity to women as childbearers that forms the basis of a specific legal and political interest in representation, and then there are others who understand maternity to be a social relation that is, under current social circumstances, the specific and cross-cultural situation of women. And there are those who seek recourse to Gilligan and others to establish a feminine specificity that makes itself clear in women's communities or ways of knowing. But every time that specificity is articulated, there is resistance and factionalization within the very constituency that is supposed to be *unified* by the articulation of its common element. In the early 1980s, the feminist "we" rightly came under attack by women of color who claimed that the "we" was invariably white, and that that "we" that was meant to solidify the movement was the very source of a painful factionalization. The effort to characterize a feminine specificity through recourse to maternity, whether biological or social, produced a similar factionalization and even a disavowal of feminism altogether. For surely all women are not mothers; some cannot be, some are too young or too old to be, some choose not to be, and for some who are mothers, that is not necessarily the rallying point of their politicization in feminism.

I would argue that any effort to give universal or specific content to the category of women, presuming that that guarantee of solidarity is required *in advance*, will necessarily produce factionalization, and that "identity" as a point of departure can never hold as the solidifying ground of a feminist political movement. Identity categories are never merely descriptive, but always normative, and as such, exclusionary. This is not to say that the term "women" ought not to be used, or that we ought to announce the death of the category. On the contrary, if feminism presupposes that "women" designates an undesignatable field of differences, one that cannot be totalized or summarized by a descriptive identity category, then the very term becomes a site of permanent openness and resignifiability. I would argue that the rifts among women over the content of the term ought to be safeguarded and prized, indeed, that this constant rifting ought to be affirmed as the ungrounded ground of feminist theory. To deconstruct the subject of feminism is not, then, to censure its usage, but, on the contrary, to release the term into a future of multiple significations, to emancipate it from the maternal or racialist ontologies to which it has been restricted, and to give it play as a site where unanticipated meanings might come to bear.

Paradoxically, it may be that only through releasing the category of women from a fixed referent that something like 'agency' becomes possible. For if the term permits of a resignification, if its referent is not fixed, then possibilities for new configurations of the term become possible. In a sense, what women signify has been taken for granted for too long, and what has been fixed as the 'referent' of the term has been "fixed," normalized, immobilized, paralyzed in positions of subordination. In effect, the signified has been conflated with the referent, whereby a set of meanings have been taken to inhere in the real nature of women themselves. To recast the referent as the signified, and to authorize or safeguard the category of women as a site of possible resignifications is to expand the possibilities of what it means to be a woman and in this sense to condition and enable an enhanced sense of agency.

One might well ask: but doesn't there have to be a set of norms that discriminate between those descriptions that ought to adhere to the category of women and those that do not? The only answer to that question is a counter-question: who would set those norms, and what contestations would they produce? To establish a normative foundation for settling the question of what ought properly to be included in the description of women would be only and always to produce a new site of political contest. That foundation would settle nothing, but would of its own necessity founder on its own authoritarian ruse. This is not to say that there is no foundation, but rather, that wherever there is one, there will also be a foundering, a contestation. That such foundations exist only to be put into question is, as it were, the permanent risk of the process of democratization. To refuse that contest is to sacrifice the radical democractic impetus of feminist politics. That the category is unconstrained, even that it comes to serve antifeminist purposes, will be part of the risk of this procedure. But this is a risk that is produced by the very foundationalism that seeks to safeguard feminism against it. In a sense, this risk is the foundation, and hence is not, of any feminist practice.

In the final part of this paper, I would like to turn to a related question, one that emerges from the concern that a feminist theory cannot proceed without presuming the materiality of women's bodies, the materiality of sex. The chant of antipostmodernism runs, if everything is discourse, then is there no reality to bodies? How do we understand the material violence that women suffer? In responding to this criticism, I would like to suggest that the very formulation misconstrues the critical point.

I don't know what postmodernism is, but I do have some sense of what it might mean to subject notions of the body and materiality to a deconstructive critique. To deconstruct the concept of matter or that of bodies is not to negate or refuse either term. To deconstruct these terms means, rather, to continue to use them, to repeat them, to repeat them subversively, and to displace them from the contexts in which they have been deployed as instruments of oppressive power. Here it is of course necessary to state quite plainly that the options for theory are not exhausted by *presuming* materiality, on the one hand, and *negating* materiality, on the other. It is my purpose to do precisely neither of these. To call a presupposition into question is not the same as doing away with it; rather, it is to free it up from its metaphysical lodgings in order to occupy and to serve very different political aims. To problematize the matter of bodies entails in the first instance a loss of epistemological certainty, but this loss of certainty does not necessarily entail political nihilism as its result.[13]

If a deconstruction of the materiality of bodies suspends and problematizes the traditional ontological referent of the term, it does not freeze, banish, render useless, or deplete of meaning the usage of the term; on the contrary, it provides the conditions to *mobilize* the signifier in the service of an alternative production.

Consider that most material of concepts, "sex," which Monique Wittig calls a thoroughly political category, and which Michel Foucault calls a regulatory and "fictitious unity." For both theorists, sex does not *describe* a prior materiality, but produces and regulates the *intelligibility* of the *materiality* of bodies. For both, and in different ways, the category of sex imposes a duality and a uniformity on bodies in order to maintain reproductive sexuality as a compulsory order. I've argued elsewhere more precisely how this works, but for our purposes, I would like to suggest that this kind of categorization can be called a violent one, a forceful one, and that this discursive ordering and production of bodies in accord with the category of sex is itself a material violence.

The violence of the letter, the violence of the mark which establishes what will and will not signify, what will and will not be included within the intelligible, takes on a political significance when the letter is the law or the authoritative legislation of what will be the materiality of sex.

So what can this kind of poststructural analysis tell us about violence and suffering? Is it perhaps that forms of violence are to be understood as more pervasive, more constitutive, and more insidious than prior models have allowed us to see? That is part of the point of the previous discussion of war, but let me now make it differently in yet another context.

Consider the legal restrictions that regulate what does and does not count as rape: here the politics of violence operate through regulating what will and will not be able to appear as an effect of violence.[14] There is, then, already in this foreclosure a violence at work, a marking off in advance of what will or will not qualify under the signs of "rape" or "government violence," or in the case of states in which twelve separate pieces of empirical evidence are required to establish "rape," what then can be called a governmentally facilitated rape.

A similar line of reasoning is at work in discourses on rape when the "sex" of a woman is claimed as that which establishes the responsibility for her own violation. The defense attorney in the New Bedford gang rape case asked the plaintiff, "If you're living with a man, what are you doing running around the streets getting raped?"[15] The "running around" in this sentence collides grammatically with "getting raped": "getting" is procuring, acquiring, having, as if this were a treasure she was running around after, but "getting raped" suggests the passive voice. Literally, of course, it would be difficult to be "running around" and be "getting raped" at the same time, which suggests that there must be an elided passage here, perhaps a directional that leads from the former to the latter? If the sense of the sentence is, "running around [looking to get] raped," which seems to be the only logical way of bridging the two parts of the sentence, then rape as a passive acquisition is precisely the object of her active search. The first clause suggests that she "belongs" at home, with her man, that the home is a site in which she is the domestic property of that man, and the "streets" establish her as open season. If she is looking to get raped, she is looking to become the property of some other, and this objective is installed in her desire, conceived here as quite frantic in its pursuit. She is "running around," suggesting that she is running around looking under every rock for a rapist to satisfy her. Significantly, the phrase installs as the structuring principle of her desire "getting raped," where 'rape' is figured as an act of willful self-expropriation. Since becoming the property of a man is the objective of her "sex," articulated in and through her sexual desire, and rape is the way in which that appropriation occurs "on the street" [a logic that implies that rape is to marriage as the streets are to the home, that is, that "rape" is street marriage, a marriage without a home, a marriage for homeless girls, and that marriage is domesticated rape], then "rape" is the logical consequence of the enactment of her sex and sexuality outside domesticity. Never mind that this rape took place in a bar, for the "bar" is, within this imaginary, but an extension of the "street," or perhaps its exemplary moment, for there is no enclosure, that is, no protection, other than the *home* as domestic marital space. In any case, the single cause of her violation is here figured as her "sex" which, given its natural propensity to seek expropriation, once dislocated from domestic propriety, naturally pursues its rape and is thus responsible for it.

The category of sex here functions as a principle of production and regulation at once, the cause of the violation installed as the formative principle of the body is sexuality. Here sex is a category, but not merely a representation; it is a principle of production, intelligibility, and regulation which enforces a violence and rationalizes it after the fact. The very terms by which the violation is explained *enact* the violation, and concede that the violation was under way before it takes the empirical form of a criminal act. That rhetorical enactment *shows* that "violence" is produced through the foreclosure effected by this analysis, through the erasure and negation that determines the field of appearances and intelligibility of crimes of culpability. As a category that effectively produces the political meaning of what it describes, "sex" here works its silent "violence" in regulating what is and is not designatable.

I place the terms "violence" and "sex" under quotation marks: is this the sign of a certain deconstruction, the end to politics? Or am I underscoring the iterable structure of these terms, the ways in which they yield to a repetition, occur ambiguously, and am I doing that precisely to further a political analysis? I place them in quotation marks to show that they are under contest, up for grabs, to initiate the contest, to question their traditional deployment, and call for some other. The quotation marks do not place into question the urgency or credibility of sex or violence as political issues, but, rather, show that the way their very materiality is circumscribed is fully political. The effect of the quotation marks is to denaturalize the terms, to designate these signs as sites of political debate.

If there is a fear that, by no longer being able to take for granted the subject, its gender, its sex, or its materiality, feminism will founder, it might be wise to consider the political consequences of keeping in their place the very premises that have tried to secure our subordination from the start.

NOTES

This paper was first presented in a different version as "Feminism and the Question of Postmodernism" at the Greater Philadelphia Philosophy Consortium in September 1990.

1. Here it is worth noting that in some recent political theory, notably in the writings of Ernesto Laclau and Chantal Mouffe (*Hegemony and Socialist Strategy*, London: Verso, 1986), William Connolly *Political Theory and Modernity* (Madison: University of Wisconsin Press, 1988), as well as Jean-Luc Nancy and Philippe Lacoue-Labarthe ("Le retrait du politique" in *Le Retrait du politique*, Paris: Editions galilée, 1983), there is an insistence that the political field is of necessity constructed through the production of a determining exterior. In other words, the very domain of politics constitutes itself through the production and naturalization of the "pre-" or "non" political. In Derridean terms, this is the production of a "constitutive outside." Here I would like to suggest a distinction between the constitution of a political field that produces *and naturalizes* that constitutive outside and a political field that produces and *renders contingent* the specific parameters of that constitutive outside. Although I do not think that the differential relations through which the political field itself is constituted can ever be fully elaborated (precisely because the status of that elaboration would have to be elaborated as well *ad infinitum*), I do find useful William Connolly's notion of constitutive antagonisms, a notion that finds a parallel expression in Laclau and Mouffe, which suggests a form of political struggle which puts the parameters of the political itself into question. This is especially important for feminist concerns insofar as the grounds of politics ('universality," "equality," 'the subject of rights" have been constructed through unmarked racial and gender exclusions and by a conflation of politics with public life that renders the private (reproduction, domains of "femininity") prepolitical.

2. Julia Kristeva, *Black Sun: Depression and Melancholy* (New York: Columbia University Press, 1989), pp. 258–59.

3. The conflation of Lyotard with the array of thinkers summarily positioned under the rubric of "postmodernism" is performed by the title and essay by Seyla Benhabib: "Epistemologies of Postmodernism: A Rejoinder to Jean-François Lyotard," in *Feminism/Postmodernism*, edited by Linda Nicholson (New York: Routledge, 1989).

4. This is abundantly clear in feminist criticisms of Jurgen Habermas as well as Catharine MacKinnon. See Iris Young, "Impartiality and the Civil Public: Some Implications of Feminist Criticisms of Modern Political Theory," in Seyla Benhabib and Drucilla Cornell, eds., *Feminism as Critique: Essays on the Politics of Gender in Late-Capitalism* (Oxford-Basil Blackwell, 1987); Nancy Fraser, *Unruly Practices: Power and Gender in Contemporary Social Theory* Minneapolis, University of Minnesota Press, 1989; especially "What's Critical about Critical Theory: The Case of Habermas and Gender." Wendy Brown, "Razing Consciousness," *The Nation*, 250:2, January 8/15, 1990.

5. See Ashis Nandy on the notion of alternative universalities in the preface to *The Intimate Enemy: Loss and Recovery of Self under Colonialism* (New Delhi: Oxford University Press, 1983).

6. Homi Bhabha's notion of "hybridity" is important to consider in this context.

7. Michel Foucault, *The History of Sexuality, Vol. I: An Introduction*, translated by Robert Hurley (New York: Random House, 1980), p. 102.

8. "Wars are no longer waged in the name of a sovereign who must be defended; they are waged on behalf of the existence of everyone; entire populations are mobilized for the purpose of wholesale slaughter in the name of life necessity: massacres," he writes, "have become vital." He later adds, "the principle underlying the tactics of battle—that one has to be capable of killing in order to go on living—has become the principle that defines the strategy of states. But the existence in question is no longer the juridical existence of sov-

ereignty; at stake is the biological existence of a population. If genocide is indeed the dream of modern powers, this is not because of a recent return of the ancient right to kill; it is because power is situated and exercised at the level of life, the species, the race, and the large-scale phenomena of population." Foucault, *The History of Sexuality*, p. 137.

9. "At the height of the revolt," Memmi writes, "the colonized still bears the traces and lessons of prolonged cohabitation (just as the smile or movements of a wife, even during divorce proceedings, remind one strangely of those of her husband)." Here Memmi sets up an analogy which presumes that colonizer and colonized exist in a parallel and separate relation to the divorcing husband and wife. The analogy simultaneously and paradoxically suggests the feminization of the colonized, where the colonized is presumed to be the subject of men, *and* the exclusion of the women from the category of the colonized subject. Albert Memmi, *The Colonizer and the Colonized*, (Boston: Beacon Press, 1965), p. 129.

10. Joan W. Scott, *Gender and the Politics of History*, (New York: Columbia University Press), 1988, introduction.

11. Gloria Anzaldua, *La Frontera/Borderlands*, (San Francisco: Spinsters Ink, 1988).

12. Gayatri Spivak, "Can the Subaltern Speak?" in *Marxism and the Interpretation of Culture*, eds. Nelson and Grossberg, (Chicago: University of Illinois Press, 1988).

13. The body posited as prior to the sign, is always *posited* or *signified* as *prior*. This signification works through producing an *effect* of its own procedure, the body that it nevertheless and simultaneously claims to discover as that which *precedes* signification. If the body signified as prior to signification is an effect of signification, then the mimetic or representational status of language, which claims that signs follow bodies as their necessary mirrors, is not mimetic at all; on the contrary, it is productive, constitutive, one might even argue *performative*, inasmuch as this signifying act produces the body that it then claims to find prior to any and all signification.

14. For an extended analysis of the relationship of language and rape, see Sharon Marcus' contribution to this volume.

15. Quoted in Catharine MacKinnon, *Toward a Feminist Theory of the State*, (Boston: Harvard University Press, 1989), p. 171.

2

"Experience"

Joan W. Scott

Becoming Visible

There is a section in Samuel Delany's magnificent autobiographical meditation, *The Motion of Light in Water*,[1] that dramatically raises the problem of writing the history of difference, the history, that is, of the designation of "other," of the attribution of characteristics that distinguish categories of people from some presumed (and usually unstated) norm.[2] Delany (a gay man, a black man, a writer of science fiction) recounts his reaction to his first visit to the St. Marks bathhouse in 1963. He describes standing on the threshold of a "gym-sized room" dimly lit by blue bulbs. The room was full of people, some standing, the rest "an undulating mass of naked male bodies, spread wall to wall." "My first response," he writes, "was a kind of heart-thudding astonishment, very close to fear."

> I have written of a space at certain libidinal saturation before. That was not what frightened me. It was rather that the saturation was not only kinesthetic but visible. (173)

Watching the scene establishes for Delany a "fact that flew in the face" of the prevailing representation of homosexuals in the 1950s as isolated perverts, subjects gone awry. The "apprehension of massed bodies" gave him (as it does, he argues anyone, "male, female, working or middle class") a "sense of political power."

> [W]hat *this* experience said was that there was a population—not of individual homosexuals . . . not of hundreds, not of thousands, but rather

22

of millions of gay men, and that history had actively and already, created for us whole galleries of institutions, good and bad, to accommodate our sex. (174)

The sense of political possibility is frightening and exhilarating for Delany. He emphasizes not the discovery of an identity, but a sense of participation in a movement; indeed it is the extent (as well as the existence) of these sexual practices that matters most in his account. Numbers—massed bodies—constitute a movement and this, even if subterranean, belies enforced silences about the range and diversity of human sexual practices. Making the movement visible breaks the silence about it, challenges prevailing notions, and opens new possibilities for everyone. Delany imagines, even from the vantage point of 1988, a future utopian moment of genuine sexual revolution ("once the AIDS crisis is brought under control").

> That revolution will come precisely because of the infiltration of clear and articulate language into the marginal areas of human sexual exploration, such as this book from time to time describes. . . . Now that a significant range of people have begun to get a clearer idea of what has been possible among the varieties of human pleasure in the recent past, heterosexuals and homosexuals, females and males will insist on exploring them even further. . . . (175)

By writing about the bathhouse Delany seeks not, he says, to "romanticize that time into some cornucopia of sexual plenty," but rather to break an "absolutely sanctioned public silence" on questions of sexual practice, to reveal something that existed but that had been suppressed. The point of Delany's description, indeed of his entire book, is to document the existence of those institutions in all their variety and multiplicity, to write about and thus to render historical what has hitherto been hidden from history.

A metaphor of visibility as literal transparency is crucial to his project. The blue lights illuminate a scene he has participated in before (in darkened trucks parked along the docks under the West Side Highway, in men's rooms in subway stations), but understood only in a fragmented way. "No one ever got to see its whole" (174). He attributes the impact of the bathhouse scene to its visibility: "You could see what was going on throughout the dorm" (173). Seeing enables him to comprehend the relationship between his personal activities and politics. "[T]he first direct sense of political power comes from the apprehension of massed bodies." Recounting that moment also allows him to explain the aim of his book: to provide a "clear, accurate, and extensive picture of extant public sexual institutions" so that others may learn about and explore them. Knowledge is gained through vision; vision is a direct, unmediated apprehension of a world of transparent objects. In this conceptualization of it, the visible is privileged; writing is then put at its service.[3] Seeing is the origin of knowing. Writing is reproduction, transmission—the communication of knowledge gained through (visual, visceral) experience.

This kind of communication has long been the mission of historians documenting the lives of those omitted or overlooked in accounts of the past. It has produced a wealth of new evidence previously ignored about these others and has drawn attention to dimensions of human life and activity usually deemed unworthy of mention in conventional histories. It has also occasioned a crisis for orthodox history, by multiplying not only stories, but subjects, and by insisting that histories are written from fundamentally different—indeed irreconcilable—perspectives or standpoints, no one of which is complete or completely "true." Like Delany's memoir, these histories have provided evidence for a world of alternative values and practices whose existence gives the lie to hegemonic constructions of social worlds, whether these constructions vaunt the political superiority of white men, the coherence and unity of selves, the naturalness of heterosexual monogamy, or the inevitability of scientific progress and economic development. The challenge to normative history has been described, in terms of conventional historical understandings of evidence, as an enlargement of the picture, a corrective to oversights resulting from inaccurate or incomplete vision, and it has rested its claim to legitimacy on the authority of experience, the direct experience of others, as well as of the historian who learns to see and illuminate the lives of those others in his or her texts.

Documenting the experience of others in this way has been at once a highly successful and limiting strategy for historians of difference. It has been successful because it remains so comfortably within the disciplinary framework of history, working according to rules which permit calling old narratives into question when new evidence is discovered. The status of evidence is, of course, ambiguous for historians. On the one hand, they acknowledge that "evidence only counts as evidence and is only recognized as such in relation to a potential narrative, so that the narrative can be said to determine the evidence as much as the evidence determines the narrative."[4] On the other hand, their rhetorical treatment of evidence and their use of it to falsify prevailing interpretations, depends on a referential notion of evidence which denies that it is anything but a reflection of the real.[5]

When the evidence offered is the evidence of "experience," the claim for referentiality is further buttressed—what could be truer, after all, than a subject's own account of what he or she has lived through? It is precisely this kind of appeal to experience as uncontestable evidence and as an originary point of explanation—as a foundation upon which analysis is based—that weakens the critical thrust of histories of difference. By remaining within the epistemological frame of orthodox history, these studies lose the possibility of examining those assumptions and practices that excluded considerations of difference in the first place. They take as self-evident the identities of those whose experience is being documented and thus naturalize their difference. They locate resistance outside its discursive construction, and reify agency as an inherent attribute of individuals, thus decontextualizing it. When experience is taken as the origin of knowledge, the vision of the individual subject (the person who had the experience or the historian who recounts it) becomes the bedrock of evidence upon which explanation is built. Questions about the constructed nature of experience, about how subjects are constituted as different in the first place, about how one's vision is structured—about language (or discourse) and history—are left aside. The evidence of experience then becomes evidence for the fact of difference, rather than a way of exploring how difference is established, how it operates, how and in what ways it constitutes subjects who see and act in the world.[6]

To put it another way, the evidence of experience, whether conceived through a metaphor of visibility or in any other way that takes meaning as transparent, reproduces rather than contests given ideological systems—those that assume that the facts of history speak for themselves and, in the case of histories of gender, those that rest on notions of a natural or established opposition between sexual practices and social conventions, and between homosexuality and heterosexuality. Histories that document the "hidden" world of homosexuality, for example, show the impact of silence and repression on the lives of those affected by it and bring to light the history of their suppression and exploitation. But the project of making experience visible precludes critical examination of the workings of the ideological system itself, its categories of representation (homosexual/heterosexual, man/woman, black/white as fixed immutable identities), its premises about what these categories mean and how they operate, its notions of subjects, origin, and cause.

The project of making experience visible precludes analysis of the workings of this system and of its historicity; instead it reproduces its terms. We come to appreciate the consequences of the closeting of homosexuals and we understand repression as an interested act of power or domination; alternative behaviors and institutions also become available to us. What we don't have is a way of placing those alternatives within the framework of (historically contingent) dominant patterns of sexuality and the ideology that supports them. We know they exist, but not how they've been constructed; we know their existence offers a critique of normative practices, but not the extent of the critique. Making visible the experience of a different group exposes the existence of repressive mechanisms, but not their inner workings or logics; we know that difference exists, but we don't understand it as constituted relationally. For that we need to attend to the historical processes that, through discourse, position subjects and produce their experiences. It is not individuals who have experience, but subjects who are constituted through experience. Experience in this definition then becomes not the origin of our explanation, not the authoritative (because seen or felt) evidence that grounds what is known, but rather that which we seek to explain, that about which knowledge is produced. To think about experience in this way is to historicize it as well as to historicize the identities it produces. This kind of historicizing represents a reply to the many contemporary historians who have argued that an unproblematized "experience" is the foundation of their practice; it is a historicizing that implies critical scrutiny of all explanatory categories usually taken for granted, including the category of "experience."

The Authority of Experience

History has been largely a foundationalist discourse. By this I mean that its explanations seem to be unthinkable if they do not take for granted some primary premises, categories, or presumptions. These foundations (however varied, whatever they are at a particular moment) are unquestioned and unquestionable; they are considered permanent and transcendent. As such they create a common ground for historians and their objects of study in the past and so authorize and legitimize analysis; indeed analysis seems not to be able to proceed without them.[7] In the minds of some foundationalists, in fact, nihilism, anarchy, and moral confusion are the sure alternatives to these givens, which have the status (if not the philosophical definition) of eternal truths.

Historians have had recourse to many kinds of foundations, some more obviously empiricist than others. What is most striking these days is the determined embrace, the strident defense, of some reified, transcendent category of explanation by historians who have used insights drawn from the sociology of knowledge, structural linguistics, feminist theory, or cultural anthropology to develop sharp critiques of empiricism. This turn to foundations even by antifoundationalists appears, in Fredric Jameson's characterization, as "some extreme form of the return of the repressed."[8]

"Experience" is one of the foundations that have been reintroduced into historical writing in the wake of the critique of empiricism; unlike "brute fact" or "simple reality," its connotations are more varied and elusive. It has recently emerged as a critical term in debates among historians about the limits of interpretation and especially about the uses and limits of post-structuralist theory for history.

The evocation of "experience" by historians committed to the interpretation of language, meaning, and culture appears to solve a problem of explanation for professed antiempiricists even as it reinstates a foundational ground. For this reason it is interesting to examine the uses of "experience" by historians. Such an examination allows us to ask whether history can exist without foundations and what it might look like if it did.

In *Keywords* Raymond Williams sketches the alternative senses in which the term "experience" has been employed in the Anglo-American tradition.[9] These he summarizes as "(i) knowledge gathered from past events, whether by conscious observation or by consideration and reflection; and (ii) a particular kind of consciousness, which can in some contexts be distinguished from reason or knowledge" (126). Until the early eighteenth century, he says, experience and experiment were closely connected terms, designating how knowledge was arrived at through testing and observation (here the visual metaphor is important). In the eighteenth century, experience still contained within it this notion of consideration or reflection on observed events, of lessons gained from the past, but it also referred to a particular kind of consciousness. This consciousness, in the twentieth century, has come to mean a "full, active awareness" including feeling as well as thought. The notion of experience as subjective witness, writes Williams, "is offered not only as truth, but as the most authentic kind of truth," as "the ground for all (subsequent) reasoning and analysis" (128). According to Williams, experience has acquired another connotation in the twentieth century different from these notions of subjective testimony as immediate, true, and authentic. In this usage it refers to influences external to individuals—social conditions, institutions, forms of belief or perception—"real" things outside them that they react to, and does not include their thought or consideration.[10]

In the various usages described by Williams, "experience," whether conceived as internal or external, subjective or objective, establishes the prior existence of individuals. When it is defined as internal, it is an expression of an individual's being or consciousness, when external, it is the material upon which consciousness then acts. Talking about experience in these ways leads us to take the existence of individuals for granted (experience is something people have) rather than to ask how conceptions of selves (of subjects and their identities) are produced.[11] It operates within an ideological construction that not only makes individuals the starting point of knowledge, but that also naturalizes categories such as man, woman, black, white, heterosexual, or homosexual by treating them as given characteristics of individuals.

Teresa de Lauretis's redefinition of experience exposes the workings of this ideology:

> Experience [she writes] is the process by which, for all social beings, subjectivity is constructed. Through that process one places oneself or is placed in social reality and so perceives and comprehends as subjective (referring to, originating in oneself) those relations—material, economic,

and interpersonal—which are in fact social, and, in a larger perspective, historical.[12]

The process that de Lauretis describes operates crucially through differentiation; its effect is to constitute subjects as fixed and autonomous, and who are considered reliable sources of a knowledge that comes from access to the real by means of their experience.[13] When talking about historians and other students of the human sciences, it is important to note that this subject is both the object of inquiry—the person one studies in the present or the past—and the investigator him- or herself—the historian who produces knowledge of the past based on "experience" in the archives or the anthropologist who produces knowledge of other cultures based on "experience" as a participant observer.

The concepts of experience described by Williams preclude inquiry into processes of subject construction; and they avoid examining the relationships between discourse, cognition, and reality, the relevance of the position or situatedness of subjects to the knowledge they produce, and the effects of difference on knowledge. Questions are not raised about, for example, whether it matters for the history they write that historians are men, women, white, black, straight, or gay; instead "the authority of the 'subject of knowledge' [is established] by the elimination of everything concerning the speaker."[14] His knowledge, reflecting as it does something apart from him, is legitimated and presented as universal, accessible to all. There is no power or politics in these notions of knowledge and experience.

An example of the way "experience" establishes the authority of the historian can be found in R. G. Collingwood's, *The Idea of History*, the 1946 classic that has been required reading in historiography courses for several generations. For Collingwood, the ability of the historian to "reenact past experience" is tied to his autonomy, "where by autonomy I mean the condition of being one's own authority, making statements or taking action on one's own initiative and not because those statements or actions are authorized or prescribed by anyone else."[15] The question of where the historian is situated—who he is, how he is defined in relation to others, what the political effects of his history may be—never enters the discussion. Indeed, being free of these matters seems to be tied to Collingwood's definition of autonomy, an issue so critical for him that he launches into an uncharacteristic tirade about it. In his quest for certainty, the historian must not let others make up his mind for him, Collingwood insists, because to do that means

> giving up his autonomy as an historian and allowing someone else to do for him what, if he is a scientific thinker, he can only do for himself. There is no need for me to offer the reader any proof of this statement.

If he knows anything of historical work, he already knows of his own experience that it is true. If he does not already know that it is true, he does not know enough about history to read this essay with any profit, and the best thing he can do is to stop here and now. (256)

For Collingwood it is axiomatic that experience is a reliable source of knowledge because it rests on direct contact between the historian's perception and reality (even if the passage of time makes it necessary for the historian to imaginatively reenact events of the past). Thinking on his own means owning his own thoughts and this proprietary relationship guarantees an individual's independence, his ability to read the past correctly, the authority of the knowledge he produces. The claim is not only for the historian's autonomy, but also for his originality. Here "experience" grounds the identity of the researcher as an historian.

Another, very different use of "experience" can be found in E. P. Thompson's *Making of the English Working Class,* the book that revolutionized social and labor history. Thompson specifically set out to free the concept of "class" from the ossified categories of Marxist structuralism. For this project "experience" was a key concept. His notion of experience joined ideas of external influence and subjective feeling, the structural and the psychological. This gave Thompson a mediating influence between social structure and social consciousness. For him experience meant "social being"— the lived realities of social life, especially the affective domains of family and religion and the symbolic dimensions of expression. This definition separated the affective and the symbolic from the economic and the rational. "People do not only experience their own experience as ideas, within thought and its procedures," he maintained. "[T]hey also experience their own experience as *feeling* . . ." (171). This statement grants importance to the psychological dimension of experience, and it allows Thompson to account for agency. Feeling, Thompson insists, is "handled" culturally as "norms, familial and kinship obligations, . . . values or . . . within art and religious beliefs." At the same time it somehow precedes these forms of expression and so provides an escape from a strong structural determination: "For any living generation, in any 'now,'" Thompson asserts, "the ways in which they 'handle' experience defies prediction and escapes from any narrow definition or determination" (171).[16]

And yet in his use of it, experience, because it is ultimately shaped by relations of production, is a unifying phenomenon, overriding other kinds of diversity. Since these relations of production are common to workers of different ethnicities, religions, regions, and trades, they necessarily provide a common denominator and they emerge as a more salient determinant of "experience" than anything else. In Thompson's use of the term, experience is the start of a process that culminates in the realization and articulation of social consciousness, in this case a common identity of class. It serves an integrating function, joining the individual and the structural and bringing together diverse people into that coherent (totalizing) whole which is a distinctive sense of class (170–71).[17]

The unifying aspect of experience excludes whole realms of human activity by simply not counting them as experience at least with any consequences for social organization or politics. When class becomes an overriding identity, other subject positions are subsumed by it, those of gender for example (or, in other instances of this kind of history, race, ethnicity, and sexuality). The positions of men and women and their different relationships to politics are taken as reflections of material and social arrangements rather than as products of class politics itself.

In Thompson's account class is finally an identity rooted in structural relations that pre-exist politics. What this obscures is the contradictory and contested process by which class itself was conceptualized and by which diverse kinds of subject positions were assigned, felt, contested, or embraced. As a result, Thompson's brilliant history of the English working class, which set out to historicize the category of class, ends up essentializing it. The ground may seem to be displaced from structure to agency by insisting on the subjectively felt nature of experience, but the problem Thompson sought to address isn't really solved. Working-class "experience" is now the ontological foundation of working-class identity, politics, and history.[18]

This use of experience has the same foundational status if we substitute women or African-American or lesbian or homosexual for working-class in the previous sentence. Among feminist historians, for example, "experience" has helped to legitimize a critique of the false claims to objectivity of traditional historical accounts. Part of the project of some feminist history has been to unmask all claims to objectivity as an ideological cover for masculine bias by pointing out the shortcomings, incompleteness, and exclusiveness of "mainstream" history. This has been achieved by providing documentation about women in the past which calls into question existing interpretations made without consideration of gender. But how authorize the new knowledge if the possibility of all historical objectivity has been questioned? By appealing to experience, which in this usage connotes both reality and its subjective apprehension—the experience of women in the past and of women historians who can recognize something of themselves in their foremothers.

Judith Newton, a literary historian, writing about the neglect of feminism by contemporary critical theorists, argues that women, too, arrived at the critique of objectivity usually associated with deconstruction or the New Historicism. This feminist critique "seemed to come straight out of reflection on our own, that is, [on] women's experience, out of the contradictions we felt between the different ways we were represented even to ourselves, out of the inequities we had long experienced in our situations."[19] Newton's appeal to experience seems to bypass the issue of objectivity (by not raising the question of whether feminist work can be objective), but it rests firmly on a foundational ground (experience). In her work the relationship between thought and experience is represented as transparent (the visual metaphor combines with the visceral) and so directly accessible, as it is in historian Christine Stansell's insistence that "social practices" in all their "immediacy and entirety" constitute a domain of "sensuous experience" (a prediscursive reality directly felt, seen, and known) that cannot be subsumed by "language."[20] The effect of these kinds of statements, which attribute an indisputable authenticity to women's experience, is to establish incontrovertibly women's identity as people with agency. It is also to universalize the identity of women and so to ground claims for the legitimacy of women's history in the shared experience of historians of women and those women whose stories they tell. In addition, it literally equates the personal with the political, for the lived experience of women is seen as leading directly to resistance to oppression, to feminism.[21] Indeed, the possibility of politics is said to rest on, to follow from, a pre-existing women's experience.

"Because of its drive towards a political massing together of women," writes Denise Riley, "feminism can never wholeheartedly dismantle 'women's experience,' however much this category conflates the attributed, the imposed, and the lived, and then sanctifies the resulting mélange."[22] The kind of argument for a women's history (and for a feminist politics) that Riley criticizes closes down inquiry into the ways in which female subjectivity is produced, the ways in which agency is made possible, the ways in which race and sexuality intersect with gender, the ways in which politics organize and interpret experience—the ways in which identity is a contested terrain, the site of multiple and conflicting claims. In Riley's words again, "it masks the likelihood that . . . [experiences] have accrued to women not by virtue of their womanhood alone, but as traces of domination, whether natural or political" (99). I would add as well that it masks the necessarily discursive character of these experiences.

But it is precisely the discursive character of experience that is at issue for some historians, because attributing experience to discourse seems somehow to deny its status as an unquestionable ground of explanation. This seems to be the case for John Toews, writing a long review article in the *American Historical Review* in 1987, called "Intellectual History after the Linguistic Turn: The Autonomy of Meaning and the Irreducibility of Experience."[23] The term "linguistic turn" is a comprehensive one used by Toews to refer to approaches to the study of meaning which draw on a number of disciplines, but especially on theories of language "since the primary medium of meaning was obviously language" (881). The question for Toews is how far linguistic analysis has gone and should go especially in view of the poststructuralist challenge to foundationalism.

By definition, he argues, history is concerned with explanation; it is not a radical hermeneutics, but an attempt to account for the origin, persistence, and disappearance of certain meanings at "particular times and in specific socio-cultural situations" (882). For him explanation requires a separation of experience and meaning, experience is that reality which demands meaningful response. "Experience" in Toews's usage, is taken to be so self-evident that he never defines the term. (This is telling in an article that insists on establishing the importance and independence—the irreducibility—of "experience." The absence of definition allows experience to take on many resonances, but it also allows it to function as a universally understood category—the undefined word creates a sense of consensus by attributing to it an assumed, stable, and shared meaning).

Experience, for Toews is a foundational concept. While recognizing that meanings differ and that the historian's task is to analyze the different meanings produced in societies and over time, Toews protects "experience" from this kind of relativism. In so doing he establishes the possibility for objective knowledge and so for communication among historians, however diverse their positions and views. This has an effect (among others) of removing historians from critical scrutiny as active producers of knowledge.

Since the phenomenon of experience itself can be analyzed outside the meanings given to it, the subjective position of historians then can seem to have nothing to do with the knowledge they produce. Toews's "experience" thus provides an object for historians that can be known apart from their own role as meaning makers and it then guarantees not only the objectivity of their knowledge, but their ability to persuade others of its importance. Whatever diversity and conflict may exist among them, Toews's community of historians is rendered homogeneous by its shared object (experience). But as Ellen Rooney has so effectively pointed out, this kind of homogeneity can exist only because of the exclusion of the possibility that "historically irreducible interests divide and define . . . communities. . . ."[24] Inclusiveness is achieved by denying that exclusion is inevitable, that difference is established through exclusion, and that the fundamental differences that accompany inequalities of power and position cannot be overcome by persuasion. In Toews's article no disagreement about the meaning of the term "experience" can be entertained, since experience itself lies somehow outside its signification. For that reason, perhaps, Toews never defined it.

Even among those historians who do not share all of Toews's ideas about the objectivity or continuous quality of history, writing the defense of "experience" works in much the same way: it establishes a realm of reality outside of discourse and it authorizes the historian who has access to it. The evidence of experience works as a foundation providing both a starting point and a conclusive kind of explanation, beyond which few questions need to or can be asked. And yet it is precisely the questions precluded—questions about discourse, difference, and subjectivity, as well as about what counts as experience and who gets to make that determination—that would enable us to historicize experience, to reflect critically on the history we write about it, rather than to premise our history upon it.

Historicizing "Experience"

How can we historicize "experience"? How can we write about identity without essentializing it? Answers to the second question ought to point toward answers to the first, since identity is tied to notions of experience, and since both identity and experience are categories usually taken for granted in ways that I am suggesting they ought not to be. It ought to be possible for historians to, in Gayatri Spivak's terms, "make visible the assignment of subject-positions," not in the sense of capturing the reality of the objects seen, but of trying to understand the operations of the complex and changing discursive processes by which identities are ascribed, resisted, or embraced and which processes themselves are unremarked, indeed achieve their effect because they aren't noticed.[25] To do this a change of object seems to be required, one which takes the emergence of concepts and identities as historical events in need of explanation. This does not mean that one dismisses the effects of such concepts and identities, that one does not explain behavior in terms of their operations. It does mean assuming that the appearance of a new identity is not inevitable or determined, not something that was always there simply waiting to be expressed, not something that will always exist in the form it was given in a particular political movement or at a particular historical moment.

> The fact is "black" has never been just there either [writes Stuart Hall]. It has always been an unstable identity, psychically, culturally and politically. It, too, is a narrative, a story, a history. Something constructed, told, spoken, not simply found. People now speak of the society I come from in totally unrecognizable ways. Of course Jamaica is a black society, they say. In reality it is a society of black and brown people who lived for three or four hundred years without ever being able to speak of themselves as "black." Black is an identity which had to be learned and could only be learned in a certain moment. In Jamaica that moment is the 1970s.[26]

To take the history of Jamaican black identity as an object of inquiry in these terms is necessarily to analyze subject positioning, in part at least, as the effect of discourses that placed Jamaica in a late-twentieth-century, international-racist political economy; it is to historicize the "experience" of blackness.[27]

Treating the emergence of a new identity as a discursive event is not to introduce a new form of linguistic determinism, nor to deprive subjects of agency. It is to refuse a separation between "experience" and language and to insist instead on the productive quality of discourse. Subjects are constituted discursively, but there are conflicts among discursive systems, contradictions within any one of them, multiple meanings possible for the concepts they deploy.[28] And subjects have agency. They are not unified, autonomous individuals exercising free will, but rather subjects whose agency is created through situations and statuses conferred on them. Being a subject means being "subject to definite conditions of existence, conditions of endowment of agents and conditions of exercise."[29] These conditions enable choices, although they are not unlimited. Subjects are constituted discursively, experience is a linguistic event (it doesn't happen outside established meanings), but neither is it confined to a fixed order of meaning. Since discourse is by definition shared, experience is collective as well as individual. Experience is a subject's history. Language is the site of history's enactment. Historical explanation cannot, therefore, separate the two.

The question then becomes how to analyze language, and here historians often (though not always and not necessarily) confront the limits of a discipline that has typically constructed itself in opposition to literature. (These limits have to do with a referential conception of language, the belief in a direct relationship between words and things). The kind of reading I have in mind would not assume a direct correspondence between words and things, nor confine itself to single meanings, nor aim for the resolution of contradiction. It would not render process as linear, nor rest explanation on simple correlations or single variables. Rather it would grant to "the literary" an integral, even irreducible, status of its own. To grant such status is not to make "the literary" foundational, but to open new possibilities for analyzing discursive productions of social and political reality as complex, contradictory processes.

The reading I offered of Delany at the beginning of this essay is an example of the kind of reading I want to avoid. I would like now to present another reading—one suggested to me by literary critic Karen Swann—as a way of indicating what might be involved in historicizing the notion of experience. It is also a way of agreeing with and appreciating Swann's argument about "the importance of 'the literary' to the historical project."[30]

For Delany, witnessing the scene at the bathhouse (an "undulating mass of naked male bodies" seen under a dim blue light) was an event. It marked what in one kind of reading we would call a coming to consciousness of himself, a recognition of his authentic identity, one he had always shared, would always share with others like himself. Another kind of reading, closer to Delany's preoccupation with memory and the self in this autobiography, sees this event not as the discovery of truth (conceived as the reflection of a prediscursive reality), but as the substitution of one interpretation for another. Delany presents this substitution as a conversion experience, a clarifying moment, after which he sees (that is, understands) differently. But there is all the difference between subjective perceptual clarity and transparent vision; one does not necessarily follow from the other even if the subjective state is metaphorically presented as a visual experience. Moreover (and this is Swann's point), "the properties of the medium through which the visible appears—here, the dim blue light, whose distorting, refracting qualities produce a wavering of the visible," make any claim to unmediated transparency impossible.[31] Instead, the wavering light permits a vision beyond the visible, a vision that contains the fantastic projections ("millions of gay men" for whom "history had, actively and already, created . . . whole galleries of institutions") that are the basis for political identification.[32] "In this version of the story," Swann notes, "political consciousness and power originate, not in a presumedly unmediated experience of presumedly real gay identities, but out of an apprehension of the moving, differencing properties of the representational medium—the motion of light in water."[33]

The question of representation is central to Delany's memoir. It is a question of social categories, personal understanding, and language, all of which are connected, none of which are or can be a direct reflection of the others. What does it mean to be black, gay, a writer, he asks, and is there a realm of personal identity possible apart from social constraint? The answer is that the social and the personal are imbricated in one another and that both are historically variable. The meanings of the categories of identity change and with them possibilities for thinking the self:

> [A]t that time, the words "black" and "gay"—for openers—didn't exist with their current meanings, usage, history. 1961 had still been, really, part of the fifties. The political consciousness that was to form by the end of the sixties had not been part of my world. There were only Negroes and homosexuals, both of whom—along with artists—were hugely devalued in the social hierarchy. It's even hard to speak of that world.[34]

But the available social categories aren't sufficient for Delany's story. It is difficult, if not impossible to use a single narrative to account for his experience. Instead he makes entries in a notebook, at the front about material things, at the back about sexual desire. These are "parallel narratives, in parallel columns."[35] Although one seems to be about society, the public, the political, and the other about the individual, the private, the psychological, in fact both narratives are inescapably historical; they are discursive productions of knowledge of the self, not reflections either of external or internal truth. "That the two columns must be the Marxist and the Freudian—the material column and the column of desire—is only a modernist prejudice. The autonomy of each is subverted by the same excesses, just as severely."[36] The two columns are constitutive of one another, yet the relationship between them is difficult to specify. Do the social and economic determine the subjective? Is the private entirely separate from or completely integral to the public? Delany voices the desire to resolve the problem: "Certainly one must be the lie that is illuminated by the other's truth."[37] And then he denies that resolution is possible since answers to these questions do not exist apart from the discourses that produce them.

> If it *is* the split—the space between the two columns (one resplendant and lucid with the writings of legitimacy, the other dark and hollow with the voices of the illegitimate)—that constitutes the subject, it is only after the Romantic inflation of the private into the subjective that such a split can even be located. That locus, that margin, that split itself first allows, then demands the appropriation of language—now spoken, now written—in both directions, over the gap.[38]

It is finally by tracking "the appropriation of language . . . in both directions, over the gap," and by situating and contextualizing that language that one historicizes the terms by which experience is represented, and so historicizes "experience" itself.

Conclusion

Reading for "the literary" does not seem at all inappropriate for those whose discipline is devoted to the study of change. It is not the only kind of reading I am advocating, although more documents than those written by literary figures are susceptible to such readings. Rather, it is a way of changing the focus and the philosophy of our history, from one bent on naturalizing "experience" through a belief in the unmediated relationship between words and things, to one that takes all categories of analysis as contextual, contested, and contingent. How have categories of representation and analysis—such as class, race, gender, relations of production, biology, identity, subjectivity, agency, experience, even culture—achieved their foundational status? What have been the effects of their articulations? What does it mean for historians to study the past in terms of these categories; for individuals to think of themselves in these terms? What is the relationship between the salience of such categories in our own time and their existence in the past? Questions such as these open consideration of what Dominick LaCapra has referred to as the "transferential" relationship between the historian and the past, that is, of the relationship between the power of the historian's analytic frame and the events that are the object of his or her study. And they historicize both sides of that relationship by denying the fixity and transcendence of anything that appears to operate as a foundation, turning attention instead to the history of foundationalist concepts themselves. The history of these concepts (understood to be contested and contradictory) then becomes the evidence by which "experience" can be grasped and by which the historian's relationship to the past she writes about can be articulated. This is what Foucault meant by genealogy:

> If interpretation were the slow exposure of the meaning hidden in an origin, then only metaphysics could interpret the development of humanity. But if interpretation is the violent or surreptitious appropriation of a system of rules, which in itself has no essential meaning, in order to impose a direction, to bend it to a new will, to force its participation in a different game, and to subject it to secondary rules, then the development of humanity is a series of interpretations. The role of genealogy is to record its history: the history of morals, ideals, and metaphysical concepts, the history of the concept of liberty or of the ascetic life; as they stand for the emergence of different interpretations, they must be made to appear as events on the stage of historical process.[39]

Experience is not a word we can do without, although it is tempting, given its usage to essentialize identity and reify the subject, to abandon it altogether. But experience is so much a part of everyday language, so imbricated in our narratives that it seems futile to argue for its expulsion. It serves as a way of talking about what happened, of establishing difference and similarity, of claiming knowledge that is "unassailable."[40] Given the ubiquity of the term, it seems to me more useful to work with it, to analyze its operations and to redefine its meaning. This entails focusing on processes of identity production, insisting on the discursive nature of "experience" and on the politics of its construction. Experience is at once always already an interpretation *and* is in need of interpretation. What counts as experience is neither self-evident nor straightforward; it is always contested, always therefore political. The study of experience, therefore, must call into question its originary status in historical explanation. This will happen when historians take as their project *not* the reproduction and transmission of knowledge said to be arrived at through experience, but the analysis of the production of that knowledge itself. Such an analysis would constitute a genuinely nonfoundational history, one which retains its explanatory power and its interest in change but does not stand on or reproduce naturalized categories.[41] It also cannot guarantee the historian's neutrality, for the choice of which categories to historicize is inevitably "political," necessarily tied to the historian's recognition of his/her stake in the production of knowledge. Experience is, in this approach, not the origin of our explanation, but that which we want to explain. This kind of approach does not undercut politics by denying the existence of subjects, it instead interrogates the processes of their creation, and, in so doing, refigures history and the role of the historian, and opens new ways for thinking about change.[42]

NOTES

A longer version of this paper appeared in *Critical Inquiry*, 17 (Summer 1991) pp. 773–97. I am grateful for their critical advice to Judith Butler, Christina Crosby, Nicholas Dirks, Christopher Fynsk, Clifford Geertz, Donna Haraway, Susan Harding, Gyan Prakash, Donald Scott, William Sewell, Jr, Karen Swann, and Elizabeth Weed.

1. Samuel R. Delany, *The Motion of Light in Water: Sex and Science Fiction Writing in the East Village, 1957–1965* (New York: New American Library, 1988). Page numbers of citations from this book are indicated in the text.

2. Martha Minow, "Foreword: Justice Engendered," *Harvard Law Review*, 101 (November 1987), pp. 10–95.

3. On the distinction between seeing and writing in formulations of identity see Homi K. Bhabha, "Interrogating Identity," in *Identity: The Real Me*, ICA Documents (London) 6 (1987), pp. 5–11.

4. Lionel Gossman, "Towards a Rational Historiography," in *Transactions of the American Philosophical Society*, 79, 3 (1989), p. 26.

5. On the "documentary" or "objectivist" model used by historians, see Dominick LaCapra, "Rhetoric and History," in Dominick LaCapra, *History and Criticism* (Ithaca: Cornell University Press, 1985), pp. 15–44.

6. On vision as not passive reflection, see Donna Haraway, "Situated Knowledges," typescript p. 9, and Donna Haraway, "The Promises of Monsters; Reproductive Politics for Inappropriate/d Others," unpublished paper, Summer 1990, p. 9. See also Minnie Bruce Pratt, "Identity: Skin Blood Heart," in *Yours in Struggle: Three Feminist Perspectives on Anti-Semitism and Racism* (Brooklyn, N.Y.: Long Haul Press, 1984) and the analysis of Pratt's autobiographical essay by Biddy Martin and Chandra Talpade Mohanty, "Feminist Politics: What's Home Got to Do with It?," in Teresa de Lauretis, *Feminist Studies/Critical Studies* (Madison: University of Wisconsin Press, 1986), pp. 191–212.

7. I am grateful to Judith Butler for discussions on this point.

8. Fredric Jameson, "Immanence and Nominalism in Postmodern Theoretical Discourse, in *Postmodernism, or, The Cultural Logic of Late Capitalism* (Durham: Duke University Press, 1991), p. 199.

9. Raymond Williams, *Keywords*, (NY: Oxford University Press, 1983) pp. 126–129. My discussion in this paragraph paraphrases much of Williams's definition. Page numbers of citations are indicated in parentheses in the text.

10. On the ways knowledge is conceived "as an assemblage of accurate representations," see Richard Rorty, *Philosophy and the Mirror of Nature* (Princeton: Princeton University Press, 1979), especially p. 163.

11. Homi Bhabha puts it this way: "*To see* a missing person, or *to look* at Invisibleness, is to emphasize the subject's *transitive* demand for a *direct* object of self-reflection; a point of presence which would maintain its privileged enunciatory position *qua subject,*" in "Interrogating Identity," p. 5.

12. Teresa de Lauretis, *Alice Doesn't,* (Bloomingtom: Indiana University Press, 1984) chapter 6, "Semiotics and Experience," p. 159.

13. Gayatri Spivak describes this as positing a metalepsis, that is, substituting an effect for a cause. See Gayatri Chakravorty Spivak, *In Other Worlds: Essays in Cultural Politics* (New York: Routledge, 1987), p. 204.

14. Michel de Certeau, "History: Science and Fiction," in *Heterologies: Discourse on the Other,* translated by Brian Massumi (Minneapolis: University of Minnesota Press, 1986), p. 218.

15. R. G. Collingwood, *The Idea of History* (New York: Oxford University Press, 1956), pp. 274–75. Page numbers of citations are indicated in parentheses in the text.

16. Raymond Williams's discussion of "structures of feeling" takes on some of these same issues in a more extended way. See his *The Long Revolution* (New York: Columbia University Press 1961), and the interview about it in Raymond Williams, *Politics and Letters: Interviews with New Left Review* (London: Verso, 1989), pp. 156–74. I am grateful to Chun Lin for directing me to these texts.

17. On the integrative functions of "experience," see Judith Butler, *Gender Trouble: Feminism and the Subversion of Identity* (New York: Routledge, Chapman and Hall, 1990), pp. 22–25.

18. For a different reading of Thompson on experience see William Sewell, Jr., "How Classes Are Made: Critical Reflections on E. P. Thompson's Theory of Working-Class Formation," in Harvey J. Kaye and Keith McClelland, eds., *E. P. Thompson: Critical Perspectives* (Philadelphia: Temple University Press 1990); see also, Sylvia Schafer, "Writing about 'Experience': Workers and Historians Tormented by Industrialization," unpublished paper, May 1987.

19. Judith Newton, "History as Usual? Feminism and the 'New Historicism,'" *Cultural Critique,* 9 (1988), p. 93.

20. Christine Stansell, "Response," *International Labor and Working Class History,* 31 (Spring 1987), p. 28. Often this kind of invocation of experience leads back to the biological or physical "experience" of the body. See, for example, the arguments about rape and violence offered by Mary Hawkesworth, "Knowers, Knowing, Known: Feminist Theory and Claims of Truth," *Signs,* 14, 3 (Spring 1989), pp. 533–57.

21. This is one of the meanings of the slogan "the personal is the political." Personal knowledge (i.e., experience) of oppression is the source of resistance to it. For critiques of this position, see Chandra Talpade Mohanty, "Feminist Encounters: Locating the Politics of Experience," *copyright,* 1 (Fall 1987), p. 32; and Katie King, "The Situation of Lesbianism as Feminism's Magical Sign: Contests for Meaning and the U.S. Women's Movement, 1968–1972," *Communication,* 9 (1986), pp. 65–91. Catharine MacKinnon's work is probably the best example of the uses of "experience" Mohanty, King, and I are criticizing; see her *Feminism Unmodified: Discourses on Life and Law* (Cambridge, Mass.: Harvard University Press, 1987).

22. Denise Riley, *'Am I That Name?' Feminism and the Category of Women in History* (Minneapolis: University of Minnesota Press, 1988), p. 100.

23. John Toews, *American Historical Review*, 92, 4 (October 1987), pp. 879–907.

24. Ellen Rooney, *Seductive Reasoning: Pluralism as the Problematic of Contemporary Theory* (Ithaca, N.Y.: Cornell University Press, 1989), pp. 5–6.

25. Gayatri Spivak, "A Literary Representation of the Subaltern: A Woman's Text from the Third World," *In Other Worlds*, p. 241.

26. Stuart Hall, "Minimal Selves," *Identity*, ICA 6, p. 45. See also Barbara J. Fields, "Ideology and Race in American History," in J. Morgan Kousser and James M. McPherson, eds., *Region, Race and Reconstruction* (New York: Oxford University Press, 1982), pp. 143–77. (Fields's article is notable for its contradictions: the way, for example, that it historicizes race while naturalizing class and refusing to talk at all about gender).

27. An excellent example of the historicizing of black women's "experience" is Hazel Carby, *Reconstructing Womanhood: The Emergence of the Afro-American Woman Novelist* (New York: Oxford University Press, 1987).

28. For discussions of how change operates within and across discourses, see James Bono, "Science, Discourse, and Literature: The Role/Rule of Metaphor in Science," in Stuart Peterfreund, ed., *Literature and Science: Theory and Practice* (Boston: Northeastern University Press, 1990), pp. 59–89. See also, Mary Poovey, *Uneven Developments: The Ideological Work of Gender in Mid-Victorian England* (Chicago: University of Chicago Press, 1988), pp. 1–23.

29. Parveen Adams and Jeff Minson, "The Subject of Feminism," *m/f*, 2 (1978), p. 52. On the constitution of the subject, see Michel Foucault, *The Archaeology of Knowledge* (New York: Harper and Row, 1972), pp. 95–96; Felicity A. Nussbaum, *The Autobiographical Subject: Gender and Ideology in Eighteenth-Century England* (Baltimore: Johns Hopkins University Press, 1989); and Peter de Bolla, *The Discourse of the Sublime: Readings in History, Aesthetics, and the Subject* (Oxford and New York: Basil Blackwell, 1989).

30. Karen Swann's comments on this paper were presented at the Little Three Faculty Colloquium on "The Social and Political Construction of Reality," Wesleyan University, 18–19 January 1991. The comments exist only in typescript. The reference cited here is p. 5.

31. Karen Swann, Comment, p. 4.

32. Samuel R. Delany, *The Motion of Light*, p. 174.

33. Karen Swann, Comment, p. 4.

34. Samuel R. Delany, *The Motion of Light*, p. 242.

35. *Ibid.*, p. 29.

36. *Ibid.*, p. 212.

37. *Ibid.*

38. *Ibid.*, pp. 29–30.

39. Michel Foucault, "Nietzsche, Genealogy, History," in D. F. Bonchard, ed., *Language, Counter-Memory, Practice* Ithaca, NY: Cornell University Press, 1977 pp. 151–52.

40. Ruth Roach Pierson, "Experience, Difference and Dominance in the Writings of Women's History," unpublished paper, 1989, p. 32.

41. Conversations with Christopher Fynsk helped clarify these points for me.

42. For an important attempt to describe a poststructuralist history, see Peter de Bolla, "Disfiguring History," *Diacritics* 16 (Winter 1986), pp. 49–58.

3

Feminism and George Sand:
Lettres à Marcie

Naomi Schor

FEMINISME: *n.m.* (1837; du lat. *fémina*). 1° Doctrine qui préconise
l'extension des droits, du rôle de la femme dans la société. *Le féminisme
politique des suffragettes.* 2° *Méd.* Aspect d'un individu mâle qui présente
certains caractères secondaires du sexe féminin.

FEMINISTE: *adj.* (1872; du précéd.). Qui a rapport au féminisme (1°).
Propagande féministe.—Subst. Partisan du féminisme. *Un, une féministe.*
—Petit Robert

The episode is well known. In 1848, at the height of pre-election fever,
a group of feminists gathered at the Club de la rue Taranne proposed the
candidacy of George Sand to the National Assembly. Two days after the
publication of that motion in *La Voix des femmes* (6 April 1848), George
Sand sent a letter to the editors of *La Réforme* and *La Vraie République*, in
which she curtly shoots down this ill-timed nomination:

[Paris, 8 April 1848]

Sir:

A newspaper edited by some women has proclaimed my candidacy to
the National Assembly. If this jest did not injure my pride, by attributing
to me a ridiculous presumption, I would let it pass, like all those of which
all of us in this world can become the object. But my silence might lead
people to believe that I support the principles of which this newspaper

41

would like to become the mouthpiece. Please receive and be kind enough
to make known the following declaration:

1) I hope that no elector will want to lose his vote by having the foolish
notion of writing my name on his ballot;

2) I do not have the honor of knowing a single one of the women who
form clubs and edit newspapers;

3) the articles that might be signed with my name or my initials in
these newspapers are not by me.

I ask these ladies to forgive me for taking these precautions against
their zeal, for they have surely treated me with much good will.

I do not claim to protest in advance against the ideas these ladies or
any other ladies will want to discuss among themselves; freedom of opinion applies equally to both sexes, but I cannot condone being taken without my consent as the standard-bearer of a female circle with which I
have never had the slighest relation either pleasant or unpleasant.

With my distinguished salutations,

George Sand[1]

Neither the tone nor the tenor of this text is designed to make of Sand
a heroine in the eyes of historians of French feminism, and it singularly
complicates the task of all those—both men and women—who insist on
enlisting Sand as a feminist and making of her an ancestress of the contemporary women's movement. In fact, opposite this disturbing, not to say frankly
antifeminist text, we could place others by the same author, texts which are
equally well known and clearly feminist, where Sand defends the equality
of women before the law, clamors for the rights of women to divorce, to
be educated, and castigates the patriarchal order and the unjust condition of
women. Or, to complicate (or simplify matters) we could consider a text
like the letter to the Members of the Central Committee, written shortly after
the letter to the editors of La Réforme and La Vraie République, and for
similar reasons—the Committee had also nominated Sand for office. In this
letter, which provides a sort of gloss on the first, Sand proclaims her lack
of solidarity with those who champion women's liberation in both the public
and the sexual arena (e.g. the disciples of Saint-Simon, Enfantin and Four-
ier) while ringingly endorsing liberation through the restoration to women
of the civil rights of which marriage deprives them, through, in short, the
reform of marriage laws.[2] The very fact that the bourgeois feminists gathered
at this club could have misunderstood the nature of Sand's involvement (*engagement*), the extent of her *representativity* clearly demonstrates how difficult it is to classify Sand when it comes to what she calls, "the women's
cause (*la cause des femmes*)."

In fact, considering the enormity of the stakes, Sand's feminism is the
pons asinorum of Sand studies. It would not be exaggerating to say that,

sooner or later, all those who are interested in Sand will be led to wonder about her feminism and to take a position pro or con, to decide the question. Sand's feminism is an obligatory and unavoidable theme of reflexion for all Sand scholars.

To say that this question is a commonplace of Sand studies is not the same as saying that the terms of the debate have not evolved over the years. If there are those who continue year-in, year-out to approach the question without demonstrating the slightest knowledge of modern feminism, as though it were sufficient to rely on common sense, some personal or journalistic knowledge of feminism to speak of Sand's feminism, there are others for whom speaking of Sand's feminism is, as it should be, simply another way of speaking of feminism.

Thus during the 1970s, at the moment when the women's-liberation movement was reborn from its ashes (as well as those of the May 1968 events), when, following either parallel or convergent tracks, both French and Anglo-American feminist thought were spectacularly productive, there is a shift in the tone, vocabulary, and even area of inquiry in the debate on Sand's feminism. Indeed, as soon as one considers the question, a new difficulty arises: the problem of the corpus. On what evidence can one make a judgment: Sand's life and/or work? the fictions and/or the letters? the social and political essays? Of course, there is no reason not to take all of these practices into account, to accord equal attention to the biographical elements and the fictional texts, but in actual fact, critics tend to privilege either the life or the work. Let us say, to anticipate, that the text I want to discuss constitutes a challenge to these distinctions, in that it is an epistolary novel, a fictional text which is also a novel of ideas, or as Sand puts it in her preface, "a sort of novel without events,"[3] the *Lettres à Marcie* (*Letters to Marcie*).

It is highly significant that, when in the 1970s American academic critics borne by the women's movement, as well as by the theoretical renewal of French neofeminism, take on the topic of Sand's feminism, they privilege the fictional texts. Because their approaches seem to me exemplary, I will cite two examples of this new Sand criticism, the articles of Leslie Rabine and Eileen Boyd Sivert.

In an article that has lost none of its currency, "Sand and the Myth of Femininity," Leslie Rabine judges Sand's feminism harshly. Not entirely excluding biography, Rabine bases herself essentially on a reading of *Indiana*, Sand's first major novel, to evaluate Sand's feminism. This choice is highly predictable in that *Indiana* is a novel that calls into question in Sand's own words, the "unjust" and "barbarous" "laws which still govern woman's existence in wedlock, in the family and in society."[4] Nevertheless, according to Rabine, it would be a mistake to confuse the critique of marriage Sand makes in her novel with a fundamental questioning of the modes of representation of women and femininity produced by the patriarchal imaginary:

> While *Indiana* appears to contest the myth of Woman as Passive Object of Male Desire and Possession, in this novel the concepts of women's freedom and of the liberated woman are themselves mythified and incorporated into the traditional established conception of womanhood.[5]

What makes Sand a bad feminist, still according to Rabine, is her way of subscribing on the plane of fiction to masculine modes of representation of desire, indeed to a conception of the subject that makes subjectivity and especially desiring subjectivity the exclusive prerogative of the masculine subject: "George Sand in this novel, reproduces the myth of Woman as Lack and Absence" (13).

The great merit of Rabine's article is that it does not gloss over the contradictions in the novel, rather, it attempts to contain them by showing how, within the framework of the novel, Sand reduces and neutralizes them:

> The message of the novel is perhaps stronger in that it is contradictory. It does not simply reproduce the stereotypes but merges feminine aspirations for freedom into them. Indiana does revolt. . . . But she runs away to Raymon only when she does it as a "sacrifice," and when "she does not in any way go to him in search of happiness." . . . Thus Indiana's revolt is contained in her resignation. . . . Thus her independence is contained in her dependence on a man, and the novel itself must rely on a fantasy ending to save Indiana from the habitual fate of women. (14)

Finally, by likening Noun's fate to that of French women in 1830, Rabine faults Sand for founding her exceptional status as a woman writer on the inferiority of other women: "She made the freedom of one woman separate from the freedom of other women" (15).

Up to a certain point Eileen Boyd Sivert shares Rabine's point of view, especially—and one can see that she too owes much to Irigaray and Kristeva—as regards the difficulty, not to say the impossibility of representing a female protagonist as a fully desiring subject, as long as one borrows the dominant linguistic codes. But, Sivert effects a significant displacement, or slippage, in relation to Rabine. To begin with, her privileged text is not *Indiana,* but *Lélia,* a text which escapes entirely the narrative schemas of nascent realism, which reduces all of women's adventures to one, marriage.[6] It is not just the starting point of the discussion, but the point of view that is radically different here. For Sivert, Sand's feminism is situated on the level of the search for a language that would be adequate to sexual difference, to femininity: "it is in writing that we must look for an opening," she writes.[7] Sivert emphasizes the open form of the text, Sand's attempt, via her character, to find her voice, her place, her position outside of the beaten paths of male discourse, to transform her exile from the order of masculine representation into the royal way to writing otherwise. For her—and Cixous's influence is clear here—*Lélia* is an example of *écriture féminine*. Here Sand/Lélia's feminism is equivalent both to a desiring subjectivity and a women's writing: "Sand's discourse, which offers so many ways of approaching woman's story, does not enclose or smother, it is strikingly open, loose, plural" (64).

At the dawn of the 1990s, the question of Sand's feminism remains very much alive and even acquires a certain urgency, in that feminist criticism—by which I mean that form of American academic criticism which is so little, so poorly known in France—is in crisis and its operating concepts—such as that of "gender"—, which enabled this form of criticism to renew the reading of literary texts and other symbolic productions, are now being interrogated.[8]

Before going on to the *Lettres à Marcie,* we can already draw three conclusions of somewhat different orders based on what precedes: first, and this seems obvious, one cannot talk about Sand's feminism without starting from a definition of feminism, without making explicit the presuppositions of the discussion. That is what most of those who have dealt with this subject end up by recognizing:

> If one defines feminism in such a way as to limit it to such traits as a scorn of domestic work, and a preference for sisterhood, organization, and politics, then one can maintain that in no way was George Sand a feminist.[9]

> [C]an one say that Sand is fundamentally feminist? I doubt it. . . . What makes Sand feminist are her personal audacities and her rebellion against the conjugal yoke and stupid bourgeois education: but she is not feminist in the modern sense of the word.[10]

> [I]n Sand's case we must agree on the meaning to give to the term "feminist" since, as soon as she takes a position with regard to concrete claims of contemporary feminists, her attitude becomes so complicated as to seem paradoxical.[11]

This entails in turn a second conclusion: if the case of Sand interpellates us, it is because it has the value of a paradigm; the contradictions Sand and her readers grapple with pose clearly the problem of feminism and perhaps especially feminism in France, for one must not under any circumstances lose sight of Sand's specific historical or national contexts. The issue is understanding why in France exceptional women who have contested their period's injustices and prejudices regarding the condition of women have in general preferred not to participate in a collective struggle for women's rights, and have so often refused to renounce their "difference." Sand is a screen onto which are projected the conflicts which oppose Marxist and psychoanalytic feminists, bourgeois individualistic and collectivist feminists, Lacanian and Althusserian feminists.

My third conclusion, which seems at first glance to contradict the first, but which in fact flows from it, is that if the debate is so unsatisfying, if the question remains forever open, it is perhaps because it is not well posed, that is, what one refuses to see is that what is problematic is the very term feminist. Instead of asking ourselves whether or not Sand is a feminist, indeed a good or a bad one, one must ask what is feminism, if there exists a definition of feminism that can account for practices and convictions that are totally heterogeneous and sometimes irreconcilable (except by oscillations of a strategic order). By posing the question in this manner, one is led to consider the hypothesis according to which in the end Sand is exemplarily feminist—if for the sake of convenience we wish to preserve this troubling term—because of her contradictions, and not despite them. In which case I would propose a definition of feminism that makes of it a sum of contradictions, the nodal point where dissatisfactions with contemporary society and the place it assigns women, claims for equality, claims for singular or plural differences, assertions of an essential and transhistorical female nature, denunciations of a subaltern condition due to specifically historical and contingent factors clash and intertwine. In all feminism in the broadest sense of the term there would then be equal parts of conservative and contestatory forces, of maternalism and antimaternalism, of familialism and antifamilialism, of separatism and assimilationism. The apparently irreconcilable debate that currently opposes essentialists and constructionists is a false debate, in that neither of the warring forces has an exclusive hold on the truth. Feminism is the debate itself. If then Sand is a feminist, it is in the sense that she bodies forth and articulates these contradictions, and not to the extent that she resolves them in a more or less satisfactory fashion. To be done with these preliminary conclusions, I would like to propose that the best way to approach Sand's feminism today is neither through her novels, nor her biography, but rather through those writings I would term theoretical. It is time to read Sand as a theoretician of sexual difference.

The distinction is crucial: it's not a matter of re-marking an opposition we have worked so hard to deconstruct, of reinstituting some sort of hierarchy between theory and practice, but of situating Sand's disparate writings on women's fate (in the form of letters, novels, essays) in the context of current theoretical work on sexual difference. Now, as I've already indicated, in this perspective—but it is not of course the only one—the *Lettres à Marcie* constitute a major document. Indeed one issue which is at stake in this text is precisely whether or not women can function in the loftiest spheres of thought, in the realm of abstraction. From the outset Sand declares in her preface that the *Lettres* are "an unfinished essay . . . an incomplete fragment and without any philosophical value whatsoever" (165). But further, the friend addresses Marcie—whose letters we don't have (these letters read as a sort of anti-*Letters of a Portuguese Nun*)—in these terms: "Women, you say, are not and cannot be philosophers. If you take the word philosophy in its primitive meaning, love of wisdom, I think you can, you must cultivate philosophy" (227). In fact the whole beginning of the sixth and last letter, to which I will return below, is devoted to the question of woman and philosophy. One of the great questions posed by the *Lettres à Marcie* is that of woman's (proper) relationship to philosophy, to theoretical activity.[12] And the nature of that relationship depends on the meaning one gives to philosophy.

The *Lettres à Marcie* were originally written as a serial novel for the newspaper *Le Monde* published by Lamennais. When Lamennais made some cuts in the third letter without consulting her, Sand informed him respectfully but firmly that if she were not free to speak about what she wanted, then she would be obliged to abandon the project and interrupt the writing of the *Letters*. In particular she asks the Abbé if he would have any objection to her speaking of divorce in a subsequent letter: "to tell you in a word all my audacities (*hardiesses*), they would involve asking for Divorce in marriage. Despite all my efforts to find a remedy for the bloody injustices, the endless miseries, the passions without remedy that trouble the union of the sexes, I don't see any other solution than the freedom to break and reform the conjugal bond."[13] When Lamennais is reticent, she continues for a while to produce copy, but ends up abandoning the text in midstream. It will then be published in a state of incompletion, which is unusual for the author.

Rarely has a text of Sand's been marked by more uncertainties, more doubts as to its legitimacy. Obviously Sand is not comfortable in the role of theoretician of sexual difference. As she admits to Lamennais, theorizing the role of women represents for her a challenge.

> What's strangest about this is that I who have written my whole life on this subject [the actual fate of women], I hardly know what to think and not having ever summarized myself, not having ever concluded anything but in the vaguest terms, I find myself today concluding from inspiration without really knowing where it's coming from, without being able not to draw the conclusions I do and finding in me I don't know what certainty, which is perhaps the voice of truth or perhaps the impertinent voice of pride. (712)

The *Lettres à Marcie* present themselves as a correspondence between a (presumably male) "friend" and a young woman who, not having a dowry, cannot marry and thus considers other possible ways of living: free love, romantic voyage, the active life, the convent. The friend eliminates them one by one to exalt the superiority of the female maternal vocation, which is somewhat paradoxical given his correspondent's situation.

At first glance, Sand's theoretical work seems to revolve around the great paradigm of feminism, the opposition *equality versus difference*. But, as Joan Scott has masterfully demonstrated, this opposition is false in that any notion of equality implies that of difference, the recognition that everyone is not identical; as Sand remarks in the *Lettres à Marcie* "equality . . . is not similarity" (229). And Scott echoes her: "The alternative to the binary construction of sexual difference is not sameness, identity or androgyny."[14] But there ends the agreement between Sand and Scott; whereas Scott's deconstruction works to replace the necessary but tacit recognition of difference in any political conception of equality by that of the multiple *differences* between women, Sand attempts to show that *difference* and equality are not incompatible. In other words: each one deconstructs the opposition, but whereas Sand seeks to reconcile both terms, Scott displaces them by a third which comes to somehow encompass the two others:

> Equality, as I told you earlier, is not identity (similitude). Equal merit does not mean that one is fit for the same jobs, and to deny man's superiority, it would have sufficed to entrust him with the domestic duties of woman. To deny the *identity* of woman's faculties with those of man, it would similarly suffice to entrust her with virile public functions; but if woman is not destined to go beyond private life that is not to say that she does not have the same degree or the same excellence of faculties applicable to the life she is assigned. (*Lettres* 229)

> Placing equality and difference in antithetical relationship has, then, a double effect. It denies the way in which difference has long figured in political notions of equality and it suggests that sameness is the only ground on which equality can be claimed. It thus puts feminists in an impossible position, for as long as we argue within the terms of discourse set up by this opposition we grant the current conservative premise that since women cannot be identical to men in all respects, they cannot expect to be equal to them. The only alternative, it seems to me, is to refuse to oppose equality to difference and insist continually on differences . . . differences as the very meaning of equality itself.[15]

The difference—or the difference of differences—between Sand and Scott is instantly apparent and brings out clearly what is for Sand the true aporia: the opposition between public and private, in other words the great opposition produced by the French Revolution and which structures Sand's thought, her theorization of sexual difference.[16] What is not so much the unthought as the *unthinkable* for Sand is the transgression by woman (as well as by man) of the bar that separates the two spheres. For Sand the separation of the spheres is sacred, inscribed in nature, and must be maintained, for social order depends on it. This brings us back in a sense to our starting point: Sand's consistent refusal (whether it be a question of the National Assembly or the French Academy) to take her place on the public scene. To speak of Sand's feminism is then to consider this opposition and the way it functions in her thought system.

What one becomes quickly aware of is that for Sand, if this opposition is essential, transhistorical, it is nonetheless inscribed in a historical continuum to whose repercussions she is subject. According to a story the friend recounts at the end of the last letter, just before he hastily concludes this interrupted correspondence, the taboo that affects the educated woman, the bluestocking, is a specifically modern fact:

> The prejudice that denies women serious intellectual occupations is of quite recent vintage. Antiquity and the Middle Ages do not to my knowledge offer us any examples of aversions and systems of abuse against those women who pursue the arts and sciences. (*Lettres* 231)

There would then have been a golden age for woman and that age coincided with a period in which man was mobilized by war: called on to leave home, man is too happy to have a companion who is capable of running the *oikos*.

> Social troubles, here the crusades, there the wars of schisms, take man far from the hearth, and leave at the head of the family a woman invested with an uncontested authority; if her responsibilities [*attributions*] are considerable, if her role is important in the society, the education she may have acquired is a real advantage for the fortune and dignity of her husband. (*Lettres* 233)

Thus, according to this curious version of women's history, the separation of spheres worked well as long as man lived far from the hearth and woman was in charge at home. What marked the decline of the condition of women is the end of wars of religion, crusades, schisms, and man's return to the hearth, in short the "ennervation of the manly character" (*Lettres* 232). The modern era must invent a new relationship between the sexes that corresponds to the end or more precisely the "suspension" of wars.

It might appear at first glance as though with this fable Sand does little more than to reinscribe the ideas of Rousseau in the *Nouvelle Héloïse* from a feminist perspective, but without calling into question Rousseau's fundamental assumptions: the separation of spheres on which the social order depends is founded on the hyperbolization of masculine and feminine roles, of masculinity (man = warrior) and femininity (woman = housewife). But, on closer inspection, it would seem that, in fact, Sand's ideal is quite different, and would be on the order of a matriarchy, a division that would do without a masculine presence altogether and leave women in full command. Paradoxically, political and economic disorders—the state of war as well as the regime of scarcity—insure the social order.

How then, Sand asks herself in 1837, maintain the separation of spheres, now that the men have come home, that is (re)invested the private and domestic sphere previously reserved for woman? This original way of posing the question sheds an unaccustomed light on postrevolutionary society. For, what the version of events given here by Sand allows us to observe is that if, as Michelle Perrot writes, "the 19th century is the golden age of the private,"[17] the same is not true for women, the supposed queens of the private. The accentuation of the separation of the so-called masculine and feminine spheres, and especially the hypertrophy of the private in bourgeois European societies in the nineteenth century, did not benefit women: while they are kept at a distance from the public arena, men are everywhere the masters, occupying simultaneously all the places, all the positions.

If Sand could neither imagine nor admit—at least in the immediate—the breakdown of the separation of spheres, if she could not find words harsh enough to condemn those women who claimed "the same attributes" as men, to wit "speech at the forum, [but] the helmet and the sword, the right to condemn to death" (201–2), it is that, like all French theorists of difference, she is more utopianist than feminist, or more precisely a utopian feminist (as one speaks of a utopian socialist). On this point I am in complete agreement with the conclusions drawn by Vareille when she summarizes her analysis of Sand's feminism:

> Far from confirming and consolidating an unjust system by aspiring to be a part of it, women must then preciously cling to their marginality, which thus becomes the visible sign of an inevitable change, the index of the necessity of creating a society founded on new principles. It's as though by refusing to endorse the most apparently radical claims of contemporary feminists, Sand was intent, on the level of mythical imagination if not that of rational reflexion, on ensuring [*conserver à*] for female marginality a function of radical interrogation of existing society.[18]

Vareille's analysis of Sand's feminism would apply just as well to that of her contemporary heirs, Cixous and Irigaray, who (just like Sand) reject the egalitarian/reformist model of feminism, indeed feminism itself, in the name of a mythical feminine that might constitute a sort of reserve of alternate and superior moral values. This comparison is meant less to demonstrate the persistent utopian temptation of French feminists—with which

I have great sympathy[19]—than to emphasize the logic which necessarily links the theory of the separation of spheres to utopian feminism. The theory of the separation of spheres reinforces utopian feminism, to the extent that it enables one to imagine a protected locus where the Ideal prevails. There is then no feminist utopia that does not on some level imply the separation of spheres, and which does not take over (*reprendre à son compte*) the separation of society set into place by the liberal system produced by the Enlightenment. French neofeminists have always been intent on marking their refusal of feminism in the restricted sense of the word, as an avatar of the (humanist) thought of the Enlightenment; but to the extent that they have surreptitiously and unknowingly reinscribed (*reconduit*) the division of the sociosymbolic space set into place by that system of thought, to the extent that they are always tempted to seek refuge in their "private garden,"[20] they remain prisoners of the (very) system they denounce. By going back to the sources of French feminism, one sees that in the future the daughters of George, herself a daughter of Jean-Jacques, will have their hands full getting rid of the cumbersome legacy of the French Revolution and going beyond the private/public split, all the while maintaining their hope of a new Revolution.[21]

NOTES

This text was originally written in French for a special issue of the *Revue des sciences humaines* (forthcoming) devoted to Sand.

1. George Sand, *Correspondance (juillet 1847–décembre 1848)* 8, edited by Georges Lubin (Paris: Garnier, 1971), pp. 391–92. All translations are mine except where otherwise noted.

2. See *Correspondance* 8, 400–08.

3. George Sand, *Lettres à Marcie* (Paris: Perrotin, 1835), p. 165.

4. George Sand, *Indiana,* translated by George Burnham Ives (Chicago: Academic Press Limited, 1976), n.p.

5. Leslie Rabine, "George Sand and the Myth of Femininity," *Women and Literature* 4, 2, pp. 2–17 (Fall 1976), p. 2.

6. See Naomi Schor, "The Scandal of Realism," in Denis Hollier, ed., *A New History of French Literature* (Cambridge: Harvard University Press, 1989), pp. 656–60.

7. Eileen Boyd Sivert, "*Lélia* and Feminism," *Feminist Readings: French Texts/American Contexts, Yale French Studies,* 62 (1981), p. 47.

8. See Judith Butler, *Gender Trouble: Feminism and the Subversion of Identity* (New York: Routledge, 1990), p. 7.

At the very moment when I began writing this text, I noted in the program of the 1990 MLA that a session was to be devoted precisely to this question. The session was entitled: "Toward a Definition of Sand's Feminism," and the titles of the talks to be given under this rubric were: 1. "*Consuelo:* the Fiction of Feminism," Pierrette Daly; 2. "The Limits of Sand's Feminism: Marriage in the Novels of Her Maturity (1857–76)," Lucy M. Schwarz; 3. "Un idéal mythique de la femme," Simone Vierne; 4. "Textual Feminism in George Sand's Early Fiction," Françoise Massarider-Kenney. One might conclude on the basis of these titles that the reading of Sand's fictional feminism remains the dominant trend in Sand studies.

9. Dennis O'Brien, "George Sand and Feminism," *George Sand Papers: Conference Proceedings 1976* (New York: AMS Press, 1980), p. 89. O'Brien's conclusion is the following: "For women of the nineteenth-century there was no dilemma as to whether or not Sand was working for the cause of women" (88). We judge her feminism according to anachronistic criteria at the risk of dehistoricizing it: "To select several tenets of feminism held in our day by some feminists and say that all who do not hold these views are inimical to the cause is ahistorical" (89). O'Brien's cautionary note is welcome though as I will attempt to show in what follows some of the problems posed by Sand's feminism have a very contemporary dimension.

10. Claudine Chonez, "George Sand et le féminisme," *Europe* 587 (mars), p. 77. What follows is worth quoting but needs no comment: "In any case today she would be a woman who votes and wears pants. . . . Some analysis would have freed her of her frigidity or naturally freed in her the expression of physical love. But a mother adoring her brood, a cautious woman in the face of violence, a good traditional housewife, she would almost surely be totally opposed to the MLF [Mouvement de Libération des Femmes]" (79).

11. Kristina Wingard Vareille, *Socialité, sexualité et les impasses de l'histoire: L'évolution de la thématique sandienne d'Indiana (1832) à Mauprat (1837)* (Uppsala: Almqvist and Wiskell, 1987), p. 397. Of all the discussions of Sand's feminisms, I find this one to be the most thoughtful and the most enlightening; my only reservation is that Vareille seems unfamiliar with contemporary feminist theorists.

12. The interdiction that affects this relationship in Sand has less to do with some intellectual deficiency in women—an argument Sand always ridicules—than with the danger that certain *bad* philosophies, such as that of the Saint-Simonians, present for female virtue. Thus in a letter to François Rollinat dated 16 October 1835, Sand writes: ". . . it is not easy for a woman to be both a philosopher and chaste at the same time," *Correspondance (juillet 1835–avril 1837)* 3, edited by Georges Lubin (Paris: Garnier, 1967), p. 58.

13. George Sand, *Correspondance* 3, p. 713.

14. Joan Wallach Scott, "The Sears Case," *Gender and the Politics of History* (New York: Columbia University Press, 1988), p. 174. Cf. Sand's analogous comments in her article on socialism: "You attempt in vain to confuse the meaning of the word equality with identity. No, men are not identical with each other. The diversity of their forms, their instincts, their faculties, their appearances, their influence is infinite. There is no parity between one man and another. But these infinite diversities consecrate equality instead of destroying it" ("Socialisme," in *Questions politiques et sociales* (Paris: Calmann Lévy, 1887), pp. 258–59).

15. Joan W. Scott, pp. 174–75.

16. See on this topic, *Histoire de la vie privée* 4, *De la Révolution à la Grande Guerre,* edited by Michelle Perrot (Paris: Seuil, 1987). It would appear according to the women historians of private life that, whereas the Revolution initially marks a rupture with the splitting off of public/private, masculine/feminine that is set into place throughout the eighteenth century—the public invading everything as the private becomes suspect—in the long run it is merely written into law, customs: "The 18th century had refined the distinction between the

public and the private. . . . The French Revolution operates in this evolution a dramatic and contradictory rupture, whose short and long term effects must incidentally (*d'ailleurs*) be distinguished. In the immediate private or 'particular interests' are suspected to be a shadow favorable to plots and treachery. . . . In the longer term, the Revolution accentuates the definition of the public and private sphere, valorizes the family, differentiates sexual roles and opposes political men and domestic women," Michelle Perrot, "Avant et ailleurs," p. 17.

17. Michelle Perrot, p. 10.

18. Kristina Vareille, pp. 410–11.

19. See my "Dreaming Dissymmetry: Barthes, Foucault, and Sexual Difference," in *Coming to Terms,* edited by Elizabeth Weed (New York: Routledge, 1989).

20. This expression was used by Hélène Cixous in the course of a debate that followed the talk given by Francine Demichel at the conference on "Lecture de la Différence Sexuelle," at the Collège International de Philosophie, 18–20 October 1990. For an (this) American listener or eavesdropper, the violence of the debate that followed the talk of a jurist who argued for the entrance of women into the "system" (by presenting themselves for the entrance exams to the "grandes écoles," notably the ENA—Ecole Nationale de l'Administration) was both very striking and significant, for it showed how much the tendency to valorize the private feminine sphere remains alive in France, whereas in the United States, however strong the separatist trends within the women's movement, one knows that refusing to enter the system amounts to playing into the hands of the most conservative, the most misogynist right wing. Which does not, of course, mean that the recuperation of the women's movement is not a permanent danger and that one must not at all times play the double game of integration and of the preservation of the revolutionary values of feminism.

The sort of horror that the word feminism inspires in France and the utopianism that accompanies its diversion (*détournement*) are illustrated by the answer Michelle Perrot gives in an interview published in a special issue of the *Nouvel Observateur* entitled, "After twenty years of struggle . . . Happy, women?" when the *Nouvel Observateur* asks her point blank the question, "Are you a feminist?": "The struggle for equality between men and women is not over. On the visible horizon of history, one sees only a male domination. Male society is not always a success. In the future, I hope that one will arrive at something else and, from this point of view, I am a feminist. That does not mean that one should impose on women masculine values. What one must aim for is an equality that preserves the difference of identities. But as soon as women assert their difference, men tend to confine them in inferiority" *Nouvel Observateur,* 1361 (6 to 12 December 1990), p. 170.

21. On the question of the difficult inheritance of the French Revolution for French feminism see Antoinette Fouque, "Femmes en mouvements: hier, aujourd'hui, demain. Entretien avec Antoinette Fouque," *Le Débat,* 59 (mars-avril 1990), pp. 126–43.

4

French Feminism Revisited:
Ethics and Politics

Gayatri Chakravorty Spivak

(Algeria has a highly diversified structure of women's movements. Interacting with part of that diversified network, starting from the now relatively venerable FLN-based national women's organization through more recent grass-roots movements, one would receive the impression that workers like Marie-Aimée Hélie-Lucas, of whom I speak in the body of my text, with their attention fixed on the Family Code, are felt by some in the interior to be more remote from other emancipatory women's issues on the domestic front, by which the former are not as deeply touched. Thus my original argument, that the face of "global" feminism is turned outward and must be welcomed and respected as such, rather than fetishized as the figure of the Other, gains confirmation from my first research visit to Algeria. Further research will, I hope, flesh out the domestic space in such a way that this postcolonial feminist will no longer need to revisit French feminism as a way in, although it might remain an exigency in academic Cultural Studies.

That way in defines the Third World as Other. Not to need that way in is, paradoxically, to recognize that indigenous global feminism must still reckon with the bitter legacy of imperialism transformed in decolonization:

> Current research on the family in Algeria and in the Maghreb cannot be
> evaluated without a retrospective view, however brief, of the movement
> of ideas that have emerged in Europe, and in Anglo-Saxon and transat-
> lantic countries. . . . The paradigms of academic intelligibility of fem-
> inism in Algeria and in the Maghreb have been, for the large part, mod-

54

ulated in the intellectual configurations of Western thought: They have offered the frame and the genesis. . . .[1]

This intelligent passage defines my charge: to see that the view is retrospective, and that the requirements are of academic intelligibility, in the service of which we write for anthologies. I must first show how the frame and the point of genesis are themselves contested; and then remind myself that within the frame, and after the genesis, is a patchwork of which I have not yet learned to speak (for ethnography/sociology must be unlearned here) without the legitimation-by-reversal of mere admiration.)

1. Second Thoughts

Texts open when you talk to groups of others, which often turn out to be classes, public audiences. Yet these openings are not beginnings, for the staging of each such talking is secured by politics; classes at least by the individualism and competition of the academy "at its best," public lectures by the politics of funding and the thematics of travel and lodging; the gender, race, and class politics of custodial staff in both arenas. No attempt such as ours can begin without a grounding mistake, cutting off the space where theory is persistently normed by politics.

Texts open when you talk to groups of others, which often turn out to be classes, public lectures. The most intimate alterity or otherness defines and offers up our so-called selves to ourselves. Most intimate, yet least accessible. So close that we cannot catch it through the self or selves that it frames for us. As for those clusters of alterity—groups of others—that we call classes or audiences, convention says that the best way to reach them is to assume them as collections of selves and adjust your pitch. (And, if you move globally—from the US via Algeria to France, for example—the imagining of pitch and collectivity inscribes the political centering of the speaker's theoretical burden).

Every craftsperson knows that unless you are sure of the effectiveness of every detail of your craft, what you are making will not hold. Assuming that classes and audiences are collections of selves ignores the details of their intimate and inaccessible alterity. These details mark the limits of teaching and talking, so that the certainty that texts are opening remains framed by a radical uncertainty. I was teaching "My chances/*Mes Chances:* A Rendezvous with Some Epicurean Stereophonics" for the first time when I wrote the first draft of this paper, and the conventionally ignored details of class and audience insistently became clear to me as they never had before.[2] And now, reading Patricia Williams's uncanny attention to the blank part of the text, I feel my affection for deconstruction grow, that it can claim such friends:

> I would like to write in a way that reveals the intersubjectivity of legal
> *constructions,* that forces the reader both to participate in the *construction*
> of meaning and to be conscious of that process. Thus, in attempting to
> fill the gaps in the discourse of commercial exchange, I hope that the gaps
> in my own writing will be self-consciously modeled, filled by the reader,
> as an act of forced mirroring of meaning-invention. To this end, I exploit
> all sorts of literary devices. . . .[3]

It is from the far end of the track which talks of intersubjectivity as forced
mirroring and the exploitation of rhetoric, even as it undoes construction,
that we can ask: What is it to write for you? What is it to teach? What is
it to learn? What is it to assume that one already knows the meaning of the
words "something is taught by me and something is learned by others"?

In one sense, this uncertainty is the ground of the academic institution,
if we consider it to be, not only an ideological apparatus, but also an apparatus with the help of which we believe we produce a critique of ideology.[4] Yet it is in the face of this felt uncertainty that we must risk the generalizations that we feel are opened up by the convenient assumption that a
class learns, an audience hears, readers read as we teach, talk, write. The
greatest fear, and the greatest hope, is that once the generalizations emerge,
the convention of taking others as collections of selves should take over only
too easily and something be grasped from whatever is offered. In that grasping, the working of the academy as ideological apparatus has an operative
role.

How can I hope that the generalizations I offer here will miraculously
escape this violating yet enabling convention? Yet how can anyone not care?
Especially since they have been opened up for me by talk with others, even,
in one case where talk was not permitted and the necessary misfiring of
teaching and learning was turned into deliberate arson.

2. Bio-Graphy

Eleven years ago I wrote "Displacement and the Discourse of Woman,"
believing that men on women could only be set right by women.[5]

Ten years ago I wrote "French Feminism in an International Frame,"
believing that no Europeanist should ignore the once and future global production of "Europe."[6]

Three years ago I wrote "Feminism and Deconstruction, Again," as a
sort of second take on "Displacement."[7] I had come to think that in the
production of feminist theoretical practice, negotiation based on acknowledgment of complicity with the male-dominated history of theory was also
in order.

And here is "French Feminism Revisited," which feels to me like a
second take on "International Frame." I have come to think that there can

be exchange between metropolitan and decolonized feminisms. A year of teaching in India, and that semi-anonymous unpublishable document, "discriminating against women in the name of racial identity," did, among many other situations of good and bad talk, open up and bring about this revision of mind for me.

When I wrote "French Feminism In An International Frame," my subject position, even if only partly assigned by the workings of the ideological apparatus, was that of an ethnic minority who had broken into the university in the United States. I was not fully aware of this, of course, just as I was not fully aware of the convictions of single-issue feminism guiding my reading in "Displacement."

"International Frame," like "Displacement," was the beginning of a certain kind of revisionary work. A decade later, what little I have learned— may I not forget to question: what it is to assume that one already knows the meaning of the words; something is taught by others and something is learned by me—seems to point at three different generalizations for this resistant reader's subject position: ethnic in in the US, racial in Britain, negotiating for decolonized space. These are generalizations that now seem good for teaching and learning in classes, lecture halls. They will not travel directly, of course, to all situations of struggle in the three arenas, as some of us, impatient with the grounding uncertainty of teaching, talking, writing, seem too quickly to presume.

After the rupture of negotiated political independence or national liberation, racialization or ethnicization of resistance is no longer the most urgent emancipatory generalization in decolonized space. As I have written elsewhere, the most urgent political claims in decolonized space are tacitly recognized as coded within the legacy of imperialism: nationhood, constitutionality, citizenship, democracy, socialism, even culturalism. "Feminism," the named movement, is also part of this so-called heritage of the European Enlightenment, although within the enclosure of the heritage it is often inscribed in a contestatory role.[8] The agenda is to wrench these regulative political signifiers out of their represented field of reference. And the instrument of such a wrenching, such a reconstellating or dehegemonizing, cannot be ethnophilosophical or race-ideological pride. Given the international division of labor of the imperialist centuries, it is quite appropriate that the best critique of the European ethico-politico-social universals, those regulative concepts, should come from the North Atlantic.[9] But what is ironically appropriate in postcoloniality is that this critique finds its best *staging* outside of the North Atlantic in the undoing of imperialism.

When I wrote "French Feminism in an International Frame" my assigned subject position was actually determined by my moment in the United States and dominated my apparent choice of a post-colonial position. For my own class in the decolonized nation vaguely conceived, I had little else

but contempt. Now it seems to me that the radical element of the postcolonial bourgeoisie must most specifically learn to negotiate with the structure
of enabling violence that produced her; and the normative narrative of metropolitan feminism is asymmetrically wedged in that structure. Simply to
resist it as white feminism is to yield privilege to the migrants' and the
diasporics' struggle, crucial *on* their terrain, and to forget that they too want
to inhabit the national subject by displacing it: Black Britain, Arab France;
it is to neglect the postcolonial's particular generalization in the vaster common space of woman.

I remain, of course, a Europeanist by training. My belief remains the
same: no Europeanist should ignore the once and future global production
of "Europe." My question has sharpened: How does the postcolonial feminist negotiate with the metropolitan feminist? I have placed three classic
texts of French feminism before an activist text of Algerian feminism that
speaks of negotiation.[10] I imagine a sympathy with Marie-Aimée Hélie-Lucas's subject position because hers too is perhaps fractured and I help to
crack it further, for use. She too is revising an earlier position. As she does
so, she speaks *of* solidarity with Islamic Women around the world. She
speaks *to* a British interviewer. And I, a non-Islamic Indian postcolonial,
use her to revise my reading of French feminism.

The texts in this essay were opened up for me in teaching; subsequently
in speeches. This, then, might be the moment to remember that, even when—
in class, in a lecture room—the other seems a collection of selves and nothing seems displaced or cracked, what "really happens" remains radically
uncertain, the risky detail of our craft. To remember both that "within the
range of our calculations we can count on certain probabilities"; and, that
"to believe in chance can just as well indicate that one believes in the existence of chance as that one does *not,* above all, believe in chance, since
one looks for and finds a hidden meaning at all costs."[11] Can it be imagined
how this mischief conducts traffic between women's solidarity across two
sides of imperialism?

3. Simone de Beauvoir

In a few paragraphs hidden in the curious chapter on "The Mother" in
The Second Sex, Simone de Beauvoir rewrote the figure of the Mother as
possible existentialist subject.[12]

We have judged Beauvoir harshly. Juliet Mitchell's remark remains
representative and definitive: "*The Second Sex,* strictly speaking, is not a
part of the second feminist movement."[13] The implications of Antoinette
Fouque's harsh words after Beauvoir's death, which Toril Moi sums up in
the following way, were quickly shared by many in France: "Now that Beauvoir is dead, feminism is finally free to move into the twenty-first century."

I want to re-open the chapter on "The Mother" in the face of the judgment of these daughters. First, and most curious, the chapter seems to focus teleologically on the child and thus frees daughters from mothers. In *our* time-space of feminism, we have kept uncertainties at bay by binding mother to daughter in our theories and strategies. But we cannot make the whole world fit forever into that devoutly wished embrace. A section of the generation of emancipated bourgeois colonial women whose daughters can be and are the agents of negotiation in decolonized feminist space, represented by Hélie-Lucas in this essay, were inspired by Beauvoir's book. Secondly, her reduced or pared-down structural picture of the Mother, so intimate that it is intuitively inaccessible (and thus protected against dominant universalizing), is theoretically inclusive of "situations" (an existentialist word) often considered beside the point of the norm: gay parenting, mothering by the gendered subaltern.[14]

"Situation" is an existentialist word. Beauvoir's chapter on "The Mother" is one among other descriptions of "situations" for the second sex. I would like to make this my point of entry into the chapter. On the threshold I place a generalization about deconstructive reading to ward off uncertainty: it is unexcusing, unaccusing, attentive, and situationally productive through dismantling.[15]

I attempt to follow the protocols of Beauvoir's text into existentialism. I sense her hesitation—as a daughter—between the role of object/Other that is offered to her. I sense her assertion of a difficult liberty—both as daughter and as the mother philosophized. And I think I am able to sketch the lineaments of a counternarrative that would bring her forward to Hélène Cixous's figuring of the Mother.

Reading against the grain of the text, then, I will suggest that, in the figure of the mother, and in the making of an anthropos, Beauvoir has set down or made visible, perhaps without intent (given her commitment to patriarchal humanism, but then, what is it to teach?), a critique of the very philosophical anthropology of which Derrida accused Sartre twenty years after the publication of *Being and Nothingness* and *The Second Sex*.[16]

In the chapter on "Existential Psychoanalysis," Sartre describes how the mother *does* create the possibility for the child to "exist." This is a much-discussed passage, but I want to quote it as if nothing had been written on it:

On the contrary it is only through another—through the words which the mother uses to designate the child's body—that he [the pronoun makes a difference in the applicability of this conceptual scheme, surely? Although it is not distinguishable in French] learns that his anus is a *hole*. It is therefore the objective nature of the hole perceived in the world which is going to illuminate for him the objective structure and the sense [*sens*]

> to the erogenous sensations which were hitherto limited to merely "ex-
> isting." In itself then the *hole* is the symbol of a mode of being which
> existential psychoanalysis must elucidate. . . . Thus to plug up a hole
> means originally to make a sacrifice of my body in order that the plenitude
> of being may exist; that is, to subject the passion of the for-itself so as
> to shape, to perfect, and to preserve the totality of the in-itself. (BN 781)

In order to frame Beauvoir's critique, I will quote a passage from the
conclusion to *Being and Nothingness*. This passage is in effect introduced
by the last sentence of "Existential Psychoanalysis": "Man is a useless passion."

"'There is' being," Sartre writes, "because the for-itself is such that
there should be being. The character of the *phenomenon* comes to being by
[way of] the for-itself" (BN 788). It is by way of a reading of the Heideggerian sentence *Es gibt Sein* (there is being), that Derrida introduces the
question of the being's prior access to the proper through sexual difference.
Es gibt Sein is guarded by the property or definitive characteristic of different languages. If you translate that German sentence into literal English,
It gives Being, the gift of Being becomes in German a *Gift* or poison. By
such ruses Derrida tries to protect the status of a sentence that can only mark
a limit by betraying it. Sartre has no such problem. He treats the "to have"
of the literal French translation *il y a* (it there has) as a verb and declines
it, and ignores the other implications of the linguistic specificity of this apparently generalizable sentence. What is it to learn?

Sartre can thus rewrite the ontico-ontological difference (what is most
intimate is also inaccessible, the lesson on my first page) in the following
way: "the phenomenon of the in-itself is an abstraction without consciousness but its *being* is not an abstraction" (BN 791). Let us proceed to examine
how, in the figure of the mother and child Simone de Beauvoir writes this
difference philosophically into the name of woman. This reduced or pared-
down structural picture of the mother, shorn of heterosexual affect, can take
on board gay parenting, or mothering by the gendered subaltern.

It is possible to read Beauvoir's description of the female body in gestation as exactly not biologism. The pregnant body here is species-life rather
than species-being, to follow Marx's famous distinction in the *Economic
and Philosophical Manuscripts*.[17] It is the site of the wholly other, rather
than the man-consolidating other that woman is supposed to be. This is where
"the whole of nature . . . is woman's *body without organs*."[18] There are
no proper names here. To read this as bio-*logy* is abreactive, for that assumes that someone reads where being is nature.[19] A bio-*logized* reading
makes this mode—if mode it can be called—merely intuitively inaccessible.
It then becomes a space before access to the properness of the species-being
of each female subject, where she is proper to herself; thus prepropriation:

"For the great difficulty is to enclose within the given frames an existence as mysterious as that of animals, turbulent and disordered like natural forces, yet human" (SS 575).

Cixous and Irigaray, in their different ways, will be concerned with an *ethics* of sexual difference. And it is in the domain of the "ethical," pointed at in the last section of *Being and Nothingness,* that Beauvoir's consideration of child *rearing* must be placed.

Here is Sartre: "Ontology allows us to catch a glimpse of what will be an ethics which will assume its responsibilities in the face of a *human reality in situation*" (BN 781; my emphasis). And then come the final questions, proved to be merely rhetorical by subsequent work:

> Is it a question of bad faith or of another fundamental attitude? And can one *live* this new aspect of being? In particular, will freedom by taking itself for an end escape all *situation?* Or on the contrary, will it remain situated? Or will it situate itself so much the more precisely and the more individually as it projects itself further in anguish as freedom on condition and accepts more fully its responsibility as an existent by whom the world comes into being? All these questions . . . can find their reply only on moral terrain. We shall devote to them a future work. (BN 798)

I have emphasized the words "human reality in situation." Derrida's strongest critique of Sartre's philosophical anthropology is contained in his rejection of Sartre's translation of *Dasein*—a catachresis to name being where it is so intimate that it is inaccessible—as "human reality." It is possible to read Beauvoir's Mother as figuring forth the fundamental difference—between proximity and accessibility to knowing—that marks *Dasein*. "Human reality in situation" stages this difference in the it-gives-being of birth.

Here the binary opposition between the "philosophical" and the "empirical" is on its way to being undone. One can read here the ontico-ontological difference being redone into the difference between species-life and species-being, as well as the scenario of mothers forever deferred in their children rather than fathers preserved in them.[20]

Here is also the assumption of care in a situation where situating oneself is not allowed. This is the "other fundamental attitude" that Sartre cannot quite imagine. It is not just another way of living, as species-being, as it were. Let us not forget that Beauvoir sees the Mother as a situation. The following passage writes the Mother as the situation that cannot situate itself but must take responsibility—the risk of a relationship in view of the impossibility of relating—*un rapport en vue de rapport sans rapport:*

> The child brings joy only to the woman capable of disinterestedly desiring without reflexion [*retour sur soi*] the happiness of another, who seeks to

exceed [*dépasser*] her own existence. To be sure, the child is an enterprise which one can validly take up [*se destiner*]; but it does not represent a ready-made justification more than any other project; and it must be willed for itself [*voulue pour elle-même*]. (SS 583)

Again,

the child does not snatch her from [*l'arrache*] her immanence. . . . [S]he can only ever create an actual situation [*situation de fait*] whose exceeding belongs to the liberty of the child alone [*appartient à la seule liberté de l'enfant de dépasser*]. (SS 585)

I have substituted "exceeding" for Parshley's misleading translation of *dépassement* as "transcendence." I find in this and comparable passages of Beauvoir the description of what Sartre calls the acceptance of "responsibility as an existent by whom the world comes into being" in a men-only universe. I must insist that, in Beauvoir's plotting, the line between philosophical and empirical begins to waver. And again, this acceptance of responsibility is radically differed-and-deferred between mother and child, rather than confined internally to men defined as self-contained beings-for-itself. (I can suggest that it is this possibility of the affirmative feminization of human ontology that Irigaray will see refracted into the thinking of women as "the envelope.")

Again, Beauvoir captures the critical potential of existentialism in the discontinuous figuration of gestation-birthing-rearing. "It is [the] perpetual failure," writes Sartre, "of the integration of the *en-soi* and *pour-soi* which explains at once the relative indissolubility of the in-itself and of the for-itself and their relative independence" (BN 792). In Beauvoir, the in-itself "is" woman in nature's laws—gestation—species-life, and the for-itself "is" the rearing mother and the child as adult.

Sartre appropriates this relative independence into the thematics of anguish and freedom: the worldly staging of the difference entailed by moral responsibility without moral authority. Beauvoir acknowledges it as the real failure that is the name of history. Convention, as I indicated at the beginning of this essay, *must* allow us to assume alterity to be another self, even the convention of mothering for the expectant mother: "justified by the presence in her womb of an other, she rejoices finally and fully in being herself." Beauvoir does not animate this with *en-soi/pour-soi* talk. But mark the final words in the French, especially the use of *jouir:* "Justifiée par la présence dans son sein d'un autre, elle jouit enfin pleinement d'être soi-même" (SS 314).

Quite apart from the restraining of the *jouissance* of the woman into the inauguration of reproduction, the inscription of the body into the species in gestation is a rupture with any model of intersubjectivity, a guardian at its margin.[21] In spite of anything the antichoice lobby might say, the pregnant mother cannot decide to desire *this* child (the "propriated" child, the child as for-itself). Beauvoir, concentrating on the existentialist project, accepts birthing as a severing from gestation into the nurturing of an intending subject, a violent origin of the possibility of intentionality. (Margaret Atwood thus questions the phrases "*giving* birth," "*delivering* a baby," and suggests that the *mother*—I presume as mother *of* daughter or son—is delivered at birth.)[22]

If, however, we turn to what is pre-originary in this scheme, the time of gestation *for* the mother, it is a peculiarly contaminated exile from herself as subject. It cannot be claimed as a pure rupture, for the physical "events" marking the progress of gestation must also be read as the body's textuality that is the daily weave of human beings pregnant with nothing but their own death. (I think Elaine Marks judges Beauvoir too harshly here by reading death with the full force of humanist passion).[23] Gestation is thus inscribed into this larger economy of death. Indeed, it undoes the binary opposition of life and death. I must consign to chance your understanding that I am saying nothing against or indeed about the feelings of joy, fulfillment, or continuity attending pregnancy and gestation. And, indeed, sonar pictures can even create a strongly anthropomorphic sense of the fetus which has become a bargaining point for the opposition in the debate about reproductive rights. In the certainty, or uncertainty, then, of not being misunderstood in that particular way I will say further, that, within this limited indeterminacy, there is also an intimation (necessarily effaced as it is disclosed) of radical exile, the only other reminder of which is the mysterious anonymity of the earth as temporary dwelling place, the anonymity of the self when newborn.

To sum up what I have said in the last few pages: Derrida criticized Sartre for anthropologizing the Heideggerian *Dasein* (and Heidegger for ignoring the question of woman as "before propriation," although the latter critique was later partially recovered in a discussion of *Geschlecht*).[24] If read with sympathy, though against the grain, Beauvoir's figure of the Mother provides an asymmetrical site of passage with the possibility of a strong framing of propriation that has been protected from a philosophical anthropology yet not preserved in transcendental talk.

4. Rights Talk

It is not possible to leave this topic without some consideration of its implication for the reproductive rights debate. Before I turn to Cixous, Hélie-Lucas, and Irigaray, then, I will engage in such a consideration briefly. I am of course aware that this issue has been part of feminist ethical philosophy for some time now. My remarks cannot possibly take into account the complexity of the legal and ethical problems here.

The reproductive rights debate can only begin after the body has been written into the normative and privative discourse of a law predicated on agency. The prepropriative description of gestation and the figure of the Mother as a site of passage *for* the Mother *from* species-life to the project of the child as species-being (rigorously to be distinguished from the patriarchal view of the person of the mother as a passageway for the child) is irreducible to that discourse. The question of agency—which in this view is distinct from the question of the subject—cannot be decided with reference to prepropriation. Indeed, the prepropriative cannot be a referent. It is rather the undecidable in view of which all decisions *must* be risked. If the prepropriative is figured into the discourse of decision, it is possible to use it to support a woman's right over her body, for it could be argued that the fetus is part of the species-life of the body. But, and this is why it remains undecidable, it would also be possible to use it against that position—for, *in the specific case of childbearing,* the question of the possibility of the origin of intention in the fetus is philosophically inaccessible to the mother, as indeed to anyone else, and therefore, for the opposition, might well have an affirmative answer. Therefore the decisions involving agency must be taken on rational grounds. The prepropriative figuration of the mother in species-life serves as a reminder that those grounds cannot be finally grounded and thus stand guard against what is perhaps the necessary possibility of failure written into all the rational abstractions of democracy: the possibility of their use as alibis, to deflect critique.

It is his lack of concern for this last position that allows Richard Rorty to dismiss deconstructive vigilance as a monotonous litany, best ignored in the field of action, a field into which he has chosen to step without much preparation because of his disappointment with philosophy.[25] I am inclined to take Zillah Eisenstein's strategic violations of what she *calls* deconstruction more seriously.[26]

There is an impasse here between rights talk and undecidability. Of course one *prefers* rights talk because of the general inscription of the globe within the culture of the European Enlightenment. Rosalind Petchesky offers a brilliant possibility of recoding here. She orchestrates the rupture between totalizing social programs and the untotalizable by suggesting, in her book *Abortion and Woman's Choice,* that abortion should be shifted from human rights talk to social need talk.[27] Coding within the rational abstraction of the rights of the sovereign subject commits feminism to a totalizing telos. Coding as a social need makes visible who does and who does not merit access to social totality. And here is how, *from within a positivist notion of self,* Petchesky reaches out to articulate the warning against a totalizable future present as a result of a constitutional guarantee for abortion:

To deny that there will always be a residual conflict between this principle—which is the *idea* of concrete individuality, or subjective reality—and that of a social and socially imposed morality of reproduction seems not only naive but dismissive of an important value. For any society, there will remain a *level of individual desire that can never be totally reconciled with social need* without destroying the individual personalities whose "self-realization" is the ultimate object of a social life.[28]

In the very last sentence of her book, she invokes "tension" rather than balance, and writes, "this very tension can be, for feminism—and through feminism, socialism—a source of political validity."

Since we are within the discourse of "French" philosophy, and for no other reason, I should mention that Derrida has recently articulated the difference between undecidability and rights talk as the *différance* between justice and the Law.[29] It is in this sense that rights talk can only be grounded in presuppositions that ignore the prepropriative, actively as well as passively. The possibility of such an ignoring/ignorance (task or event) is not derived from any accessible model of faithfulness.[30]

I should, however, also mention that any discussion of abortion outside of the entire network of the necessarily normative and privative discourse of rights talk operates on more situational principles that will engage (disclose/efface) the prepropriative as figure, in different ways. Simone de Beauvoir's own words on the *affective* coding of abortion in the French society of the time must be read with this in mind. In quite another context, the sharp break between the arena of abortion and sterilization issues and the well-organized movement against reproductive engineering in some Third World countries with well-developed women's activist organizations are pertinent examples here.[31]

5. Hélène Cixous. Giving the Mother

Back now to the mysterious thickets of French feminist philosophy. I want to touch briefly upon Hélène Cixous's use of the figure of the mother and her staging of plurality. If Simone de Beauvoir belongs basically to the language of the very Enlightenment that she questions, Cixous belongs to that stream of French writing announced as having happened by Stéphane Mallarmé in the 1880s: *on a touché au vers*—   She calls, therefore, for a somewhat different style of reading.

She calls for a different style of reading also because she writes as a writer, not as a philosopher, although she is deeply marked by her own version of the philosophies of writing and of the Other. We must attend more closely to the detail of her style as we attempt to explain her positions.

I want to look at the moment of the mother and of plurality in the famous essay, written many years ago, "The Laugh of the Medusa."[32] This essay falls into two modes of address—one where, addressing one woman intimately as *"tu,"* Cixous gives advice about writing and publishing on the then current French scene. By using the second-person *style indirect libre,* Cixous characterizes this person fairly accurately. The bit about mothering is still in the *"tu-toi"* form, but it seems to dissolve the lineaments of the character of the addressee. By the time the talk moves on to the historical plurality of woman, the mode of "address," if one can even use such a term for this part of the essay, is the implicit and impersonal one of expository prose. Let us consider the two moments without ignoring their mode of presentation.

Whatever Cixous's intent in *arranging* the modes of address in her essay in quite this way, here is a *reading* of it. Strictly speaking, an ethical relationship with the Other entails universalizing the singular. And there is no room for an ethico-theological I-thou in the space where the mother is in species-life rather than species-being, as the prepropriative figure. In the first part of the I-thou situation of "The Laugh of the Medusa," by contrast, it is the extreme specificity of the situation—the Parisian publishing scene in the mid-1970s—that will not allow a transposition into an ethical exchange.

But what of the moment when the Parisian literary scene unobtrusively fades out and, although the *"tu"* is retained, the usefulness of the addressee's characterization is also dissolved by an entry into a strange injunction?

"It is necessary and sufficient," Cixous writes first, "that the best be given to woman by another woman for her to be able to love herself and return in love the body that was 'born' to her." (LM 252). And "Mother" is the name of this "giving." Then she moves to the injunction: "You [*toi*], if you wish, touch me, caress me, give me you the living no-name, even me as myself." I would like to suggest that by thus framing the moment, Cixous releases the peculiar threshold of an ethical "I-thou" which has nothing to do with the theological. Such devices of foregrounding are not uncommon in practice that is recognizably "literary" and is routinely noticed in minimally efficient literary criticism. By releasing this threshold, Cixous might be bringing into the feminine familiar that space described by Heidegger as a space of prior interrogation, "a vague average understanding of Being . . . [which] up close, we cannot grasp at all."[33]

We know that Derrida has reread such passages as the effaced/disclosed trace (not a past present), and the differed/deferred end (not a future present), inscribing what we must stage as our present, here and now, here only insofar as it is also away, elsewhere. Cixous's genius is to take these ways of thinking and straining to turn them into something doable. I think she is helped in this by her somewhat unexamined belief in the power of poetry and art in general which she has never lost. To be sure, in the hands of essentialist enthusiasm, this doability can turn into precious posturing.

But, then, in the hands of rationalist convictions, attempts to bring the aesthetic into the *Lebenswelt* can lead to interminable systems talk bent on the simple task of proving that the aesthetic is coherent. And, in the grip of *anti*-essentialist enthusiasm, the Derridean maneuvers can *also* turn into precious posturing. I think it is in this spirit that Cixous has recently written: "I believe the text should establish an ethical relation to reality as well as textual practice."[34] The task here is not to suspend reading until such a time as a text is out of quarantine.

All precautions taken, then, we can say that Cixous is staging the thought that, even as we are determined in all kinds of other ways—academic, philosopher, feminist, black, homeowner, menstruating woman, for example— we *are* also *always* in the peculiar being-determination that sustains these. She is staging that dimension in the name of the place of mother-and-child. This is not really a space accessible to political determinations, or to specific determinations of mothering in specific cultural formations. Following a chronological notion of human psychobiography, this is where, at the same *time* as we mature into adulthood and responsibility, we continue to exist in a peculiar being-determination to which the name "child" can be lent:

> The relation to the "mother," in terms of intense pleasure and violence,
> is curtailed no more than the relation to childhood (the child that she was,
> that she is, that she makes, remakes, undoes, there at the point where,
> the same she mothers herself).[35]

I have argued at length elsewhere that this sort of post-structuralist nominalism brings with it the burden of "paleonymy," imposed by the fact that the name belongs to the imbrication of a so-called empirical-historical account which is the condition and effect of the role of the word in the history of the language.[36] Cixous makes a selective use of the paleonymy of the name "mother," comparable to Derrida's selective use of the paleonymy of words such as "writing" or "justice." *Not* the narrow sense: "Listen to me, it is not the overbearing clutchy 'mother' but, rather, it is, touching you, the equivoice that affects you" (LM 252).

It is almost as if Beauvoir's female child is beginning to take responsibility toward the situation of the mother.

Notice that determinative essentialisms become irrelevant here. No matter if I have no children and therefore no experience of "giving the mother to the other woman." It is a general sense of mothering—its minimal definitive and presupposed cultural predication as self*less* love, re-inscribed in Beauvoir as the species-other passing into loved subject—that is supposedly also a defining characteristic of woman in the narrow sense—that Cixous is turning into a relationship with the other woman—who is precisely not a child of my body. If read seriously, this must be rigorously distinguished from being motherly or maternal, matronizing, et cetera. The other woman's age is not specified, only that she is other. As a formulation, this is rather better than what I wrote a couple of years ago:

> Incanting to ourselves all the perils of transforming a "name" to a refer-
> ent—making a catechism, in other words, of catachresis—let us none the
> less name (as) "woman" that disenfranchised woman whom we strictly,
> historically, geo-politically, *cannot imagine* as literal referent.[37]

Try to think of what Cixous is actually asking you to do and you will begin to see what an amazing formulation of responsibility this is, especially since the dimension is inaccessible and therefore the responsibility is effortful. If you want to reduce to conceptual logic some of the more obviously metaphoric passages, there are handles, such as "woman does not defend herself against these unknown women whom she's surprised at becoming, pleasuring [*jouissant*] in this gift of alterability" (LM 258). We must be able to read this "present tense" in that nondimensional verbal mode of which I spoke earlier: not a future present but a persistent effortfulness that makes a "present." This practice "does and will take place in areas other than those subordinated to philosophico-theoretical domination." Up close, we cannot grasp it at all. The undecidable in view of which decisions *must* be risked.

6. Marie-Aimée Hélie-Lucas. Flash

Is this of any use to Hélie-Lucas? Yes, because she lives in a classed space of power as well.

Should Hélie-Lucas listen to Hélène Cixous? Not necessarily. But I don't know how many of you can imagine the extraordinary cultural politics of asking Hélie-Lucas to listen only to purely "traditional" Algerian things. Remember, Hélie-Lucas is not a member of an Algerian minority in the United States. In decolonization, she has to negotiate actively with the trace of the French until it becomes unrecognizable, with Hélène Cixous, or indeed with much worse, especially when unacknowledged. And Cixous's text has put a limit to its *own* power in the field of negotiation. The ethical field of the I-thou requires that the I earn the right to *tutoyer* the interlocutor. Indeed, that felicitous *tu-toi*-ing is itself a case of what she is speaking of: "Everything will be changed once woman gives woman to the other woman" (LM 260). In "Laugh of the Medusa," Cixous earns the right by narrowing the entry—a published feminist writer speaking to a novice woman writer upon the Parisian scene of writing.

In the heritage of imperialism, one of the peculiar by-products is the emancipated woman *in* the decolonized nation, not her sister in metropolitan space, whom we know much better. However unwilling she may be to acknowledge this, part of her historical burden is to be in a situation of *tu-toi*-ing with the radical feminist in the metropolis. If she wants to turn away from this, to learn to "give woman to *the other woman*" in her own nation-state is certainly a way, for it is by no means certain that, by virtue of organizational and social work alone, she is in touch with the Algerian gendered subaltern in the inaccessible I-thou.[38]

At any rate, my agenda is not to recommend Hélène Cixous to Marie-Aimée Hélie-Lucas or to prescribe Hélène Cixous for Marie-Aimée Hélie-Lucas, but in a sense to judge Hélène Cixous's text to see if it can live in Hélie-Lucas's world, which is not the grass-roots world of Algeria. This is a particularly interesting challenge because, like Derrida, Cixous is, in the strictest sense, a Creole, a Frenchwoman born and raised in early childhood in Oran in the days before the Revolution.[39] It is in that spirit that I have lingered on this moment in "The Laugh of the Medusa." I want now to pass on to the thought of plurality, which is lodged in one of the islands of comparatively expository prose coming immediately after the passage I have read.

7. Back to Cixous. Subject for History

> As subject for history [*sujet à l'histoire*], woman always occurs simultaneously in several places. Woman un-thinks or squanders the unifying, ordering history that homogenizes and channels forces, herding contradictions into the practice of a single battlefield. In woman, the history of all women blends together with her personal history, national and international history. *As a fighter,* woman enlists [*fait corps*] in all liberations. She must be far-sighted. Not blow for blow. She foresees that her liberation will do more than modify relations of force or toss the ball over to the other camp; she will bring about a mutation in human relations, in thought, in all practices: it is not only the question of a class struggle, which she sweeps along in fact into a much vaster movement. Not that in order to be a woman-in-struggle(s) one must leave the class struggle or deny it; but one must open it up, split it, push it, fill it with the fundamental struggle so as to prevent the class struggle, or any other struggle for the liberation of a class or people, from operating as an agent of repression, pretext for postponing the inevitable, the staggering alteration in relations of force and in the production of individualities. (LM 252–253)

In her exchange with Catherine Clément, later published as *La Jeune née,* Cixous shows herself to be somewhat ethereal in her take on "hard" politics.[40] But perhaps Catherine Clément is not her best interlocutor. Here, under the surface of an often-read passage, some surprising points are being made. Certain seeming generalizations are being advanced about woman's role as subject *for* history. Remember the ordinary-language double charge of the word "histoire" in French. It is almost as if Cixous is speaking of a narrativization or figuration of woman that would be appropriate *for* this new story. This is not, in other words, an account of woman as world-historical subject or, in a humbler vein, subject *of* history.

The "is," "will," "must" of the passage are articulated within *this* framework. Thus these straightforward lines do not necessarily mark a forgetfulness of the deconstructive lesson of timing that Cixous seems to know elsewhere. The general point is that the appropriate subject *for* such a new story is the one that makes visible all the plural arenas that are suppressed when history is written with the representative man as its subject. This temporality operates within the task of producing a subject *for* a story—at the other end from ethical intimacy. Within this peculiar time, then, woman as subject *for* history will not merely modify but mutate and alter relations of force. This is not a liberatory promise but a feminist alliance with relevant bits in Foucault/Derrida and, later, Lyotard's position, a development out of Nietzsche via Heidegger which freezes and takes a distance from Marxism. If the manifold, irreducibly plural, and incessantly shifting strategic exclusions required by a coherent systematic account of history, are incessantly attended to, power/knowledge (*pouvour/savoir*) relations are thoroughly displaced and productively disrupted, framing in undecidability the sure ground of decision. This feminism is a persistent critique of history.

Cixous finesses the question of agency delicately. Not for her the Derridean unfleshed figuration/nomination, but rather the task of conceiving an agent of pluralization, alteration. This is unusual in metropolitan feminism, yet may be a requirement in decolonized feminism. Thus Cixous *opposes* single-issue feminism. *If* and *when* woman as subject *for* storying or history is conceived as militant, she must be faithful to the subversive logic or graphic of plurality and thus become part of the body of all struggles (*faire corps* in French is more charged, especially in military metaphors, than the English "integrate").[41] Like most French radicals, Cixous sees the class struggle as the only *struggle* that operates out of a coherent narrative.[42] Therefore it presupposes exclusions and invites supplementation by repression. Yet the fundamental struggle as such is not woman's struggle alone. It is to split, open, and fill all generalized, unified struggles with plurality. Within the framing of the putting together of a subject for a new story, the status of the last phrase "production of individualities" is rhetorically charged. An "individuality" here is not merely an exclusionist repressive construction, but a necessary underived fiction, the springboard for a decision in the face of radical undecidability, affirmative deconstruction performed in the way of a writer rather than a philosopher.

Is Cixous able to become part of the body of the struggle for national liberation, or against imperialism? That struggle too is pluralized—traveling up and down, and in a discontinuous way—from the familiar to the aggregative and out, from the epistemic to the legal and away. The way in which Cixous attaches to this moving base is, inevitably, interpretable. When she writes her Indian and Indonesian plays, her take on the complexity and hybridity of so-called postcolonial nations is shaky. Her work with the *Theater of the Sun* can unfortunately be seen as perpetuating a kind of inspired, too-admiring ethnography.[43] If one understands the serviceability of underived fictions, one is obliged to know more intimately the contaminated fictions of the empirical, and for this we must turn to Marie-Aimée Hélie-Lucas.

8. Marie-Aimée Hélie-Lucas

As I have often insisted, deconstructive subversion when affirmed in the political sphere can perhaps find its best theater outside of the Atlantic tradition. With all the reservation that I have already stated, it is still to be noted that the argument from plurality becomes something different in the hands of Marie-Aimée Hélie-Lucas.

Her statement engages two arenas of generalization—the first a national liberation movement that is also a revolution in the strictest sense of the word—the establishment of a "more progressive" mode of production through armed struggle; and the second the coding of gender difference. The second arena is also the field of play of two sets of normative and privative discourses—the extended French Law on personal status under French rule, the Islamic Code under Algerian.

I have written elsewhere about the historical discursive spaces of the possible socialization of the two great monotheisms: the Judaeo-Christian and the Islamic.[44] Hélie-Lucas does not concern herself with that problem of choice here. She comments rather on the repressive logic of a race and class struggle not open to plurality. She treats the women monumentalized in the earlier struggle for decolonization with sympathy but also instrumentally, as do other Algerian postrevolutionary feminist women: "Usually any kind of demonstration is just crushed, but this time we had in the front line six women who had been condemned to death under the French, so the police didn't beat them" (BG 4).

Cixous's register can be roughly described as the European literary romantic, deployed to release the intimate-ethical as well as the fictive-historical in a woman-defined field. This register has been as often used to question as to supplement the more recognizable, reasonable discourse of philosophy. The relationship between Cixous's mother and plurality and Beauvoir's mother and passage can be plotted on this circuit as well. By contrast, Hélie-Lucas's register is postcolonial where the nation cannot be taken for granted. Here is her tabulation of a repressive homogenization:

(It is never, has never been the right moment [to protest . . . in the name of women's interests and rights]: not during the liberation struggle against

colonialism, because all forces should be mobilised against the principal
enemy: French colonialism; not after Independence, because all forces
should be mobilised to build up the devastated country; not now that racist
imperialistic Western governments are attacking Islam and the Third World,
etc.). Defending women's rights "now" (this "now" being ANY historical
moment) is always a betrayal—of the people, of the nation, of the revolution, of Islam, of national identity, of cultural roots, of the Third World
. . . according to the terminologies in use *hic et nunc*. . . . (HL 13)

What Hélie-Lucas is speaking of is, clearly, the *postponement* of the
production of individualities. "There is a constant ideological confusion,"
she reminds us, "between religion, culture and nationality" (HL 15). But if
Cixous's individuality is short of the "real individual" because it is posited
in the possibility of fiction, Hélie-Lucas's is beyond the "real individual"
because posited *as* the possibility of collectivity. Each should presuppose
the other. When Cixous imagines collectivity, Hélie-Lucas must thicken it.
When Hélie-Lucas naturalizes individuality, Cixous can stand as a warning.
The enabling violation of imperialism laid the line for a woman's alliance
in decolonization. Hélie-Lucas can only ever animate that line with the implicit metaphor of sisterhood. Cixous's impossible dimension of giving woman
to the other woman can split up and fill that thought of sisterhood so that
it does not become the repressive hegemony of the old colonial subject. To
imagine that Hélie-Lucas's distance from the subaltern Algerian woman is
any less than Cixous's from the scared novice writer or Beauvoir's from the
French peasant or working class unmarried mother in need of abortion is to
decide to forget the plurality of the Third World. From within decolonized
space, Hélie-Lucas productively uses her specific subject-production and calls
out to women around the world: "We should link our struggles from one
country to the other for reasons of *ethics*. . . . We have everything to gain
in being truly internationalist" (HL 14).

The word "true" in truly internationalist can be read as an affirmative
"misuse," a wrenching away from its proper meaning. The Oxford Dictionary provides this among the important meanings of "catachresis." One
of the offshoots of the deconstructive view of language is the acknowledgment that the *political* use of words, like the use of words, is irreducibly
catachrestic. Again, the possibility of catachresis is not derived. The task
of a feminist political philosophy is neither to establish the proper meaning
of "true," nor to get caught up in a regressive pattern to show how the proper
meaning always eludes our grasp, nor yet to "ignore" it, as would Rorty,
but to accept the risk of catachresis.

A "true internationalism." The antagonist here is clearly the strained
Marxist ideal of internationalism-after-national-liberation. It is only when
we see that that we can begin further to see that the word being really put

into question here is "nation." Everyone who gets embroiled in the real politics and history of nationalism begins to get the uneasy sense that the nation-state, spring and source of nationalisms, is not altogether a good thing. This is not really an unease for the North Atlantic radical when it comes to the history and development of nationalism in that part of the world. When it comes to the development of national identity in the Third World, it is harder to acknowledge the mysterious anonymity of space, to acknowledge that all nationalism is, in the last instance, a mere inscription on the earth's body.[45] Yet this is where, to use two of the formulas I use most, the persistently critical voice must be raised at the same time as a strategic use of essentialism—in other words this is the crucial scene of the usefulness of catachresis. Hélie-Lucas is using the historical empirical definitive predication of women in exogamous societies—a woman's home is radical exile, fixed by her male owner. A woman's *norm* is a persistent passive critique of the idea of the *miraculating* agency or identity produced by a home, whose rational aggregative consolidation is the apparatus of the nation, presupposed by the great aggregative teleological system of internationalism. *This* is the telos that Hélie-Lucas shakes up through the *pouvoir-savoir* of the feminine. And this is the perspective that is almost always lacking in North Atlantic calls for female solidarity, whether metropolitan or migrant. This is an internationalism that takes a distance from the project of national identity when it interferes with the production of female individualities. And the *critique* of individualities, not merely individualism, will bring us back to Cixous.

This model of true inter-nationalism is also in an oblique relationship with the diversified Algerian womanspace (the northern, predominantly urban, class-hatched socius, the South predominantly rural, subalternity shared by Arab, Kabyle, Berber women) with all its discontinuous and sometimes contradictory relationships to the culture of Islam and the culture of imperialism, because the model belongs to the organization called Women Living Under Muslim Law.[46] Although the impetus in the organization is clearly against Islamic patriarchy, what it signals by sheer opposition is the (gendered) internationality of Islam, rather different from the (masculinist) demonized image that is projected in the West. This internationality is, on one plane, written in the civil machinery of many different forms and stages of nation-state consolidation, in many different economic and political alignments, stretching from Morocco through Bangladesh to Indonesia: on another plane, this inter-nationalism is not among nations, not *inter* but *antre* whatever is hyper-realized as "nation" in the "real world."[47] And woman/individuality is crucial here. These women persistently and affirmatively deconstruct political theory on the ground, although they are not identical with women on ground level.

9. Luce Irigaray

Earlier I suggested a supplementary and contrastive relationship between the literary-romantic and the recognizably reasonable discourses of Cixous and Beauvoir respectively. By some accounts, the general critique of humanism in France has summoned up a style of philosophizing which would use both. I believe that Luce Irigaray writes more and more in that style. The usual critique of Irigaray, that she is an "essentialist," generally springs from an ignoring of the aggressive role of rhetoricity in her prose. Derrida has framed his remark about writing and woman in the possibility that he is himself acting out the male fetish, *if* Freud were right.[48] Those precautions taken, *if* Derrida were right, the writing of the woman called Luce Irigaray is written like writing and should be read that way, although the other way of reading, involving the history of the language, should also be taken into account.

Any consideration of Irigaray as a feminist philosopher should consider her extended reading of Plato in "Plato's *Hystera*."[49] Here I will point at its rhetorical conduct in passing.

Like Derrida, Irigaray as philosopher defines herself as critic within the enclosure of Western metaphysics. Any argument about how deconstructively she in-habits this enclosure should look at the rhetorical detailing of the timing of "Plato's *Hystera*." Here let me simply quote the passage that might be read as the name of the mother being used to homogenize multiplicity into intelligibility. Please remember that this comes toward the end of a spectacular reading of, among other texts, *Republic* V, that I *cannot* summarize:

> The dilemmas of Plato's *hystera* will . . . have concealed the fact that there is no common measure with the unrepresentable *hystera protera,* [think of the virtuoso play of use and mention in this catachrestic, because pluralized, invocation of, of all things, the *rhetorical* figure of *hysteron proteron,* putting last things first, here] the path that might lead back to it and the diaphragm that controls the cavity opening . . . the mother.[50]

Then a section break. Then: "The confused and changing multiplicity of the other thus begins to resolve itself into a system of intelligible relationships." And so on.

In the lectures collected under the general title "Ethics of Sexual Difference," the question of the maternal-feminine (mistranslated mother-woman) is reopened. I will read you two passages to outline cryptically how, from within the problematic that Beauvoir and Cixous can be made to inhabit, Irigaray wants to move to a final dialogue with the passive-masculinist philosopher Emmanuel Levinas in "The Fecundity of the Caress," the last piece in the book.[51]

The maternal-feminine is a limit, an envelope, the other place consolidated into *her* norm. The maternal-feminine must incessantly envelop herself twice, as mother and woman. Yet the *ethical* question for woman is played out in the realms of nudity and a perverse self-decoration through envelopes. Let me cite the text.

> If, traditionally, in the role of mother, woman represents *place* for man [Sartre's silence about the French version of *Es gibt Sein—il y a* (it has *there*)—comes to mind], the limit signifies that she becomes a *thing*, undergoing resultant mutations from one historical period to another. She finds herself caged as a thing. Moreover, the maternal-feminine is also used as *envelope* in terms of which man limits things. *The relationship between the envelope and things* constitutes . . . the aporia of Aristotelianism and the philosophical systems which are derived from it. . . . The mother woman remains the *place separated from "its" place*, deprived of "its" place she ceaselessly is or becomes the place for the other who cannot separate himself from it. . . . She would have to re-envelop herself by herself, and do so at least twice: as a woman and as a mother. This would entail a modification in the entire economy of space-time. In the mean time, this ethical question is played out in the realms of *nudity* and *perversity*. Woman is to be nude, since she cannot be situated in her place. She attempts to envelop herself in clothes, make-up and jewelry. She cannot use the envelope that she is, and so must create artificial ones.[52]

Taking a distance from the entire problematic of claiming a proper place within this tradition, Irigaray thinks sexual difference as the separation from the *absolutely* other. Commenting on Descartes's passage on wonder, she writes:

> Who or what the other is, I never know. But this unknowable other is that which differs sexually from me. This feeling of wonder, surprise and astonishment in the face of the unknowable ought to be returned to its proper place: the realm of sexual difference. (SD 124)

This is no separatist politics, but a full-blown plan for an ethics where sexual difference, far from being located in a decisive biological fact, is posited as the undecidable in the face of which the now displaced "normal" must risk ethico-political decisions. An ethical position must entail universalization of the singular. One can wish not to be excluded from the universal. But if there is one universal, it cannot be inclusive of difference. We must therefore take the risk of positing two universals, one radically other to the other in one crucial respect. If Derrida had dared to think of minimal idealization, Irigaray dares minimal alterity. Each is a same-sexed ethical universal, operating in a social cooperation that must conventionally assume others to be collectivities of othered selves. This is to provide ingredients for an ethical base to rewrite gendering in the social sphere.

For Irigaray, sexual *difference* is the limit to ethics. As in Derrida's essay on Levinas, so also for her, there can be no ethics of ethics.[53] But for her that impossibility is determined (an "impossible determination," for alterity cannot determine) by the alterity of sexual difference. Thus, if coded within reproductive ethics, the fecund caress can become indistinguishable from violence. This is the supplement to Cixous's imagination of the alteration of fields of force in the family.

For Levinas the erotic accedes neither to the ethical nor to signification. In Beauvoir, it is in gestation that the mother/child in species-life is prepropriative, but intended, in so far as the Mother is a "situation," toward the rupture of the proper in species-being: mother *and* child. Since, as we shall see, "fecundity" for Levinas is the "transubstantiation" of paternity, it is in the male-dominant heterosexual embrace that he locates the issueless prepropriative which,

> prior to the manifestation of attributes . . . qualifies alterity itself. . . . [In it] *the essentially hidden throws itself toward the light, without becoming signification.* . . . The relationship established between lovers in voluptuosity, fundamentally refractory to universalization, is the very contrary of the social relation. . . . Only the being that has the frankness of the face can be "discovered" in the non-signifyingness of the wanton.[54]

However subtle Levinas's thought of the impossible "subject"-ship of ethics in general, upon the heterosexist erotic scene, the subject-ship of ethics is certainly male. I have been speaking of the "empirical" narrative with which these catachrestic morphologies secure themselves. I intend no disrespect to the grandeur of Levinas's thought when I say that the empirical scene of sexual congress behind Levinas's "Phenomenology of Eros" is almost comically patriarchal, so generally so that the bourgeois male colonial subject from various parts of the world can be fitted into the slot of "the lover." The "forever inviolate virginity of the feminine," "frail and animal-like," is completely excluded from the public sphere: "It excludes the third party . . . [and is] the supremely non-public" (TI 258, 263, 265). Being prior to attribution, this scene is supposedly before the emergence of value. Yet value drips from words such as "profanation," "indecency," "obscenity," "interdiction," "indiscretion," "exhibitionism," ubiquitously part of the descriptive vocabulary of the phenomenology of eros. As for "fecundity," it defines the "distinction within identification" (TI 267). Here "the *encounter* with the Other [not *Autre* but *Autrui*—"all around?"] as feminine is required" so that the father's "*relation* with the future [may be trans-formed] into a *power* of the subject" (TI 267, emphases mine).

In this patriarchal discourse, "equivocation" is not the activation of Cix-ous's delicate "equivoice" of the mother but simply the old-fashioned nasty word describing woman's civil duplicity, her only access to power (over men), her only access to the public sphere, indeed to phenomenality itself, her epiphany:

> Equivocation constitutes the epiphany of the feminine—at the same time interlocutor, collaborator, and master superiorly intelligent, so often dom-inating men in the masculine civilization it [the feminine as master] has entered, and woman having to be treated as woman, according to rules *imprescriptible* by an orderly [*policé*] society. The face, all straightfor-wardness and frankness, in its feminine epiphany dissimulates allusions, innuendos. It laughs under the cloak of its own expression, without lead-ing to any specific meaning, alluding to it in empty space [*en faisant allusion dans le vide*], signaling the less than nothing. (TI 264).

Just as I find it difficult to believe that Hegel's virulent racism is written off (not by Derrida) when we worship at the shrine of the dialectic; so do I find it difficult to take this prurient heterosexist, male-identified ethics seriously.[55] Irigaray is more generous. She undoes Levinas's sexism by de-gendering the active-passive division. The lover is *amant and amante,* the beloved *aimé and aimée.* She does indeed also notice the features of Levi-nas's treatment of the erotic that I mention above: "Infantile and animal, for him? Irresponsible in order to give him back freedom" (FC 240). Iri-garay's rhetoric makes the question apply not only to the invariably male-gendered lover in Levinas's scheme, but to Levinas the philosopher; he makes the invariably female-gendered beloved infantile and animal in order to win back his freedom. Let us read the next few paragraphs with this robust phi-losophical equivocation in mind: "the lover leads her back to the *not yet* of the infant, the *never like that* of the animal—outside human becoming. This gesture perpetrated [*ce geste perpétré*], [he] separates himself to return to his ethical responsibilities" (FC 241); as well as her comment on the sur-reptitious equivocation of the philosopher:

> the seduction of the loved one makes a bridge [*fait pont*] between the Father and the son. . . . In the [female] loved one's fragility and weak-ness the [male] lover loves himself as a [male] loved one without power [*en lesquelles l'amant s'aime comme aimé sans pouvoir*]. (FC 244)

Voluptuousness, in this reading, is irreducibly male, that which "does not know the other. That which seduces itself of her [*d'elle*] in order to return to the abyss and take up ethical seriousness again" (FC 246).

The most noticeable thing about Irigaray's "Fecundity of the Caress" is the practical crispness of its tone. It is obviously a text that assumes that both partners do things, and are not inevitably heterosexual. Again, it is not surprising that, in the world of this text, although the scene of sexuality is prior and exterior to the son or daughter, there is such a thing as pregnancy, the womb, and its ontological inaccessibility to some mother's son and some mother's daughter, as they meet in the fecundity of the caressing hands. Their faces are not the only ethical surfaces. Their hands take part in shaping otherness. And each one reminds the other of that prepropriative site, the impossible origin of the ethical that can only be figured, falsely, as the subject as child-in-mother:

> The fecundity of a love whose gesture or the most elementary gesture remains caress [*dont le geste ou le geste le plus élémentaire demeure caresse*]. . . . The other's hand, these palms with which he approaches me without crossing me [*m'approche sans me traverser*], give me back the borders of my body and call me to the remembrance of the most profound intimacy [of the child-in-the-mother]. Caressing me, he bids me neither to disappear nor to forget, but to rememorate [*rémémorer*] the place where, for me, the most secret life holds itself in reserve. . . . Plunging me back into the maternal entrails [*entrailles*] and, before that conception [*en deça de cette conception*], awakening me to another—amorous—birth. (FC 232)

This is not a past present, this act of rememoration that we are all mothers' children. This is "birth that has never taken place, unless one remains a substitute for the father and the mother. Which signifies a gesture radically non-ethical" (FC 233). If Beauvoir had spoken only of the child as project, and Cixous had only exhorted women to give the mother to the other woman, and Hélie-Lucas had spoken of the female individual in a political rather than a familial collectivity, then Irigaray exhorts lover *and* beloved to give the woman to the other, indeed to rememorate being-in-the-mother as the impossible threshold of ethics, rather than inaugurate it as the Law of the Father. Not all of us are mothers, but we have all been children.

What is it that is born in the sexual embrace? The possibility of two spaces, un-universalizable with each other:

> A (time) to come [*à venir*] which is not measured by the surmounting of death but by the call to birth for self and other [*naissance pour soi et l'autre*]. Of which each arranges and rearranges the environment, the body, and the cradle without closing up anything at all of a room, a house, an identity. (FC 232)

For Irigaray the fecund caress gives birth to the (im)possible threshold of the ethical:

[T]he most intimate perception of the flesh escapes every sacrificial substitution. . . . This memory of the flesh as the place of approach is ethical fidelity to incarnation. To destroy it risks suppressing alterity, both God's and the Other's. (FC 256)

Otherwise, "the aporia of a tactility which cannot caress itself and needs the other to touch itself" gives itself the usual alibi: ethics as such. The scene of the caress is in fact porous to the (im)possibility of ethics.

This is not just philosophical or literary talk, but Christian talk, of incarnation. This talk will have to be fleshed out in the future with a consideration of Derrida's current work: *aimer/manger l'autre*—to love/eat the other.[56] Irigaray would restore the (im)possible garden—therefore the threshold of the garden—where woman's sin does not make man's difficult access to knowledge possible: "Not perceptible as profanation. The threshold of the garden, a welcoming cosmic home, remaining open. No guard other than love itself. Innocent of the knowledge of the display and the fall" (FC 244).

Is this a new regulative narrative? Perhaps so. It is hard for me to enter this garden. But can Hélie-Lucas?

In principle, yes. Muslims, Christians, and Jews are all "people of the book," as the recent effort of the *Intersignes* group would show.[57] This attempt to see two different ethical worlds, opened up by the gender divided caress is, I believe, operative in Farhad Mazhar's "To Mistress Khadija," a poem I have translated and quoted elsewhere.[58]

Yet in *Intersignes* I, which deploys the impulse to transfer discourses from one Book to another by correcting the errors of Freud's *Moses and Monotheism* in the text of the life of Muhammad, the one discordant note is struck by Martine Medejel, a Frenchwoman married to a Moroccan who bitterly complains about the loss of her name.[59] And therefore simply redoing the stories will, again, not suffice. If the new Irigaray, revising Levinas, tries to restore a sexual encounter that is the threshold of ethics, it is still true that, in acceding to the agency of the caress, the woman must *violate* the historical narrative—time as sequence, told in numbers—in which she is written:

But there is time [*il y a le temps*]. Too linked [*trop lié*] to numbers, and to what has already been. And how repair, in a second, an evil that has lasted for such a long time? . . . And if others continually meddle with this expectation of alliance [*alliance*], how to maintain a candor that neither cries out for remission nor burdens the lover with the weight [*poids*] of the healing of wounds? (FC 243)

This is a serious question: how indeed? The ethics of sexual difference are persistent and to come. In *all* patriarchal cultures, *all* classes, it is an immense move for the wife to become the fecund agent of the caress. Nawal el-Saadawi recently made the point that one could not raise a collective voice against the war if one could not raise an individual voice against a husband.[60] How much more immense to inscribe the agency of the fecund caress in "woman" collectively, rather than in site- and situation-specific exceptions. In fact, it is not excessive to say that this ethical charge illuminates every immediate practical undertaking for women's liberation. There is even something like an analogy between Saadawi/Irigaray and Hélie-Lucas/Cixous. Saadawi exhorts women to be the sovereign agent of resistance; Irigaray, having learned from (by learning resisting) Freud and the Marx of Ideology and commodity-hieroglyph, reminds us that this future (*à venir*) is not totally under our control, for we spell out the truth there as if our being were a rebus. If Levinas had relegated eros to a short-circuiting of signification, Irigaray shows the couple as being written, *être-écrit*. Here face and hand come together in the structural possibility of writing rather than articulation in a language. Once again that intimate (ontic) space:

> The [female] loved one's face radiates the secret that the lover touches.
> . . . It says [*dit*] the hidden [*le caché*] without exhausting it in a meaning [*un vouloir dire*]. . . . A giving of form to matter [*mise en forme de la matière*] that precedes any articulation in a language. (FC 251)

What have I said so far but that Irigaray has rewritten the fecundity of the caress as the figuring of the prepropriative into an (im)possible appropriation? What is it, indeed, to learn the agency of the caress? Perhaps to keep on unlearning agency in the literal sense and allowing space for the blankness of the *être-écrit(e)*, even in the pores of struggles recognizably "political." To acknowledge that, however urgent the need of time measured in numbers, "the limit to the abyss [or the abyssal; *la limite à l'abîme*] is the unavoidable alterity of the other" (FC 246).

The discourse of the clitoris in the mucous of the lips still remains important in Irigaray's work. Trying to think the international from within a metropolized ethnic minority, I had given this discourse a general structural value a decade ago. Much talk, flying, and falling, from known and unknown women, has shown me that that evaluation runs no more than the usual risks of intelligibility. It is just that the generalization of a *bicameral* universal, or even two universals, to provide the impossible differed/deferred grounding of the ethics of sexual difference in the fecund caress seems to respond to the call of the larger critique of humanism with which postcoloniality must negotiate, even as it negotiates daily with the political and cultural legacy of the European Enlightenment.

What of the Irigaray who rereads Plato and Levinas? Can Hélie-Lucas have no use for her?

On the contrary. Here again we revert to the task of decolonizing the mind through negotiating with structures of violence. One cannot be sure that, in a specific cluster of others (such as the readership of this book), with all its attendant insecurities, there will be someone who is in that peculiar subject position—a feminist citizen of a recently decolonized nation concerned with its domestic/international political claims, not merely its ethno-cultural agenda. To such a person I would say—whenever the teleological talk turns into unacknowledged, often travestied, articulations of the Plato of *The Republic* or *Laws;* or, indeed to the rights of the self-consolidating other, Irigaray's readings must be recalled in detail. If such a person—I must assume her without alterity—holds a reproduction of this page, she will know, alas, that such occasions will not be infrequent. But how can I be certain? And what is it to know, or be sure that a knowing has been learned? To theorize the political, to politicize the theoretical, are such vast aggregative asymmetrical undertakings; the hardest lesson is the impossible intimacy of the ethical.

NOTES

1. Chafika Marouf, "Etat de la recherche sur le monde féminin et la famille en Algérie et au Maghreb," in *Femme, famille et société* (Oran: URASC, 1988), p. 5; translation mine.

2. In Joseph N. Smith and William Kerrigan, eds., *Taking Chances: Derrida, Psychoanalysis and Literature* (Baltimore: Johns Hopkins University Press, 1984).

3. Patricia J. Williams, *The Alchemy of Race and Rights* (Cambridge Mass.: Harvard University Press, 1991), p. 8; emphasis mine.

4. Pierre Bourdieu defines it as risk, in somewhat more aggressive language: "It is on condition that they take what is indeed the greatest possible risk, namely that of bringing into question and into danger the philosophical game itself, the game to which their own *existence* as philosophers, or their own participation in the game, is linked, that philosophers can assure for themselves the privilege that they almost always forget to claim, that is to say their freedom in relation to everything that authorizes and justifies them in calling themselves and thinking of themselves as philosophers." "The Philosophical Institution," in Alan Montefiore, ed., *Philosophy in France Today* (Cambridge: Cambridge University Press, 1983), p. 8. I quote this passage in full so that my position is not identified with the position stated in it. For me the line between freedom and uncertainty is itself uncertain.

5. Gayatri Spivak, "Displacement and the Discourse of Woman," in Mark Krupnick, ed., *Displacement: Derrida and After* (Bloomington: Indiana University Press, 1983), pp. 169–95.

6. Gayatri Spivak, "French Feminism In An International Frame," in Gayatri Spivak, *In Other Worlds: Essays in Cultural Politics* (New York: Methuen, 1987), pp. 134–53.

7. Gayatri Spivak, "Feminism and Deconstruction, Again," in Teresa Brennan, ed., *Between Feminism and Psychoanalysis* (London: Methuen, 1989), pp. 206–24.

8. Most recently restated in the headnote to this piece. See also the final section of Gayatri Spivak, "More on Power/Knowledge," in Thomas E. Wartenburg, ed., *Rethinking Power* (Stony Brook: SUNY Press, forthcoming). It is obvious that these positions, logically defined, swirl in the inaccessible intimacy of the everyday, giving hue to being. To fix it in paint is to efface as much as to disclose.

9. Richard Rorty attempts to recode these fruits of historico-economic chance for the North Atlantic as grounds for rewriting universalism (objectivity) as solidarity in, for example, "Solidarity," in Richard Rorty, *Contingency, Irony, and Solidarity* (Cambridge: Cambridge University Press, 1989), pp. 189–98. It is this historical advantage that allows contemporary US imperialism its attempts to consolidate itself in spite of relative economic decline.

10. Marie-Aimée Hélie-Lucas, "Bound and Gagged by the Family Code," in Miranda Davies, ed., *Third World Second Sex: Women's Struggles and National Liberation* (London: Zed Books, 1983), Vol. 2, pp. 3–15. Hereafter cited in text as BG.

11. Jacques Derrida, "My Chances," in *Taking Chances: Derrida, Psychoanalysis and Literature*, pp. 3, 4.

12. Simone de Beauvoir, *The Second Sex*, trans. H. M. Parshley (New York: Vintage Books, 1952), pp. 540–88. Hereafter cited in text as SS.

13. Toril Moi, unpublished manuscript. I am grateful to Professor Moi for letting me see this work. See also Anne Tristan and Annie de Pisan, "Tales from the Women's Movement," and Michèle Le Doeuff, "Women and Philosophy," in Toril Moi, ed., *French Feminist Thought: A Reader* (New York: Basil Blackwell, 1987), pp. 197–221.

14. The reason for retaining this awkward phrase may be found in Gayatri Spivak, "Subaltern Studies: Deconstructing Historiography," in *In Other Worlds*, p. 14. The argument is made in "Woman in Difference: Mahasweta Devi's 'Douloti the Bountiful,'" in *Cultural Critique* (Winter 1989–90), pp. 105–28.

15. This summary most specifically distills Derrida, "The Ear of the Other," in Christie Vance McDonald, trans., *The Ear of the Other: Otobiography, Transference, Translation* (New York: Schocken Books, 1985).

16. Jean-Paul Sartre, *Being and Nothingness*, trans. Hazel E. Barnes (New York: Pocket Books, 1966). Hereafter cited in text as BN. Derrida's critique is in "The Ends of Man," in *Margins of Philosophy*, trans. Alan Bass (Chicago: University of Chicago Press, 1982), pp. 114–17.

17. Karl Marx, *Early Writings*, trans. Rodney Livingstone and Gregor Benton (New York: Vintage-Penguin, 1976), pp. 327–30.

18. *Ibid.*, p. 328.

19. *Ibid.*

20. For Derrida's version of Nietzsche's distinction between the scenes of the father and the mother, see Jacques Derrida, "The Ear of the Other."

21. For an extended discussion of guardians at the margin, see Gayatri Spivak, "Versions of the Margin: J. M. Coetzee's *Foe* reading Defoe's *Crusoe/Roxana*," in Jonathan Arac and Barbara Johnson, eds., *Theory and Its Consequences* (Baltimore: Johns Hopkins University Press, 1990) pp. 154–80.

22. Margaret Atwood, "Giving Birth," in *Dancing Girls* (New York: Simon and Schuster, 1977), pp. 225–40.

23. Elaine Marks, "Feminism's Wake," in *Boundary 2* 12, 2 (Winter 1984), pp. 99–110.

24. Jacques Derrida, "*geschlecht:* différence sexuelle, différence ontologique," in *Psyche* (Paris: Galilée, 1983), pp. 395–414.

25. Richard Rorty, "Private Irony and Liberal Hope," in *Contingency,* pp. 73–95.

26. Zillah Eisenstein, *The Female Body and the Law* (Berkeley: University of California Press, 1988), pp. 6–41.

27. Rosalind Petchesky, *Abortion and Woman's Choice* (London: Verso, 19), pp. 241–276.

28. Rosalind Petchesky, *Abortion,* p. 395.

29. Jacques Derrida, "Force of Law: 'the Mystical Foundation of Authority,'" trans. Mary Quaintance, *Cardozo Law Review,* 11, 5–6 (July/August 1990), p. 963. Reprinted in *Deconstruction and the Possibility of Justice,* ed. Drucilla Cornell, Michel Rosenfeld, and David Gray Carlson (New York and London: Routledge, forthcoming, 1992).

30. This last sentence is by now either familiar to you via Derrida's rather notorious text *Limited, Inc.,* ed. Gerald Graff (2d edition; (Evanston: Northwestern University Press, 1988) p. 96), or it would take too lengthy an exposition. The operative sentence in the Derrida text is, of course, "the possibility of fiction cannot be derived."

31. The work of Farida Akhter is exemplary here. Since she is primarily a field activist rather than a writer, the best I can do is give a reference to her as mentioned in Yayori Matsui, *Women's Asia* (London: Zed Books, 1989), pp. 16–17. She runs *UBINIG* in Dhaka, Bangladesh.

32. Hélène Cixous, "The Laugh of the Medusa," in Elaine Marks and Isabelle de Courtivron, eds., *New French Feminisms: An Anthology* (New York: Schocken Books, 1981), pp. 245–64. Hereafter cited in text as LM. As Verena Conley and others point out, this piece is not representative of the current Cixous (Verena Andermatt Conley, *Hélène Cixous: Writing the Feminine,* expanded ed. (Lincoln: University of Nebraska Press, 1991), pp. xi–xxiii). It is, however, representative of that moment in "French" feminism which has become a flashpoint for feminist intellectuals.

33. Martin Heidegger, *Being and Time,* trans. John Macquarrie and Edward Robinson (New York: Harper, 1962), p. 25.

34. *"Coming to Writing" and other essays*/Helene Cixous; with a foreword by Susan Rubin Suleiman, edited by Deborah Jensen, trans. Sarah Cornell . . . [et al.] Cambridge, Mass.: Harvard University Press, 1991.

35. The word "lent" comes from Foucault's powerful remark that one must be a nominalist when thinking power. In such nominalism, names are "lent" to networks. The word is quite correctly translated "attributed" in *History of Sexuality,* trans. Robert Hurley (New York: Vintage Books, 1980), Vol. 1, p. 93. But I think the literal translation for *prêter* is more apposite here.

36. In Gayatri Spivak, "Poststructuralism, Marginality, Postcoloniality, and Value," in Peter Collier and Helga Geyer-Ryan, eds., *Literary Theory Today* (Cambridge: Polity Press, 1990), p. 242.

37. Gayatri Spivak, "Feminism and Deconstruction, Again," p. 220.

38. There is a peculiar relevancy to this because, in the French that has been dehegemonized by the underclass or rural Algerian, the *vous* ("you" as opposed to "thou") hardly exists, all exchange is in the "thou" or *tu*. It is only half fanciful to say that the language of imperialism loses its power to achieve the ethical distinction outside of the culture of imperialism, in subalternity.

39. It is a mistake, I think, to call Cixous, simply, an "Algerian," as does Conley in her otherwise interesting book (*Cixous*, p. 4); for my argument against such a gesture, see Gayatri Spivak, "Imperialism and Sexual Difference," in *Oxford Literary Review*.

40. Hélène Cixous and Catherine Clément, *The Newly Born Woman*, trans. Betsy Wing (Minneapolis: University of Minnesota Press, 1986).

41. For a discussion of the significance of the French "*corps*," see Jacques Derrida, "Ou commence et comment finit un corps enseignant," in Dominique Grissoni, ed. *Politiques de la philosophie* (Paris: Grasset, 1976), pp. 55–97.

42. For the French intellectuals of 1968, this conviction found strict theoretical focus in the useful idea of Capital as the abstract as such, one of the operative persuppositions of Gilles Deleuze and Felix Guattari, *Anti-Oedipus: Capitalism and Schizophrenia*, trans. Robert Hurley, Mark Seem, and Helen R. Lane (Minneapolis: University of Minnesota Press, 1983).

43. *L'Histoire terrible mais inachevée de Norodom Sihanouk roi de Cambodge* (1985); and *L'Indiade où l'Inde de leurs rêves* (1988): both published by Paris, Théâtre du soleil.

44. Gayatri Spivak, "Reading *The Satanic Verses*," in *Third Text*, 11 (1990), pp. 68–69.

45. The complex and contrastive relationships between Benedict Anderson, *Imagined Communities*, rev. ed. (London: Verso, 1991), Partha Chatterjee, *Nationalist Thought and the Colonial World: A Derivative Discourse?* (London: Zed Books, 1986), and Andrew Parker, ed., *Nationalisms and Sexuality* (New York: Routledge, 1991) are instructive here.

46. For a report on the organization, see Hélie-Lucas, "Women Living Under Muslim Laws," in *South Asia Bulletin*, 10, 1 (1990), p. 73.

47. For *antre*, see Jacques Derrida, "Dissemination," in Barbara Johnson, trans. *Disseminations* (Chicago: University of Chicago Press, 1981), p. 212. I am obliged to report an unverifiable anecdote here, as part of the social textiling of feminism. On a panel on the Gulf War at the 1990 Socialist Scholars' Conference in New York, I had suggested that although secularism was absolutely to be supported in the legal sphere, and the consolidation of theocracies to be opposed in every way, it must also be acknowledged that it is, in former colonies, a class-internalized position, belonging to the very class that had had "free" access to the culture of imperialim; that it was not a *moral* position; and finally that, for precisely these reasons, it could not be effectively used as ethical persuasion against religious violence. In the corridor after the session, a secularist Muslim academic woman based in the US bitterly rebuked me and remarked, "Islam is against women like *me*!" That is precisely the aporia of secularism that I was and am pointing to.

48. Rather: "if the style were (just as the penis would be according to Freud 'the normal prototype of the fetish') the man, writing would be the woman" (Jacques Derrida, *Spurs: Nietzsche's Styles*, trans. Barbara Harlow (Chicago: University of Chicago Press, 1979)), p. 57; translation modifed.

49. Luce Irigaray, "Plato's *Hystera*," in *Speculum of the Other Woman*, tr. Gillian C. Gill, Ithaca: Cornell University Press, 1985, pp. 243–364.

50. Luce Irigaray, "*Hystera*," p. 358.

51. Luce Irigaray, "The Fecundity of the Caress: A Reading of Levinas, *Totality and Infinity section IV, B*, 'The Phenomenology of Eros,'" in *Face to Face With Levinas*, trans. Carolyn Burke, ed. Richard A. Cohen (Albany: SUNY Press, 1986), pp. 231–56; hereafter cited in text as FC.

52. Luce Irigaray, "Sexual Difference," in Toril Moi, ed., *French Feminist Thought: A Reader* (London: Basil Blackwell, 1987), p. 122; hereafter cited as SD.

53. In Derrida, "Violence and Metaphysics: An Essay on the Thought of Emmanuel Levinas," in *Writing and Difference*, tr. Alan Bass (Chicago: University of Chicago Press, 1978), p. 79–153.

54. Emmanuel Levinas, *Totality and Infinity: An Essay on Exteriority*, tr. Alphonso Lingis (Pittsburgh: Duquesne University Press, 1969), p. 256, 264, 261. Hereafter cited in text as TI.

55. See Derrida's treatment of Hegel on the fetish in *Glas*, tr. John P. Leavey, jr. *et. al.* (Lincoln: University of Nebraska Press, 1986), pp. 207ai–211ai and passim. The importance of coming interminably to terms with Heidegger's involvement with National Socialism and Paul de Man's wartime journalism is also important in this context (see Derrida, *Of Spirit*, tr. Geoffrey Bennington and Rachel Bowlby, Chicago: Univ. of Chicago Press, 1989); and "Like the Sound of the Sea Deep Within A Shell: Paul de Man's War," in Werner Hamacher *et al.*, eds., *Responses: On Paul de Man's Wartime Journalism* (Lincoln: Univ. of Nebraska Press, 1989), p. 127–164.) The position is stated most forcefully in "Ear of the Other," pp. 25f.

56. Still in seminar form.

57. For "people of the book," see Mark Shell, "Marranos (Pigs), or from Coexistence to Toleration," *Critical Inquiry* 17, 2 (winter 1991) pp. 306–335. For the effort to transcribe psychoanalysis into Islam, see *Cahiers Intersignes* I, Spring 1990.

58. Spivak, "Reading *The Satanic Verses*," in *Third Text*. 71, 9 (summer 1990), p. 47.

59. Medejel, "L'exil d'un prenom étranger," *Intersignes* I, p. 63–70.

60. Remarks made at Conference on "Decolonizing the Imagination: the New Europe and its Others," Amsterdam, May 6, 1991.

5

Ecce Homo, Ain't (Ar'n't) I a Woman, and Inappropriate/d Others: The Human in a Post-Humanist Landscape

Donna Haraway

I want to focus on the discourses of suffering and dismemberment. I want to stay with the disarticulated bodies of history as figures of possible connection and accountability. Feminist theory proceeds by figuration at just those moments when its own historical narratives are in crisis. Historical narratives are in crisis now, across the political spectrum, around the world. These are the moments when something powerful—and dangerous—is happening. Figuration is about resetting the stage for possible pasts and futures. Figuration is the mode of theory when the more "normal" rhetorics of systematic critical analysis seem only to repeat and sustain our entrapment in the stories of the established disorders. Humanity is a modernist figure; and this humanity has a generic face, a universal shape. Humanity's face has been the face of man. Feminist humanity must have another shape, other gestures; but, I believe, we must have feminist figures of humanity. They cannot be man or woman; they cannot be the human as historical narrative has staged that generic universal. Feminist figures cannot, finally, have a name; they cannot be native. Feminist humanity must, somehow, both resist representation, resist literal figuration, and still erupt in powerful new tropes, new figures of speech, new turns of historical possibility. For this process, at the inflection point of crisis, where all the tropes turn again, we need ecstatic speakers. This essay tells a history of such a speaker who might figure the self-contradictory and necessary condition of a nongeneric humanity.

I want here to set aside the Enlightenment figures of coherent and masterful subjectivity, the bearers of rights, holders of property in the self, legitimate sons with access to language and the power to represent, subjects endowed with inner coherence and rational clarity, the masters of theory, founders of states, and fathers of families, bombs, and scientific theories—in short, Man as we have come to know and love him in the death-of-the-subject critiques. Instead, let us attend to another crucial strand of Western humanism thrown into crisis in the late twentieth century. My focus is the figure of a broken and suffering humanity, signifying—in ambiguity, contradiction, stolen symbolism, and unending chains of noninnocent translation—a possible hope. But also signifying an unending series of mimetic and counterfeit events implicated in the great genocides and holocausts of ancient and modern history. But, it is the very nonoriginality, mimesis, mockery, and brokenness that draw me to this figure and its mutants. This essay is the beginning of a project on figurations that have appeared in an array of internationalist, scientific, and feminist texts, which I wish to examine for their contrasting modernist, postmodernist, and amodernist ways of constructing "the human" after World War II. Here, I begin by reading Jesus and Sojourner Truth as Western trickster figures in a rich, dangerous, old, and constantly renewed tradition of Judeo-Christian humanism and end by asking how recent intercultural and multicultural feminist theory constructs possible postcolonial, nongeneric, and irredeemably specific figures of critical subjectivity, consciousness, and humanity—not in the sacred image of the same, but in the self-critical practice of "difference," of the I and we that is/are never identical to itself, and so has hope of connection to others.

The larger project that this essay initiates will stage an historical conversation among three groups of powerfully universalizing texts:

1) two versions of United Nations discourses on human rights (the UNESCO statements on race in 1950 and 1951 and the documents and events of the UN Decade for Women from 1975–85);

2) recent modernist physical-anthropological reconstructions of the powerful fiction of science, species man, and its science-fiction variant, the female man (pace Joanna Russ) (i.e., Man the Hunter of the 1950s and 1960s and Woman the Gatherer of the 1970s and 1980s); and

3) the transnational, multi-billion-dollar, highly automated, postmodernist apparatus—a language technology, literally—for the production of what will count as "the human" (i.e., the Human Genome Project, with all its stunning power to recuperate, out of the endless variations of code fragments, the singular, the sacred image of the same, the one true man, the standard—copyrighted, catalogued, and banked).

The whole tale might fit together at least as well as the plot of Enlightenment humanism ever did, but I hope it will fit differently, negatively, if you will. I suggest that the only route to a nongeneric humanity, for whom specificity—but emphatically not originality—is the key to connection, is through radical nominalism. We must take names and essences seriously enough to adopt such an ascetic stance about who we have been and might yet be. My stakes are high; I think "we"—that crucial material and rhetorical construction of politics and of history—need something called humanity. It is that kind of thing which Gayatri Spivak called "that which we cannot not want." We also know now, from our perspectives in the ripped-open belly of the monster called history, that we cannot name and possess this thing which we cannot not desire. Humanity, whole and part, is not autochthonous. Nobody is self-made, least of all man. That is the spiritual and political meaning of poststructuralism and postmodernism for me. "We," in these very particular discursive worlds, have no routes to connection and to noncosmic, nongeneric, nonoriginal wholeness than through the radical dis-membering and dis-placing of our names and our bodies. So, how can humanity have a figure outside the narratives of humanism; what language would such a figure speak?

Ecce Homo! The Suffering Servant as a Figure of Humanity[1]

Isaiah 52.13–14:
Behold, my servant shall prosper, he shall be exalted and lifted up, and shall be very high. As many were astonished at him—his appearance was so marred, beyond human semblance, and his form beyond that of the sons of men—so shall he startle many nations.

Isaiah 53.2–4:
He had no form or comeliness that we should look at him, and no beauty that we should desire him. He was despised and rejected by men; a man of sorrows, and acquainted with grief, and as one from whom men hide their faces he was despised, and we esteemed him not. Surely he has borne our griefs and carried our sorrows; yet we esteemed him stricken, smitten by God, and afflicted. But he was wounded for our transgressions, he was bruised for our iniquities; upon him was the chastisement that made us whole, and with his stripes we are healed.

Isaiah 54.1:
For the children of the desolate one will be more than the children of her that is married, says the Lord. ("Is this a threat or a promise?" ask both women, looking tentatively at each other after a long separation.)

John 18.37–38:
Pilate said to him, "So, you are a king? Jesus answered, "You say that

I am a king. For this I was born, and for this I have come into the world, to bear witness to the truth. Everyone who is of the truth hears my voice." Pilate said to him, "What is truth?"

John 19.1–6:
Then Pilate took Jesus and scourged him. And the soldiers plaited a crown of thorns, and put it on his head, and arrayed him in a purple robe; they came up to him, saying, "Hail, King of the Jews!" and struck him with their hands. Pilate went out again, and said to them, "Behold I am bringing him out to you, that you may know I find no crime in him." So Jesus came out, wearing the crown of thorns and the purple robe. Pilate said to them, "Behold the man!" When the chief priests and officers saw him, they cried out, "Crucify him, crucify him!" Pilate said to them, "Take him yourselves and crucify him, for I find no crime in him."

John staged the trial before Pilate in terms of the suffering-servant passages from Isaiah. The events of the trial of Jesus in this nonsynoptic gospel probably are not historical, but theatrical in the strict sense: from the start, they *stage* salvation history, which then became the model for world history in the secular heresies of the centuries of European colonialism with its civilizing missions and genocidal discourses on common humanity. Pilate probably spoke publicly in Greek or Latin, those languages that became the standard of "universal" European scholarly humanism, and his words were translated by his officials into Aramaic, the language of the inhabitants of Palestine. Hebrew was already largely a ceremonial language, not even understood by most Jews in the synagogue. The earliest texts for John's gospel that we have are in Greek, the likely language of its composition (the Koiné, the common Greek spoken and understood throughout the Roman Empire in the early centuries of the Christian era). We don't have the first versions, if there ever were such things; we have endless, gap-filled, and overlaid transcriptions and translations that have grounded the vast apparatus of biblical textual and linguistic scholarship—that cornerstone of modern scholarly humanism, hermeneutics, and semiology and of the human sciences generally, most certainly including anthropology and ethnography. We are, indeed, peoples of the Book, engaged in a Derridean writing and reading practice from the first cries of prophecy and codifications of salvation history.

From the start we are in the midst of multiple translations and stagings of a figure of suffering humanity that was not contained within the cultures of the origin of the stories. The Christian narratives of the Son of Man circulated rapidly around the Mediterranean in the first century of the present era. The Jewish versions of the suffering servant inform some of the most powerful ethical cautions in Faustian transnational technoscience worlds. The presentation to the people of the Son of Man as a suffering servant, arrayed mockingly and mimetically in his true dress as a king and salvation figure, became a powerful image for Christian humanists. The suffering servant figure has been fundamental in twentieth-century liberation theology and Christian Marxism. The guises of the suffering servant never cease. Even in Isaiah, he is clothed in the ambiguities of prophecy. His most important counterfeit historically was Jesus himself, as John appropriated Isaiah into a theater of salvation history that would accuse the Jews of demanding the death of their king and savior in the root narrative of Christian anti-Semitism. The "Ecce homo!" was standardized in the Latin vulgate after many passages through the languages and transcriptions and codifications of the gospels. Jesus appears as a mime in many layers; crowned with thorns and in a purple cloak, he is in the mock disguise of a king before his wrongful execution as a criminal. As a criminal, he is counterfeit for a scapegoat, indeed, *the* scapegoat of salvation history. Already, as a carpenter he was in disguise.

This figure of the Incarnation can never be other than a trickster, a check on the arrogances of a reason that would uncover all disguises and force correct vision of a recalcitrant nature in her most secret places. The suffering servant is a check on man; the servant is the figure associated with the promise that the desolate woman will have more children than the wife, the figure that upsets the clarity of the metaphysics of light, which John the Evangelist too was so enamored of. A mother's son, without a father, yet the Son of Man claiming *the* Father, Jesus is a potential worm in the Oedipal psychoanalytics of representation; he threatens to spoil the story, despite or because of his odd sonship and odder kingship, because of his disguises and form-changing habits. Jesus makes of man a most promising mockery, but a mockery that cannot evade the terrible story of the broken body. The story has constantly to be preserved from heresy, to be kept forcibly in the patriarchal tradition of Christian civilization, to be kept from too much attention to the economies of mimicry and the calamities of suffering.

Jesus came to figure for Christians the union of humanity and divinity in a universal salvation narrative. But, the figure is complex and ambiguous from the start, enmeshed in translation, staging, miming, disguises, and evasions. "Ecce homo!" can, indeed must, be read ironically by "post-Christians" and other post-humanists as "Behold the man, the figure of humanity (Latin), the sign of the same (the Greek tones of homo-), indeed, the Sacred Image of the Same, but also the original mime, the actor of a history that mocks especially the recurrent tales that insist that 'man makes himself' in the deathly onanistic nightdream of coherent wholeness and correct vision."

But, "Ain't I a Woman?"

> Well, children, whar dar is so much racket der must be something out o' kilter. I tink dat 'twixt de niggers of de Souf and de women at de Norf

all a talkin 'bout rights, de white men will be in a fix pretty soon. But what's all dis here talkin' 'bout? Dat man ober dar say dat women needs to be helped into carriages, and lifted ober ditches, and to have de best places—and ain't I a woman? Look at me! Look at my arm! . . . I have plowed and planted and gathered into barns, and no man could head me— and ain't I a woman? I could work as much as any man (when I could get it), and bear de lash as well—and ain't I a woman? I have borne five children and I seen 'em mos all sold off into slavery, and when I cried with a mother's grief, none but Jesus hear—and ain't I a woman?[2]

Sojourner Truth is perhaps less far from Isaiash's spine-tingling proph- ecy than was Jesus. How might a modern John, or Johanna, stage her claim to be—as a black woman, mother, and former slave—the Son of Man, the fulfillment of the promise to unite the whole people under a common sign? What kind of sign is Sojourner Truth—forcibly transported, without a home, without a proper name, unincorporated in the discourses of (white) wom- anhood, raped by her owner, forcibly mated with another slave, robbed of her children, and doubted even in the anatomy of her body? A powerful speaker for feminism and abolitionism, Sojourner Truth's famous lines from her 1851 speech in Akron, Ohio, evoke the themes of the suffering servant in order to claim the status of humanity for the shockingly inappropriate/d figure[3] of New World black womanhood, the bearer of the promise of hu- manity for womanhood in general, and indeed, the bearer of the promise of humanity also for men. Called by a religious vision, the woman received her final names directly from her God when she left her home in New York City in 1843 for the road to preach her own unique gospel. Born a slave around 1797 in Ulster County, New York, her Dutch master named her Isabella Baumfree. "When I left the house of bondage I left everything be- hind. I wa'n't goin'to keep nothin' of Egypt on me, an' so I went to the Lord an' asked him to give me a new name."[4] And Sojourner Truth emerged from her second birth a prophet and a scourge.

Sojourner Truth showed up repeatedly at women's suffrage and abo- litionist meetings over the last half of the nineteenth century. She delivered her most famous speech at the women's rights convention in Ohio in 1851 in answer to white male antisuffrage provocateurs who threatened to disrupt the meeting. In another exchange, she took on the problem of the gender of Jesus—whose manhood had been used by a heckler, a clergyman, to argue against women's rights. Sojourner Truth noted succinctly that man had nothing to do with Jesus; he came from God and a woman. Pilot was not this vagrant preacher's unwilling and evasive judge; but another man authorized by the hegemonic powers of his civilization stood in for him. This free white man acted far more assertively than had the colonial bur- eaucrat of the Roman Empire, whose wife's dreams had troubled him about his queer prisoner.[5] Pilot's ready surrogate, an irate white male physician, spoke out in protest of her speaking, demanding that she prove she was a woman by showing her breasts to the *women* in the audience. Difference (understood as the divisive marks of authenticity) was reduced to anatomy;[6] but even more to the point, the doctor's demand articulated the racist/sexist logic that made the very flesh of the black person in the New World indecipherable, doubtful, out of place, confounding—ungrammatical.[7] Remember that Trinh Minh-ha, from a different diaspora over a hundred years later, wrote, "Perhaps, for those of us who have never known what life in a vernacular culture is/was and are unable to imagine what it can be/could have been, gender simply does not exist otherwise than grammatically in language."[8] Truth's speech was out of place, dubious doubly; she was female and black; no, that's wrong—she was a black female, a black woman, not a coherent substance with two or more attributes, but an oxymoronic singularity who stood for an entire excluded and dangerously promising humanity. The language of Sojourner Truth's body was as electrifying as the language of her speech. And both were enmeshed in cascading questions about origins, authenticity, and generality or universality. This Truth is a figure of nonoriginality, but s/he is not Derridean. S/he is Trinhian, or maybe Wittigian, and the difference matters.[9]

When I began to sketch the outlines of this essay, I looked for versions of the story of Sojourner Truth, and I found them written and rewritten in a long list of nineteenth-century and contemporary feminist texts.[10] Her famous speech, transcribed by a white abolitionist—*Ain't I a Woman?*—adorns posters in women's studies offices and women's centers across the United States. These lines seem to stand for something that unifies "women," but what exactly, especially in view of feminism's excavation of the terrible edifice of "woman" in Western patriarchal language and systems of representation—the one who can never be a subject, who is plot space, matrix, ground, screen for the act of man? Why does her *question* have more power for feminist theory 150 years later than any number of affirmative and declarative sentences? What is it about this figure, whose hard name signifies someone who could never be at home, for whom truth was displacement from home, that compels retelling and rehearing her story? What kind of history might Sojourner Truth inhabit?

For me, one answer to that question lies in Sojourner Truth's power to figure a collective humanity without constructing the cosmic closure of the unmarked category. Quite the opposite, her body, names, and speech—their forms, contents, and articulations—may be read to hold promise for a never-settled universal, a common language that makes compelling claims on each of us collectively and personally, precisely through their radical specificity, in other words, through the displacements and resistances to unmarked identity precisely as the means to claiming the status of "the human." The essential Truth would not settle down; that *was* her specificity. S/he was not everyman; s/he was inappropriate/d. This is a "postmodern" reading from some points of view, and it is surely not the only possible reading of her story. But, it is one that I hope to convince the reader is at the heart of the inter- and multicultural feminist theory in our time. In Teresa de Lauretis's terms, this reading is not so much postmodern or poststructuralist, as it is specifically enabled by feminist theory:

> That, I will argue, is precisely where the particular discursive and epistemological character of feminist theory resides: its being at once inside its own social and discursive determinations, and yet also outside and excessive to them. This recognition marks a further moment in feminist theory, its current stage of reconceptualization and elaborations of new terms; a reconceptualization of the subject as shifting and multiply organized across variable axes of difference; a rethinking of the relations between forms of oppression and modes of resistance and agency, and between practices of writing and modes of formal understanding—of doing theory; an emerging redefinition of marginality as location, of identity as disidentification. . . . I will use the term feminist theory, like the term consciousness or subject, in the singular as referring to a process of understanding that is premised on the historical specificity and the simultaneous, if often contradictory, presence of those differences in each of its instances and practices. . . .[11]

Let us look at the mechanisms of Sojourner Truth's exclusions from the spaces of unmarked universality (*i.e.*, exclusion from "the human") in modern white patriarchal discourse in order to see better how she seized her body and speech to turn "difference" into an organon for placing the painful realities and practices of de-construction, dis-identification, and dis-memberment in the service of a newly articulated humanity. Access to this humanity will be predicated on a subject-making discipline hinted at by Trinh:

> The difficulties appear perhaps less insurmountable only as I/i succeed in making a distinction between difference reduced to identity-authenticity and difference understood also as critical difference from myself. . . . Difference in such an insituable context is *that which undermines the very idea of identity,* deferring to infinity the layers whose totality forms "I." . . . If feminism is set forth as a demystifying force, then it will have to question thoroughly the belief in its own identity.[12]

Hazel Carby clarified how in the New World, and specifically in the United States, black women were not constituted as "woman," as white women were.[13] Instead, black women were constituted simultaneously racially and sexually—as marked female (animal, sexualized, and without rights), but not as woman (human, potential wife, conduit for the name of the father)—in a specific institution, slavery, that excluded them from "culture" defined as the circulation of signs through the system of marriage. If kinship vested men with rights in women that they did not have in themselves, slavery abolished kinship for one group in a legal discourse that produced whole groups of people as alienable property.[14] MacKinnon defined woman as an imaginary figure, the object of another's desire, made real.[15] The "imaginary" figures made real in slave discourse were objects in another sense that made them different from either the Marxist figure of the alienated laborer or the "unmodified" feminist figure of the object of desire. Free women in U.S. white patriarchy were exchanged in a system that oppressed them, but white women *inherited* black women and men. As Hurtado noted, in the nineteenth century prominent white feminists were *married* to white men, while black feminists were *owned* by white men. In a racist patriarchy, white men's "need" for racially "pure" offspring positioned free and unfree women in incompatible, asymmetrical symbolic and social spaces.[16]

The female slave was marked with these differences in a most literal fashion—the flesh was turned inside out, "add[ing] a lexical dimension to the narratives of woman in culture and society."[17] These differences did not end with formal emancipation; they have had definitive consequences into the late twentieth century and will continue to do so until racism as a founding institution of the New World is ended. Spillers called these founding relations of captivity and literal mutilation "an American grammar" (68). Under conditions of the New World conquest, of slavery, and of their consequences up to the present, "the lexis of reproduction, desire, naming, mothering, fathering, etc. [are] all thrown into extreme crisis" (76). "Gendering, in its coeval reference to African-American women, *insinuates* an implicit and unresolved puzzle both within current feminist discourse *and* within those discursive communities that investigate the problematics of culture" (78).

Spillers foregrounded the point that free men and women inherited their *name* from the father, who in turn had rights in his minor children and wife that they did not have in themselves, but he did not own them in the full sense of alienable property. Unfree men and women inherited their *condition* from their mother, who in turn specifically did not control their children. They had no *name* in the sense theorized by Lévi-Strauss or Lacan. Slave mothers could not transmit a name; they could not be wives; they were outside the system of marriage exchange. Slaves were unpositioned, unfixed, in a system of names; they were, specifically, unlocated and so disposable. In these discursive frames, white women were not legally or symbolically *fully* human; slaves were not legally or symbolically human *at all*. "In this absence from a subject position, the captured sexualities provide a physical and biological expression of 'otherness'" (67). To give birth (unfreely) to the heirs of property is not the same thing as to give birth (unfreely) to property.[18]

This little difference is part of the reason that "reproductive rights" for women of color in the United States prominently hinge on comprehensive control of children—for example, their freedom from destruction through lynching, imprisonment, infant mortality, forced pregnancy, coercive sterilization, inadequate housing, racist education, drug addiction, drug wars, and military wars.[19] For American white women the concept of property in the self, the ownership of one's own body, in relation to reproductive freedom, has more readily focused on the field of events around conception, pregnancy, abortion, and birth because the system of white patriarchy turned on the control of legitimate children and the consequent constitution of white females as women. To have or not have children then becomes literally a subject-defining choice for such women. Black women specifically—and the women subjected to the conquest of the New World in general—faced a broader social field of reproductive unfreedom, in which their children did not inherit the status of human in the founding hegemonic discourses of U.S. society. The problem of the black mother in this context is not simply her own status as subject, but also the status of her children and her sexual partners, male and female. Small wonder that the image of uplifting the race and the refusal of the categorical separation of men and women—without flinching from an analysis of colored and white sexist oppression—have been prominent in New World black feminist discourse.[20]

The positionings of African-American women are not the same as those of other women of color; each condition of oppression requires specific analysis that both refuses the separations and insists on the nonidentities of race, sex, sexuality, and class. These matters make starkly clear why an adequate feminist theory of gender must *simultaneously* be a theory of racial and sexual difference in specific historical conditions of production and reproduction. They also make clear why a theory and practice of sisterhood cannot be grounded in shared positionings in a gender system and the cross-cultural structural antagonism between coherent categories called women and men. Finally, they make clear why feminist theory produced by women of color has constructed alternative discourses of womanhood that disrupt the humanisms of many Western discursive traditions. "[I]t is our task to make a place for this different social subject. In so doing we are less interested in joining the ranks of gendered femaleness than gaining the *insurgent* ground as female social subject. Actually *claiming* the monstrosity of a female with the potential to 'name,' . . . 'Sapphire' might rewrite after all a radically different text of female empowerment."[21] And, perhaps, of empowerment of the problematic category of "humanity."

While contributing fundamentally to the breakup of any master subject location, the politics of "difference" emerging from this and other complex reconstructings of concepts of social subjectivity and their associated writing practices is deeply opposed to leveling relativisms. Nonfeminist poststructuralist theory in the human sciences has tended to identify the breakup of "coherent" or masterful subjectivity as the "death of the subject." Like others in newly *unstably* subjugated positions, many feminists resist this formulation of the project and question its emergence at just the moment when raced/sexed/colonized speakers begin "for the first time," to claim, that is, with an "originary" authority, to represent themselves in institutionalized publishing practices and other kinds of self-constituting practice. Feminist deconstructions of the "subject" have been fundamental, and they are not nostalgic for masterful coherence. Instead, necessarily political accounts of constructed embodiments, like feminist theories of gendered racial subjectivities, have to take affirmative *and* critical account of emergent, differentiating, self-representing, contradictory social subjectivities, with their claims on action, knowledge, and belief. The point involves the commitment to transformative social change, the moment of hope embedded in feminist theories of gender and other emergent discourses about the breakup of masterful subjectivity and the emergence of inappropriate/d others.

"Alterity" and "difference" are precisely what "gender" is "grammatically" about, a fact that constitutes feminism as a politics defined by its fields of contestation and repeated refusals of master theories. "Gender" was developed as a category to explore what counts as a "woman," to problematize the previously taken for granted, to reconstitute what counts as "human." If feminist theories of gender followed from Simone de Beauvoir's thesis that one is not born a woman, with all the consequences of that insight, in the light of Marxism and psychoanalysis (and critiques of racist and colonial discourse), for understanding that any finally coherent subject is a fantasy, and that personal and collective identity is precariously and constantly socially reconstituted,[22] then the title of bell hooks' provocative 1981 book, echoing Sojourner Truth, *Ain't I a Woman,* bristles with irony, as the identity of "woman" is both claimed and deconstructed simultaneously. This is a woman worthy of Isaiah's prophecy, slightly amended:

> S/he was despised and rejected by men; a wo/man of sorrows, acquainted with grief, and as one from whom men hide their faces s/he was despised, and we esteemed him/her not. . . . As many were astonished at him/her—his/her appearance was so marred, beyond human semblance . . . so shall s/he startle many nations.

This decidedly unwomanly Truth has a chance to refigure a nongeneric, nonoriginal humanity after the breakup of the discourses of Eurocentric humanism.

However, we cannot leave Sojourner Truth's story without looking more closely at the transcription of the famous *Ain't I a Woman* speech delivered in Akron in 1851. That written text represents Truth's speech in the white abolitionist's imagined idiolect of The Slave, the supposedly archetypical black plantation slave of the South. The transcription does not provide a southern Afro-American English that any linguist, much less actual speaker, would claim. But it *is* the falsely specific, imagined language that represented the "universal" language of slaves to the literate abolitionist public, and this is the language that has come down to us as Sojourner Truth's "authentic" words. This counterfeit language, undifferentiated into the many Englishes spoken in the New World, reminds us of a hostile notion of difference, one that sneaks the masterful unmarked categories in through the back door in the *guise* of the specific, which is made to be not disruptive or deconstructive, but typical. The undifferentiated black slave could figure for a humanist abolitionist discourse, and its descendants on the walls of women's studies offices, an ideal type, a victim (hero), a kind of plot space for the abolitionists' actions, a special human, not one that could bind up the whole people through her unremitting figuring of critical difference— that is, not an unruly agent preaching her own unique gospel of displacement as the ground of connection.

To reinforce the point, this particular former slave was not southern. She was born in New York and owned by a Dutchman. As a young girl, she was sold with some sheep to a Yankee farmer who beat her for not understanding English.[23] Sojourner Truth as an adult almost certainly spoke an Afro-Dutch English peculiar to a region that was once New Amsterdam. "She dictated her autobiography to a white friend and lived by selling it at lectures."[24] Other available transcriptions of her speeches are printed in "standard" late-twentieth-century American English; perhaps this language seems less racist, more "normal" to hearers who want to forget the diasporas that populated the New World, while making one of its figures into a "typical" hero. A modern transcription/invention of Sojourner Truth's speeches has put them into Afro-Dutch English; her famous question retroubles the ear, "Ar'n't I a woman?"[25] The change in the shape of the words makes us rethink her story, the grammar of her body and life. The difference matters.

One nineteenth century, friendly reporter decided he could not put Truth's words into writing at all: "She spoke but a few minutes. To report her words would have been impossible. As well attempt to report the seven apocalyptic thunders."[26] He went on, in fact, to transcribe/reconstruct her presentation, which included these often-quoted lines:

When I was a slave away down there in New York [was New York *down* for Sojourner Truth?!], and there was some particularly bad work to be done, some colored woman was sure to be called upon to do it. And when

I heard that man talking away there as he did almost a whole hour, I said
to myself, here's one spot of work sure that's fit for colored folks to clean
up after.[27]

Perhaps what most needs cleaning up here is an inability to hear Sojourner Truth's language, to face her specificity, to acknowledge her, but
not as the voice of the seven apocalyptic thunders. Instead, perhaps we need
to see her as the Afro-Dutch-English New World itinerant preacher whose
disruptive and risk-taking practice led her "to leave the house of bondage,"
to leave the subject-making (and humanist) dynamics of master and slave,
and seek new names in a dangerous world. This sojourner's truth offers an
inherently unfinished but potent reply to Pilate's skeptical query—"What is
truth?" She is one of Gloria Anzaldúa's *mestizas*,[28] speaking the unrecognized hyphenated languages, living in the borderlands of history and consciousness where crossings are never safe and names never original.

I promised to read Sojourner Truth, like Jesus, as a trickster figure, a
shape changer, who might trouble our notions—all of them: classical, biblical, scientific, modernist, postmodernist, and feminist—of "the human,"
while making us remember why we cannot not want this problematic universal. Pilot's words went through cascades of transcriptions, inventions,
and translations. The "Ecce homo!" was probably never spoken. But, no
matter how they may have originated, these lines in a play about what counts
as humanity, about humanity's possible stories, were from the beginning
implicated in permanent translation and reinvention. The same thing is true
of Sojourner Truth's affirmative question, "Ain't/Ar'n't I a (wo)man?" These
were tricksters, forcing by their constant displacements, a reconstruction of
founding stories, of any possible home. "We, lesbian, *mestiza,* inappro-
priate/d other are all terms for that excessive critical position which I have
attempted to tease out and rearticulate from various texts of contemporary
feminism: a position attained through practices of political and personal displacement across boundaries between sociosexual identities and communities, between bodies and discourses, by what I like to call the "eccentric
subject."[29] Such excessive and mobile figures can never ground what used
to be called "a fully human community." That community turned out to
belong only to the masters. However, these eccentric subjects can call us
to account for our imagined humanity, whose parts are always articulated
through translation. History can have another shape, articulated through differences that matter.

NOTES

This paper was originally presented at the American Anthropological Association meetings,
Washington, D.C., 19 November 1989. Its rhetorical shuttling between the genres of scholarly

writing and religious speech is inspired by, and dedicated to, Cornel West. Thanks to grants from the Academic Senate of the University of California at Santa Cruz.

1. Thanks to Gary Lease for biblical guidance.

2. Quoted in bell hooks, *Ain't I a Woman: Black Women and Feminism* (Boston, Mass.: South End Press, 1981), p. 160.

3. I borrow Trinh's powerful sign, an impossible figure, the inappropriate/d other. Trinh T. Minh-ha, "She, the Inappropriate/d Other," *Discourse*, 8 (1986–87).

4. Gerda Lerner, in *Black Women in White America: A Documentary History*, edited by Gerda Lerner (New York: Random House, 1973), pp. 370–75.

5. Matthew 27.19.

6. Trinh T. Minh-ha, *Woman, Native, Other: Writing, Postcoloniality, and Feminism* (Bloomington: Indiana University Press, 1989).

7. Hortense Spillers, "Mama's Baby, Papa's Maybe: An American Grammar Book," *Diacritics*, 17, 2 (1987), pp. 65–81.

8. Trinh T. Minh-ha, *Woman, Native, Other*, p. 114.

9. I am using "matter" in the way suggested by Judith Butler in her work in progress, *Bodies That Matter*. See also Monique Wittig, *The Lesbian Body*, translated by David LeVay (New York: Avon, 1975). The marked bodies and subjects theorized by Trinh, Butler, and Wittig evacuate precisely the heterosexist and racist idealism-materialism binary that has ruled in the generic Western philosophical tradition. The feminist theorists might claim a siblingship to Derrida here, but not a relation of derivation or identity.

10. A sample: bell hooks, *Ain't I a Woman;* Trinh T. Minh-ha;, *Woman, Native, Other;* Angela Davis, *Women, Race, and Class* (New York: Random House, 1981); Gerda Lerner, *Black Women*; Paula Giddings, *When and Where I Enter: The Impact of Black Women on Race and Sex in America* (New York: Bantam Books, 1984); Bettina Aptheker, *Woman's Legacy: Essays on Race, Sex, and Class in American History* (Amherst: University of Massachusetts Press, 1982); Olive Gilbert, *Narrative of Sojourner Truth, a Northern Slave* (Battle Creek, Mich.: Review and Herald Office, 1884; reissued New York: Arno Press, 1968); Harriet Carter, "Sojourner Truth," *Chautauquan*, 7 (May 1889); Lillie B. Wyman, "Sojourner Truth," in *New England Magazine* (March 1901); Eleanor Flexner, *Century of Struggle: The Woman's Rights Movement in the United States* (Cambridge, Mass.: Harvard University Press, 1959); Edith Blicksilver, "Speech of Woman's Suffrage," in *The Ethnic American Woman* (Dubuque, Iowa: Kendall/Hunt, 1978), p. 335; Hertha Pauli, *Her Name Was Sojourner Truth* (New York: Appleton-Century-Crofts, 1962).

11. Teresa de Lauretis, "Eccentric Subjects," in *Feminist Studies*, 16 (Spring 1990), p. 116

12. Trinh T. Minh-ha, *Woman, Native, Other*, pp. 89, 96.

13. Hazel V. Carby, *Reconstructing Womanhood: The Emergence of the Afro-American Woman Novelist* (New York: Oxford University Press, 1987).

14. Hortense Spillers, "Mama's Baby."

15. Catharine MacKinnon, "Feminism, Marxism, Method, and the State: An Agenda for Theory," *Signs*, 7, 3 (1982), pp. 515–44.

16. Aida Hurtado, "Relating to Privilege: Seduction and Rejection in the Subordination of White Women and Women of Color," *Signs*, 14, 4 (1989), pp. 833–55, 841.

17. Hortense Spillers, "Mama's Baby," pp. 67–68.

18. Hazel V. Carby, *Reconstructing Womanhood* p. 53.

19. Aida Hurtado, "Relating to Privilege," p. 853.

20. Hazel V. Carby, *Reconstructing Womanhood*, pp. 6–7; bell hooks, *Ain't I a Woman*; bell hooks, *Feminist Theory: From Margin to Center* (Boston, Mass.: South End Press, 1984).

21. Hortense Spillers, "Mama's Baby," p. 80.

22. Rosalind Coward, *Patriarchal Precedents: Sexuality and Social Relations* (London: Routledge and Kegan Paul, 1983), p. 265.

23. Gerda Lerner, *Black Women*, p. 371.

24. *Ibid.*, p. 372; Olive Gilbert, *Narrative of Sojourner*.

25. Edith Blicksilver, "Speech."

26. Quoted in Bettina Aptheker, *Woman's Legacy*, p. 34.

27. *Ibid.*, p. 34.

28. Gloria Anzaldúa, *Borderlands/La Frontera* (San Francisco: Spinsters, 1987).

29. Teresa de Lauretis, *Feminist Studies*, p. 145.

6

Postmodern Automatons

Rey Chow

for A . . .

Modernism and Postmodernism: Restating the Problem of "Displacement"

If everyone can agree with Fredric Jameson that the unity of the "new impulse" of postmodernism "is given not in itself but in the very modernism it seeks to displace,"[1] exactly how modernism is displaced still remains the issue. In this paper, I follow an understanding of "modernism" that is embedded in and inseparable from the globalized and popularized usages of terms such as "modernity" and "modernization," which pertain to the increasing technologization of culture. I examine this technologization in terms of the technologies of visuality. In the twentieth century, the preoccupation with the "visual"—in a field like psychoanalysis, for instance—and the perfection of technologies of visuality such as photography and film take us beyond the merely physical dimension of vision. The visual as such, as a kind of dominant discourse of modernity, reveals epistemological problems that are inherent in social relations and their reproduction. Such problems inform the very ways social difference—be it in terms of class, gender, or race—is constructed. In this sense, the more narrow understanding of modernism as the sum total of artistic innovations that erupted in Europe and North America in the spirit of a massive cultural awakening—an emancipation from the habits of perception of the past—needs to be bracketed within an understanding of modernity as a force of cultural expansionism whose foundations are not only emancipatory but also Eurocentric and patriarchal.

The displacement of "modernism" in what we now call the postmodern era must be addressed with such foundations in mind.

Generally speaking, there is, I think, a confusion over the status of modernism as theoretical determinant and modernism as social effect. The disparagement of modernism that we hear in First World circles—a disparagement that stems from the argument of modernism as "mythical," as "narrative," or as what continues the progressive goals of the European Enlightenment—regards modernism more or less as a set of beliefs, a particular mode of cognition, or a type of subjectivity. The rewriting of history by way of the postmodern would hence follow such lines to say: such and such were the governing *ideas* that characterize modernism which have been proven to be grand illusions in the postmodern era, and so on. If "modernity" is incomplete, then, postmodernism supplements it by shaking up its foundations. Therefore, if one of the key characteristics of modernism is the clear demarcation of cognitive boundaries—a demarcation that occurs with the perceptual hegemony of physical vision in the modern period—then postmodernism is full of talk about boundaries dissolving, so that that which sees and that which is seen, that which is active and that which is passive, and so forth, become interchangeable positions. The profusion of discourse and the illusion that every discourse has become permissible make it possible to associate postmodernism with a certain abandonment, such as is suggested in the title of a recent anthology edited by Andrew Ross, *Universal Abandon?*[2]

Once we view the modernism-postmodernism problematic not in terms of a succession of ideas and concepts only, but as the staggering of legacies and symptoms at their different stages of articulation, then the "displacement" of modernism by postmodernism becomes a complex matter, and can vary according to the objectives for which that displacement is argued. For instance, for the cultures outside the Berlin-Paris-London-New York axis, it is not exactly certain that modernism has exhausted its currency or, therefore, its imperialistic efficacy. Because these "other" cultures did not dominate the generation of modernism theoretically or cognitively, "displacement" needs to be posed on very different terms.

On the one hand, modernism is, for these other cultures, always a displaced phenomenon, the sign of an alien imprint on indigenous traditions. In Asia and Africa, modernism is not a set of beliefs but rather a foreign body whose physicality must be described as a Derridean "always already"—whose omnipresence, in other words, must be responded to as a given whether one likes it or not. On the other hand, the displacement of modernism in postmodernity as it is currently argued in the West, in the writings of François Lyotard, Jürgen Habermas, Jameson, and so on, does not seem right either, for modernism is still around as ideoelogical legacy, as habit, and as familiar, even coherent, way of seeing. If the First World has rejected modernism, such rejection is not so easy for the world which is still living through it as cultural trauma and devastation. In the words of Masao Mioshi and H. D. Harootunian:

> The black hole that is formed by the rejection of modernism is also apt to obliterate the trace of historical Western expansionism that was at least cofunctional, if not instrumental, in producing epistemological hegemonism. Thus a paradox: as postmodernism seeks to remedy the modernist error of Western, male, bourgeois domination, it simultaneously vacates the ground on which alone the contours of modernism can be seen. Furthermore, colonialism and imperialism are ongoing enterprises, and in distinguishing late post-industrial capitalism from earlier liberal capitalism and by tolerating the former while condemning the latter, postmodernism ends up by consenting to the first world economic domination that persists in exploiting the wretched of the earth.[3]

In the Third World, the displacement of modernism is not simply a matter of criticizing modernism as theory, philosophy, or ideas of cognition; rather it is the emergence of an entirely different problematic, a displacement of a displacement that is in excess of what is still presented as the binarism of modernism-postmodernism. It is in the light of this double or multiple displacement that a feminist intervention, in alliance with other marginalized groups, can be plotted in the postmodern scene. If what is excluded by the myth-making logic of modernism articulates its "existence" in what looks like a radically permissive postmodern era where anything goes, postmodernism (call it periodizing concept, cultural dominant, if you will, after Jameson) is only a belated articulation of what the West's "others" have lived all along.[4]

Because vis-à-vis the dominant modern culture of the West, feminism shares the status with other marginalized discourses as a kind of "other" whose power has been the result of historical struggle, the relationship between feminism and postmodernism has not been an easy one. Even though feminists partake in the postmodernist ontological project of dismantling claims of cultural authority that are housed in specific representations, feminism's rootedness in overt political struggles against the subordination of women makes it very difficult to accept the kind of postmodern "universal abandon" in Ross's title. For some, the destabilization of conceptual boundaries and concrete beliefs becomes the sign of danger that directly threatens their commitment to an agenda of social progress based on the self and reason.[5] While I do not agree with the espousal of humanistic thinking as such for feminist goals, I think the distrust of postmodern "abandon" can be seen as a strategic resistance against the dismantling of feminism's "critical regionalism" (to use a term from postmodern architectural criticism[6]) and its local politics.

In the collection *Universal Abandon?,* Nancy Fraser and Linda Nicholson voice this understanding of the conflict between postmodernism and
feminism in terms of philosophy and social criticism. While they criticize
the essentialist moves feminists have had to make to stage the primacy of
gender in social struggles, they are equally distrustful of the abstract philosophical frameworks in which theorists of postmodernism often begin their
inquiry. Lyotard's "suspicion of the large," for instance, leads him to reject
"the project of social theory *tout court*"; and yet "despite his strictures against
large, totalizing stories, he narrates a fairly tall tale about a large-scale social
trend."[7]

The conflicts as to what constitutes *the social* amount to one of the
most significant contentions between postmodernism and feminism. *Poststructuralism* plays a role in both's relation to the social. For those interested
in postmodernism, the decentering of the logos and the untenability of structuralism as a mode of cognition provide the means of undoing modernism's
large architectonic claims. Once such claims and their hierarchical power
are undone, the meaning of the "social" bursts open. It is no longer possible
to assume a transparent and universal frame of reality. Instead, "tropes" and
"reality" become versions of each other,[8] while aporias and allegories play
an increasingly important role in the most "natural" acts of reading. And
yet, precisely because the subversive thrust of poststructuralism consists in
its refusal to name its own politics (since naming as such, in the context of
political hegemony, belongs to the tactics of doctrinaire official culture) even
as it deconstructs the language of established power from within, it does not
provide postmodernism with a well-defined agenda nor with a clear object
of criticism other than "the prison house of language." Instead, the persistently negative critique of dominant culture in total terms produces a vicious
circle that repeats itself as what Jean Baudrillard calls "implosion"—the
"reduction of difference to absolute indifference, equivalence, interchange-
ability."[9] Since positions are now infinitely interchangeable, many feel that
postmodernism may be little more than a "recompensatory 'I'm OK, you're
OK' inclusion or a leveling attribution of subversive 'marginality' to all."[10]

The difficulty feminists have with postmodernism is thus clear. Although feminists share postmodernism's poststructuralist tendencies in dismantling universalist claims, which for them are more specifically defined
as the claims of the white male subject, they do not see their struggle against
patriarchy as quite over. The social for feminists is therefore always marked
by a clear horizon of the inequality between men and women; the social,
because it is mediated by gender with its ideological manipulations of biology as well as symbolic representations, is never quite "implosive" in the
Baudrillardian sense. With this fundamental rejection of indifference by an
insistence on the cultural effects of sexual and gendered difference,[11] feminists always begin, as the non-Western world must begin, with the legacy

of the constellation of modernism *and* something more. While for the non-Western world that something is imperialism, for feminists it is patriarchy. They must begin, as Fraser and Nicholson put it, with "the nature of the social object one wished to criticize" rather than with the condition of philosophy. This object is "the oppression of women in its 'endless variety and monotonous similarity.' "[12]

Visuality, or the Social Object "Ridden with Error"[13]

One of the chief sources of the oppression of women lies in the way they have been consigned to visuality. This consignment is the result of an epistemological mechanism which produces social difference by a formal distribution of positions and which modernism magnifies with the availability of technology such as cinema. To approach visuality as the object of criticism, we cannot therefore simply attack the *fact* that women have been reduced to objects of the "male gaze," since that reifies the problem by reifying its most superficial manifestation.[14]

If we take visuality to be, precisely, the nature of the social object that feminism should undertake to criticize, then it is incumbent upon us to analyze the epistemological foundation that supports it. It is, indeed, a foundation in the sense that the production of the West's "others" depends on a logic of visuality that bifurcates "subjects" and "objects" into the incompatible positions of intellectuality and spectacularity.

To illustrate my point, I will turn briefly to Chaplin's *Modern Times,* a film which demonstrates by its use of cinematic technology the modernist production of the space of the other.

There are, of course, many ways to talk about this film, but what makes it so fascinating to watch (and this is a point that can be generalized to include other silent movies) is the way it exaggerates and deconstructs prefilmic materials, in particular the human body. What becomes clear in the film is how a perception of the spectacular cannot be separated from technology, which turns the human body into the site of experimentation and mass production. No audience would forget, for instance, the scenes in which the Chaplin character, an assembly line worker, is so accustomed to working with his lug wrenches that he automatically applies his twisting motions to everything that meets his eyes. This *automatizing* of the human body fulfils *in a mechanized manner* a typical description about a debased popular form, melodrama, that its characters are characters "who can be guaranteed to think, speak and act exactly as you would expect."[15] Cinema, then, allows us to realize in an unprecedented way the mediated, that is, technologized, nature of "melodramatic sentiments." The typical features of melodramatic expression—exaggeration, emotionalism, and Manichaeanism—can thus be redefined as the eruption of the machine in what is presumed to be spontaneous. Gestures and emotions are "enlarged" sentimentally the way reality is "enlarged" by the camera lens.

In Chaplin's assembly-line worker, visuality works toward an automatization of an oppressed figure whose bodily movements become excessive and comical. Being "automatized" means being subjected to social exploitation whose origins are beyond one's individual grasp, but it also means becoming a spectacle whose "aesthetic" power increases with one's increasing awkwardness and helplessness. The production of the "other" is in this sense both the production of class and aesthetic/cognitive difference. The camera brings this out excellently with mechanically repeated motions.

What these moments in *Modern Times* help foreground in a densely meaningful way is the relationship between the excess of spectacle and the excess of response that Freud explores in his discussion of the comic in *Jokes and Their Relation to the Unconscious*. Freud's question is: why do we laugh in the face of the comic? Similarly, in *Modern Times*, how is it that the automatizing of "the other" in the ways we have described becomes the source of our pleasure?

Early on in his essay, Freud indicates that the problem of the comic exists "quite apart from any communication."[16] For him the chief interest of the comic lies in *quantitative* terms. The comic is the "ideational mimetics" that involves "somatic enervation." The expenditure of energy that occurs constitutes the origin of culture in the form of a differentiation or division of labor:

> The comic effect apparently depends . . . on the difference [*Differenz*] between the two cathectic expenditures—one's own and the other person's—as estimated by "empathy"—and not on which of the two the difference favors. But this peculiarity, which at first sight confuses our judgement, vanishes when we bear in mind that a restriction of our muscular work and an increase of our intellectual work fit in with the course of our personal development toward a higher level of civilization. By raising our intellectual expenditure we can achieve the same result with a diminished expenditure on our movements. Evidence of this cultural success is provided by our machines.[17]

Although Freud's statements are ostensibly about the comic, what they reveal is the hierarchical structuring of energies which are distributed between "spectacle" and "spectator" in the intellectual endeavors which form the basis of culture. If the comic as such makes apparent a human being's dependence on bodily needs and social situations, then it also means that the moment of visualization coincides, in effect, with an inevitable dehumanization in the form of a physically automatized object, which is *produced as spectacular excess*. Freud's ironic remark that this is "cultural success" which is evidenced by our machines suggests that this process of dehumanization is accelerated by the accelerated sophistication of intellectual culture itself.

In *Modern Times,* the "increase of intellectual work" does not involve psychology in the popular sense of an interiorization of dramatic action. Rather, it involves a confrontation with the cruelties of industrial exploitation through our laughter, the response that Freud defines as the discharge of that unutilized surplus of energy left over from the difference between the two "cathectic expenditures." If the body of the assembly-line worker is seen in what Freud calls its "muscular expenditure," it is also seen in a way that was not possible before mass production, including the mass production that is the filmic moment. The "human body" as such is already a *working body automatized,* in the sense that it becomes in the new age an automaton on which social injustice as well as processes of mechanization "take on a life of their own," so to speak. Thus, the moment the "human body" is "released" into the field of vision is also the moment when it is made excessive and dehumanized. This excess is the *mise-en-scène* of modernity *par excellence.*

If Freud's reading captures formally the capacity and the limit of the camera's eye, this formalism is itself a symptom of the modern history to which it tries to respond. This is the history of the eruption of "mass culture" as the site both of increasingly mechanized labor and of unprecedentedly multiplied and globally dispersed subjectivities. As Freud analyzes the comic as a spectacle and in quantifiable terms, he is reading human "subjectivity" the way a camera captures "life." The automatized mobility of the spectacularized "other" happens within a frame of scopophilia.

That this scopophilia is masculinist becomes clear when we turn to another one of Freud's texts, "The Uncanny." [18] In this essay, Freud wants to talk about emotions that pertain to inexplicable patterns of psychic repetition. Central to his argument is his reading of E. T. A. Hoffmann's tale, "The Sandman," in which the student Nathaniel falls in love with a doll, Olympia. For Freud, the interest of the story does not so much lie in this heterosexual "romance" as it does in the Sandman and the "father series" in which Nathaniel's tragic fate is written.

But Freud's emphatically masculinist reading—that is, a reading that produces a cultural and psychic *density* for the male subject—becomes itself a way of magnifying the visual object status in which woman is cast. Hoffmann's tale, of course, provides material for Freud's camera eye by highlighting two elements in Nathaniel's fall for Olympia. One: that he first sees her from afar, whereby her beauty, blurred and indistinct, takes on a mesmerizing aura. Two: when they finally meet, the collapse of the physical distance which gives rise to his pleasure at first is now replaced by another equally gratifying sensation—her mechanistic response to everything he says in the form of "Ah, ah!" The combination of these two elements—visuality and automatization—leads to Freud's reading: "Olympia . . . the automatic doll, can be nothing else than a personification of Nathaniel's feminine attitude towards his father in his infancy. . . . Olympia is, as it were, a dissociated complex of Nathaniel's which confronts him as a person. . . ."[19]

Freud's two arguments, the comic and the uncanny, are arguments about mass culture even though they are not stated explicitly as such. The two arguments intersect at the notion of the automatized other, which takes the form either of the ridiculous, the lower class, or of woman. The meaning of woman here is inseparable from the meaning of intellectual class struggle by virtue of the fact that woman is "produced" the way the lower class in Chaplin is produced. The sight of woman is no less mechanized than the sight of the comic, and both embody the critical, indeed repressed, relationship between modernist scopophilia and the compulsive and repetitive "others" which confront Modern Man.

As the ruin of modernism, mass culture is the automatized site of the others, the site of automatized others, the site of automatons. Automatization as such is the "social object" which defines the critical field for feminism. But it is not an object which exists in any pure form; rather, its impurity as cultural construct with historical weight means that feminists need constantly to seize it and steer it in a different direction from other types of politics which can lay equal claim to it. The struggles here are among (1) the perpetuation of masculinist modernism, (2) *feminized* postmodernism, and (3) *feminist* postmodernism. To understand this, let us discuss the term "abandon" in Andrew Ross's title.

"Abandon" belongs to that corpus of concepts which are explicitly or implicitly associated with the devaluation of women since the eighteenth century. If the certainty of a masculinist culture can only be erected by policing the behavior of men's conventional sexual other, women, then any suggestion of women's "misbehavior" amounts to a threat to the dominant culture's foundational support. Traditionally, any departure from the virtues demanded of females becomes the occasion both for male moralistic pedagogy (which asserts social control) and for male romantic musings (which celebrate acts of social transgression). The notion of "abandon" belongs to an economy in which male hegemony relies on the "loose woman" and its cognates of "looseness-as-woman" and "woman-as-looseness" for a projection of that which is subversive, improper, marginal, unspeakable, and so forth. Teresa de Lauretis has called this the "violence of rhetoric" and criticized the masculinism which informs Nietzsche's and Derrida's appropriation of the feminine for their deconstruction of established power.[20] What Nietzsche and Derrida accomplish in philosophy, others accomplish through the notions of mass culture. This historical inscription of the feminine on the notion of mass culture, Andreas Huyssen argues, is problematic primarily because of "the persistent gendering as feminine of that which is devalued."[21] The case of Emma Bovary, that "avid consumer of pulp,"[22] is the most paradigmatic. In Huyssen's argument, the equation of woman with mass culture is a threat to the serious purity of high modernism.

Once the implications of gender are introduced, it becomes possible to see how the twentieth-century debates about "mass" culture—what is now called postmodern culture—have been conducted over categories which bear the imprint of hierarchically defined sexual difference. For example, we can now view the classic case of Theodore Adorno and Max Horkheimer's devastating denunciation of American mass culture in terms of a politically astute and uncompromising masculinism. Adorno and Horkheimer define the "culture industry" as what "robs the individual of his function." This individual is the autonomous human being who holds a critically resistant relationship to the stultifying effects of undifferentiated mass culture. This critically resistant individualism is meanwhile extended to the work of art. The commitment to the possibility of autonomy and liberation is expressed negatively, in the form of an "in spite of": in spite of the deafening, blinding, and numbing powers of the mass, autonomy and liberation exist for the ones who remain sober, alert, and clear-sighted. This of course leaves open the question of how the impure nature of social history can even begin to be approached, and how social transformation can take place in a communal or collective sense.

The rigidity and pessimism of the Frankfurt School "stamp" on mass culture have been criticized on many fronts. My point in mentioning it is rather to emphasize that, precisely because Adorno and Horkheimer's argument has had such an indelible impact on our conception of the culture industry for so long, it paradoxically enables the equally problematic "postmodern" descriptions of mass culture given by Jean Baudrillard to have great seductive powers.[23] In Baudrillard, the nonresisting activities of the reputedly passive consumer now take on an "implosive" dimension. The mass(es), in its (their) stubborn, somnambulent silence, in its (their) simulated or simulating acquiescence to the media, become(s) abandoned and "feminine" in the ruin of representation. Baudrillard's theory does not reverse Adorno and Horkheimer's view of the masses; rather, it exaggerates it and pushes it to the extreme by substituting the notion of an all-controlling "industry" with that of an all-consuming mass, a mass that, in its abandon, no longer allows for the demarcation of clear boundaries, such as between an above and a below. Huyssen writes: "Baudrillard gives the old dichotomy a new twist by applauding the femininity of the masses rather than denigrating it, but his move may be no more than yet another Nietzschean simulacrum."[24]

From Object to Strategy

Be it the repudiation of or the abandonment to the feminized mass, then, the modernism-postmodernism problematic continues the polarized thinking produced by the logic of visuality. Visuality in Freud works by displacement, which makes explicit (turns into external form) what are interiorized states called "neuroses" and "complexes." The site occupied by woman, by the lower classes, by the masses, is that of excess; in Freud's reading their specularity—their status as the visual—is what allows the clarification of problems which lie outside them and which need them for their objectification. Beyond this specularity, what can be known about the feminized "object"?

The answer to this question is "nothing" if we insist that this object is a pure phenomenon, a pure existence. However, if this object is indeed a *social* object which is by nature "ridden with error," then criticizing it from within would amount to criticizing the social sources of its formation. Albeit in fragmented forms, such criticisms can lead to subversions which do not merely reproduce the existing mechanism but which offer an alternative for transformation.

For feminists working in the First World, where relatively stable material conditions prevail, criticism of the oppression of women can adopt a more flamboyantly defiant tone as the affirmation of female power *tout court*. The availability of food, living space, mechanical and electronic forms of communication, institutionalized psychoanalytic treatment, and general personal mobility means that "automatization" *can* turn into autonomy and independence. Hélène Cixous's challenge to Freud's reading of Hoffmann, for instance, represents this defiant automaton power: "what if the doll became a woman? What if she *were* alive? What if, in looking at her, we animated her?"[25]

These First World feminist questions short-circuit Freud's neurotic pessimism by rejecting, as it were, the reductionism of the modernist logic of visuality and the polarity of masculine-human-subject-versus-feminized-automaton it advances. It retains the notion of the automaton—the mechanical doll—but changes its fate by giving it life with another look. This is the look of the feminist critic. Does her power of animation take us back to the language of God, a superior being who bestows life upon an inferior? Or is it the power of a woman who bears the history of her own dehumanization on her as she speaks for other women? The idealism of First World feminism would have us believe the latter. The mythical being of this idealism is the "cyborg," that half-machine, half-animal creature, at once committed and transgressive, spoken of by Donna Haraway.[26]

For those feminists who have lived outside the First World as "natives" of "indigenous cultures" (for such are the categories in which they are put, regardless of their level of education), the defiance of a Cixous is always dubious, suggesting not only the subversiveness of woman but also the more familiar, oppressive discursive prowess of the "First World." The "post-modern" cultural situation in which non-Western feminists now find them-selves is a difficult and cynical one. Precisely because of the modernist epis-temological mechanism which produces the interest in the Third World, the great number of discourses that surround this "area" are now treated, one feels, as so many Olympias saying "Ah, ah!" to a Western subject de-manding repeated uniform messages. For the Third World feminist, the question is never that of asserting power as woman alone, but of showing how the concern for women is inseparable from other types of cultural oppression and negotiation. In a more pronounced, because more technol-ogized/automatized manner, her status as postmodern automaton is both the subject and object of her critical operations.

In this light, it is important to see that the impasse inherent in Freud's analytic insights has to do not only with visuality and the ontological po-larities it entails, but also with the *instrumentalism* to which such a con-struction of the visual field lends itself. Because Freud privileges castration as a model, he is trapped in its implications, by which the "other" that is constructed is always constructed as what completes what is missing from our "own" cognition. But the roots of "lack" lie beyond the field of vision,[27] which is why the privileging of vision as such is always the privileging of a fictive mode, a veil which remains caught in an endless repetition of its own logic.

On the other hand, Freud's analysis of the comic remains instructive because in it we find a resistance to the liberalist illusion of the autonomy and independence we can "give" the other. It shows that social knowledge (and the responsibility that this knowledge entails) is not simply a matter of empathy or identification with the "other" whose sorrows and frustrations are being made part of the spectacle. Repetition, which is now visibly rec-ognized in the field of the other, mechanistically establishes and intensifies the distintions between spectacular (kinetic) labor and cognitive labor, while the surplus created by their difference materializes not only in emotional (or imaginary) terms but also in economic terms. This means that *our* attempts to "explore the 'other' point of view" and "to give it a chance to speak for itself," as the passion of many current discourses goes, must always be dis-tinguished from the other's struggles, no matter how enthusiastically we as-sume the nonexistence of that distinction. "Letting the 'other' live" with a liveliness never visible before is a kind of investment whose profits return, as it were, to those who watch. Freud puts it this way:

> In "trying to understand," therefore, in apperceiving this movement [the comic], I make a certain expenditure, and in this portion of the mental

process I behave exactly as though I were putting myself in the place of the person I am observing. But at the same moment, probably, I bear in mind the aim of this movement, and my earlier experience enables me to estimate the scale of expenditure required for reaching that aim. In doing so I disregard the person whom I am observing and behave as though I myself wanted to reach the aim of the movement. These two possibilities in my imagination amount to a comparison between the observed movement and my own. If the other person's movement is exaggerated and inexpedient, my increased expenditure in order to understand it is inhibited in *statu nascendi,* as it were in the act of being mobilized . . .; it is declared superfluous and is free for use elsewhere or perhaps for discharge by laughter. This would be the way in which, other circumstances being favorable, pleasure in a comic movement is generated—an innervatory expenditure which has become an unusable surplus when a comparison is made with a movement of one's own.[28]

The task that faces Third World feminists is thus not simply that of "animating" the oppressed women of their cultures, but of making the automatized and animated condition of their own voices the conscious point of deprture in their intervention. This does not simply mean they are, as they must be, speaking across cultures and boundaries; it also means that they speak with the awareness of "cross-cultural" speech as a limit, and that their very own use of the victimhood of women and Third World cultures is both symptomatic of and inevitably complicitous with the First World. As Gayatri Spivak says of the American university context: "the invocation of the pervasive oppression of Woman in every class and race stratum, indeed in the lowest sub-cast, cannot help but justify the institutional interests of the (female) academic."[29] Feminists' upward mobility in the institution, in other words, still follows the logic of the division of labor and of social difference depicted by Freud in his analysis of the comic. The apparent receptiveness of our curricula to the Third World, a receptiveness which makes full use of non-Western human specimens as instruments for articulation, is something we have to practice and deconstruct at once. The Third World feminist speaks of, speaks to, and speaks as this disjuncture:

> The privileged Third World informant crosses cultures within the network made possible by socialized capital, or from the point of view of the indigenous intellectual or professional elite in actual Third World countries. Among the latter, the desire to "cross" cultures means accession, left *or* right, feminist *or* masculinist, into the elite culture of the metropolis. This is done by the commodification of the particular "Third World culture" to which they belong. Here entry into consumerism and entry into "Feminism" (the proper named movement) have many things in common.[30]

By the logic of commodified culture, feminism shares with other marginalized discourses which have been given "visibility" the same type of destiny—that of reification and subordination under such terms, currently popular in the U.S. academy, as "cultural diversity." As all groups speak like automatons to the neurotic subject of the West, an increasing momentum of instrumentalism, such as is evident in anthologies about postmodernism and feminism, seeks to reabsorb the differences among them. Our educational apparatuses produce ever "meta" systems, programs, and categories in this direction. Feminism has already become one type of knowledge to be controlled expediently through traditional epistemological frameworks such as the genre of the "history of ideas."

Awareness of such facts does not allow one to defend the purity of feminism against its various *uses*. Here, the Third World feminist, because she is used as so many types of automatons at once, occupies a space for strategic alliances.

One such alliance is worked out by foregrounding the political significance of theoretical feminist positions, even if they may have ostensibly little to do with politics in the narrower sense of political economy. The refusal, on the part of many feminists, to give up what may be designated as "feminine" areas, including the close attention to texts, can in this regard be seen as a refusal to give up the local as a base, a war front, when the cannon shots of patriarchal modernism are still heard everywhere. Although this base is also that "social object" which feminists must criticize, to abandon it altogether would mean a complete surrender to the enemy. Naomi Schor puts it this way:

> Whether or not the "feminine" is a male construct, a product of a phallocentric culture destined to disappear, in the present order of things we cannot afford not to press its claims even as we dismantle the conceptual systems which support it.[31]

Elizabeth Weed comments:

> Schor's insistence on the need for a feminine specificity is political. It represents a recognition on the part of some feminists . . . that much of post-structural theory which is not explicitly feminist is simply blind to sexual difference or, in its desire to get beyond the opposition male/female, underestimates the full political weight of the categories.[32]

Thus the "social object" for feminist discourse in general—the oppression of women—becomes both object and agent of criticism. Vis-à-vis postmodernism, the question that feminists must ask *repeatedly* is: how do we deal with the local? Instead of the local, accounts of postmodernism usually provide us with lists that demonstrate what Jean-François Lyotard says literally: "Not only can one speak of everything, one must."[33] The impossibility of dealing with the local except by letting everyone speak/everything be spoken at the same time leads to a situation in which hegemony in the Gramscian sense always remains a danger. But with this danger also arises a form of opportunity, which feminists take hold of by way of situating themselves at every point in a constellation of political forces without ever losing sight of women's historical subordination.

Pressing the claims of the local therefore does not mean essentializing one position; instead it means using that position as a parallel for allying with others. For the Third World feminist, especially, the local is never "one." Rather, her own "locality" as construct, difference, and automaton means that pressing its claims is always pressing the claims of a form of existence which is, by origin, coalitional.

By contrast, the postmodernist list neutralizes the critical nature of such coalitional existences. The list allows "the others" to be seen, but would not pay attention to what they say. In the American university today, the rationale of the list manifests itself in the wholehearted *enlisting* of women, blacks, Asians, and so forth, into employment for their "offerings" of materials from non-Western cultures. Those who have been hired under such circumstances know to what extent their histories and cultures manage to make it to significant international forums, which are by and large still controlled by topics such as "modernism" and "postmodernism." Those who want to address the local must therefore always proceed by gesturing toward the forum at large, or by what we nowadays call, following the language of the market, "packaging." One knows that as long as one deals in First World abstractions—what Fraser and Nicholson mean by "philosophy"—one would have an audience. As for local specificities—even though such are buzz words for a politics of abandonment—audiences usually nod in good will and turn a deaf ear, and readers skip the pages.

It is in resistance against postmodernist enlistment, then, that various strategies for coalition between feminism and postmodernism, which all partake of a "critical regionalism," have been explored. Donna Haraway and Teresa Ebert define postmodern feminist cultural theory as "oppositional" practice;[34] Craig Owens argues the necessity to genderize the formalisms of postmodern aesthetics and to revamp the substance of postmodern thought;[35] Jane Flax speaks of "the embeddedness of feminist theory in the very social processes we are trying to critique."[36] Perhaps what is most crucial about the meeting of feminism and postmodernism is that, after refusing to be seduced into abandonment, feminists do not put down the "pulp novel" that is postmodernism, either. Instead, they extract from the cries of abandonment the potential of social criticism that might have been lost in the implosions of simulacra. The careful rejection of postmodernist abandon as a universalist politics goes hand in hand with its insistence on the need to *detail* history, in the sense of cutting it up, so that as it gains more ground in social struggle, sexual difference becomes a way of engaging not simply with women but with other types of subjugation. The future of feminist postmodern automatons is described in this statement by Weed: "If sexual difference becomes ever more destabilized, living as a female will become an easier project, but that will result from the continued displacement of 'women,' not from its consolidation."[37]

NOTES

This paper was originally written for the International Symposium on "Feminism and Theory of Discourse" in Valencia, Spain, January 1990. It has appeared as "Autómatas postmodernos," in the symposium volume, *Feminismo y teoría del discurso*, edited by Giulia Colaizzi (Madrid: Ediciones Cátedra, Colección Teorema, 1990), pp. 67–85. I am grateful to Amitava Kumar and Peter Canning for their comments on an early version of this paper.

1. Fredric Jameson, "Postmodernism and Consumer Society," in *The Anti-Aesthetic: Essays on Postmodern Culture*, edited and with an introduction by Hal Foster (Port Townsend, Washington; Bay Press, 1983), p. 112.

2. Andrew Ross, ed., *Universal Abandon?: The Politics of Postmodernism* (Minneapolis: University of Minnesota Press, 1988).

3. Introduction to *The South Atlantic Quarterly*, Special Issue on Postmodernism and Japan, 87, 3 (Summer 1988), p. 388.

4. I argue this in the context of modern Chinese literature in "Rereading Mandarin Ducks and Butterflies: A Response to the 'Postmodern' Condition," *Cultural Critique*, 5 (Winter 1986–87) pp. 69–93.

5. See, for instance, Daryl Mcgowan Tress's response (*Signs*, 14, 1, p. 200) to Jane Flax's "Postmodernism and Gender Relations in Feminist Theory" (*Signs*, 12, 4, pp. 621–43): "Postmodernism, with its 'deep skepticism' and 'radical doubts' is not the medicine required to cure intellectual and social life of the afflictions of various orthodoxies (e.g., Marxist, Enlightenment, Freudian). What is sorely needed instead of theory that denies the self and integrity or reason is theory that permits us to achieve appropriate and intelligent trust in the self and in its various abilities to come to know what is real."

6. See Kenneth Frampton, "Towards a Critical Regionalism: Six Points for an Architecture of Resistance," in Hal Foster, pp. 16–30.

7. Nancy Fraser and Linda Nicholson, "Social Criticism without Philosophy: An Encounter between Feminism and Postmodernism," in Andrew Ross, pp. 88, 90.

8. Hayden White's argument about history in *Tropics of Discourse: Essays in Cultural Criticism* (Baltimore and London: Johns Hopkins University Press, 1978) remains exemplary in this regard.

9. Craig Owens, "The Discourse of Others: Feminists and Postmodernism," in Hal Foster, p. 58.

10. George Yúdice, "Marginality and the Ethics of Survival," in Andrew Ross, p. 215.

11. See Naomi Schor's argument in "Dreaming Dissymmetry: Barthes, Foucault, and Sexual Difference," in Alice Jardine and Paul Smith, eds., *Men in Feminism* (New York: Methuen, 1987), pp. 98–110.

12. In Andrew Ross, pp. 91, 102. The phrase "endless variety and monotonous similarity" is from Gayle Rubin, "The Traffic in Women," in *Toward an Anthropology of Women,* edited by Rayna R. Reiter (New York: Monthly Review Press, 1975), p. 160.

13. This notion is Walter Benjamin's.

14. A similar point can be made about pornography. Attacks on pornography that focus only on its abuse of women cannot deal with the question of why pornography always exists.

15. James Smith, *Melodrama* (London: Methuen 1973), p. 18.

16. Freud, *Jokes and Their Relation to the Unconscious,* translated and edited by James Strachey (New York and London: Norton, 1963), p. 193.

17. Freud, *Jokes,* p. 195.

18. Freud, "The 'Uncanny,'" *Collected Papers,* vol. IV, trans. Joan Riviere (London: The Hogarth Press, 1946), pp. 368–407.

19. Freud, "The 'Uncanny,'" p. 385, note 1.

20. Teresa de Lauretis, "The Violence of Rhetoric: Considerations on Representation and Gender," *Semiotica,* 54, 1–2 (1985), Special Issue on "The Rhetoric of Violence," edited by Nancy Armstrong; rpt. in *Technologies of Gender: Essays on Theory, Film, and Fiction* (Bloomington: Indiana University Press, 1987), pp. 31–50.

21. Andreas Huyssen, *After the Great Divide: Modernism, Mass Culture, Postmodernism* (Bloomington: University of Indiana Press, 1986), p. 53.

22. Andreas Huyssen, p. 46.

23. See especially Jean Baudrillard, *In the Shadow of the Silent Majorities or the End of the Social and Other Essays,* translated by Paul Foss, Paul Patton, and John Johnston (New York: Semiotext(e), 1983), and *Simulations,* translated by Paul Foss, Paul Patton, and Philip Beitchman (New York: Semiotext(e), 1983).

24. Andreas Huyssen, p. 62.

25. Hélène Cixous, "Fiction and Its Phantoms: A Reading of Freud's *Das Unheimliche* (The 'uncanny')," *New Literary History,* VII, 3, p. 538; emphasis in the original.

26. Donna Haraway, "A Manifesto for Cyborgs: Science, Technology, and Socialist Feminism in the 1980s," *Socialist Review,* 80 (March-April 1985); rpt. in Elizabeth Weed, ed., *Coming to Terms: Feminism, Theory, Politics* (New York and London: Routledge, 1989), pp. 173–204.

27. De Lauretis deals with this problem by reintroducing narrative. See especially her chapter on "Imaging" in *Alice Doesn't: Feminism, Semiotics, Cinema* (Bloomington: University of Indiana Press, 1984). Neil Hertz makes a similar argument about Freud's reading of Hoffmann by showing the necessity of "literature" for "psychoanalaysis": "we know that the relation between figurative language and what it figures cannot be adequately grasped in metaphors of vision. . . ." See "Freud and the Sandman," in *Textual Strategies: Perspectives in Post-Structuralist Criticism,* edited and with an introduction by Josué V. Harari (Ithaca: Cornell University Press, 1979), p. 320.

28. Freud, *Jokes,* p. 194.

29. Gayatri Spivak, "The Political Economy of Women As Seen by a Literary Critic," in Elizabeth Weed, p. 220.

30. Gayatri Spivak, p. 221; emphases in the original.

31. Naomi Schor, *Reading in Detail: Aesthetics and the Feminine* (New York and London: Methuen, 1987), p. 97.

32. Elizabeth Weed, "Introduction: Terms of Reference," in Weed, ed. *Coming to Terms,* pp. xvii–xviii.

33. Jean-François Lyotard, "Presentations," in *Philosophy in France Today,* edited by Alan Montefiore (Cambridge: Cambridge University Press, 1983), p. 133; quoted by Warren Montag, "What is at Stake in the Debate on Postmodernism?," in E. Ann Kaplan, ed., *Postmodernism and Its Discontents: Theories, Practices* (London and New York: Verso, 1988), p. 91.

34. See Donna Haraway, "Cyborgs," and Teresa Ebert, "The Romance of Patriarchy: Ideology, Subjectivity, and Postmodern Feminist Cultural Theory," *Cultural Critique,* 10 (Fall 1988) pp. 19–57.

35. ". . . women's insistence on difference and incommensurability may not only be compatible with, but also an instance of postmodern thought." in Hal Foster, pp. 61–62.

36. See Jane Flax, p. 638.

37 Elizabeth Weed, p. xxiv.

II

Signifying Identity

7

A Short History of Some Preoccupations

Denise Riley

Part of a polemical essay I published a couple of years ago, *Am I That Name?*,[1] suggested that feminism had necessarily inherited those ambiguities heavy in the ordinary collective noun, "women." That "women" could be used as a coinage in any political currency ensured that its face value had to be deciphered carefully. But to examine both that and the many other peculiarities of "women" didn't undermine feminism, as some might feel, but was on the contrary an aspect of understanding the historical and the contemporary strains upon, and the alliances of, various kinds of feminism. In brief, both historical and political interpretations needed some scrutiny of "women," and this could only be taken as postfeminist or antifeminist if you believed that a celebration of women *en masse* was the only permissible strategy.

To distinguish the levels of indeterminacy which characterized "women" was a rather artificial task—but it seemed that three could be roughly picked out. The individual's indeterminacy (when am I a woman?), the historical indeterminacy (what do "women" mean, and when?), and the political indeterminacy (what can "women" do?) are, however, variously blurred, and the nature of their overlappings was what I had in mind when I wrote about the peculiar temporality of "women." This generated an anxiety, I think, for some readers who felt that if the whole category of women took on the aspect of a problem, then the self-identity was under attack, and feminism as a politics was consequently being eroded by thoughtless theory. About this problem of "identity," I'd say that it's important to try to know the resonances, for as many hearers as possible, of what you are claiming. So that part of replying to that worry—"How can you simultaneously query the cohesion and the constancy of 'women' and retain any politics of women, be a feminist? Don't you need the security of the identity in order to have the politics at all?"—would be to say that the politics would be more effective if you knew the different ways in which *you were likely to be heard*, what your assertion of identity was *doing*. My own feeling is that "identity" is an acutely double-edged weapon—not useless, but dependent on the context, sometimes risky—and that the closeness between an identity and a derogatory identification may, again always in specific contexts, resemble that between being a subject and the process of subjectification. "Women" can also suffer from too much identification. Yet an aspect of any feminism in formation *is* that collective self-consciousness of "being women," and to deny the force of that elective identification would be mistaken, as mistaken as the supposition of its necessary fixity.

The question of the politics of identity could be rephrased as a question of rhetoric. Not so much of whether there was for a particular moment any truthful underlying rendition of "women" or not, but of what the proliferations of addresses, descriptions, and attributions were doing. The dizziness induced by seeing "women" named from the political left or the right in a morass of opinion, journalese, sociological observation, or family-policy statement, will be familiar to anyone immured in libraries and archives. Earlier feminisms, whose stock in trade was also women, were also necessarily busied with elaborating or refuting the thickets of labor statistics, departmental minutes, or bright articles about women's real wants and aspirations. Where to turn for clarity? I looked for but did not find any accounts of rhetoric which would be helpful, and it was hard to devise any boundaries between the formally rhetorical and the rest, the generally discursive deployments of "women." Perhaps the former was merely an intensification of the latter, at once more and less self-conscious than it. During these library years, which were not undisturbed, I had read Michel Foucault's earlier work; *The Archaeology of Knowledge* appeared in translation in 1972. I can't say that I recognized what would become more valuable to me later; it was, then, the streaks of sheer obstinacy in his refusals to make reductions of discourse to history or vice versa, and the theatrical drive toward self-obliteration that I liked—the introduction says of the text:

> It rejects its identity, without previously stating: I am neither this nor that. It is not critical, most of the time; it is not a way of saying that everything else is wrong. It is an attempt to define a particular site by the exteriority of its vicinity, rather than trying to reduce others to silence by claiming that what they say is worthless. I have tried to define this blank space from which I speak, and which is slowly taking shape in a discourse which I feel to be so precarious and so unsure . . . .. I am no doubt not the only one who writes in order to have no face.[2]

A few years later, studying the history of developmental psychology and of psychoanalysis and their ramifications in the hope of grasping more about childcare and "the State," I went back to the tentative formulations of *The Archaeology of Knowledge*. These tried to replace the smoothness of "the history of ideas" with something more jagged, more demanding, but also curiously more prosaic; the aim was "to substitute for the enigmatic treasure of 'things' anterior to discourse, the regular formation of objects that arise only in discourse."[3] There were, of course, new difficulties, and these were laid out by Foucault in his book: where and how were the "edges" of a discursive formation to be traced? Or did this matter; but then how could you give any delineation of change, not of what Foucault denounced as "the general empty category of change" but of modest local alterations? Were you at risk of ending up in a positivist position where everything simply was as it was, and did this antiheroic flatness have anything much to commend it beyond the silent charm of stoicism? Nevertheless, and with acknowledgment to such tenacious complexities and to Foucault's suggestions for their resolutions, there was an immediate helpfulness about the idea of discursive formations. When the first volume of *The History of Sexuality* appeared in 1976, not only did it characterize the nineteenth-century construction of "homosexuality" but also, in placing "sex" in the modern sense as an aspect of the history of the present, it opened the way to the historicizing of any category, including that of "women." And given that people understand their lives discursively, the point therefore wouldn't be to trace a history of rhetoric as if this were a layer plastered over the strata of real silent lives underneath; but to distinguish what different forms of description were active at what levels. This was surely a fully historical and indeed a materialist undertaking, if the latter term is used in a more modest and less canonical sense.

My object, however, isn't a defense of Foucault, but to set out why someone engaged with feminism, especially socialist feminism and its possibilities, would have been drawn to Foucault's early work at all. This is an awkward undertaking, to hint at some of the intellectual background to the work of people of "my generation," now over forty years old—the aim isn't to be chauvinistic for a group, but just to suggest some sources which will be different from those available to others of different ages, convictions, and national educational and political backgrounds. I am deliberately and artificially omitting reference to political campaigns and to changes in the women's movement, since my brief is to touch only on the sort of reading which preoccupied me and many others. This is really a skeletal history of mottoes. Certain phrases and formulations take on a talismanic quality, rattle at the back of one's brain for years. Perhaps, or even probably, they are not deployed, not formally worked up and digested into a coherent theory; none the less they keep a powerful presence on top of which later "influences" lie only lightly.

I'd gone to the archives originally in search of illumination for the problems of the State and family policy which occupied the women's liberation movement in the early 1970s; what was then called the politics of childcare or of welfare was especially pertinent for a young single mother; was it true that in the Second World War, the State had deployed psychology to justify its closing of nurseries, or was that a misconceived way of stating the problem? This reflected a general uncertainty about what "the State" was, and what "rights" might be; the British women's liberation movement formulated demands to a (solidly unresponsive) State, so that there was nothing academic about this interest; it was understood to be sharply political. Those of us who could somehow manage to research these questions saw our investigations as "at the service of "feminist politics and campaigns. In this we continued an aspiration of the late-1960s libertarian socialism which hoped for critical intellectual work to be done outside of the universities, to have an independent base.

We (and this "we" is a difficulty, as I want to avoid being autobiographical, but am uncertain of who else I can properly speak for) followed a self-imposed countereducation of reading Marx and Hegel, Engels, Althusser, Freud—among a great many other European socialists and theorists of society. What worried us was how to understand the individual-society relation and how that drew on psychology and psychoanalysis and biology, vis-à-vis various collective theories, sociology, and socialism. Translations of European socialist writers, several of whom were made available through the New Left Books series, fuelled these discussions; among these Timpanaro's *On Materialism*, which tried to retrieve questions of life and, literally, death for socialist argument, stood at a tangent to self-consciously antihumanist writings. Much of this debate gyrated around the poles of humanism and antihumanism.[4] In brief, it was argued that the historical anthropology of Marxist humanism placed "man" at the center but that this was a hindrance to political clarity; the counterattack, the dethronement of "man," turned on different theories of the human subject. These variously displaced the sovereignty of "man," in part through Lacanian and other readings of Freud's psychoanalysis. Juliet Mitchell's *Psychoanalysis and Feminism*, published in 1973, was a masterful work of synthesis whose drawbacks echoed those of its sources. The chief inspiration for the feminism of the early 1970s (which did not then use the term, preferring "women's liberation") was probably Simone de Beauvoir's *The Second Sex*, of 1946, and Virginia Woolf's *A Room of One's Own*. Doris Lessing's earlier novels were also strong background presences. This history of progressive politics of "the personal" was being dug out by Sheila Rowbotham and Jeffrey Weeks, among others; their work was in the libertarian-socialist tradition where "theory" and "politics" were intimately bound together; and Lenin's formulae on that topic were quoted extensively (and by those whose ideas about the sexual would have been as repugnant to him as were Alexandra Kollontai's). Most of the arguments were waged through small press leaflets, articles in new journals, and polemical pamphlets; and the more historical or philosophical writings also placed themselves under the banner of politics, and were occupied with campaigns about unionization, or abortion legislation, or other contemporary issues.

I mention these things, glancingly, to suggest a little of the discussion which buoyed up the then-embryonic feminism of the early 1970s. In this flux, everyone hung onto a set of references perhaps of their own, perhaps held in common with others. I imagine that many of "us," especially the bookish ones, felt ourselves to be hung around with talismans or mottoes which we'd collected and which could be fingered like rosaries for guidance in the tumult. The new feminism gave us the ubiquitous "the personal is the political" and the slogans (like "No women's liberation without socialism! No socialism without women's liberation!") but these were new accretions which fell upon the older layers; the formulations about the State and the individual, Marx and Freud and why 1917 had failed. It is these formulations, these talismanic memories, which possess a powerful and continuing presence in the work done perhaps a decade or fifteen years later, even where they are not consciously remembered, or are refined, or indeed are repudiated.

A hunt through old notebooks and pencilled underlinings turned up a few of the mottoes which determined, however obscurely, my own directions. I don't want to be portentous, or self-important; the point is simply to set out the kind of readings and fragments which might have been present to anyone leaving higher education in the years shortly after 1968. Marx, above all, was studied scrupulously. From his *Theses on Feuerbach* (a critique of the author of, among other works, *The Essence of Christianity*), we took his objection to the abstracted and isolated human individual who also figured in classical political economy: "Feuerbach resolves the religious essence into the *human* essence. But the human essence is no abstraction inherent in each single individual. In its reality it is the ensemble of social relations."[5] In Feuerbach's account, wrote Marx, the human essence could be conceived only as an inner, mute generality, naturally uniting the many individuals. Whereas, Marx held in 1845, supposedly abstract individuals belonged to particular forms of society; by 1857–58, his *Grundrisse* elaborated on this concept of "social individuals." These were, in short, produced historically, first as clan beings, then as political city dwellers. "Exchange itself is a chief means of this individuation."[6]

What mattered about this was not so much the problems inherent in Marx's designation of the mode of exchange as the main source of individuation, but the implied transformation of a timeless society-individual antagonism. The publication of *Reading Capital* (in 1968 in Paris, two years later in London), by Louis Althusser and Etienne Balibar, let loose more speculation about what this historical individuality was, and how it could be differentiated from a "historicist humanism" of Man through the ages. Balibar criticized the conception of "men" as miniature centers or concentrated representations of the social structure, from which the whole might be read off. Instead, just as there were different kinds of time at work within the social structure, so "there are different forms of political, economic, and ideological individuality in the social structure, too, forms which are not supported by the same individuals, and which have their own relatively autonomous histories."[7] Whatever the difficulties of this formulation, it had the great usefulness of insisting that "historical individuation" implied elaborate and nonunified, and nonunifying processes, and that was what interested me.

Before the machinations of the humanist versus antihumanist allegiances occupied the presses, a writer less familiar to the Left lexicon had described the inevitable ambiguity between collectivity and individuality. Merleau-Ponty's principled working between and against the standard reductive versions of both Marxism and liberal humanism did not result in any unassailable "synthesis" of the two, but returned, in the end, to the perspectival character of knowledge, its necessary unfinishedness. His *Phenomenology of Perception*, written in 1945, translated into English in 1962, is in part an extended battle with received psychologies of sensory knowing, and with their supporting philosophies which assumed an antagonism between the "inner" and "outer" worlds.

> I am a psychological and historical structure, and have received, with existence, a manner of existing, a style . . . .. The fact remains that I am free, not in spite of, or on the hither side of, these motivations, but by means of them. For this significant life, this certain significance of nature and history which I am, does not limit my access to the world, but on the contrary is my means of entering into communication with it . . . .. Nothing determines me from outside, not because nothing acts upon me, but on the contrary because I am from the start outside myself and open to the world.[8]

The indeterminacy and multiply signifying quality of thought and action "does not stem from some imperfection of our knowledge, and we must not imagine that any God could sound our hearts and minds and determine what we own to nature and what to freedom."[9] History could neither transcend nor be reduced to economics; historical materialism "consists just as much in making economics historical as in making history economic" and if, Merleau-

Ponty wrote, "Man is a historical idea and not a natural species,"[10] the resulting uncertainties were hardly weaknesses. "An existential theory of history is ambiguous, but this ambiguity cannot be made a matter of reproach, for it is inherent in things."[11]

Again, my object in repeating these quotations isn't to expound or to defend or obliterate the difficulties which arise from the philosophies of their authors. I cite them, as I said, as energetic fragments which reverberated behind the later reading and writing which I, among many others, attempted; and perhaps similar cuttings from theories of politics, history, and psychology will occur in others' memories. They have some force for thinking about feminism and what a history of "women" might be.

A final cluster of talismanic quotations here, again of use in considering the nature of political rhetoric: Wittgenstein, in his *Philosophical Investigations*, first published in 1953, describes the intelligibility of words as depending on their positioning: ". . . a great deal of stage-setting in the language is espoused if the mere act of naming is to make sense. And when we speak of someone's having given a name to 'pain', what is presupposed is the existence of the grammar of the word "pain;" it shews the post where the new word is stationed."[12] The uniform appearance of printed or spoken words may mislead, "for their application is not presented to us so clearly" and the myriad uses of language remind us "to make a radical break with the idea that language always functions in one way, always serves the same purpose: to convey thoughts—which may be about houses, pains, good and evil, or anything else you please."[13] Wittgenstein gives the example of a sketch of a vaguely letter-like cipher, which could be from a foreign alphabet, or a poor rendition of a familiar pattern, or a mere flourish; "I can see it in various aspects according to the fiction I surround it with. And here there is a close kinship with 'experiencing the meaning of a word'."[14]

Isn't one essential aspect of any archival historical work, including work on "women," just this "stage-setting in the language," the business of assessing the surrounding conventions and the political "grammar?" This is *not* an alternative or a vague preliminary to studying the history of a "reality" set against "discourse"—but it is simply and immediately studying history. Foucault (whose conception of discursive formations is not reducible to a synonym for "language") insists, again in *The Archaeology of Knowledge*, on the historicity of his task. Not to produce one great universal discourse common to all for some particular period, but

> to show what the differences consisted of, how it was possible for men, within the same discursive practice, to speak of different objects, to have contrary opinions, and to make contradictory choices; my aim was also to show in what way contradictory choices; my aim was also to show in what way discursive practices were distinguished from one another; in

short, I wanted not to exclude the problem of the subject, but to define
the positions and functions that the subject would occupy in the diversity
of discourse.[15]

There was, it followed, no grand empire of discourse which ruled a
cloudy realm above, set in opposition to "the real"; there were—only, and
demandingly—local transformations at different levels. Foucault's "archaeology" here means the historical formation of discourses:

> [T]he archaeological description of discourses is deployed in the dimen-
> sion of a general history; it seeks to discover that whole domain of in-
> stitutions, economic processes, and social relations on which a discursive
> formation can be articulated; it tries to show how the autonomy of dis-
> course and its specificity nevertheless do not give it the status of pure
> ideality and total historical independence; what it wishes to uncover is the
> particular level in which history can give place to definite types of dis-
> course, which have their own type of historicity, and which are related
> to a whole set of various historicities.[16]

> Archaeology does not deny the possibility of new statements in correlation
> with "external" events. Its task is to show on what conditions a correlation
> can exist between them, and what precisely it consists of . . .. It does
> not try to avoid that mobility of discourses that makes them move to the
> rhythm of events; it tries to free the level at which it is set in motion
> . . ..[17]

This characterization, although it has some awkwardness of translation,
seemed an accurate and sympathetic account of the discoveries that historical
work generates. I have set it out, as it has been present for years for me,
as a benevolent and conscientious analysis of how things seem to be.

NOTES

1. *Am I That Name? Feminism and the Category of "Women" in History* (London:
Macmillan, and Minneapolis: University of Minnesota Press, 1988).

2. Michel Foucault, *The Archaeology of Knowledge,* translated by A.M. Sheridan Smith
(London: Tavistock Publications, 1972), Introduction, p. 17.

3. *Ibid.*, p. 46.

4. Kate Soper in *Humanism and Anti-Humanism* (London: Hutchinson, 1986) gives a
very useful summary of the arguments and their settings.

5. Karl Marx, *Theses on Feuerbach*, in *Karl Marx and Frederick Engels, Selected
Works*, translated by Richard Dixon & others (London: Lawrence & Wishart, 1968), p. 29.

6. Karl Marx, *Grundrisse: Foundations of the Critique of Political Economy*, translated by Martin Nicolaus (London: Allen Lane, New Left Review, 1973), p. 496.

7. Louis Althusser and Etienne Balibar, *Reading Capital* (London: New Left Books, 1970), p. 252.

8. Maurice Merleau-Ponty, *The Phenomenology of Perception* (London: Routledge & K. Paul, 1962), p. 455.

9. *Ibid.*, p. 169.

10. *Ibid.*, p. 170–71.

11. *Ibid.*, p. 172.

12. Ludwig Wittgenstein, *Philosophical Investigations* (1953; these references all from 1963 edition (Oxford: Oxford University Press, 1963), p. 92e.

13. *Ibid.*, p. 102e.

14. *Ibid.*, p. 210e.

15. Michel Foucault, p. 200.

16. *Ibid.*, p. 164–65.

17. *Ibid.*, p. 168.

8

Dealing with Differences

Christina Crosby

Things change. First written in 1989 for a session of the annual conference of the International Association for Philosophy and Literature titled "Identity at the Limits of Dialectic," this essay is marked by its occasion. Focused on women's studies, the paper argues that feminists need to theorize difference and think again about history if feminist scholarship is to escape the circularity of simply recognizing a preconceived, pregiven "women's identity." A mere two years later it seems that no one is talking about identity; everyone is talking about differences—and about history. Diversity is said to be a fact of life which, like it or not, will transform the academy; history is thought to show the facts of race, class, and gender long obscured, even actively repressed, by scholarship. Yet, *plus ça change, plus c'est la même chose.* That is, as I set about the task of revising the essay in light of these changes, I concluded that "differences" work now more or less as "identity" did before. What remains obscured is the problem of the production of knowledge at the level of theory, despite all the talk about theory which has gone on in the past decade. So what follows is still about women's studies and identity, but it is also about the university and differences. And it is still about theory.

In 1978 the feminist literary critic Helene Moglen spoke at a conference on "the novel," and in an anecdote explained the genesis of her decision to do a biographical-critical study of Charlotte Brontë.[1] She had been teaching *Villette*, a story of emotional suffering and fleetingly realized satisfaction told retrospectively by the first-person narrator, Lucy Snowe. At the end of the last class, one of her students—a woman—made her way to Moglen's

130

side, burst into tears and declared, "I *am* Lucy Snowe!" This striking testimony of recognition and identification moved Moglen to study Brontë's life and works to discover how "the self" is "conceived" in her writings, to discover how Lucy represents an identity recognized intuitively, assumed viscerally, by women readers. In 1978, then, the founding moment of a certain feminist self-consciousness is the discovery of an identity common to all women, woman's identity as "the other."

A year later, in 1979, a major international feminist conference was held in New York City celebrating the thirtieth anniversary of the publication of *The Second Sex*. That event may serve to mark the emergence of a sharp and strenuous critique of feminist criticism and theory, a critique developed largely by women of color. Speaking at that conference, Audre Lorde asked why white feminists didn't address the differences between women:

> If white american feminist theory need not deal with the differences between us, and the resulting difference in our oppressions, then how do you deal with the fact that the women who clean your houses and tend your children while you attend conferences on feminist theory are, for the most part, poor women and women of Color? What is the theory behind racist feminism?[2]

These questions, and others along the same lines, have had profound effects. As Donna Haraway puts it, "white women . . . discovered (i.e. were forced kicking and screaming to notice) the non-innocence of the category 'woman'." "Differences" has become a given of academic feminisms; feminism has been modified and pluralized. No longer one, feminisms are marked by nation and race (Lorde's "white american" feminism), by class, ethnicity, sexuality: black feminism, latina feminism, lesbian feminism, middle-class "mainstream" feminism, and so on. It would seem that dealing with the fact of differences is *the* project of women's studies today.

Moreover, "differences" are now spoken everywhere in the academy. The demand to specify, to mark the (now familiar) differences of race, class, and gender is part of a general call for diversity, pluralism, for a multicultural academy. In research and teaching, in writing or awarding grants, in admitting students, in hiring and promoting faculty, one must now deal with differences.

What does this mean? Those of use in the academy who are devoted, as Gayatri Spivak puts it, to "building for difference,"[3] might well reflect on how "differences" works at this moment when diversity is spoken by students, faculty, college presidents and blue-ribbon committees, is the subject of National Endowment of the Humanities reports, and is a featured topic in the press and on the radio.[4] Lorde says that the *fact of differences* is a problem for *theory*, specifically for white American feminist theory which cannot deal with differences. Further, differences are not formal, but political, a matter of "oppression." How, then, have differences been theorized? How have the relations of "fact" and "theory," politics and theory, been thought? These questions are especially pressing given the widespread attention now accorded to diversity and the fractious debates over the "politicizing" of the university. To approach these questions I will return to women's studies, taking this field not as marginal to the academy as a whole but rather as an exemplary instance of an academic discourse in which "difference" and "differences" have had a long career, and in which theory has always been articulated with politics.

White academic feminism of the 1970s stressed identity, as in Moglen's work on Brontë. Yet this identity is of course inseparable from difference. That is, to be woman is to be different from man, from normative masculinity. Recognizing one's identity with Brontë's heroine—"I am Lucy Snowe"—is the discovery that to be a woman is to be "the other," the second sex. It is to see that, in Beauvoir's famous phrase, "one is not born, but rather becomes, a woman." For Moglen, Brontë's life and writing embody the difficulty of that becoming in ways that bear directly on women's lives today. "[T]he world in which Charlotte Brontë lived is the world which we have ourselves inherited," she writes, and "as we too strive for autonomous definition, we see ourselves reflected in different aspects of Brontë's struggle. . . . I have pursued my own shadow through the beckoning recess of another's mind, hoping to discover its substance at the journey's end." Reflecting the present, history reveals to Moglen the facts of womanhood: the trials of conceiving a self, of becoming a substantive subject when one is systematically objectified, positioned as the other. Her first-person plural, then, is the "we" of a feminism founded on an identity common to all women, uniting past and present, the feminist critic and her object of study.

There is a circularity to this conception. To know women one must be a woman, to know the other one must be the other. While Moglen doesn't elaborate the theoretical dimension of her study, it assumes the central tenet of "standpoint epistemology": that the "subjugated social location" women share is an epistemologically privileged position. Developed by Nancy Hartsock and others, the idea of the standpoint has been widely discussed in women's studies. Given Lorde's pointed question about "theory," a look at Hartsock's work is in order.

In an essay published in a collection titled *Discovering Reality* (1983), Hartsock sets out to "develop the ground for a specifically feminist historical materialism."[5] This ground is "a feminist standpoint." Working on what she takes to be "the methodological base provided by Marxian theory," Hartsock assumes a "distinction between appearance and essence, circulation and production, abstract and concrete" in which "the deeper level or essence both includes and explains the 'surface' or appearance, and indicates the logic by means of which the appearance inverts and distorts the deeper reality" (283, 285). Seeing the deeper level and comprehending its logic is possible only from a particular perspective, she argues, since "material life structures understanding" (287). Thus whether one can see the reality of capitalism depends on where one is positioned. Exchange only is visible to the capitalist, while workers can see both the reality of exchange relations and the deeper reality of production which includes exchange. Hartsock holds that women are similarly privileged by the sexual division of labor of patriarchy. Women experience a lived reality of materiality, process, and change in the daily reproduction of life; a woman's "immersion in the world of use," while a fact of her subjection, is also the condition which enables her to see more clearly the deeper reality of life: "sensuous activity," not a series of abstractions. "The experience of continuity and relation—with others, with the natural world, of mind and body—provides an ontological base for developing a non-problematic social synthesis," she writes (303). From this base, the reality of being a woman, emerges a feminist standpoint, "a mediated rather than immediate understanding" (288). That is, the feminist standpoint "expresses female experience at a particular time and place, located within a particular set of social relations," but experience alone is not enough. The source for the feminist standpoint and the critique of patriarchy it makes possible is "found in political activity itself" (285). The historically specific experience of subjugation, then, mediated by political struggle, is the ground for discovering an adequate—rather than partial and mystified—knowledge of reality as a whole.

This is a "theory," then, in which knowledge follows from and leads to identity, in which an experience unique to women is prior to thought, and in which the history of women is continuous—in "Western cultures," at least (303). The fact of "differences" is mentioned, but only to be bracketed: "In addressing the institutional sexual division of labor, I propose to lay aside the important differences among women across race and class boundaries and instead search for central commonalities" (290). Lorde's pointed question about feminist theory addresses the failure of this structure of knowledge to see anything other than its own preconceptions, the pre-existing category of woman-as-other. In short, this is not theory, but rather "the vicious circle of the mirror relation of ideological reflection," in Louis Althusser's phrase. That is, a feminism which looks to history to find "women" and always finds what it is looking for is bound to be ideological—falsely universalizing and dehistoricizing—despite its appeals to history (and to Marx). The question, then, is whether feminisms which "deal with the differences between us" break out of this vicious circle in which women are self-evident and history mirrors the present.

Before approaching this question, I will go a bit further with Althusser and his analysis of the circularity of ideology. In *Reading Capital* he develops a detailed reading of ideology as historicism; his critique is important for women's studies since feminisms turn to history to see the political, to see the facts of hierarchical differences ideology obscures. Everything, then, depends on how history is thought if history is to be the way out of ideology.

Althusser analyzes two variants of historicism, speculative and empiricist, demonstrating that both are closed, circular systems. The structure of mirror reflection is what marks historicism as ideological, a repetition of what is, rather than a theoretical reading of process. In speculative (Hegelian) historicism, "the speculative genesis of the concept is identical with the genesis of the real concrete itself, i.e. with the process of empirical history" and "history . . . culminates and is fulfilled in the present of a science [knowledge] identical with consciousness. . . ."[6] Conversely, in empirical historicism, "knowledge . . . is completely *inscribed in the structure of the real object.* . . . Knowledge is therefore already *really* present in the real object it has to know. . . ." (38). Thus "the empirical-speculative thesis of all historicism [is] the identity of the concept and the *real* (historical) object," and empiricism and idealism are two sides of the same ideological coin (130).

Speculative historicism is, as Althusser points out, a "religious model," a recognition of essence in existence. At the End of History, "the concept at last becomes visible, present among us in person, tangible in its sensory existence" (16). Theory, then, is the retrospective representation of revealed truth—the owl of Minerva which flies only at the end of the day. Knowledge is the recognition of the realized concept.

If in speculative historicism the objective real is but the realization of the concept, in empiricist historicism the real object determines the concept. Both reduce theory to reflection, guaranteeing that theory will only recognize and repeat an essential pre-existent "history." History is homogeneous, an "historical bloc" with its own enclosing logic—even dialectical contradiction is seen as cumulative and progressive. Theory, or philosophy, is stripped of its power to "see" anything truly different, Althusser argues in a reading of Gramsci:

> Since all philosophy is history, the "philosophy of praxis" can, as philosophy, only be the philosophy of the philosophy-history identity. . . . [P]hilosophy . . . is reduced . . . to a mere "historical methodology," i.e., to the mere self-consciousness of the historicity of history, to a reflection on the presence of real history in all its manifestations. . . . (136–37).

The circularity of historicism is evident in Moglen's work on Brontë. There the mirror of the past reflects the present; past and present are the same, as are the investigating subject and the object of knowledge, as are history and theory; one can only reflect on the historical reality of women as a woman. History is knowledge, and according to history "I am Lucy Snowe." So, too, in Hartsock's epistemology history gives women an experience of subjection which is the ground for knowledge. Mediated through political practice—which is the immediate "source" of critique—the "subjected social location" women have in common is conceptually and temporally prior to theory; knowledge is given by that material reality. As Sandra Harding explains, in standpoint epistemology "the woman inquirer interpreting, explaining, critically examining women's condition is simultaneously explaining her own condition."[7]

Women's studies so conceived sees the concept of identity realized in the facts of history (speculative historicism) *and* takes the historical facticity of identity as an a priori fact (empiricist historicism), so that theorizing is but the recognition of what one has already become: "woman." Theory is but ideology, a repetition of the already known; theory cannot transform the field, produce a different object of knowledge, see something other than women's identity as the negative.

Has dealing with the fact of differences broken the vicious circle of ideological reflection? Things change—how much? Certainly Hartsock's more recent work shows her readiness to modify her concept of the feminist standpoint and to criticize its exclusiveness. If in 1983 she brackets "the important differences among women" to "search for central commonalities," in 1987 she declares that "most important . . . are questions about difference, especially differences among women. We need to develop our understanding of difference. . . ."[8] She argues that until recently theory has been the province of "white men of a certain class background" who have constituted their experience as central and universal, marginalizing all who differ as the devalued Other. Hartsock finds most pressing the need to "build an account of the world as seen from the margins, an account which can transform these margins into centers" (204). Here the standpoints from which an analysis of falsely universalizing Theory (to use her critical capital) can be mounted are plural, although united by the fact of living as the Other. The "history of marginalization" protects against a falsely "totalizing discourse" since it is the basis of knowledge and "marginal groups are far less likely to mistake themselves for the universal 'man'" (205). "When the various 'minority' experiences have been described and when the significance of those experiences as a ground for the critique of the dominant institutions and ideologies of society is better recognized," Hartsock writes, "we will have at least the tools with which to begin to construct an account of the world sensitive to the realities of race and gender, as well as class" (206). "[W]e need to sort out who we really are" (204).

What was once singular is now plural. Hartsock's work may stand as exemplary of a major shift in women's studies, a move to greatly increased specificity and diversity. It is impossible to exaggerate the importance of the critique of feminism's (*white* feminism's) exclusions, the ways in which the supposedly universal category of "woman" was constituted. Dealing with the fact of difference has broken up the singular standpoint of an earlier women's studies and the universalizing identity of women visible from that standpoint. Women's studies, which was founded on the ontological question "what is woman?" and its corollary "who am I?" has changed.

But only to "who are we?" However importantly feminism has been modified, specifying differences and "describing minority experiences" is not going to transform women's studies at the level of theory, that is, enable it to break through the circle of ideology. For that circle is vicious precisely because it is elastic and expansive though resolutely closed. While Hartsock has taken seriously Lorde's call for a theory which can deal with differences, Lorde herself, in appealing to the "fact" of "the differences between us" as the corrective to feminist theory, is suggesting, however polemically, that facts speak for themselves. The *relationship*, then, between "the real" and knowledge of the real, between "facts" and theory, history and theory is occluded even as women's studies seeks to address the problem of theoretical practice. Lorde's intervention, and a host of other critiques of "racist feminism," have broken up an oppressively singular feminism, but much of U.S. women's studies is still bound to an empiricist historicism which is the flip side of the idealism scorned and disavowed by feminisms.

"[E]very reading . . . reflects in its lessons and rules . . . the conception of knowledge underlying the object of knowledge which makes knowledge what it is," Althusser argues (34). What can be seen in a field of knowledge is a function of the way the field is conceived, the way knowledge itself is conceived, and what can be seen also determines what must remain unseen. Althusser's formulation of the problem of the production of knowledge in terms of vision and oversight has been followed by Foucault's archaeology of knowledge and Paul de Man's reading of blindness and insight, so the general issues seem old and familiar. Yet as Foucault remarked in 1983:

> [W]e come to summarize a work, or a problem in terms of slogans. . . .
> [A] fairly evolved discourse, instead of being relayed by additional work
> which perfects it (either with criticism or amplification), rendering it more
> difficult and even finer, nowadays undergoes a process of amplification
> from the bottom up . . . philosophical thought, or a philosophical issue,
> becomes a consumer item.[9]

Foucault's *oeuvre* could arguably be considered a critical amplification of Althusser's work on the problem of the production of knowledge (he was, after all, Althusser's student), but in many respects his thought has become a consumer item—especially the concept of "subjugated knowledges." Focusing on Foucault's interest in what he called "local popular knowledges. . . . that have been disqualified," many have overlooked "the fairly evolved discourse" on epistemological issues in which he participates, his work on the systematic limits of knowledge and the violence inherent in any "will to know." As for de Man, the gleeful dismissal on the evidence of "history" of his complex and corrosive theory of reading may be said to speak for itself. So the problem of the production of knowledge is still often overlooked, even with all the talk of "theory" in the last decade.

Women's studies is no exception. Despite efforts to historicize, women's studies often runs willy-nilly in the circles of historicism. Overlooking the ways that "history," the "real," even "the fact of difference" necessarily reflect the conception of knowledge by which they are available to thought, much of women's studies proceeds as though reality itself can be—must be—mirrored in thought. This avoids "the question of a theory of the production of knowledge, which as the knowledge of its object . . . is the grasp or appropriation of the *real* object, the real world."[10]

Thus in responding to Lorde's call for a theory which can deal with the reality of the differences which divide women, feminist theory nonetheless is too often "reduced . . . to a reflection on the presence of real history in all its manifestations" (Althusser). The problem is that differences are taken to be self-evident, concrete, *there*, present in history and therefore the proper ground of theory. Theory is identical with history; theory becomes, as Althusser says, nothing but "historical methodology," a circularity in which only what is already known—"differences," for example—can be seen. It is impossible to ask how "differences" is constituted as a concept, so "differences" become substantive, something in themselves—race, class, gender—as though we knew already what this incommensurate triumvirate means!

To specify is not necessarily to historicize. Lorde writes, "As a forty-nine-year old Black lesbian feminist socialist mother of two, including one boy, and a member of an interracial couple, I usually find myself a part of some group defined as other, deviant, inferior, or just plain wrong" (114). Such specifying statements are now *de rigueur* and serve to locate one implicitly in relation to others, a useful exercise that does guard against certain presumptions of universality. But consciously assuming a specific standpoint, reflecting on the facts of history which place one in a particular way, leaves the problem of identity intact and the concept of history uninterrogated. It is to assume that ontology is the ground of epistemology, that who I am determines what and how I know. But how do I know who I am? That's obvious: I am my differences, which have been given to me by history. In this circle, the differences which seem to refract and undo a substantive identity actually reflect a multifaceted, modified but all-too-recognizable subject.

In concluding a critical yet fundamentally sympathetic discussion of standpoint epistemology, Sandra Harding asks, "Why should we be loath to attribute a certain degree of, if not historical inevitability, at least historical possibility to the kinds of understandings arrived at in feminist science and epistemology?"[11] This, however, is a weak form of the claim she is committed to, that "feminist theory is nothing but the reflex in thought of these conflicts [the development of cheap and effective birth control, the growth in service sectors which drew women into wage labor, the civil-rights movement and radicalism of the 1960s, the increase in divorce, the escalation in international hostilities revealing the overlap between masculine domination and nationalist domination] in fact, their ideal reflection in the minds first of the class most directly suffering under them—women" (160). Paraphrasing Engels, Harding like Hartsock thinks to avoid the dangers of idealist speculation only to repeat the same problem from its other side, that of an empiricism in which "knowledge . . . is completely *inscribed in the structure of the real object*" and philosophy is but "a reflection on the presence of real history in all its manifestations." The subject in its mirror relation remains intact.

One of the great virtues of Donna Haraway's work, which is in some ways associated with Hartsock's and Harding's, is that the subject is at first unrecognizable. "By the late twentieth century, our time, a mythic time, we are all chimeras," she writes, "theorized and fabricated hybrids of machine and organism; in short, we are cyborgs. The cyborg is our ontology; it gives us our politics."[12] In her "Manifesto for Cyborgs," "an effort to build an ironic political myth faithful to feminism," Haraway argues that the "integrated circuit" of multinational late capitalism, a technological wonder in a nuclear age that may be the end of the world, a network of exhaustive exploitation and fragmentation, is ironically the condition of possibility for understanding gender, race, and class—indeed ontology "itself"—as effects:

> There is nothing about 'being' a female that naturally binds women. There is not even such a state as 'being' female, itself a highly complex category constituted in contested sexual scientific discourses and other social practices. Gender, race or class consciousness is an achievement forced on us by the terrible historical experience of the contradictory social realities of patriarchy, colonialism, and capitalism. (179)

Social reality, which of course includes the reality of living as women, is "lived social relations, our most important political construction, a world-changing fiction" (174). In her mythic manifesto Haraway declares that the circuits of the "informatics of domination," the military/industrial complex of microelectronic sophistication, can be both known and transformed, but only by giving up faith in pretechnological innocence and unified being.

Cyborgs are by definition fabricated, part this and part that. In this partiality Haraway sees "the promise of objectivity: a scientific knower seeks the subject position not of identity, but of objectivity, that is, partial connection."[13] Any other claim to objective knowledge is false, either the "godtrick" of totalizing scientific authority ("whose power depends on systematic narrowing and obscuring") or of relativism ("a way of being nowhere while claiming to be everywhere equally") (584). "There is no way to 'be' simultaneously in all, or wholly in any, of the privileged (i.e. subjugated) positions structured by gender, race, nation, and class," she writes in response to theories of standpoint epistemology (586). Knowledge, then, is not founded on a standpoint which in turn depends on an ontology, but on shifting, mobile, simultaneous, multiple positions, critical positions which are taken up in response to domination. That is, political positions. Haraway's concept of "situated knowledges" is fully political; as she says, "admitted or not, politics and ethics ground struggles over knowledge projects in the exact, natural, social, and human sciences; otherwise rationality is simply impossible, an optical illusion projected from nowhere comprehensively" (587). Arguing that the "politics of positioning" grounds knowledge shifts Haraway's theoretical project away from the circularity of ontological claims, the vicious circle in which subject and object are predetermined, linked by the copula "to be": "I am _____," "we are _____." Further, in its energetic emphasis on partiality it makes differences—the differences among positions, and the different positions any one person must assume—the condition of any knowledge.

Yet Haraway's startlingly inventive work, which so exuberantly transforms many of the shibboleths of U.S. women's studies, nonetheless does not break decisively with the structure of reflection and recognition which is historicism. The cyborg, that assemblage of different parts which is the late-twentieth-century subject, "gives us our politics," and politics ground knowledge. And the cyborg "itself"?—"an achievement forced on us by the terrible historical experience of the contradictory social realities of patriarchy, colonialism, and capitalism." That is, history gives us politics, and politics gives us knowledge, which is the same basic structure standpoint epistemology assumes, though importantly modified to emphasize differences rather than identity.

The question remains of how to deal with difference and how to work for difference—how to think difference as a problem for theory and not a solution. These questions must be asked, especially now when the politicization of the academy is a given, the call to historicize is insistent, and diversity is on everyone's lips. "Differences" has passed into the realm of the slogan which makes it even harder to think, of course, since slogans are by their very nature self-evident: you are either for or against differences, for or against diversity. Thus in the academy we are confronted with a duopoly, a structure of "simultaneous opposition" which seems agonistic but is remarkably stable.[14] What is foreclosed is the possibility of thinking differently about differences, yet that is precisely what is to be done. Otherwise differences will remain as self-evident as identity once was, and just as women's studies once saw woman everywhere, the academy will recognize differences everywhere, cheerfully acknowledging that since everyone is different, everyone is the same. Such is the beauty of pluralism.

Foucault has argued that

> knowledge, even under the banner of history, does not depend on 'rediscovery,' and it emphatically excludes the 'rediscovery of ourselves.' History becomes 'effective' to the degree that it introduces discontinuity into our very being—as it divides our emotions, dramatizes our instincts, multiplies our body and sets it against itself.[15]

Such history has little to do with historicist projects which see a beautifully diverse humanity everywhere and is equally hostile to historicist feminisms which see women and differences everywhere, reflected in "history." Effective history, which is to say knowledge which is not a reflection of the already known, the taken for granted, the obviously true, introduces discontinuity into knowledge, not only "being." That is, knowledge, if it is to avoid the circularity of ideology, must read the processes of differentiation, not look for differences. As Gayatri Spivak has argued, the necessary condition for knowledge is "irreducible difference," unknowable "itself" because difference is not a thing to be recognized but a process always underway. A return to the text of Marx will indeed be useful in this project, but Marx after Althusser and Derrida doesn't look the same as the Marx of Hartsock's "feminist historical materialism" or even Haraway's cyborgian feminism of situated knowledges. As Etienne Balibar writes in an essay on ideology, theory, and politics,

> [t]he materialist critique of ideology, for its part, corresponds to the discovery that the reality of the real is not a being identical to itself but is, in a sense, a specific abstraction the individual can only at first perceive as an abstraction twice-removed—speculative or, as Marx puts it, inverted and rendered autonomous. It is not individuals who *create* this abstraction, for they are themselves basically only relations or the product of relations. The whole science of history is virtually the distinction between these two antithetical abstractions, which is to say that it breaks up or deconstructs their identification. It is in this that the science of history is "concrete."[16]

Things change. Let us look again, then, at *Villette*, that novel of the white-feminist canon, written by a middle-class Englishwoman. Differences, it would seem, hardly figure here. I will argue to the contrary, beginning with some old questions.[17] How does the text produce a representation of a woman's experience so powerful as to induce readers to identify with the heroine ("I am Lucy Snowe") and find in the book a reflection of their own lives? What does history have to do with this representation of experience? First, Brontë appeals directly to an historical discourse in her characterization of Lucy Snowe and in Lucy's narration of the events of her life. In order to invest her heroine and her story with a significance beyond the uniquely individual Brontë appropriates the discourse of typology, a hermeneutical method which finds in the events, people, and prophecies of the Old Testament "types and shadows" which are fulfilled in the new. This "Christian historicism" is evoked by Brontë to make poor, plain, and unattached Lucy a representative figure, to place her in an all-encompassing history: she must pass through the trials of the Old to arrive at the New, must suffer materially to advance spiritually. Brontë thus invests her protagonist with substantial ideological value, and in the process invests the Scriptures with new significance, as Lucy narrates the story of her life—a secular story—in sacred, universalizing terms. Brontë achieved dramatic effects; no less a reader than George Eliot found the effect of *Villette* to be "preternatural," and her response is representative of the strong reactions the novel generated. Many objected to the "toying" with the Word of God to tell a secular tale, but few of Brontë's reviewers were indifferent to the book.

Feminist critics today tend to forget the theological question, displacing the questions of history and ideology the novel raises. In general, feminists have interpreted the novel in psychological, experiential terms: Lucy's effort to read and then to write the Book of Life is a matter of discovering an order of intelligibility which she must simultaneously produce herself. This is a project of self-authorship, fraught with difficulties for women who are positioned as objects, not subjects. Lucy's search for herself is thus taken to be emblematic of the universal process of becoming a woman (an objectified subject), and the excessively symbolic dimensions of the text are said to be part of a necessary and even heroic struggle with the patriarchal order to make visible the truths of women's lives.

I would argue that, on the contrary, such a realization of Lucy's inner essence in her existence is an impossibility, and that *Villette* actually displays this impossibility for the reader who doesn't take the text at face value. Brontë's appropriation of typological discourse already indicates a contest over the meanings of history and the representation of history. But there is more, for the rhetoric of the text—the very extended figures which establish Lucy as a Type and her story as Typical—defeats the progressive realization of a transcendental design. *Villette* is an intensely figurative text which promises semantic depth, but which develops instead bizarrely allegorical passages in which "correspondences" do not hold and passages extend to extravagant lengths as a wild metonymy overwhelms any hope of resemblance or resolution. The text undoes the order of intelligibility to which it is committed in a radical dissolution of identity and an equally radical disruption of the unified, continuous, progressive history of historicism. To see this *Villette*, one must avoid the seductive circularity of historicist explanation to read the proliferation of difference in the text, the ways the text elaborates typology only to explode the possibility of historicist coherence.

"Building for difference," Spivak says, is difficult in a "very personalist culture," because such a project requires continual vigilance against taking anything, especially anything marked as "the personal," for granted. It also means foregoing the satisfying search for error in favor of reading how truths are produced, including the truth one holds most dear, and sustaining a critique of something which is both dangerous and indispensable.[18] Like identity and history, difference and differences. The challenge is not to purify women's studies or the academy, but to question constantly our most powerful concepts.

NOTES

1. A conference sponsored by *Novel: A Forum on Fiction* at Brown University in 1976.

2. Audre Lorde, *Sister Outsider* (Trumansburg, New York: The Crossing Press, 1984), p. 112.

3. Gayatri Spivak, with Ellen Rooney, "In a Word. Interview," *differences*, 1, 2 (Summer 1989), p. 128.

4. A few examples: Juniata College, a small liberal arts college in central Pennsylvania, has recently declared an emphasis on diversity, both in student life and in teaching; Brown University, a major Ivy League institution, published an internal report titled "The American University and the Pluralist Ideal," a response to student agitation for more attention to diversity in the curriculum and throughout the university; Wesleyan University is offering a faculty seminar in "multiculturalism"; first William Bennett and now Lynn Cheney, as heads of the National Endowment for the Humanities, have released reports on the state of the Humanities in the U.S. which explicitly call for a recentering of humanistic education on what they call the Western tradition (*To Reclaim a Legacy* (1984); *Humanities in America* (1988)); The *New York Times* ran a piece in the ideas and trends section headlined "A Campus Forum on Multiculturalism: Opening Academia Without Closing It Down" (December 1990); The *Chronicle of Higher Education* (28 November 1990, A5) reported on the 1989 American Studies Association meeting in an article headed "Proponents of 'Multicultural' Humanities Research Call for a Critical Look at Its Achievements"; and *All Things Considered*, the Na-

tional Public Radio news show, had as part of the program on 3 January 1991 a report on "ethnic studies" in the university.

5. Nancy C. M. Hartsock, "The Feminist Standpoint: Developing the Ground for a Specificially Feminist Historical Materialism," in Sandra Harding and Merill B. Hintikka, eds., *Discovering Reality: Feminist Perspectives on Epistemology, Metaphysics, Methodology, and Philosophy of Science* (Boston: D. Reidel, 1983), p. 283. Future references to this work appear in the text.

6. Louis Althusser, *Reading Capital*, translated by Ben Brewster (London, NLB, 1977), pp. 126, 125.

7. Sandra Harding, *The Science Question in Feminism* (Ithaca: Cornell University Press, 1986), p. 147.

8. Nancy Hartsock, "Rethinking Modernism: Minority vs. Majority Theories," *Cultural Critique*, 7 (Fall 1987), p. 189. Since then Hartsock has published "Postmodernism and Political Change: Issues for Feminist Theory," *Cultural Critique*, 14 (Winter 1989–90), which she says "builds on and may be read in conjunction with "Rethinking Modernism."" . . . (15). In this essay she turns to Eduardo Galeano, Gabriel Garcia Márquez, Kum Kum Sangari, Gloria Anzaldúa, Sylvia Wynter, Audre Lorde, and others; she concludes, "Attention to the epistemologies contained in our various subjugated knowledges can allow us to shift the theoretical terrain in fundamental ways . . ." (33).

9. Michel Foucault, *Politics, Philosophy, Culture: Interviews and Other Writings 1977–1984*, translated by Alan Sheridan (New York, Routledge, 1988), pp. 44–45.

10. Althusser, *Reading Capital*, p. 54.

11. Sandra Harding, p. 161.

12. Donna Haraway, "A Manifesto for Cyborgs: Science, Technology, and Socialist Feminism in the 1980s," in Elizabeth Weed, ed., *Coming to terms: Feminism, Theory, Politics* (New York: Routledge, 1989), p. 174.

13. Donna Haraway, "Situated Knowledges: The Science Question in Feminism and the Privilege of Partial Perspective," *Feminist Studies* 14, 3 (Fall 1988), p. 586.

14. Jean Baudrillard, *Simulations*, translated by Paul Foss, Paul Patton, and Philip Beitchman (New York: Semiotext(e), 1983), p. 134.

15. Michel Foucault, *Language, Counter-Memory, Practice*, translated by Donald F. Bouchard and Sherry Simon (Ithaca, N.Y.: Cornell University Press), pp. 153–54.

16. Etienne Balibar, "The Vacillation of Ideology," in Cary Nelson and Lawrence Grossberg, eds., *Marxism and the Interpretation of Culture* (Urbana, Ill.: University of Illinois Press, 1988), p. 164.

17. The reading of *Villette* which follows is developed in detail in my book, *The Ends of History: Victorians and "The Woman Question"* (New York: Routledge, 1991), pp. 110–143.

18. Gayatri Spivak, pp. 127, 129.

9

Speaking in Tongues: Dialogics Dialectics, and the Black Woman Writer's Literary Tradition

Mae Gwendolyn Henderson

I am who I am, doing what I came to do, acting upon you like a drug
or a chisel *to remind you of your me-ness, as I discover you in myself.*
    —Audre Lorde, *Sister Outsider* (emphasis mine)

> There's a noisy feelin' near the cracks
> crowdin' me . . . slips into those long, loopin' "B's"
> There's a noisy feelin' near the cracks
> crowdin' me . . . slips into those long, loopin' "B's"
> of Miss Garrison's handwritin' class;
> they become the wire hoops I must jump through.
> It spooks my alley, it spooks my play,
> more nosey now than noisy,
>   lookin' for a tongue
>   lookin' for a tongue
>   to get holy in.
> Who can tell this feelin' where to set up church?
> Who can tell this noise where to go?
> A root woman workin' . . . a mo-jo,
> Just to the left of my ear.
>
>   —Cherry Muhanji, *Tight Spaces*

Some years ago, three black feminist critics and scholars edited an anthology entitled *All the Women Are White, All the Blacks Are Men, But Some of Us Are Brave,*[1] suggesting in the title the unique and peculiar dilemma of black women. Since then it has perhaps become almost commonplace for literary critics, male and female, black and white, to note that black women have been discounted or unaccounted for in the "traditions" of black, women's, and American literature as well as in the contemporary literary-critical dialogue. More recently, black women writers have begun to receive token recognition as they are subsumed under the category of woman in the feminist critique and the category of black in the racial critique. Certainly these "gendered" and "racial" decodings of black women authors present strong and revisionary methods of reading, focusing as they do on literary discourses regarded as marginal to the dominant literary-critical tradition. Yet the "critical insights" of one reading might well become the "blind spots" of another reading. That is, by privileging one category of analysis at the expense of the other, each of these methods risks setting up what Fredric Jameson describes as "strategies of containment," which restrict or repress different or alternative readings.[2] More specifically, blindness to what Nancy Fraser describes as "the gender subtext" can be just as occluding as blindness to *the racial subtext* in the works of black women writers.[3]

Such approaches can result in exclusion at worst and, at best, a reading of part of the text as the whole—a strategy that threatens to replicate (if not valorize) the reification against which black women struggle in life and literature. What I propose is a theory of interpretation based on what I refer to as the "simultaneity of discourse," a term inspired by Barbara Smith's seminal work on black feminist criticism.[4] This concept is meant to signify a mode of reading which examines the ways in which the perspectives of race and gender, and their interrelationships, structure the discourse of black women writers. Such an approach is intended to acknowledge and overcome the limitations imposed by assumptions of internal identity (homogeneity) and the repression of internal differences (heterogeneity) in racial and gendered readings of works by black women writers. In other words, I propose a model that seeks to account for racial difference within gender identity and gender difference within racial identity. This approach represents my effort to avoid what one critic describes as the presumed "absolute and self-sufficient" *otherness* of the critical stance in order to allow the complex representations of black women writers to steer us away from "a simple and reductive paradigm of 'otherness.' "[5]

Discursive Diversity: Speaking in Tongues

What is at once characteristic and suggestive about black women's writing is its interlocutory, or dialogic, character, reflecting not only a relationship with the "other(s)," but an internal dialogue with the plural aspects of self that constitute the matrix of black female subjectivity. The interlocutory character of black women's writings is, thus, not only a consequence of a dialogic relationship with an imaginary or "generalized Other," but a dialogue with the aspects of "otherness" within the self. The complex situatedness of the black woman as not only the "Other" of the Same, but also as the "other" of the other(s) implies, as we shall see, a relationship of difference and identification with the "other(s)."

It is Mikhail Bakhtin's notion of dialogism and consciousness that provides the primary model for this approach. According to Bakhtin, each social group speaks in its own "social dialect"—possesses its own unique language—expressing shared values, perspectives, ideology, and norms. These social dialects become the "languages" of heteroglossia "intersect[ing] with each other in many different ways. . . . As such they all may be juxtaposed to one another, mutually supplement one another, contradict one another and be interrelated dialogically."[6] Yet if language, for Bakhtin, is an expression of social identity, then subjectivity (subjecthood) is constituted as a social entity through the "role of [the] word as medium of consciousness." Consciousness, then, like language, is shaped by the social environment. ("Consciousness becomes consciousness only . . . in the process of social interaction.") Moreover, "the semiotic material of the psyche is preeminently the word—*inner speech.*" Bakhtin in fact defines the relationship between consciousness and inner speech even more precisely: "Analysis would show that the units of which inner speech is constituted are certain *whole entities . . . [resembling] the alternating lines of a dialogue.* There was good reason why thinkers in ancient times should have conceived of inner speech as *inner dialogue.*"[7] Thus consciousness becomes a kind of "inner speech" reflecting "the outer word" in a process that links the psyche, language, and social interaction.

It is the process by which these heteroglossic voices of the other(s) "encounter one another and coexist in the consciousness of real people— first and foremost in the creative consciousness of people who write novels,"[8] that speaks to the situation of black women writers in particular, "privileged" by a social positionality that enables them to speak in dialogically racial and gendered voices to the other(s) both within and without. If the psyche functions as an internalization of heterogeneous social voices, black women's speech/writing becomes at once a dialogue between self and society and between self and psyche. Writing as inner speech, then, becomes what Bakhtin would describe as "a unique form of collaboration with oneself" in the works of these writers.[9]

Revising and expanding Teresa de Lauretis's formulation of the "social subject and the relations of subjectivity to sociality," I propose a model that is intended not only to address "a subject en-gendered in the experiencing of race," but also what I submit is *a subject "racialized" in the experiencing of gender.*[10] Speaking both to and from the position of the other(s), black women writers must, in the words of Audre Lorde, deal not only with "the external manifestations of racism and sexism," but also "with the results of those distortions internalized within our consciousness of ourselves and one another."[11]

What distinguishes black women's writing, then, is the privileging (rather than repressing) of "the other in ourselves." Writing of Lorde's notion of self and otherness, black feminist critic Barbara Christian observes of Lorde what I argue is true to a greater or lesser degree in the discourse of black women writers: "As a black, lesbian, feminist, poet, mother, Lorde has, in her own life, had to search long and hard for *her* people. In responding to each of these audiences, in which a part of her identity lies, she refuses to give up her differences. In fact she uses them, as woman to man, black to white, lesbian to heterosexual, as a means of conducting creative dialogue."[12]

If black women speak from a multiple and complex social, historical, and cultural positionality which, in effect, constitutes black female subjectivity, Christian's term "creative dialogue" then refers to the expression of a multiple *dialogic of differences* based on this complex subjectivity. At the same time, however, black women enter into a *dialectic of identity* with those aspects of self shared with others. It is Hans-Georg Gadamer's "dialectical model of conversation," rather than Bakhtin's dialogics of discourse, that provides an appropriate model for articulating a relation of mutuality and reciprocity with the "Thou"—or intimate other(s). Whatever the critic thinks of Gadamer's views concerning history, tradition, and the like, one can still find Gadamer's emphases—especially as they complement Bakhtin's—to be useful and productive. If the Bakhtinian model is primarily adversarial, assuming that verbal communication (and social interaction) is characterized by contestation with the other(s), then the Gadamerian model presupposes as its goal a language of consensus, communality, and even identification, in which "one claims to express the other's claim and even to understand the other better than the other understands [him or herself]." In the "I-Thou" relationship proposed by Gadamer, "the important thing is . . . to experience the 'Thou' truly as a 'Thou,' that is, not to overlook [the other's] claim and to listen to what [s/he] has to say to us." Gadamer's dialectic, based on a typology of the "hermeneutical experience," privileges tradition as "a genuine partner in communication, with which we have fellowship as does the 'I' with a 'Thou.'" For black and women writers, such an avowal of tradition in the subdominant order, of course, constitutes an operative challenge to the dominant order. It is this rereading of the notion of tradition within a field of gender and ethnicity that supports and enables the notion of community among those who share a common history, language, and culture. If Bakhtin's dialogic engagement with the Other signifies conflict, Gadamer's monologic acknowledgment of the Thou signifies the potential of agreement. If the Bakhtinian dialogic model speaks to the other within, then Gadamer's speaks to *the same within*. Thus, "the [dialectic] understanding of the [Thou]" (like the dialogic understanding of the other[s]) becomes "a form of self-relatedness."[13]

It is this notion of discursive difference and identity underlying the simultaneity of discourse which typically characterizes black women's writing. Through the multiple voices that enunciate her complex subjectivity, the black woman writer not only speaks familiarly in the discourse of the other(s), but as Other she is in contestorial dialogue with the hegemonic dominant and subdominant or "ambiguously (non)hegemonic" discourses.[14] These writers enter simultaneously into familial, or *testimonial* and public, or *competitive* discourses—discourses that both affirm and challenge the values and expectations of the reader. As such, black women writers enter into testimonial discourse with black men as blacks, with white women as women, and with black women as black women.[15] At the same time, they enter into a competitive discourse with black men as women, with white women as blacks, and with white men as black women. If black women speak a discourse of racial and gendered difference in the dominant or hegemonic discursive order, they speak a discourse of racial and gender identity and difference in the subdominant discursive order. This dialogic of difference and dialectic of identity characterize both black women's subjectivity and black women's discourse. It is the complexity of these simultaneously homogeneous and heterogeneous social and discursive domains out of which black women write and construct themselves (as blacks and women and, often, as poor, black women) that enables black women writers authoritatively to speak to and engage both hegemonic and ambiguously (non)hegemonic discourse.

Janie, the protagonist in Zora Neale Hurston's *Their Eyes Were Watching God,* demonstrates how the dialectics/dialogics of black and female subjectivity structure black women's discourse.[16] Combining personal and public forms of discourse in the court scene where she is on trial and fighting not only for her life but against "lying thoughts" and "misunderstanding," Janie addresses the judge, a jury composed of "twelve more white men," and spectators ("eight or ten white women" and "all the Negroes [men] for miles around" [274]). The challenge of Hurston's character is that of the black woman writer—to speak at once to a diverse audience about her experience in a racist and sexist society where to be black and female is to be, so to speak, "on trial." Janie not only speaks in a discourse of gender and racial difference to the white male judge and jurors, but also in a discourse of gender difference (and racial identity) to the black male spectators and a discourse of racial difference (and gender identity) to the white women spectators. Significantly, it is the white men who constitute both judge and jury, and, by virtue of their control of power and discourse, possess the authority of life and death over the black woman. In contrast, the black men (who are convinced that the "nigger [woman] kin kill . . . jus' as many niggers as she please") and white women (who "didn't seem too mad") read and witness/oppose a situation over which they exercise neither power nor discourse (225, 280).

Janie's courtroom discourse also emblematizes the way in which the categories of public and private break down in black women's discourse. In the context of Janie's courtroom scene, testimonial discourse takes on an expanded meaning, referring to both juridical, public, and dominant discourse as well as familial, private, and nondominant discourse. Testimonial, in this sense, derives its meaning from both "testimony" as an official discursive mode and "testifying," defined by Geneva Smitherman as "a ritualized form of . . . communication in which the speaker gives verbal witness to the efficacy, truth, and power of some experience in which [the group has] shared." The latter connotation suggests an additional meaning in the context of theological discourse where testifying refers to a "spontaneous expression to the church community [by whomever] feels the spirit."[17]

Like Janie, black women must speak in a plurality of voices as well as in a multiplicity of discourses. This discursive diversity, or simultaneity of discourse, I call "speaking in tongues." Significantly, glossolalia, or speaking in tongues, is a practice associated with black women in the Pentecostal Holiness church, the church of my childhood and the church of my mother. In the Holiness church (or as we called it, the Sanctified church), speaking unknown tongues (tongues known only to God) is in fact a sign of election, or holiness. As a trope it is also intended to remind us of Alice Walker's characterization of black women as artists, as "Creators," intensely rich in that spirituality which Walker sees as "the basis of Art."[18]

Glossolalia is perhaps the meaning most frequently associated with speaking in tongues. It is this connotation which emphasizes the particular, private, closed, and privileged communication between the congregant and the divinity. Inaccessible to the general congregation, this mode of communication is outside the realm of public discourse and foreign to the known tongues of humankind.

But there is a second connotation to the notion of speaking in tongues—one that suggests not glossolalia, but heteroglossia, the ability to speak in diverse known languages. While glossolalia refers to the ability to "utter the mysteries of the spirit," heteroglossia describes the ability to speak in the multiple languages of public discourse. If glossolalia suggests private, nonmediated, nondifferentiated univocality, heteroglossia connotes public, differentiated, social, mediated, dialogic discourse. Returning from the trope to the act of reading, perhaps we can say that speaking in tongues connotes both the semiotic, presymbolic babble (baby talk), as between mother and child—which Julia Kristeva postulates as the "mother tongue"—as well as the diversity of voices, discourses, and languages described by Mikhail Bakhtin.

Speaking in tongues, my trope for both glossolalia and heteroglossia, has a precise genealogical evolution in the Scriptures. In Genesis 11, God confounded the world's language when the city of Babel built a tower in an attempt to reach the heavens. Speaking in many and different tongues, the dwellers of Babel, unable to understand each other, fell into confusion, discord, and strife, and had to abandon the project. Etymologically, the name of the city Babel sounds much like the Hebrew word for "babble"—meaning confused, as in baby talk. Babel, then, suggests the two related, but distinctly different, meanings of speaking in tongues, meanings borne out in other parts of the Scriptures. The most common is that implied in I Corinthians 14—the ability to speak in unknown tongues. According to this interpretation, speaking in tongues suggests the ability to speak in and through the spirit. Associated with glossolalia—speech in unknown tongues—it is ecstatic, rapturous, inspired speech, based on a relation of intimacy and identification between the individual and God.

If Genesis tells of the disempowerment of a people by the introduction of different tongues, then Acts 2 suggests the empowerment of the disciples who, assembled on the day of Pentecost in the upper room of the temple in Jerusalem, "were filled with the Holy Spirit and began to speak in other tongues." Although the people thought the disciples had "imbibed a strange and unknown wine," it was the Holy Spirit which had driven them, filled with ecstasy, from the upper room to speak among the five thousand Jews surrounding the temple. The Scriptures tell us that the tribes of Israel all understood them, each in his own tongue. The Old Testament, then, suggests the dialogics of difference in its diversity of discourse, while the New Testament, in its unifying language of the spirit, suggests the dialectics of identity. If the Bakhtinian model suggests the multiplicity of speech as suggested in the dialogics of difference, then Gadamer's model moves toward a unity of understanding in its dialectics of identity.

It is the first as well as the second meaning which we privilege in speaking of black women writers: the first connoting polyphony, multivocality, and plurality of voices, and the second signifying intimate, private, inspired utterances. Through their intimacy with the discourse of the other(s), black women writers weave into their work competing and complementary discourses—discourses that seek both to adjudicate competing claims and witness common concerns.[19]

Also interesting is the link between the gift of tongues, the gift of prophecy, and the gift of interpretation. While distinguishing between these three gifts, the Scriptures frequently conflate or conjoin them. If to speak in tongues is to utter mysteries in and through the Spirit, to prophesy is to speak to others in a (diversity of) language(s) which the congregation can understand. The Scriptures would suggest that the disciples were able to perform both. I propose, at this juncture, an enabling critical fiction—that it is black women writers who are the modern day apostles, empowered by experience to speak as poets and prophets in many tongues. With this critical gesture, I also intend to signify a deliberate intervention by black women writers into the canonic tradition of sacred/literary texts.[20]

A Discursive Dilemma

In their works, black women writers have encoded oppression as a discursive dilemma, that is, their works have consistently raised the problem of the black woman's relationship to power and discourse. Silence is an important element of this code. The classic black woman's text *Their Eyes Were Watching God* charts the female protagonist's development from voicelessness to voice, from silence to tongues. Yet this movement does not exist without intervention by the other(s)—who speak for and about black women. In other words, it is not that black women, in the past, have had nothing to say, but rather that they have had no say. The absence of black female voices has allowed others to inscribe, or write, and ascribe to, or read, them. The notion of speaking in tongues, however, leads us away from an examination of how the Other has written/read black women and toward an examination of how black women have written the other(s)' writing/ reading black women.

Using the notion of "speaking in tongues" as our model, let us offer a kind of paradigmatic reading of two works which encode and resist the material and discursive dilemma of the black woman writer. Sherley Anne Williams's *Dessa Rose* and Toni Morrison's *Sula* are novels that emphasize respectively the *inter*cultural/racial and *intra*cultural/racial sites from which black women speak, as well as the signs under which they speak in both these milieus.[21] Artificial though this separation may be—since, as we have seen, black women are located simultaneously within both these discursive domains—such a distinction makes possible an examination of black women's literary relations to both dominant and subdominant discourse. These works also allow us to compare the suppression of the black female voice in the dominant discourse with its repression in the subdominant discourse.[22] Finally, they provide models for the disruption of the dominant and subdominant discourse by black and female expression, as well as for the appropriation and transformation of these discourses.

The heroine of Sherley Anne Williams's first novel, *Dessa Rose,* is a fugitive slave woman introduced to the reader as "the Darky" by Adam Nehemiah, a white male writer interviewing her in preparation for a forthcoming book, *The Roots of Rebellion in the Slave Population and Some Means of Eradicating Them* (or, more simply, *The Work*). The opening section of the novel is structured primarily by notations from Nehemiah's journal, based on his interactions with the slave woman during her confinement in a root cellar while awaiting her fate at the gallows. The latter section, describing her adventures as a fugitive involved in a scam against unsuspecting slaveholders and traders, is narrated primarily in the voice of Dessa (as the slave woman calls herself) after she has managed, with the assistance of fellow slaves, to escape the root cellar. At the end of the novel, the writer-interviewer, Adam Nehemiah, still carrying around his notes for *The Work,* espies the fugitive Dessa.

Brandishing a poster advertising a reward for her recapture, and a physical description of her identifying markings (an R branded on the thigh and whip-scarred hips), Adam Nehemiah coerces the local sheriff into detaining Dessa for identification. Significantly, Adam Nehemiah, named after his precursor—the archetypal white male namer, creator, and interpreter—attempts not only to remand Dessa into slavery but to inscribe her experiences as a slave woman through a discourse that suppresses her voice. Like the Adam of Genesis, Nehemiah asserts the right of ownership through the privilege of naming. Not only is his claim of discursive and material power held together symbolically in his name, but his acts and his words conflate: Nehemiah not only wishes to capture Odessa (as he calls her) in words that are instructive in the preservation of slavery, but he wishes to confine her in material slavery. Just as the biblical Nehemiah constructed the wall to protect the Israelites against attack by their enemies, so Williams's Nehemiah sets out to write a manual designed to protect the American South against insurrection by the slaves. Ironically, the character of Nehemiah, a patriot and leader of the Jews after the years of Babylonian captivity, is reread in the context of the Old South as a racist and expert on the "sound management" of the slaves.[23]

Dessa fears that exposure of her scars/branding will confirm her slave status. As she awaits the arrival of Ruth, the white woman who abets in the perpetration of the scam, Dessa thinks to herself, "I could feel everyone of them scars, the one roped partway to my navel that the waist of my draws itched, the corduroyed welts across my hips, and R on my thighs." (223). What interests me here is the literal inscription of Dessa's body, signified by the whip marks and, more specifically, the branded R, as well as the white male writer-cum-reader's attempt to exercise discursive domination over Dessa. Seeking to inscribe black female subjectivity, the white male, in effect, relegates the black woman to the status of discursive object, or spoken subject. The location of the inscriptions—in the area of the genitalia—moreover, signals an attempt to inscribe the sign *slave* in an area that marks her as *woman* ("Scar tissue plowed through her pubic hair region so no hair would ever grow there again" [154]). The effect is to attempt to deprive the slave woman of her femininity and render the surface of her skin a parchment upon which meaning is etched by the whip (pen) of white patriarchal authority and sealed by the firebrand. Together, these inscriptions produce the meaning of black female subjectivity in the discursive domain of slavery.[24] Importantly, the literal inscription of the flesh emphasizes what Monique Wittig, insisting on "the *material* oppression of individuals by discourses," describes as the "unrelenting tyranny that [male discourses] exert upon our *physical* and *mental* selves" (emphasis mine).[25] Dessa is ordered by the sheriff to lift her skirt so that these inscriptions can be "read" by her potential captors. (Perhaps we should read the R on Dessa's thigh as part of an acrostic for *Read*.) The signifying function of her scars is reinforced when Dessa recognizes that "[Nehemiah] wouldn't have to say nothing. Sheriff would see [i.e., read] that for himself" (223). Her remarks also suggest the mortal consequence of such a reading, or misreading:[26] "This [the scars] was what would betray me . . . these white mens would kill me" (223).

If Williams's *Dessa Rose* contains a representation of the inscription of *black female* in the dominative white and male discourse, then Morrison's *Sula* contains a representation of *female* ascription in black subdominative discourse. If in the context of the white community's discourse Dessa is suppressed as woman *and* black, in the discourse of the black community she is repressed as woman.

Like Dessa, Sula is marked. Unlike Dessa, Sula is marked from birth. Hers is a mark of nativity—a biological rather than cultural inscription, appropriate in this instance because it functions to mark her as a "naturally" inferior female within the black community.[27] The birthmark, "spread[ing] from the middle of the lid toward the eyebrow" (45), is associated with a series of images. For her mother, Hannah, Sula's birthmark "looked more and more like a stem and a rose" (64). Although in European and Eurocentric culture the rose is the gift of love as well as the traditional romantic symbol of female beauty and innocence (lily-white skin and rose blush), it is a symbol that has been appropriated by black women writers from Frances Harper, who uses it as a symbol of romantic love, to Alice Walker, who associates it with sexual love.[28]

Jude, the husband of Nel, Sula's best friend, refers to the birthmark as a "copperhead" and, later, as "the rattlesnake over her eye." If the image of the rose suggests female romantic love and sexuality, then the snake evokes the archetypal Garden and the story of Eve's seduction by the serpent.[29] The association is significant in light of the subsequent seduction scene between Jude and Sula, for it is Jude's perception of the snake imagery which structures his relationship with Sula, suggesting not only that the meaning he ascribes to the birthmark reflects the potential of his relationship with her, but that, on a broader level, it is the "male gaze" which constitutes female subjectivity. At the same time, Morrison redeploys the role of Other in a way that suggests how the black woman as Other is used to constitute (black) male subjectivity.

The community, "clearing up," as it thought, "the meaning of the birth-mark over her eye," tells the reader that "it was not a stemmed rose, or a snake, it was Hannah's ashes marking Sula from the very beginning" (99). (That Sula had watched her mother burn to death was her grandmother's contention and the community gossip.) If Jude represents the subject con-stituted in relation to the black woman as Other, the community represents a culture constituted in relation to the black woman as Other:

> Their conviction of Sula's evil changed them in accountable yet myste-rious ways. Once the source of their personal misfortune was identified, they had leave to protect and love one another. They began to cherish their husbands and wives, protect their children, repair their homes and in general band together against the devil in their midst. (102)

Sula signifies, for the community, the chaos and evil against which it must define and protect itself. Convinced that she bears the mark of the devil because of her association with Shadrack, the town reprobate, the com-munity closes ranks against one who transgresses the boundaries prescribed for women.

For Shadrack, the shell-shocked World War I veteran who has become the community pariah, Sula's birthmark represents "the mark of the fish he loved"—the tadpole (134). A symbol of the primordial beginnings of life in the sea, the tadpole represents potential, transformation, and rebirth. Such an image contrasts with the apocalyptic ending of life by fire suggested by the community's perception of Hannah's ashes.[30] As an amphibious crea-ture, the tadpole has the capacity to live both terrestrially and aquatically. Etymologically, Sula's name is derived from the designation of a genus of seabird, again an image associated with a dual environment—aquatic and ariel. These contrasts suggestively position Sula at the crossroads or inter-section of life and death, land and sea, earth and air. Thus both the mark and the designation are particularly appropriate for the black woman as one situated within two social domains (black and female) and, as such, impli-cated in both a racial and gendered discourse.

But it is the black community—the Bottom—which provides the setting for the action in Morrison's novel, and it is the men who have the final say in the community: "It was the men," writes the narrator, "who gave [Sula] the final label, who *fingerprinted* her for all time" (emphasis mine; 197). The men in the community speak a racial discourse that reduces Sula finally to her sexuality: "The word was passed around" that "Sula slept with *white* men" (emphasis mine; 97). It is thus her sexuality, read through the race relation, which structures her subjectivity within the male-dominated discourse of the black community.

The power of male discourse and naming is also suggested in the epithet directed to the twelve-year-old Sula as she, along with her friend Nel, saunters by Edna Finch's ice cream parlor one afternoon, passing the old and young men of the Bottom:

> Pigmeat. The words were in all their minds. And one of them, one of the young ones, said it aloud. His name was Ajax, a twenty-one-year-old pool haunt of sinister beauty. Graceful and economical in every movement, he held a place of envy with men of all ages for his magnificently foul mouth. In fact he seldom cursed, and the epithets he chose were dull, even harmless. His reputation was derived from the way he handled words. When he said "hell" he hit the *h* with his lungs and the impact was greater than the achievement of the most imaginative foul mouth in town. He could say "shit" with a nastiness impossible to imitate. (43)

Not only does the language itself take on a special potency when exercised by males, but the epithet "pigmeat" which Ajax confers on Sula still has a powerful hold on her seventeen years later, when at twenty-nine, having traveled across the country and returned to the Bottom, she is greeted by the now thirty-eight-year-old Ajax at her screen door: "Sula . . . was curious. She knew nothing about him except the word he had called out to her years ago and the feeling he had excited in her then" (110).

The images associated with Sula's birthmark connote, as we have seen, a plurality of meanings. These images become not only symbols of opposition and ambiguity associated with the stemmed rose, snake, fire, and tadpole, but they evoke the qualities of permanence and mutability (nature and culture) inherent in the sign of the birthmark, the meaning and valence of which changes with the reading and the reader. At one point, Nel, Sula's complement in the novel, describes her as one who "helped others define themselves," that is, one who takes on the complementary aspect of the Other in the process of constituting subjectivity. As if to underscore Sula's signifying function as absence or mutability, Sula is described as having "no center" and "no ego," "no speck around which to grow" (103). The plurality and flux of meaning ascribed to the birthmark share some of the characteristics of the Sign or, perhaps more precisely, the Signifier. Sula's association with the birthmark gradually evolves, through synecdoche, into an identification between the subject/object and the Sign. Thus her entry into the subdominative discursive order confers on her the status of "a free-floating signifier," open to diverse interpretations.

The inscription (writing) of Dessa and the ascription (reading) of Sula together encode the discursive dilemma of black women in hegemonic and ambiguously (non)hegemonic discursive contexts. However, these works also embody a code of resistance to the discursive and material domination of black women. To different degrees and in different ways, Williams and Morrison fashion a counterdiscourse within their texts.

Disruption and Revision

In negotiating the discursive dilemma of their characters, these writers accomplish two objectives: the self-inscription of black womanhood, and the establishment of a dialogue of discourses with the other(s). The self-inscription of black women requires disruption, rereading and rewriting the conventional and canonical stories, as well as revising the conventional generic forms that convey these stories. Through this interventionist, intertextual, and revisionary activity, black women writers enter into dialogue with the discourses of the other(s). Disruption—the initial response to hegemonic and ambiguously (non)hegemonic discourse—and revision (rewriting or rereading) together suggest a model for reading black and female literary expression.

Dessa's continued rejection of Adam Nehemiah's inscription suggests that we must read with some measure of credence her claims of being misrecognized. ("I don't know this master, Mistress," she says. "They mistook me for another Dessa, Mistress" [226–227].) Ultimately, Dessa's insistence on *meconnaissance* is vindicated in the failure of Nehemiah's attempts either to *con*fine her in the social system or *de*fine her in the dominant discourse.

Dessa not only succeeds in rupturing the narrator's discourse at the outset of the novel through a series of interventionist acts—singing, evasion, silence, nonacquiescence, and dissemblance—but she employs these strategies to effect her escape and seize discursive control of the story.[31] Moreover, Dessa's repeated use of the word *track* (a term connoting both pursuit and inscription) in reference to Nehemiah takes on added significance in the context of both her inscription and revision. Tracking becomes the object of her reflections: "Why this white man *track* me down like he owned me, like a bloodhound on my *trail*," and later, "crazy white man, *tracking* me all cross the country like he owned me" (emphasis mine; 225). In other words, Nehemiah *tracks* Dessa in an attempt to establish ownership—that is, the colonization—of her body. Yet tracking also suggests that Dessa's flight becomes a text that she writes and Nehemiah reads. His tracking (i.e., reading of Dessa's text) thus becomes the means by which he attempts to capture her (i.e., suppress her voice in the production of his own text).

If the pursuit/flight pattern emblematizes a strategic engagement for discursive control, Dessa's tracks also mark her emergence as narrator of her own story. It is her escape—loosely speaking, her "making tracks"— that precludes the closure/completion of Nehemiah's book. The story of

Dessa's successful revolt and escape, in effect, prefigures the rewriting of *The Work*—Nehemiah's projected treatise on the control of slaves and the prevention of slave revolts. The latter part of the novel, recounted from Dessa's perspective and in her own voice, establishes her as the successful author of her own narrative. Tracking thus becomes a metaphor for writing/reading from the white male narrator's perspective, and a metaphor for re-vision (*re*writing/*re*reading) from Dessa's. Creating her own track therefore corresponds to Dessa's assumption of discursive control of the novel, that is, the telling of her own story. In flight, then, Dessa challenges the material and discursive elements of her oppression and, at the same time, provides a model for writing as struggle.

Nehemiah's inability to capture Dessa in print is paralleled, finally, in his failure to secure her recapture. As Dessa walks out of the sheriff's office, Nehemiah cries: "I know it's her . . . I got her down here in my book." Leaving, Dessa tells the reader, "And he reach and took out that little black-bound pad he wrote in the whole time I knowed him" (231). But the futility of his efforts is represented in the reactions of the onlookers to the unbound pages of Nehemiah's notebook as they tumble and scatter to the floor:

> [Sheriff] Nemi, ain't nothing but some scribbling on here. . . . Can't no one read this.
>
> [Ruth] And these [pages] is blank, sheriff. (232)

Finally, in two dramatic acts of self-entitlement, Dessa reaffirms her ability to name herself and her own experience. In the first instance, she challenges Nehemiah's efforts to capture her—in person and in print: "Why, he didn't even know how to call my name—talking about *O*dessa" (emphasis mine; 225). And in the second, after her release she informs Ruth, her white ac-complice and alleged mistress, "My name Dessa, Dessa Rose. Ain't no O to it" (232). She is, of course, distinguishing between Odessa, an ascription by the white, male slave master and used by both Nehemiah and Ruth, and Dessa, her entitlement proper. Her rejection of the *O* signifies her rejection of the inscription of her body by the other(s). In other words, Dessa's re-pudiation of the *O* (Otherness?) signifies her always already presence—what Ralph Ellison describes as the unquestioned humanity of the slave. She de-letes nothing—except the white, male other's inscription/ascription.[32]

At the conclusion of the novel, Dessa once again affirms the importance of writing oneself and one's own history. It is a responsibility that devolves upon the next generation, privileged with a literacy Dessa herself has been denied: "My mind wanders. This is why I have it down, why I has the child say it back. I never will forget Nemi trying to read [and write] me, knowing I had put myself in his hands. Well, *this* the childrens have heard from our own lips" (236). Yet, as Walker might say, the story bears the mother's signature.[33]

While Dessa, through interventions and rewriting, rejects white, male attempts to write and read black female subjectivity, Sula, through disruption and rereading, repudiates black male readings of black female subjectivity. (Significantly, black males, like white females, lack the power to *write*, but not the power to *read* black women.) If it is her sexuality which structures Sula within the confines of black (male) discourse, it is also her sexuality which creates a rupture in that discourse. It is through the act of sexual intercourse that Sula discovers "the center of . . . silence" and a "loneliness so profound *the word itself had no meaning*" (emphasis mine; 106). The "desperate terrain" which she reaches, the "high silence of orgasm" (112), is a nodal point that locates Sula in the interstices of the closed system of (black) male signification. She has, in effect, "[leapt] from the edge" of discourse "into soundlessness" and "[gone] down howling" (106). Howling, a unitary movement of nondifferentiated sound, contrasts with the phonic differentiation on which the closed system of language is based. Like the birthmark, which is the symbolic sign of life, the howl is the first sound of life—not yet broken down and differentiated to emerge as intersubjective communication, or discourse. The howl, signifying a prediscursive mode, thus becomes an act of self-reconstitution as well as an act of subversion or resistance to the "network of signification" represented by the symbolic order. The "high silence of orgasm" and the howl allow temporary retreats from or breaks in the dominant discourse. Like Dessa's evasions and interventions, Sula's silences and howls serve to disrupt or subvert the "symbolic function of the language." It is precisely these violations or transgressions of the symbolic order that allow for the expression of the suppressed or repressed aspects of black female subjectivity. The reconstitutive function of Sula's sexuality is suggested in the image of the "post-coital privateness in which she met herself, welcomed herself, and joined herself in matchless harmony" (107). The image is that of symbiosis and fusion—a stage or condition represented in psychoanalysis as pre-Oedipal and anterior to the acquisition of language or entry into the symbolic order.[34]

It is through the howl of orgasm that Sula discovers a prediscursive center of experience that positions her at a vantage point outside of the dominant discursive order. The howl is a form of speaking in tongues and a linguistic disruption that serves as the precondition for Sula's entry into language. Unless she breaks the conventional structures and associations of the dominant discourse, Sula cannot enter through the interstices.[35] (This reading of *Sula*, in effect, reverses the biblical movement from contestorial, public discourse to intimate, familial discourse.)

In contrast to the howl, of course, is the stunning language of poetic metaphor with which Sula represents her lover and the act of love:

If I take a chamois and rub real hard on the bone, right on the ledge of
your cheek bone, some of the black will disappear. It will flake away into
the chamois and underneath there will be gold leaf. . . . And if I take a
nail file or even Eva's old paring knife . . . and scrape away at the gold,
it will fall away and there will be alabaster. . . . Then I can take a chisel
and small tap hammer and tap away at the alabaster. It will crack then
like ice under the pick, and through the breaks I will see the [fertile] loam.
(112)

It is an eloquent passage—not of self-representation, however, but of representation of the male other. If Sula cannot find the language, the trope,
the form, to embody her own "experimental" life, she "engage[s] her tremendous curiosity and her gift for metaphor" in the delineation of her lover.
The poetic penetration of her lover through the layers of black, gold leaf,
alabaster, and loam signals that her assumption of a "masculine" role parallels the appropriation of the male voice, prerequisite for her entry into the
symbolic order. (Such an appropriation is, of course, earlier signaled by the
association of the birthmark with the stemmed rose, the snake, the tadpole—
a series of phallic images.)

I propose, however, in the spirit of the metaphor, to take it one step
further and suggest that the imagery and mode of the prose poem form a
kind of model for the deconstructive function of black feminist literary criticism—and to the extent that literature itself is always an act of interpretation, a model for the deconstructive function of black women's writing—
that is, to interpret or interpenetrate the signifying structures of the dominant
and subdominant discourse in order to formulate a critique and, ultimately,
a transformation of the hegemonic white and male symbolic order.

If Williams's primary emphasis is on the act of rewriting, then Morrison's is on the act of rereading. Perhaps the best example of Sula's deconstructive rereading of the black male text is exemplified in her refor-
mulation of Jude's "whiny tale" describing his victimization as a black man
in a world that the "white man running":

I don't know what the fuss is about. I mean, everything in the world loves
you. White men love you. They spend so much time worrying about your
penis they forget their own. The only thing they want to do is cut off a
nigger's privates. And if that ain't love and respect I don't know what is.
And white women? They chase you all to every corner of the earth, feel
for you under every bed. . . . Now ain't that love? They think rape soon's
they see you, and if they don't get the rape they looking for, they scream
it anyway just so the search won't be in vain. Colored women worry
themselves into bad health just trying to hang on to your cuffs. Even little
children—white and black, boys and girls—spend all their childhood eat-
ing their hearts out 'cause they think you don't love them. And if that

ain't enough, you love yourselves. Nothing in this world loves a black
man more than another black man. (89)

Adrienne Munich points out that "Jude's real difficulties allow him to maintain his male identity, to exploit women, and not to examine himself." Sula,
she argues, turns "Jude's story of powerlessness into a tale of power." Through
a deconstructive reading of his story, Sula's interpretation demonstrates how
Jude uses "racial politics [to mask] sexual politics."[36]

If Sula's silences and howls represent breaks in the symbolic order, then
her magnificent prose poem looks to the possibilities of appropriating the
male voice as a prerequisite for entry into that order. Dessa similarly moves
from intervention to appropriation and revision of the dominant discourse.
As the author of her own story, Dessa writes herself into the dominant discourse and, in the process, transforms it. What these two works suggest in
variable, but interchangeable, strategies is that, in both dominant and subdominant discourses, the initial expression of a marginal presence takes the
form of disruption—a departure or a break with conventional semantics and/
or phonetics. This rupture is followed by a rewriting or rereading of the
dominant story, resulting in a "delegitimation" of the prior story or a "displacement" which shifts attention "to the other side of the story."[37] Disruption—the initial response to hegemonic and ambiguously (non)hegemonic
discourse—and the subsequent response, revision (rewriting or rereading),
together represent a progressive model for black and female utterance. I
propose, in an appropriation of a current critical paradigm, that Sula's primal
scream constitutes a "womblike matrix" in which soundlessness can be
transformed into utterance, unity into diversity, formlessness into form, chaos
into art, silence into tongues, and glossolalia into heteroglossia.

It is this quality of speaking in tongues, that is, multivocality, I further
propose, that accounts in part for the current popularity and critical success
of black women's writing. The engagement of multiple others broadens the
audience for black women's writing, for like the disciples of Pentecost who
spoke in diverse tongues, black women, speaking out of the specificity of
their racial and gender experiences, are able to communicate in a diversity
of discourses. If the ability to communicate accounts for the popularity of
black women writers, it also explains much of the controversy surrounding
some of this writing. Black women's writing speaks with what Mikhail Bakhtin
would describe as heterological or "centrifugal force" but (in a sense somewhat different from that which Bakhtin intended) also unifying or "centri-
petal force."[38] This literature speaks as much to the notion of commonality
and universalism as it does to the sense of difference and diversity.

Yet the objective of these writers is not, as some critics suggest, to
move from margin to center, but to remain on the borders of discourse,
speaking from the vantage point of the insider/outsider. As Bakhtin further

suggests, fusion with the (dominant) other can only duplicate the tragedy or misfortune of the other's dilemma. On the other hand, as Gadamer makes clear, "there is a kind of experience of the 'Thou' that seeks to discover things that are typical in the behaviour of [the other] and is able to make predictions concerning another person on the basis of [a commonality] of experience."[39] To maintain this insider/outsider position, or perhaps what Myra Jehlen calls the "extra-terrestial fulcrum" that Archimedes never acquired, is to see the other, but also to see what the other cannot see, and to use this insight to enrich both our own and the other's understanding.[40]

As gendered and racial subjects, black women speak/write in multiple voices—not all simultaneously or with equal weight, but with various and changing degrees of intensity, privileging one *parole* and then another. One discovers in these writers a kind of internal dialogue reflecting an *intrasubjective* engagement with the *intersubjective* aspects of self, a dialectic neither repressing difference nor, for that matter, privileging identity, but rather expressing engagement with the social aspects of self ("the other[s] in ourselves"). It is this subjective plurality (rather than the notion of the cohesive or fractured subject) that, finally, allows the black woman to become an expressive site for a dialectics/dialogics of identity and difference.

Unlike Bloom's "anxiety of influence" model configuring a white male poetic tradition shaped by an adversarial dialogue between literary fathers and sons (as well as the appropriation of this model by Joseph Skerrett and others to discuss black male writers), and unlike Gilbert and Gubar's "anxiety of authorship" model informed by the white woman writer's sense of "dis-ease" within a white patriarchal tradition, the present model configures a tradition of black women writers generated less by neurotic anxiety of disease than by an emancipatory impulse which freely engages both hegemonic and ambiguously (non)hegemonic discourse.[41] Summarizing Morrison's perspectives, Andrea Stuart perhaps best expresses this notion:

> I think you [Morrison] summed up the appeal of black women writers when you said that white men, quite naturally, wrote about themselves and their world; white women tended to write about white men because they were so close to them as husbands, lovers and sons; and black men wrote about white men as the oppressor or the yardstick against which they measured themselves. Only black women writers were not interested in writing about white men and therefore they freed literature to take on other concerns.[42]

In conclusion, I return to the gifts of the Holy Spirit: 1 Corinthians 12 tells us that "the [one] who speaks in tongues should pray that [s/he] may interpret what [s/he] says." Yet the Scriptures also speak to interpretation as a separate gift—the ninth and final gift of the spirit. Might I suggest that if black women writers speak in tongues, then it is we black feminist critics who are charged with the hermeneutical task of interpreting tongues?

NOTES

This article was first published in *Changing Our Own Words,* edited by Cheryl A. Wall, (New Brunswick: Rutgers University Press, 1991), reprinted here with permission.

1. Gloria Hull, Patricia Bell Scott, and Barbara Smith, eds., *All the Women Are White, All the Blacks Are Men, But Some of Us Are Brave* (Old Westbury, N.Y.: Feminist Press, 1982).

2. Fredric Jameson, *The Political Unconscious: Narrative as a Socially Symbolic Act* (Ithaca N.Y.: Cornell University Press, 1981), p. 53.

3. The phrase "gender subtext" is used by Nancy Fraser (and attributed to Dorothy Smith) in Fraser's critique of Habermas in Nancy Fraser, "What's Critical about Critical Theory?" in Seyla Benhabib and Drucilla Cornell, eds. *Feminism as Critique* (Minneapolis: University of Minnesota Press, 1987), p. 42.

4. See Barbara Smith, ed., *Home Girls: A Black Feminist Anthology* (New York: Kitchen Table: Women of Color Press, 1983), p. xxxii.

5. John Carlos Rowe, "To Live Outside the Law, You Must Be Honest: The Authority of the Margin in Contemporary Theory," *Cultural Critique,* 1 2, pp. 67–68.

6. Mikhail Bakhtin, "Discourse in the Novel," reprinted in Michael Holquist, ed., *The Dialogic Imagination: Four Essays by M. M. Bakhtin* (Austin: University of Texas Press, 1981), p. 292. Bakhtin's social groups are designated according to class, religion, generation, region, and profession. The interpretative model I propose extends and rereads Bakhtin's theory from the standpoint of race and gender, categories absent in Bakhtin's original system of social and linguistic stratification.

7. V. N. Volosinov [Mikhail Bakhtin], *Marxism and the Philosophy of Language* (New York: Seminar Press, 1973), pp. 11, 29, 38. Originally published in Russian as *Marksizm I Filosofija Jazyka* (Leningrad, 1930). Notably, this concept of the "subjective psyche" constituted primarily as a "social entity" distinguishes the Bakhtinian notion of self from the Freudian notion of identity.

8. Bakhtin, "Discourse in the Novel," p. 292.

9. According to Bakhtin, "The processes that basically define the content of the psyche occur not inside but outside the individual organism. . . . Moreover, the psyche "enjoys extraterritorial status . . . [12] a social entity that penetrates inside the organism of the individual personal" (*Marxism and Philosophy of Language,* pp. 25, 39). Explicating Caryl Emerson's position on Bakhtin, Gary Saul Morson argues that selfhood "derives from an internalization of the voices a person has heard, and each of these voices is saturated with social and ideological values." "Thought itself," he writes, "is but 'inner speech,' and inner speech is outer speech that we have learned to 'speak' in our heads while retaining the full register of conflicting social values." See Gary Saul Morson, "Dialogue, Monologue, and the Social: A Reply to Ken Hirshkop," in Morson, ed., *Bakhtin: Essays and Dialogues on His Work* (Chicago: University of Chicago Press, 1986), p. 85.

10. Teresa de Lauretis, *Technologies of Gender* (Bloomington: Indiana University Press, 1987), p. 2.

11. Audre Lorde, "Eye to Eye," included in *Sister Outsider* (Tramansburg, N.Y.: Crossing Press, 1984), p. 147.

12. Barbara Christian, "The Dynamics of Difference: Book Review of Audre Lorde's *Sister Outsider,*" in *Black Feminist Criticism: Perspectives in Black Women Writers* (New York: Pergamon Press, 1985), p. 209.

13. While acknowledging the importance of historicism, I can only agree with Frank Lentricchia's conclusion that in some respects Gadamer's "historicist argument begs more questions than it answers. If we can applaud the generous intention, virtually unknown in structuralist quarters, of recapturing history for textual interpretation, then we can only be stunned by the implication of what he has uncritically to say about authority, the power of tradition, knowledge, our institutions, and our attitudes." See Frank Lentricchia, *After the New Criticism* (Chicago: University of Chicago Press, 1980), p. 153. Certainly, Gadamer's model privileges the individual's relation to history and tradition in a way that might seem problematic in formulating a discursive model for the "noncanonical" or marginalized writer. However, just as the above model of dialogics is meant to extend Bakhtin's notion of class difference to encompass gender and race, so the present model revises and limits Gadamer's notion of tradition. See Hans-Georg Gadamer, *Truth and Method* (New York: Seabury Press, 1975), pp. 321–25. My introduction to the significance of Gadamer's work for my own reading of black women writers was first suggested by Don Bialostosky's excellent paper entitled "Dialectic and Anti-Dialectic: A Bakhtinian Critique of Gadamer's Dialectical Model of Conversation," delivered at the International Association of Philosophy and Literature in May 1989 at Emory University in Atlanta, Georgia.

14. I extend Rachel Blau DuPlessis's term designating white women as a group privileged by race and oppressed by gender to black men as a group privileged by gender and oppressed by race. In this instance, I use "ambiguously (non)hegemonic" to signify the discursive status of both these groups.

15. Black women enter into dialogue with other black women in a discourse that I would characterize as primarily testimonial, resulting from a similar discursive and social positionality. It is this commonality of history, culture, and language which, finally, constitutes the basis of a tradition of black women's expressive culture. In terms of actual literary dialogue among black women, I would suggest a relatively modern provenance of such a tradition, but again, one based primarily on a dialogue of affirmation rather than contestation. As I see it, this dialogue begins with Alice Walker's response to Zora Neale Hurston. Although the present article is devoted primarily to contestorial function of black women's writing, my forthcoming work (of which the present essay constitutes only a part) deals extensively with the relationships among black women writers.

16. Zora Neale Hurston, *Their Eyes Were Watching God* (1937; rpt., Urbana: University of Illinois Press, 1978). All subsequent references in the text.

17. Geneva Smitherman, *Talkin and Testifyin: The Language of Black America* (Detroit: Wayne State University Press, 1986), p. 58.

18. Alice Walker, "In Search of Our Mothers' Gardens," in *In Search of Our Mothers' Gardens: Womanist Prose* (New York: Harcourt Brace Jovanovich, 1984), p. 232.

19. Not only does such an approach problematize conventional categories and boundaries of discourse, but, most importantly, it signals the collapse of the unifying consensus

posited by the discourse of universalism and reconstructs the concept of unity in diversity implicit in the discourse of difference.

20. The arrogant and misogynistic Paul tells us, "I thank God that I speak in tongues more than all of you. But in church I would rather speak five intelligible words to instruct others [i.e., to prophesy] than ten thousand words in a tongue." Even though we are perhaps most familiar with Paul's injunction to women in the church to keep silent, the prophet Joel, in the Old Testament, speaks to a diversity of voices that includes women: "In the last days, God says, I will pour out my Spirit on all people. Your sons and *daughters* will prophesy. . . . Even on my servants, both men and *women*, I will pour out my Spirit in those days, and they will prophesy" (emphasis mine). I am grateful to the Rev. Joseph Stephens whose vast scriptural knowledge helped guide me through these and other revelations.

21. Sherley Anne Williams, *Dessa Rose* (New York: William Morrow, 1986), and Toni Morrison, *Sula* (New York: Alfred A. Knopf, 1973; rpt., Bantam, 1975). Page references for these two works are given in the text.

22. I draw on the distinction between the political connotation of *suppression* and the psychological connotation of *repression*. Suppression results from external pressures and censorship imposed by the dominant culture, while repression refers to the internal self-censorship and silencing emanating from the subdominative community.

23. Nehemiah, a minor prophet in the Old Testament, is best remembered for rebuilding the walls around Jerusalem in order to fortify the city against invasion by hostile neighbors of Israel. Under his governorship, Ezra and the Levites instructed the people in the law of Moses "which the Lord had commanded for Israel." He is represented as a reformer who restored the ancient ordinances regarding proper observance of the Sabbath and the collection of the tithes; he also enforced bans against intermarriage with the Gentiles. He is perhaps most noted for the reply he sent, while rebuilding the walls, to a request from his enemies, Sanballat and Gesham, to meet with him: "I am doing a great *work* and cannot go down" (emphasis mine). William's Nehemiah, like his prototype, is devoted to the completion of a project he calls *The Work*—in this instance a book entitled *The Roots of Rebellion in the Slave Population and Some Means of Eradicating Them*. Significantly, the name of William's character, Adam Nehemiah, reverses the name of Nehemiah Adams, author of *A South-side View of Slavery* (1854), and a Boston minister who wrote an account of his experiences in the South from a point of view apostate to the northern antislavery cause.

24. The mark of the whip inscribes Dessa as a slave while she remains within the discursive domain of slavery—a domain architecturally figured by the prison from which she escapes, but also a domain legally and more discursively defined by the Fugitive Slave Act, the runaway ads, and the courts and depositions of the nation. Note, however, that within the northern lecture halls and the slave narratives—the spatial and discursive domains of abolitionism—the marks do not identify an individual, but signify upon the character and nature of the institution of slavery.

25. Monique Wittig, "The Straight Mind," *Feminist Issues*, 1 (Summer 1980), pp. 105–106.

26. Although the status of slave is not a "misreading" within the discursive domain of slavery, it is clearly a misreading according to Dessa's self-identification.

27. One might describe Sula's birthmark as an iconicized representation rather than, strictly speaking, an inscription. For our purposes, however, it has the force of a sign marking her birth or entry into black discourse.

28. Morrison's epigram to the novel highlights the cultural significance of the birthmark by quoting from Tennessee Williams's *The Rose Tattoo:* "Nobody knew my rose of the world but me. . . . I had too much glory. They don't want glory like that in nobody's heart." In "The Mission of the Flowers," Harper describes the rose as "a thing of joy and beauty" whose mission is to "lay her fairest buds and flowers upon the altars of love." Walker's protagonist Celie compares her own sex to the "inside of a wet rose." See Frances E. W. Harper, *Idylls of the Bible* (Philadelphia: George S. Ferguson, 1901), quoted in Erlene Stetson, ed., *Black Sister* (Bloomington: Indiana University Press, 1981), pp. 34–36, and Alice Walker, *The Color Purple* (New York: Harcourt Brace Jovanovich, 1982), p. 69. In naming her own character Dessa *Rose,* Williams not only plays on the above connotations, but links them, at the same time, to the transcendence implicit in "arising" and the insurgence suggested in "uprising."

29. Signifying perhaps on Hawthorne's short story "The Birthmark," Sula's mark can be reread as a sign of human imperfection and mortality, a consequence of Eve's seduction by the serpent in the Garden.

30. The fire and water image, associated with the tadpole and ashes, respectively complement and contrast with that of the snake—a symbol of death and renewal—and that of the stemmed rose—an image suggesting not only love and sexuality, but the beauty and brevity of life as a temporal experience.

31. I do not develop here the interviewer's misreadings of Dessa in the early part of the novel, nor the specific insurgent strategies with which Dessa continually outwits him. These details are treated extensively, however, in my article on Williams's "Meditations on History," the short story on which the novel is based. It appears in Linda Kauffman, ed., *Gender and Theory: A Dialogue between the Sexes,* vol. 2 (London: Basil Blackwell, 1989).

32. Williams also uses onomastics to signify upon a less rebellious female heroine, somewhat more complicitous with female ascription by the Other. See Kaja Silverman's excellent discussion of Pauline Reage's *The Story of O,* in her article "Histoire d'O: The Construction of a Female Subject," in Carole S. Vance, ed., *Pleasure and Danger: Exploring Female Sexuality* (Boston: Routledge and Kegan Paul, 1984).

33. Williams, in her earlier version of this story, "Meditations on History," privileges orality (rather than writing)—as I attempt to demonstrate in my article "W(R)iting *The Work* and Working the Rites," in Kauffman, *Gender and Theory,* vol. 2.

34. Positing a kind of "mother tongue," Julia Kristeva argues that "language as symbolic function constitutes itself at the cost of repressing instinctual drive and continuous relation to the mother." This order of expression, she contends, is presymbolic and linked with the mother tongue. According to Nelly Furman's interpretation, the existence of this order "does not refute the symbolic but is anterior to it, and associated with the maternal aspects of language. This order, which [Kristeva] calls 'semiotic,' is not a separate entity from the symbolic, on the contrary, it is the system which supports symbolic coherence." Continuing, Furman quotes Josette Feral in establishing a dialogical relationship between the semiotic and symbolic orders "which places the semiotic *inside* the symbolic as a condition of the symbolic, while positing the symbolic as a condition of the semiotic and founded on its repression. Now it happens that the Name-of-the-Father, in order to establish itself, needs the repression of the mother. It needs this otherness in order to reassure itself about its unity and identity, but is unwittingly affected by this otherness that is working within it." Nelly Furman, "The Politics of Language: Beyond the Gender Principle?" in Gayle Greene and Coppelia Kahn, eds., *Mak-*

ing A Difference: Feminist Literary Criticism (London and New York: Methuen, 1985), pp. 72–73.

35. In contrast to Dessa, who disrupts the dominant discourse, Sula would seem to disrupt not only discourse but, indeed, language itself.

36. Adrienne Munich, "Feminist Criticism and Literary Tradition," in Greene and Kahn, *Making a Difference,* pp. 245–54.

37. Rachel Blau DuPlessis uses these terms to describe the "tactics of revisionary mythopoesis" created by women poets whose purpose is to "attack cultural hegemony." "Narrative displacement is like breaking the sentence," writes DuPlessis, "because it offers the possibility of speech to the female in the case, giving voice to the muted. Narrative delegitimation 'breaks the sequence'; a realignment that puts the last first and the first last has always ruptured conventional morality, politics, and narrative." Rachel Blau DuPlessis, *Writing Beyond the Ending* (Bloomington: Indiana University Press, 1985), p. 108.

38. Bakhtin, "Discourse in the Novel," pp. 271–72.

39. Gadamer, *Truth and Method,* p. 321.

40. Myra Jehlen, "Archimedes and the Paradox of Feminist Criticism," reprinted in Elizabeth Abel and Emily K. Abel, eds., *The Signs Reader: Women, Gender* and *Scholarship* (Chicago: University of Chicago Press, 1983).

41. See Harold Bloom, *The Anxiety of Influence: A Theory of Poetry* (New York: Oxford University Press, 1973); Sandra M. Gilbert and Susan Gubar, eds., *The Madwoman in the Attic: The Woman Writer and the Nineteenth-Century Literary Imagination* (New Haven: Yale University Press, 1979); and Joseph T. Skerrett, "The Wright Interpretation: Ralph Ellison and the Anxiety of Influence," *Massachusetts Review,* 21 (Spring 1980), pp. 196–212.

42. Andrea Stuart in an interview with Toni Morrison, "Telling Our Story," *Sparerib* (February 1988), pp. 12–15.

10

The Real Miss Beauchamp: Gender and the Subject of Imitation

Ruth Leys

Jacqueline Rose has remarked that resistance to psychoanalysis within feminism has recently tended to express itself in two different but complementary ways. On the one hand, "the terms of the objections have shifted from the critique of phallocentricism to the argument that feminism needs access to an integrated subjectivity more than its demise." On the other, the resistance "takes the form of a new asserted politics of sexuality in all its multiplicity, but one from which any idea of the psychic as an area of difficulty has been dropped."[1] What does Rose mean by the psychic as an "area of difficulty"? And what are the political implications of such a notion?

For Rose, the psychic as an "area of difficulty" is important for feminism because it involves a concept of the subject as structured by unconscious fantasies that always exceed the rigid gender positions that are defined as the norm for women and men. This is the political purchase of Rose's Lacanian defense of psychoanalysis, and her argument in this regard is directed as much against Nancy Chodorow's object-relations account of sexual difference as it is against those British and American theorists, such as Elizabeth Wilson, Shulamith Firestone, and Kate Millett, who dismiss psychoanalysis as irrelevant to a feminist politics. "What distinguishes psychoanalysis from sociological accounts of gender (and hence for me the fundamental impasse of Nancy Chodorow's work)," Rose writes, "is that whereas for the latter, the internalization of norms is assumed roughly to work, the basic premise and indeed starting-point of psychoanalysis is that it does not":

The unconscious constantly reveals the "failure" of identity. Because there is no continuity of psychic life, so there is no stability of sexual identity, no position for women (or for men) which is ever simply achieved. Nor does psychoanalysis see such "failure" as a special-case inability or an individual deviancy from the norm. "Failure" is not a moment to be regretted in a process of adaptation, or development in normality, which ideally takes its course. . . . Instead, "failure" is something endlessly repeated and relived moment by moment throughout our individual histories.[2]

For Rose, the necessary "failure" of identity—the inability of the patriarchal "law" fully to determine human actions and beliefs—is also virtually a condition of possibility for a feminist politics such as she understands it.

Not the least of Rose's claims is that psychoanalysis radically contests the binary oppositions—subject/object, inside/outside, fantasy/real, public/private, victim/aggressor—that almost invariably inform biological, sociological, and Marxist accounts of sexual difference and that tend to reintroduce those normative and totalizing assumptions about gender that such accounts ostensibly contest and subvert. Rose's argument is especially helpful for theorizing the location of violence. I am thinking, for example, of the challenge she poses to Catharine MacKinnon, Jeffrey Masson, and others who, rejecting the notion of unconscious conflict, embrace instead a rigid dichotomy between the internal and the external such that violence is imagined as coming to the subject entirely from the outside—a point of view that inevitably reinforces a politically retrograde stereotype of the female as a purely passive victim.[3] Even more crucially for my purposes, Rose's work allows us to critique the reductive terms in which the theory of the trauma, understood as an external historical event that befalls the already-constituted female subject, is being deployed today to explain dissociation or multiple personality—a concept whose invention at the end of the nineteenth century I plan to analyze here,[4] and whose recent revival in the United States has reached epidemic proportions.

In sum, Rose's psychoanalytic perspective lends itself powerfully to a certain sort of feminist politics. But it's at least arguable that the advent of psychoanalysis in the early twentieth century was associated historically with the displacement of a very different account of the psyche that held and in a sense holds again radical implications for a theory of the female subject, implications whose specifically political resonances remain to be explored. The account of the psyche I have in mind is bound up with a problematic of *hypnosis* or *suggestion,* understood as involving a kind of *imitation* or *mimesis.* Recent deconstructive readings of Freud have stressed the extent to which Freud's thought continually struggled to distinguish itself from the hypnosis-suggestion paradigm, which he is seen as having regarded as undermining the very concept of the subject defined, in a tradition going back

to Descartes, as the subject of representation. In this account, the basic impulse of psychoanalysis, "for all its assertion of primordial alterity," was to
preserve more or less intact what Lacan was later to call the "scandal of the
subject thought as 'unifying unity.'"[5] These are difficult matters, but they
are ones which—for reasons that will become clear—I have no choice but
to confront.

What makes the confrontation inevitable is my sense of the issues at
stake in a once-famous text, Morton Prince's *The Dissociation of a Personality: A Biographical Study in Abnormal Psychology* (1905). The moment of its writing returns us to the beginnings not only of psychoanalysis
but of modern American psychology as well, when the problem of hypnosis
and with it the phenomenon of multiple personality were first engaged. And
as we shall see, in Prince's text the quest for a patient's "real" or "original"
identity is, I shall argue, intimately if covertly entangled not only with notions of suggestion or mimesis but also, equally importantly, with questions
of sexual difference. Eventually, too, we shall want to ask what relation, if
any, obtains between the early history of multiple personality as exemplified
by Prince's text and the use of the multiple-personality concept in both medical and feminist discourse today. Is it possible that the recently revived idea
of the multiple self functions, as it did in the past, to "repress" the hypnotic-
mimetic paradigm? What are the implicit or strategic sexual politics of such
a development? These are questions I shall be attempting to answer in the
light of my reading of a key moment in the theorization of the modern subject.

Mimesis, Identification, and Multiple Personality

In the spring of 1898 a young woman of modest Irish-American background and education came to Morton Prince, a well-known New England
psychotherapist, for the treatment of a condition he diagnosed as a typical
if extreme example of neurasthenia or hysteria. Almost immediately, the
case took an unexpected turn when, failing to improve his patient's health
by "conventional" methods of treatment, Prince began to use hypnotic suggestion.[6] The patient, when awake and when hypnotized, was usually weary,
depressed, and extremely passive. One day, however, under deep hypnosis,
she suddenly changed: she became lively, bold, saucy—and difficult to control. In this new state, she insisted that she was an entirely different person
from the morbidly conscientious, reticent, anxious, self-sacrificing, and pious
individual whose body she shared and from whom she differentiated herself
by referring to the latter contemptuously in the third person as "She." Soon
convinced that this second vivacious personality's claim to independence
was genuine, Prince named her "BIII," "Chris," or "The Devil," in order
to distinguish her from her other self, whom he called "BI," "Christine,"

or "The Saint" (BII was merely BI in the hypnotic state). Subsequently, "of her own accord," Chris in a "spirit of fun" adopted the name "Sally Beauchamp" after "a character in some book" (29–30). Nor was this the end of the multiplication of the patient's selves, for about a year later still another personality emerged, "BIV," someone whose independence, "frailties of temper, self-concentration, ambition, and self-interest" (17) led Prince to call her "The Woman" or "The Realist," and whom Sally scornfully dubbed "The Idiot." (Prince uses the name "Beauchamp" for all three of the personalities.)

The social complications, embarrassments, and quarrels that resulted from the dramatic appearances and disappearances of the three major personalities in the case furnish the plot of Prince's book. The case only came to an end six years later when Prince succeeded through his hypnotic powers in identifying or "resurrecting" Miss Beauchamp's "real, original or normal self" (1) by annihilating Sally and preserving the other personalities by synthesizing or "integrating" them into a single, stable identity. At last restored to the self "that was born and which she was intended by nature to be," (1) Miss Beauchamp—"like the traditional princess in the fairy story"—was awakened by her Prince and "soon married and 'lived happily ever afterward.' "[7]

Prince's text invokes the genres of the detective and the adventure story. But as the last quotation suggests, the narrative also belongs to the genre of the fairy tale. As in all fairy tales, *The Dissociation of a Personality* is preoccupied with change, with the magical transformation of the self. (Hypnotism functions in the case as a kind of magic: Sally's metamorphosis is invoked at one point by the image of a butterfly emerging from its chrysalis (93).) And as in a fairy tale, the narrative's resolution is at once conventional, enforcing a social and political moral (the destiny of women is marriage), and arbitrary. One feels this arbitrariness above all in the way the text comes to an abrupt stop. It would be tempting to say that the abruptness of the ending amounts to a kind of violence, epitomized by the narrative's representation of Prince's relentless, Svengali-like struggle for Miss Beauchamp's soul as a war to the death and the suppression of his patient's various alter egos as "psychical murder" (248). Moreover, in one of the many intertextual moments in the case, Prince compares Miss Beauchamp's condition as a psychological double to that of the ape in Kipling's story, Bertran and Bimi, who had "half of a human soul" and "too much Ego in his Cosmos" and whose death at the hands of his human "father" and sexual rival warrants our thinking of Sally's disappearance in similar terms.[8] Yet it might be truer to say that the abruptness of the ending is a way of *avoiding* violence. Sally must be made to "go back to where she came from" (414, 138–39, 405, 524), an ambiguous expression that could be a euphemism for her murder or suicide but that could also be taken to suggest that she isn't ex-

actly dead—as if Prince had contrived at once to eliminate and to spare the
playful, flirtatious, heartless, rebellious, dangerous Sally (one reviewer
compared her to an unruly city mob)[9] without whom the case would lose
much of its narrative drive and interest and whom Prince finds "delightfully
attractive" (53), indeed "irresistible" (110). (It was typical of such cases
that the most prominent of the selves to emerge during treatment was more
athletic, outgoing, spontaneous, reckless, and irresponsible—in short, more
juvenile—than the patient's primary self.)[10] The great, even excessive length
of Prince's narrative—it goes on for more than 500 pages, while another
American case-history closely modeled on the Beauchamp case is a numbing
1,500 pages long[11]—also suggests the author's reluctance if not inability to
bring the narrative to a close. Prince's friend and colleague, William James,
was also fascinated by Sally: "But *who* and *what* is the lovely Sally? That
is a very dark point."[12] I too would like to know what the enthralling but
threatening Sally represents in the case.

Now a major assumption of Prince's narrative is that the different personalities in the case are autonomous subjects whom he understands as having emerged as a consequence of an emotional shock and the patient's pathological condition. But his text is also haunted by the fear or possibility that
Sally and the others have been created by the physician's own hypnotic or
suggestive powers. What complicates matters further, what makes it extremely difficult to achieve something like a univocal reading of the construction of identity and gender in the case, is that Prince's book is written
under the sign of, and in relation to, a paradigm of *mimetic identification*
in which he himself is necessarily implicated.

But what is identification? Explicitly or implicitly, that question haunts
recent feminist efforts to think through the construction of sexual identity
and sexual difference. Indeed a central aim of this paper is to urge a new
understanding of the mechanism of identification as that mechanism has come
to be understood in the wake of psychoanalysis. In particular, I want to
propose that we not uncritically follow Freud's tendency to regard identification as the result of the subject's unconscious desire for a loved *object*.
Rather, we must reverse the ostensible terms of Freud's analysis by treating
identification as involving the imitation by one "self" of an "other" that to
all intents and purposes is indistinguishable from the first and as a result of
which desire is provoked or *induced*. "In the beginning is mimesis: as far
back as one goes in anamnesis (in self-analysis, we might say, if the *self*
were not precisely what is in question here), one always finds the identification from which the 'subject' dates, (the 'primary identification,' as Freud
later puts it)," Mikkel Borch-Jacobsen writes in his philosophically acute
reading of the critique of the subject and the theory of unconscious desire
associated with Freud's attempted repudiation of hypnosis.

This is why the chronology Freud most frequently indicates has to be inverted. Desire (the desiring subject) does not come first, to be *followed* by an identification that would allow the desire to be fulfilled. What comes first is a tendency toward identification, a primordial tendency which then gives rise to a desire; and this desire is, from the outset, a (mimetic, rivalrous) desire to oust the incommodious other from the place the psuedo-subject already occupies in fantasy.

"If desire is satisfied in and through identification," Borch-Jacobsen adds in acknowledging the (partial) convergence of his analysis with René Girard's mimetic theory, "it is not in the sense in which a desire somehow precedes its 'gratification,' since no desiring subject (no 'I,' no ego) precedes the mimetic identification: identification brings the desiring subject into being, and not the other way around." The hypnotic rapport precisely exemplifies the workings of this "primordial," unconscious, identification.[13]

Hypnosis threatens to dissolve the distinction between self and other to such a degree that the hypnotized subject comes to occupy the place of the "other" in an unconscious identification so profound that the other is not apprehended *as other*. We might put it that in hypnosis the mimesis is unrepresentable to the subject. Yet as Borch-Jacobsen has argued, this lack of distinction between self and other "has to be acted out."[14] This means that for Prince no less than for Freud, although in different terms, mimesis is continually relegated to a secondary position: the hypnotized person is conceived not as imitating the "other" in a scene of unconscious, *nonspecular identification* unavailable to subsequent recall, but as occupying the vantage point of a *spectator* who, being distanced from the scene, can *see herself* in the scene, can represent herself to herself *as other,* and hence can distinguish herself from the model. In short, mimesis—the coalescence of self and other that takes place in hypnosis—is converted into the specular order of the hated double or rival. (I draw attention here to the idea that mimesis always produces a sadistic, paranoid desire to annihilate the "other" who is also "myself": "I hate her, I just hate her" (130) says Sally Beauchamp of her alter ego, Miss Beauchamp. "I wish she were dead!" (169).[15] The identity between self and other that is constitutive of mimesis inevitably succumbs to the requirement that there be *a subject or foundation* which precedes mimesis and out of which identification is produced.

On this reading, Freud seeks to evade the radical dedifferentiation implicit in hypnotic suggestion by reinterpreting the effects of hypnosis as the product, not of the relationship between hypnotist and subject, but of the subject's sexual desire. What Freud finds uncanny or scandalous about hypnosis-suggestion, and what therefore he struggles to suppress, is the idea that in suggestion my thoughts do not come from my own mind or self but are produced by the "imitation" or suggestion of another—the hypnotist or, in psychoanalytic practice, the analyst. Freud's theory of the unconscious is thus an attempt to solve the problem of the hypnotic rapport by *transforming suggestion into desire*. For Borch-Jacobsen, therein lies precisely its originality and historical specificity. "Always [Freud] imputed to an improbable hypnotised *subject* the responsibility and the initiative for this unappropriable, unimputable 'rapport,'" Borch-Jacobsen writes.

> Of suggestion, of the "transmission" or "transference of thoughts" . . . of magic and hypnotic demonism in general, he simply wanted to know nothing: "She, the hysteric, is not me." Or again: "It is not I who influence her, it is she who influences herself—her or her unconscious." And above all: "It is not I who speaks with her mouth, not I the demon who possesses her—it is her, or Another in her."[16]

In relation to Prince, the implications of such a rereading of Freud are no less charged, for it suggests that an analogous tendency toward the suppression of the mimesis-suggestion paradigm might powerfully if silently be at work in the writings of Prince and the American school of imitation-suggestion. Thus Prince and his colleagues marveled both at the multiple roles or "impersonations" that their patients were capable of performing while under deep hypnosis and at the fact that those patients afterwards remembered nothing of what they had said or done. Such a radical self-estrangement or psychic splitting is the hallmark of posthypnotic suggestion, in which the awake patient carries out, as if in a trance, actions that have been suggested in a previous hypnotic state and that are characteristically attributed to another person, "another me" who is present to the hypnotic order in a way the patient never is. "They speak of this person as of a stranger," Alfred Binet wrote;[17] or as Prince remarks of Miss Beauchamp: "I was startled to hear her, when hypnotized, speak of herself in her waking state as 'She'" (26). From this standpoint the notion of hypnotic suggestion as involving a somnambulistic, unconscious identification with the hypnotist so deep that the patient "blindly" or unconsciously, without the possibility of subsequent recollection or narration, takes the place of or incarnates the other ("who at the same moment isn't an 'other,' but 'myself,' in my undecidable identity of the somnambulistic ego"),[18] can scarcely if at all be distinguished from the phenomenon of multiple personality as it was experienced in the early twentieth century. Understood in this way, multiple personality is the mimetic idea *par excellence*.[19]

But this is not how Prince and his fellow hypnotists tend to understand the concept of multiple personality. Instead, they interpret the scandalous estrangement or splitting of the "self" in hypnosis not as the effect of mimetic identification but as the sign of *another subject or personality*—that is, as the manifestation of a part of the self that has hitherto been latent or concealed (William James's "subliminal" or "hidden self") but that has now been revealed or "dissociated" by a trauma or by suggestion.[20] The hypnotized person is conceived not as a sleepwalker given over body and soul to the hypnotist's suggestions such that she *is* the other, but rather as a subject who can distance herself from the scene and hence can observe the other *as* other, that is, can distinguish the model from the copy. That is why the act of naming assumes such importance in cases of this kind, for conferring a name on the patient's second self helps establish and reinforce the idea that the patient's actions are not the effect of hypnotic or mimetic identification but are produced by component parts of the patient's consciousness each of which under normal (James) or abnormal (Prince) circumstances may thus constitute a distinct identity or "personality."

"If the concept of an unconscious is to be retained," Borch-Jacobsen has written, "it needs to be definitively liberated from the phantom of the *other subject* and the *other consciousness* inherited from late-nineteenth-century psychology and psychiatry (Azam's 'somnambulistic' or 'hypnotic consciousness,' Binet's 'personality alterations,' Breuer's 'hypnoid state,' the early Freud's 'dissociation of consciousness,' and so on)."[21] But this is to suggest that *both* Prince and Freud may be viewed as seeking to provide a solution to the historical-theoretical problem of imitation-suggestion: the later Freud through a theory of unconscious sexual desire, and both the earlier Freud and Prince through a theory of the "dissociation of consciousness"— that is, multiple personality. But perhaps it would be more accurate to say that *The Dissociation of a Personality* stages a struggle in which the multiple-personality concept functions as a switch point between two competing models—the first mimetic and the second antimimetic—of personal identity and, I will argue, gender formation. Therein would lie *its* originality and historical specificity.

I need hardly add that if this is correct we can't simply use Freud to interpret Prince. Deliberately written for a general audience, Prince's book "created a sensation wherever English was read,"[22] quickly went through two editions and many more printings, and provided the theme for more than five hundred plays, one of which drew capacity audiences on Broadway.[23] Yet already by 1905, the by-then-familiar terms of its analysis, derived chiefly from Prince's friend Janet—hypnotic suggestion, traumatic shock, dissociation of the mind—were under challenge from Freud (the Dora case appeared the same year), which is one reason why hypnosis and with it the multiple personality concept were progressively abandoned in the years that followed.[24] And in fact it's difficult to read the Beauchamp case without placing it in a psychoanalytic frame—without thinking, for example, of Sally's investment in Prince in libidinal-conflictual terms,[25] or of Prince's desire to hunt down the "real" Miss Beauchamp in Lacanian terms as a wish to recover a presence or origin that in principle cannot be recuperated but only fantasized or displaced. But this is what I want to resist.

The Birth of the Subject

My thesis is that Prince's analysis of the Beauchamp case simultaneously instantiates and suppresses what I shall call the mimesis-suggestion paradigm. It follows that we might expect to find scenes of mimetic identification and of their virtually immediate denial by way of effects of distance and "originary" difference at strategic junctures in his text. Or to put this the other way round, we might expect the narrative to contain scenes of specular representation that, even as they appear to prove the spontaneity and independence of the subjects in question, silently depend on the very structure of mimetic identification they appear to deny. One such scene may be regarded as representative in this regard. One day early on, Chris, the patient's recently named second self, who until then had always had her eyes closed in conformity with Prince's hypnotic command, *opens her eyes*. For some time, Chris—who, unlike the passive, "very suggestible" (15) Miss Beauchamp, "from the outset showed a will and individuality of her own, which was in no way subject to anybody else's influence" (56–57)— had been rubbing her closed eyelids with her hands, asserting that it was "her deliberate purpose to get her eyes open," and even going so far as to "threaten insubordination, insisting that she *would* see, and that she 'had a right to see.' She complained rather piteously that it was not fair Miss Beauchamp should be allowed to see, while she was forbidden" (91). Prince was determined to prevent Chris from opening her eyes, on the theory that if she were to see she "might become educated into an independent personality" (92). But in this contest of wills Prince's attempts to "limit the mental experiences of Chris" were "hopeless" for as he says with admiration: "She proved herself made of different stuff" (92–93). Prince emphasizes the willful character of Chris's—or, as she comes to be called, Sally's—disobedience by adding that the mechanical movement of rubbing her eyes was not in itself sufficient for her to achieve her goal:

> Besides rubbing her eyes she was obliged to "will" to come. "Willing," as a part of her conscious processes, plays a very prominent part in the psychological phenomena manifested by this personality, particularly in those which are the effect of her influence upon the others.
> "How did you make her do this or that?" I frequently asked.
> I just "willed," was the reply. (93)

Here is how Prince describes the scene in which Chris/Sally succeeds in opening her eyes:

One day toward the end of June Miss Beauchamp was sitting by the open window reading. She fell into what Chris afterward called a half "mooning" state. She would read a bit, then look out of the window and think; then turn to her book and again read. Thus she would alternately read and dream,—day-dreaming, it was. All her life she had been in the habit of falling into these states of abstraction (for such they were), when she lived in the clouds. Here was Chris's opportunity. The physical and mental conditions were ripe. Chris was not one to let such a golden chance slip by. So while Miss Beauchamp was dreaming in her chair, Chris took both her hands,—Miss Beauchamp's hands,—rubbed her eyes, and "willed"; then, for the moment, Miss Beauchamp disappeared and "Sally" came, mistress of herself, and, for the first time, able to see. From this time on we shall call Chris by the name of Sally; for though it was much later that Chris took the name, the complete independent existence of this personality dates from this event.

Sally had gotten her eyes open at last, and with the opening of her eyes she may be said to have been truly born into this world, though she claimed to have really existed before. Sally was delighted with her success, so she must celebrate her birthday by smoking two cigarettes. Her belief in the naughtiness of it all, and a consciousness of the displeasure which it would occasion Miss Beauchamp, added to her enjoyment. (95–96)

Sally's delight was tempered by the fear that she had somehow killed Miss Beauchamp and perhaps would not be able to bring her back. But, ever ingenious, she remembered that Prince sometimes used a "strong Faradic battery" (96) to wake up the hypnotized Miss Beauchamp when she (Chris) herself would not disappear on his command. Accordingly, she took her lighted cigarette and, imitating Prince, (sadomasochistically) burned her (alter–ego's) arm so that Miss Beauchamp "woke up" (96).

The significance of this scene is that it marks Sally's birth as an independent person, which is to say that it marks the birth of the subject *as a subject*. If sleep is the sign of the hypnotic trance,[26] then when Sally opens her eyes she proves (or rather, demonstrates) her claim that she's not an artifact of suggestion, not merely a version of Miss Beauchamp when the latter is asleep or hypnotized, but a genuinely independent person. It's not just the fact that Sally opens her eyes, but *how* she does it that matters: she opens her eyes in an act of volition that not only establishes her difference from the Miss Beauchamp's "aboulia" or lack of will (15) but is so powerful that henceforth she appears to defeat even Prince's most determined efforts to control her. *Willing* is here conjoined with *looking* (more broadly, with *specularity*) as that which defines personal identity, and one is not surprised to learn later in Prince's text that Sally plans to write a "willing book" (340).[27]

Another point that should be stressed is that this ostensible scene of origins really constitutes a *second* birth, for Prince had already devoted a previous chapter to the "Birth of Sally," when he had first conferred a name, Chris, on his patient's hypnotic self. Yet as Prince recognizes, the act of naming in itself can't secure Sally's autonomy as a subject, because the very fact that she adopts her name at Prince's suggestion casts doubt on her genuineness as a second personality. "How did you get the name of Chris?," Prince asks. "'You suggested it to me one day, and I remember everything'" (41). Moreover, Prince doesn't think it's sufficient to appeal, as James, Janet, Binet, and others do, to the phenomena of automatic writing and post-hypnotic suggestion as evidence for the existence of a second or hidden self, for these are experimental phenomena which may also be artifacts of suggestion (26–27). Similarly, Chris's/Sally's testimony as to her ignorance of the literature of multiple personality, her ability to assert her will by hypnotizing Miss Beauchamp into telling outrageous lies (58–60), drinking wine (59), and doing many other things distasteful to the latter's moral standards, and her personal conviction that she's a completely different personality from Miss Beauchamp (42–49)—all might be adduced as evidence in favor of Sally's independence as a subject, yet, as Prince himself argues, these too might be the product of suggestion or simply delusions. "Spontaneous phenomena were essential for proof" (50).[28] And perhaps the most dramatic demonstration of Sally's "spontaneity"—the event that marks her (re)birth as a stable character and genuinely independent subject—is her ability to successfully will her eyes open.

What makes Sally's act of volition all the more interesting to the historian is that it seems to contradict William James's assertion in the *Principles of Psychology* that "no creature not endowed with divinatory power can perform an act voluntarily for the first time."[29] Until we have performed an action at least once, James argues, "we can have no idea of what sort of a thing it is like, and do not know in what direction to set our will to bring it about." That is, a randomly occurring or reflex movement must, through the "kinesthetic" impressions associated with it, first leave an image of itself in the memory before the movement can be "desired again, proposed as an end, and deliberately willed." The idea or representation of the movement must always precede its execution. "We need to know at each movement just *where we are in it*," James writes, "if we are to will intelligently what the next link will be," noting in this regard that if a suitably predisposed person is told during the hypnotic trance that he can't feel his limb, "he will be quite unaware of the attitudes into which you may throw it."[30] This is precisely Sally's condition, for, until she wills her eyes open, like many hysterics she is completely anaesthetic and so lacks the guiding sensations James believes are necessary for voluntary movement. When her eyes are shut, Sally can "feel nothing" (147), with the result that Prince can place a limb in any posture he chooses without her being able to recognize the position it's in. "In reality the movement cannot even be *started* correctly in some cases [of hysteria] without the kinesthetic impression," James observes, adding: "M. Binet suggests . . . that in those [hysterics] who cannot move the hand at all the sensation of light is required as a 'dynamogenic' agent."[31] Prince seems to have the same idea in mind when he observes of Sally: "But let her open her eyes and look at what you are doing, let her join the visual sense with the tactile or other senses, and the lost sensations at once return. The association of visual perceptions with these sensations brings the latter into the field of her personal consciousness" (147–48).

But this leaves unexplained how Sally *first* voluntarily opens her eyes, an action whose origin thus appears to be utterly mysterious. It's as if Sally achieves a state of personhood *ex abrupto,* to use James's expression,[32]— as she puts it, "I just willed." The absoluteness of this feat of willing is for Prince the hallmark of Sally's authenticity as a distinct personality, which is to say of the repudiation of mimesis-suggestion as an explanation of her existence. Yet the possibility can't be ignored that in that scene of origins Sally succeeds in authorizing herself as a subject (parthenogenetically giving birth to herself by willing her eyes open) precisely by identifying mimetically with the hypnotist, Prince himself, who enjoys a privileged position of spectatordom and who is described (by BIV) as seeing everything with his "'eagle eye'" (244). Sally's action is thus simultaneously and irreducibly mimetic and antimimetic, her birth as a subject at once a product of mimetic repetition and an act of self-production.[33] (Sally "dates her whole independent existence from this day, and she always refers to events as being 'before' or 'after she got her eyes opened.' That is the central event in her life, just as mothers date periods before or after the birth of a child," Prince wrote in a preliminary account of the case.[34] The scene as Prince thematizes it thereby announces the problematic of the mother, to which I'll return.) Understood in these terms, Sally's celebration of her birth by smoking not one but two cigarettes is highly significant. For even before she gets her eyes open Sally (still Chris), in a "Bohemian" (55) act designed to provoke the disapproval of Miss Beauchamp, to whom smoking is "absolutely repugnant" (55), imitates Prince by smoking one of his cigarettes (54). (Thereafter cigarettes mark both Sally's difference from her other selves and her male-identified transgression of conventional standards of female behavior.) It's as if James was right after all—as if in order for Sally successfully to will to smoke she had to have *already* smoked, not as a willed action but rather as one of involuntary or mimetic identification. Indeed for James hypnotic suggestion and the will turn out to be virtually indistinguishable from one another: to illustrate what he considers the simplest or most fundamental type of voluntary action—that which follows "unhesitatingly and immediately the notion of it in the mind"—James cites the example of hypnotized subjects who "repeat whatever they hear you say, and imitate whatever they see you do"[35]—a point of view that Prince, for reasons that are already plain, could hardly afford to make his own.

The shift from mimetic identification to specularity exemplified by Sally's opening her eyes is accompanied in Prince's text by a thematics of surface and depth that also works to establish if not always the autonomy of the subject in question at any rate the antimimetic nature of certain subject-*effects*. Thus Sally is a brilliant mimic who repeatedly deploys her mimetic skills in order to get her own way. Sally used to "impersonate Miss Beauchamp," Prince writes, "copying as far as she was able her mannerisms and tone" (117). "When blocked in some design I have seen Sally over and over again attempt to pass herself off as Miss Beauchamp" (118). But if Sally can fool her friends, she can't deceive Prince, for she's incapable of feeling the inner emotions that involuntarily determine Miss Beauchamp's outward expression. "In connection with the matter of detecting Sally when masquerading as Miss Beauchamp, I have often been asked how one personality differs from the other," Prince remarks.

> Of course the mode of speech and mannerisms of each differ, but more than this, it is a very interesting fact that with both Miss Beauchamp and Sally every mood, feeling, and emotion is accompanied automatically by its own facial expression, so that, as each individuality has a dominant, and for the most part continuous state of mind, each wears a corresponding expression.

As this expression is "purely automatic," it's impossible for one personality to completely simulate the other. "When Sally tries to impersonate Miss Beauchamp the best she can do is to look serious; but as she does not *feel* serious . . . her face does not assume the expression of that personality" (123). Not that Miss Beauchamp is perceived by Prince as a paragon of psychic independence—on the contrary, for the most part she epitomizes passivity, obedience, indeed suggestibility. But Prince's unease with suggestion and mimesis is such that he is at pains to emphasize what might be called Miss Beauchamp's *limited* autonomy in the face of Sally's efforts to mimic her persuasively. At the same time, there is a sense in which Sally's failure to deceive Prince serves to dramatize her own (relatively) *absolute* autonomy or say her sheer psychic distinctness, the specific individuality that sets her apart from the other selves and that Prince finds so attractive. And of course it also further establishes Prince as the master of internal/external relations, the one person in the text in whose eyes Miss Beauchamp and Sally cannot fail to look like themselves, in their irreducible difference from each other.

Further light is thrown on the dynamics of specularity in Prince's text by a scene that occurs much later in the book. BIV, who has been locked in a "life and death struggle" (476) with her hated rival, Sally, had a "very remarkable experience" (360). A day or two earlier she had written an "ultimatum" (359) to Sally, threatening to have her banished to an asylum if she did not comply with BIV's demands for control. Now BIV, in a "depressed, despondent, rather angry frame of mind," looks at herself in a mirror. She was combing her hair, and at the time thinking deeply, when suddenly she saw, "notwithstanding the seriousness of her thoughts, a curious, laughing expression—a regular diabolical smile—come over her face. It was not her own expression, but one that she had never seen before. It seemed to her devilish, diabolical, and uncanny." Prince identifies this expression as the peculiar smile of Sally. "BIV had a feeling of horror come over her at what she saw. She seemed to recognize it as the expression of the thing that possessed her. She saw herself as another person in the mirror and was frightened by the extraordinary character of the expression." Realizing that her attempt to question the "thing" was "absurd," BIV hits on the idea of using automatic writing to get Sally to respond. Placing some paper on her bureau, and taking a pencil in her hand, "she addressed herself to the face in the glass. Presently her hand began to write" and an exciting interrogation of Sally began—"for, of course, the 'thing' was Sally" (360–61).

On the one hand, the scene in question represents a moment of identification as BIV confronts her own image in a mirror. On the other (and more importantly), it dramatizes the constitutive instability of *all* moments of identification in Prince's strongly antimimetic text, as Sally's image— more precisely, her *expression* (both less and more than an image in its own right)—instantly takes the place of BIV's own. Of course what makes this displacement uncanny, what gives it its horrifying force, is that difference is established only on the basis of a fundamental likeness (the image in the mirror is of BIV but its "expression" is different). Here again we must reverse the terms of Freud's analysis. On this reading, the uncanny double is not the product of the subject's repressed infantile desires, as it is for Freud, but arises directly out of the mimetic relationship itself, as the person with whom I identify is immediately converted into my rival who is *seen* to occupy *my* place.[36]

A closely related aspect of the mirror scene is that it reinforces the idea, thematized though never theorized throughout the book, that from the perspective of mimesis the specular as such is linked to the assertion of difference, of essential otherness, indeed of *violent rivalry* with that other who is, as the scene makes clear, a version of the same. The annexation of automatic writing, elsewhere in the text a means of suspending conscious control and therefore associated with suggestion-imitation, in order to give expression to a rival will is consistent with this idea: BIV's brilliant stratagem allows Sally to make use of her, BIV's, hand as an instrument for expressing her, Sally's "independent" personality (I imagine this automatic writing as *dependent* on the framing context of the mirror). The scene thus converts the automatic into the volitional, BIV's loss of control into Sally's intentions. "The fact that the writing was spontaneous . . . deserves to be emphasized," Prince observes, "because this spontaneity removes it from the class of artifacts unwittingly manufactured by the observer." Then, as if to reassure himself and the reader on this point, Prince adds:

> BIV, as she testifies, was not in an abstracted state while the writing was done, but was alert, conscious of her surroundings, excited, and extremely curious to know what the hand was writing. *It is to be regretted that she was not under observation at the time,—though this would have given rise to the suspicion that the doubling of consciousness was an artifact,— but I have seen the same feat performed under substantially similar conditions.* (364, emphasis added)

Prince wishes he had something more than BIV's word to go on, but he also insists that the fact that she was alone (with Sally, so to speak) guarantees the antimimetic nature of the events she describes. At the same time, he wants us to know that he has witnessed equivalent scenes—as if the reassurance this offers can somehow escape the taint of mimesis he correctly recognizes is inseparable from his presence.

Gender and Mimesis

Sally gets her eyes open at last and thereby gains her full independence as a very special kind of subject. For Prince, what makes her special, what for him defines her as psychologically the most interesting of all the personalities in the case—"the one who has to be reckoned with" (266)—is that she's what he calls a "co-consciousness": not only does she alternate with the other selves, appearing in their place when they disappear, but she permanently coexists with them. Unlike Miss Beauchamp, "The Idiot," and other multiples, all of whom when submerged are unaware of what the other personalities are thinking and doing, Sally has a continuous, uninterrupted existence: "It meant the co-existence of two different combinations at one and the same time, each with a self-consciousness. There were two I's then in existence."[37]

Being a co-consciousness, ·Sally is able to observe the other personalities at all times and hence can see, hear, and know things of which they are entirely unaware. "I am always present," she says (158). "I am always alive" (339). As a permanent "spectator of their lives" (147), Sally serves as Prince's surrogate by providing him with crucial information about the case that he is unable to obtain for himself. "I can't conceive of things being done without my knowledge, even in hypnosis," she says. "They never have been, you know, since that very, *very* early time when I used to sleep" (318).[38] Always conscious, Sally claims never to sleep and hence never to dream. But precisely because she's always conscious she knows the dreams of her other selves, even those the latter are unable to remember on waking, which is why she can produce a "unique" account of Miss Beauchamp's dream life.[39] Similarly, Sally's co-consciousness permits her to write out for Prince a remarkable "Autobiography" providing a record of two independent sets of thoughts, memories, and wills, her own and Miss Beauchamp's, going back to earliest childhood, that are known in their entirety only to herself; for unlike Miss Beauchamp and BIV, who have gaps in their memories corresponding to their condition as alternating states, Sally has a remarkably comprehensive and continuous memory (238)—along with volition, the very mark of personal identity according to Pierre Janet and Théodule Ribot.[40] "Perhaps it would be better if I divided the page [into parallel columns] and carried it on that way," Sally suggests in her first attempt to express her duality of thought in a suitable literary form. "That really was the way the thought went, you know, until I got my eyes open" (316).

It follows that Sally is internally divided in ways the other personalities in the case are not. Whereas Miss Beauchamp and "The Idiot" differ from each other (and from all the other selves), Sally differs *from herself* in ways that make her virtually incarnate the notion of double or multiple personality as such.[41] Sally's internal heterogeneity finds expression in a variety of ways, starting with her choice of a last name, "Beauchamp," which is marked by a discrepancy between its (French) spelling and its (English) pronounciation, "*Beecham*" (1). But the aspect of her heterogeneity that I want to focus on in this section is the fact that she is gendered both female and male.

Prince's commitment to the idea that the various personalities in the case are not artifacts of suggestion but are genuinely (if unequally) autonomous subjects motivates his attempt to draw sharp lines between them by differentiating their tastes, educational attainments, feelings, morals, and other traits (even their writing differs). He thereby creates what amounts to a virtual typology of early-twentieth-century concepts of the feminine. In Prince's analysis, the morbidly impressionable, passive, modest, and self-sacrificing Miss Beauchamp, who has a history of somnambulism, daydreaming and trance-like states, represents a neurasthenic version of traditional womanhood. She is the antithesis of the self-reliant, realistic, enormously strong-willed, indeed "belligerent" (324) and emphatically unmaternal BIV (293), who imagines that she is "quite capable of running the world" (292) and who in Prince's disapproving, misogynistic description amounts to a parody of the "New Woman." Between these extremes, Sally occupies the position of the untutored, irresponsible young girl whose love of adventure, play, and excitement and dislike of books and the passive, scholarly life declare her unmistakably to be the adolescent of Stanley Hall's recent, influential definition.[42] "[O]ne of the most marked peculiarities of Sally's personality is its *childlike immaturity*. Sally is a child" (152, emphasis his), Prince writes, characterizing her as a young girl of about twelve or thirteen (112). "[S]he looked at everything from a child's point of view. Her general attitude of mind and her actions were those of a very young girl, as were her some of her ideas of fun, and particularly her love of mischief" (112).

As an adolescent, Sally is highly labile in mood and character, representing that unique moment of pubescent transition from relatively undifferentiated sexuality to gender decision, when according to Hall youth is "plastic and suggestible to an amazing degree" and when girls especially are prone to gender confusion and even complete role reversal.[43] Flirtatious and saucy, Sally acts her heterosexual feminine role to the hilt as she plays (the safely married) Prince off against the other important male in the story, the mysterious "William Jones," whose dramatic intervention in Miss Beauchamp's life I shall examine in a moment. "Know all men by these presents that I, Sally, being of sound mind and in full possession of all my senses, do hereby most solemnly promise to love, honor, and obey Morton Prince, M.D., situate in the city of Boston, state of Massachusetts, from this time forth, *toujours*. Amen, amen, amen. *Toujours* is French, you know," Sally writes Prince in a mock imitation of a marriage vow (138). Yet she is also "faithless" to Prince by repeatedly making forbidden "engagements" to meet her "caro amico" Jones, with whom she hopes to run off and love "for always" (111). At the same time, in conformity with Hall's concept of the pervasiveness of homosexuality in adolescent girls, Sally is also very attached to several older women, mother substitutes as she recognizes, who make shadowy appearances in the text. For Hall, this otherwise normal homosexual phase of development risks progressing to, what he refers to as, outright lesbian masculinization if not properly checked.[44] Just so, Sally is insistently phallicized throughout Prince's text, starting with her name "Chris" (the masculine version of "Christine")[45] and her liking for Prince's "masculine" cigarettes. At moments of conflict with Miss Beauchamp, Sally's voice, coming like an explosion "suddenly out of the depths," changes to a "bass note" (157). Resembling her father in looks (12), she is careless of her appearance, threatening to "ape" a man by cutting off Miss Beauchamp's hair. "You will cut off your own hair; it is your hair," Prince points out. "[Laughing.] 'I don't care. She will look like a guy—just like one of those monkeys. I don't care how I look'" (169). (At one point, Prince compares Sally to a monkey (313).) Like a "guy," she is unafraid of the spiders, snakes, toads, and mice with which she torments the terrified, conventionally feminine Miss Beauchamp (71, 161, 208). More generally, Sally's male-coded refusal to be "one small victim" (98), her enormously energetic and powerful will,[46] and her love of practical jokes, of "an outdoor, breezy life;

sports, amusements, physical activity, games, and the theatre" and of "tales of adventure, and of outdoor life, of hunting and riding" which the playful, energetic, and athletic Prince often has to tell her "to satisfy her longing" (129)—all of this signals Sally's identification with Prince's virile, if similarly "adolescent" or "boyish," modes of behavior.[47] This is especially apparent in Sally's "Autobiography." Written at Prince's suggestion and designed, like the *Journal* of Marie Bashkirtseff (for Hall the very type of the "exaggerated adolescent confessionalist"),[48] to reveal "every little secret emotion of her soul" (365), Sally's "Autobiography" provides further evidence for Hall's alarming claim that nearly half of American adolescent girls reject the role of wife and mother and much prefer the freer life of the male sex.[49] "[N]asty squally little thing" is how the unmaternal Sally describes a baby sister who died in her arms (387). Whereas the bookish Miss Beauchamp had enjoyed school, Sally had "wanted to play 'hookey.' I thought it would be awfully exciting because the boys did it" (373). Like the ambitious Bashkirtseff who rebels against the restrictions imposed on women and frequently cries out "If only I were a man,"[50] Sally longs for the opportunities and mobility of the male sex, even to the extent of "donning boys' clothes on several occasions in search of adventure."[51]

Sally's monkey-like ability to imitate gender roles is in keeping with contemporary notions of the fluidity of identity in the prenubile state. Thus Hall appeals to the "new psychology of imitation" in order to explain what belongs to adolescence as "one of its most intrinsic traits," namely, its disposition to "ape positions, expressions, gait and mien" so that "every peculiarity is mimicked and parodied" and every youth has a "more or less developed stock of phrases, acts, and postures, expressive of mimetic love, anger, and fear." According to Hall, this mental plasticity explains the frequency, especially in young girls, of somnambulism, reverie, "transliminal modes of psychic action," and "multiplex personality." It also explains why, at a time before full sexual differentiation, both girls and boys are "more or less plastic" to the will not only of persons of the opposite sex but somewhat older persons of the same sex. Carrying the theory of suggestion, as embodied in contemporary notions of sexual fetishism, to its logical conclusion, Hall draws the "momentous inference" that in adolescence *"the sexual glow may come to be associated with almost any act or object whatever and give it an unique and otherwise inexplicable prominence in the life of the individual,* and that even the Platonic love of the eternally good, beautiful, and true is possible because of this early stage of indetermination and plasticity" (emphasis his).[52]

In other words, desire for an object is secondary to mimesis, which comes first. What's particularly interesting in this connection is that, the very year he first encountered Miss Beauchamp, Prince himself had analyzed the origin of sexual identity in mimetic terms. In a paper of 1898,

Prince agreed with Schrenck von Notzing, Binet, and others that homosexuality was a "vice" and not a disease because it was acquired by corrupt habits and wasn't the expression of a congenitally diseased nervous system, as Krafft-Ebing, Moll, Kiernan, Lydston, and the majority of sexologists believed. As a vice it deserved to be condemned; but as a vice it might also be cured or prevented. To give renewed credibility to a position that risked being viewed as moralizing and hence as unscientific, Prince made use of recent studies of hypnotism to argue that the sexual aberrations might originate in accidental, external suggestions that were subsequently forgotten, just as hysterical symptoms might be caused by forgotten subconscious influences. Within a general framework that always tended to represent homosexuality as involving gender role "inversion" of various degrees of severity, Prince rejected the view that there are fixed, essential male, female, or homosexual identities in nature, as the congenitalists maintained. Instead, he envisaged a continuum of sexual possibilities, ranging from the "strong, vigorous, masculine characters" at one end, through the intermediate types— the "men with female personalities" and the "masculine females"—to the "strongly marked feminine personalities" at the other end. For Prince in 1898, the differentiation between the sexes was a product of the "total environment" or "education" broadly defined, including the effects of "intentional education," "unconscious mimicry," "external suggestion," and "example" in determining the "tastes and habits of thought and manners" of the child. Nor did he shrink from the transgressive implications of this claim, which was that the homosexual option was equally available to all men and women. It is "extremely probable," he writes, "that if a boy were brought up as a girl or a girl as a boy" under conditions that were absolutely free of counter influences, "each would have the non-sexual [i.e., the characterological-erotic or nonanatomical] tastes and manners of the other sex."[53]

As Prince sees it, the process of education by which sexuality is molded isn't a matter of simple social conditioning, since each person is complicit in the "cultivation" of his or her desires. But nor is it a matter of inherent moral corruption, since healthy people develop normal heterosexuality precisely becuase they *are* healthy, whereas the homosexual's willful opposition to society's unwritten social laws involves a weakened resistance to external influence that is itself grounded in a congenital nervous taint. This double determination in "culture" and "nature," in "character" and the body, completely obscures the opposition between vice and disease with which Prince begins. It also produces a narrative that works to undermine the text's official condemnation of homosexuality. For in the mimetic scenario of origins that Prince now develops, homosexuality turns out to be the most "natural," heterosexuality the most "unnatural," forms of sexual desire.

"It is questionable whether only abnormally the vita sexualis of the male is excited by the *female*, and conversely" (94, emphasis mine), Prince declares. But doesn't he mean to say that it's questionable whether it's only abnormally that the male is sexually aroused by the *male*? That even under normal conditions a male may be excited to desire another *man*? Prince's extraordinary gender slip has the effect of making it appear doubtful whether the male is *ever* naturally excited by the female, as if heterosexuality is always superinduced on an authentic form of homosexual desire. And this is exactly what Prince immediately goes on to imply, remarking that there is "every reason to believe" that in "some perfectly healthy individuals" erotic feelings may be excited by the "sight or touch" of the sexual organs of a person of the "same sex," and that "at any rate, thoughts (pertaining to anatomy) so excited may very naturally awaken secondarily associated sexual feelings." As Prince explains: "[T]he vita sexualis in a boy is first associated with his own sexual organs. Later, the sight of those of another boy awaken the association of ideas by the well-known law, and then, in a degenerate, cultivation does the rest" (94, emphasis added). Nor is the origin of homosexual desire in suggestion restricted to the male sex, since Prince claims that Krafft-Ebing's first case of homosexuality in a girl may "readily" be explained in the same way. Thus in Prince's scenario of origins, the initial sexuality of both boys and girls is equally not heterosexual but homosexual, in the sense that it first arises in the form of an autoeroticism that develops via suggestion into a homosexual love of the same before it is later transformed into heterosexual desire.

From one point of view the scene Prince alludes to is a scene of representation, because in order to imitate the other boy the child must recognize the latter *as other,* that is to say, must *represent the other to himself.* But from another perspective, the scene in question takes place outside all "specular" representation, for—like the hypnotized subject to whom Prince compares him—the child is so in the grip of the "blind," unconscious reflex of suggestion—so caught up in a mimetic identification with the other boy— that in effect he becomes the other boy without being able to represent him to himself.[54] One might say that the child's hypnotically or mimetically induced homosexual response isn't truly "sexual" at all. Rather, it's an automatic, involuntary response of the body that has no psychical, representational, or cultural meaning in that the child is unaware of the significance of his act or that society considers it wrong. In fact, this is exactly what Prince immediately goes on to argue, quoting his opponent Krafft-Ebing to the effect that at the beginning of the child's sexual development "'the psychical relation to persons of the opposite sex is still absolutely wanting, and the sexual acts during this period partake more or less of a reflex spinal nature.'" (94). Here we can appreciate the ambiguity of Prince's narrative, for although the passage from Krafft-Ebing seems to concern the reflex nature of heterosexual love, Prince cites it in order to confirm the reflex character of homosexual desire. Thus it's not until adolescence, Prince claims, again quoting Krafft-Ebing, that these purely reflex reactions acquire a psychological dimension. For it's not until the anatomical and functional maturation of the "'generative organs'" associated with puberty and the "'differentiation of form belonging to each sex'" that the child develops "'rudiments of a mental feeling corresponding with the sex'" and begins to feel the "'powerful effect'" of "'education and external influence'" (94). We again note Prince's inability to decide between the primacy of biology or social training in the production of gender: it's not clear whether these rudimentary feelings associated with physical maturation are what determine desire, in which case the effects of society are secondary to those of biology, or whether external influences and education are decisive. Nothing seems more fragile than this distinction between the two causes. "Now, in a person of perfectly healthy mind and body," Prince continues, "all social customs, habits of thought, unwritten laws, and moral precepts tend to suppress any existing homosexual feeling and its gratification, and to encourage hetero-sexual feeling" (94). On the other hand, a person of "tainted constitution" does everything in his power to "foster, indulge and cultivate the perverse instinct" (94) which may, as in the female hysteric, through constant repetition acquire the "monstrous force" of a compulsive psychosis. Hence his conclusion:

> Thus may arise a perversity that had its origin in a normal reflex, but the accidental cause of which is forgotten with much else of the psychical life of childhood, or, if not forgotten, considered abnormal because of its future monstrous development. . . . What is really pathological in this aberration is the extraordinary intensification of the sexual feelings and the unbridled lack of restraint with which the subject indulges his senses and seeks every opportunity for gratification. These, without doubt, depend upon the neuropathic constitution. (95)

But the inescapable implication of this scenario is that a violent act of cultural repression is required to force desire away from its natural origins in a mimetically induced homosexual desire. Figuring the order of authority, law, and difference, culture produces a split in the self between a youthful, presexual homosexuality and an adult, reproductive heterosexuality that has to be brutally imposed because it has no simple basis in natural desire. In a text that never stops reinscribing the biological in the cultural, the natural becomes "monstrous" and corrupt only *because* it's socially prohibited, as if it's only this violent social prohibition that gives a natural and normal homosexuality its unnatural, pathological power of growth.

In sum, according to Prince's mimetic hypothesis, sexual identity is a consequence or effect of mimetic identification and not, as Freud will argue, the other way round. But this mimetically induced multiplicity of desire and identity is precisely what must be repudiated. For doesn't imitation-suggestion threaten to dissolve the boundaries between the sexes? Prince's writings, like those of Hall, thus join the increasingly abrasive turn-of-the-century debate over the "crisis" of masculinity associated with the New Woman's appropriation of male roles and the breakdown of the traditional separation between male and female spheres.[55] A tactical retreat from mimesis and imitation is therefore required, an antimimetic gesture that will reassert the radical difference between the sexes and will involve an attack on feminism for encouraging the homogenization of sexual identity associated with the mimetic-suggestion hypothesis. Thus in *Adolescence* Hall undercuts his own appeal to the mimetic lability of gender by condemning the women's movement for ignoring the natural, innate differences between the sexes. Criticizing coeducation for creating exhausted, effeminate males and dominant, masculine females, Hall characterizes three types of dysfunctional women produced by "the new woman movement," the "witch," the "egoist," and the "saint," in terms that strikingly resemble Prince's portraits of Sally, "The Idiot" (or "Realist"), and Miss Beauchamp respectively.[56] Similarly, if in certain passages sexologists Havelock Ellis and others appear to accept the modifiability of sexual identity, in other passages it's precisely because this presumed modifiability makes heterosexual desire as accidental as homosexuality that they (on antifeminist grounds) object to the theory of acquired sexual perversion, emphasizing instead the role of inborn factors in the origin of desire.[57]

But what I want to stress here is less the sexologists' appeal to biology or instinct as a means of containing mimesis than the antimimetic tendencies within the structure of mimesis itself. Thus in his 1898 scenario of the mimetic origins of sexual desire and sexual difference, Prince surreptitiously grounds that difference in a scene that presumes the existence of the *desiring subject* whose origin his theory of imitation-suggestion is designed to explain. The child first autoerotically desires himself, Prince tells us: his "vita sexualis is first associated with his own sexual organs." But in a specular logic that is nowhere made explicit, in order to love himself the child must get outside himself—more precisely, he must imitate or identify with another boy *in whom he sees an image of himself,* that is, whom he *resembles.* In Prince's scene of origins, the child can only love himself if he is penetrated by an internal difference that is itself produced by the child's analogical perception of resemblance or identity: "Later, the sight of those [sexual organs] of another boy awakens the association of ideas by the well-known law, and then, in a degenerate, cultivation does the rest." The child is already object-oriented, he already autoerotically loves his own genitals, and desires only doubles—objects that resemble his own (or himself). (Resemblance so understood is an antimimetic relation.) Thus the ambiguity I spoke of earlier, as to whether this is a scene of specular representation or not is, by virtue of the grounding of desire in the perception of the similarity between the child's genital organs and those of the other boy, silently resolved in favor of the former. In the process, Prince makes the desiring subject, which is to say the very phenomenon of gender, not the consequence or effect of identification, as his theory of suggestion-imitation ostensibly maintains, but rather its basis and origin. He thus proposes a version of Freud's thesis that an autoerotic or narcissistic stage followed by a homosexual stage is the normal sequence in the origin of heterosexual desire.[58]

I think we can see in this compulsion to defeat mimesis why homosexuality paradoxically occupies a privileged position in Prince's 1898 account of the mimetic origin of desire. It's as if the *homosexual subject* is present in Prince's text as an answer to—one might say it serves to suppress—the far greater scandal of dedifferentiation that structures mimesis itself. *And whereas mimesis can't be cured* (if for no other reason than that it is what makes subjecthood possible), the homosexually desiring subject, like the female hysteric, can: for what abnormal "cultivation" may achieve in the way of consolidating a perverse desire, hypnotic suggestion may undo, as Prince believes Schrenck von Notzing's treatment of the perversions demonstrates.[59] The scandal of homosexuality can thus be averted, according to Prince's normalizing narrative, by appealing to the benefits of a hypnotic therapy designed to undo the homogenization implicitly at work in his account of the mimetic origins of desire by mesmerizing—or scaring—the male and female population straight.[60]

Moreover—and this is a crucial point—Prince's retreat from mimesis is all the more necessary because mimesis has primarily to do with the *mother*. Thus, to return to the Beauchamp case, it may be argued that a problematic of maternal identification is central to its genesis and unfolding. As Sally reveals in her "Autobiography" over the objections of Miss Beauchamp and BIV (375, 427), the patient as a child was "terrified" of her violent father, "worshipping, literally worshipping" instead her unhappily married mother, "who, however, did not care for her and paid her slight attention" (374). "C.[hristine Beauchamp]'s whole life, all her thought and action and feeling, centred about her mother," Sally reports. "She believed that God wanted her to save mamma from some dreadful fate, and that in order to do this she must, before the day should come, have attained a certain ideal state, mentally, morally and . . . spiritually" (380). "[A]s for mamma, she never wanted C. near her after we grew older, but was always saying, 'Keep out of my sight'" (387). "*Haunted*" (380) by this impossible ideal day and night, the thirteen-year-old chld became "half delirious" or "disintegrated" (12) when her mother died and, consumed with guilt, believed herself to be "the victim of fierce persecution" (389). (Miss Beauchamp's subsequent choice of a career in nursing, which Sally detests, may be linked to the theme of maternal identification, as may her "Madonna worship" and religious conversion).

Now, as these citations suggest, the child's identification with the mother is ambivalent from the start: there is no purely libidinal relation to the maternal figure. The child's idealization of the mother, self-reproaches, and paranoia conceal a murderous aggressiveness toward the maternal figure. As Melanie Klein has argued, the child's ambivalence is especially intense when, as in the case of Miss Beauchamp, its love for the mother has been prohibited or refused.[61] "Since at the time of incorporation it is the very first 'object' of the very first identification, the womb-mother is also the site of the very first erotic war," Borch-Jacobsen writes in a passage that stresses the hidden mimetism of Freud's (and Klein's) account of the child's envious, destructive identification with the mother:

> To identify oneself with the object is to put oneself in its place or to place it within oneself, to kill it and live off its death. If I *am* the breast, then that breast *is nothing*—outside of myself, who have always already swallowed it up (and consequently *I* shall never come back to that place where *it* was before I was). This first bond, this first *copula* that makes me what I am, is also the first unbonding, the first annihilation of alterity (a forgetting of the other, prior to any remembering): a matricidal Oedipus.[62]

In other words, the subject is mimetically "born" or engendered as a desiring subject through a melancholic process of identification and incorporation by which the maternal imago is fantasmatically devoured and encrypted within the self.[63] In this context it is curious, though hardly surprising, that according to Sally just such an image of herself as an entombed living corpse or "Egyptian mummy"—"for to kill the double is of course to kill oneself"[64]—haunts the paranoid Miss Beauchamp's dreams (338).[65]

Mimesis is grounded in maternal dependency, which is why it is so threatening, especially for the male, for whom the original maternal "subjection" connotes passivity, feminization. Note that in this account, the child's identification with the mother isn't a question of libidinal desire: the mother is not initially a sexual object in the Freudian sense of the term. Rather, the relation of *both* sexes to the mother is "homophilic," that is, mimetic. Incarnating or "being" the mother, both boy and girl love and envy *her* objects of desire, whatever these may be. Just as, under the paternal law and as a consequence of her maternal identification, the girl will love and envy the father in a rivalry of the mimetic type, so too will the boy: a (culturally prohibited) homosexual desire for the father—a "feminization" of the homosexual type—is thus one consequence of the boy's initial identification with the mother. Nor are the gender consequences of mimesis simply triangular, as Girard tends to insist. The dual child-mother relationship may have gender consequences of its own: the maternal model may herself become the object of mimetic passion with the result that the girl may come to love her mother with a (culturally prohibited) homosexual love, just as the boy may come to desire her heterosexually. Of course, the fact that both sexes also identify with the father—among other objects—further complicates this scenario. We are both near to and far from Freud's libidinal, object-oriented description of the positive and negative Oedipus complex in boys and girls. In short, the subject is "born" or produced in a melancholic incorporation of the mother which provokes a highly labile desire that from its inception is infused with rivalry and hatred and that, as Prince intuitively recognizes, can only be disavowed by an emphasis on difference and autonomy.

The concept of multiple personality will be harnessed to that project of maternal disavowal by way of three closely related developments. First, the malleability and radical heterogeneity of the "subject" that is so threatening in mimesis will be countered by an antimimetic concept of the self conceived as the sum or aggregate of more or less fixed component parts (Prince's "traits" or "dispositions," Janet's psychical "elements," McDougall's "instincts," etc.,) that can be shuffled together in a variety of different combinations—Prince employs the metaphor of a pack of cards[66]—to produce the more or less unified, functionally adapted personality. And whereas the mimetic paradigm expressly holds that no "real" self exists prior to mimesis, the concept of the self as a multiple of component traits or dispositions lends itself to the common-sense, essentialist idea that there exists a "real" or "normal" self that can be identified and recuperated. As Prince states: "Common experience shows that, philosophize as you will, there is an empirical self which may be designated the real normal self" (233).

Second, the concept of the self as a multiple of traits or dispositions will be assimilated to a theory of *psychic hermaphroditism* or *bisexuality* that functions antimimetically to reinforce a compulsory heterosexuality. Thus the political and social threat of imitation-suggestion is staved off by assuming that, according to Charles Godfrey Leland, men and women are "radically different as regards both body and mind" and that

> in proportion to the female organs remaining in man, and the male in woman, there exists also in each just so much of their peculiar mental characteristics. . . . [W]hat of late years occupied much thought as the Subliminal Self, the Inner Me, the Hidden Soul, Unconscious Cerebration, and the like, may all be reduced to or fully explained by the Alternate Sex in us.[67]

In this process of assimilation, the theory of bisexuality, hitherto associated with a reprobated homosexuality, will be largely stripped of its perverse connotations and put to heterosexual uses. Thus again according to Leland, the male or female "alternate" in us invariably desires its heterosexual opposite. The female in the male loves the male in the female and *vice versa,* for within the structure of bisexuality there can be no same-sex desire.[68] In short, the concept of bisexuality emerges as a *solution* to the problem of mimesis by virtue of its positing the existence of a *bisexual subject* in whom two heterosexual desires coincide. Furthermore, this reheterosexualization of desire is accompanied by a denial of the character inversion previously associated with the theory of bisexuality: since all men and women have second selves or traits of the opposite sex, the existence of a bisexual constitution or alternately gendered self is normal and, at least in the case of the man, does not compromise his virility. Indeed, according Edward Carpenter, theorist of inversion or the "intermediate sex," even the male homosexual remains completely masculine in his nonsexual behavior.[69] "Among the loosely organized complexes in many individuals, and possibly in all of us," Prince writes in 1914,

> there are certain dispositions towards views of life which represent natural inclinations, desires, and modes of activity which, for some reason or other we suppress or are unable to give fully play to. Thus a person is said to have "many sides to his character," and exhibits certain alternations of personality which may be regarded as normal prototypes of those which occur in abnormal mental states.

A favorite example of Prince's in this regard is the Scottish writer, William Sharp (1855–1905), the creative and imaginative side of whose personality Sharp "distinctly felt to be feminine in type" and whose writings he published under the name "Fiona Macleod." Such an example, Prince observes, "brings home to us the recognition of psychological facts which we all, more or less, have in common."[70]

Third, the concept of the self as a composite of male and female traits will be placed in the service of a misogyny that functions to contain the threat of mimesis by scapegoating the female. On the one hand, the theory of the alternate self contributes to a dissolution of gender boundaries by expanding the definition of masculinity and femininity to include aspects of the self that had previously been excluded. On the other hand, in such an expanded definition of the self, specifically in the "more interesting case of the male," the "alternate" self is described in such stereotypical terms that it—she—comes to lack all the attributes by which subjecthood is defined. The theory of bisexuality that accords a feminine side to the male thus reconfigures masculinity and femininity in such starkly oppositional terms as not only to reinforce the traditional superiority of the former but to do so by representing the latter as pure plasticity or negativity. Thus if, according to Weininger's well-known theory of bisexuality, only the male can claim absolute difference and originality, if only the male can resist the influence of the model (for he "objects to being thought a mere echo"), this is because only man possesses the will, the superior, continuous memory, and consciousness on which the existence of an incommensurable and permanent ego depends. By contrast woman, for Weininger absolute mother or absolute prostitute, lacks all originality—she's the very essence of the undifferentiated, of the same. Mindless (for she is nothing but sexual unconsciousness), un-moral (for being incapable of conceptual thought she is incapable of morality), lacking a continuous memory (which is why she is a liar and has no sense of time), and without a will of her own (for she is slavishly imitative and impressionable, which is why she can be so easily hypnotized), she has no permanent identity. "The absolute female has no ego." Like the soulless Undine of Fouqué's fairy tale whom Weininger characterizes as the "platonic idea" of the female, women have no individuality or character: "Personality and individuality (intelligible), ego and soul, will and (intelligible) character, all these are different expressions of the same actuality, an actuality the male of mankind attains, the female lacks." "Multiplex," "diffused," "undifferentiated," "changeable," "heartless," "nameless," and endlessly double, woman is the bearer of everything that man excludes: she's the absence of "property," of subjective identity—she's mimeticism itself.[71]

Just so, like the "half-person" Undine, to whom Prince's friend the neurologist James Jackson Putnam compares her, or the all-too-human ape Bimi, Sally is a representative of the "monstrous" danger of mimesis—the danger of that disturbing undifferentiation out of which the subject is born.[72] By the same token, it is mimesis itself which *produces* the powerful subjectivity effects that Prince and his contemporaries associate with the most fully developed examples of independent personhood. Sally's combative will is a subjectivity effect of exactly this kind; it is both an artifact of her mimetic identification with Prince, hence gendered male, and it is what is crucial to Prince's (and our) sense of her as the most dynamic, appealing, and autonomous of all the personalities in the case. Much the same might be said of her internal heterogeneity, which gives to her actions and statements—for all their jejune character—an interest and complexity that are missing in BI and BIV. Sally is the "self" who is most internally split because mimetic "self-division" is what gives rise to the most forceful and authoritative instatement of the subject. At once lacking a personality (for she's merely a morbid, suggestible group of dissociated states) and a fascinating personality in her own right (for she has a formidable will, a "sane" (396) intelligence, and a remarkably comprehensive memory), Sally is the site where the mimetic and the antimimetic irreducibly meet.

Which is why, like Weininger's woman, she must be made to disappear.[73] A decision must be made against mimesis and in favor of difference and autonomy, although, as William McDougall almost alone among Prince's commentators appears to recognize,[74] Sally's disappearance can't be motivated within the theoretical terms of Prince's analysis, and although the attempt to master mimesis will be of dubious success. A ritual "exorcism" (137) then, one that depends on the violent imposition of Prince's hypnotic will and that can, therefore, only redouble the mimesis. Worse, isn't Sally a version of Prince, and isn't to kill Sally therefore in a sense to kill himself?

The Subject of Trauma

One of the ways in which Sally remains occult to Prince—in which she exceeds his interpretive frame—is that she can't be accommodated within Prince's theory of the trauma. In agreement with Janet, James, and the early Freud, Prince holds that multiple personality is the result of a mental shock that dissociates or splits the personality into its component elements; therapy consists in using hypnosis like a neutral experimental instrument to probe the patient's past in an attempt to identify the precipitating trauma. In the case of Miss Beauchamp, Prince concludes that neither BI, BIV, nor Sally is the "real" or "normal" self; rather, the original self is the one that fell apart under the impact of a dramatic encounter that occurred several years earlier, in 1893, between his patient and the mysterious "William Jones." Jones is an older man who served as spiritual guide to the adolescent Miss Beauchamp after her mother's death and whom the patient revered and adored almost as much as she had previously revered and adored her mother (he is, in those respects, a mother substitute). It turns out, though, that Jones "unintentionally, and perhaps all unconsciously" (89) is responsible for the "psychical catastrophe" (109) that caused Miss Beauchamp to disintegrate.

Here is Prince's description of Miss Beauchamp's catastrophic encounter with Jones. The scene is set in southern Massachusetts, in a town he calls Providence (actually Fall River, a small industrial town on the Rhode Island border), where Miss Beauchamp has been pursuing a career as a medical nurse:

> One night, while in the nurses' sitting-room conversing with a friend, Miss K., she was startled, upon looking up, to see a face at the window. It was the face of her old friend, William Jones, a man whom with the idealism of girlhood she worshipped as a being of a superior order. He was much older than she, cultivated, and the embodiment of the spiritual and the ideal.

Miss Beauchamp goes downstairs to meet Jones:

> It transpired that he had stopped over in Providence, en route to New York, and had wandered up to the hospital. Seeing a ladder (which had been left by workmen) leaning against the side of the building, he had,

in a spirit of fun, climbed up and looked into the window. At the hospital door an exiting scene occurred. It was to Miss Beauchamp of an intensely disturbing nature, and gave her a tremendous shock. . . . The surroundings, too, were dramatic. It was night, pitch dark. A storm was passing over, and great peals of thunder and flashes of lightning heightened the emotional effect. It was only by those flashes that she saw her companion. (214–15)

The scene as a whole shares with the one in which Sally opens her eyes and with the mirror scene an unmistakable emphasis on seeing and specularity. Like the earlier scenes, this one is virtually cinematic in its intensity, despite the fact that it remains unclear exactly what took place between the patient and Jones at the hospital door. (And despite its inherent implausibility: it's one or two o'clock in the morning (219), and Jones happens to find a ladder that allows him, in the middle of a violent thunderstorm, to climb to a second floor window in order to play a joke on his young friend.)

Prince repeatedly emphasizes the importance of this scene for his interpretation of the case; in particular the image of Jones's face framed in the window and illuminated by flashes of lightning is the last thing BIV remembers of the episode when she first "recalls" it in a trance-like state (171–77, 220–22). But there are insuperable difficulties here, starting with the fact that according to Sally's account (to which Prince gives considerable credence) she has existed from earliest childhood, that is, well before the catastrophic encounter with Jones. In addition, although in certain passages Prince seems to imply that the restoration of Miss Beauchamp's "real" or "normal" personality involves the reabsorption of Sally into BI and BIV, no proof is given that this is in fact what has taken place.[75] Another, graver source of difficulty is that Miss Beauchamp's reconstruction of the traumatic encounter occurs under the influence of suggestion and moreover involves a sequence of dramatically enacted scenes of the decisive event, in which at one crucial juncture Prince stands in for—plays the role of—the elusive Jones (173). In other words, the patient's reconstruction takes place more in the mode of a quasi-hypnotic, emotionally charged acting-in-the-present than in the mode of a conscious memory of a past event. (Prince obtains the first, comprehensive account of the scene from Sally and then turns to his patient's other selves for corroboration that the reconstruction is accurate, which would of course count as persuasive evidence only if the independence as witnesses of all the selves were beyond question.) But despite these and other problems, Prince never thereafter questions the reality of the scene at the hospital. And I suggest that this is because the function of scene, like that of the scene in which Sally opens her eyes, is to *guarantee the status of the subject as a subject.* In particular, the specular staging of the scene, Jones's disembodied face framed and frozen in the window, the mutual facing off between the patient and Jones—all serve to *validate Miss Beauchamp's separateness as a personality even as she is shattered into multiplicity*. Similarly, I suggest that Sally can't be comprehended within Prince's theory of the trauma because she personifies *the very production of the subject in and by a mimetic dynamic that the theory of the trauma as a historical, external event coming to the already-constituted subject functions to evade*. No wonder the scene at the window never ceases to resonate in our minds throughout our reading of Prince's long, convoluted narrative; it is the key, not as Prince believes to the "secret" (214) of Miss Beauchamp's condition, but rather to his attempt to stabilize that condition even as he struggles to do justice to its protean manifestations.

More might be said about the functions of the scene of the encounter with Jones in Prince's text. More might be said, too, about how Prince never abandons this schema of the subject even as in the years that follow he compulsively returns to the Beauchamp case in an effort to negotiate his relationship to Freud.[76] But rather than pursue these topics further I want to turn now to the present-day revival of the multiple-personality diagnosis. For without realizing it, don't current medical theories of multiple personality tend simply to replicate Prince's theory of the subject by positing a dichotomy between the already-constituted subject and the external trauma? And doesn't that dichotomy serve to rule out of court—to make unthinkable—the mimetic dynamic I've been analyzing here? What are the political implications of my account of the history of the multiple-personality concept for feminism today?

The recent revival of the multiple-personality diagnosis, or Multiple Personality Disorder (MPD), is a remarkable phenomenon. After virtually disappearing in the 1930s, the "movement" has been growing rapidly since the 1970s.[77] According to Humphrey and Dennett, two hundred cases of multiple personality had been reported prior to 1980, one thousand were known to be in treatment by 1984 and four thousand in 1989. Estimates of the total number of cases in the United States go as high as twenty-five thousand. The number of personalities in a given case has also been growing rapidly; in 1989 the median was eleven, but as many as forty or more "alters" have been reported. Now, as then, the majority of cases are female.[78] Although in the past most cases were found in America, the phenomenon was a distinctly European-American development; today, the diagnosis appears to be restricted to the United States.[79] Typical cases, involving splitting or dissociation, memory lapses, time distortions, and the use of the third person are attributed to emotional and physical trauma, especially childhood sexual abuse, and the therapy of choice is hypnosis.[80] Prince's text is widely considered a classic in the field.

At the same time, the proliferation of cases has been met with considerable skepticism, largely because of the crucial role of hypnosis in diagnosis and treatment. For the most part, such skepticism has taken the unhelpful form of regarding the phenomenon in its entirety as art "iatrogenic condition" or "*folie à deux*"[81] between patient and physician, or hypnosis itself as a "cultural delusion."[82] But my reading of the Beauchamp case suggests another approach. On the one hand, I take the phenomena of psychical trauma, hypnosis, and dissociation very seriously. On the other, I am suspicious of the simple polarity between the external trauma and passive female—between absolute aggressor and absolute victim—that underwrites much current theorizing about multiple personality. What I want to know instead is how my interpretation of the Beauchamp case—specifically, the understanding of mimetic identification as I have deployed it in this paper— might help us retheorize the articulation between violence and female subjectivity. In this regard, I will make the following provisional and necessarily highly schematic observations:

1) Like Prince's account of the Beauchamp case, present-day theories of multiple personality assume a notion of the already-constituted female subject, understood as comprising a functional plurality of component parts to which violence comes entirely from the outside to shatter its functional unity into dysfunctional multiplicity. As in Prince's text, such a notion serves to evade the mimetic dimension and to do so on the basis of a normalization of gender roles that represents the female subject as a passive or innocent victim. Indeed this familiar sexual coding finds reverse expression in the often-repeated theory that if there are far fewer reported cases of male multiples this is because, being more active or violent than women, male multiples are more likely to end up in jail than in the therapist's waiting room. So that the same arguments I began this essay by bringing, on psychoanalytic grounds, against MacKinnon and other theorists of women's victimage also apply here with equal force. (The tendency among certain feminists to ignore mimesis by theorizing the female subject as a multiplicity of attributes risks being essentialist in the same way.)

2) With respect to the question of the location of violence, however, my account of the origin of gender identity differs from—better, it inflects—that of psychoanalytic theory in certain regards. Thus one major implication of my argument is that identification, including identification with the mother, is never a matter of pure pleasure: *negativity* and *ambivalence* are constitutive of subjectivity or alterity, as Jacqueline Rose on somewhat different grounds has recently argued in her re-evaluation of the work of Melanie Klein.[83] In my view, those who ignore or seek to efface the psychic ambivalence of the earliest mother-child relationship tend either to idealize the mother as the all-loving maternal imago or, in an almost unavoidable reversal, to externalize that negativity by denigratating the mother as the source of all hatred and destruction. On the mimetic hypothesis, by contrast, both subject and desired object are *constituted by* the child's ambivalent

mimetic identification with and fantasized incorporation (loss) of the maternal breast or figure. Mimesis thus lies "beyond" the pleasure principle and "before" unpleasure,[84] a notion that poses momentous difficulties not only for Freud's attempt to derive a pacific sociality from a primary identification between "self" and "other," as Borch-Jacobsen has compellingly argued, but also for the American theorists of the social bond such as James Mark Baldwin, Charles Cooley, and George Herbert Mead.[85]

Note that under the pressure of a mimetic reading of Freud the psychoanalytic concept of the "object" of desire is implicitly reformulated. The object is not something that the subject would like to "have" as distinct from something it would like to "be": rather, the object coincides with the identificatory "model" itself.[86] On this interpretation the subject may be said to identify with the "object" of desire even in the most "anaclitic" (heterosexual, genital) relationships, as the very common fantasies of fusion and devouring testify. As Freud himself said, "identification is the original form of emotional tie with an object,"[87]—a claim that holds for any relationship with another (human sexuality is thus permeated with mimesis and hence fundamentally "perverse").

3) The concept of psychic negativity has of course been central to the work of Julia Kristeva—indeed, there are certain obvious parallels between her description of the pre-Oedipal, mother-child relationship in terms of "abjection" and the theory of mimetic identification postulated here. But as I understand her, she does not move out of the orbit of the triangular or "ternary" structure of desire dictated by the paternal law. In Kristeva's account of the origin of the signifying process, the bar of signification is produced through the infant not-yet ego's identification with the gap between it and the threateningly chaotic, maternal not-yet object or "abject." The gap is described as "an archaic modality of the paternal function, anterior to the Name, to the Symbolic but also to the 'mirror' . . . a modality that one can call that of the Imaginary Father,"[88] which is to say it is constituted by the mother's desire for something or someone other than the child. In other words, according to Kristeva the maternal "object" is (produced and) lost not directly, out of an enraged mimetic identification with the abjected mother, but because the mother always already desires something other than the child, a "not-me," or is imagined to do so.[89] A mimetic analysis of desire points rather to the way in which Freud's speculations, in *The Ego and the Id* and related writings on the "prehistory" of the ego, lead him to posit the existence of affective ties or identifications that are irreducible to object love and the first theory of the drives.

Another way of expressing my distance from Kristeva is to say that on the mimetic paradigm love and hate—conflict—emerge prior to the point where we are used to locating them, not between subject and subject, or subject and object, as both Prince and recent theorists of multiple personality tend to assume, but at the very moment of the mimetic installation of the subject on a constitutively abyssal ground. It is to Nicholas Abraham's analysis of the *non-separé-separé* or "dual union" between child and mother and of the fort/da game that we might look for an account of the origin of the symbolic order in the child's identification with and loss of the abjected m(other).[90] The power relations involved here can be understood in Foucauldian terms. Thus one advantage of the mimetic paradigm for feminism as I see it is that it allows us to understand the production of the gendered subject as the effect of paranoid identifications with mimetic rivals whose status as such is determined by a "subjugating" law in the Foucauldian sense. By now I need hardly add that by interpreting the origin of subjectivity in these terms we avoid any naively recuperative or utopian politics that imagines the female subject not as produced by power but as existing "before" the law or "after" its revolutionary overthrow.

4) The grounding of the subject in mimesis poses yet another challenge to Prince's and recent interpretations of multiple personality. As already noted, such accounts tend to theorize the trauma as an external event that shatters or splits the pregiven female subject into her several constitutent parts. As in the Beauchamp case, the aim of hypnotic treatment is to get the patient to recover the memory of the abuse and thereby to restore her to a condition of adaptive wholeness. A contemporary of Prince figured dissociation as a "city blockaded, like a great empire dying at the core" such that the reunification of the subject was conceived to be necessary for the *polis*.[91] In a related fashion, the goal of therapy in cases of multiple personality has recently been described as follows: "It seems to me that after treatment you want to end up with a functional unit, be it a corporation, a partnership, or a one-owner business."[92] As the bearer of that threatening lack of "property" or subjective identity that is mimesis, the female multiple—like Weininger's woman—defeats economic calculations: getting her back to being a subject means restoring the very condition for there being an economy—ownership—at all.

But the use of hypnosis or suggestion to elicit recollections of past traumatic events and to cure patients is problematic, as Prince's case demonstrates and as even some of today's most ardent supporters of the multiple-personality diagnosis recognize. Patients tend to relapse and, just as significant, "true" recollections of the traumatic event are hard to come by. As one influential architect of the multiple-personality diagnosis has recently warned:

> The therapist must learn to interpret and restructure dissociation rather than try to suppress, ignore, or medicate it. He must remain aware as well that material influenced by intrusive inquiry or iatrogenic dissociation may be subject to distortion. In a given patient, one may find episodes of pho-

tographic recall, confabulation, screen phenomena, confusion between dreams or fantasies and reality, irregular recollection, and willful misrepresentation. One awaits the goodness of fit among several forms of data, and often must be satisfied to remain uncertain.[93]

The difficulty of deciding whether events recollected under hypnosis are fact or fantasy is one major reason why the use of hypnosis to recover memories has proven so controversial in the courts of law.[94]

Freud faced the same difficulty. On the one hand, Freud's concept of "psychic reality," as put forward in the "Wolfman case" and other texts, at once elides and displaces the opposition between external event and internal fantasy in such a way that the status of the event as conscious recollection cannot and need not be decided. On the other hand, it is also the case that Freud in subsequent texts continues to express a desire to ground "psychical reality" in an origin antecedent to or independent of that "reality"—whether the origin is conceived as an historical event or as a "primal fantasy" which is itself derived from a phylogenetic or archetypical "truth" transcending individual experience.[95] Even more crucially from my point of view, under the pressure of a deconstructive reading of Freud the question of the trauma is also reopened. For the force of that deconstructive reading is similarly to propose that in his attempt to distinguish psychoanalysis from suggestion, Freud risks succumbing to the same desire to establish an origin or foundation by grounding the patient's neurosis in (real or fantasized) repressed infantile representations whose recovery through recollection or construction is the task of analysis. The unconscious, for Freud, is the repository of those repressed infantile representations, and it is the latter that, transferred secondarily to the person of the analyst, are held to become accessible to consciousness in the form of the patient's self-narration (*diegesis*). The patient's speech during the hypnotic trance does not constitute such a *diegesis* for that verbalization occurs precisely in the absence of consciousness. Borch-Jacobsen therefore seems to me right when he claims that it is over the issue of remembering that Freud attempts to break with suggestion.[96]

However, as Freud soon discovers, the transference, far from facilitating recollection, proves rather to be its major stumbling block. Instead of remembering, patients *repeat* the earlier scenes or memories in the present, in a "positive" emotional transference onto the analyst that, for all the absence of overt suggestion, or rather precisely because of the analyst's deliberate self-effacement, manifests all the more clearly that rapport without rapport to "another," that "affective tie" to the "other" that for Freud is primary identification—or mimesis. In other words, following Borch-Jacobsen we can say that if Freud continues to believe that the transference constitutes a resistance to rememoration by dissimulating a prior Oedipal affective tie, his own writings on the second topography strongly suggest that no such dissimulation is involved. This is because the atient's transferential resistance rests on an affect that, as Freud observes, cannot be unconscious or repressed but can only be felt and experienced in the immediacy of an acting or *repetition* in the present that is unrepresentable to the subject and that—like the unconscious itself—knows no delay, no time, no doubt, and no negation.

In short, where the notion of remembering becomes problematic in Freud is where he states, in his speculations on the child's earliest object-attachments, that the Oedipal tie which is supposed to be recalled in transference is itself a derivative of an even more archaic "affective tie" or "primary identification"—an identification that can never be remembered by the subject precisely because it precedes the very distinction between "self" and "other" on which the possibility of self-representation and hence of recollection depends. It follows that the origin is not present to the "subject" but is on the contrary the condition of the latter's "birth":

> The origin, if it's of the "primary identification" type, never *presents* itself to a "me," since on the contrary it is the condition of that "me's" coming-to-itself, "before" itself, "before" all memorable events: the other that I incorporate [in order] to be a "me" disappears from the origin in a "past that was never present." That is why this "past" is forgotten before all repression and all rememoration (narration) is possible. And why it is repeated, in such an insistent manner in the transference and/or in hypnosis: never having occurred *in* time . . . it takes "place" all the time.[97]

5) If this is true of the origin, is it also true of the trauma? Ever since the work of Sandor Ferenczi we have become accustomed to think of the identification with the aggressor as one of the subject's characteristic responses to, or defenses against, psychic trauma.[98] But what if we understand the trauma to consist in *identification (mimesis) itself,* which is to say in "the subject's *originary* 'invasion' [*envahissement*]"?[99] This would explain why the traumatic event cannot be remembered, indeed why it is "relived" in the transferential relationship not in the form of a recounting of a past event but of a mimetic identification with another (who is no other) *in the present*—in the timelessness of the unconscious—that is characterized by a profound amnesia or absence from the self.

It is this absence from the self that Sandor Ferenczi, in his remarkable late reflections on the trauma, psychic splitting, and the transference or trance state, repeatedly calls attention to. In these and related texts, even as he appears to remain committed to an ontology of repressed representations that calls for the "conversion"[100] of the repetition tendency into a memory of the traumatic scene, Ferenczi attests on the contrary to the absolute inability of the patient to recollect the scene in question.

More precisely, on the one hand Ferenczi often appears to theorize the psychical trauma as a violent event that, repressed into the unconscious in the form of a mnemonic trace, ideally can be brought into the victim's consciousness in the analytic relationship.[101] From this only a short step is required, which he takes, to attribute neurosis to the reality of a trauma that comes to the completely innocent, unambivalent, and autonomous child in the form of an absolute exteriority, that is, in the form of a brutal and erotic adult aggressivity. "It is hatred that traumatically surprises and frightens the child while being loved by an adult, that changes him from a spontaneously and innocently playing being into a guilty love-automaton imitating the adult anxiously, self-effacingly"[102]—an argument that brings in its train the simultaneous idealizing and scapegoating of the mother that we find in his own work as well as in that of Michael Balint, John Bowlby, and others.

Yet Ferenczi also repeatedly testifies not to the possibility of converting those mnemonic traces into conscious recollections but to the (inevitable) failure of memory. "If the patient makes a cathartic plunge to the phase of emotional experience, then, in this trance, he experiences his sufferings again, but remains unaware of what is happening," Ferenczi writes. "Of the series of sensations from the object and the subject, only those on the side of the subject are accessible. If he wakes from the trance, the immediate evidence instantly vanishes; the trauma is again seized only externally, through reconstruction, without any feeling of conviction."[103] In recognition of the significance of this observation, Ferenczi in a posthumously published passage attributes the patient's lack of memory of a trauma not to the repression of a representation, but to the vacancy of the subject in a radical openness to "impressions"—call them identifications—that occurs prior to all representation and hence to all rememoration.[104] So that if the subject of a trauma identifies with the aggressor, she does so not as a defense of the ego that represses the violent event into the unconscious, but on the basis of a dissociation that connotes an abyssal, though ambivalent, openness to all identification. "It is unjustifiable to demand in analysis that something should be *recollected consciously* which has never been conscious [which has never been represented]," Ferenczi writes[105]—an argument that leads to him (in terms psychoanalysis has found unacceptable and nor do I endorse) to retheorize the role of suggestion ("encouragement") in psychoanalysis as a technique not for obtaining the memory of an event that has passed but for countercommanding the effects of a trauma that is, as it were, logically unavailable to recollection.

This is emphatically not to dispute the reality of violence, sexual or otherwise. But it is to suggest an explanation, grounded in the very nature of the architrauma of mimetic identification, of why the victim's memory of the traumatic event is so often difficult if not impossible to recover. It is also to redefine the traumatic "event" as that which, precisely because it triggers or reactivates the "trauma" that is identification, strictly speaking cannot be described as an event since it does not happen to a pregiven subject.

6) My remarks point in another direction as well. If the memory of the traumatic "event" cannot be lifted from the unconscious because that memory has never been "in" the unconscious; if the "ground" or origin of identity is an abyssal mimesis that is unrepresentable to the subject; if, accordingly, the transference or hypnotic "rapport" cannot be dissolved; if, most radically, mimesis is the condition of the production of the subject—what is the goal of treatment?

Certainly, my purpose is not to recommend a simple rehabilitation of hypnosis, understood as a technique that stands in a relation of opposition to psychoanalysis. On the contrary, it is the use of hypnosis, conceived on the model of Prince and his contemporaries as a neutral scientific instrument to *objectify* mimesis in a medical symptomatology of "Multiple Personality Disorder," that I am calling into question here. From my perspective, it is hardly surprising that the more psychotherapists look for cases of multiple personality (characteristically under hypnosis) the more they claim to find them, or that Satan is now being invoked as the evil cause of multiple personality—or "possession."[106]

Is it possible, rather, that the efficacy of psychoanalysis and hypnosis lies *in mimesis itself*—in the "acting out" of the indistinction between "self" and "other" that is mimesis? This has been proposed by Borch-Jacobsen, who has argued that if psychoanalysis has a therapeutic effect it is because it is a "pharmakon" in Derrida's sense: not because, in Lacanian terms it demands that the subject accede to the symbolic order by distinguishing her demand from that of the Other, but because it ritually "cures" our familiar (and in a sense "normal") troubles of social identity *by mimesis*—by giving symbolic recognition to the loss of differentiation between "self" and "other" that takes place in the "light trance" of the psychoanalytic transference.[107] This is no doubt a disquieting proposition, especially if it is seen as an attempt to avoid the negativity of the self/other analytic scenario by simply expelling that negativity in a more or less violent acting out. Yet perhaps the proposition can be understood differently, perhaps within the framework I have presented in this paper we can understand that proposition to mean not that mimesis—suggestion—is the (possibly more "efficacious") antagonist or "other" of psychoanalysis, but rather its most intimate interiority. In such an understanding—which at present can be no more than provisional—hypnotic suggestion would not occupy a new place of truth but instead would be situated "within" psychoanalytic discourse as that which defines the unconscious itself. But of course this would in turn imply a transformation of psychoanalysis that at present is only barely imaginable.

NOTES

I thank Jonathan Crewe, Milad Doueihi, and François Roustang for valuable discussions at the beginning of this project. In addition I thank the following for their helpful comments on my paper: Mikkel Borch-Jacobsen, Judith Butler, Frances Ferguson, Michael Fried, Neil Hertz, Walter Benn Michaels, Jacqueline Rose, Joan Scott, and Judy Walkowitz. Research for this project was supported by a Ford Fellowship from the American Council of Learned Societies.

1. Jacqueline Rose, *Sexuality in the Field of Vision* (London: Verso, 1986), p. 15.

2. *Ibid.*, pp. 90–91.

3. When MacKinnon treats women as "raped, battered, pornographed, defined by force, by a world that begins, at least, entirely outside us" (*Feminism Unmodified: Discourses on Life and Law* (Cambridge: Harvard University Press, 1987), p. 57), she implicitly subscribes to a notion of the female subject defined as external to the very power that in Foucaultian terms produces them as such. She thus fails to recognize the political violence of her own discourse, a discourse which in effect denies the female subject all possibility of agency.

4. Ian Hacking, "The Invention of Split Personalities," in Alan Donagan, Anthony N. Perovich, Jr., and Michael V. Wedin, eds., *Human Nature and Natural Knowledge, Boston Studies in the Philosophy of Science*, 89 (1989), pp. 63–85.

5. Stephen Melville, "On Mood, Time, and The Freudian Subject," *Oxford Literary Review*, 12, (1990), pp. 215–226.

6. Morton Prince, *The Dissociation of a Personality. A Biographical Study in Abnormal Psychology*, 2nd edition (London: Longmans, Green, and Co., 1910), p. 20 (subsequent page references are cited in parentheses in the text). By conventional methods of treatment, Prince was probably referring to hydrotherapy and electrotherapy.

7. Morton Prince, "Miss Beauchamp: The Theory of the Psychogenesis of Multiple Personality" (1920), in his *Clinical and Experimental Studies in Personality* (Cambridge, Mass.: Sci-Art Publishers, 1929), p. 208. Hereafter "Miss Beauchamp." Soon after the end of her treatment, the upwardly-mobile Miss Beauchamp (actually Clara Norton Fowler) managed to obtain the rudiments of a college education by enrolling as a special student for three semesters at Radcliffe; in 1912, aged thirty-nine, she married Dr. George A. Waterman, a leading Boston psychotherapist who had been an assistant of Prince's friend, the well-known neurologist James Jackson Putnam, and was a close associate of Prince himself.

8. *Ibid.*, p. 133. Kipling's tale, "Betran and Bimi," first published in 1891, tells the story of Bimi, a great orang-outan, who is found as an infant by the "beast-tamer" Bertran and raised in the latter's house as his child or brother ("He was *not* a beast; he was a child"; "He was not a beast; he was a man"). But the day comes when Bertran marries a pretty half-caste French girl. Mad with jealousy, Bimi murders Bertran's bride (there is also more than a hint of sexual violence); Betran then strangles Bimi with his own hands but is himself killed in the struggle.

9. Cited by Otto Marx, "Morton Prince and the Dissociation of a Personality," *Journal of the History of the Behavioral Sciences*, 6, 2 (1970), p. 124.

10. A point stressed by Hillel Schwarz, "The Three-Body Problem and the End of the World," in *Fragments For a History of the Human Body*, edited by Michael Feher, Ramona Naddaff, Nadia Tazi, et al., Part II, vol. 4 (New York, NY: Zone Publications, 1989), pp. 420–24.

11. Walter Franklin Prince (and James Hervey Hyslop), *The Doris Case of Multiple Personality; A Biography of Five Personalities in Connection with One Body* (New York: Proceedings of the American Society for Psychical Research, 1915–17).

12. James's letter to Prince, 28 September 1906, cited by Saul Rosenzweig, "Sally Beauchamp's Career: A Psychoarchaeological Key to Morton Prince's Classic Case of Multiple Personality," *Genetic Social and General Psychology Monographs*, 113, 1 (1987), p. 8. Two days later Prince wrote James: "And to think that Sally has 'gone back to where she came from' when she might have told me so much that I wished I knew!"—a remark that testifies to Prince's sense that the case might be over but that it was not *resolved*. Prince's letter to James is cited by Michael G. Kenny, "Multiple Personality and Spirit Possession," *Psychiatry*, 44 (1981), p. 347, note 19.

13. Mikkel Borch-Jacobsen, *The Freudian Subject*, translated by Catherine Porter (Stanford: Stanford University Press, 1988), p. 47. My analysis owes a great deal to this study, as well as to the other publications by Borch-Jacobsen cited in my text. I am also indebted to the work of Philippe Lacoue-Labarthe and Jean-Luc Nancy, especially Lacoue-Labarthe's "Typography" and "The Echo of the Subject," in *Typography: Mimesis, Philosophy, and Politics*, edited by Christopher Fynsk (Cambridge: Harvard University Press, 1989), Lacoue-Labarthe and Nancy's "La Panique politique," *Cahiers confrontation*, 2 (1980), pp. 33–54, and François Roustang's *Dire Mastery: Discipleship from Freud to Lacan*, translated by Ned Lukacher (Baltimore: Johns Hopkins University Press, 1976).

Note that Borch-Jacobsen employs the term "mimesis" rather than "imitation" for hypnotic suggestion and identification, on the grounds that mimesis has nothing to do with the simple imitation of a *model* or with fictive simulation, both of which presume the very subject that is in question here (Mikkel Borch-Jacobsen, "Dispute," in Leon Chertok ed., *Hypnose et psychanalyse* (Paris: Dunod, 1987), pp. 203–6). His point is well taken: as will become evident, I'm convinced that a mimetic structure of identification is at work in the texts I shall be examining. But I have chosen not to follow systematically Borch-Jacobsen's terminological strategy, for the simple reason that the texts in question use the terms "imitation," "suggestion," and "mimicry" interchangeably to denote the same phenomena.

Two further points: First, Borch-Jacobsen's phrase "primordial tendency to identification," in the quotation just cited above, may appear to reintroduce the idea of a pre-existing subject, which is exactly what he aims to deconstruct. But it would, I think, be truer to say that the subject is "born" in an identification with or (non)relation to the "other" that involves an active "receptivity" (suggestibility, affectibility) or passive "spontaneity" in which the very distinction between active and passive is called into question. Cf. in this connection Jacques Derrida, "Introduction: Desistance," in Philippe Lacoue-Labarthe, *Typography*, pp. 21–22.

Second, I want to emphasize that the deconstructive interrogation of the subject proposed here treats the commitment to a thematics of specularity or vision in the constitution of the subject (in a tradition that reaches from Plato through Descartes and Freud) as a philosophical "mistake," in the sense that it issues from and is beholden to a theory of the subject according to which representation can only be understood as representation *to or for a subject*, as in a mirror. See in this regard Mikkel Borch-Jacobsen's *The Freudian Subject*, pp. 32–34, 118, 228–33, and his analysis and critique of Michel Henry's phenomenological interpretation of Freud in "The Unconscious, Nonetheless," translated by Douglas Brick, *Stanford Literature Review* 6, 2 (Fall 1989), 261–95.

14. Mikkel Borch-Jacobsen, *The Freudian Subject*, p. 40.

15. A hypnotized patient gave the following account of himself: "I appeared to myself to act automatically, by an impulsion foreign to myself. It was certainly another who had taken my form and assumed my functions. I hated, I despised this other; he was perfectly odious to me" (reported by Boris Sidis, *The Psychology of Suggestion: A Research into the Subconscious Nature of Man and Society* (New York and London: D. Appleton and Company, 1927) p. 66). The same animosity between "alters" is frequently reported in recent cases of multiple personality.

16. "In statu nascendi," in Mikkel Borch-Jacobsen, Eric Michaud, and Jean-Luc Nancy, eds., *Hypnoses* (Paris: Editions Galilée, 1984), p. 71 (translation mine).

17. Alfred Binet, *Les Alterations de la personnalité*, (Paris: Alcan), 1890, p. 75 (translation mine).

18. Mikkel Borch-Jacobsen, "L'Hypnose dans la psychanalyse," in *Hypnose et psychanalyse*, p. 42 (translation mine). Hence this marvellous example: "We have not to wonder that to the question 'Where are you?' the subject [of hypnosis] sometimes gives the seemingly absurd reply of Krafft-Ebing's patient—'In your eye'" (Boris Sidis, *The Psychology of Suggestion*, p. 65).

19. Freud himself came close to describing multiple personality in these terms: "If they [the ego's identifications] gain the upper hand and become too numerous, unduly powerful and incompatible with one another, a pathological outcome will not be far off. It may come to a disruption of the ego in consequence of the different identifications becoming cut off from one another by resistances; perhaps the secret of the cases of what is described as 'multiple personality' is that the different identifications seize hold of consciousness in turn" (Sigmund Freud, *The Ego and the Id*, The Standard Edition of the Complete Psychological Works, vol. XIX (London: The Hogarth Press, 1966–74), pp. 30–31).

20. "It is therefore to no 'automation,' in the mechanical sense, that such [posthypnotic] acts are due: a self presides over them, a split-off, limited, and buried, but yet fully conscious self" (William James, "The Hidden Self," *Papers on Psychology* (Cambridge, Mass.: Harvard University Press), p. 263).

21. Mikkel Borch-Jacobsen, *The Freudian Subject*, p. 41.

22. Henry A. Murray, "Dr. Morton Prince. A Founder of Psychology," *Harvard Alumni Bulletin*, 32 (1930), p. 491.

23. See Nathan G. Hale, Jr., *James Jackson Putnam and Psychoanalysis. Letters Between Putnam and Sigmund Freud, Ernest Jones, William James, Sandor Ferenczi, and Morton Prince, 1877–1917* (Cambridge: Harvard University Press, 1971), p. 17.

24. It's not my purpose to rehearse here the general history of the multiple-personality concept. The most useful sources are Henri Ellenberger, *The Discovery of the Unconscious. The History and Evolution of Dynamic Psychiatry* (New York: Basic Books, 1970); Jacques Quen, ed., *Split Minds/Split Brains* (New York and London: New York University Press, 1984); Michael G. Kenny, *The Passion of Anselm Bourne. Multiple Personality in American Culture* (Washington, D.C.: Smithsonian Institution Press, 1986); and Ian Hacking, "The Invention of Split Personalities."

25. For an early instance of this approach see Harold Grier McCurdy, "A Note on the Dissociation of a Personality," *Character and Personality*, 10 (1941), pp. 35–41.

26. The most common method of hypnotism involved getting the subject or patient to close her eyes, usually by concentrating her attention on the hypnotist's own eyes, telling her that she was feeling sleepy and that she would close her eyes. "Look right at me and think

only of falling asleep" orders Bernheim, whom Prince visited in 1893 (*De la suggestion dans l'état hypnotique et dans la veille* (Paris: Octave Doin, 1884), p. 5, my translation). Perhaps it would be more accurate to say that the hypnotic trance depended on a combination of the hypnotist's authoritative gaze and the command of his voice. Thus Freud says that the hypnotist exerts his hypnotic power by "telling the subject to look him in the eyes; his most typical method of hypnotizing is by his look" (Sigmund Freud, *Group Psychology and the Analysis of the Ego,* Standard Edition, VIII, p. 125). Similarly, when Sally wants to hypnotize the "Idiot" she imitates Prince by stating: "'[A]s you read, slowly, slowly, your lids grow heavy—they droop, droop, droop; you're going, going, gone'" (320); similarly, when she's trying to be cooperative, she promises Prince she'll go to sleep.

27. "I will, therefore I am," Maine de Biran declared in a statement that became the starting point of Pierre Janet's psychology (cited by Henri Ellenberger, "Pierre Janet and his American Friends," in George E. Gifford Jr., ed. *Psychoanalysis, Psychotherapy, and the New England Medical Scene,* (New York: Science History Publications, 1978) p. 64).

28. "I emphasize the word 'spontaneous,' because, by artificial means (hypnotic suggestion) a mental dissociation in some apparently *healthy* people can be experimentally induced which is capable of exhibiting such automatic phenomena (post-hypnotic suggestion, etc.)" (Morton Prince, *Dissociation,* p. 284).

29. William James, *The Principles of Psychology* (Cambridge: Harvard University Press, 1983), p. 1099.

30. Quotations from James's "What the Will Effects," in *Essays in Psychology* (Cambridge: Harvard University Press, 1983), pp. 218–19, and *Principles of Psychology,* p. 1102.

31. William James. *The Principles of Psychology,* pp. 1102–3.

32. William James. "What the Will Effects," p. 219.

33. More broadly, the problem of multiple personality cannot, in my view, be reduced to the problem of suggestion, understood simply as the demonic, external imposition of the hypnotist's will. As I have remarked in note 13, mimetic identification must be understood as involving a paradoxical inmixing of "activity" and "passivity" or a mimetic "invention" of the subject that tends to exceed the dual relationship between the analyst-hypnotist and the patient.

34. Morton Prince, "The Development and Genealogy of the Misses Beauchamp: A Preliminary Report of a Case of Multiple Personality 1900–01," in Morton Prince, *Psychotherapy and Multiple Personality: Selected Essays,* ed. Nathan G. Hale, Jr. (Cambridge: Harvard University Press, 1975), p. 142.

35. William James, *Principles of Psychology,* pp. 1130, 1132. In James's account the relation of will to automatism is reversible: if volition is essentially a matter of suggestion, consciousness is inherently dynamic or impulsive.

36. Freud in one passage describes the double in mimetic terms, stating that the relation to the double is "accentuated by mental processes leaping from one of these characters to another—by what we should call telepathy—so that the one possesses knowledge, feelings, and experiences in common with the other. Or it is marked by the fact that the subject identifies himself with someone else, so that he is in doubt as to which his self is, or substitutes the extranous self for his own" (Sigmund Freud, "The Uncanny," Sigmund Freud Standard Edition, XVII, p. 234). Cited by Mikkel Borch-Jacobsen, "In statu nascendi," p. 68.

37. Morton Prince, "Miss Beauchamp," p. 133.

38. Actually, Sally can't read BIV's thoughts until, late in the case, through the strength of her hypnotic will she mesmerizes BIV into revealing the "secret chamber" of her mind (Morton Prince, *Dissociation,* pp. 435–43).

39. Prince doubts Sally's claim that she never sleeps, observing that it is "probable that she is unaware of the lapse of time during which she sleeps"—for, like a child, Sally has no sense of time. Nevertheless, he wants to believe Sally's assertion that she is always awake, for it helps establish the case for her permanent spectatorship, that is, for her continuity as an independent personality (see Morton Prince, *Dissociation,* pp. 153–54, 330–33). As Erickson has observed, disturbances in the sense of time (and space) are characteristic of the hypnotic trance (Milton H. Erickson, *The Nature of Hypnosis and Suggestion,* ed. Ernest Rossi (New York: John Wiley and Sons, 1980), p. 380); indeed, the trance state epitomizes the timelessness of the unconscious and the primary process as described by Freud.

40. "It is memory that establishes the continuity of psychological life" (Pierre Janet, *L'Automatisme psychologique,* (Paris: Alcan, 1894), p. 323, translation mine). "It would seem that the identity of the self rests entirely on memory" writes Theodule Ribot in his *Maladies de la memoire* (1881), cited by Michael S. Roth, "Remembering Forgetting: *Maladies de la memoire* in Nineteenth-Century France," *Representations,* 26 (1989), p. 54.

41. In this regard, Sally personifies a particular form of what in another essay I've described as an emerging, barely theorizable, concept of individuality based on a relation of "self"-difference—or "type of one" (Ruth Leys, "Types of One: Adolf Meyer's Life Chart and the Representation of Individuality," *Representations,* 34 (Spring 1991), pp. 1–28.)

42. Stanley Hall, *Adolescence: Its Psychology and Its Relations to Physiology, Anthropology, Sociology, Sex, Crime, Religion, and Education,* 2 vols. (New York: D. Appleton and Company, 1904).

43. Stanley Hall, *Adolescence,* vol. I, pp. 316–17.

44. *Ibid.,* vol. II, pp. 107–8.

45. Saul Rosenzweig suggests that the patient—or rather, Sally—took the name "Beauchamp" from the hero of George Meredith's novel, *Beauchamp's Career,* which if true would mean that she identifies with its male protagonist ("Sally Beauchamp's Career," p. 24).

46. Charles Godfrey Leland treats a strong will in a woman as a "virile" manifestation (*The Alternate Sex* (New York: Funk and Wagnalls Company, 1904), p. 35). Somewhat too schematically from my perspective, John H. Smith has identified the failure of the will or "aboulia" as primarily a male disorder of the *fin de siècle* ("Abulia: Sexuality and Diseases of the Will in the Late Nineteenth Century," *Genders,* 6 (Fall 1989), pp. 102–24).

47. A friend described Prince as "boyish" in his enthusiasm (Michael G. Kenny, *The Passion of Anselm Bourne,* p. 131); and Ernest Jones characterized him as having a "boyish love of fighting" (Nathan Hale Jr., *James Jackson Putnam,* p. 263). On Prince's love of sports, especially riding and yachting, see Henry Murray, "Dr. Morton Prince," p. 294.

48. Stanley Hall, *Adolescence,* vol. I, p. 554. The *Journal* of the aspiring painter (dead from tuberculosis at 25) caused a sensation in Europe and especially in the United States when it appeared, not least because, at a time of intense debate over the "woman question," Bashkirtseff was perceived, in Hall's words, as a "veritable spy upon woman's nature" (p. 629).

49. *Ibid.,* vol. II, pp. 391–92.

50. *The Journal of Marie Bashkirtseff,* translated by Mathilde Blind, introduction by Rozsika Parker and Griselda Pollock (London: Virago Press, 1985), p. ix.

51. Morton Prince, "Miss Beauchamp," p. 180. Thus Sally daydreams about "the things I would like to do if I could. When some men who were quarrelling passed, I thought of them for a long while, and envied them, for it was very late . . . and they had the street to themselves" (Morton Prince, *Dissociation*, pp. 340–41).

52. These citations are from Stanley Hall, *Adolescence*, I, pp. 239–40, 286–87, 316–37; vol. II, pp. 105–8n.

53. Morton Prince, "Sexual Perversion or Vice? A Pathological and Therapeutic Inquiry" (1898), reprinted in Prince, *Psychotherapy and Multiple Personality*, edited by Nathan G. Hale, Jr. (Cambridge: Harvard University Press, 1975), pp. 93–94. Subsequent page references are cited in parentheses in the text.

54. As Mikkel Borch-Jacobsen puts it: "[M]imesis is unrepresentable for the subject in the mode of *Vorstellung:* ungraspable, inconceivable, unmasterable, because unspecularizable (even if it is always already specularized)" (*The Freudian Subject*, p. 40). Cf. note 13, above.

55. In a large literature see especially Joe L. Dubbert, "Progressivism and the Masculinity Crisis," *The Psychoanalytic Review*, 61 (1974), pp. 443–55; Carroll Smith–Rosenberg, *Disorderly Conduct* (New York: A. A. Knopf, 1985); Harry Brod, ed. *The Making of Masculinities* (Boston: Allen and Unwin, 1987); J. A. Mangan and James Walvin, eds., *Manliness and Morality. Middle-Class Masculinity in Britain and America, 1800–1940* (New York: St. Martin's Press, 1987); Gail Bederman, " 'The Women Have Had Charge of the Church Work Long Enough': The Men and the Religion Forward Movement of 1911–1912 and the Masculinization of Middle-Class Protestantism," *American Quarterly*, 41 (September 1989), pp. 432–65.

56. Stanley Hall, *Adolescence*, II, pp. 561–646.

57. Havelock Ellis, "Sexual Inversion: With an Analysis of Thirty-Six New Cases," *Medico-Legal Journal*, 13 (1895–96), pp. 261–62. Like many congenitalists, Ellis retains the notion of a "pseudo" homosexuality of the classroom, the prison, etc., conceived as the effect of a "spurious imitation."

58. Sigmund Freud, *Three Essays on the Theory of Sexuality*, Standard Edition, VII.

59. Prince's reference is to the American translation of Albert Philibert Franz Schrenck von Notzing's book, *Therapeutic Suggestion in Psychopathia Sexualis*, translated by Charles Gilbert Chaddock (Philadelphia: Davis, 1895).

60. Or to rephrase this: in my reading of Prince's text, a notion of the genesis of homosexuality as the result of (specular) *resemblance* displaces the greater "scandal" of *de-differentiation or sameness* in the mimetic relation to the other. I put the term "scandal" in quotation marks here to indicate that, although from the point of view of mimesis the scandal is indeed the blurring of gender boundaries and hence of identity, the figuration of homosexuality as love of the same may be seen as fully domesticating—for homosexuality can and does involve highly complex modes of differentiation.

61. Melanie Klein, "A Contribution to the Psychogenesis of Manic-Depressive States" (1935) and "Mourning and Its Relation to Manic-Depressive States" (1940), in *Love, Guilt and Reparation and Other Works, 1921–1945* (New York: Delta Publishing Company, 1977).

62. Mikkel Borch-Jacobsen, *The Freudian Subject*, p. 181. Cf. Philippe Lacoue-Labarthe *Typographies*, p. 129.

63. On incorporation defined as the refusal or inability to mourn the loss of the mother, who is thus fantasmatically encrypted or preserved as the "living dead" in a secretly main-

tained topography, see especially Nicholas Abraham and Marie Torok, "Introjection-Incorporation, *Mourning* or *Melancholia*" (1972), in *Psychoanalysis in France,* edited by Serge Lebovici and Daniel Widlocher (New York: International Universities Press, 1980), pp. 3–16.

64. Mikkel Borch-Jacobsen, *The Freudian Subject,* p. 92.

65. "Then she dreamed of being dead, and in a coffin lined with hands which tried to clutch at her. Suddenly they all doubled up and seemed to be watching. C.[hristine] wondered, but was so tired struggling to get away from them . . . that she leaned back, in her dream, on her brain, which was her pillow, to rest a minute. But the pillow moved—long . . . worms wriggled out of it, covering her from head to foot, and she screamed with terror. When she tried to escape the worms, the hands clutched her. When she would avoid the hands, the worms went through and through her. Finally she awoke as C., whole shuddering and cold, though . . . simply dripping with perspiration" (Morton Prince, *Dissociation,* p. 338). (Sally's account of the dream is interrupted by a dialogue with BIV that raises the topic of language and Sally's inability adequately to speak English or the "mother tongue.") Sally states that as a child Miss Beauchamp's terrifying dreams were "usually about her mother" (376) and associates the particular dream in question to "Egyptian mummy images" (341). (In Kleinian terms, the proliferation of the Egyptian mummy images may be said to function as a hyperbolic defense against maternal incorporation and loss.)

It is also relevant to the theme of the fantasy of the incorporated mother that at a very early moment, before her second self acquires the name Chris, Miss Beauchamp tentatively identifies her "other self" with the all-powerful, two-thousand-year-old, murderous matriarch "She" of *Rider Haggard's* immensely popular novel of the same name (Morton Prince, *Dissociation,* p. 28). "She"—or "She-Who-Must-Be-Obeyed"—rules over a city ("Kor") of murdered, entombed bodies and at the end of the narrative is herself withered to the condition of an Egyptian mummy. For the place of *H. Rider Haggard's* text in the *fin de siècle* imagination see Sandra M. Gilbert, "Rider Haggard's Heart of Darkness," in *Coordinates: Placing Science Fiction and Fantasy,* edited by George E. Slusser, Eric S. Rabkin, and Robert Scholes (Carbondale: Southern Illinois University Press, 1983), pp. 124–38.

In connection with the same maternal problematic it is worth observing that Sally, who is ambivalent about letting Prince read her "Autobiography" and eventually refuses to complete it, states that "All I care for is my precious manuscript, which I beg you will return to me. . . . I will be reasonable, I will indeed, but it is hard to refrain from 'My daughter! Oh my daughter!'" (468). Nothing could more demonstrate the instability of identification than that the very manuscript that reveals the mother's lack of affection for her daughter is used by Sally to figure a loved daughter whom the mother-Sally doesn't want to lose. If the "Autobiography" discloses the negative aspect of maternal identification, this passage reveals its positive one. Moreover, the violence of identification is expressed in the *form* of Sally's utterance, as if the distance of representation that would have been conveyed by the words "it is hard to refrain *from saying* 'My daughter! Oh my daughter!'" is here collapsed as Sally at least verbally becomes the mother "herself."

66. Morton Prince, "Why We Have Traits—Normal and Abnormal: An Introduction to the Study of Personality" (1929), in *Clinical and Experimental Studies in Personality,* p. 129.

67. Charles Godfrey Leland, *The Alternate Sex,* p. v.

68. As Judith Butler has emphasized in connection with Freud's theory of bisexuality (*Gender Trouble*, p. 61). Otto Weininger appears to be an exception to this rule. Thus while he insists that opposites attract, his theory of complementarity supposes that the man in the man loves the man in the woman and *vice versa*, i.e., he posits a homosexual structure of desire. However, the result is just as normalizing as it is in the case of Leland and others. First, he insists that in spite of our inherent bisexuality, each of us belongs only to *one* sex, male or female; and second, in opposition to those who maintain that homosexuality is an acquired trait, he antimimetically grounds that inversion in anatomy (*Sex and Character*, authorized German translation (London: William Heinemann, 1906), pp. 45, 188).

Weininger's claim that "one must *be* either man or woman" (*Ibid.*, pp. 188–89) is consistent with Michel Foucault's observation that in the modern period "everybody was to have one and only one sex . . . as for the elements of the other sex that might appear, they could only be accidental, superficial, or even quite simply illusory" (*Herculine Barbin: Being the Recently Discovered Memoirs of a Nineteenth-Century French Hermaphrodite* (New York: Pantheon Books, 1980), p. viii.) For useful discussions of the history of the concept of bisexuality see George Chauncey, Jr., "From Inversion to Homosexuality: Medicine and the Changing Conceptualization of Female Deviance," *Salmagundi*, 57 (Summer 1982), pp. 114–46; Michel Foucault, *Herculine Barbin*, pp. vii–xvii; and Frank Sulloway, *Freud: Biologist of the Mind* (London: Burnett Books, 1979), pp. 183ff.

69. Edward Carpenter, *The Intermediate Sex. A Study of Some Transitional Types of Men and Women* (London: George Allen and Unwin, 1921 (first published as an essay entitled "The Intermediate Sex" in 1896)), pp. 126–27.

70. Morton Prince, *The Unconscious: The Fundamentals of Human Personality Normal and Abnormal* (New York: MacMillan Company, 1914), pp. 296–99. In a gesture which serves to stave off the sexual dangers of mimetic identification with Freud, Prince, in 1910 in a letter to James Jackson Putnam expresses his rivalry with Freud by adopting the persona of "Fiona MacCleod."

71. Otto Weininger, *Sex and Character, passim.* "If a woman possessed an 'ego' she would have a sense of property both in her own case and that of others," Weininger writes (p. 205), and: "[N]o animal is made afraid by seeing its reflection in a glass, whilst there is no man who could spend his life in a room surrounded with mirrors. . . . It is in striking harmony with the ascription to men alone of an ineffable, inexplicable personality, that in all the authenticated cases of double or multiple personality the subjects have been women. The absolute female is capable of subdivision; the male . . . is always an indivisible unit" (pp. 210–11).

72. James Jackson Putnam, Review of *Dissociation, Journal of Abnormal Psychology*, 1 (1906), pp. 236–39. Putnam treats the Beauchamp case as a "caricature, a monstrosity."

73. "Woman, as woman, must disappear, and until that has come to pass there is no possibility of establishing a kingdom of God on earth" (Otto Weininger, *Sex and Character*, p. 343). Weininger's vision of a male homosocial world that would be purified not only of women but of the demands of genital sexuality altogether is consonant with the structure of twentieth-century homosexual panic as described by Eve Kosoksky Sedgwick in her *Between Men. English Literature and Male Homosocial Desire* (New York: Columbia University Press, 1985).

74. William McDougall, "The Case of Sally Beauchamp," *Proceedings of the English Society for Psychical Research*, 19 (1907), pp. 410–31.

75. On this basis, William McDougall concludes that Sally must be a spirit ("The Case of Sally Beauchamp," p. 430), a popular turn-of-the-century interpretation of multiple personality that is alluded to in the Beauchamp case but is rejected by Prince. Prince used a Dr. Richard Hodgson, a leading Boston spiritualist and James's collaborator in the investigation of the medium Mrs. Leonore Piper, to serve as Miss Beauchamp's physician when he himself was unavailable and there are signs of Hodgson's influence on the patient: "I am a spirit. You know it is true," Sally provocatively exclaims at one moment in the text (Morton Prince, *Dissociation*, p. 377); at another, Prince characterizes Sally as a medium. But on antimimetic grounds Prince appears to have severely limited Hodgson's role in the case, and nowhere in his text does he discuss the spiritualist hypothesis.

76. In his writings on psychoanalysis, Prince will simultaneously identify with Freud by admitting the role of childhood conflict in the origin of dissociation, and will reassert his difference by simultaneously appealing to a concept of the *subject's auto-suggestion* in the determination of psychic splitting. This however leaves a remainder or supplement, in the form of a footnote deferring once again a "fuller explanation" of the case, signaling that the interpretation hitherto given is, if not inadequate, incomplete (Morton Prince, "Miss Beauchamp," p. 172).

77. Nicholas Humphrey and Daniel C. Dennett report that the phenomenon of multiple personality is now referred to as The Movement or Cause ("Speaking for Ourselves: An Assessment of Multiple Personality Disorder," *Raritan*, 9 (Summer 1989), p. 69). The International Society for the Study of Multiple Personality was founded in 1984. The movement's journal is *Dissociation*. In 1980, for the first time the *Diagnostic and Statistical Manual* recognized multiple personality as a clinically distinct dissociative disorder.

78. *Ibid*. Humphrey and Dennett report that the female to male ratio for all reported cases is 8:1. For an interesting recent analysis of multiple personality see Ian Hacking, "Two Souls in One Body," *Critical Inquiry* 17 (Summer 1991), pp. 838–67.

79. Michael G. Kenny, *The Passion of Anselm Bourne*, p. 161.

80. *Childhood Antecedents of Multiple Personality*, edited by Richard P. Kluft (Washington, D.C.: American Psychiatric Press, 1985).

81. These are Humphrey and Dennett's characterizations, "Speaking for Ourselves," p. 89.

82. Michael G. Kenny, *The Passion of Anselm Bourne*, p. 168.

83. Jacqueline Rose, "Psychopolitics I: Negation," and "Psychopolitics II: Controversial Discussions: Anna Freud and Melanie Klein," papers delivered at the Humanities Center, Johns Hopkins University, Spring 1989.

84. Mikkel Borch-Jacobsen, *The Freudian Subject*, p. 32.

85. *Ibid*., pp. 156ff. Cf. his "The Freudian Subject, From Politics to Ethics," *October*, 39 (Winter 1986), pp. 125–26.

86. "'Having' and 'being' in children," Freud writes in a posthumously published note. "Children like expressing an object-relation by identification: 'I am the object.' 'Having' is the later of the two: after loss of the object it relapses into 'being.' Example: the breast. 'The breast is a part of me, I am the breast.' Only later: 'I have it,' that is, 'I am not it'" (Sigmund Freud, "Findings, Ideas, Problems," Standard Edition, XXIII, p. 299). Cited by Mikkel Borch-Jacobsen, *The Freudian Subject*, p. 28.

87. Freud, *Group Psychology and the Analysis of the Ego*, Standard Edition, XVIII, p. 107.

88. Julia Kristeva, "L'Abjet d'Amour," *Tel Quel*, 91 (1982), p. 18 (translation mine).

89. For helpful analyses of Kristeva's paper see Cynthia Chase's review in *Criticism*, 26 (1984), pp. 193–201, and her "Desire and Identification in Lacan and Kristeva," in *Feminism and Psychoanalysis*, Richard Feldstein and Judith Roof, eds. (Ithaca: Cornell University Press, 1989), pp. 65–83; Neil Hertz, *The End of the Line. Essays on Psychoanalysis and the Sublime* (New York: Columbia University Press, 1985), pp. 231–33. Cf. Jacqueline Rose's valuable discussion of Kristeva's work, "Julia Kristeva: Take Two," in *Sexuality in the Field of Vision*, pp. 141–64.

90. Nicholas Abraham, "Notes du seminaire sur l'unité duelle et le fantôme," and "Notules sur le fantôme," in Nicholas Abraham and Maria Torok, *L'Écorce et le Noyau* (Paris: Flammarion, 1978), pp. 393–433.

91. Frederic W. H. Myers, "Multiplex Personality," *Proceedings of the Society for Psychical Research*, 4 (1889), p. 502.

92. D. Caul, quoted by Richard P. Kluft, "Treatment of Multiple Personality Disorder: A Study of 33 Cases," *Psychiatric Clinics of North America*, 7 (March 1984), p. 11.

93. *Ibid.*, pp. 13–14.

94. See in this connection Jean-Roch Laurence and Campbell Perry, *Hypnosis, Will, and Memory: A Psycho-Legal History* (New York and London: The Guilford Press, 1988).

95. The classical analysis here is Jean Laplanche and J.-B. Pontalis, "Fantasy and the Origin of Sexuality," *The International Journal of Psychoanalysis*, 49 (1968), pp. 1–17.

96. The next three paragraphs are based especially on Mikkel Borch-Jacobsen's "L'Hypnose dans la psychanalyse" and "The Unconscious, Nonetheless."

97. Mikkel Borch-Jacobsen, "Dispute," p. 203 (translation mine).

98. Although it is usually attributed to Anna Freud's *The Ego and the Mechanisms of Defence* (1937), the concept of identification (or what he also calls introjection) with the aggressor occurs for the first time in Sandor Ferenczi's article "Confusion of Tongues Between Adults and the Child" (*Final Contributions to the Problems and Methods of Psychoanalysis*, edited by Michael Balint (New York: Basic Books, 1955), p. 162.)

99. Mikkel Borch-Jacobsen, "Dispute," p. 203.

100. Sandor Ferenczi, "The Principle of Relaxation and NeoCatharsis," *Final Contributions*, p. 124.

101. "Of course the task of analysis is not fulfilled when we have reactivated the infantile level and caused the traumas to be reenacted. The material re-enacted in play or repeated in any other way has to be thoroughly worked through analytically. Of course, too, Freud is right when he teaches us that it is a triumph for analysis when it succeeds in substituting recollection for acting out" ("Child-Analysis in the Analysis of Adults," *Final Contributions*, p. 131). Ferenczi's highly controversial concept of "mutual" analysis was supposed to help bring about this transformation.

102. Sandor Ferenczi, "Confusion of Tongues Between Adults and the Child," p. 167.

103. Sandor Ferenczi, *Journal Clinique* (Paris: Payot, 1985), p. 88 (translation mine).

104. "An unexpected, unprepared for, overwhelming shock acts like, as if it were, an anaesthetic. How can this be? Apparently by inhibiting every kind of mental activity and thereby provoking a state of complete passivity devoid of any resistance. The absolute paralysis of motility includes also the inhibition of perception and (with it) of thinking. The shutting off of perception results in the complete defencelessness of the ego. An impression which is not perceived cannot be warded off. The results of this complete paralysis are: (1)

The course of sensory paralysis becomes and remains permanently interrupted; (2) while sensory paralysis lasts every mechanical and mental impression is taken up without resistance; (3) no memory traces of such impressions remain, even in the unconscious, and thus the causes of the trauma cannot be recalled from memory traces" (Sandor Ferenczi, "Notes and Fragments. On the Revision of The Interpretation of Dreams," *Final Contributions*, pp. 239–40).

105. Sandor Ferenczi, "Notes and Fragments. Psychic Infantalism," in *Final Contributions*, pp. 261, 255.

106. Michael G. Kenny, *The Passion of Anselm Bourne*, pp. 175–76. Cf. Ralph Allison, *Minds in Many Places* (1980).

107. Mikkel Borch-Jacobsen, "Dispute," p. 212, "Analytic Speech: From Restricted to General Rhetoric," in *The Ends of Rhetoric. History, Theory, Practice*, edited by John Bender and David E. Wellbery (Stanford: Stanford University Press, 1990), and "L'Efficacité mimétique," unpublished paper presented to a colloquium entitled "Autour de l'hypnose: suggestion, influence, identifications, individuelles et collectives," held September 1989 at Cerisy-la-Salle. On Derrida's notion of the pharmakon see "Plato's Pharmacy," in *Dissemination*, translated with an introduction by Barbara Johnson (Chicago: University of Chicago Press, 1981), pp. 61–171.

11

Toward an Agonistic Feminism: Hannah Arendt and the Politics of Identity

B. Honig

Hannah Arendt is an odd, even awkward figure to turn to if one is seeking to enrich the resources of a feminist politics. Notorious for her rigid and uncompromising public/private distinction, Arendt protects the *sui generis* character of her politics and the purity of her public realm by prohibiting the politicization of issues of social justice and gender. These sorts of occupations belong not to politics but to the traditional realm of the household as Aristotle theorized it. In short, the "Woman Problem," as she called it, was not one that Arendt thought it appropriate to pose, politically.[1]

Why turn to Arendt, then? I turn to her not as a theorist of gender, nor as a woman, but as a theorist of a politics that is potentially activist, certainly dynamic, an agonal and performative politics that might stand a feminist politics in good stead.[2] I turn to Arendt because of what she *does* include in her vision of politics, and also because (*not* in spite) of what she excludes from it: The terms of that exclusion are instructive for a feminist politics that confronts and seeks to contest entrenched and often paralyzing distinctions between a public and a private realm. In spite of Arendt's insistent reliance on her public/private distinction, the resources for its politicization are present within her account of politics and action: A reading of Arendt that grounds itself in the agonistic and performative impulse of her politics must, for the sake of that politics, resist the *a priori* determination of a public/private distinction that is beyond contestation and amendment. This resistance is itself an important and component part of Arendt's account of politics and political action.

I begin by arguing that resistibility is a *sine qua non* of Arendt's politics. Next, I briefly examine the terms of her exclusion of the body from the realm of politics, focusing first on the univocally despotic and irresistible character of the body, as Arendt sees it, and then on the multiplicity of the acting self whose performative speech acts win for it the politically achieved identity that Arendt valorizes. On Arendt's account, identity is the performative production, not the expressive condition or essence of action. This feature of Arendt's work, combined with the public/private distinction upon which it is mapped, have led feminist critics of Arendt to fault her for theorizing a politics that is inhospitable to women and women's issues.[3] In my view, however, it is precisely in Arendt's rejection of an identity-based politics that her value to a feminist politics lies. The problem is that Arendt grounds that rejection in a refusal to treat private-realm identities, like gender, as potential sites of politicization. I note, however, that Arendt's famous engagement with Gershom Scholem over the terms of her Jewish identity and its responsibilities illustrates her failure strategically to contain (so-called) private identities to a "prepolitical" realm and suggests the need for alternative strategies that are more empowering.

I conclude that Arendt's performative politics can serve as a promising model for a feminist politics that seeks to contest (performatively and agonistically) the prevailing construction of sex and gender into binary and binding categories of identity, as well as the prevailing binary division of political space into a public and private realm. Arendt herself would undoubtedly have been hostile to this radicalization of her work but I believe that, as an amendment of her (founding) texts, it is very much in keeping with her politics.

Political Action and Resistibility

Arendt's most brief and most pointed discussion of her vision of politics and action comes to us by way of her reading of the American Declaration of Independence. Here we have all the basic elements of Arendt's account. The Declaration is a political act, an act of power, because it founds a new set of institutions and constitutes a new political community; it "brings something into being which did not exist before," it "establishes new relations and creates new realities."[4] It is a "perfect" instance of political action because it consists "not so much in its being 'an argument in support of an action'" as in its being an action that appears in words; it is a speech act, performed among and before equals in the public realm; it is, in short, a performative utterance.[5]

Focusing on the famous phrase, "We hold these truths to be self-evident," Arendt argues that the new regime's power, and ultimately its authority, derive from the performative "we hold" and not from the constative reference to self-evident truths.[6] Both dramatic and nonreferential, the performative brings a new political community into being; it *constitutes* a "we." This speech act, like all action, gives birth, as it were, to the actor(s), in the moment(s) of its utterance (and repetition).

In contrast to the performative "we hold," the constative reference to self-evident truths expresses not a free coming together but an isolated acquiescence to compulsion and necessity. A self-evident truth "needs no agreement"; it "compels without argumentative demonstration or political persuasion"; it is "in a sense no less compelling than 'despotic power'. . . ." Constatives are "irresistible"; they "are not held by us, but we are held by them."[7] For the sake of politics, for the sake of free political action, Arendt cleanses the Declaration and the founding of their violent, constative moments, of the irresistible anchors of God, self-evident truth, and natural law. There is to be no "being" behind this doing. The doing, the performance, is everything.[8]

On Arendt's account the real source of the authority of the newly founded republic was the performative not the constative moment, the action in concert not the isolated acquiescence, the "we hold" not the self-evident truth. And the real source of authority in the republic, henceforth, would be the style of its maintenance, its openness to refounding and reconstitution:

> Thus, the amendments to the Constitution augment and increase the original foundations of the American republic; needless to say, *the very authority of the American Constitution resides in its inherent capacity to be amended and augmented.*[9]

A regime so favorably disposed to constitutional amendment and augmentation, to refounding, must reject the foundational anchors of god, natural law, and self-evident truth because it knows that God defies augmentation, that God is what does not need to be augmented. God, natural law, self-evident truth are, all three, irresistible and complete. As constatives, they petrify power. Their reification of performativity into constation closes the spaces of politics and deauthorizes a regime by diminishing its possibilities of refounding and augmentation. Resistibility, openness, creativity, and incompleteness are the *sine qua non* of this politics. And this is why Arendt insists on the inadmissibility of the body, and its needs, to the public realm.

The Single, Univocal Body

The human body is, for Hannah Arendt, a master signifier of necessity, irresistibility, imitability, and the determination of pure process. The body is a univocal instance of complete closure. As Arendt puts it:

The most powerful necessity of which we are aware in self-introspection is the life process which permeates our bodies and keeps them in a constant state of a change whose movements are automatic, independent of our own activities, and *irresistible*—i.e., of an overwhelming urgency. The less we are doing ourselves, the less active we are, the more forcefully will this biological process assert itself, impose its inherent necessity upon us, and overawe us with the fateful automatism of sheer happening that underlies all human history.

One of the reasons for action in the public realm, then, is to escape the pure process that afflicts laboring, working, and (most of all) impoverished beings in the private realm. At least this is what Arendt says in *On Revolution* where she documents the horrific failures of the French Revolution and attributes them to the fact that "the poor, driven by the needs of their bodies, burst onto the scene" and effectively closed the spaces of politics by making the "social question" the center of political attention.[10] When demands are made publicly on behalf of the hungry or poor body, then the one individuating and activating capacity that humans possess is silenced. There can be no speech, no action, unless and until the violently pressing, indeed irresistible, needs of the body are satisfied.

Elsewhere, in *The Human Condition,* Arendt's emphasis is different: Here her hostility to the political consideration of the "social" is unabated but the "rise of the social" is theorized in terms of the usurpation of political space by behaviorism, mass society, and the administration of "housekeeping" concerns that are no less obtrusive than the body's urgency but which seem to be less urgently irresistible. Here, the social *rises,* it does not *burst,* onto the scene.

In contrast to *On Revolution, The Human Condition* tends not to discuss the body directly. And when things of the body are addressed, the emphasis is less on the irresistibility of the body than on its imitability.[11] For example, Arendt says that in the political speech and action that distinguish him, man "communicate[s] himself and not merely something—thirst or hunger, affection or hostility or fear."[12] Thirst or hunger are "merely something" because they are common, shared features of our biological existence and as such they are incapable of distinguishing us from each other in any significant way. This feature of commonality is exaggerated in modernity as the social develops into a strongly conformist set of arrangements which, "by imposing innumerable and various rules, . . . tend to 'normalize' its members, to make them behave, to exclude spontaneous action or outstanding achievement."[13] Here, the reason to act is not situated in a need to escape the body and be freed, episodically, from its urgency; instead, Arendt focuses on the need to escape or contain the normalizing impulse of the social through the antidotal but also *sui generis* goods of politics and action. The reason to act is situated in action's unique, individuating power, and in the self's agonal passion for distinction and outstanding achievement.

When they act, Arendt's actors are reborn.[14] Through innovative action and speech, they "show who they are, reveal actively their unique personal identities and thus make their appearance in the human world."[15] Their momentary engagement in action in the public realm grants to them identities that are lodged forever in the stories told of their heroic performances by the spectators who witness them. Prior to or apart from action, this self has no identity; it is fragmented, discontinuous, indistinct, and most certainly uninteresting. A life-sustaining, psychologically determined, trivial, and imitable biological creature in the private realm, this self attains identity— becomes a "who"—by acting. For the sake of "who" it might become, it risks the dangers of the radically contingent public realm where anything can happen, where the consequences of action are "boundless" and unpredictable, where "not life but the world is at stake."[16] In so doing, it forsakes the comforting security of "what" it is, the roles and features that define (and even determine) it in the private realm, the "qualities, gifts, talents and shortcomings, which [it] may display or hide," and the intentions, motives, and goals that characterize its agency.[17] Thus, Arendt's actors are never self-sovereign. Driven by the despotism of their bodies (and their psychologies) in the private realm, they are never really in control of what they do in the public realm, either. This is why, as actors, they must be courageous. Action is spontaneous, it springs up *ex nihilo* and, most disturbing, it is self-surprising: "[I]t is more than likely that the 'who' which appears so clearly and unmistakably to others, remains hidden from the person himself."[18]

There is nothing interesting nor distinct about "what" we are, nothing remarkable about the psychological and biological self. The features of the private self are, like our inner organs, "never unique."[19] Arendt says of the biological self: "If this inside were to appear, we would all look alike."[20] Here the silence that is opposed to the performative speech acts valorized by Arendt is not the muteness that is provoked by violently urgent bodily need, but rather a kind of silent communication, a constative speaking that is strictly communicative and narrowly referential, so narrowly referential that it need not even be spoken. Here, "speech plays a subordinate role, as a means of communication or as a mere accompaniment to something that could *also be achieved in silence*."[21] Since the point of language in the private realm is "to communicate immediate identical needs and wants" (of the body), this can be done mimetically. The single, univocal body is capable of handling this task without the aid of speech: "signs and sounds," Arendt says, "would be enough."[22]

The Multiple, Acting Self

By contrast with the single, univocal body, the acting self is multiple. Indeed, this bifurcated self can be metaphorized in terms of the illicit and oppositional constative and performative combination that structures the Declaration of Independence, on Arendt's account. Constatives and bodies are both despotic, irresistible, univocal, singular. Neither is creative. Both are disruptive, always threatening to rise, or burst, onto the scene and close the spaces of politics. Because of this ever-present threat, we must be vigilant and guard the public realm and performativity against the intrusion of the bodily or constative compulsion.

The acting self is like the performative moments of the Declaration: free, (self-)creative, transformative, and inimitable. Arendt's performatives postulate plurality and her actors postulate multiplicity. The power of the performative "we hold" is actualized by distinct and diverse individuals with little in common prior to action except a care for the world and an agonal passion for distinction.[23] Likewise, Arendt's actors do not act because of what they already are, their actions do not express a prior, stable identity; they presuppose an unstable, multiple self that seeks its, at best, episodic self-realization in action and in the identity that is its reward.

This multiple self is characterized by Arendt as the site of a struggle that is quieted, temporarily, each time the self acts and achieves an identity that is a performative production. The struggle is between the private and the public self, the risk-aversive stay-at-home and the courageous, even rash, actor in the contingent public realm. This bifurcation between its private and public impulses marks the self but does not exhaust its fragmentation. In the private realm alone, this self is also animated and conflicted by three distinct, rival, and incompatible mental faculties—thinking, willing, and judging—each of which is "reflexive," recoiling "back upon itself." Always, Arendt says "there remains this inner resistance."[24] This is why Arendt insists that autonomy is an impositional construction. It imposes a univocity on a self that is fragmented and multiple; it involves "a mastery which relies on domination of one's self and rule over others"; it is a formation to which the self, on Arendt's account, is resistant.[25] This self is not, ever, one. It is itself the site of an agonistic struggle that Arendt (sometimes) calls politics.[26] And Arendt approves of this because, like Nietzsche, she sees this inner multiplicity of the self as the source of its power and energy, as one of the conditions of creative performative action.[27]

These bifurcations, between the univocal body and the multiple self, are presented as attributes of individual selves, but they actually operate to distinguish some selves from others in the Ancient Greece that is Arendt's beloved model. Here the experience of action is available only to the very few. The routine and the urgency of the body are implicitly identified in

The Human Condition, as they were explicitly in ancient Greece, with women and slaves (but also with children, laborers, and all non-Greek residents of the polis), the laboring subjects who tend to the body and its needs in the private realm where "bodily functions and material concerns should be hidden."[28] These inhabitants of the private realm are passively subject to the demands that their bodies and nature make upon them, and to the orders dictated to them by the master of the household to which they belong as property. As victims of both the tiresomely predictable, repetitious, and cyclical processes of nature, and the despotism of the household, they are determined, incapable of the freedom that Arendt identifies with action in the public realm. Free citizens, by contrast, could tend to their private needs in the private realm (or, more likely, have them tended to) but they could then leave these necessitarian, life-sustaining concerns behind to enter the public realm of freedom, speech, and action. Indeed their ability to leave these concerns behind is the mark of their capacity to act. In politics, after all, "not life but the world is at stake."

This passage, made periodically by free citizens from the private to the public realm, indicates that the chasm between the two realms is not non-negotiable.[29] But this is true only for citizens, only for those who are not essentially identified with their condition of embodiment, for those who can be other than only, and passively, embodied beings. This is, in effect, the criterion for their citizenship. For "others," whose very nature prevents them from ever becoming citizens because their identity *is* their embodiment (and this is the criterion for their barbarism), there is no negotiating the public/private impasse.

This problematic feature of political action is certainly one that Arendt attributes to the polis, but is it right to attribute it to Arendt herself?[30] Arendt does often speak as if her private realm and its activities of labor and work were to be identified with particular classes of people, or bodies, or women in particular. But, as Hanna Pitkin points out, at other times the private realm and its activities of labor and work seem to represent not a particular class or gender but "particular *attitude[s]* against which the public realm must be guarded."[31] Labor, for example, "the activity which corresponds to the biological process of the human body," is a mode in which the necessitarian qualities of life and the instrumental character of a certain kind of rationality dominate us so thoroughly that the freedom of politics and its performativity cannot surface.[32] Since Arendt's real worry about labor and work is that they require and engender particular sensibilities that hinder or destroy action, Pitkin suggests that "Perhaps a 'laborer' is to be identified not by his manner of producing nor by his poverty but by his 'process'-oriented outlook; perhaps he is driven by necessity not objectively, but because he *regards* himself as driven, incapable of action."[33]

Or, better, perhaps it is the laboring sensibility that is excluded from political action, a sensibility that is taken to be characteristic of laboring as an activity but which may or may not be characteristic of the thinking of any particular laborer, a sensibility that is certainly not taken to signal a laboring nature or essence that is expressed when the laborer labors. There is no "being" behind this doing. The same analysis applies to work. On this account, there is no determinate class of persons that is excluded from political action. Instead, politics is protected from a variety of sensibilities, attitudes, dispositions, and approaches all of which constitute *all* selves and subjects to some extent, all of which engage in a struggle for dominion over the self, and all of which are incompatible with the understanding(s) of action that Arendt valorizes. In short, the construal of labor, work, and action as sensibilities *could* de-essentialize or denaturalize them. Each would be understood as itself a performative production, not the expression of the authentic essence of a class, or a gender, but always the (sedimented) products of the actions, behaviors, norms and institutional structures of individuals, societies, and political cultures.

This reading of labor, work, and action as (rival) sensibilities is compatible with Arendt's view of the self as multiplicity. And it might point the way to a gentle subversion of Arendt's treatment of the body as a single, univocal, master signifier of irresistibility, imitability, and the closure of constation. Labor is, after all, a bodily function, on Arendt's account, as well as being the mode in which the body is tended to, the mode which is preoccupied with things that are "needed for the life process itself."[34] If labor (that determining sensibility by which all are sometimes driven) can be a performative production, why not the body itself? Why not allow this reading of labour, work, and action as sensibilities to push us to de-essentialize the body, perhaps pluralize it, maybe even see it as a performative production, a possible site of action, in Arendt's sense?

Distinguishing Public and Private

If there is one thing in the way of this radicalization of Arendt's account, it is Arendt's reliance on that series of distinctions which I have grouped together under the heading of performative versus constative. Arendt treats these distinctions as binary oppositions, nonnegotiable and without overlap, and she maps them onto a (historically invidious) public/private distinction that lies at the (shifting) center of her work. Indeed, as it turns out, there is more than one thing in the way since Arendt secures her public/private distinction with a multilayered edifice. The distinction spawns numerous binaries, each one a new layer of protective coating on the last, each one meant to secure, that much more firmly, the distinction that resists the ontologizing function that Arendt assigns to it. Performative versus constative,

"We hold" versus "self-evident truth," self versus body, male versus female, resistible versus irresistible, courageous versus risk-aversive, multiple versus univocal, speech versus silence, active versus passive, open versus closed, power versus violence, necessity versus freedom, action versus behavior, extraordinary versus ordinary, inimitable versus imitable, disruption versus repetition, light versus dark, in short, public versus private.

Why so many? In the very drawing of the distinction, where the drawing is an extraordinary act, in Arendt's sense (it has the power to create new relations and new realities), Arendt is caught in a cycle of anxious repetition. Binary distinctions and adjectival pairs are heaped, one upon another, in a heroic effort to resist the erosion of a distinction that is tenuous enough to need all of this. Tenuous, indeed. There are, in Arendt's account, numerous instances of the permeation of these distinctions. Arendt is quite straightforward about the fact that the public realm is all too easily colonized by the private (it is to this problem that she responds in *The Human Condition* and in *On Revolution*). Her straightforwardness tempts us to think that these distinctions are, above all else, drawn to protect the public from the private realm's imperialism. But the converse is also true. It is equally important to Arendt to protect the private realm's reliability, univocality, and ordinariness from the disruptions of action and politics.[35] In short, Arendt domesticates not only behavior but also action itself: She gives action a place to call home and she tells it to stay there, where it belongs. But, of course, it refuses.

Here is the real risk of action—in this refusal. The self-surprising quality of action is not limited to the fact that action does not always turn out as we would have intended it to; nor even to the fact that we, as actors, are never quite sure "who" it is that we have turned out to be. Action is self-surprising in another sense as well, in the sense that it happens to us; we do not decide to perform, then enter the public realm, and submit our performance to the contingency that characterizes that realm: Often, political action comes to us, it involves us in ways that are not deliberate, willful, or intended. Action produces its actors; episodically, temporarily, we are its agonistic achievement. On Arendt's account, the American Revolution happened to the American revolutionaries ("But the movement which led to the revolution was not revolutionary except by inadvertence."[36]) And, sometimes, particularly in her account of willing, action happens to the private self, initially in the *private* realm.

Arendt treats willing as an antecedent of action but it is a funny kind of antecedent because it actually defers action. Caught in a reflexive, internal, and potentially eternal dynamic of willing and nilling, a dynamic which it is incapable of arresting, the will awaits redemption. And when that redemption comes, it comes in the form of action itself. *Action* liberates the self from the will's paralysing "disquiet and worry," by disrupting the compulsive repetitions of the will. Action comes in, as it were, to the private realm; it happens to the as yet unready and not quite willing (because still also nilling) subject in the private realm. Like a *"coup d'état,"* action "interrupts the conflict between *velle* and *nolle,"* and redeems the will. "In other words," Arendt adds, "the Will is redeemed by ceasing to will and starting to act and *the cessation cannot originate in an act of the will-not-to-will* because this would be but another volition."[37]

Examples of public/private realm cross-fertilizations abound; they are as manifold as the distinctions that are supposed to account for their impossibility, their perversion, their monstrosity. What is to prevent us, then, from applying "performativity to the body itself," as one feminist theorist of gender performance does?[38] What prohibits the attenuation of the public/private distinction? What would be the punishment for unmasking the private realm's constative identities as really the (sedimented) products of the actions, behaviors, and institutional structures and norms of individuals, societies, and political cultures? What is at stake?

At stake, for Arendt, is the loss of action itself, the loss of a realm in which the actionable is vouchsafed. This is a real cause of concern, especially given the astonishing and disturbing success of the "innumerable and various rules" of the social in producing normal, well-behaved subjects. But in order to vouchsafe it, Arendt empties the public realm of almost all content. Things possessed of content are constatives, after all, sites of closure, in Arendt's theorization, irresistible obstacles to performativity. Hence Hanna Pitkin's puzzled wonderment at what those citizens "talk about together in that endless palaver of the *agora.*"[39] Arendt's effective formalization of action, her attempts to safeguard action with her nonnegotiable public/private distinction, may contribute more to the loss or occlusion of action than any rise of the social, than any bursting forth of ostensibly irresistible bodies.

The permeability, inexactness, and ambiguity of the distinction between public and private, however, are not reasons to give it up. Instead, they suggest the possibility of attenuation. What if we took Arendt's own irresistibly lodged public/private distinction to be a line drawn in the sand, an illicit constative, a constituting mark or text, calling out, agonistically, to be contested, augmented, and amended? And what if we began by dispensing with the geographic and proprietary metaphors of public and private? What if we treated Arendt's notion of the public realm not as a specific *topos,* like the *agon,* but as a metaphor for a variety of (agonistic) spaces, both topographical and conceptual, that might occasion action?[40] We might be left with a notion of action as an event, an agonistic disruption of the ordinary sequence of things, a site of resistance of the irresistible, a challenge to the normalizing rules that seek to constitute, govern, and control various behaviors. And we might then be in a position to identify sites of political action in a much broader array of constations, ranging from the self-evident truths of God, nature, technology, and capital to those of identity, of gender, race, and ethnicity. We might then be in a position to *act*—in the private realm.

Arendt would no doubt be concerned that these amendments of her account politicize too much, that (as Nancy Fraser puts it on her behalf) "when everything is political, the sense and specificity of the political recedes."[41] For Fraser, Arendt's theorization of politics highlights a paradox: If politics is everywhere then it is nowhere. But not everything *is* political on this (amended) account; it is simply the case that nothing is ontologically protected from politicization, that nothing is necessarily or naturally or ontologically *not* political. The distinction between public and private is seen as the performative product of political struggle, hard won and always temporary. Indeed, the paradox is reversible. The impulse to secure, foundationally, the division between the political and the nonpolitical is articulated as a concern for the preservation of the political but is itself an antipolitical impulse. Arendt knew this; this was the basis of her critique of the constative, foundational ground of the Declaration of Independence. This is what motivated her to apply performativity to the self-evidence of the Declaration. And the same impulse can motivate the application of performativity to Arendt's public/private distinction itself.

This dispersal of the agon is also authorized by another, somewhat different moment in Arendt's theorization of politics. Arendt understood that there were times in which the exigencies of a situation forced politics to go underground. She looks to the underground politics of occupied France, and valorizes its proliferation of sites of resistance, its network of subversive political action.[42] Occupation might not be a bad term for what Arendt describes as the "rise of the social" and the displacement of the political by routinized, bureaucratic, and administrative regimes. In the absence of institutional sites, a feminist politics might well go underground, looking to locate itself in the rifts and fractures of identities, both personal and institutional, and doing so performatively, agonistically, and creatively, with the hope of establishing new relations and realities.

Acting in the Private Realm

This notion of an agonistic politics of performativity situated in the self-evidences of the private realm is explored by Judith Butler, who focuses in particular on the construction and constitution of sex and gender. Butler unmasks the constation—described by Arendt as the mindless, tiresome, and oppressive repetition of the univocal cycles of nature—in the private realm, as performativities that daily produce sex and gender identities. These performances, Butler argues, are the enforced products of a regulative practice of binary gender constitution centered on and by a "heterosexual contract."

But these acts are "internally discontinuous"; the identities they produce are not "seamless." The "multiplicity and discontinuity of the referent [the self] mocks and rebels against the univocity of the sign [sex/gender]." This means that there are "possibilities of gender transformation" in these spaces of mockery and rebellion, "in the arbitrary relation between such acts, in the possibility of a different sort of repeating."[43] A subversive repetition might performatively produce alternative sex and gender identities that would proliferate and would, in their proliferation (and strategic deployment), contest and resist the reified binaries that now regulate and seek to constitute, exhaustively, the identities of sex and gender.

The strategy, then, is to unmask identities that aspire to constation, to deauthorize and redescribe them as performative productions by identifying spaces that escape or resist administration, regulation, and expression. These are spaces of politics, spaces (potentially) of performative freedom. Here action is possible in the private realm because the social and its mechanisms of normalization consistently fail to achieve the perfect closures which Arendt attributes to them, too readily, without resistance. This failure of the social to realize its ambitions means that it is possible to subvert the concretized, petrified, reified, and naturalized identities and foundations that paralyze politics and to broaden the realm of the actionable, to resist the sedimentation of performative acts into constative truths and to stand by the conviction that in politics and in identity, it is not possible to get it right. This impossibility structures the needs and the repressions of Arendt's public *and* private realms. And it provides good reasons to resist and to problematize any politics of identity.

Hanna Pitkin energetically criticizes Arendt's refusal to theorize politics as a practice or venue of the representation of interests, and of shared material needs and concerns.[44] She rightly worries that Arendt's politics is so formal as to be left without import or content. But Pitkin fails to appreciate the promise in Arendt's vision. There is promise in Arendt's unwillingness to allow political action to be a site of the re-presentation of "what" we are, of our reified private-realm identities. In Arendt's view, a politics of representation projects a commonality of identity and interests that is imagined, impositional, and ill-fitting, and it obstructs an important alternative: A politics of performativity that, instead of reproducing and re-presenting "what" we are, agonistically generates "who" we are by episodically producing new identities, identities whose "newness" becomes "the beginning of a new story, started—though unwittingly—by acting [wo]men [and] to be enacted further, to be augmented and spun out by their posterity."[45]

Identity Politics

The centrality of performativity to Arendt's theory of action accounts for Arendt's opposition to attempts to conceive of politics as expressive of shared (community) identities such as gender, race, ethnicity, or nationality. Performativity and agonism are not coincidentally connected in Arendt's account. Arendt's politics is always agonistic because it always resists the attractions of expressivism for the sake of her view of the self as multiplicity, of identity as a performative production, and of action as creative of new relations and new realities.

From Arendt's perspective, a political community that constitutes itself on the basis of a prior, shared, and stable identity threatens to close the spaces of politics, to homogenize or repress the plurality and multiplicity that political action postulates. Attempts to overcome that plurality or multiplicity, Arendt warns, must result in "the abolition of the public realm itself" and the "arbitrary domination of all others," or in "the exchange of the real world for an imaginary one where these others would simply not exist."[46] The only way to prevent such an exchange is by protecting the spaces of politics in the nonidentity, the heterogeneity and discontinuity of political communities, and also in the resistances of the self to the normalizing constructions of subjectivity and the imposition of autonomy (and perhaps even to the formation of sex/gender identities into binary categories of male and female, masculine and feminine). The self's agonistic ill-fittedness is a source of the generation of power, a signal that there are sites from which to generate (alternative) performativity(ies).

It is this care for difference and plurality as conditions of politics and action that accounts for Arendt's hostility to the nation-state, whose repugnant "decisive principle" is its "homogeneity of past and origin."[47] And it might also account for her silence on the subject of a feminist politics: Arendt would have been quite wary of any proclamation of homogeneity in "women's experience," or in "women's ways of knowing." She would have been critical of any feminist politics that relies on a category of woman that aspires to or implies a universality that belies (or prohibits, punishes, or silences) significant differences and pluralities within—and even resistances to—the bounds of the category itself.

These remarks are speculative because Arendt did not address the issues of feminism or a feminist politics in her theoretical work. I myself have been reluctant to pose gender questions to Arendt, directly, because those questions tend to be posed by Arendt's feminist critics in a mode of ethical responsibility: The assumption is that, as a woman, Arendt had a responsibility to pose the "woman question" or at least to theorize a politics that showed that she had women in mind. Her failure to do so marks her as a collaborator. The charge is made most bluntly and forcefully by Adrienne Rich who describes *The Human Condition* as a "lofty and crippled book," exemplary of the "tragedy of a female mind nourished on male ideology."[48] I am less certain about the ethical responsibilities assumed here and so I seek to pose these questions, but not in that mode, that is, without assigning or even implying that responsibility. In fact, I feel a certain respect for Arendt's refusal to be a "joiner," for her wariness of identity politics and of membership in identity communities, for the startling perversity that led her to say of Rosa Luxemburg (but also, I think, of herself) that: "Her distaste for the women's emancipation movement, to which all other women of her generation and political convictions were irresistibly drawn, was significant. In the face of suffragette equality, she might have been tempted to reply, *Vive la petite différence.*"[49]

An odd remark; certainly unfair to the suffragists whose political dedication is dismissed as a product of an "irresistible" identification with a "movement," not a politics; but an intriguing remark nonetheless. What is this *"petite différence"* which Arendt imagines Luxemburg celebrating? It is not sexual difference—that is *la différence,* nothing *petite* about it. *La petite différence* is an intra–sex/gender difference: It is the difference that sets Luxemburg apart from these other women. Arendt admires in Luxemburg a quality that she herself strived for, the refusal of membership, the choice of difference over a certain kind of equality.[50] The "suffragette equality" to which she refers in this passage is not the civic equality with male voters for which these women were still striving; it is the equality among the suffragettes, their devotion to a common cause in the name of which (Arendt alleges) differences among them are effaced. Arendt constructs and celebrates a Rosa Luxemburg who was "an outsider," a "Polish Jew in a country she disliked," a member of a political "party she came soon to despise," and "a woman," the sort of excellent woman who resisted the "irresistible" allure of a women's movement, called other contests her own, and won for herself, thereby, an identity of distinction, not homogeneity.[51]

The same sentiments, the same distancing techniques and distaste for identity politics are evident in Arendt's exchange with Gershom Scholem, an exchange which professed to be about Arendt's controversial book on Eichmann but which was really a contestation of the terms of Arendt's (would-be private realm) identity as a Jew.[52] Indeed, this short exchange is an instructive and provocative study in identity politics. Scholem's letter to Arendt is an exercise in identification, and in politicization: He tells Arendt that her book has little in it of the "certainty of the believer," that it manifests "weakness" and "wretchedness, and power-lust," that it leaves *"one* with a sense of bitterness and shame . . . for the compiler," that he has a "deep respect" for her and that that is why he must call to her attention the "heartless" and "almost sneering and malicious tone" of her book; he can find "little trace" in her ("dear Hannah") of any *"Ahabath Israel:* 'Love of the Jewish People . . .,'" and this absence is typical of "so many intellectuals who came from the German Left." What licenses Scholem to say all of these things, and to mark them as moral failings, is the fact that he regards Arendt "wholly as a daughter of our people and in no other way."[53]

Arendt responds with two strategic refusals: First, she contests Scholem's claim that she is "wholly" Jewish and is constituted by no other differences or identities; and second, she contests Scholem's assumption that Jewish identity is expressive, that it has public effects and carries with it certain responsibilities, that particular sorts of action, utterance, and sentiment ought necessarily to follow from the fact that she is Jewish. Throughout, however, she assumes, as does Scholem, that Jewish identity is an "indisputable," univocal, and constative "fact" (like the other facts of her multiple, but private, identity), "not open to controversy" nor to "dispute." Thus, many of Scholem's statements about her "are simply false" and Arendt is in a position to correct them. For example, she is not "one of the 'intellectuals who come from the German Left'"; if Arendt "can be said to 'have come from anywhere,' it is from the tradition of German philosophy."

To Scholem's "I regard you wholly as a daughter of our people, and in no other way," Arendt responds cryptically: "The *truth* is I have never pretended to be anything else or to be in any other way than I am and I have never even felt tempted in that direction." The point is not that she has not pretended to be anything other than "a daughter" of the Jewish people; she has simply not pretended to be anything other than what she is. But Arendt never *says* what she *is,* she never identifies herself, affirmatively.[54] All she says is that to pretend "to be anything . . . other than I am . . . would have been like saying that I was a man and not a woman—that is to say, kind of insane." Again, there is no affirmative identification of herself, in this case, as a woman, just the claim that to assert its contrary would be "insane." (What would it be to assert it affirmatively?)

Where Scholem *regards* her "*wholly* as a daughter of our people and in no other way," Arendt has "always *regarded*" her own "Jewishness as *one of* the indisputable factual data of my life." She does not regard her Jewishness as the "wholly" constitutive identity that Scholem projects it to be. Arendt is constituted by other "facts," as well, two of which she mentions here—sex/gender, and her schooling in German philosophy.[55] Thus, Scholem's depiction of her as "wholly" a "daughter of our people," is a "label" that he "wish[es] to stick" on her, but it has "never fitted in the past and does not fit now."[56] The label is a label, ill-fitting and stuck on, because Arendt's Jewishness is a fragment of a complex identity.

For Arendt, nothing follows from the fact of her Jewishness as she understands that fact. Her Jewishness is a private matter; because it is a fact, it is not at all actionable. And for that, for its facticity, Arendt is grateful: "There is such a thing as a basic gratitude for everything that is as it is; for what has been *given* and was not, could not be, *made;* for things that are *physei* and not *nomoi,*" for things that are "beyond dispute or argument."

This insistence on her ethnic, religious, cultural identity as a given, a private fact, not to be made or acted upon, is structurally figured in Arendt's letter to Scholem. Arendt begins the letter with a discussion of the facts of her private identity, presented as a series of corrections aimed at what she treats as factual errors. These matters of fact are uninteresting, "not open to controversy"; Arendt sets this part of the letter up as a preamble; it is "pre-political," separate from the political debate that follows. Only the latter treats "matters which merit discussion" and speech. She underscores this distinction by beginning the paragraph that marks the start of the debate and the end of the identity-centered preliminaries with the heading: "To come to the point."

But the very thing for which Arendt expresses her gratitude in this letter is the one thing that Scholem will not grant her in this encounter. Scholem will not treat her Jewish identity as a private affair. For Scholem, certain identifiable and incontestable public responsibilities and implications follow from the indisputable and univocal fact of Arendt's Jewishness. This is why Arendt resists Scholem's inclusions, this is why she resists his writing of her "wholly as a daughter" of the Jewish people: She treasures difference, even a *petite différence,* over and above the equality or sameness that Scholem ascribes to, or demands from Jews. She sees in his identity politics insidious resources for the homogenizing control of behavior and the silencing of independent criticism. And that is why she resists. Her resistance, however, is not all it could be.

Instead of insisting on the privacy of Jewish identity, a privacy that is already problematized by Scholem's charges and by this very public, highly politicized, identity debate, Arendt would have done better to contest the terms of Scholem's construal of Jewishness as identity. This strategy was not available to Arendt, however, because she agrees with Scholem on the most important point. Both she and Scholem treat Jewish identity as a univocal, constative fact. They disagree on whether it is a public or a private fact, on whether any prescriptions or requirements for action follow from it, but both agree that Jewishness is a fact that "could not be made," nor, indeed, unmade; it is unaffected by what the subject *does*. This is why Scholem can regard Arendt as, in spite of all the things that she has written, in spite of her apparently total lack of any *Ahabath-Israel,* "wholly" a "daughter of our people." Arendt's authentic identity as a Jew is unaffected by her actions; she could not deny or subvert it no matter what she did. And with all this, Arendt is in perfect agreement. Her defense strategy mimes the basic premise of Scholem's accusations: Nothing she does can call into question or subvert the indisputable, constative fact of her Jewishness.

In claiming that Jewish identity is constative, Arendt relinquishes the opportunity to engage or even subvert Jewish identity performatively, to explore its heterogeneity, to dislodge and disappoint its aspirations to univocity, to proliferate its differentiated possibilities, and this leaves her without any resources with which to respond, critically, to Scholem's portrayal of Jewishness as a homogeneous, univocal thing that implies certain incontestable responsibilities and claims certain loyalties. Scholem's constative criterion for distinguishing good Jews from bad is left intact. The same would be true for Adrienne Rich's strategy for distinguishing healthy women from those who are crippled, loyal women from those who are treasonous. After all, Rich's approach mirrors Scholem's: It is because she regards Arendt "wholly as a" woman "and in no other way," that she can treat Arendt's other constituting identities (like her schooling in German philosophy) as betrayals of Arendt's authentic and univocal identity as a woman.

The more powerful and empowering defense against Scholem, or Rich, or, indeed, against any identity politics, is to resist the irresistible, not by privatizing it but by unmasking the would-be irresistible, homogeneous, constative and univocal identity in question as a performative production, fractured, fragmented, ill-fitting, and incomplete, the sedimented and not at all seamless product of a multitude of performances and behaviors, the naturalized product of innumerable repetitions. This is Arendt's strategy for empowering the "We hold" of the Declaration against the coercive violence of that document's "self-evident truths." Why not usurp this strategy of empowerment to unmask, subvert, and resist the violent closures of the univocity and self-evidence assumed by some Jewish and feminist politics of identity?

The strategy here is to theorize a Jewishness that is not homogenizing and a feminism that does not efface difference for the sake of an equality of sameness. The strategy here is to proliferate difference rather than reify it and the result might be the empowering discovery or insistence that there are many ways to do one's Jewishness, many ways to do one's gender.[57] The homogenizing impulse of some (so-called) private-realm identities would be weakened and that would allow for greater differentiation and contestability within the frame of the "identities" themselves.

This constitutes an important alternative to the notion of a pariah, and of a pariah perspective, so celebrated by Arendt.[58] Arendt treats the conscious pariah's position of outsider (personified by Rosa Luxemburg as well as by others whom Arendt admired) as a privileged site from which one can secure the distance necessary for independent critique, action, and judgment. But Arendt's celebration of the pariah position is fueled by her problematic assumption that there is no critical leverage to be had from inside formed identities. Arendt celebrates the pariah because she believes that identities succeed, that they do attain seamlessness and closure, that they are necessarily homogenizing and univocally constating. The politics of performativity that I extend and explore here assumes instead that identities are never seamless, that there are sites of critical leverage within the ruptures and inadequacies, in the ill-fittedness, of existing identities. It assumes, therefore, that the position of the pariah is itself unstable, that the pariah is never really an outsider, and that its sites are multiple.

The premise of this performative politics is that in matters of identity, no less than in politics, it is not possible to get it right. The conception of the self presupposed in all this is an agonistic, differentiated, multiple, non-identitied being that is always becoming, always calling out for augmentation and amendment. And the politics truest to all this is likewise agonistic (resistant but still responsive to the expressive aspirations of any identity) and performative, potentially subversive, and always seeking to create new relations and establish new realities . . . even in the private realm.

NOTES

For their comments and criticisms, I am indebted to Judith Butler, Marcie Frank, Sara Gibbons, and, especially, to Tom Keenan and Kirstie McClure.

1. *Rahel Varnhagen: The Life of a Jewish Woman* (revised edition), translated by Richard and Clara Winston (New York: Harcourt, Brace, Jovanovich, 1974), p. xviii.

2. Of course there are some feminists who take issue precisely with this agonal and performative dimension of Arendt's politics. They accuse Arendt's political actors of "boyish posturing," and of membership in a "romanticised" and "agonistic male warriors' club." See Hanna Pitkin, "Justice: On Relating Public and Private," in *Political Theory*, vol. 9 (1981), pp. 303–26; Patricia Springborg, "Hannah Arendt and the Classical Republican Tradition," in *Thinking, Judging, Freedom*, edited by G. T. Kaplan and C. S. Kessler (Sydney: Allen and Unwin, 1989); Wendy Brown, *Manhood and Politics* (N.J.: Rowman and Littlefield, 1988). One of the goals of this paper is to disrupt these identifications of the agonal with masculinism and of performativity with an aggressively vain practice of self-display.

3. The most hostile charges are in Adrienne Rich's *On Lies, Secrets, and Silence: Selected Prose 1966–1978* (New York: W.W. Norton and Co., 1979) and Mary O'Brien's *The Politics of Reproduction*, (Boston and London: Routledge and Kegan Paul, 1981). I discuss Rich's charges, briefly, below; see pp. 227–31.

4. Hannah Arendt, *The Human Condition* (Chicago: University of Chicago Press, 1958), pp. 155, 200.

5. Hannah Arendt, *On Revolution* (New York: Penguin Books, 1963), p. 130.

6. Henceforth, I allow J. L. Austin's terms, performative and constative, to play an integral role in my reading of Arendt.

7. Hannah Arendt, *On Revolution*, pp. 192–93.

8. I am paraphrasing Nietzsche to whom Arendt is greatly, albeit ambivalently, indebted. See Friedrich Nietzsche, *On the Genealogy of Morals*, edited by Walter Kaufmann; translated by Walter Kaufmann and R. J. Hollingdale (1887; New York: Vintage Books, 1969), I, p. xiii.

9. Hannah Arendt, *On Revolution*, p. 202 (emphasis added). I discuss Arendt's provocative theorization of authority as a practice of augmentation and amendment in more detail

in "Declarations of Independence: Arendt and Derrida on the Problem of Founding a Republic," *American Political Science Review*, 85, 1 (March 1991).

10. Hannah Arendt, *On Revolution*, p. 59 (emphasis added). For a much more sustained treatment of this topic, see Norma Moruzzi, "The Social Question, the Mask, and the Masquerade," in *Speaking Through the Mask: The Construction of the Body in the Political Thought of Hannah Arendt*, PhD Diss. Johns Hopkins University, 1990.

11. Hanna Pitkin notes this difference but reads it differently. She argues that *On Revolution* is "franker," presumably a more genuine expression of Arendt's *real* views on the body and the social ("Justice," p. 334), but her conclusion is unwarranted; it implies that *The Human Condition* is reticent in a way that is uncharacteristic of any of Arendt's texts. Moreover, Pitkin's treatment of one of Arendt's accounts of the body as a thin veil for the other obscures the fact that Arendt *strategically layers* distinct characterizations of the body, one on top of the other.

12. Hannah Arendt, *The Human Condition*, p. 176.

13. *Ibid.*, p. 40.

14. *Ibid.*, p. 176.

15. *Ibid.*, p. 179.

16. Hannah Arendt, *Between Past and Future*, enlarged ed. (New York: Penguin, 1977), p. 156.

17. Hannah Arendt, *The Human Condition*, p. 179 and *Between Past and Future*, 151–52. Arendt reads these attributes of agency behaviorally, as *causes* of action that compromise its freedom.

18. Hannah Arendt, *The Human Condition*, p. 179.

19. *Ibid.*, p. 206.

20. Hannah Arendt, *Thinking*, Vol. I of *The Life of the Mind*, edited by Mary McCarthy (New York: Harcourt, Brace, Jovanovich, 1978), p. 29. This claim is clearly false. Arendt probably meant not that all "insides" look identical but that biological differences are not interesting or significant: As bodies we are all alike.

21. Hannah Arendt, *The Human Condition*, p. 179 (emphasis added).

22. *Ibid.*, p. 176.

23. Hannah Arendt, *On Revolution*, p. 118, *passim*.

24. Hannah Arendt, *Willing*, Vol. II of *The Life of the Mind*, p. 69. Arendt makes this claim specifically with reference to willing but it is characteristic of a recoiling that affects all three of the mental faculties.

25. Hannah Arendt, *The Human Condition*, p. 244.

26. I mean to say that Arendt terms "political" the phenomenon of agonistic struggle, not that she herself would use the term "political" to describe these internal struggles. She would not.

27. Elisabeth Young-Bruehl is the only reader of Arendt to note the multiplicity of Arendt's self, but she does not pursue the connections between this view of the self as multiplicity and Arendt's treatment of action as performative, not expressive. Nor does Young-Bruehl see this multiple self as itself a site of agonistic struggle. On the contrary, she refers to the "checks and balances existing within an individual," implying an overarching unity which is inapt, in this context. See Elisabeth Young-Bruehl, *Mind and the Body Politic* (New York: Routledge, 1989), p. 23.

28. Hannah Arendt, *The Human Condition,* p. 73. In *The Human Condition,* Arendt describes "the laborers who 'with their bodies minister to the (bodily) needs of life' [here quoting Aristotle's *Politics* 1254b25] and the women who with their bodies guarantee the physical survival of the species" (72).

29. *Ibid.,* p. 24.

30. Arendt often fails to distinguish clearly her (admittedly admiring) descriptions of the practice of agonal politics in the polis from her account of her own vision of politics and her critics often mistake the first for the second: For example, Pitkin notes that Arendt's account of action is "individualistic" but the citation upon which Pitkin relies (from *The Human Condition,* p. 41) is one in which Arendt describes the *agon* of the polis; where Arendt describes her *own* view of action, even in the early, some say too agonal, text, *The Human Condition,* she says that it is always "in concert" (200).

31. Hanna Pitkin, "Justice," p. 342.

32. Hannah Arendt, *The Human Condition,* p. 7.

33. Hanna Pitkin, "Justice," p. 342. I borrow the term "sensibilities" from Shiraz Dossa, who makes a case quite similar to Pitkin's. Both he and Pitkin, however, stop short of arguing that, as sensibilities, labor, work and action are characteristic of *all* selves. See *The Public Realm and the Public Self: The Political Theory of Hannah Arendt* (Waterloo: Wilfred Laurier University Press, 1989), chapter 3; and my review of Dossa in *Political Theory,* 17, 2, p. 322.

34. Hannah Arendt, *The Human Condition,* p. 96.

35. Arendt insists that "this whole sphere" of politics be "limited," that it "not encompass the whole of man's and the world's existence" (Hannah Arendt, *Between Past and Future,* p. 264).

36. Hannah Arendt, *On Revolution,* p. 44.

37. Hannah Arendt, *Willing,* pp. 37–38, 101–2 (emphasis added). I have argued elsewhere that, on Arendt's account, the will is both self-generating *and* capable of bringing its own activity to an end. (See "Arendt, Identity, and Difference," in *Political Theory,* 16, 1 (Feb. 1988), p. 81.) However, the phrase highlighted in the text here has persuaded me that Arendt did not attribute the latter feature to the will, but to action.

38. Judith Butler, "Performative Acts and Gender Constitution: An Essay in Phenomenology and Feminist Theory," in *Performing Feminisms,* edited by Sue-Ellen Case (Baltimore: Johns Hopkins University Press, 1990), p. 273.

39. Hanna Pitkin, "Justice," p. 336.

40. Seyla Benhabib also metaphorizes Arendt's public realm, but Benhabib metaphorizes only the discursive moment in Arendtian action and leaves its agonistic other behind. For Benhabib, agonistic public space is a *place,* but discursive public space, Arendt's more "modernist" notion, "is a space not necessarily in any topographical or institutional sense." (It "emerges whenever and wherever men act together in concert," (p. 193–94). Because Benhabib limits the metaphorization, because she does not identify spaces of politics *in* the (so-called) private self, she continues to treat Arendt's notion of political space as, literally, a *public* (intersubjective) space. And because she cleanses Arendtian action of its agonistic character, she renders Arendt's concept of political action into more of a conversation and less of an event; there is less for action to disrupt and it becomes, once again, difficult to imagine what the topics of "political" conversations might be. See Seyla Benhabib, "Hannah Arendt and the Redemptive Power of Narrative," *Social Research,* 57, 1 (1990).

41. Nancy Fraser, *Unruly Practices: Power, Discourse and Gender in Contemporary Social Theory* (Minneapolis: University of Minnesota Press, 1989), p. 76.

42. Hannah Arendt, *Between Past and Future*, pp. 3–4.

43. Judith Butler, "Performative Acts," pp. 276, 271, 280, and 271.

44. Hanna Pitkin, "Justice," p. 336.

45. Hannah Arendt, *On Revolution*, p. 47. Cf. Judith Butler, "Performative Acts," p. 274.

46. Hannah Arendt, *The Human Condition*, pp. 220, 234.

47. Hannah Arendt, *On Revolution*, p. 174.

48. Adrienne Rich, *On Lies, Secrets, and Silence*, pp. 211–12. Readers of Arendt have been recirculating these citations for some time. Less often noted is the fact that Rich's essay, on "The Conditions of Work," also opens with a citation from Arendt's *The Human Condition*, which is, after all, a "lofty" even if also a "crippled" book.

49. Hannah Arendt, *Men in Dark Times* (New York: Harcourt, Brace, Jovanovich, 1968), p. 44. Arendt never considers the possibility that politically active women were drawn, almost exclusively, to suffragist activities because the suffragist movement was the only institutionally available opportunity for political action open to women at the time.

50. The story is probably apocryphal, but Arendt is reported to have refused to appear at an American Political Science Association Women's Caucus panel devoted to her work, saying "I do not think of myself as a woman."

51. Hannah Arendt, *Men in Dark Times*, p. 45.

52. The controversy surrounding the publication of Arendt's *Eichmann in Jerusalem* is well documented in Dagmar Barnouw's *Visible Spaces: Hannah Arendt and the German-Jewish Experience* (Baltimore, Johns Hopkins University Press, 1990).

53. Gershom Scholem, "'Eichmann in Jerusalem:' An Exchange of Letters between Gershom Scholem and Hannah Arendt," *Encounter* (Jan. 1964), pp. 51–52 (emphasis added). All citations from Scholem, henceforth, are from pp. 51–52. All citations from Arendt in this section are from pp. 53–54.

54. Even when she identifies herself with "the tradition of German philosophy" the identification is conditional: "*If* I can be said to have come from anywhere, it is from the tradition of German philosophy" (emphasis added).

55. And so is Scholem, of course, constituted by facts other than his Jewish and Zionist identities. Arendt reminds him of this (and retaliates in kind for his own projections of her identity) by addressing *her* letter to "Dear Gerhard," even though Scholem signs his letter with his Hebrew name, "*Gershom* Scholem."

56. I treat Scholem's use of the term "daughter" in this context less as a recognition that Arendt is (distinctly) constituted also by sex/gender difference than as a means of invoking a sense of obligation to the paternal figure "our people." In short, the term "daughter" in Scholem's phrase, seeks to assimilate Arendt's sex/gender *unproblematically* into her Jewish identity.

57. I borrow the notion of "doing one's gender" from Judith Butler; cf. "Performative Acts," p. 276.

58. Hannah Arendt, *The Jew as Pariah*, edited by Ron H. Feldman (New York: Grove Press 1978).

III

Subjects Before the Law

12

The Abortion Question and the Death of Man

Mary Poovey

In this essay I'm going to offer what I hope will be an extremely controversial argument—even to those who support, as I do, the availability of
safe and legal abortions for all women, regardless of age, race, income, or
special needs, on demand and without apology. I expect the controversy
about this argument to center on my effort to bring poststructuralist assumptions about the "death of man" to bear on the formulation of the abortion question, for, in practice, this conjunction calls into question the basic
tenets of liberal individualism—choice, privacy, and rights. I understand
that the implications of questioning these cherished ideals extend far beyond
the abortion debate, but my argument is that unless feminists who support
abortion on demand begin to rethink the gendered assumptions to which
these ideals are historically and metaphysically wed, we will inadvertently
reinforce the discriminatory legal concepts to which antiabortionists so effectively appeal.

Let me begin by discussing very briefly the two most common defenses
currently advanced in support of legal abortion—the privacy defense and
the defense of equality.[1] The first of these defenses, the privacy argument,
derives its authority from the Fourteenth Amendment's guarantee of due
process. As the Supreme Court has interpreted the due-process clause, individuals have been granted the right "to decide for themselves ethical and
personal issues arising from marriage and procreation."[2] Among these "personal issues," argue prochoice advocates, is a woman's right to decide whether
or not to carry a pregnancy to term. The second defense, the defense of
equality, recognizes that there is a "gender dimension" to the abortion issue.
As a consequence, advocates argue, antiabortion laws violate the equal-pro-

tection clause of the Fourteenth Amendment because they impose upon women burdens that men do not have to bear. Here is the commentary of one feminist lawyer:

> Although nature, not the state, has determined that women and not men shall become pregnant, innumerable state actions either mitigate or exacerbate the physical burdens of pregnancy that women alone bear. . . . Women's reproductive function does not make them unequal or oppressed; rather, the social demands placed upon them in connection with their reproductive functions oppress women. When state laws "den[y] women access to abortion, both nature and the state impose upon women burdens of unwanted pregnancy that men do not bear" [as well as] "very significant discomfort and health risks."[3]

Each of these defenses has much to recommend it. The privacy defense is appealing because it stresses the equality of women and men: like men, women should have the right to govern their own bodies. By contrast, the defense of equality is appealing because it acknowledges that, given the systemic oppression and devaluation of women in American society, women may not be *able* to act as autonomous agents in the "private" area of their sexuality. The legal notion of "privacy," in other words, may actually exacerbate sexual oppression because it protects domestic and marital relations from scrutiny and from intervention by government or social agencies.[4] The defense of equality combats the abuses to which women have been subjected in the *name* of sexual freedom by identifying reproductive difference as a difference that mandates protective interference.

The relative merits of these two positions have been discussed extensively in the literature on abortion.[5] Instead of going over this well-covered ground again, I want to direct my attention to the problems the two defenses introduce, for the heart of the assumption they share seems to me to be behind the impasse at which the abortion debate has now stalled. Only by identifying the reason for this impasse can advocates of abortion on demand understand what is really at stake in the abortion issue; only in the light of this understanding can we begin to forge a new political vocabulary in which to conduct the struggle.

The primary difficulty with the privacy defense, to my mind, is that, in postulating a realm of the "private" and an autonomous model of the individual, it ignores the extent to which social relations permeate the home and even such "personal" realms as sexual activity. In postulating an individual capable of "free choice," in other words, the privacy defense ignores the extent to which women have been subjected to violence, *especially* in relation to their sexuality.[6] The primary difficulty with the defense of equality seems to me to be the flip side of this blindness. In focusing on reproductive capacity as that which subjects women to systemic oppression, the equality defense makes reproductive capacity *the* defining characteristic of every woman.[7] The effect of this is not only to reinforce the *grounds* of sexism (i.e., the primacy *of* sexual difference), but also to marginalize all other forms of difference that exist among women—including race, income, and religious and sexual preference. In its attempt to protect all women from unequal treatment in relation to *men,* in other words, the defense of equality inevitably leaves some women subject to the unequal treatment virtually guaranteed in this society by their racial or class difference. The principle of exclusion inherent in the equality defense helps explain why race and class are rarely given extensive attention by advocates of this position; the fact that, even though they are not recognized by advocates of *sexual* equality, other differences are recognized in socioeconomic practice helps explain why race and class always return to haunt would-be supporters of equality.

Both of these defenses, in their attempts to draw upon and conform to legal reasoning, derive their authority from the Fourteenth Amendment to the United States Constitution. In so doing, they remain entrenched in a discourse about rights, which that document codifies as the basis of United States law. But using the language of rights exacts its price, for the language of rights coincides with—indeed, is inextricable from—a set of assumptions about the nature of the individual who is possessed of those rights, which is, in turn, intimately bound to a set of assumptions about gender.[8] My argument is that the problems introduced by the defenses of abortion I have just described are the inevitable consequences of retaining this discourse of rights, choice, and privacy. In order to explain why this is true, I need to elaborate the assumption basic to the discourse of rights, an assumption that philosophers describe as "the metaphysics of substance."[9]

The basic assumption of the metaphysics of substance is that every subject has a substantive being or "core" that precedes social and linguistic coding. This substantive "core," which is the philosophical and putatively "natural" ground for legal "personhood" and therefore for rights, is characterized by the capacity to reason, to exercise moral judgment, and to acquire language. By extension, the social contexts or relationships in which the person engages are understood to be external and incidental to the inner essence. Theoretically, the law simply recognizes the substantive core that pre-exists it and makes effective the rights that that core naturally possesses by virtue of its capacities. Despite the fact, however, that the law seems to recognize something that already exists, it actually creates that which it claims to recognize. The law creates the *effect* of a substantive core by "basing" rights on (the fiction of) that core. "Legal recognition is a real and circular process," according to Parveen Adams. "It recognizes the things that correspond to the definitions it constructs."[10]

One further dimension to the metaphysics of substance is crucial to understanding the abortion debate: this metaphysics is intimately bound to the social system of gender. Although the substantive being "recognized" by law seems to be merely human and therefore to precede gender, the "coherence" and "continuity" of the person are actually socially instituted and guaranteed only *by* the regulatory matrix of coherent gender norms. As Judith Butler has argued, the *"regulatory practices* of gender formation and division constitute identity, the internal coherence of the subject, indeed, the self-identical status of the person. . . . In other words, the 'coherence' and 'continuity' of the 'person' are not logical or analytic features of personhood, but, rather, socially instituted and maintained norms of intelligibility" that are anchored by "'intelligible' genders."[11] Coherence, in other words, is a property that belongs to our ideas about gender and to many of the institutionalizations of those ideas, *not* a property of the human subject.

"'Intelligible' genders," Butler continues, "are those which in some sense institute and maintain relations of coherence and continuity among sex, gender, social practice, and desire."[12] Thus the appearance of a coherent "core" within the "person" is not the reflection of something essential that is really there, but merely the *effect* of a set of social institutions that differentiate between people on the basis of a binary system of coherent genders. In order to attain its own internal coherence, moreover, this system of gender falsely and inadequately homogenizes each term of the binary opposition by reference to the supposedly natural "ground" of biological sex. The connection between gender, sex, sexual practice, and desire is socially constructed, of course, not natural, but, despite the fact that the slippage that can occur among these terms has become evident to almost everyone, the metaphysics of substance to which this equation is crucial remains largely invisible—partly because it is institutionalized and reinforced by the system of law that I have already discussed, a system based on individual identity and individual rights. The appearance of a "core" may be only the effect of the representational system of gender, in other words, but because it is the ground of one's legal status as a "person," it has real, institutional incarnations—including a set of "rights," some of which are inevitably differential according to sex because gender is a differential structure in our society.

Here it is important to see that there are actually two, overlapping differential structures at work. The very concept of rights is differential, as Wai-Chee Dimock explains: "a right exists only because there is something to which one is entitled, and entitled by virtue of something else; it exists only because there are others who must honor that entitlement, and the performance of whose obligation one can demand."[13] This differential structure of entitlement is mapped onto the differential structure of gender, which grants women identity and personhood *only in relation to* the identity and personhood of "man." In the metaphysics of substance, then, the idea of individual rights is not separable from the idea of individual identity, and this, in turn, is inextricably bound to a binary system of gendered norms that seems to but does not derive from sexual difference. When one uses the discourse of rights, one necessarily mobilizes this entire binary system of substantive, sexed difference, which necessarily introduces the two "problems" I identified in the abortion defenses: it establishes a system of rights that is differential according to sex and it subsumes one group of people into the falsely homogenized category "men" and sets this group in opposition to (and superiority over) another falsely homogenized category, "women."

The metaphysics of substance that is implicit in the discourse of rights is historically related to the basic tenets of individualism, from which the discourse of rights is derived. A cardinal feature of individualism as it was elaborated in the late seventeenth century and institutionalized in the eighteenth and nineteenth centuries was the constitution of maternity as the essence of the female subject. As Michel Foucault and others have argued, during the eighteenth and nineteenth centuries, the female body was constituted as a maternal body because the ideology of bourgeois individualism required maternity as a social practice over and above simple reproduction.[14] From this, it has seemed to follow not only that mother-love emanates from the body, in the form of maternal instinct, but also that the desire to be a mother motivates and lies at the heart of all female desire. Despite the changes that have occurred since the nineteenth century in family size, birth rate, and the frequency of women's paid employment (not to mention attitudes), this assumption about female nature persists in the laws that embody the metaphysics of this historical development. The institutionalization of this assumption in an entire battery of contemporary social practices, moreover, reinforces the feeling that the laws that were developed alongside it are ahistorical—simply natural and right. Behind it lies a set of entailments with dramatic implications for women–and men. For, if the normative woman is a mother, then the mother-nature of woman is one of the linchpins of sexed identity and therefore, by the oppositional logic of gender, one ground of the intelligible masculinity of men. If women are allowed to question or to reject their maternity, then not only is the natural (sexed) basis of rights in jeopardy, but so is the natural basis of female identity and, by implication, of masculine identity as well. From this perspective, in other words, the abortion debate is about what it means to accept–or reject–the notion that there is a "natural" basis for individual identity and therefore for individual rights and sexual identity.

I want to turn now to the two landmark constitutional decisions that have brought these issues before United States citizens and that have thus far set the terms of the abortion debate–*Roe v. Wade* (decided in 1973) and

Webster v. Reproductive Health Services of Missouri (1989). My reason for focusing on these two texts rather than elaborating the defenses of abortion I have already discussed is that these two decisions not only set out the metaphysics of substance that the defenses of abortion rights share, but also contain the terms upon which a new politics could be built.

The class-action suit brought by Jane Roe in 1971 was a challenge to the Texas criminal abortion statute, which criminalized any abortion not considered necessary to save the pregnant woman's life. The ruling handed down by the United States Supreme Court on 22 January 1973 essentially overturned the Texas law, thereby guaranteeing women the right to seek a legal, medically supervised abortion during the first trimester of pregnancy. For my purposes, the crucial articles of the decision are the following: (4) "the right to privacy encompasses a woman's decision whether or not to terminate her pregnancy"; (5) "a woman's right to terminate her pregnancy is not absolute, and may to some extent be limited by the state's legitimate interests in safeguarding the woman's health, in maintaining proper medical standards, and in protecting potential human life"; (6) "the unborn are not included within the definition of 'person' as used in the Fourteenth Amendment"; and (8) "from and after the end of the first trimester, and until the point in time when the fetus becomes viable, the state may regulate the abortion procedure only to the extent that such regulation relates to the preservation and protection of maternal health."[15] One leading interpretation of the core of this decision, as I have already pointed out, is the issue of individual privacy, which was further elaborated in *Roe* as follows: the United States Supreme Court recognizes that "certain areas or zones of privacy" are guaranteed by the Constitution, even though the Constitution does not specify this; that the "guarantee of a right of personal privacy" extends only to those "personal rights that can be deemed 'fundamental' or 'implicit in the concept of ordered liberty'"; and that "the right to privacy, founded upon the Fourteenth Amendment's concept of personal liberties and restrictions upon state action, is broad enough to encompass a woman's decision whether or not to terminate her pregnancy."[16]

Along the way toward reaching this definition of privacy, the Court also made two, related but potentially contradictory, decisions. The first was that the privacy of a pregnant woman could not be absolute. Her biological condition means not only that she is never really alone, but also that, at some point in the pregnancy, the state's interest in "potential human life" will rival its interest in the woman's right to privacy. "Because a pregnant woman cannot be isolated in her privacy," the majority decision reads, "carrying, as she does, an embryo and later a fetus, it is reasonable and appropriate for a state to decide that, at some point in time, another interest, such as the health of the mother or the interest in potential human life, becomes significantly involved, that the woman's right to privacy is no longer sole, and that any right to privacy which she possesses must be accordingly measured against such other interests" (*Roe* 154). This ruling necessitated the second decision I want to highlight: the determination of that "point in time" at which another interest—most problematically, that of the state on behalf of the fetus—becomes sufficiently "involved" to mandate curtailing the pregnant's woman's "fundamental" right to privacy.

Despite the Court's elaborate refusal to decide "when life begins,"[17] the question of the "point in time" at which the fetus acquires rights clearly had to be addressed, for the Court's strategy was to subsume the right of the pregnant woman to seek an abortion into the right to privacy that every "person," including the fetus at that critical point, is guaranteed. In a ruling remarkable for its rhetorical equivocations, the Court decided that the critical "point in time" was the moment of fetal "viability." "Viability," the Court declared, "is usually placed at about seven months (28 weeks) but may occur earlier, even at 24 weeks" (*Roe* 181). The basis for the Court's decision was declared to be "present medical knowledge": "at viability . . . the fetus . . . presumably has the capacity of meaningful life outside the mother's womb" (*Roe* 183). Elsewhere the Court added the further qualification: "albeit with artificial aid" (*Roe* 181).

Even before the Rehnquist Court pried open the ambiguity of fetal "viability" in the *Webster* decision, the language of *Roe* acknowledged that viability could never be stabilized as a precise "point." If the ambiguity of "meaningful" were not enough, all kinds of rhetorical qualifications surround the Court's descriptions of the timing and the likelihood of survival: "usually," "about," "may occur," "presumably." Despite this deliberate imprecision in defining fetal personhood, the Burger Court clearly intended to bring all of the thorny problems of the abortion issue into the relative clarity of the "fundamental" rights guaranteed by the Fourteenth Amendment. To do so, the Court had to simplify the pregnant woman into a single subject during the first trimester of the pregnancy, at the same time that it elaborated the viable fetus into a "person" during the last. The period in between the two was governed by considerations for the admittedly ambiguous category of "maternal health," and here we should note that in this phrase, as elsewhere in *Roe*, the pregnant woman has already begun to be represented as a mother. Since the temporal process that subsumes these trimesters is continuous, the Court further had to draw lines, which ought to but could not be exact, through this continuum in order to divide one period of time into three and one legal person into two.

However torturous the logic of *Roe*, its effect was to uphold for the woman the model of individual (sexed) identity that lies at the heart of the metaphysics of substance. Since the legal person that follows from (but seems to ground) this ruling can presumably exercise reason, the pregnant woman— like any other legal "person"—has the capacity and therefore the right to "choose." For the fetus, by contrast, *Roe* tried to reify another status, which is related to but not the same as legal personhood. Viability is defined as the potentiality for personhood, although the relationship between "meaningful life" and "personhood" remains unexamined. Presumably, viability is not identical to legal personhood, because the fetus does not have the biological capacity to reason, make decisions, or acquire language. The fetus, in short, is not autonomous physically (despite the illusions produced by laser imaging): nothing can be done for or to the viable fetus except through the medium of the woman's body or whatever technology stands in for the woman's body. The fetus, therefore, does not acquire the right to choose. Instead, it acquires the right to protection. The problem with this reasoning is that the Court was trying both to differentiate between and to connect a sociolegal status—that of personhood—and a biological state—that of viability. The Aristotelian concept it used to separate and link these two—the metaphysical concept of "potential"—naturalizes the relations among conception, gestation, and birth. As a teleological concept, "potential" assumes that the fetus will be brought to term; in so doing, it forecloses not only other possible outcomes of the pregnancy (such as a miscarriage) but also, and as a consequence, any effective differentiation between the biological state of "viability" and the sociolegal status of "person." The concept of "potential," in other words, actually undermines the very distinction it seems to create because it collapses the two states it wants to keep separate. Sixteen years after *Roe v. Wade,* the *Webster* decision elaborated and extended *Roe*'s paradoxical logic.

In many senses, the *Webster* decision was not so much a decision as a series of deferrals and refusals to decide. The case involved a Missouri statute, enacted in June 1986, and the successful challenge to this statute by five health-care professionals, who argued that the Missouri statute was unconstitutional because its various provisions violated a woman's Fourteenth Amendment rights.[18] Upon appeal, the United States Supreme Court reversed the lower court's reversal of the statute, arguing as follows: (1) the Supreme Court does not need to decide whether the Missouri preamble declaring that life begins at conception is constitutional; (2) the statute's injunction against using public facilities and employees to provide abortions places no governmental obstacles in the path of a woman who wants an abortion; and (3) that, as a consequence of (2), the question about the constitutionality of using public funds to counsel a woman about abortion is moot (*Webster* 412–13). Individual Justices concurred with and dissented from parts of this decision, as well as adding more opinions, including the opinion expressed by three Justices that *Roe's* trimester-and-viability framework should be struck down and the judgment expressed by one Justice that *Roe* should be explicitly overruled, instead of being evaded, as the *Webster* decision was so clearly doing.

The first point I want to make about *Webster* concerns its refusal to address the constitutionality of the Missouri preamble. This preamble, which set forth the "findings" of the Missouri legislature, stated "that the life of each human being begins at conception and that unborn children have protectable interests in life, health, and well-being." It further declared that the laws of Missouri were "to be interpreted to provide unborn children with all the rights, privileges, and immunities available to other persons . . . subject to the Federal Constitution" (*Webster* 410). In refusing to address the constitutionality of this preamble, *Webster* implicitly decided that a legislative body could proclaim the fetus—or "unborn child"—to be a person from conception. In other words, it explicitly politicized the decision about what constitutes life. At the same time, *Webster* implicitly extended *Roe's* bridge of "potential," which the Burger Court had used as much to distinguish between the sociolegal and the biological states as to connect them, in order to close the gap between conception and personhood. In so doing, the Rehnquist Court eliminated the requirement that a legal person be an autonomous, embodied individual.

In their ancillary opinion, Justices Rehnquist, White, and Kennedy explicitly attacked the trimester-and-viability rubric that *Roe* had used to block this extension. Their reasoning drew upon a number of issues: the (presumably) medical ambiguity of *Roe's* "rigid" trimester scheme, reflected in the fact that an error of as much as four weeks can be made in estimating gestational age; the legal incompatibility of *Roe's* pseudoexact language of "trimesters" and "viability" with the "general terms" of the Constitution; and the fact that it was not socially necessary for *Roe* to remove the abortion issue from the states by "balanc[ing] once and for all, by reference only to the calendar, the State's interest in protecting human life against the claims of a woman to decide whether or not to abort" (*Webster* 421). The burden of these Justices' complaints, in other words, concerned *Roe's* creation of distinctions. In all three instances, Rehnquist declared—the interpretive schema of trimesters and viability, the language of trimesters and viability, and the delineation of "fundamental rights" that underwrote *Roe's* protection of choice—*Roe* created distinctions that were not necessary in principle and that have proved unworkable in fact. In a passage that summarizes their overall objections, Rehnquist stated that "since the bounds of inquiry are essentially indeterminate, the result has been a web of legal rules that have become increasingly intricate, resembling a code of regulations rather than a body of constitutional doctrine" (*Webster* 420).

The authors of *Roe* had spun this "web of legal rules" in their attempt to contain the two ambiguous entities with which they dealt—the pregnant woman and the "potential human"—within the category of the individual "person" as recognized by the Fourteenth Amendment. In cutting through *Roe's* skein of fine distinctions, the authors of *Webster* implicitly acknowl-

edged the anomalous, nonunitary nature of these entities and therefore implicitly exposed the fact that the Constitution's language of individualized
rights is not adequate to cover all of the guises in which so-called persons
appear. Rather than pursuing the inadequacy of constitutional individualism,
of course, *Webster* took the opposite tack: it shored up the category of the
individual person by allowing states to extend their interest in "potential
human life" *throughout* a woman's pregnancy, as if the fetus were, from
the moment of conception, an individual with rights commensurate to those
of the pregnant woman. Whereas *Roe* had drawn a distinction not only between viable and nonviable, but also, at least implicitly, between viable and
autonomous or embodied, *Webster* obliterated both distinctions, in part through
appropriating and redeploying the critical concept of "potential."[19] In doing
so, *Webster* reinforced the constitutional groundwork for contests of interest
between a pregnant woman and the fetus she carries and, thus, between a
pregnant woman and the state acting on behalf of the fetus and the state's
own interest in "potential human life."

But such fetal rights contests had already begun to pepper state and
appellate courts before the 1989 *Webster* decision. In the 1977 case of *Simon
v. Mullin,* for example, the Connecticut Superior Court ruled that a "child
born alive" could sue for "prenatal injuries suffered at any time after conception, without regard to viability of fetus."[20] In 1978, a Missouri law
extended fetal rights even further, to a point *before* conception. In *Berstrasser v. Mitchell,* the United States Court of Appeals ruled that a child born
with brain damage because of injury inflicted to his mother's uterus during
a caesarian section for a prior delivery had an independent cause of action
against the physicians who performed the surgery before the child's conception.[21]

The timing of these cases, as well as the emphasis placed on fetal rights
by opponents of abortion even before *Webster,* reveals that the basis for
shifting the discussion about abortion to the issue of fetal rights was laid
not by *Webster* but by *Roe v. Wade.*[22] For, in locating the "point in time"
at which an individual acquires rights at a moment *before* birth through the
concepts of viability and "potential" life, *Roe* implicitly called attention to
the arbitrariness of relying on the biological state of embodiment for a definition of the social concept of "meaningful life" and, by extension, the
sociolegal concept of legal personhood. The ambiguity *Roe* left unexplored
in the relationship between "viability" and "meaningful" life therefore set
the stage for arguments that the fetus can be interpreted as a legal person,
and also, since even a viable fetus cannot act independently, for doctors and
the state to restrict a pregnant woman's rights in the name of the potential
child. *Roe's* attempt to stabilize the biological ambiguities of pregnancy and
to subsume these ambiguities into a sociolegal argument about "privacy"
and the right of an individual to "choose" obscured the importance of two

debates, which the abortion issue reveals to be crucial to renewing the legitimacy of the United States legal system: one is a debate about the political dimensions of the deployment of such metaphysical concepts as "rights" or "potential" life; the other is a discussion about the relationship between the biological and sociolegal concepts that underwrite the concept of a "person." In effect, *Roe* reasserted the metaphysics of substance without examining either the extent to which the assumptions inherent in this metaphysics are always political or the fact that one of the entities the decision endowed with legal personhood was not substantive in the biological sense that the social rules of gendered identity assume: *Roe* implicitly granted the fetus some of the properties of a gendered subject even though this subject does not have an autonomous, sexed body. Following this logic, there is no reason not to grant personhood to an egg or a sperm or, for that matter, to an organ or tissue that one wants (or does not want) to donate or sell to someone else.[23] By the same token, unless the relationship between biological embodiment and sociolegal personhood can be worked out there is no obvious reason to grant personhood to an infant upon birth, since a neonate is no more capable of independent life than is the fetus. Pregnancy, abortion, and the fierce debates that have materialized around the latter make it clear that these issues need to be aired. Indeed, the crisis of legitimacy that now torments the legal community may well result from the profession's continued reluctance to subject these problems to a public discussion.

I am not arguing that the *Webster* decision was somehow "better" than *Roe,* either in its legal exactness or in its implications for women, just as I would not argue that the equality defense is a better defense of legalized abortion than the privacy argument. I do think, however, that the *Webster* decision has begun to reveal why the metaphysics of substance constitutes an inadequate basis for all the arguments thus far advanced for the right to legal abortions. Most obviously, *Webster* has disclosed the fact that the central terms abortion advocates have tried to defend are susceptible to appropriation and reactionary redeployment by abortion opponents. In the mouths of antiabortionists, "choice," "privacy," and "rights" invert effortlessly into their opposites, precisely because, regardless of who uses them, these terms belong to a single set of metaphysical assumptions. In its attempt to avoid a head-on confrontation with *Roe,* for example, the Rehnquist Court argued that cutting off funding to all public facilities and employees did not really limit a woman's right to choose an abortion. Curtailing public funds, the Justices argued, "left a pregnant woman with the same choices as if the state had chosen not to operate any public hospitals at all" (*Webster* 411). The strategy here was obviously to preserve the individual's right to choose guaranteed by the Fourteenth Amendment. This, of course, is the same strategy proprivacy advocates have used to defend abortion. Even though the meaning of "choice" has significantly altered, the *Webster* decision makes it clear that, once the concept of individual choice is granted, it is very difficult to decide what choices will be declared legitimate.

Beyond this, the *Webster* ruling also exposes the limitation inherent in the very notion of individualized, "free" choice. If the state "chooses" to operate no public hospitals, after all, the individual will only be "free" to "choose" a private hospital. This means, in effect, that only women who have enough money to hire a private doctor can "choose" to abort an unwanted pregnancy and then only if private doctors are trained and willing to perform abortions. The *Webster* ruling also exposes the limitations of the privacy defense by demonstrating the unreliability of that concept. The statute effectively limits abortions to clinics that are so private that they do not even lease land from the state (or, some lawyers argue, use public water or sewers), thereby once more making abortion an option only for women whose "private" income is sufficient to hire physicians with no sources of public funding at all (if any exist). The *Webster* decision's combined emphasis on rights and restrictions, then, brings into stark relief the instability of the abstractions contained in the metaphysical concept of rights. Because this inherent instability must always be stabilized in practice by the socioeconomic circumstances in which individuals and social institutions exist, moreover, the *Webster* decision also reveals that the argument for abstract rights will always simultaneously mask and assume a set of social conditions that actually defines those rights and delimits who has access to them. Once exercised, "rights" and "choice" cannot remain abstract, and the concrete situation in which they are embedded limits what these concepts mean and who will be able to exercise them. It is because of the situatedness of practice, not incidentally, that the differences of race and class always return to haunt the abortion issue once an abortion statute has been implemented, for in practice and in everyday situations, race and class are determinants that often make more difference than sex.

The individualism implied by the metaphysics of substance is a dead end for supporting abortion on demand for two reasons: first, because the appeal to individual rights *in the absence of* an interrogation of the metaphysical assumptions behind the idea of rights leads almost inevitably to a proliferation of those considered to have rights—in other words, to a defense of fetal personhood; second, because appeals to this metaphysics obscure the fact that both the metaphysics and legal persons are always imbricated in a system of social relations, which, given the existence of social differences, are also inevitably politicized. Indeed, under the United States Constitution, human beings can be legal persons only as a *consequence* of their place in at least one system of social relations—the system of gender, which is, but does not seem to be, the basis for the metaphysics of substance. My argument, then, is that we need to change not just the terms but the tenor of the abortion debate. As long as we engage in what is essentially a metaphysical debate about abstract rights, choice, and privacy, we will remain blind to the fact that metaphysics can be used to reify and rationalize a set of social practices that prohibit access to concrete rights, choices, and privacy. Once we acknowledge the embeddedness of these categories in the social fabric, we will be able to develop another set of arguments, which appeals not to the metaphysics of substance and the individualized, autonomous subject, but to the discursive and institutional networks of social relations that destabilize this individualized subject even as they extend our analysis of subjectivity beyond the autonomous "person."

I will sketch out one version of this alternative politics, but I need to preface my suggestions with two caveats. In the first place, given the antiessentialist position I have been arguing, it would be hypocritical for me to claim absolute authority for my own ideas. If practice, as I have been suggesting, always reflects its embeddedness in the system of social meanings and relations, then no theoretical argument that imports or derives its authority from a metaphysical position should be used to pass judgment on all practices as if they were interchangeable. At most, the kind of suggestion I will offer has the status of a self-consciously politicized contribution to a cultural debate that should have many participants.

In the second place, and following from my antiessentialist position, I suggest that no individual can know what is best or fair for every other individual (including the people she deems to be "like herself"). Indeed, I suggest that no individual who conceptualizes herself as an isolated unit can even know what is best for herself, since the differential concept of "best" implies knowing all the possible options and their outcomes in advance—a knowledge that would inevitably have to extend to the social relations that help structure those options and outcomes. Beyond this, the claim that the individual knows what is best for herself implies that no one ever wanted two, mutually exclusive things at the same time—that, in other words, desire is singular and consciousness the center of the individual. These comments should prepare the way for the shift I now want to make from a mode of thinking that focuses on the individual to one that proposes another conceptualization of the legal unit.

Ironically, the terms of the alternative politics I will outline here have already been introduced into the abortion debate by its most conservative participants—those people who endorse the idea of fetal personhood. The fetal personhood argument, after all, makes it clear that the embodied individual is only one of many possible interpretations of what counts as a legal person possessed of rights. This position therefore introduces the possibility that legal personhood might be assigned to some unit that is lesser or greater than the embodied individual. Beyond this, the attempts by *Roe* and *Webster* to salvage the individualized, sexed, legal subject while suspending the requirement that this "person" be physically autonomous have inadvertently called attention to two other possible conceptualizations of the subject—one that emphasizes the heterogeneity or nonunitary nature of the individual (and therefore equates personhood with a subset of the embodied individual) and another that stresses the social nature of personhood (and therefore assigns the status of "person" to a unit greater than the individual). If the law acknowledged that it has already upon occasion suspended the necessity of linking personhood to embodiment, then a politics that was not based on the individual, sexed body would make legal as well as practical sense. This politics would not be based on the individual, sexed body. It would not consider one's biological sex the most important determinant of some unitary identity, nor would it imagine the individual to be separable from the social relations in which every person is inevitably bound. Instead of attempting to ensure abstract rights for the individualized legal subject, this politics would strive to create the social conditions in which the heterogeneity of the individual could be accommodated and in which community debates would determine what is considered socially acceptable and fair behavior in the light of the recognition that all behaviors—including those that seem to involve only the individual body—are expressions of relationships that entail difference as well as community. Basically, this nonindividualistic politics would work to complicate and elaborate our commonsense notion of "self." It would emphasize not the ways in which subjects are isolatable, autonomous, centered individuals, but the ways in which each person has conflicting interests and complex ties to other, apparently autonomous individuals with similar (and different) interests and needs.

In terms of the abortion issue more specifically, this nonindividualistic politics would emphasize two things: first, the fact that every woman experiences many reproductive opportunities in her life, not all of which she wants to eventuate in a child; and second, the fact that any pregnancy, perhaps especially an unwanted pregnancy, affects the network of social relations in which the pregnant woman is involved (not just her relation to an individual man, but also to her family, her employer or employees, the health-care system, the social-welfare system and, through that, the tax system that indirectly involves every taxpayer). The first of these emphases would place abortion in the context of contraception, not murder. The second would place it alongside other services that recognize social needs—such services as prenatal care, child day-care for working parents, and medical care for those unable to care for themselves. Far from making the abortion issue more arcane or difficult to identify with, this repositioning of abortion within the landscape of contemporary issues might well increase the number of people willing to support abortion on demand, for it would align advocates of safe and legal abortions with the millions of women and men who support safe and effective birth control and with the growing numbers of people who endorse plans for day care and parental leave, as well as some system of subsidized health care capable of guaranteeing affordable medical service to everyone.

Casting the abortion issue in these terms represents a critical alternative to the metaphysics of substance because dispensing with the body as the necessary and sufficient criterion for legal personhood forecloses the possibility that sex will be isolated as the determining feature of one's identity. In so doing, of course, it also works against subsuming all women into the homogeneous category "woman," juxtaposing this falsely homogenized category to the generic "man," and—perhaps most importantly—marginalizing or erasing other kinds of difference, including race, class, age, and sexual preference. In refusing the assumption that "identity" is based on some "core" that the law recognizes, this suggestion dispenses with the (unrealistic) expectation that any human being will want the same thing throughout a lifetime or that desire will necessarily be aligned with reproductive potential. By returning the individual, who is now conceptualized as a heterogeneous rather than homogeneous entity, to its place within social relations, moreover, this solution insists that for a concept like "choice" to make sense, it will have to be conceptualized as a social issue and in a social arena: that is, a variety of options will have to be made available and supported with equal social resources. In the case of reproductive choice, these options would include not only access to safe and legal abortions but also to pre- and postnatal care and to day-care facilities.

The reconceptualization I am suggesting would entail fundamental alterations in the way most people now think of themselves and others, because it ultimately challenges what seems to be the primacy of one's immediate experience of (and fantasies about) the body. It also challenges the system of legal entitlements that is not only tied to the concept of an isolatable body but also wedded to the contradictory notion that the majority of these bodies are ruled by self-aware, self-consistent faculties of reason, which will act for the greater good of society even if this means sacrificing personal pleasure or gain. Such a reconceptualization is obviously difficult to campaign for; in all its ramifications, it is even difficult to imagine, given all the institutional and representational bulwarks that shore up the individualistic status quo. I do not, however, think that the details of this reconceptualization are difficult to imagine. When I argue that one's reproductive potential is not the only, or the most important constituent of one's being, after all, I am agreeing with everyone who believes that a woman's place should not be limited to the home, that mother should not be the only role a woman is allowed, and that legal discrimination should not follow sexual difference. When I argue that an unwanted pregnancy warrants the same level of health care as a pregnancy that will be brought to term—and that the same woman can experience both in a lifetime—I am agreeing with everyone who wants to combat the kind of moralization and individualization of women's sexual activity that holds only the woman responsible for sexual self-control. In practice, the details of the antiessentialist position I have outlined are attacks on the sexual double standard, which lies at the heart of the metaphysics of substance and therefore lurks in the concept of rights as it has been institutionalized in this country.

I confess that I'm not sure that the discourse of rights could—or even should—be jettisoned completely at this moment. Given the political capital this discourse has accrued in the history of the United States, perhaps it should simply be reworked—as some feminists are now trying to do—so as to serve as a bridge between the old, absolutist metaphysics, whose politics remain masked but not inoperative, and a new, situational or conditional conceptualization of entitlements and restraints.[24] I am certain, however, that the discourse of rights needs to be subjected to a rigorous interrogation, not just by legal scholars and academics but by everyone involved in the political process that is theoretically legitimized by the discourse of rights. The abortion issue has brought crucial questions about entitlement and the politics of the law to the attention of more United States citizens than any issue since civil rights. Perhaps the passion that now attends the debate about whether or not the fetus is a person could be redirected toward the issues that lie behind this single question. I hope that whatever controversy this essay provokes will become part of the debate that will make some new conceptualization of these issues possible.

NOTES

For their help with this essay I would like to thank Judith Butler, Jane Caplan, Ruth Leys, Norma Moruzzi, Joan W. Scott, and the audiences at Queen's University and the Columbia Society for the Study of Medicine and Society.

1. An extremely helpful overview of these arguments is provided by Frances Olsen, "Unraveling Compromise," *Harvard Law Review*, 103 (November 1989), pp. 105–35. In several places, my own analysis of these arguments echoes Olsen's.

2. Ronald Dworkin, "The Great Abortion Case," *New York Review of Books*, 29 June 1989, p. 51. See also Ronald Dworkin, "The Future of Abortion," *New York Review of Books*, 28 September 1989, pp. 47–51.

3. Frances Olsen, "Unraveling," p. 119, n. 68. Olsen is discussing Sylvia Law's "Rethinking Sex and the Constitution," *University of Pennsylvania Law Review* (1984).

4. See Frances Olsen, "Unraveling," pp. 111–13.

5. In addition to the essays and books cited elsewhere in this essay, I especially recommend the following recent studies of the abortion issue and gender and the law: Catharine A. MacKinnon, "Privacy v. Equality: Beyond Roe v. Wade," in *Feminism Unmodified: Discourses on Life and Law* (Cambridge, Mass.: Harvard University Press, 1987), pp. 93–116; Martha Minow, "Justice Engendered," *Harvard Law Review*, 101 (November 1987), pp. 10–

95; Rosalind Pollack Petchesky, *Abortion and Woman's Choice: The State, Sexuality, and Reproductive Freedom* (Boston: Northeastern University Press, 1985); and Lawrence H. Tribe, *Abortion: The Clash of Absolutes* (New York: W. W. Norton & Co., 1990).

6. Catharine MacKinnon also criticizes the privacy argument, stating that the very concept of privacy assumes that "injuries arise in violating the private sphere, not within and by and because of it" (*Feminism Unmodified*, p. 100).

7. See Jed Rubenfeld, "The Right of Privacy," *Harvard Law Review*, 102 (1989), p. 782; and Frances Olsen's criticism of Rubenfeld, "Unraveling," pp. 112–13, note 32.

8. A very thoughtful analysis of the contemporary debate about rights within the legal community is provided by Martha Minow, "Interpreting Rights: An Essay for Robert Cover," *Yale Law Journal*, 96 (1987), pp. 1860–1915.

9. For a discussion of the metaphysics of substance, see Judith Butler, *Gender Trouble: Feminism and the Subversion of Identity* (New York and London: Routledge, 1990), pp. 10, 16–21, 141.

10. Parveen Adams and Jeff Minson, "The 'Subject' of Feminism," *m/f*, 2 (1978), p. 50.

11. Judith Butler, *Gender Trouble*, pp. 16, 17.

12. Judith Butler, *Gender Trouble*, p. 17.

13. Wai-Chee Dimock, "Rightful Subjectivity," *Yale Journal of Criticism*, 4, 1 (1990), p. 28. I take the term "differential structure" from Dimock's provocative discussion.

14. See Michel Foucault, *The History of Sexuality, Part I: An Introduction*, translated by Robert Hurley (New York: Vintage Books, 1980), and Jacques Donzelot, *The Policing of Families*, translated by Robert Hurley (New York: Random House, 1979).

15. *Roe v. Wade*, 93 *Supreme Court Reporter* 705 (U.S. Supreme Court 1973), p. 148.

16. *Roe*, p. 153; see also p. 177. See also Justice Douglas's concurring opinion, pp. 185–89.

17. Here is the famous passage: "We need not resolve the difficult question of when life begins. When those trained in the respective disciplines of medicine, philosophy, and theology are unable to arrive at any consensus, the judiciary, at this point in the development of man's knowledge, is not in a position to speculate as to the answer" (*Roe* 181).

18. *William L. Webster v. Reproductive Health Services et al.*, 106 *United States Supreme Court Reports*, pp. 410–71.

19. See Joanna Weinberg, "Feeling the Chill Wind," *Women's Review of Books* (October 1989), p. 18.

20. *Simon v. Mullin*, 380 A. 2d 1353 (Conn. 1977). For discussions of this and other fetal-rights cases, I am indebted to Katherine A. White, "Precedent and Process: The Impending Crisis of Fetal Rights," unpublished paper, University of Illinois (1989).

21. *Berstrasser v. Mitchell*, 577 f. 2d 22 (1978).

22. See Joanna Weinberg, "Feeling the Chill Wind," p. 19.

23. The case of Moore v. The Regents of the University of California has raised the question of an individual having the right to his or her own body in this sense. The California Supreme Court ruled in July 1990 that John Moore did not have proprietary rights to the spleen that was surgically removed in 1976. By contrast, in September 1989, a Tennessee state court ruled that frozen embryos did have a special legal status—in fact, they were awarded the status of "potential life" when the court granted custody of these embryos to Mary Sue Davis, the woman who produced the eggs. For a discussion of the implications of such decisions for

women, see Rex B. Wingerter, "Fetal Protection Becomes Assault on Motherhood," *In These Times,* 10–23 June 1987, pp. 3, 8.

24. For one legal theorist's attempt to reconsider rights from a feminist point of view, see Minow, "Interpreting Rights." In her essay, Wai-Chee Dimock proposes that we consider the concept of *prima facie* rights. "These are rights which are more or less provisional, which remain sovereign while left to themselves, but can be overridden should a superior right intervene." This notion challenges the "stability of the concept of rights, because, in making rights relative rather than absolute, conditional rather [than] universal, [it] also eliminate[s] the ground from which rights derive their transcendent authority. In a contingent universe, rights are very much a situational variant: less than inalienable, and hence less than natural" ("Rightful Subjectivity," p. 33).

13

"Shahbano"

Zakia Pathak and *Rajeswari Sunder Rajan*

In April 1985, the Supreme Court of India, the highest court of the land, passed a judgment in favor of Shahbano in the case of Mohammad Ahmed Khan, appellant, versus Shahbano and others, respondents.[1] The judgment created a furor unequaled, according to one journal, since "the great upheaval of 1857."[2]

The Supreme Court confirmed the judgment of the High Court awarding Shahbano, a divorced Muslim woman, maintenance of Rs 179.20 (approximately $14) per month from her husband, Mohammad Ahmed Khan, and dismissed the husband's appeal against the award of maintenance under section 125 of the 1973 Code of Criminal Procedure.[3]

For Shahbano this victory came after ten years of struggle. A lower court had awarded her only Rs 25 a month (the average daily wage of a laborer in India is Rs 11.50, or roughly a dollar). Shahbano was not the first Muslim woman to apply for (and be granted) maintenance under the 1973 Code of Criminal Procedure.[4] The repercussions of the Supreme Court judgment therefore took many, including the government, by surprise. When some by-elections fell due in December 1985, the sizable Muslim vote turned against the ruling party (the Congress-I) partly because it supported the judgment. Its candidate at Kishengunj, although a Muslim, was defeated by the opposition's Muslim candidate, Syed Shahabuddin, who would play a major role in the events that followed. When an independent member of Parliament, a Muslim, introduced a bill to save Muslim personal law (with the support of the Muslim Personal Law Board), the ruling party reversed its earlier position and resorted to a whip to ensure the bill's passage. The bill was passed in May 1986 and became the Muslim Women (Protection of Rights in Divorce) Act.

The relationship of state or secular law to personal or religious law has always been a vexed one in India. Although Hinduism is the majority religion, there are sizable minority populations.[5] Most rulers, including the British, recognizing that interference in religious issues could be explosive in its consequences, respected the traditional laws of religious communities in personal matters relating to family and inheritance rights. As a result, matters relating to the family (such as marriage, divorce, maintenance, succession to property, inheritance, and custody and guardianship of children, as well as adoption), which came to be known as "personal laws" and would vary from one religious community to another, remained uncodified. During the nineteenth century, however, several British acts and legislative measures empowered the courts to recognize and apply local customs and usages; these often prevailed uniformly over an area, irrespective of religion. In fact, in some instances, they were less liberal than religious laws, as in the case of Muslim women and property inheritance. It was largely due to this conflict that the Shariat Law was passed in 1937. The Shariat Law provides that Muslims in India will be governed by Muslim religious laws in matters relating to the family.

In 1949, when the Constitution of Independent India was framed, the founding fathers saw the necessity of continuing to recognize personal law at the same time that, moved by the unifying secular impulse, they also declared as an objective of the state the adoption of a uniform civil code (art. 44). (Other articles of the constitution that relate to religious freedom are art. 14, which guarantees the right to equal protection of laws; art. 15, which forbids discrimination on grounds only of religion, race, caste, sex, place of birth, and so forth; art. 25, which guarantees freedom of religion and conscience; and art. 29, which guarantees to minorities the right to conserve their culture.)

The interests of women in this dual legal structure are particularly vulnerable to exploitation by alliance of religious and secular interests. Personal law concerns women intimately, pronouncing as it does on marriage, divorce, maintenance, adoption, succession, and inheritance. Women's-rights activists in India have long been protesting against the gender-discriminatory nature of the personal laws of all religious communities which regulate most spheres of women's activity. Under all personal laws, the male is the head of the family and succession is through the male line—women have no right to inherit an equal share of property, and the father is the natural guardian of minor children.[6] Since 1872, divorced and abandoned women of all faiths have been regularly applying for maintenance under the Criminal Procedure Code (which relates to "maintenance of wives, children and parents").[7]

The religion of the divorced woman seeking maintenance under section 488 of the 1872 code piloted by Sir James Fitzjames (forerunner to sec. 125 of the Code of Criminal Procedure, 1973) was immaterial. Since criminal-law procedures are quicker and more effective than civil-law procedures, many divorced women of all communities (by appealing under a legal provision intended primarily to prevent vagrancy) bypassed the personal law of their religions.

Muslim fundamentalists have been disturbed by what they perceive as a trend away from honoring religious law. The Shahbano judgment gave them an opportunity to mount an attack on what they perceived as the Hindus' homogenizing influence, an influence that would eventually lead to the assimilation and destruction of Muslim identity. The Muslim Personal Law Board intervened in the Shahbano case on behalf of the husband and, having been unsuccessful in the Supreme Court, carried the battle to Parliament.

Under the provisions of the Muslim Women (Protection of Rights in Divorce) Act, divorced Muslim women would fall outside the purview of section 125 of the Code of Criminal Procedure. According to this newly codified Muslim personal law, the divorced woman's husband is obliged only to return the *mehr* (dower, or marriage settlement) and pay her maintenance during the period of *iddat* (the period of three months following the divorce). If the divorced woman is not able to maintain herself after the *iddat* period, her maintenance will be the responsibility of her children, or parents, or those relatives who would be entitled to inherit her property upon her death; if she has no relatives or if they have no means to pay her maintenance, the magistrate may direct the State *Wakf* Boards (administrators of Muslim trust funds) to pay the maintenance determined by him.

This has not resolved the crisis sparked by the Supreme Court judgment in favor of Shahbano, however. The Muslim community continues to find itself divided into "progressives" (those supporting the judgment) and "fundamentalists" (those opposing it). The act has been challenged in the courts. The government of India, possibly in an attempt to appease feminists and Muslim progressives and to refurbish its secular image, is engaged in drafting a uniform civil code.

The terms "fundamentalist" and "progressive" have been used both descriptively and pejoratively in this debate when referring to the positions of Muslim groups on their personal law. Syed Shahabuddin, the acknowledged spokesman for the Muslim-fundamentalist position and president of the Muslim *Majlis-e-Mushawarat,* accepts the term "fundamentalist" as accurately descriptive of his allegiance to the Quran: "Historically, the Quran was revealed to the Prophet 1400 years ago but it is the final message of God to mankind. Not one syllable is subject to change. . . . It is in this sense that the Muslim is by definition a fundamentalist."[8]

Arif Mohammed Khan, Muslim minister in the government of India, who, at its behest, initially defended the Supreme Court judgment and subsequently refused to follow the government when it reversed its position, rejects such fundamentalism: "My faith has always been progressive on matters relating to women. . . . The Prophet's grandson gave his wife 10,000 *dirhams* while divorcing her. It was to clear doubts on this that God revealed verse 11.241 that says: 'And for the divorced women let there be a fair provision.'" He goes on to say: "Gandhi was shown black flags across the country when he spoke against untouchability. Any suggestion of change or reform upsets fundamentalists and that should not deter any progressive person, least of all a right thinking Muslim."[9] Thus the term "progressives" defines those Muslims who endorse reform in the personal law.

Some experts on Islamic law, however, deride those Muslims who demand the uniform civil code: "They want to project their image as progressives and support the demand without knowing what they are talking about."[10] The term "fundamentalist" is also applied to extremist members of the Hindu religious parties who, as part of a sustained anti-Muslim campaign, opposed the Muslim Women Bill.

In what follows, we explore the sense of crisis produced in a society through a women's issue and the possibilities for change that it may provoke. From the narrative of Shahbano we describe the formation of a discontinuous female subjectivity in response to the displacement of the Muslim woman question onto several discourses. These discourses are marked, and unified, by the assumptions of an ideology of protection. We explore the possibilities of resistance within such a discourse. Our notion of a "subaltern consciousness" assumes an operative "will" that functions as resistance; it destabilizes the family's ideology of protection and the law's ideology of evolution. Thus a space is created from which a woman can speak.

Discursive Displacements

To be framed by a certain kind of discourse is to be objectified as the "other," represented without the characteristic features of the "subject," sensibility and/or volition.[11] The Muslim woman, as subject, is either absent or fragmented in the various legal, religious, sexual, and political texts that develop into a discourse supposedly about her. Discourse, in this conceptual sense, works in fact only by significantly excluding certain possibilities (in this case full representation of the subject). It achieves its internal coherence by working within parameters which are ideologically fixed. The different textual strands achieve discursive coherence by these two related procedures, that is, exclusion and limitation within ideologically fixed boundaries. Working within the contours of a conceptually unified field, discourse seeks to produce knowledge. Such knowledge is implicated in the structures of power.

At this level, social action itself is textualized into legal, religious, political, and other texts. In any stable society, the texts must exist harmoniously. This harmony is disturbed and a crisis results when a proposition accommodated in one text is displaced onto another.

We do not want to invoke an actual Freudian/psychoanalytic narrative of history. But we do wish to suggest, analogically, that both the decentering and the substitution of the "truth" of a situation, which are characteristics of the "disguise" that the dream wears,[12] are diagnosable in the route traveled by the plea for maintenance initiated by Shahbano.

The narrative of displacement begins when this plea for maintenance moved out of domestic discourse into the realm of law and law courts, when Shahbano, a woman of seventy-three, after over forty years of marriage, was driven out of her house by the triple pronouncement of *talaq* (oral and unilateral divorce) by her husband.

The narrative intersects with religious discourse when the Muslim Personal Law Board intervenes for the husband in the Supreme Court. Daniel Latifi, counsel for Shahbano, located the significance of the case in the elevation of the Muslim Personal Law Board:

> Why was the Bill brought forward at all? . . . Some Machiavelli seems to have masterminded this entire operation. . . . The act that preceded the Bill, the recognition of the so-called Muslim Personal Law Board as a College of Cardinals for Indian Muslims is not only against Islam but is also the most flagrant exercise of a power-drunk autocracy since Caligula installed Incitatus, his favourite horse, as Governor of Rome. The Muslim intelligentsia who have opposed this Act will continue the struggle against this illegitimate Papacy.[13]

The discourse now appears in the area of electoral politics. A cover story of the influential magazine, *India Today,* traced the trajectory of the case: "[Shahbano's] search for a small sustenance has led to an unprecedented Islamic resurgence, not seen in the country for decades. . . . More vitally, it threatens to upset the very electoral equation on which the arithmetic of national political fortunes has been based since Independence." The article goes on to detail the reverses suffered by the Congress-I in the by-elections in Uttar Pradesh, Assam, and Gujarat.[14]

After the judgment, the battle is joined in Parliament. Reformists and activists continued the debate into the liberal discourse of secularism and constitutional rights. Kuldip Nayar, a leading journalist who pressed for a secular solution, asked: "Should the country join issue with the community on a point which is a non-issue? Some argue that one thing will lead to another; probably it will if we continue to concentrate our attention and energy on non-issues like maintenance of a divorced woman in Muslim society."[15]

Fundamentalists, both Muslim and Hindu, take up positions. Syed Shahabuddin, M. P., depersonalized Shahbano completely while relocating her predicament within a Muslim identity problematic:

> In the current turmoil, the Shahbano case, celebrated as it became, recedes into the background and pales into insignificance. Stripped to its bones, the case was no more than a conflict of opinion among the Muslims on whether what is desirable can be made obligatory, whether a recommendation [in the Quran] to treat the divorcees generously can be made into a legal mandate. Thus it was a very limited issue though the Muslim Indians saw it as the beginning of state interference with the Shariat.[16]

Once the disturbances of the peace break out, the discourses can no longer be kept clear of each other.

The displacements nonetheless continue. In an attempt to assert her faith and restore communal harmony, Shahbano is driven to announce her rejection of the Supreme Court's judgment, asserting her Muslim loyalty. (We see in this the attempt to highlight the Muslim identity problematic at the expense of all others.) The counterattempt to anchor the crisis in a limited legal discourse has resulted in a challenge to the Muslim Women Act in the Supreme Court. The drafting of a common civil code is promised by the government.

Where, in all these discursive displacements, is Shahbano the woman?[17] Has the discourse on the Muslim woman, torn away from its existential moorings, sucked her in and swallowed her up? Though, as the pronouncements above show, the several discourses attend to only one or the other dimension of her identity, the dominant consciousness tends to homogenize the subaltern subject for its purposes:[18] here as that which is to be "protected."

The Discourse of Protection

All the parties to the discourse share the common assumption that they are protecting the Muslim woman; but statements from the discourse reveal the ubiquity of this argument, either as a claim or as a rebuttal:

> This Government will never deviate from the path of protecting the legitimate interests of the minority. (Asoke Sen, law minister)

> The Bill intends to safeguard the majority voice of the community. (Syed Shahabuddin, Opposition Muslim member of Parliament)

> The Bill protects the husbands who would divorce their wives. (Zoya Hassan, Muslim women's-rights activists)

We have to protect ourselves from such protection. (Justice Chowdhary,
Supreme Court judge)[19]

"Protection" can confer upon the protector the right to interfere in areas
hitherto out of bounds or the authority to speak for the silent victim; or it
can serve as a camouflage for power politics. An alliance is formed between
protector and protected against a common opponent from whom danger is
perceived and protection offered or sought, and this alliance tends to efface
the will to power exercised by the protector. Thus the term conceals the
opposition between protector and protected, a hierarchical opposition that
assigns higher value to the first term: strong/weak, man/woman, majority/
minority, state/individual.

At the propositional level, we understand the discourse of protection as
meaning-in-use. By this we mean language in a contextual frame, that is,
as having a certain meaning in communication which cannot be accounted
for by its grammatical or objective properties.[20] Considered thus, utterances
are explicable only in terms of the activities in which they play a role and
in the way they negotiate relationships (therefore, to ask whether these propositions are true or false is to miss the force which informs the sentences).
Three such propositions from the discourse of protection that show sentential
force are:

Hindu men are saving Muslim women from Muslim men.
Islam is in danger.
The perceptions of the minority community must govern the pace of change.

The attack of Hindu fundamentalists (often members of communalist
political parties like Shiv Sena, Vishwa Hindu Parishad, Rashtriya Swayam
Sevak Sangh) upon the proposed Muslim Women Act, upon Muslim religious law in general, and upon the Muslim community at large on behalf
of oppressed Muslim women translates into the proposition "Hindu men are
saving Muslim women from Muslim men."[21] It is a bizarre as well as sinister
claim. It invokes the stereotypes of the Muslim woman as invariably destitute, and the Muslim male as polygamous, callous, and barbaric. This scenario clears the way for Hindu intervention in the form of a demand for
reform or outright removal of the Muslim personal law. The protection of
women of a minority community thus emerges as the ploy of a majority
community to repress the religious freedom of that minority and ensure its
own dominance.

When the interventionary intentions of the protection of Muslim women
became clear, the cry "Islam is in danger!" was sounded from within the
community. Some Muslim women's organizations also opposed the judg-

ment for the same reason. The government gave primacy to the Muslims' perception that their community identity was threatened.[22]

When the government somersaulted and supported the bill that created the Muslim Women Act, it came under pressure to explain its *volte face,* which was widely seen as panicked capitulation to the fundamentalist lobby in order to ensure the ruling party's political future. Speaking on its behalf in Parliament, Minister K. C. Pant declared that what mattered was not whether the Supreme Court was right or wrong, but how the Muslims perceived it. Law Minister Sen also emphasized this.[23]

By adopting "perception theory," the government was able to present the situation as a conflict of two minority interests, that is, Muslim versus woman. Calling upon all the power of Solomon to adjudicate in the matter, it assumed its traditional benevolent role, its commitment to the protection of all minorities. The real exigencies of power struggles in party politics were successfully down-played in this deployment of the ideology of protection. When the government emerged to take up its role, it was as deus ex machina. In response to the accusation implicit in the Supreme Court judgment, as well as in Hindu-fundamentalist attacks, that Islam offered inadequate protection to women, influential members of Parliament argued that the provisions for women in Muslim religious laws were liberal and farsighted. The proposed Muslim Women Act was persuasively presented as a means of protecting women's rights: instead of being dependent on the whims of a recalcitrant and hostile ex-husband, the Muslim woman by the provisions of the new act would be able to fall back on the affection and duty of the natal family, and failing that, the *Wakf* Board. In this way her protection would be guaranteed. By passing the bill and foregrounding these arguments in favor of the progressiveness of the provisions for divorced women in Muslim religious law, the government successfully "protected" both Muslims in general and Muslim women in particular.[24]

The government's strategy of reconciling these conflicts is not one that liberal intellectuals have been able to adopt, since the act is clearly regressive. Yet, the sensitivity of the minority community to any form of interference in their personal law makes a primarily feminist position, that is, outright condemnation of the act, equally difficult to adopt. An article in *Manushi,* a leading feminist journal, expressed it this way:

> [A] minority community's reactions have a logic of their own and cannot be lightly dismissed, especially if the minority has been a disadvantaged community. . . .

> The most important task is to prevent the Hindu communalists from using what is essentially a women's rights issue for the purpose of stirring up communal hatred against the Muslims and other minorities.[25]

The indulgence toward a minority's insecurity cannot altogether avoid the aspect of liberal "protection." Feminist discourses have tried to steer clear of choosing between supporting a minority community or condemning them on feminist grounds by emphasizing the shared predicament of all Indian women within the personal laws of all religious communities—thus displacing the religious identity of Muslim women by highlighting their gender identity.

Shahbano's emergence from and retreat into the family suggest that the family is a site and an ideology that need to be considered in relation to the law and the state. The state is sensitive about issues relating to the family, first, because of their regulation by religious law (as we have already pointed out). For religion, too, is a "protected" sphere in India (the constitutional commitment to secularism does not imply, as in many western countries, a separation of church and state, or a state in which "religion or religious considerations are not only ignored but also purposely excluded from the sphere of State activities"; on the contrary, it has meant "the co-existence of various religions under the benevolent supervision of the State").[26] Second, the demarcation of the spheres of influence of family and state into the private and the public, respectively, enables them to work together in a collaborative hegemony. Since the entitlement of the family to privacy and autonomy is widely recognized and granted, any rights granted to the woman as an individual citizen by the state can only be imperfectly enforced within that state-within-a-state. When women become victimized within the family—and the most significant site of violence against women in India today is the household—the state (read: police) is reluctant to move in to prevent or punish the crime.[27] The conflict between the state and the patriarchal family over the rights of women is caught up in the problematic of "protection." In the Muslim woman's case, her legal right to maintenance from her estranged husband has resulted in an act that has not only taken away that right but driven her back to total dependence upon (the protection of) her natal family. The family has reclaimed the erstwhile "vagrant." Thus the discourse of women's rights becomes implicated in a discourse of protection, shifting imperceptibly from a question of establishing that to which women are entitled to that to which women have (for the moment) the privilege.

Protectionist arguments would then appear to be inherent in any women's issue. They are not altogether easy to avoid, as the predicament of women's groups outlined earlier suggests, nor are they invariably "insincere." We only argue that the will to power contaminates even the most sincere claims of protection. There are multifarious relations of dominance and subordination that circulate within the term "protection," so that its meaning is always deferred.

A protectionist argument succeeds in effacing the protector's will to power, but it also effaces the recalcitrant (nonsubmissive) will of the protected. The register of the discourse on Muslim women thus needs to be shifted to take into account the possibility of the operation of such a will.

Subjectivity

To counter a discourse about women that operates with the subtext "protection," we consider how a gendered subaltern subjectivity is constructed to express resistance. It is not our intention to recreate a "Shahbano" who is the origin and repository of her story, whose actions are interpretable through her motives, which in turn may be ascertained through interviews and other modes of transcription of her "inner" being. Nor do we wish to construct an individualized and individualistic "heroine" who single-handedly provoked a nation into crisis. Our mode of access to Shahbano will be through the actions she initiated in the law courts: these will be our text. Law, like language, "objectifies, typifies, anonymises."[28] Thus we move beyond a biographical dimension.

Shahbano gave two interviews, one to an Urdu newspaper *Inquilab* and the other on national television. We have not privileged these as sources of her subjectivity. Shahbano's multiple identities—as Muslim (a minority religious community), lower class (the daughter of a police constable), and woman—are severally and compositely subaltern and do not make for a symmetrical distribution of dialogue-constitutive universals.[29] In the best of circumstances, the notion of an ideal speech situation is contrafactual.[30] In the charged political and religious situation in which the media sought and were given the interviews, her freedom to apply regulative and representative speech acts was further and drastically curtailed. So that while we agree generally that speech provides an important access to self-representation, it is not always the case that "to speak is to become a subject."[31] Moreover, a direct interview with Shahbano would not have resolved this problem for us. Since she does not speak English, the politics of translation would, in any case, be deeply implicated in the "retrieval" of her speech.

In contrast, legal actions and other forms of social protest, while problematically subject to issues of mimeticism and referentiality, and still contained within discursive frames, are more "open" and recognizable as combative social action than are personal narratives. In broadly distinguishing between "speech" and "action" in this way, we hope to make the terms of our representation of Shahbano clearer. In what follows, we interpret Shahbano from the crises her legal actions produce. We create her subjectivity in terms of a series of discontinuous and exteriorized actions rather than, as in classic systems of representation, through "depth" characterization. We tentatively trace below the formation of a gendered subjectivity through its discontinuous actions and argue for a Foucaultian notion of resistance in this refusal of subjectification.

Primary socialization for an Indian is effected in terms of religion and class. Gender intersects this general ideological formation to articulate subjectivity. Shahbano's identity as Muslim and woman was gradually formed over a period of childhood. We need to distinguish this process from the violent constitution of the subject as it occurs later. Power is recognized as such only when it is exercised. When Shahbano was ejected from her home after forty years of marriage and several children, the ejection problematized the values that were embedded in the daily routines of life. And when this was followed by her husband's pronouncement of oral and unilateral divorce (as prevails in Islam), she moved to the courts. The ejection and divorce provided Shahbano with the lived experience that leads to a sharp consciousness of gender in a patriarchal culture. The litigant who approached the lower courts was a poor female Muslim subject made painfully aware of being disadvantaged by her religion and her sex and in need of economic assistance. The maintenance award of the lower court of a sum less than the daily wages of a laborer sharply constituted her economic-caste identity. She appealed to the High Court in protest against this meager award. Her upper-class Muslim sisters (coreligionists) accused her of a lack of self-respect in fighting for money from a man who, by viture of the divorce, had become a stranger. She was estranged by class division from women of her religion. We can see class and religion delicately poised in the struggle for dominance in her response. When Hindu fundamentalists offered to "protect" her from Muslim men, her religious identity won, as her subsequent action shows. In an open letter, she denounced the Supreme Court judgment

> which is apparently in my favour; but since this judgment is contrary to the Quran and the *hadith* and is an open interference in Muslim personal law, I, Shahbano, being a muslim, reject it and dissociate myself from every judgement which is contrary to the Islamic Shariat. I am aware of the agony and distress to which this judgment has subjected the muslims of India today.[32]

Her apparent inconstancy or changeability must be interpreted as her refusal to occupy the subject position offered to her. When the battle was carried to Parliament and the government of India passed the bill that threw her on the mercy of the male relatives of her natal family, her gender status was again activated. She became a Muslim woman pursuing the case for the return of her *mehr* (dower) under the provisions of the new act.

It is clear that every discursive displacement is matched by a violent movement of religion/class/gender attributes to the foreground of the identity. This process of writing and erasure cannot construct that unified and freely choosing individual who is the normative male subject of Western bourgeois liberalism. The consciousness we have been describing that comes into being in response to and through the investments of a hegemonic or dominant consciousness can perhaps only be described as a subject-effect.[33] To live with what she cannot control, the female subaltern subject here responds with a discontinuous and apparently contradictory subjectivity. Shahbano's legal actions—her appeal for maintenance, her ten-year struggle in the courts, her victory, her denunciation of the judgment and renunciation of the compensation, her quest for restitution of the dower under the new act—may appear within the normative paradigm of subjectivity to conform to the male image of woman as inconstant. So deeply internalized is this notion that when Rajiv Gandhi veered around from acclaiming the judgment to supporting the Muslim Women Act, a member of the opposition attacking the bill in Parliament declaimed: "Frailty, thy name is Rajiv!"[34] But if the inconstancy that is proverbially ascribed to woman is deconstructed, we shall find not a unified, freely choosing, purposefully changing subject, but a palimpsest of identities, now constituted, now erased, by discursive displacements.[35]

The episodic narrative of Shahbano's actions we have traced has no center and no closure. If we retraverse its trajectory, we find that for every constituted "effect" there is a simultaneous act of resistance. This for us exemplifies that refusal of subjectification that Foucault recommends, the refusal of "the simultaneous individualization and totalization of the modern power structures."[36] Shabano's multiple identities must be read in a differential relation to each other. None of them is a positive term but exists in combination with other terms to produce meaning. We greet the resistance offered by this spacing, temporalizing self "with a certain laughter, a certain dance."[37]

The Subject in Law

Whether this spacing, temporalizing self is a deferral of the unified, freely choosing subject or whether the latter is itself only a metaphysic remains outside our concern here. Certainly the Constitution of India, following Western constitutional models, did envisage this unity of the Indian subject within the legal system.

While there was no specific reference to secularism in the Constitution in 1949, article 25(2) empowered the state to make laws "regulating or restricting any economic, financial, political or other secular activity which may be associated with religious practice."[38] So while the division into secular and personal law might seem to concede that the subject was split, at the time of the framing of the Constitution this division was only envisaged as a temporary accommodation of contemporary reality (the partition of the country attended by large-scale communal riots). The Constitution signals the desired coexistence of secular and personal law; and, in the hierarchical relationship between the two, we are left in no doubt that "secular" is the upper term.

This was the narrative perspective which made the telos of an eventual uniform civil code "natural," a promised goal toward which the social and legal system would evolve. Until the goal was achieved, personal law would be temporarily harbored under the overarching secular law which promises this achievement: "The State shall endeavour to secure for the citizens a Uniform Civil Code throughout the territory of India" (art. 44).

This assumption emerged unambiguously in the discussions about a comprehensive Criminal Procedure Code that was framed in 1974. When the question of the maintenance of Muslim women had similarly threatened to become an issue, the government was able to satisfy the objections of Muslims without unsettling the hierarchy of the law: "If post-divorce entitlement under personal law was realized by the divorced wife, this should be taken into account, and if maintenance had been granted earlier, it could be cancelled." In this way, Muslim personal law was given recognition at the same time that, by allowing Muslim women to have recourse to sections 125–28 of the Criminal Procedure Code, the economic, religious, and common secular identity of the female Indian subject was ensured in law.

However, with the passage of the Muslim Women Act, this ideology of the law has been jeopardized. An interesting concession in the act now makes possible the Muslim woman's continued recourse to section 125, but only with the consent of the husband:

> If a divorced woman and her former husband declare by affidavit or any other declaration in writing in such form as may be prescribed, either jointly or separately, that they would prefer to be governed by the provisions of Section 125 to Section 128 of the Code of Criminal Procedure, 1973, and file such affidavit or declaration in the court hearing the application, the magistrate shall dispose of such application accordingly.

That the husband's consent to such a declaration is unlikely is widely recognized. In a reversal of the previous legal hierarchy, the common Code of Criminal Procedure has now become merely an optional or special case of the personal law.

In any relationship of two terms, an implicit or explicit hierarchy prevails, where one of the terms is viewed as the "supplement," the marginal, extraneous, gratuitous, temporary, or subsidiary element—these approximate to the terms in which personal law was viewed in the Directive Principles. But the passing of the bill has sharply illustrated the workings of "the logic of the supplement,"[39] whereby the supplement moves out of its space and deconstructs the uneasy hierarchy of the governing terms and the metaphysic of the unified subject of legal discourse that it supports. The intervention of religion in politics, or of politics in religion, exacerbates the conflict between the categories of secular and personal. Such exacerbation might eventually result in the translation of the legal division into a split in the psyche of the Indian subject.

In a climate of political and religious controversy, the progress toward a uniform civil code falters. There is a fear among minority communities that, instead of being uncompromisingly secular, a common code would only enshrine some form of codified personal law, most probably that of the majority.[40] Many conceptualizations of a common civil code are unproblematically based on a notion of modernization which, in its turn, is nothing more than a scenario of Westernization, out of keeping with the complex historical reality of the situation in India today.[41] The historical narrative of national evolution and progress, for which the uniform civil code has been projected as the "happy ending," over-simplifies. Under the pressures and exigencies of the times, we might even ask whether the attempt to exchange the present significatory function of the uniform civil code for textual status will block the accommodation of future changes.[42] The passage of the bill has vividly raised the ghosts who haunt attempts at codifications that historically have not necessarily benefited women.[43] In this case the passage of the bill has led to the collaborative hegemony of government and the Muslim Personal Law Board. For purposes of framing the law, stereotypes of the Muslim woman (and man) have been invoked and substituted for the actual socioeconomic reality of the situation of divorced Muslim women, the regional differences in *Wakf* funding, and the statistical variations in the rate of divorce. Therefore, the question of the ability of the Uniform Civil Code to (re-)construct the unified Indian subject in law is open to debate.

Nevertheless, the aim must be to close eventually the split between secular and religious law in the interests of legal equality (art. 14 of the Constitution). Perhaps reform of religious law would obviate the need for a uniform civil code.[44] Revisionary readings (similar to those already undertaken by feminist scholars in literature and the social sciences) and "interested" translations of religious texts are clearly needed. By these means, religious law may be creatively interpreted to accommodate the reality of women's contemporary situation. These are initiatives that have already begun in the wake of the Shahbano crisis. Until such a merging of the two systems takes place, the Uniform Civil Code must continue to function as the site of desire and the sign of the unified legal subject.

The identity of legal subjectivity for Indian women, even if a metaphysic, is necessary in order to counter their identity as the "protected" within the family. Accordingly, section 125 might be looked at as an enabling provision: ostensibly "negative" as to the subject position it offers, it is in practice one mode of access to a public space, a forum for combative legal action, a strategy for countering absorption and containment in the family. By being categorized as a vagrant, the destitute woman—widow, divorcee, or abandoned wife—is envisaged as a potential threat to the public peace. It would seem that ironically it is only when a woman threatens the public realm as an excluded figure, as criminal, prostitute, or vagrant, that she fulfills her (anti-)social role.[45] The psychological damage of potential vagrant status is partially minimized by the depersonalizing effects of legal action. Section 125 offers women a "negative" subjectivity: the new act responds by reinserting the divorcee within the family, this time as dependent on her natal family and sons.

In the ideal, subjects in law are undifferentiated, nondescript, equal, and singular. The Shahbano case points to the contradictions inherent in such "ideal" subjectification.

Resistance

Multiple intersections of power, discursive displacements, discontinuous identities refusing subjectification, the split legal subject: to read this multiple plot is to recognize that the space of the other has no permanent occupant. When translated into an oppositional strategy, this situation seems to lend itself to a free play of alliances between reformist groups, to a politics of association which is oriented to specific issues; and as one views the scene of resistance to the Muslim Women Bill, this possibility is confirmed. In the nationwide response first to the Supreme Court's judgment and then to the bill, the politics of coalition are most striking; there was no attempt by different groups to merge into a homogeneous oppositional identity. What one finds instead is a "multiplicity of voices of liberation [which] remain autonomous."[46]

A selective summary of events in 1985–86 shows a coming together of several feminist and reformist groups in spite of basic ideological differences among them, as well as differences on specific issues like the desirability of a common civil code, of foreign funding, of male participation, or of enactment of further reform (instead of implementing existing laws). That the groups shared a common platform which was open to women's wings of political parties, university teachers and lawyers' collectives, was significant.

Five organizations presented a joint memorandum to the Prime Minister: "Given the fact that the dismally low status of women is a reality for all sections of women regardless of caste or community, the necessity for affording minimum legal protection to all women is self-evident. . . .

The unseemly controversy over Section 125 aims at excluding a large section of women from minimum legal protection in the name of religion." The organizations were the All India Democratic Women's Association, the National Federation of Indian Women, the All India Lawyers' Association, the Young Women's Christian Association, and the Mahila Dakshata Samiti.[47]

On January 30, 1986, the women's wing of the Rashtriya Ekjoot held a *dharna* (demonstration) in Bombay to demand a common civil code.

Between September 1985 and May 1986 Muslim women organized similar *dharnas* in all parts of the country from Darbhanga in Bihar to Pune in Maharashtra; outside the offices of the district magistrates and collectors, hundreds of Muslim divorcees supported by various organizations agitated against the bill.

A Muslim reformist organization of Maharashtra, the Muslim Satyashodak Mandal (some of whose programs are not popular with other Muslim reformists), brought a delegation of women, chiefly divorcees, to Delhi to plead their cause to the government on February 22, 1986.

About fifteen women's organizations, consisting of hundreds of women, held a rally in New Delhi on March 6, 1986, to protest the bill.

A statement published on March 8, 1986, in the journal *Mainstream* to protest the bill had 118 signatures from the Muslim intelligentsia, including eminent journalists, educationists, filmmakers, writers, and painters.

Thirty-five women's organizations joined together for a rally organized by the Women's Liberation Movement in Bombay on March 21, 1986, to demand a secular code.

Senior members of the legal profession took part in a public meeting in New Delhi in March 1986, organized by Karmikar, a women's organization.

In West Bengal, a seminar on Women's Right of Equality before the Law was held in April 1986 and was addressed by the Marxist chief minister of the state. The Socialist leader, Raj Narain, began a seventy-two hour hunger strike to protest the bill on May 3, 1986.

On May 5, 1986, while the bill was being passed, women's organizations in the capital protested outside Parliament, chaining themselves to the iron gates of the building to symbolize their plight. Over a hundred women courted arrest.[48]

Muslim women in Delhi, including university teachers and other professionals, formed the Committee for the Protection of Rights of Muslim
Women and held a convention on April 26, 1986, in New Delhi. The
speakers included Asghar Ali Engineer (who led a revolt against the lead-
ership of the Muslim Bohra community); Saifuddin Chowdhry, Muslim
and leftist member of Parliament; Reshma Arif, wife of Minister Arif
Mohammed Khan and an advocate (lawyer) of the Supreme Court; Shahnaz
Shaikh, who challenged the Muslim personal law to obtain her divorce;
Zoya Hassan, professor at Jawaharlal Nehru University; Daniel Latifi,
Shahbano's counsel; and Moonis Raza, vice-chancellor of Delhi University.

A group of young women students of the Mass Communication Centre at
Jamia Milia University, New Delhi, made a video film called "In Secular
India." The inaugural screening was held on September 14, 1986. Calling
themselves Mediastorm, the group interviewed some major figures in the
controversy and also poor Muslim divorcees, and wove these interviews
into the film.

The tempo was kept up in the press by articles by well-known feminist
journalists like Neeraja Chowdhury, Bacchi Karkaria, Nandita Haksar,
Madhu Kishwar, Vasudha Dhagamvar, and so on.[49] Women's rights activists and women lawyers are actively engaged in drafting acceptable
versions of a common civil code, keeping in mind the basic demand of
women's equality with men.

In October 1986, the Third National Conference of Women's Studies held
a session on the Shahbano case.[50]

In February 1987, the Joint Women's Programme, a national women's
organization (which had earlier organized nationwide protests against the
bill), collaborated with Asghar Ali Engineer, of the Institute of Islamic
Studies, to publish a book, *The Shahbano Controversy*.[51]

We are well aware that the resistance initiated by the individual subject,
as in Shahbano's case, can frequently move out of her control, and even
out of the area of her concerns, so that any aggrandizement of her individual
resistance would reduce her to a bone of contention among conflicting groups.
The Shahbano crisis was not allowed to be defused in this fashion. The
feminist collectivity, by embracing the individual woman's cause, converted
her resistance into a significant operation within a (collective) feminist politics. We have noted how women's groups have been able to reconcile two
contradictory aims: to attend to the specificity of the problem of Shahbano
as a woman living in poverty, in order to focus on concrete, pragmatic, end-
directed action; and also to subsume the specific issue in the larger context

of Indian women's secondary social and legal status, in order to avoid the danger of isolating women of the community, of targeting their religious identity as regressive, speaking therefore on their behalf, even usurping their victim status, and ending by offering "protection." As we have detailed above, not only have women's groups formed different alliances in response to such complexities, but they have also chosen varied strategies of protest and resistance. Some groups have resorted to active consciousness-raising programs, such as demonstrations, petition drives, signature campaigns, or courting arrest. Other women have been campaigning in the press, on cinema and television, as well as in legal, religious, and academic forums.

It will be clear by now that our decentered subject is not that "post-structuralist ideal . . . the 'man without qualities' (Musil), the Reichian subject without 'character armour,' the Deleuzian schizophrenic subject."[52] Instead, by allowing a strategic redefining of her subject position in accordance with the exigencies of the shifting political situation, she engages with the collectivity. The fragmented subject, refusing to be protected, seeks access to the public realm by erupting into its discourses, problematizing the shared assumptions across those discourses, and disrupting their harmony. "Shahbano" is to be found in the transformative power of gender operating in such analytic categories as "minorities," "citizens," and "working classes." The contradictions of the gendered situation cease to be socially inert at historical junctures. Shahbano activated these contradictions, even as other women have pushed them toward a crisis.

It is this view of gender as social force that allows us to express an "optimism of the will" that counters the "pessimism of the intelligence"[53] inevitable in tracing a narrative that concludes with the passage of a retro-gressive law. Some developments following the passing of the bill further permit a certain cautious optimism.

The act was challenged in the Supreme Court by the *Anjuman-e-Taraqqi Pasand* Muslim group on May 22, 1986.[54]

The first two legal verdicts under the new act have gone in favor of the divorced women. In January 1988, Rekha Dixit, a woman magistrate in the Lucknow court, ordered Shafat Ahmed to pay his divorced wife Fahmida Sardar Rs 30,000 as "reasonable and fair provision" plus Rs 3,000 as *iddat* (maintenance) and Rs 52,000 as *mehr* (dower). Eight days later she directed Mohammed Khalid Ahmed to pay his divorced wife Shahida Khatoon Rs 11,000 (*mehr*), Rs 1,500 (*iddat*), and Rs 69,000 as "reasonable and fair provision." In making these generous settlements, Rekha Dixit was interpreting liberally the statutory provision regarding "reasonable and fair provision" as laid down in the act.[55]

There is hope that the shape of new legislation relating to women's issues, including the drafting of a uniform civil code, may show a greater awareness of the interests of women.[56]

So we read deliberately against the grain: the narrative that concludes with the Muslim Women Act is also a beginning which has opened a space in the public realm for women. It is in our attempt to retain Shahbano within the concerns of a feminist project—to ensure that the crisis initiated by her does not move away from the issue of destitute women—that the question we posed at the beginning, Where is Shahbano the woman?, finds its tentative answer.

NOTES

This paper was presented at the Third National Conference on Women's Studies in Chandigarh, India, in October 1986, at the invitation of Uma Chakravorty and Sudesh Vaid. Our thanks to them. Our special gratitude to our colleague Rashmi Bhatnagar for her indefatigable enthusiasm and support. This article was first published in *Signs* 14 (Spring 1989), and is reprinted here with permission.

1. Mohd. Ahmed Khan, Appellant, v. Shah Bano and others, Respondents. The Supreme Court of India, Criminal Appellate Jurisdiction. Criminal Appeal No. 103 of 1981, D/ -23.4.1985. A.I.R. 1985 Supreme Court 945 = 985 Cri.L.J. 875 = M.L.R. (1985) p. 202.

2. Shekhar Gupta with Farzand Ahmed and Inderjit Badhwar, "The Muslims, a Community in Turmoil," *India Today* 3 (January 1986), pp. 90–104, esp. 90.

3. Section 125 is an "order for maintenance of wives, children, and parents." "If any person having sufficient means neglects or refuses to maintain" his wife, children, or parents in need, a magistrate may "upon proof of such neglect, or refusal, order such person to make a monthly allowance for the maintenance . . . at such monthly rate not exceeding five hundred rupees in the whole"; see Ratanlal Ranchhoddas and Dhirajlal Keshavlal Thakore, *The Code of Criminal Procedure* (Nagpur: Wadwa, 1987), pp. 94–112, esp. 110.

4. The Supreme Court judgment (A.I.R. 1985 SC) quotes two earlier decisions of the Court confirming the applicability of sec. 125 of the code to Muslims: Bai Tahira v. Ali Hussain Fidaalli Chotia, 1979, and Fazlunbi v. V. Khader Vali, 1980 (946).

5. There are 75 million Muslims, forming 11.35 percent of India's population.

6. Some other examples of personal law relating to women, taken from Indira Jaisingh, "Personal Law: A Matter of Politics," *Bombay,* 7–21 March 1986, pp. 56–57. In spite of the Hindu Succession Act, 1956, Hindu daughters cannot be coparceners in a Hindu undivided family. The Travancore Christian Succession Act, 1916, totally disinherits a daughter who has received a dowry and limits her share to Rs 5,000. Under Parsi law, daughters get only half the share of a son in inheritance. Under Muslim law, a Muslim male can marry four wives and can divorce a wife by unilateral pronouncement of the triple *talaq.*

7. Vasudha Dhagamvar has described the code as one "whose universal applicability has never been challenged"; see "Uniform Civil Code: Don't We Have It Already?," *Mainstream* (6 July 1985), pp. 15–17, 34, esp. 16.

8. Syed Shahabuddin, "The Turmoil in the Muslim Mind," *Onlooker* (16–31 March 1986), pp. 32–37, esp. 36.

9. Arif Mohammed Khan in an interview with Shekhar Gupta, *India Today* (16–31 Januaary 1986), p. 94.

10. See, e.g., Tahir Mahmood's comments in an interview with Kuldeep Kumar, *Sunday Observer* (9 March 1986).

11. It seems to us that much historical as well as religious narrative represses the subject. For a discussion of the repression of female subjectivity in *Paradise Lost,* see Christine Froula, "When Eve Reads Milton: Undoing the Canonical Economy," *Critical Inquiry,* 10, 2 (December 1983), pp. 321–47.

12. Richard Wollheim explains the place of displacement in Freud's dream theory: "By 'displacement' . . . Freud meant two distinct but related processes. One is that whereby the dream is differently 'centered' from the dream thoughts, so that it does not reflect the relative importance of these thoughts. The other is that whereby elements in the dream do duty for elements in the dream thoughts, the substitution being in accordance with a chain of association. Displacement is peculiarly connected with the disguise that the dream wears" (*Sigmund Freud* (New York: Viking, 1971), p. 65).

13. Daniel Latifi, "The Unfriendly Act," *Sunday* (8–14 June 1986), pp. 32–37, esp. 37.

14. Shekhar Gupta, Farsand Ahmed, and Inderjit Badhwar, "The Muslims," p. 90.

15. Kuldip Nayar, "Separate Personal Laws Do Not Dilute Secularism," *Telegraph* (15 March 1986).

16. Syed Shahabuddin, p. 34.

17. We use here the argument put forward by Gayatri Chakravorty Spivak, "Subaltern Studies: Deconstructing Historiography," in *Subaltern Studies IV: Writings on South Asian History and Society,* edited by Ranajit Guha (Delhi: Oxford University Press, 1985), pp. 330–63. She uses the phrase "discursive displacement" to mean "functional changes in sign systems." Our indebtedness to the work of Gayatri Spivak goes beyond the actual quotations used in this essay.

18. Subaltern: Of inferior rank: A particular not a universal (OED). Of inferior rank: A particular in relation to a universal of the same quality. Therefore, here, a subject relating to the societal universal norm of a unified, freely choosing subject—tangentially or marginally, or in opposition to, or opaquely.

19. Asoke Sen, 5 May 1986; Syed Shahabuddin, May 1986; Zoya Hassan, March 1986; Justice Chowdhary, 22 March 1986; as cited in a publicity pamphlet issued by Mediastorm at the inaugural screening, 14 September 1986, of "In Secular India," a video film on the Muslim Women (Protection of Rights in Divorce) Bill.

20. This theory of language was propounded by Ludwig Wittgenstein, *Philosophical Investigations,* translated by G. E. M. Anscombe (New York: Macmillan, 1985); and J. L. Austin, *How to Do Things with Words* (Cambridge, Mass.: Harvard University Press, 1962), and is fully formulated in the speech-act theory of language.

21. This sentence is analogous to "white men are saving brown women from brown men" in Spivak's essay on *Sati,* "Can the Subaltern Speak? Speculations on Widow Sacrifice," *Wedge* 7/8 (Winter/Spring 1985), pp. 120–30, esp. 121.

22. Through a strategy of synedochic substitution, the Muslim Personal Law Board has claimed to represent the sentiments of the entire Muslim population. "Progressive" Muslims have felt alienated from their community because their call for Islamic reform has been dismissed either as irrelevant or as opposed to mass opinion. Women of the Muslim community have also been ignored; no referendum on the bill among Muslims was held, though it was repeatedly promised.

23. In an article in *Statesman* (8 May 1986), the editor described the law minister as an acknowledged legal luminary who could argue both sides of a case with equal facility. He pointed out that "perception theory" had not been applied to the Sikh minority's demand for a separate state, or to their perception that Sikh temples were sacred places which the army could not enter. Castigating the perception theory as dangerous, the article held: "In a plural society such as ours, the rulers, though not impervious to public opinion, are expected to lead society—to mould it, rather than surrender to its darker mood. If the 'perception theory' were to prevail, no reform would ever be possible. . . . Dowry is considered a necessary evil among the Hindus. Will the Government make it a ground for not reforming society?"

24. Seema Mustafa, "Behind the Veil," points out how the prime minister, Rajiv Gandhi, himself defended the bill in Parliament "on the grounds that it was secular, that it did not deprive Muslim women of their rights but was superior to even Section 125, Cr.P.C., and that, as Hindus, Parsis and Christians had modified bills why should this be denied to Muslim women" (see The *Telegraph* (2 March 1986).

25. Madhu Kishwar, "Pro Women or Anti Muslim? The Shahbano Controversy," *Manushi*, 32 (1986, pp. 4–13, esp. 12–13.

26. See K. K. Wadhwa, *Minority Safeguards in India* (Delhi: Thomson, 1975), 85, 96.

27. In recent times, it has been the task of women's groups to question the sanctified space of the family and to demand that women's cries for help be heard and addressed.

28. Peter Berger and Thomas Luckmann, *The Social Construction of Reality* (Harmondsworth: Penguin Books, 1967), 53.

29. Jurgen Habermas, quoted in T. A. McCarthy, "A Theory of Communicative Competence," in *Critical Sociology,* edited by Paul Connerton (Harmondsworth: Penguin, 1976), pp. 473–78.

30. *Ibid.*

31. Catherine Belsey, *The Subject of Tragedy: Identity and Difference in Renaissance Drama* (London and New York: Methuen, 1985), p. 191.

32. "Open Letter to Muslims," *Inquilab* (13 November 1985). The letter is signed by Shahbano with her thumb impression, attested by the signatures of four witnesses; translated into English by A. Karim Shaik, in *Radiance* (24–30 November 1985); reprinted in Asghar Ali Engineer, ed., *The Shahbano Controversy* (Hyderabad: Orient Longman, 1987), 211.

33. Gayatri Spivak, "Subaltern Studies," p. 341.

34. M. S. Gurupadaswamy, "In Focus," *Sunday Observer* (11 May 1986).

35. Palimpsest: A parchment from which writing has been partially or completely erased to make room for another text.

36. Herbert Dreyfus and Paul Rabinow, *Michel Foucault: Beyond Structuralism and Hermeneutics* (Brighton: Harvester Press, 1982), p. 216.

37. Jacques Derrida, "Difference," in *"Speech and Phenomena" and Other Essays on Husserl's Theory of Signs* (1967), translated by David B. Allison (Evanston, Ill.: Northwestern University Press, 1973), p. 159.

38. When, in 1948, an attempt was made to introduce a clause to save personal law, Dr. B. R. Ambedkar, one of the framers of the Constitution, argued as follows against it: "The religious conceptions in this country are so vast that they cover every aspect of life from birth to death. There is nothing which is not religious, and, if personal law is to be saved, I am sure about it, that in social matters we shall come to a standstill. . . . After all, what are we having liberty for? We are having this liberty to reform our social system which is so full of inequalities, discriminations and other things which conflict with our fundamental rights." Ambedkar, like other liberal secularists, postulated an Indian-hood which would hold together in unity identities grounded in gender, class, language, and religion; see P. C. Chatterjee, *Secular Values for Secular India* (New Delhi: Lola Chatterjee, 1984), 13.

39. Jacques Derrida has explained the functioning of the supplement thus: "But the supplement supplements. It adds only to replace. It intervenes or insinuates itself *in-the-place-of;* if it fills, it is as if one fills a void. If it represents and makes an image, it is by the anterior default of a presence. Compensating . . . and vicarious, the supplement is an adjunct, a subaltern instance which *takes-(the)-place*" (see *Of Grammatology,* translated by Gayatri Chakravorty Spivak (Baltimore and London: Johns Hopkins University Press, 1976), p. 145).

40. As Asghar Ali Engineer points out, "Whatever the merit of a common civil code . . . when the demand for it comes from communalist Hindus, it arouses deep suspicion even among the Muslim intelligentsia and they begin to perceive it as a Hindu Code" (18).

41. On the ideology of modernization with special reference to Islamic law, see Iqbal Masood, "Islam and 'Word Politics,'" *Express Magazine* (1 June 1986).

42. By "significatory function," we refer to the invocation of art. 44 as a sign: it has served until now as both threat and promise, as that which has to be fulfilled in an indeterminate future, a "deferred presence." "The circulation of signs," as Derrida points out, "defers the moment in which we can encounter the thing itself" (see *Margins of Philosophy* (Chicago: University of Chicago Press, 1982), p. 9). It is this free play of the sign that will be curtailed in actualizing the code.

43. In "The Production of an Official Discourse on *Sati* in Early Nineteenth-Century Bengal," *Economic and Political Weekly,* Review of Women Studies 21, no. 17 (April 26, 1986): pp. 32–40, Lata Mani has argued that increasing textualization of Hindu laws by colonial rulers reduced the heterogeneity, contextualization, and variety of traditional interpretations, and produced "consequences of domination" (39).

44. The closeness of personal and secular laws already exists in some cases. Some of the personal laws of the Hindus, codified since 1955, such as the Hindu Adoption and Maintenance Act and the Hindu Marriages Act, have no specific *shastric,* i.e., religious, sanction. There exist also several uniform laws covering personal matters, such as the Special Marriage Act, 1955, the Indian Succession Act, 1875, the Guardians and Wards Act, 1890, the Indian Majority Act, and the Medical Termination of Pregnancy Act, 1971; see Dhagamvar (n. 7 above), p. 15.

45. The Supreme Court judgment makes this recategorization clear: "The liability imposed by sec. 125 to maintain close relatives who are indigent is founded upon the individual's obligation to the society to prevent vagrancy and destitution. . . . Sir James Fitz-James . . . piloted the Code of Criminal Procedure, 1872 . . . as a mode of preventing vagrancy or at least of preventing its consequences. In Jagir Kaur v. Jaswant Singh . . . Subba Rao J. speaking for the court said that [sec. 125] 'intends to serve a social purpose'" (n. 1 above). Foucault's study of a society through its procedures of exclusion is an insightful one and useful

in this context; see, esp., *Madness and Civilization: A History of Insanity in the Age of Reason,* trans. R. Howard (New York: Random House, 1973), and *Discipline and Punish: The Birth of the Prison,* trans. Alan Sheridan (New York: Random House, 1979).

46. Stanley Aronowitz, *The Crisis in Historical Materialism: Class, Politics and Culture in Marxist Theory* (New York: Praeger, 1981), p. 131.

47. Janak Raj Jai, *Shah Bano* (New Delhi: Rajiv Publications, 1986), 119.

48. These events have been listed in Asghar Ali Engineer, ed., *The Shabhano Controversy* pp. 237–42.

49. In addition to articles already cited in this essay, see also Nandita Haksar, "And Justice for All," and Madhu Kishwar, "Losing Sight of the Real Issue: Another Look at the Shahbano Controversy," both in a special supplement, "Woman," *Times of India* (8 March 1986), 1, 4; Shahida Lateef, "Indian Muslim Women: Caught in a Time Warp," *Express Magazine* (30 March 1986); Rasheeda Bhagat, "How Poor Muslim Women Look at Maintenance" (a report from Madras), *Indian Express* (11 April 1986); Neeraja Chowdhury, "The Communal Divide" (three-part article), in *Statesman* (18, 19, and 20 April 1986), "Muslim Women Bill: Trail of Errors," *Statesman* (28 April 1986), and "Shortsighted Move to Appease Communities," *Statesman* (1 May 1986).

50. The National Conferences on Women's Studies are organized by the Indian Association of Women's Studies (CWDS, B–43, Panchsheel Enclave, New Delhi, 110 017). This paper, and two others on the "Shahbano" issue, were part of a workshop on religion, secularism, and women's rights convened by Uma Chakravorty and Sudesh Vaid.

51. This book, cited in n. 32 above, is a collection of documents relating to the issue and reprints of several newspaper and periodical articles.

52. Leonard Green, Jonathan Culler, and Richard Klein, "Interview: Frederic Jameson," *Diacritics,* 12 (Fall 1982), pp. 72–91, esp. 82.

53. Antonio Gramsci, *Selections from Prison Writings, 1910–1920,* edited by Quintin Hoare, translated by John Mathews (London: Lawrence & Wishart, 1977), 175n.

54. Asghar Ali Engineer, ed., *The Shabhano Controversy,* p. 242.

55. Minu Jain, "Curious Role Reversal," *Sunday Observer* (24 January 1988).

56. The three supposedly prowomen acts passed in 1987—the Dowry Amendment Act, the Prevention of Immoral Traffic Act, and the Indecent Representation of Women Act—"were intended to soften the negative impact of the politically motivated Muslim Women (Protection of Rights in Divorce) Act" (see unsigned editorial, "Women versus Women," *Statesman* (2 September 1988)). These acts have nevertheless been widely perceived not only as powerless to effect real changes but also as impinging upon civil rights. The Commission of Sati (Prevention) Act, 1987 (which bans the celebration of *Sati*), has also come in for the same criticism (*see The Current Indian Statutes,* June 1988, pt. 6, pp.7–12). The pressure from women's groups for effective legal reform therefore continues.

14

Gender, Sex, and Equivalent Rights

Drucilla L. Cornell

In a recent article in *Dissent,*[1] Seyla Benhabib argued that the alliance between feminism and so-called poststructuralism is, at best, uneasy. Her worry—and it is a worry frequently articulated in feminist political critiques of deconstruction and postmodern philosophy more generally—is that Jacques Derrida's deconstruction of gender identity[2] reinstates the patriarchal view of Woman as the mysterious Other, without a knowable essence, substance, or identity. Feminists, on the other hand, have militantly rejected the so-called nonidentity of Woman as one more mystification that justifies the subordination of actual women. Derrida, on this reading, is accused of the restoration of feminine stereotypes through his very deconstruction of gender identity and, more particularly, of a graspable female identity which could provide us with a basis for a specifically feminist politics.

Ultimately, however, this reading misunderstands the ethical and political significance of Derrida's deconstruction of the structures of gender identity, as it is defined as a hierarchy which privileges the masculine. I emphasize the ethical and political significance of this deconstruction because my purpose is less to set the record straight than to show instead what we, as feminists and civil-rights activists, stand "to gain" from a reinterpretation of Derrida's specific deconstructive intervention into the psychoanalytic theory of Jacques Lacan. This deconstructive intervention demonstrates the irreducibility of sex and sexuality to the imposed structures of the gender hierarchy.

It is correct, then, to observe that Derrida does not attempt to resolve the dilemma of femininity—the dilemma that Freud believed haunted psychoanalytic theory—through an appeal to an authentic concept of female identity. In fairness to Derrida's critics, it is also important to note that the early feminist criticism of Freud did appeal to a unique female identity and, more specifically, to a unique female libido, that had purportedly been erased by the masculine bias of the profession.[3] This attempt to conceptualize female identity, and thus to solve the dilemma of femininity, is also reflected in the ethical and political versions of object-relations theory that have dominated recent debates in American feminism. The advantage of such an approach, which Benhabib notes, is that it allows us to speak of and to affirm what is unique to women. A popular example that has had significant impact in the legal literature is Carol Gilligan's "ethic of care" that attempts to locate what is different about women's moral reasoning.[4] But the political disadvantage of this version of object-relations theory is that it once again identifies sex, sexuality, and gender identity, and thereby reinforces *conventional* stereotypes of the feminine as defined by the current gender structure, and potentially constrains women and men in their fashioning of their individual lives as sexuate beings.

To better understand the political and legal implications of the deconstruction of gender identity, as conceived within gender hierarchy, I want to turn to the law of "sex" discrimination. My first purpose in this article is to suggest that we should understand the wrong in sex discrimination as the imposed law of gender identity on lived possibilities, whether those oppressed are women who seek to be truck drivers or prison guards, or homosexual men who want to be fathers or to have access to desperately needed medical treatment such as AZT. My second purpose is to argue that the deconstruction of the *conventional* structures of gender identity as either biologically necessary or as culturally desirable not only does not erase the "reality" of women's suffering, but demands instead the affirmation of feminine sexual difference as irreducible to the dominant definition of the feminine within the gender hierarchy as man's other or as his mirror image.[5] In other words, sexual difference and more specifically feminine sexual difference, is not being erased; instead, the rigid structures of gender identity which have devalued women and identified them with the patriarchal conventions of the gender hierarchy are being challenged.

The respect for difference, including feminine sexual difference, as continually reimagined by actual women, becomes the basis for the two types of equivalent rights I will advocate. The first type of equivalent rights recognizes the legitimacy of nontraditional, intimate relationships, particularly the arrangements of those who engage in homosexual rather than heterosexual love and sexual encounters. The second type of equivalent rights addresses the value of feminine sexual difference. These rights demand the acceptance of one fundamental premise, perhaps the most basic premise of feminism, which is that what is called human is only too often in patriarchal culture the genre of the male, which implicitly erases the other genre of the human species: the female. Equivalent rights recognize that the human species as currently constituted is composed of two genres, irreducible to one another. As Luce Irigaray has explained:

> I know that some men imagine that the great day of the good-for-everyone universal has dawned. But what universal? What new imperialism is hiding behind this? And who pays the price for it? There is no universal valid for all women and all men outside the natural economy. Any other universal is a partial construct and, therefore, authoritarian and unjust. The first universal to be established would be that of a legislation valid for both sexes as a basic element in human culture. That does not mean forced sexual choices. But we are living beings, which means sexuate beings, and our identity cannot be constructed without a vertical and horizontal horizon that respects difference.[6]

The deconstruction of rigid gender structures delegitimates "forced sexual choices" in the name of the recognition of the respect for difference, which is why I argue that it must play a role in feminist theory. The "legislation valid for both sexes as a basic element in human culture" to which Irigaray refers, must include equivalent rights as rights, not just as privileges needed to correct the imposed inequality of women. Neither are they merely a means to help women become more like men in the name of promoting one species undivided by sexual difference. Sexual difference is recognized and valued, even if at the same time deconstruction also challenges the inevitability of the current division of sexuate beings into only two genres, male or female.

Equivalent rights, in other words, do not have as their sole or even their main goal creating a space for women in a male world from which they have previously been shut out. As I will suggest, the vision of equality most consistent with both types of equivalent rights I advocate is Amartya Sen's equality of capability and well-being.[7] As Sen reminds us, "[c]apability reflects a person's freedom to choose between different ways of living."[8] I would add that the valuation of difference implicit in equivalent rights is essential if we are to actually make these choices of different lifestyles possible without the tremendous suffering of being treated as an outcast or as inferior because one's life, and in this case "one's sex" and sexual relationships, are devalued. There is one further basic assumption that must be made here and that is that capability not only includes functioning in the world of social achievements,[9] but also includes sexual expression as an important aspect of human life and the appreciation and affirmation of "one's sex" as necessary for well-being. And, in the case of women, more specifically, of living without shame of their "sex."[10]

"Equivalence," is defined in the Standard Oxford Dictionary as "of equal value," but not necessarily of equal value because of likeness. Equivalence, as a result, does not demand that the basis of equality be likeness to men. Such a view would once again deny that we are indeed sexuate beings currently divided into two genres, male and female, and not one species without differentiation. Equivalent rights can then be distinguished from the dominant analysis of sex discrimination that has been reflected in current opinions in the federal courts and in the United States Supreme Court.

Under current sex-discrimination law, as conventionally interpreted,[11] the wrong of discrimination is the imposition of a universal on an individual who does not match that universal. The wrong is not the imposition of stereotypes *per se*, but the imposition of stereotypes when they are not "true"— that is, when the stereotypes are not an adequate description of the actual life of the person. So, for example, if a job requires that the employee lift two hundred pounds, and a woman can lift two hundred pounds, she should be able to take on the job even if women generally could not meet the job requirements. Difference, in the sense of being unable to meet the norm, must be shown, not just assumed on the basis of generalizations about gender. Equality, on this definition of discrimination, turns on the demonstration that if a women is *like* her male counterparts for the purposes of a specific job she should be treated as such. Discrimination, so defined, is based on an inherently comparative evaluation between men and women which implicitly assumes the validity of the standards of an already-established world of work.

Thus, discrimination results from a comparison *between* the genders under previously established norms. Under this conception of discrimination, heterosexual white men can sue because of the imposition of an inaccurate stereotype by which they are judged exclusively and incorrectly on the basis of their gender. In sex-discrimination cases, white heterosexual men have been granted jurisdiction under Title VII of the Civil Rights Act of 1964.[12] The irony is that gay men have been denied jurisdiction under the statute because their complaints have been found to involve only discrimination on the basis of what is called sexual preference. Thus, their complaints as gay men have not been understood as sex discrimination for Title VII purposes. This supposedly follows from the comparative analysis that focuses on the relationship between the genders rather than within the genderized group. Under this reasoning, the differential treatment would be between two groups of men, heterosexual and homosexual, and not between men and women. But, of course, to point to the established definition of discrimination only pushes the problem one step further back. We still need to question a conception of the relationship between sex, sexuality, and gender that denies a gay man the right to seek redress under Title VII. We also have to question why, when women are "truly" different, they cannot claim that they have been discriminated against or treated unequally. This issue is not merely a question of why women should have to meet an already-established male norm which, of course, as I have already argued, assumes that in a patriarchal society what appear as neutral or human standards will often implicitly assume the male as the norm. The first question is how can difference be taken into account when that difference is an "accurate" stereotype? The second question is how can women's reproductive capacity, which is a difference irreducible to imposed conventions, be valued and legally protected?

The deconstruction of rigid gender identities can give us a new approach to the two questions I have just posed because, as suggested, it can help us reconceptualize the wrong of "sex" discrimination and to justify the two types of equivalent rights I have defined. Of course, to suggest the relevance of deconstruction to an analysis of "sex" discrimination is to also indicate the necessity of psychoanalytic theory in political thought more generally, and to a feminist politics more specifically. But let me turn now to what this deconstruction entails within the context of psychoanalytic theory. To do so, we have to look more specifically at Derrida's intervention into the theory of Jacques Lacan.[13]

Lacan's central insight provides a corrective to the biologistic readings of Freud's account of gender differentiation through the castration complex, and corrects the American object-relations stress on the mother/child relation rather than on the Oedipal complex.[14] According to Lacan, the genesis of linguistic consciousness occurs when the infant recognizes itself as having an identity separate from the mother, because the mother is other to himself. The primordial moment of separation is experienced by the infant both as a loss as well as the gaining of an identity. The pain of this loss results in a primary repression that simultaneously buries the memory of the relationship to the mother in the unconscious and catapults the infant into the Symbolic realm to fulfill its desire for the Other. Once projected into language, this primary identification with the mother is experienced only through the disruptive force of the unconscious. The unrepresentable desire for the Phallic Mother[15] is only remembered in the fantasy projection that compensates for Her absence. It is the Phallic Mother and what She represents—not the actual mother and what she wants—that cannot be spoken in the conventional language of the Symbolic. So far on this account, it would seem that both sexes suffer a primordial separation from the mother and would be marked by this separation in the same way.

Although Lacanians maintain the difference between the penis and the phallus[16] (the phallus represents the supposed lost symbiotic connection that triggers desire in both sexes), it remains the case that the value given to the penis in patriarchal culture allows the penis to appear to stand in for the would-be neutral phallus. This establishes the basis of the illusion that having the penis is having the phallus, with all its symbolic power. In this culture based on gender hierarchy, the male child "sees" his mother's lack, which gains significance as her castration.[17] Sexual difference and gender identity are based on the cultural significance attributed to this experience of "sighting." Having the penis is identified with being potent, able to satisfy the mother's desire and, therefore "bring her back."[18] Woman, on the other hand, is now identified as the castrated Other.[19] If the penis, at least on the level of fantasy, is identified with the phallus, then Woman, who lacks the penis, is also seen as lacking the affirmative qualities associated with the phallus. As a result, Woman is devalorized. The assumption of a masculine gender identity thus turns on the devalorization of Woman which, in turn, explains the repudiation of the feminine as the basis of culture. The result for women is that we are left in a state of *dereliction*, which technically means that given the definition of Woman as the castrated Other, the little girl cannot positively represent her relationship to the mother and, thus, to her own "sex." In this way, Lacan's account of gender differentiation into "two" sexes explains why the gender divide becomes a hierarchy in which the feminine is repudiated.

But for my purposes here, it is important to note three aspects of Lacan's own analysis of the division of human beings into two "sexes," which also defines Woman as the castrated Other. The first is that Lacan's recognition of the constitutive force of language denies any attempt to root sex, sexuality, and gender identity in a pregiven nature or a set of libidinal drives, as Freud is conventionally interpreted to have done. Thus, there is no biologically based sex and, correspondingly, no normal, mature sexuality or gender identity that can be understood as the culmination of the proper development of the libidinal drives. Gender identity, in other words, is understood as imposed by normative injunction, not given by biology or ontology. In this sense, Lacanianism undermines the traditional Freudian conception of sexual perversion, which turns on an account of the "normal" maturation of sexuality into heterosexuality.

Secondly, Lacan understands male superiority as a "sham," meaning that it is not mandated by a person's "sex," but instead rests on the fantasy identification that having the penis is having the phallus. This fantasy lies at the very base of patriarchal culture and justifies gender hierarchy. Lacan undermines the claim that gender identity as currently defined is in any way mandated by the nature of sex or sexuality. Sex and sexuality are, instead, determined and *limited* by the structures of gender identity, not the other way around. Third, because Lacan recognizes the role of fantasy in the assumption of gender identity, he also understands that there can be no perfect identification of oneself with one's gender. The very idea of gender is itself always shifting, because there can never be any end to the divergent interpretations of the meaning of gender in an "accurate" description of sex or sexuality. Yet, in spite of his recognition that gender as a cultural structure determines sex and sexuality, Lacan's analysis emphasizes the way the law of gender identity and hierarchy perpetuates itself. Thus, even if Lacan understands the situation of women within patriarchal culture and society as an unnecessary subjugation—if by unnecessary we mean not mandated by a biologically determined inferiority of her sex—he still sees change in the gender structure and in gender identity as well nigh impossible.

Derrida's intervention into Lacanianism is precisely against the conclusion that the problem of Woman is "insoluble," because her definition as lack is continually reinforced given the meaning of sexual difference in our current structures of gender identity. Even if Lacan recognizes the fantasy dimension of sexual difference, he emphasizes the power of gender structures to give significance to the reality that women do not have a penis. Derrida, on the other hand, emphasizes the political and ethical significance of the way in which lived sexuality never perfectly matches the imposition of gender identity. He does so first by showing us how Lacan fails to take note of the implications of his own insight into the constitutive force of language in the assumption of gender identity. Second, he gives us another interpretation of Lacan's infamous statement, "Woman does not exist," which, within Lacan's own framework, means that the libidinal relationship to the Phallic Mother cannot be represented precisely because it has been repressed into the unconscious.

Lacan teaches us that any concept of sex and sexuality cannot be separated from what shifts in language, what he calls *significance*.[20] For Lacan, as already argued, there is no outside referent in which the process of interpretation of sexuality comes to an end, such as nature or biology, or even conventional gender structures. As a result, we can never discover the "true," authentic ground of female identity to counter the masculine erasure or devaluation of the feminine.[21] Derrida reinterprets Lacan's insight into what is perceived as the inability to separate the truth of Woman from the fictions in which she is represented and in and through which she portrays herself.[22] For Derrida, Lacan's insight into the unconscious as a linguistic code not simply based on repressed biological drives undermines his own pessimistic political conclusions. As Derrida shows us again and again, this linguistic code cannot be frozen because of the slippage of meaning inherent in the performative aspect of language. As a result, Derrida can also demonstrate that within Lacanian understanding of the linguistic structure of gender identity, Woman cannot just be reduced to the lack of the phallus because the metaphors through which she is represented produce an always-shifting reality. Against Lacan, Derrida shows us that what shifts in language, including the definition of gender identity and the designation of the feminine as the lack of the phallus, cannot definitively be stabilized.

Derrida also shows us that the phallus takes on the significance it does for the child only as the metaphor for what the mother desires. Because the erection of the phallus as the "transcendental signifier" is based on a reading or an interpretation, the significance of the phallus can be reinterpreted.[23] Thus, the significance of the discovery of anatomical sexual difference can also be reinterpreted (if the phallus is not read through the fantasy projection of what it means to have a penis). As a result, the current divide into two genders may also yield to other interpretations, including one not based on the devaluation of the feminine "sex."

For Derrida, heterosexuality and homosexuality are only given the meaning they are within this current structure of gender hierarchy. The possibility of reinterpretation of the meaning of the feminine, as well as of the significance of the standardized gender divide itself, which implies heterosexuality as crucial to a normal gender identity, is what keeps open the space for Derrida's "new choreography of sexual difference,"[24] a choreography which, however, in no way denies that we are sexuate beings never simply to be reduced to the category of the "human." Thus, the emphasis on the performative power of language, in and through which gender identity is constituted, allows for the transformation and reinterpretation of current structures of gender identity which devalues the feminine and defines heterosexuality as the norm.

It is a mistake, then, to think that Derrida reduces Woman to the definition of lack or fundamental nonidentity. Rather, he argues that "sex" and "gender" are not identical. In the space of that separation we can open up further transformative possibilities. Moreover, the recognition of the constitutive, performative power of language means that Woman cannot be imprisoned in the current definitions of herself as lack, as the castrated "other," because such an analysis of Woman turns on the assumption that the phallus will *necessarily* be erected as the "transcendental signifier." The reading of Derrida that insists that he advocates Woman's nonidentity conflates his position with Lacan's and fails to appreciate the full political and ethical significance of Derrida's "dream of a new choreography of sexual difference," in which feminine sexual difference would not be violated by the gender hierarchy and the existence of human beings as sexuate creatures sexually differentiated from one another would not be denied.

Put in the context of a model of equality of capability and well-being, the very devalorization of the feminine and the definition of heterosexuality as "normal," makes it difficult for women and homosexuals to participate in their community without shame of their "sex" or their sexuality, and this very shame, I am arguing, could and should be considered an important inequality in women's and homosexuals' well-being. Without a challenge to the very definition of the feminine as the "castrated other" and heterosexuality as the norm, there is no true possibility of overcoming that shame. In this sense, the need to deconstruct the current gender hierarchy is necessary for equality of capability, once we redefine it to explicitly include questions of "sex" and sexuality. Given the connection in the Lacanian analysis between sex, gender identity, and heterosexuality, this experience of shame is not only that of women, as already suggested, but is also shared by those who live outside the heterosexual matrix. As a result, the need to rethink the relationship between gender identity, sex, and sexuality is connected to the reconceptualization of equality beyond the likeness model that has dominated the courts.

We can now begin to see why both Lacan and Derrida's intervention into the Lacanian analysis of the gender hierarchy can help us rethink the wrong in discrimination and, more specifically, help us solve the two problems in discrimination law I indicated earlier. First, let us take the problem of whether or not the gay man's denial of jurisdiction under the statute can be justified, because the discrimination of which they complain is supposedly not based on "sex." As we have seen, the argument is that the complaint is not based on "sex" or gender, but on a division within the group of men themselves due to sexual preference. The psychoanalytic perspective I have developed here can help us think differently about "sex" discrimination against gay men. As we have seen, Lacan's own denial that there is a pregiven sexual nature which determines gender rejects the validity of the concept of homosexuality as perversion. Therefore, the division between normal, heterosexual and abnormal, homosexual "sexual identity"—as long as that identity is based on consent between adults—is a cultural construction. In other words, heterosexuality can only justify itself as normal by an appeal to the past history in which heterosexuality has been established as normal.

The best example of this tautology is Justice White's majority opinion in *Bowers v. Hardwick*.[25] There, White concludes that the "privacy right" established in the line of cases from *Griswold v. Connecticut*[26] through *Roe v. Wade*[27] and *Carey v. Population Services International*[28] did not cover homosexual activity.[29] He also argued that there was nothing in the Constitution or the Bill of Rights, in spite of the interpretation of precedent, that guaranteed any fundamental right to homosexual activity. As a result, Justice White rejects the Eleventh Circuit's holding that the Georgia statute violated the respondent's fundamental rights "because his homosexual right is a private and intimate association that is beyond the reach of state regulation by reason of the Ninth Amendment and the Due Process Clause of the Fourteenth Amendment."[30] Clearly suspicious of the basis of the privacy right itself, White further concludes:

> Accepting the decisions in these cases and the above description of them, we think it evident that none of the rights announced in those cases bears any resemblance to the claimed constitutional right of homosexuals to engage in acts of sodomy that is asserted in this case. No connection between family, marriage, or procreation on the one hand and homosexual

activity on the other has been demonstrated, either by the Court of Appeals or by respondent.[31]

Of course, if one is a homosexual, the right to engage in homosexual activity has everything to do with "family, marriage, and procreation," even if the standard rights of heterosexual engagement have been denied to gay and lesbian couples, and even if gay and lesbian couples seek other forms of intimate association. Can Justice White's blindness to this obvious reality be separated from his own acceptance of an implied heterosexuality as the "natural" and, therefore, right way to live? As Thomas Nagel has correctly pointed out in a more general discussion of sexual perversion, the condemnation of homosexuality as perversion often implicitly, if not explicitly, rests on a conceptualization of homosexual activity as unnatural. To quote Nagel:

> What is regarded as unnatural admittedly varies from culture to culture, but the classification is not a pure expression of disapproval or distaste. In fact, it is often regarded as a *ground* for disapproval, and that suggests that the classification has an independent content.[32]

In White's opinion, we see how implicit conceptions of human nature and, more specifically, natural, sexual identity, effect a concrete decision, precisely because White's "reasoning" can only make sense if the ground for the constitutional recognition of the legitimacy of the Georgia statute is that homosexuality is unnatural. Without such an implicit appeal, Justice White can only rely on the "fact" that most states—and this remains true today—impose sanctions on homosexual activity. But when one turns to the statutes cited in the opinion, the language of legal condemnation of homosexual activity is that such engagement is unnatural. Without an appeal to good, because natural, versus bad, because unnatural, sexual identity, White's reasoning represents the mistake of deriving an "ought" from an "is," without any justification for why homosexuality should be normatively devalued, let alone criminally punished.

This is why Justice White returns us to the state statutes and to the explicit appeal to what is natural and, therefore, "right" or "good" in terms of sexual identity. Homosexual activity is outlawed by the state statutes because it is "unnatural" and, therefore, "abnormal" or "perverted." It is precisely this appeal to a natural sexual identity as the basis of a clear-cut distinction between "perversion" and normal, mature sex and sexuality that Lacanian psychoanalysis challenges. Without this distinction, we can see more clearly the validity of Justice Blackmun's conclusion in his dissent. For Blackmun, the right involved in *Bowers* is the right of all consenting adults to be left alone in their intimate associations.[33] For Blackmun, this right for homosexuals could not legitimately be withheld without some jus-

tification, other than it had always been so.[34] If, however, we go one step
further and say that there is no identity based in our natural sexual difference
that makes homosexuality "unnatural," then there can be no such justification for "outlawing" such engagement as perversion and, worse yet,
"wicked."

We now turn to the first type of equivalent rights. Homosexuals should
be given the *equivalent right* to be left alone in their intimate associations,
whether or not they choose to mimic the life patterns of traditional hetero-
sexuals. The topicality of this issue is evident from a recent *New York Times*
article which reported that a lesbian is suing A.T.&T. for refusing, after the
death of her lesbian partner, to pay her death benefits that they would have
paid a husband.[35] Under the analysis I am offering, she is being denied her
equivalent rights. Under the equality of capability and well-being conception
of equality, she is being treated unequally for her choice of a different,
because nonheterosexual, relationship. The recognition of the equivalent rights
of homosexuals is, to my mind, the best interpretation of Blackmun's dissent
in *Bowers*. I advocate *equivalent* rather than *equal* rights to recognize the
difference of homosexuality, which should not have to match itself to heterosexual arrangements in order to justify itself.

Equivalent rights stress the value of different lifestyles and forms of
intimate association. In terms of the problem of jurisdiction under Title VII,
if gay men do not fit into the traditionally defined properties of the masculine—and they are discriminated against for not doing so—they are discriminated against because of their supposedly "aberrant" sexuality. They
are being condemned for not being "real" men. Thus, this condemnation
should be understood as "sex" discrimination. Derrida shows us in his intervention into Lacanianism not only that such a rigid designation of human
being is ontologically arbitrary, but that it also curtails possibilities of a
sexuality lived differently. As such, it is normatively suspect for limiting
possibilities when this limit is not only unjustifiable by reference to a pregiven nature or gender identity, but also "causes the misery."[36] In order to
argue that the limit "causes the misery," we need only a very "thin" theory
of the good, which assumes that to be denied sexual expression is severely
detrimental to a persons's well-being.

Against the possibility of a "new choreography of sexual difference"
that can never be foreclosed, and which, at the same time, recognizes the
human species as composed of sexuate beings irreducible to one gender, we
can also redefine the wrong in discrimination. The wrong in discrimination
is the imposition of rigid gender identities on sexual beings who can never
be adequately captured by any rigid definition of gender identity. On this
definition, gay men suffer "sex" discrimination precisely because the reality
of their "sex" and sexuality is denied in the name of a normative gender
identity that is imposed upon them and defines them as not "real" men.

We can now turn to our second problem in discrimination law: the difficulty of finding discrimination under Title VII when women seem to be actually different and, thus, accurately stereotyped. I have already discussed how the standard definitions of discrimination define the illegal harm as the imposition of a "false" stereotype. But if we accept the wrong in discrimination as the imposition of gender identity when it cannot be adequate to enjoyed sexuality or the lived individuality of a sexuate being, and which, more specifically, in patriarchal culture devalues the specificity of feminine sexual difference as the castrated "other," we can begin to think through this problem differently too. The imposition of rigid gender structures may well mean that women have been forced to define their lives within those structures. In other words, women are imprisoned by stereotypes because their options are limited by forced sexual choices. Thus, against the backdrop of a new choreography of sexual difference, which respects sexuate beings as different, the very reinforcement of stereotypes can be understood as discrimination because these stereotypes of feminine difference cannot be separated from the gender hierarchy. The "purpose" of Title VII can then be understood to disrupt the status quo of gender hierarchy rather than to establish its reinforcement.[37] The very process of stereotyping can be understood itself as a wrong because it forecloses individual possibilities in the name of rigid gender identity and forces women to have to operate within an unsatisfactory either/or, inseparable from gender hierarchy in which the female sex is devalued. As Irigaray explains:

> Women themselves are caught in a cleft stick between the minimum of social rights they can obtain: getting out of the house, acquiring economic autonomy, having some social visibility, etc., and the psychological or physical price they have to pay for that minimum, whether they know it clearly or not.[38]

Under this reading, the "mommy track"[39] would be wrong because it reinforces the very gender hierarchy in which "mommies"—and mommies are identified as women—mother, and yet this activity of mothering is not valued enough to demand changes in the structure of work. This is a classic example of how, as Irigaray explains:

> [T]he contemporary social order, including the order defining the professions, is not neutral from the point of view of the difference between the sexes. Working conditions and the production techniques are neither equally invented by both sexes nor equally adapted in terms of sexual difference. The goals of work, its modalities, are not defined equally by or for women and men.[40]

The "mommy track" is one way of allowing women to have limited rights within the job market, given the imposed truth of the stereotypes. But, of course, women are still expected to make sacrifices in their lives because they mother. As a result, such "rights" are not "equivalent." An equivalent right would be much closer to what Irigaray has called the right to motherhood and to the conditions in which maternity is possible without sacrifice imposed only upon the mother. For Irigaray, and I agree with her, this right would not only include the protection of guarantees such as maternity leave and prenatal care, but also the right to choose to be pregnant and to decide the number of these pregnancies.

Why is this an equivalent right rather than an equal right? It is an equivalent right because the biological potential for motherhood is an aspect of being female for a woman in a way it cannot be for a man. Also, if "mothering" is a valued social activity, then there should be no sacrifice of either status or pay and, of course, in the name of collapsing the gender divide, we should encourage men to take up this activity. I am obviously accepting that if mothering is understood as a social activity, not exclusively tied to reproductive capacity, then men can also be "mommies."

Yet, even if we can interpret Title VII to challenge gender stereotypes, we still have to face those circumstances in which the difference between men and women, masculine and feminine, cannot be reduced to imposed convention, even the imposed convention that women are and will remain the primary caretakers of children. The obvious examples, one of which I have already indicated, are those that seem inevitably to characterize sexual difference as anatomical difference, not just role difference. As of now, women and men must still have a different relationship to reproduction because it is women who physically bear children and who must live with the constant risk of unwanted pregnancy. How can we take this actual difference into account? We are returned to the way in which gender hierarchy leaves women in a state of *dereliction,* in which feminine difference is ignored, repudiated, or stereotypically limited. The only way in which feminine difference can gain legal status under the current standards is, ironically, to obliterate itself—we are like men—or to define itself in already-accepted conventions like the "mommy track."

We continually have to analogize our experience to men's if we want it legally "recognized" as unequal treatment. For example, if we can show that a pregnancy is like a hernia, we can legitimately claim that we are discriminated against as women when our insurance program covers hernias and not pregnancies, because under this understanding sex-specific male disabilities are covered while female "disabilities" are not. The discrimination so understood under this analysis is that female "disabilities" are not being recognized and, therefore, women are being treated unequally because men and their "special" physical problems are being privileged. But then, of course, we have defined pregnancy as a disability, a definition hardly worthy of the richness of the experience.

The political struggle against *dereliction* in the name of equality of well-being involves the recognition of feminine difference in those circumstances when we are different, as in our relationship to pregnancy, while simultaneously not reinforcing the stereotypes through which patriarchy has attempted to make sense of that difference and has limited our power because of it. If, however, we challenge the devalorization of childbearing, including its definition as a disability, as itself a sign of *dereliction,* then we can insist that the recognition of feminine difference should not be interpreted to devalue us as different from them, setting them up as the standard of the person. Here we are returned to the second category of equivalent rights, now understood to cover those aspects of life and lived sexuality which allow women to live full lives. These rights are equivalent because they allow difference to be recognized and equally valued without women having to show that they are like men for legal purposes or having to make sacrifices because of the specificity of our "sex" which makes us "unlike" men. The right of abortion is a classic example of equivalent rights for women, and should be included in what Irigaray has called the right to "motherhood" (as should such rights as maternity leave and prenatal care). Without such a right women cannot aspire to achieve the most basic sense of well-being because we are denied control over our reproductive capacity and the power to live pregnancy and motherhood with joy and without sacrifice of other aspects of our lives. Men clearly do not need the right of abortion. But that does not mean that women should not have such a right guaranteed if they are to have equality of capability and well-being. Very simply, rights should not be based on what men, as conventionally defined under the gender hierarchy, need for their well-being, as if there was only one genre of the human species.

Postmodern philosophy and, more particularly, its intervention into psychoanalytic theory, can help us, then, to challenge the categories of the person, sexual difference, and gender identity that have blocked our thinking about what constitutes sex discrimination and limited our thinking about the conditions of what would constitute equality of capability and well-being for women, homosexuals, and others who choose to live outside the dominant heterosexual matrix. Very simply put, equality of well-being in the area of sex and sexuality can only be protected by equivalent rights which value our difference as sexuate beings while, at the same time, breaking down and delegitimizing—and I have suggested this deconstruction engages in precisely this delegitimization—the imposed sexual choices of our current gender hierarchy.

NOTES

1. Seyla Benhabib, "On Contemporary Feminist Theory," *Dissent* 36 (Summer 1989), pp. 366, 369–70.

2. See generally, Jacques Derrida, "Choreographies," in *The Ear of the Other: Otobiography, Transference, Translation,* edited by Christie McDonald, translated by Peggy Kamuf (Lincoln and London: University of Nebraska Press, 1985).

3. This was the project of some earlier feminist Freudians and post-Freudians who wanted to salvage the truth of femininity so as to understand our unique identity. See, e.g., Karen Horney, *New Ways in Psychoanalysis* (New York: W. W. Norton & Co., 1939).

4. Carol Gilligan, *In a Different Voice: Psychological Theory and Women's Development* (Cambridge, Mass.: Harvard University Press, 1982), p. 73. Benhabib herself has made a significant contribution to the way in which the ethic of care should be thought about in conjunction with the ethic of right. See generally, Seyla Benhabib, "The Generalized and the Concrete Other: The Kohlberg-Gilligan Controversy and Feminist Theory in *Feminism as Critique: On the Politics of Gender,* edited by Seyla Benhabib and Drucilla Cornell (Minneapolis: University of Minnesota Press, 1987), p. 77.

5. See Simone de Beauvoir, *The Second Sex,* translated by H. M. Parshley (New York: Random House, 1974), originally published as *Le Deuxieme sexe* (Paris: Gallimard, 1949), pp. xv–xxxiv.

6. Luce Irigaray, "How to Define Sexuate Rights?" (provisional title), p. 3 (hereinafter referred to as "Sexuate Rights").

7. This is a reference to Amartya Sen's piece, "Inequality Reexamined: Capability and Well-Being," a paper prepared for a conference on the Quality of Life, organized by the World Institute of Development Economics Research (WIDER) held at Helsinki, Finland, July 1988.

8. *Ibid.,* p. 5.

9. See *ibid.,* pp. 5–6.

10. E. Galenson and H. Roiphe, "The Impact of Early Sexual Discovery on Mood, Defensive Organization and Symbolism," *The Psychoanalytic Study of the Child,* 26 (1971), pp. 195–216.

11. I say conventionally interpreted, because there are dissident circuits and judges who not only do not make this mistake, but who also strive to expose the dangers inherent in the imposition of these kinds of stereotypes in the area of sex-discrimination law.

12. 42 U.S.C.A. Sections 2000e–2000e–17. Title VII prohibits the use of discriminatory employment practices on the part of an employer. The statute states, in relevant part, that : "(a) It shall be an unlawful employment practice for an employer (1) to fail or refuse to hire or to discharge any individual, or otherwise to discriminate against any individual with respect to his compensation, terms, conditions, or privileges of employment, because such individual's race, color, religion, sex, or national origin; or (2) to limit, segregate, or classify his employees or applicants for employment in any way which would deprive or tend to deprive any individual of employment opportunities or otherwise adversely affect his status as an employee, because of such individual's race, color, religion, sex, or national origin" (42 U.S.C.A. Section 2000e–2).

13. For insight into Lacan's basic theories, see generally, Jacques Lacan, *Feminine Sexuality: Jacques Lacan and the Ecole Freudienne,* edited by Juliet Mitchell and Jacqueline Rose, translated by Jacqueline Rose (New York and London: W. W. Norton & Company,

1982); Jacques Lacan, *Ecrits: A Selection,* translated by Alan Sheridan (New York and London: W. W. Norton & Company, 1977), originally published as *Ecrits* (Paris: Editions du Seuil, 1966). In addition, for a detailed explanation of the Lacanian framework, see Drucilla Cornell and Adam Thurschwell, "Feminism, Negativity, Intersubjectivity," in Seyla Benhabib and Drucilla Cornell, eds., *Feminism as Critique,* p. 145, note 2.

For Derrida's intervention into Lacan's psychoanalytic theories, see generally, Jacques Derrida, "Choreographies," in *The Ear of the Other: Otobiography, Transference, Translation,* edited by Christie McDonald, translated by Peggy Kamuf (Lincoln and London: University of Nebraska Press, 1985); Jacques Derrida, *Spurs: Nietzsche's Style/Eperons: Les Styles de Nietzsche* (Chicago and London: University of Chicago Press, 1978).

14. See Jacques Lacan, *Feminine Sexuality,* p. 75.

15. *Ibid.,* p. 76.

16. *Ibid.,* p. 82.

17. *Ibid.,* p. 102.

18. The classic example of this attempt to "bring the mother back" is Freud's story of his grandson Ernst assuaging his desire for the lost mother through the Fort/Da game with the spool.

19. E. Galenson and H. Roiphe, "The Impact of Early Sexual Discovery," pp. 195–216.

20. Throughout his work, Lacan uses the term *significance* to refer to that "movement in language against, or away from, the positions of coherence which language simultaneously constructs" (Jacques Lacan, "Introduction–II, in *Feminine Sexuality,* pp. 51--52.). As Jacqueline Rose goes on to explain, "[t]he concept of *jouissance* (what escapes in sexuality) and the concept of *significance* (what shifts in language) are inseparable" (*Ibid.,* p. 52).

21. As I have argued in "The Doubly Prized World: Myth, Allegory and the Feminine," 75 *Cornell Law Review* 644 (1990), this attempt to base feminism on an authentic female identity or nature is precisely Robin West's fundamental mistake. 75 *Cornell Law Review,* pp. 646–50.

22. For a fuller exploration of Derrida's deconstructive reading of Lacan and his reversal of Lacan's insistence on separating the Truth of Woman from the fictions that surround her in the name of a remetaphorization and restylization of the Feminine, see D. Cornell, "The Doubly Prized World," 75 *Cornell Law Review,* pp. 673–85 (1990).

23. See Cynthia Chase, "Desire and Identification in Lacan and Kristeva," in *Feminism and Psychoanalysis,* edited by Richard Feldstein and Judith Roof (Ithaca: Cornell University Press, 1989).

24. This phrase is the keynote of Derrida's "Choreographies."

25. 478 U.S. 186 (1986).

26. 381 U.S. 479 (1965).

27. 410 U.S. 113 (1973).

28. 431 U.S. 678 (1977).

29. 478 U.S., pp. 190–91.

30. *Ibid.,* p. 189. The Ninth Amendment reads: "The enumeration in the Constitution, of certain rights, shall not be construed to deny or disparage others retained by the people" (U.S. Const. amend. IX). The Due Process Clause of the Fourteenth Amendment provides that : "No State shall . . . deprive any person of life, liberty, or property, without due process of law."

31. 478 U.S., pp. 190–91.

32. Thomas Nagel, "Sexual Perversion," in *The Philosophy of Sex: Contemporary Readings*, edited by Alan Soble (Totowa, NJ: Rowman and Littlefield, 1980), p. 77.

33. 478 U.S., p. 199 (Blackmun, J. dissenting).

34. See *ibid*. Quoting Justice Holmes, Blackmun reminds us that: "It is revolting to have no better reason for a rule of law than that so it was laid down in the time of Henry IV. It is still more revolting if the grounds upon which it was laid down have vanished long since, and the rule simply persists from blind imitation of the past." (*Ibid.*)

35. *See* Tamar Levin, *Suit Over Death Benefits Asks, What is a Family?*, New York *Times*, 21 September 1990, p. B7, col. 3.

36. Wilhelm Reich, *Reich Speaks of Freud: Conversations With Kurt Eissler*, edited by Mary Higgins and C. M. Raphael (New York: Farrar, Strauss & Giroux, 1967), pp. 42–43.

37. It should be noted that this purpose is consistent with Title VII's intervention into a world of rigid race and sex stereotypes.

38. Luce Irigaray, "Sexuate Rights," p. 6.

39. The term "mommy track" refers to an arrangement whereby women who need a flexible schedule to meet the needs of their families are given the "opportunity" to work part-time. Unfortunately, in terms of career goals, this accommodation serves only to relegate these women to positions where they have no hope of reaching senior management positions or achieving partnership. Some women have taken the position that corporations ought to recognize two different groups of women managers: those who put career first and those who need a flexible schedule for personal reasons. See, e.g., Felice Schwartz, "Management Women and the New Facts of Life," *Harvard Business Review* 67 (January-February 1989), p. 65. Others take a stronger stance, demanding equal pay and an equal sense of entitlement for women. See, e.g., Judy Mann, "The Demeaning 'Mommy Track': Separate and Unequal," *Washington Post*, 15 March 1989, p. C3.

40. Luce Irigaray, "Sexuate Rights," p. 5.

15

Women "Before" the Law: Judicial Stories about Women, Work, and Sex Segregation on the Job

Vicki Schultz

It is not enough to inquire into how women might become more fully represented in language and politics. Feminist critique ought also to understand how the category of "women," the subject of feminism, is produced and restrained by the very structures of power through which emancipation is sought. Indeed, the question of women as the subject of feminism raises the possibility that there may not be a subject who stands "before" the law, awaiting representation in or by the law. Perhaps the subject, as well as the invocation of a temporal "before," is constituted by the law as the fictive foundation of its own claim to legitimacy.

—Judith Butler, *Gender Trouble*[1]

How do we make sense of that most basic feature of the world of work, sex segregation on the job? That it exists is part of our common understanding. Social science research has documented, and casual observation confirms, that men work mostly with men, doing "men's work," and women work mostly with women, doing "women's work."[2] We know also the serious negative consequences segregation has for women workers. Women's jobs offer lower wages, less status, and fewer opportunities for advancement.[3] Despite this shared knowledge, however, we remain deeply divided in our attitudes toward sex segregation. What divides us is how we interpret this reality, the stories we tell about its origins and meaning. Why does sex segregation on the job exist? Who is responsible for it? Is it an injustice, or an inevitability?

Because the courts are one of the few arenas in which working women have been able to contest segregation, the legal system has been at the center of this controversy. For two decades, women have been bringing lawsuits under Title VII of the Civil Rights Act to challenge their stratification into low-paying, undesirable, traditionally female jobs. Like all employment discrimination plaintiffs, women rely heavily on statistical evidence to prove their claims.[4] Typically, the statistical evidence shows that women have been significantly underhired for nontraditional jobs, relative to their distribution in some larger pool of eligible workers. But some employers argue that the statistical evidence proves nothing, for the segregation is attributable to women's own choice. According to these employers, women "lack interest" in the more lucrative jobs done by men. "It's not our fault," say the employers. "We don't exclude women from the men's jobs. The trouble is, women won't apply for them—they just aren't interested. They grow up wanting to do women's work, and we can't force them to do work they don't want to do."[5] In this account, employers are not responsible for segregation; they are guilty only of honoring the preexisting employment preferences of working women themselves.

Many readers will be familiar with this "lack-of-interest" argument from *EEOC v. Sears, Roebuck & Co.* In *Sears* the court refused to find that the company had discriminated against women in hiring and promotion into commission sales jobs, and instead attributed segregation in Sears's salesforce to women sales applicants' own preference for much lower paying noncommission sales positions.[6] Although *Sears* has provoked a great deal of attention and controversy,[7] it was by no means the first case in which an employer has dared to argue—or a court has deigned to affirm—that sex segregation is attributable to women's own choice. Employers have raised the lack-of-interest argument in at least 54 sex discrimination claims, spanning from 1972 to 1989.[8] Furthermore, in almost three-quarters of the claims (39, or 72.2%), women plaintiffs were seeking relatively low-level blue-collar jobs, mostly in factories.[9] Thus, the women whose job preferences have been questioned in these cases are working-class women who work mostly due to economic necessity. Yet, in almost half the cases (23, or 42.6%), courts accepted the employer's argument and interpreted sex segregation as the expression of women's own lack of interest in higher-paying nontraditional jobs.

Cases raising the lack-of-interest argument are rich terrain for exploring the relationship between law and identity. They illustrate how the legal system can reproduce the very categories of gender that women are struggling to subvert through law. In these cases, courts are called upon to characterize the work aspirations and identities of "women" as a group. To resolve the

lack-of-interest argument, judges must decide whether eligible women workers are systematically less interested than their male counterparts in more-
highly-rewarded nontraditional work. The legal system defines this as a
question of "fact," which implies that the answer can be discovered through
empirical investigation and revealed through evidence. But the evidence does
not and cannot reveal a verifiable answer to this question. To resolve the
interest issue and assign sex segregation a legal cause, courts must draw on
larger cultural assumptions about women and work. Judges cannot avoid the
problem of interpretation.

Consciously or unconsciously, the courts have created a framework for
interpreting segregation that obscures and limits the law's potential to transform it. Most centrally, courts have assumed that women's work interests
and identities are shaped exclusively in private realms of life that are independent of and prior to the workworld.[10] This "pre-labor market" view
separates the "public" world of wage work from "private" non-work realms
and relegates the formation of gender to the private side. Women develop
stable aspirations for traditional or nontraditional employment before they
ever begin working or searching for work; their job preferences constitute
predetermined "inputs" into the labor market. Once this assumption is accepted, there is no room for employers to participate in creating women
workers in their images of who "women" are supposed to be. As a consequence, there is little role for the law in constituting—or changing—the
dynamics that lead to sex segregation. Women's interests and identities are
fixed "before" the law, and the most courts can do to is to ensure that employers do not erect specific barriers to prevent women from exercising their
preexisting preferences.

To inspire more promising legal interpretations, feminists must expose
and challenge the foundational assumption that women have static interests
and identities that precede the influence of employers and the law. This
paper takes up that project. Part I traces how the courts have relied on the
pre-labor market assumption to create an unduly narrow framework for evaluating the evidence and interpreting sex segregation in sex discrimination
cases. Part II explores how judges tell stories about women and work to
legitimate interpretations of segregation that limit the law's capacity to dismantle it. Part III draws on sociological research to challenge the pre-labor
market view and propose an alternative account of the formation of women's
work aspirations that holds greater promise for legal transformation. In this
new account, women develop their work aspirations and identities only within
the context of, and in response to, structural features of the workworld. By
arranging work and workplace relations in ways that disempower women
from ever aspiring to nontraditional jobs, employers create the gendered
preferences that they use to justify sex segregation.

From this perspective, it becomes clear that the legal system can and does influence the interests and identities of women that courts purport to merely describe. Through the exercise of their institutional and interpretive authority, courts approve or alter the workplace arrangements out of which women's work aspirations arise. When courts impose liability, they can prompt employers to make changes that will dramatically increase women's representation in nontraditional jobs. That large numbers of women pursue such jobs in response to court decrees shows that women's interests are subject to legal transformation.[11] Whether or not courts impose liability, their decisions establish the terms within which women and employers will perceive and bargain over sex segregation in the future. Thus, judges have the potential power to create the conditions that make their stories about sex segregation come true.

The Interpretive Framework

Within the law expounded by federal courts in Title VII cases, there are two mutually exclusive explanations for sex segregation. The conservative explanation accepts the lack-of-interest argument and interprets sex segregation as women's own "choice," while the more liberal explanation rejects the lack-of-interest argument and interprets segregation as employer "coercion" (or discrimination). Although these interpretations lead to different outcomes, the fact that they are conceptualized as mutually exclusive reveals that they are premised on a shared assumption that women form their choices about work, independently of employer action or coercion, in private pre-work realms. Both conservative and liberal courts have relied on, and reinforced, this pre-labor market assumption in evaluating the evidence in sex discrimination cases. Through their assessments of the probative value of the evidence presented on the interest issue, the courts have created an anti-historical, anti-institutional approach to defining discrimination and interpreting segregation in sex discrimination cases.

This approach was not inevitable. Before the first sex discrimination case raising the lack-of-interest argument was decided, the courts had already decided a landmark series of race discrimination cases addressing the same argument. In these early race discrimination cases, the courts acknowledged that human choices are never formed in a vacuum and that people's work aspirations are inevitably shaped by the opportunities that have historically been available to them, as well as by their experiences in the workplaces of which they have been a part. The early race discrimination cases illustrate what the courts can accomplish when they have the vision to acknowledge their own power and responsibility to dismantle oppressive workplace arrangements.[12] That the courts have never taken such an approach in sex discrimination cases testifies to the degree to which judges have accepted the dominant cultural image of women as marginal workers: subjects formed in and for the private domestic order, rather than actors who shape their own identities and aspirations in relation to the public world of work (as men are assumed to do).

Early Race Discrimination Cases

Before 1972, the courts almost universally rejected employers' attempts to attribute racial segregation in their work forces to racial minorities' own job choices.[13] The courts created the "futility doctrine," which held that minorities' failure to apply for higher-paying predominantly white jobs was not due to any lack of interest but instead to a sense of futility created by the employer's history of discrimination. As early as 1967, the Fourth Circuit rejected a hospital's attempt to attribute the absence of Black physicians to their own lack of interest in joining the staff. "That so few Negro physicians have applied is no indication of a lack of interest, but indicates, we think, a sense of the futility of such an effort in the face of the notoriously discriminatory policy of the hospital, and may even reflect a fear of reprisals should they seek to attain their rights."[14]

The futility doctrine confronted the legacy of historical racial discrimination in the workworld. Early courts crafted a three-part evidentiary approach that facilitated plaintiffs' ability to invoke this doctrine and to counter the lack-of-interest argument. First, although the doctrine required a finding that the employer had engaged in past racial discrimination, judges were willing to infer past discrimination from statistical evidence of historic underrepresentation alone. This was an important principle, for many employers had implemented systems of segregation through informal customs so deeply ingrained that they did not require being openly stated. Judges acknowledged this phenomenon early on; they refused to require plaintiffs to produce "smoking-gun" evidence that the employer had once operated an overt system of segregation in order to prove that long-standing disparities were attributable to historical discrimination rather than to minorities' own past preferences.[15]

Second, the courts imposed on employers with historically segregated work forces an affirmative duty to attract minorities to formerly segregated jobs.[16] Judges evaluated whether employers had fulfilled this duty with reference to results— and not merely alleged efforts. When employers tried to exonerate themselves by claiming that they had made "special efforts" to recruit minorities, courts held that such efforts, however laudable, did not absolve employers of liability.[17] Judges refused to infer that the failure of employers' efforts was due to minorities' lack of interest, and instead condemned employers' efforts for "fall[ing] short of what is necessary."[18]

Third, and finally, the courts refused to individualize the problem of segregation. Employers tried to discredit the statistical proof by pointing to plaintiffs' failure to produce anecdotal evidence showing that individual minorities had been discriminatorily rejected or discouraged from applying. The courts concluded, however, that plaintiffs need not present individual victims of discrimination to refute the contention that minorities lacked interest in the work.[19] This approach followed from judges' recognition of the history of labor market discrimination. If a people's aspirations have been formed in the context of historical oppression, it is unreasonable (even cruel) to ask them to prove that they have not chosen their lot.

Taken as a whole, the evidentiary approach established in this body of cases reflected a strong judicial commitment to the view that minorities' work aspirations posed no impenetrable barrier to their full integration into the mainstream of economic life. This commitment, in turn, reflected an underlying assumption that minorities' current work interests were neither permanent nor inevitable, but rather only provisional preferences formed and expressed in the context of a historically racist workworld. If these work interests had been formed by employers' historically discriminatory practices, then they could also be altered through employer's persistent efforts. Judges pressed forward in the belief that they could prompt employers to "persuade the doubtful and the skeptical that the discriminatory bars have been removed,"[20] and thus free minorities to aspire to work many had never before dreamed of being able to do. By acknowledging that people's work aspirations are shaped in the context of what larger institutional and legal environments define as possible, early courts refused to allow employers to escape responsibility for the collective history of labor market discrimination by pinning the blame on its victims.[21]

Sex Discrimination Cases

In sex discrimination cases, the lower courts have never taken an approach parallel to the one taken in the early race discrimination cases.[22] In fact, judges have evaluated each type of evidence presented in connection with the lack-of-interest argument differently in sex discrimination cases than they did in the early race discrimination cases.

Most importantly, the courts have failed to situate women's work aspirations within a context of historical labor market discrimination. Sex-discrimination plaintiffs have not been able to overcome the lack-of-interest argument with evidence that the employer discriminated against women historically. In fact, evidence of past discrimination has actually decreased plaintiffs' likelihood of winning. Whereas plaintiffs prevailed on the lack-of-interest argument in only 48.6% (17 out of 35) of the cases in which they presented evidence of past employer discrimination, they prevailed on the argument in 73.7% (14 out of 19) of the cases in which they presented no such evidence. This result is the opposite of the one we would expect if courts had been relying on the futility doctrine to counter the lack-of-interest argument. The futility doctrine invokes the employer's past discrimination to explain historically disadvantaged group members' failure to apply.

Conservative courts have refused to invoke the futility doctrine because they do not believe that employers ever discriminated against women. These judges interpret even long-standing, near-complete patterns of job segregation as the expression of past women's own freely made choices; they invoke "common sense" as proof that women have always found nontraditional work unappealing. As one judge stated, "[C]ommon sense tells us that certain work in a bakery operation is not attractive to females. *This is a fact of life that an Act of Congress cannot overcome.*"[23] Or, as another judge put it, "There has been no showing that any female has ever wanted to work for the Hardwood Division. . . . Although the plaintiff may call this stereotype classification, the Court has not seen females clamoring to work in such jobs. . . ."[24] This conservative vision is ultimately ahistorical, for history reveals only the expression of an unchanging "truth" that gender and gendered work aspirations are so deeply ingrained that they may be considered part of human nature.

While conservative courts have denied the history of sex discrimination in the labor market, even more sympathetic liberal courts have not relied on the futility doctrine to counter the lack-of-interest argument.[25] Liberal judges acknowledge that employers historically denied women the opportunity to enter nontraditional jobs, but they remain skeptical that past generations of women would have taken those jobs even if the opportunity had been available.[26] The liberal approach rests on a story of historical progress that imagines a "modern" woman whose aspirations for nontraditional work represent a sharp break from those of most women in the past. Unlike the conservative vision, the liberal one is not completely ahistorical, for it acknowledges that human consciousness is subject to historical change. Yet, it traces the shift in women's work aspirations to unspecified "societal" forces in the private order, rather than to expanded opportunities in the labor market prompted in large part by law.

The conservative and liberal approaches converge for Title VII purposes, for neither clearly acknowledges the power of historical discrimination in shaping women's work aspirations and identities.[27] The courts' antihistorical vision, of course, denies the reason women needed Title VII's protection in the first place.[28] Like any civil rights statute, Title VII's prohibition of sex discrimination has meaning only if it is understood to symbolize a commitment to ending a history of oppression for a disadvantaged group.[29] The courts' failure to recognize that women's work aspirations and identities have been shaped collectively and historically by their experience of discrimination in the workworld has both grounded and reinforced the assumption that women's work preferences are formed freely and individually within private pre-work realms. This view has, in turn, led judges to rely heavily on the two types of evidence that they rejected in early race discrimination cases.

First, judges have accepted uncritically employers' assertions that they made special efforts to attract women to nontraditional work. Whereas courts accepted the lack-of-interest argument in 57.1% (12 out of 21) of the cases in which employers claimed to have made such special efforts, they accepted the argument in only 33.3% (11 out of 33) of the cases in which employers claimed no such efforts. These employers claimed that women's failure to respond to their overtures proved that women lacked interest in nontraditional work. Yet, most of the employers' alleged efforts lacked substance. In only one-third of the cases had employers even adopted written affirmative action plans with goals for women,[30] and none of the employers had directed any recruiting efforts specifically toward women's networks. Furthermore, employers offered little or no evidence that their efforts failed due to women's lack of interest. Of the twenty-one employers who claimed to have tried to "woo" women into nontraditional work, not one presented documentation that women had declined actual job offers at a higher rate than men. In most cases, employers offered only the self-serving testimony of managers that when they had approached women about the possibility of doing nontraditional work, the women said they found the work unappealing.[31]

The courts' reliance on such evidence reflects and reproduces a narrow conception of discrimination that is premised on the pre-labor market assumption. If women's work aspirations have been shaped not by a labor market that has taught them their place, but instead by prior "social" forces, then one cannot really expect employers to succeed in attracting many women to nontraditional work. As one court stated, "[T]he job preferences of females may be born of attitudes conditioned by *societal* sexist values. But frustration with the realization that equality of opportunity untouched by gender remains a *social* goal and not an achieved reality must not be visited on this employer in the form of liability."[32] Once this pre-labor market view is accepted, there is little role for employers in creating segregation and little role for the courts in dismantling it. Prohibiting discrimination means only ensuring that employers do not withhold formal opportunities from (the few exceptional) women who have already managed to form and express preferences for nontraditional work. But empowering most women to aspire to such work remains only a "social" goal, beyond the reach of managers or judges.

This same narrow view is manifest in the courts' reliance on anecdotal evidence of discrimination against individual "victims."[33] Whereas courts accepted the lack-of-interest argument in 59.1% (13 out of 22) of the cases in which plaintiffs failed to present anecdotal evidence of discrimination, they accepted the argument in only 31.3% (10 out of 32) of the cases in which plaintiffs did present anecdotal evidence.

Conservative judges explicitly berate plaintiffs for failing to produce evidence of discrimination against individual women. According to these courts, the absence of live "victims" serves only to confirm that women lack interest in nontraditional work.[34] Liberal courts, too, however, have looked to anecdotal evidence to decide how to interpret segregation. Although many liberal judges seemed ambivalent about whether the eligible women workers were, as a group, as interested as men in the work, the fact that a few live women stood before them to proclaim their interest persuaded the judges to reject the lack-of-interest explanation.[35]

The courts' reliance on anecdotal evidence is paradoxical, for anecdotal evidence does not suffice logically to confirm or controvert the lack-of-interest argument. The lack-of-interest argument is a *group-based* defense. Its validity depends on the assertion that, within the pool of eligible workers, the women are sufficiently less interested than the men to account for the degree of female underrepresentation.[36] Just as this assertion is not proved by offering a few women to testify that they were not interested in the work, neither is it disproved by offering a few women to testify that they were interested. With enough resources, lawyers can always find individual women to testify on both sides of this issue. Because judges have no way of discovering which group of witnesses is representative of the larger group of women in the eligible pool, and because testimony from such women witnesses reveals nothing about the level of interest among the men in the eligible pool, anecdotal evidence gets courts no closer to determining the validity of the lack-of-interest argument. In the end, judges cannot avoid the problem of interpretation.

In the early race discrimination cases, courts approached this same problem of interpretation with a sensitivity to the fact that minorities' work aspirations had been formed in the context of historical discrimination. Courts filled in the evidentiary "gap" by assuming that minorities were no less interested than whites in higher-paying, more challenging work. The courts' attribution of minorities' work aspirations to forces within the world of work—rather than private pre-labor market influences—grounded the presumption that there were no systematic racial differences in work preferences. If judges had been unwilling to take such an approach, employers would have simply rationalized the status quo as the expression of minorities' own work choices.

To a large extent, this rationalization of the status quo has occurred in sex discrimination cases. Courts have been unwilling to take an approach that analyzes women's work aspirations in the context of historical labor market discrimination and have instead attributed those aspirations to women's pre-work socialization. Like the focus on employers' claimed efforts, the courts' focus on anecdotal evidence simultaneously expresses and creates a narrow definition of discrimination that is based on this pre-labor market assumption. The courts rely on anecdotal evidence not because of its analytical persuasiveness, but for its symbolic value. Anecdotal evidence signifies that that society has progressed sufficiently to produce (at least a few exceptional) women who emerge from pre-work socialization with aspirations for nontraditional work. The individual victim has come to symbolize the "modern" woman, that "ungendered" creature who is entitled to the law's protection. But the focus on the individual victim has left the majority of women lying in the wake of the law. In the interpretive framework adopted by conservative and liberal courts alike, employers' practices are deemed discriminatory only insofar as they prevent individual women from exercising what are imagined to be their preexisting preferences for nontraditional work—and not because those practices are embedded in a larger web of workplace relations in which most women have never been able to dream of the possibility of such work.

Judicial Stories about Women and Work

Although both the conservative and liberal explanations rest in a common interpretive framework, they each legitimate a different legal outcome. To justify accepting the lack-of-interest argument, courts tell the conservative story of choice; to justify rejecting that argument, courts tell the liberal story of coercion. Each of these rhetorical justifications may be envisioned as a story with a beginning, middle, and end. There is dramatic tension, and resolution, as each story draws on particular images of women and work to explain women's underrepresentation in nontraditional work. Each story ends with a "moral" that makes sense of and legitimates a certain way of understanding sex segregation.

Both the conservative and liberal stories are stories about women, work, and segregation; they are not explicitly about law. But intertwined with their representations of women and work are implicit messages or "morals" about the transformative potential of Title VII law. The conservative story implies that law does not, and cannot, influence women's work aspirations and identities. The liberal story, too, however, suppresses law's constitutive capacity. By proceeding from the pre-labor market assumption, it posits a female subject whose identity is formed, and fixed, before the law. Neither story acknowledges the law's influence over the workplace structures out of which women's work aspirations and identities develop. Ultimately, both stories legitimate sex segregation by refusing to recognize the law's power to change it.

The Conservative Story

The conservative story rests on a simple syllogism: women are "feminine," nontraditional work is "masculine," and therefore women do not want to do it. Even though the story always follows this same logic, the story changes along class lines depending on whether women are challenging their exclusion from blue-collar or white-collar jobs.[37]

In cases involving blue-collar jobs, the story begins by describing the work in heavily masculinized terms. Nontraditional jobs in bakeries are "hot, heavy, and hard work."[39] Males, of course, do this "heavy work," while females do the "lighter," "less demanding work."[39] Work in a cardboard box factory is "dirty and somewhat heavy"; the factory is located in a "very poor section of the city" where (apparently even poor) women fear to tread.[40] Work as a food inspector is characterized as "nocturnal prowling in railroad years inspecting rotten food" that is not "attractive" to young women.[41] In these cases, the courts do not bother to question whether the work fits the gendered characteristics ascribed to it.[42] Within the story of coercion, work is simply reified, endowed with characteristics thought of as masculine as though there were a natural connection between heavy, dirty work, and manhood itself.

Once the work is represented in reified, masculinized terms, women's lack of interest follows merely as a matter of "common sense." "Common sense tells us that few women have the skill or the desire to be a welder or a metal fabricator," said one judge.[43] "Common practical knowledge tells us that certain work in a bakery operation is not attractive to females. . . .," said another.[44] Interestingly, in the blue-collar context, employers and courts almost never invoke women's domestic roles to explain their alleged lack of interest in nontraditional work. They appeal instead to a much broader, naturalized conception of femininity that draws on physical images of weakness and cleanliness and applies even to women with no family responsibilities.

In cases involving white-collar work, by contrast, the story begins by describing women as "feminine," and courts invoke social and psychological characteristics rather than physical images to ground their conceptions of femininity. In particular, employers appeal to domesticity to explain women's lack of interest in nontraditional work,[45] and conservative courts accept this explanation. In some cases, courts explicitly describe women as secondary-wage earners whose domestic responsibilities preclude a genuine commitment to wage work.[46] In other cases, the appeal to women's domestic roles is less direct, but even broader in its implications. In the *Sears* case, for example, the court invoked women's experience in the family as the source of a whole host of "feminine" traits and values that implied an aversion to commission sales jobs.[47] The implicit premise is, of course, that nontraditional work is inherently "masculine." In *Sears,* women were romanticized as friendly and noncompetitive, but this mattered only because such traits were the opposite of the ones allegedly needed to succeed in commission selling. Despite evidence suggesting that Sears had deliberately constructed the commission sales jobs in masculinized terms,[48] the court simply took for granted that the gendered characteristics Sears ascribed to the commission-sales position were an inherent, necessary part of the job.[49] Once the court endowed the job with these reified masculine characteristics, it became a foregone conclusion that women would find it unappealing.

The conservative story appeals to "masculinity" and "femininity" as oppositional, essentialist categories. The story is powerful precisely because it begins from the widely shared perception that the sexes are different, and translates this perception into an account of gendered work aspirations. If women have different physical characteristics or different domestic experiences than men, then this implies automatically that they have different job interests as well. In this story, gender is totalizing. The content of the "feminine" role is so monolithic and so all-encompassing that it dictates women's attitudes and behavior across all areas of life. Women's preferences for female work are so central to feminine identity that they remain unchanged and unchangeable regardless of what women experience in the workworld. The flip side of the coin is that work itself is inherently "masculine" or "feminine," apart from anything employers do to construct it that way.

With the world neatly compartmentalized into gendered people and jobs, sex segregation becomes easy to explain. Women bring to the labor market their preordained preferences for traditionally female work, and employers merely honor those preferences. In the story of choice, sex segregation implies no oppression or even disadvantage for women. Indeed, courts telling this story sometimes describe women's jobs as "more desirable" than men's jobs.[50] The moral of the conservative story is that working women choose their own economic disempowerment. The implicit message is that sex segregation is impervious to legal authority. It is simply the natural order that even "an Act of Congress cannot overcome."[51]

The Liberal Story

Like their conservative counterparts, liberal courts assume that women's job aspirations and identities are fixed in advance of their experiences in the workworld. This shared assumption drives liberal courts to a rhetoric that is the opposite of conservative rhetoric. While the conservative story totalizes gender, the liberal story suppresses gender, for liberal courts' acceptance of the pre-labor market assumption means that they can hold employers responsible for segregation only by representing women as ungendered subjects.

The liberal story centers around the prohibition against stereotyping. Liberal courts reject the lack-of-interest argument by reasoning that "Title VII was intended to override stereotypical views" of women.[52] "[T]o justify failure to advance women because they did not want to be advanced is the type of stereotyped characterization which will not stand."[53] By invoking the image of the individual woman who does not "share the characteristics generally attributed to her group,"[54] courts signify the presence of a new private social order in which the sexes are equal and ungendered. In this brave new world free of gender, young women emerge from pre-work realms with the same life experiences and values as men. If women approach the labor market with the same experiences and values as men, they must have the same job preferences as men; and if women end up severely underrepresented in nontraditional jobs, then the employer must have discriminated. The liberal story thus suppresses gender difference *outside* the workworld in order to attribute sex segregation *within* the workworld to employer coercion.

Conceptually, however, the liberal story only reinforces the conservative one. Because it begins from the pre-labor market assumption, the liberal story accepts the proposition that only women who are socialized the same as men can aspire to nontraditional work. To secure victory under the liberal approach, working women must present themselves as having no distinctive history, experience, or identity; they must pose as subjects ungendered before the law. But this approach only validates the conservative notion that women who are "different" ("feminine") in non-work aspects automatically have "different" ("feminine") work aspirations as well. It perpetuates the conservative view that defines "woman" and "worker" as contradictions in terms.[55]

The EEOC's position in the *Sears* case illustrates this dynamic. On appeal, the EEOC emphasized that contrary to the district court's findings, it had not assumed that female sales applicants were as interested as males in commission sales jobs. Instead, the EEOC recognized that women were less interested than men, and it had controlled for sex differences in interest by identifying the subset of female applicants who were similar to the males on a number of different background characteristics and who therefore could be presumed to be equally interested in commission sales.[56] Judge Cudahy, in a dissent from the Seventh Circuit's decision, agreed. Although he condemned the majority for "stereotyping" women,[57] his acceptance of the EEOC's position implied that the only women whose job interests were being inaccurately "stereotyped" were those whose personal histories resembled men's. This position assumed that women sales applicants approached Sears with definite preferences for commission or noncommission sales jobs firmly in mind. Indeed, Judge Cudahy stated this assumption explicitly, emphasizing that the EEOC's case would have been much stronger if it had produced "even a handful of witnesses to testify that Sears had frustrated their *childhood dreams* of becoming commission sellers.[58] Once this assumption was accepted, it became impossible to consider the extent to which Sears had contributed to shaping its workers' preferences along gendered lines. The only alternative was to identify the elusive group of women whose personal histories were so similar to men's that one might safely presume that they had been socialized to prefer the same jobs.

This leads to a second, related difficulty with the liberal story. By denying gender difference, the liberal approach obscures the processes through which employers draw upon existing gender relations to produce sex segregation at work. The liberal approach to discriminatory recruiting exemplifies this problem. Through recruiting, employers do more than simply publicize job vacancies to people who are already interested; they actually stimulate interest among those they hope to attract to the jobs. The harm of discriminatory recruiting practices such as sex-biased advertising or word-of-mouth recruiting is thus not only, or even primarily, that they fail to convey information about nontraditional job opportunities to already-interested women. The deeper harm of such practices is that they invest nontraditional jobs with such a masculinized image and culture that many women will never be able to picture themselves as the sort of person the employer has in mind.[59] Most liberal courts, however, have failed to recognize the deeper nature of the harm. They have analyzed the problem as one of passively failing to disseminate job information on a sex-neutral basis,[60] rather than as one of actively constructing people's work aspirations along gendered lines. Insofar as the liberal approach fails to identify the gender-producing dynamics of employers' practices, more conservative courts are able to turn the liberal rhetoric of gender neutrality against itself—to transform it into a defense of sex segregation.[61]

Ultimately, the liberal story is an inadequate alternative to the conservative one. The partial truth of the conservative story is that people and jobs are gendered; but they are not naturally or inevitably so. To explain sex segregation, one must account for how employers actively shape people's work aspirations and identities along gendered lines. In failing to account for the processes through which gender is socially constructed at work, the liberal story fails to confront the major problem Title VII should be addressing and fails to come to terms with the transformative potential of the law. For if women approach the workworld with pre-ordained, permanent job preferences, then neither employers nor courts can contribute much toward creating a world in which women aspire to and at tain the more-highly-valued work that the law has long been promising them.

An Alternative Account of Gender and Work

There is no need to posit women's "choice" and employer "coercion" as mutually exclusive, dichotomous explanations for sex segregation. A rich body of sociological and ethnographic research suggests an alternative account of sex segregation which rejects and reveals the fallacy of such oppositional thinking. Unlike the liberal story, this alternative account recognizes the reality of gender in social life. But unlike the conservative story, this account does not find sex-role socialization so monolithic or powerful that it dictates irrevocably gendered work aspirations. Girls and women may be taught to be "feminine," but this does not imply that they will aspire only to traditionally female jobs throughout their lives. Rather, women form, create and recreate their work preferences throughout their lives in response to changing conditions at work.

This new account traces gendered work attitudes and identities to organizational structures and social relations within the workplace. Like all workers, women adapt their work aspirations and orientations rationally and purposefully, but always in the context of and in response to the constraints of organizational arrangements not of their own making. It is not enough to provide women formal labor market opportunity, because deeper aspects of organizational life provide powerful disincentives for women to aspire to and succeed in nontraditional employment.

The new account suggests a more transformative role for the law in dismantling sex segregation. If women's work aspirations are shaped not solely by amorphous "social" forces operating in pre-work realms, but primarily by structural features of work organizations, then it is clear that Title VII can help bring about the needed changes. Title VII lawsuits promise to alter the very conditions that keep women from developing and realizing ambitions for higher-paid, more challenging jobs. The new account thus exposes the fictional character of the female subject fixed before the law, and encourages courts to take responsibility for their own role in creating and changing women's work aspirations and identities.

The Inadequacy of the Pre-labor Market Explanation

Both the conservative and liberal legal approaches proceed from the premise that women approach the labor market with stable preferences for traditional or nontraditional work; sex segregation persists because women are socialized to choose traditionally female jobs. On both empirical and theoretical grounds, however, this explanation is insufficient. Gender conditioning in pre-work realms is simply too slender a reed to sustain the weight of sex segregation.

On average, young women are more likely to articulate preferences for traditionally female jobs than young men; this is hardly surprising, given that girls and boys are continually bombarded with messages that link "femininity" and "masculinity" to sex-appropriate work.[62] Despite this conditioning, however, women's early job preferences do not remain stable but shift dramatically over time. Over eighty percent of all young women change their preferences after they begin working, and the sex-type of the jobs to which they initially aspire does not predict the sex-type of the jobs they desire—or actually do—as their careers unfold.[63] Even the sex-type of women's early jobs does not predict the sex-type of their later ones; both younger and more mature women move between female-dominated and male-dominated occupations over time.[64] These patterns controvert the claim that sex segregation is attributable to women's pre-work socialization. Even if women's early preferences predicted perfectly the sex-type of their first jobs, women's preferences evolve over time and do not explain where they end up in the occupational hierarchy.

Furthermore, the fact that women in nontraditional jobs often begin in traditionally female ones undercuts the view that nontraditional women workers are an anomalous group of women who somehow managed to escape early socialization to feminine sex roles. Indeed, women in nontraditional and traditional employment have similar personal histories, which suggests that nothing in the backgrounds of nontraditional women workers caused them to veer away from the "feminine" course that allegedly steered their sisters into more traditional jobs. Studies have shown that women's probability of moving across sex-typed occupational boundaries does not vary significantly by race, age, marital status, or parental status.[65] Other studies have shown that a woman's likelihood of being employed in a nontraditional occupation at any given time cannot be explained by such personal, family-related characteristics as marital status,[66] continuity of labor-force participation,[67] or number of children.[68] Despite the fact that women assume disproportionate family responsibilities,[69] these studies show that sex segregation cannot be attributed to women's domestic roles.[70] Contrary to conventional wisdom, sex segregation does not exist because women's family commitments lead them to "choose" to consign themselves to lower-paid, female-dominated jobs.[71]

If empirical evidence refutes the view that sex segregation is a function of women's early socialization, it also challenges the theoretical account of gender implicit in that view. Because it posits that women have "chosen" traditionally female work, the pre-labor market explanation appears at first to portray women as agents actively involved in constructing their own work aspirations and identities. Instead, however, this explanation eliminates women's capacity for agency. It presumes that the content of early sex-role conditioning is so coherent and its hold on women so permanent that it predetermines what they do throughout their lives. In adopting a static view of women's work aspirations, the pre-labor market explanation reduces women to little more than walking embodiments of other people's early role expectations for them. Adult women are limited to acting out scripts others wrote for them when they were children.

This view suppresses the dynamism and complexity that characterizes the development of female subjectivity. The content of early socialization is neither monolithic nor uniform. Girls receive ambiguous and inconsistent signals that encourage them in stereotypically masculine behavior as well as stereotypically feminine behavior. In addition, children do not always conform to even the clearest expectations, but respond to parental and other messages with their own interpretations.[72] It is not surprising, then, that young women emerge from early socialization with work preferences that are open and subject to revision. Neither life nor people are static; socialization is not a straightjacket that predetermines that adult women will aspire only to work that the dominant culture defines as feminine.[73] As they confront life's exigencies, women contest the content of femininity by drawing upon multiple, often contradictory systems of meaning.

Christine Williams's recent study of female Marines illustrates this point. One would be hard-pressed to think of an occupation American culture defines as more quintessentially masculine than the U.S. Marine Corps. Yet, Williams found that women in the Marines were no different from—no less "feminine"—than other women.[74] Female Marines "value[d] femininity and identif[ied] themselves as feminine,"[75] but they had a complex sense of gender identity that did not preclude them from engaging in occupational pursuits deemed appropriate for men. Indeed, they challenged the cultural construction of the military as inherently masculine, many of them insisting that the Marine Corp's basic training in discipline and deference was no different from Catholic schoolgirls' education.[76] Although these women did not evade gender identification, they did disrupt the dominant definition of feminine identity by expanding it to encompass aspirations and activities traditionally defined in opposition to it.

Like the quantitative studies, Williams's research refutes the notion that only unusual women who managed to escape early conditioning to traditional sex roles can aspire to nontraditional work. It is only within the context of their work experiences that women come to develop their work aspirations and identities. Mary Walshok's *Blue-Collar Women* provides a vivid portrait of this process. Like other nontraditionally employed women, the women in Walshok's study moved to nontraditional work from traditionally female work.[77] They began in female jobs "not because of a strong preference for that kind of work, but because there were no alternatives."[78] As a result of limited opportunities, both the college graduates and the less-educated women had erratic and unstable work histories—moving in and out of low-paying, dead-end, female-dominated jobs. Before they began working in nontraditional trades, these women had formed no real preference for any type of work. More than half the women had no prior interest in nontraditional jobs; indeed, most knew little or nothing about the trades they entered before they were trained for them.[79] They discovered their love for the trades, and their identities as committed workers, only as a result of encountering opportunities that became available after they had been in the labor force for years.

These women's experiences suggest that the direction of causation in the pre-labor market explanation is reversed. Rather than prior work interests and commitments leading women to jobs, women's work aspirations and commitments evolve and stabilize only in response to their opportunities and experiences in the workworld.[80] At one level, this observation is astonishingly simple. It seems obvious that gender conditioning does not grind to a halt when young women emerge from childhood, but continues behind the office door or factory gate to influence their aspirations and identities as adult workers. At another level, however, this point challenges much of what has been taken for granted about the reproduction of gender. If female identities remain in flux, then the workworld is no mere passive reflector of preexisting properties of gender, but rather a central site where the category of "woman" is contested and created.

The Construction of Gender at Work

An emerging perspective in the social science literature provides an alternative to the pre-labor market explanation. This perspective begins from the premise that people's work aspirations and identities are shaped by their experiences in the workplace—by the positions they occupy within larger structures of opportunities, rewards and social relations at work.[81] As Rosabeth Moss Kanter has written,

> [T]o a very large degree, organizations make their workers into who they are. . . . [O]rganizations act as though it is possible to predict people's job futures from the characteristics they bring with them [to] a recruiting interview. What really happens is that predictions get made on the basis of stereotypes and current notions of who fits where in the present system; poeple are then "set up" in positions which make the predictions come true.[82]

In contrast to the pre-labor market view, this perspective endows human beings with an ongoing capacity for agency. People act reasonably and strategically within the context of their organizational positions to make the best of them; their work aspirations and identities are "the result of a sense-making process involving present experiencing and future projecting, rather than of psychological conditioning in which the dim past is a controlling force."[83]

This perspective sheds light on the workplace dynamics that drive sex segregation. Women's patterns of occupational movement suggest that there are powerful disincentives for women to enter and remain in nontraditional employment. Recent research shows that women in higher-paying male-dominated occupations are leaving them at disproportionate—and alarming—rates.[84] Thus, just as employers appear to have begun opening the doors to nontraditional occupations, almost as many women have been leaving those occupations as have been entering them.[85] To the extent that women have been given formal opportunity to enter nontraditional work, something is preventing them from realizing that opportunity.

The new perspective demands that we look beyond formal labor market opportunity to inquire what it is about the workplace itself that disempowers women from permanently seizing that opportunity. Research in this tradition directs us toward the culture-producing aspects of work organizations, examining whether there is "something in the relations of employment, in work culture, the way jobs are defined and distinguished from each other, that conspires to keep women from even aspiring to [nontraditional] work."[86] For example, two structural features of work organizations that contribute to sex segregation are the structures of mobility and reward for traditionally female jobs and the work cultures of traditionally male jobs. These two features interact dynamically to construct work and workers along gendered lines—the first on the "female" side and the second on the "male" side.

Female-dominated jobs are structured in ways that encourage those who do them to develop work orientations that employers attribute to pre-existing gender attributes. It is, of course, an old insight that people who are placed in jobs that offer little opportunity for mobility and challenge will adapt to their situations by lowering their work aspirations and looking for satisfaction elsewhere. Decades ago, researchers documented this phenomenon among male workers. Men in low-mobility positions display work attitudes and behaviors that conventional stereotypes reserve for women. They do not define work as a central life interest, but focus instead on non-work activities. They interrupt their careers and dream of escape from their jobs. They value extrinsic features of their jobs such as sociability with their coworkers more highly than the intrinsic aspects of the work. They also insist that they are content not to be promoted.[87]

It was not until fairly recently, however, that this same insight began to be applied to women workers.[88] Female-dominated jobs tend to be on separate-but-unequal career ladders that offer far less opportunity for advancement than male-dominated jobs.[89] In addition, female-dominated jobs are often characterized by paternalistic forms of authority and evaluation.[90] In response to these unequal incentive structures, "[w]omen in low mobility . . . situations develop attitudes and orientations that are sometimes said to be characteristic of those people as individuals or 'women as a group,' but that can more profitably be viewed as universal *human* responses to blocked opportunities."[91]

Kanter's study of secretaries in a major industrial corporation vividly illustrates this point. The secretaries had little opportunity to move upward; they could not switch to the managerial track. Their own career ladder was short, with their rank derivative of their bosses' position in the organizational hierarchy. Bosses rewarded secretaries for their attitudes instead of their skills, their loyalty instead of their talent. An analysis of their performance evaluations showed that secretaries were valued most highly for "enthusiasm" and "personal-service orientation." In exchange, secretaries were offered symbolic rewards—such as "praise" and "love"—in lieu of higher wages or career advancement. As a consequence, the secretaries tended to display work attitudes and behaviors that are commonly perceived to be attributes of "femininity." Many were narrowly devoted to their bosses, timid and self-effacing, dependent on flattery, and given to gossip. But it was their position within the organization and the structure of incentives attached to their jobs that led them to develop these orientations. To be good secretaries, they were required to display the "feminine" behaviors that were attributed to their womanhood.[92]

Like the blue-collar men studied by an earlier generation of sociologists, Kanter's secretaries adjusted to their realistically nonexistent possibility of advancement by rating the desirability of promotion relatively low. They began to value relations with their coworkers over the intrinsic aspects of their jobs, developing a counterculture that valued mutual aid and loyalty over mobility and "success." The corporation's "folk wisdom" maintained that only women would be worried about taking a promotion because it would mean leaving their friends. But the men in low-opportunity positions exhibited the same concern.[93] Thus, like their male counterparts, the women's work aspirations and identities were shaped by the structures of incentives and rewards for their jobs.

The experiences of blue-collar tradeswomen illustrate the converse effect on women's aspirations created by their position in jobs offering higher wages, challenge, and the chance for advancement. These women's interest and commitment to nontraditional work seemed almost fortuitous, the by-product of being lucky enough to encounter the opportunity to move into jobs offering greater personal growth and rewards. The fact that they were confronted with such opportunities was not mere happenstance, however, but a direct consequence of the fact that their employers felt legal pressures to hire women.[94]

The tradeswomen's stories are a testimonial to the law's power to inspire transformation in women's work aspirations and identities. Many of the women cited the significance of affirmative action in influencing them to pursue nontraditional work. It was important for them to hear that the employer was actively seeking *women* workers—not just looking for workers in general (which they would have understood to mean men). When they heard that nontraditional jobs were opening up specifically for women ("I didn't think about nontraditional work until I heard the carpenters were looking for women. . . . But as soon as the possibility was mentioned, my imagination went with it");[95] or saw other women doing nontraditional work ("[T]hey had some potlucks for women in the building trades and I went there and I saw all these women and I was real excited—I thought, 'Oh, yeah, that's who I am, I'm like those women over there'");[96] or made contact with community-based programs designed to attract and support women in nontraditional work ("[I]t wasn't until I moved to Seattle when I was surrounded by organizations and groups that seemed encouraging of this— just seeing flyers about workshops on women in nontraditional trades. . . . That's when it became a real possibility"),[97] it occurred to many of them for the first time that they could aspire to and attain nontraditional jobs.

Once they began working in the trades, these women became highly motivated workers who defined their work as a central life interest and source of identity. Although many of the women had originally moved into nontraditional work because they needed the money, the job quickly became more than a paycheck. The women in Walshok's study valued four things most highly about their work: (1) productivity, or "a feeling of having done something constructive, of having accomplished something with one's time";[98] (2) challenge, or "a new or unusual experience, that requires a woman to stretch herself, to reach, to grow";[99] (3) autonomy, or the opportunity to work independently and to exercise discretion about how to control the timing and sequencing of one's work;[100] and (4) relatedness, or "feeling as if one's' in the swim of things,' in the 'mainstream' of life."[101] Indeed, women may appreciate these features of nontraditional jobs even more than men do, because they contrast so favorably with the characteristics of female-dominated jobs available to working-class women.[102]

If there is tragedy in this account of how people's work aspirations and behaviors come to be gendered, there is also potential for hope. If women's work orientations are attributable not to their preexisting "feminine" characteristics, but largely to the structures of mobility and rewards attached to their jobs, then the obvious solution is to change those structures. Title VII suits challenging sex discrimination in promotion hold the promise to do just that. In alleging that women on the female job ladder are systematically being denied promotion into better jobs on the male job ladder, plaintiffs are seeking to restructure internal career ladders so as to create new paths up and out of entry-level female jobs for all women (and not just an exceptional few). Courts can order remedies that will prompt employers to restructure those ladders in ways that will infuse women workers with new hopes and aspirations.[103] In doing so, they may also stimulate employers to redefine the content of entry-level jobs held by women in less patronizing, less sexist terms.[104]

To liberate working women to pursue nontraditional jobs, however, the work cultures surrounding those jobs would also have to be changed. While separate-but-unequal job structures encourage women to lower their work aspirations, they also create the appearance that segregation is natural in a way that encourages male workers to adopt proprietary attitudes toward "their" jobs. These attitudes encapsulate male-dominated jobs in a web of social relations that are hostile and alienating to women who dare to upset the settled order of segregation. Although the legal system focuses on conduct that is explicitly sexual in nature,[105] sexual overtures are only a small part of a wide-ranging set of harassing behavior and attitudes by male coworkers and supervisors that threaten women in nontraditional jobs.[106] The following statement by a woman welder captures a sense of what is involved:

> It's a form of harassment every time I pick up a sledgehammer and that prick laughs at me, you know. It's a form of harassment when the journeyman is supposed to be training me and it's real clear to me that he does not want to give me any information whatsoever. . . . It's a form of harassment to me when the working foreman puts me in a dangerous situation and tells me to do something in an improper way and then tells me, Oh, you can't do that! It's a form of harassment when someone takes a tool out of my hand and said, Oh, I'm going to show you . . . and he grabs the sledgehammer from my hand and proceeded to . . . show me how to do this thing . . . you know, straighten up a post . . . it's nothing to it, you just bang it and it gets straight. . . . It's a form of harassment to me when they call me honey and I have to tell them every day, don't call me that, you know, I have a name printed right on my thing . . . . Ah, you know, it's all a form of harassment to me. It's not right. They don't treat each other that way. They shouldn't treat me that way.[107]

This type of harassment is no isolated occurrence; it is a structural feature of the workplace that sex segregation engenders.[108] Although even overtly sexual harassment is widespread,[109] the broader form of harassment is so much a part of the "normal" environment of nontraditional jobs that many researchers do not even attempt to measure it. Walshok observed, for example, that it is "normal" for men in blue-collar trades to "question the sincerity of the woman's interest and commitment to a man's job," "to question whether the woman had technical or mechanical competence of the physical strength and agility to do the job," and "to resent women because they perceived them as taking away a job from one of their own."[110]

The hostile environments of nontraditional jobs create a serious disincentive for women to enter and remain in them. Women in male-dominated occupations are more likely to be subjected to harassment than are women in other occupations.[111] Women in female-dominated jobs understand that they will be likely to experience hostility if they attempt to cross the gender divide,[112] and they may conclude that the price of deviance is too high. Harassment is also helping drive the small number of women in nontraditional jobs away.[113] Blue-collar tradeswomen report that women are leaving the trades because they cannot tolerate the animosity and alienation,[114] and there are signs that this is occurring in male-dominated professions as well.[115]

One of the most debilitating forms of harassment is conduct that undermines a women's ability to do her job. In nontraditional blue-collar occupations, virtually all the training is acquired informally on the job. Thus, a woman's ability to succeed depends on the willingness of her supervisors and coworkers to teach her the relevant skills. Yet, women's stories of being denied proper training are legion.[116] Indeed, it is sometimes difficult to distinguish inadequate training from deliberate sabotage of women's work performance, both of which can endanger a woman's physical safety. Stories like carpenter Susan Eisenberg's are still too common:

> For some men, getting rid of the invaders was a personal mission. Ron, one of my first foremen, constantly warned me of the ways I might get killed in this dangerous trade: be electrocuted, have my head severed from my body, be boiled alive by steam. Without giving any instruction on how to do it safely, he told me one day to open up a 200-foot-long snake. . . . A snake is a thin piece of steel, used by electricians to pull wires through pipes. It comes tightly coiled, bound with wire ties, and if not opened carefully, will spring apart with great force. "I had a Chinese kid open one up," Ron told the crew, laughing. "He got it caught up his nose and would up in the hospital. Quit right after that." I haven't opened up a snake since without remembering how I sweated through it that first time, while my coworkers hid.[117]

In white-collar occupations, male workers—including elite professionals—also guard their territory against female incursion. Their conduct, too, runs the gamut from overtly sexual behavior,[118] to discriminatory work assignments and performance evaluations, to day-to-day personal interactions that send women the message that they are "different" and "out of place."[119] The white-collar equivalent of work sabotage may lie in evaluating women's work by differential and sexist standards, as *Price-Waterhouse v. Hopkins* illustrates. Among other outstanding achievements, accountant Ann Hopkins had secured a multi-million dollar contract with the Department of State, an accomplishment none of her peers had matched. Yet, when it came time to consider her for partnership, she was evaluated by criteria by which no man would be judged:

> One partner described her as "macho" . . .; another suggested that she "over-compensated for being a woman" . . .; a third advised her to take "a course at charm school." . . . Several partners critized her use of profanity. . . . [Another advised her] to "walk more femininely, talk more femininely, wear make-up, have her hair styled, and wear jewelry."[120]

Whatever male workers' motivations or sources of insecurity, harassment is a central process through which the image of nontraditional work as "masculine" is sustained. If there are no women in the job, the work's content can be described exclusively in terms of the "manly" personal characterstics of the men who do it. On the other hand, if women can do the work, it becomes far more difficult to define the job with reference to masculinized imagery.[121] As one female pipefitter explained:

> For a long time I wasn't allowed to do certain types of jobs. . . . Some of the men would take the tools out of my hands. You see it is just very hard for them to work with me because they're really into proving their masculinity and being tough. And when a woman comes on a job that can work, get something done as fast and efficiently, as well, as they can, it really affects them. Somehow if a woman can do it, it ain't that masculine, not that tough.[122]

By driving women away and undermining their ability to perform nontraditional jobs, harassment reinforces the idea that women are inferior workers who cannot meet the demands of a "man's job." By exaggerating gender difference to remind women that they are deviants and simultaneously pressuring them to conform to the dominant male culture, harassment mediates the contradiction posed by the presence of women doing "masculine" work. Thus harassing conduct enables men to continue to define "their" work (and themselves) in masculine terms.

Cynthia Cockburn's study of engineers illustrates this process. By defining women as inherently incapable of possessing technological competence, the men appropriated engineering as a masculine preserve. They viewed the relationship between manhood and technology in essentialist terms, as a natural affinity between "man" and "machine."[123] "In contrast to the way the men [perceived] themselves—as striving, achieving, engaging in the public sphere of work—they [viewed] women as static, domestic, private people, as nonworkers."[124] They defined women as "aspects of the decor" who "create a pleasant atmosphere,"[125] as interested in and good at "boring and repetitive tasks" that would drive men crazy,"[126] and as soft, weak creatures who "'couldn't do' the manhandling" required to master technology.[127] They exceptionalized the few women engineers as "performing seals," who must have been "train[ed] . . . up a bit" by some man behind the scene.[128] They also created an occupational culture built around "sexual stories, references and innuendo that are directly objectifying and exploitative of women."[129] By creating such a hostile work culture, the men ensured that few women would try to invade "their" jobs. They could then point to the absence of women as evidence that these jobs demand "masculine" skills and abilities not possessed by women.[130]

This analysis of the relationship between harassment and the "masculinity" of nontraditional work makes clear why so many women are reluctant to apply for such work. Women understand that behind the symbolism of masculinized job descriptions lies a very real force: the power of men to harass, belittle, ostracize, dismiss, marginalize, discard, and just plain hurt them as workers. The legal system does not adequately protect women from this harassment and abuse. Courts have erected roadblocks to recovery, abandoning women to cope with hostile work environments on their own. The general attitude of the legal system seems to mirror that held by many male workers and managers:[131] if women want to venture into a man's workworld, they must take it as they find it. As one court recently stated,

> [I]t cannot seriously be disputed that in some work environments, humor and language are rough hewn and vulgar. Sexual jokes, sexual conversation and girlie magazines may abound. Title VII was not meant to—or can—change this. Title VII is the federal court mainstay in the struggle for equal employment opportunity for the female workers of America. But . . . Title VII was [not] designed to bring about a magical transformation in the social mores of American workers.[132]

The legal system thus places women workers in a catch-22 situation. Women are disempowered from pursuing or staying in higher-paid nontraditional jobs because of the hostile work cultures surrounding those jobs. The best hope for making those work cultures more hospitable to women lies in dramatically increasing the proportion of women in the jobs. Eliminating those imbalances is, of course, what Title VII suits promise to accomplish. But when women workers bring these suits, too often the courts tell them they are underrepresented in nontraditional jobs not because the work culture is threatening or alienating, but rather because their own internalized sense of "femininity" has led them to avoid those jobs.

And so, the cycle continues. A few women continue to move in and out the revolving door, with little being done to prevent them from being pushed back out almost as soon as they enter. The majority of working women stand by as silent witnesses, their failure to enter used to confirm that they "chose" all along to remain on the outside.

Conclusion

This account of the dynamics of work and gender brings us back full circle to where we began: to the role of interpretation in creating meaning and power. Judicial stories about sex segregation simultaneously flow from and feed back into a larger stream of cultural understandings and practices. To characterize women's job interests and assign responsibility for sex segregation, judges must draw from larger cultural assumptions about gender and work and their interrelation. Once cast, however, judicial interpretations circle back to affect the very reality they purport to describe. By portraying women as already-fixed subjects who approach the labor market with preordained work preferences, courts reinforce sexist views of women as marginal workers fit only for the lowest-paying, least-challenging jobs. By portraying jobs as inherently "masculine" or "feminine," courts legitimate the structures through which employers construct work and workers' aspirations along gendered lines. By refusing to intervene, courts permit and even encourage employers to continue to organize work and work relations in ways that disempower women from claiming the more highly valued nontraditional jobs the law has promised them. When courts interpret sex segregation as women's own choice they negate the very "choice" they purport to defend.

What does this analysis mean for feminists, working women, and others who wish to challenge sex segregation on the job? The legal system remains one of the few arenas in which segregation may be contested. As such, it is simply too important for us to abandon. Just as workers adapt their aspirations and behavior within organizational constraints not of their own making, so too must we work within a legal framework not of our own invention. Still, the project is not hopeless. If workplace structures are open to revision, legal discourse also permits some room to maneuver.[133] Even under the existing legal framework, women have managed to achieve some gains. In fact, ironically, victories from within this framework expose its contradiction. Legal doctrine assumes that women's work interests are fixed in advance of organizational or legal action; yet, in response to legal intervention, women have developed new vocational interests and pursued nontraditional work in unprecedented numbers.

I have sketched an alternative account of work and gender in the hope of providing a new theoretical starting point for formulating strategies to expose this contradiction and to reveal the law's transformative capacity.

This new account has three implications that we might draw upon to expand the existing legal framework for interpreting sex segregation.

First, the new account provides a framework for educating judges that they can reject the fatalistic "choice" interpretation without resorting to the liberal suppression of gender. Once we acknowledge that women's early job preferences remain tentative and temporary, we need not ignore the force of gender in social life in order to hold employers responsible for sex segregation at work. Courts may acknowledge that our society pressures girls to conform to appropriate sex roles, that is women who assume the lion's share of the load of caring for families, and even that it is important to most women to think of themselves as "feminine," for none of these observations imply that women will aspire only to less highly valued female jobs. To put it more positively, judges may acknowledge that women (and particular groups of women) have a distinctive history, culture, and identity without concluding as a corollary that they are marginal workers content to do only unremunerative, unchallenging tasks. The meaning of feminine identity is never fixed but always fluid, and so we need not represent women as ungendered in order to recognize them as authentic workers. Indeed, it is only by recognizing the complexities and contradictions in gender identity that it can ultimately be subverted.

Second, we must elaborate upon and demand deeper judicial scrutiny of the internal culture-producing aspects of work organizations. Once we abandon the assumption that women approach the labor market with stable job preferences, it will no longer do to conceptualize discrimination in terms of whether employers have erected "barriers" to prevent women from exercising their preexisting preferences. Employers do not simply erect "barriers" to already-formed preferences; they create the workplace structures and relations out of which those preferences arise in the first instance. Thus, we must look beyond whether the employer has provided women formally equal opportunity to enter nontraditional jobs. Even well-intentioned recruiting efforts will fail if the firm manages only to convey an all-too-accurate picture of organizational life that serves more as a warning than a welcome to women. Through its hiring criteria, training programs, performance evaluation standards, mobility and reward structures, response to harassment, and the myriad, day-to-day actions and attitudes of its managers and male workers, the firm may have spun a web of social relations that debilitate most women from aspiring to nontraditional jobs. Disempowering work cultures can be changed, but only if courts are taught to recognize them as creators rather than reflectors of gender difference.

This leads to the third and most fundamental point: that the legal system is itself inevitably implicated in creating women's work preferences. Once we acknowledge that women's work interests are always unstable and potentially in transition depending on conditions at work, it will no longer do to imagine that women have a static set of "true" preferences that courts can discover as a factual matter and use to ground legal decision making. Indeed, the notion that women have stable work aspirations and identities becomes a legal fiction that is plausible only by taking as given the very structural features of the workplace that women are seeking to dismantle through law. Once we understand this, it becomes clear that preference-shaping is an unavoidable part of the law's domain. Every time a plaintiff brings such a case, a court must decide whether to affirm or alter the status quo. When courts accept the lack-of-interest argument, they permit employers to organize their workplaces in ways that disable women from becoming interested in nontraditional work. When judges impose liability instead, they can prompt employers to restructure their workplaces in ways that empower women to aspire to nontraditional jobs. Thus, legal decisions are embedded in the fabric of organizational life through which women's hopes and dreams as workers are woven.

By elaborating the new account, feminists can remind judges that they too are the architects of women's work aspirations and identities. Courts can acknowledge their own constitutive power and use it to create a workworld in which working women are able to choose the more highly rewarded work that Title VII has promised them. To create that world, they must abandon the fiction of the female subject already-fixed "before" the law.

NOTES

The notes to this essay follow the standard form of legal journals.

1. Butler, Gender Trouble: Feminism and the Subversion of Identity 2–3 (1990).

2. Throughout the 1980's, around 60% of all workers would have been required to switch to occupations atypical for their sex in order to eliminate occupational segregation. *See, e.g.,* J. Jacobs, Revolving Doors: Sex Segregation and Women's Careers 20, 28–29 (1989); Beller, *Trends in Occupational Segregation by Sex and Race 1960–1981,* in Sex Segregation in the Workplace: Trends, Explanations, Remedies 11 (B. Reskin ed. 1984) [hereinafter Sex Segregation in the Workplace]. Of course, estimates of occupational segregation understate the degree of segregation, because workers in apparently sexually integrated occupations are often employed in industries, firms, departments, and job titles that are highly stratified by sex. *See, e.g.,* Gutek & Morasch, *Sex-Ratios, Sex-Role Spillover, and Sexual Harassment of Women at Work,* J. Soc. Issues, Winter 1982, at 55, 61–62 (finding that in a representative sample of 1632 Los Angeles workers, 42% of the women employed in male-dominated occupations nonetheless worked in female-dominated jobs). According to some reports, the degree of job segregation by sex remains near complete. *See* Bielby & Baron, *A Woman's Place Is with Other Women: Sex Segregation Within Organizations,* in Sex Segregation in the Workplace, at 27, 35 (finding that in a random sample of 393 California firms, 90% of the workers were in job titles to which only men or women were assigned).

3. For a summary of these and other negative consequences of sex segregation for working women, see Women's Work, Men's Work: Sex Segregation on the Job 9–17 (B. Reskin & H. Hartmann eds. 1986).

4. Statistical evidence is the cornerstone of group-based Title VII litigation. Plaintiffs make a prima facie case of discrimination by demonstrating a significant disparity between the number of protected class members hired by the employer and the number of protected class members qualified and available for hire in the absence of discrimination. *See, e.g., Hazelwood School Dist. v. United States*, 433 U.S. 299, 307–08 (1977); *International Bhd. of Teamsters v. United States*, 431 U.S. 324, 339 n.20 (1977).

5. For examples of employers' use of this argument to justify sex segregation outside the litigation context, see C. Cockburn, Machinery of Dominance: Women, Men and Technical Know-How 165 (1985); and V. Beechey & T. Perkins, A Matter of Hours: Women, Part-Time Work and the Labour Market 102–19 (1987).

6. The EEOC's multiple regression analyses showed that Sears had significantly underhired women sales applicants for commission sales jobs, even after controlling for a number of potential sex differences in qualifications. *See EEOC v. Sears, Roebuck & Co.*, 628 F. Supp. 1264, 1296–98 (N.D. Ill. 1986) *aff'd*, 839 F.2d 302 (7th Cir. 1988). The median hourly wages for first year commission salesworkers were approximately twice as high as those for all noncommission salesworkers. *See* Plaintiff's Pretrial Brief—Commission Sales Issues at 27, EEOC v. Sears Roebuck & Co., 628 F. Supp. 1264 (N.D. Ill. 1986) (No. 79-C-4373). Nonetheless, the district judge concluded that the EEOC's statistical analyses were "virtually meaningless," for they were based on the faulty assumption that females sales applicants were as "interested" as male applicants in commission sales jobs. *See Sears*, 628 F. Supp. at 1305. According to the judge, women shunned the "big ticket," "hard" lines of merchandise likely to be sold on commission at Sears; they felt more comfortable with the "small ticket," "soft" products sold on a noncommission basis. *See id.* at 1306. In addition, women "disliked the perceived dog-eat-dog competition" and "financial risk" of commission sales, preferring the "security" and "more enjoyable and friendly nature" of noncommission sales. *See id.* at 1307. The U.S. Court of Appeals for the Seventh Circuit affirmed the district court's acceptance of the lack-of-interest argument. *See Sears*, 839 F.2d 302 (7th Cir. 1988).

7. The news media reported on developments in the case from its inception, and speculated about its effect on the future of Title VII enforcement. *See, e.g.*, Hunter, *U.S. Files Five Suits Charging Sears with Job Bias*, N.Y. Times, Oct. 23, 1979, at A1, col. 4; Williams, *Despite Class-Action Doubts, EEOC Presses Sears Bias Case*, Wash. Post, July 9, 1985, at A1, col. 1; Greenhouse, *Federal Judge Rules for Sears in Sex Bias Case*, N.Y. Times, Feb. 4, 1986, at A21, col. 2. Numerous scholars have analyzed the *Sears* case, discussing its implications for feminist theory and practice. *See, e.g.*, Kessler-Harris, *Equal Employment Opportunity Commission v. Sears, Roebuck & Company: A Personal Account*, 1986 Radical Hist. Rev. 57; Milkman, *Women's History and the Sears Case*, 12 Feminist Stud. 375 (1986); Scott, *Deconstructing Equality-Versus-Difference: Or, the Uses of Poststructuralist Theory for Feminism*, 14 Feminist Stud. 33, 38–47 (1988); Z. Eisenstein, The Female Body and the Law 110–16 (1988).

8. I searched systematically for every published Title VII decision since 1965 in which a federal district court or court of appeals addressed the lack-of-interest argument. For a more detailed description of the search strategy and the resulting set of cases, see Schultz, *Telling Stories About Women and Work: Judicial Interpretations of Sex Segregation in the Workplace*

in Title VII Cases Raising the Lack of Interest Argument, 103 Harv. L. Rev. 1749, 1766–69 (1990). *Telling Stories* describes and documents more fully most of the analyses presented in this essay; interested readers should consult that piece for more comprehensive legal and statistical evaluation of the cases.

9. Of the 39 claims involving blue-collar jobs, 22 (56.4%) involved factory work. The remaining blue-collar claims involved laborer jobs, jobs in the baking or transportation industries, or law enforcement positions. Even most of the white-collar claims did not involve professional or other high-prestige jobs. Of the 15 claims in which women challenged their underrepresentation in white-collar work, 10 (66.7%) involved relatively non-elite positions as sales agents or supervisors.

10. I use the term "workworld" here to refer to all aspects of wage work as a sphere of activity or interest. It encompasses both people's experience of searching for work in particular labor markets and their experience of working in specific jobs in particular workplaces. In stating that courts assume that women form their work aspirations and identities in private realms that are "prior to" the workworld, I mean to capture a dimension of both temporal and metaphysical priority. The temporal dimension is reflected in the view that women form stable work aspirations through biological influences or early-sex role socialization that is completed before they ever begin working or searching for work. This in turn implies an almost metaphysical dimension: women's job preferences are "fixed" in advance, so that they constitute predetermined inputs to the labor market. Throughout this essay, I refer to the realms in which courts imagine women's job preferences to be formed as "pre-work" or "pre-labor market" realms. I refer to the view that women form stable job preferences in such realms as the "pre-labor market" explanation for job segregation.

11. Several case studies document dramatic increases in female representation in nontraditional jobs in response to court-ordered or court-supervised decrees. *See, e.g., Appendix D,* in Equal Employment Opportunity and the AT&T Case 343 (P. Wallace ed. 1976) (recording a 119% increase in female participation in craft jobs and a 46% increase in female participation in managerial jobs between 1973 and the end of 1974); K. Deaux & J. Ullman, Women of Steel: Female Blue-Collar Workers in the Basic Steel Industry 85 (1983) (recording a 170% increase in female participation in production and maintenance and craft positions in two steel mills between 1976 and 1979); Council on Economic Priorities, Women and Minorities in Banking: Shortchange/Update 68 (1976) (recording a 166% increase in female participation in managerial, professional, technical and salesworker jobs, and an even greater increase in female participation in nontraditional blue-collar jobs, between 1971 and 1975). *See also,* Law, *"Girls Can't Be Plumbers"—Affirmative Action for Women in Construction: Beyond Goals and Quotas,* 24 Harv. C.R.-C.L. L. Rev. 45, 54 n.33 (1989) (documenting examples in which women applied in great numbers in response to announcements that construction jobs were open to them).

12. This vision is receding from the courts' view. In a forthcoming piece, I analyze how the federal courts have treated the lack-of-interest argument in race discrimination cases over time. Since the late 1970's, judges have become increasingly willing to attribute racial segregation to minorities' own lack of interest in higher-paying jobs. *See* V. Schultz & Petterson, Race, Gender, Work and Choice: An Empirical Study of the Lack of Interest Defense in Title VII Cases Challenging Job Segregation (unpublished manuscript on file with author).

13. Between 1967 and 1972, the lower federal courts decided twelve race discrimination cases in which employers raised the lack-of-interest argument. In all but two of the

cases, the courts rejected the argument. Even in the two remaining cases, the plaintiffs won at least a partial victory. *See* Schultz, *supra* note 8, at 1771 n.88.

14. Cypress v. Newport News Gen. & Nonsectarian Hosp. Ass'n, 375 F.2d 648, 653 (4th Cir. 1967).

15. *See, e.g.*, Parham v. Southwestern Bell Tel. Co., 433 F.2d 421, 426–27 (8th Cir. 1970); Jones v. Lee Way Motor Freight, 431 F.2d 245, 247 (10th Cir. 1970), *cert. denied*, 401 U.S. 954 (1971); *Cypress*, 375 F.2d at 653–55; United States v. Plumbers Local 73, 314 F. Supp. 160, 161–63 (S.D. Ind. 1969).

16. Many courts stated this affirmative duty explicitly, holding that employers were required to overcome their "reputations for discrimination" in the African-American community. *See, e.g.*, United States v. Sheet Metal Workers Int'l Ass'n, Local Union No. 36, 416 F.2d 123, 139 (8th Cir. 1969); United States v. Central Motor Lines, 338 F.Supp. 532, 551, 559–60 (W.D. N.C. 1971); United States v. Local 86, Int'l Ass'n of Ironworkers, 315 F.Supp. 120, 1236 (W.D. Wash. 1970), *aff'd sub nom.* United States v. Ironworkers Local 86, 443 F.2d 544 (9th Cir.), *cert. denied*, 404 U.S. 984 (1971).

17. *See, e.g.*, *Parham*, 443 F.2d at 425, 429; *Central Motor Lines*, 338 F.Supp. at 549–50, 565–66.

18. *Sheet Metal Workers*, 416 F.2d at 139; *accord Jones*, 431 F.2d at 248; *Ironworkers*, 315 F.Supp. at 1235; *Plumbers*, 314 F.Supp. at 163–64.

19. *See, e.g.*, *Jones*, 431 F.2d at 247 ("True, no specific instances of discrimination have been shown. However, because of the historically all-white makeup of the Company's [job] category, it may well be that Negroes simply did not bother to apply."); *Sheet Metal Workers*, 416 F.2d at 127 (containing a similar statement).

20. *Sheet Metal Workers*, 416 F.2d at 139.

21. This body of law probably took sex segregation as a given, however. Most of the cases involved jobs held by white men, and the courts do not seem to have envisioned women of color as among those who had been discriminatorily denied the jobs. *See, e.g.*, Rios v. Enterprise Ass'n Steamfitters Local 639, 501 F.2d 622, 632 (2d Cir. 1974) (noting that "women have never sought to become steamfitters," and vacating a 30% minority hiring goal because it was based on the entire minority population in the area and thus included women); United States v. Central Motor Lines, 338 F.Supp. 532, 548–52 (W.D. N.C. 1971) (mentioning African-American women in connection with clerical jobs, but not in connection with truck-driver jobs).

22. The relevant provisions of Title VII make no distinction between race and sex discrimination. *See* 42 U.S.C. § 2000e-1(a)(1)-(2) (1982). Moreover, the Supreme Court has never suggested that race and sex discrimination are to be analyzed differently under Title VII. Indeed, in the only sex discrimination case in which the Supreme Court has addressed the lack-of-interest argument, the Court supported its analysis of the interest issue with a reference to its earlier analysis of the same issue in a race discrimination case. *See* Dothard v. Rawlinson, 433 U.S. 321, 330 (citing International Brotherhood of Teamsters v. United States, 431 U.S. 324, 365–67 (1977)). In addressing other Title VII issues, the Court has consistently used the same approaches to analyze race and sex discrimination, citing precedent from the two context interchangeably. *See, e.g.*, Johnson v. Transportation Agency, 480 U.S. 616, 631 (1987) (citing United Steelworkers of America v. Weber, 443 U.S. 193, 197 (1979), to uphold an affirmative action plan for women).

23. EEOC v. Mead Foods, Inc., 466 F.Supp. 1, 3 (W.D. Okla. 1977) (emphasis added).

24. EEOC v. Korn Industries, 17 Fair Empl. Prac. Cas. (BNA) 954, 958 (D.S.C. 1978), *aff'd on other grounds and remanded*, 662 F.2d 256 (4th Cir. 1981).

25. Of the 31 sex discrimination cases in which the courts rejected the lack-of-interest argument, only one court explicitly invoked the principle, developed in early race discrimination doctrine, that an employer has affirmative duty to remedy the effects of his own past discrimination by attracting women to formerly segregated jobs. *See* Chrapliwy v. Uniroyal, Inc., 458 F.Supp. 252, 262 (N.D. Ind. 1977). In most cases, the courts did not rely on the employer's history of discrimination to explain women's recent reluctance to apply.

26. In *Catlett v. Missouri Highway & Transp. Comm'n*, for example, the evidence showed that until 1976, the State had never hired a single woman for its road "maintenance-man" job, and women continued to be severely underrepresented. 589 F.Supp. 929, 933–34 (W.D. Mo. 1983), *aff'd in part and rev'd in part*, 828 F.2d 1260 (8th Cir. 1987), *cert. denied*, 485 U.S. 1021 (1988). Although the Eighth Circuit affirmed the district court's rejection of the lack-of-interest argument, the appellate court did not even mention the possibility that the state's long history of exluding women may have discouraged them from applying. *Id.* at 1266. Furthermore, despite the district court's conclusion that the State's "long history of discrimination" necessitated numerical relief, *see Catlett*, 589 F. Supp. at 1020, the Eighth Circuit held that that the state's past record failed to warrant such relief and concluded that there was no need for the trial court even to maintain jurisdiction over the case to ensure that the State ceased its discriminatory practices. *See Catlett*, 828 F.2d at 1268–69.

27. Indeed, one cannot always distinguish clearly between the conservative and liberal approaches in judicial decisions. There is slippage between the view that women aspire to "women's work" because they are women and the view that women aspire to "women's work" because society has socialized them to be women. The allegedly more historical liberal approach converges with the ahistorical conservative approach insofar as the former attributes the historical change in women's work aspirations and identities to "societal" forces that are so vague and ill-defined as to constitute essentialist explanations. On this sort of essentialism, see Scott, Gender: A Useful Category of Historical Analysis, 91 Am. Hist. Rev. 1053, 1065 (1986).

28. Those who spoke in favor of the amendment adding the prohibition against sex discrimination to the original 1964 Act focused on the injustice of sex segregation in the labor market. *See, e.g.,* 110 Cong. Rec. 2579–80, 2580–81 (1964) (remarks of Reps. Griffiths and St. George). Furthermore, when Congress amended Title VII in 1972, both the House and the Senate made clear that they considered sex segregation to be a primary evil that the statute was designed to address. *See* H.R. Rep. No. 92-238, 92nd Cong., 1st Sess. 4–5, *reprinted in* 1972 U.S. Code Cong. & Admin. News 2137, 2140 [hereinafter House Report] ("[W]omen are placed in the less challenging, the less responsible, and the less remunerative positions on the basis of their sex alone. Such blatantly disparate treatment is particularly objectionable in view of the fact that Title VII has specifically prohibited sex discrimination since its enactment in 1964."); S. Rep. No. 415, 92nd Cong., 1st Sess. 7 (1971) [hereinafter Senate Report] (including similar statements). Finally, both the House and the Senate stated that they intended the courts to treat discrimination based on sex with the same seriousness as discrimination based on any other protected status. *See* Senate Report, at 7; House Report, at 5.

29. A voluminous literature documents historical labor market discrimination against women, including employer practices restricting women to lower-paying, less desirable jobs. For examples, see M. Greenwald, Women, War, and Work: The Impact of World War I on

Women Workers in the United States (1980); J. Jones, Labor of Love, Labor of Sorrow: Black Women, Work, and the Family From Slavery to the Present (1985); A. Kessler-Harris, Out to Work: A History of Wage-Earning Women in the United States (1982); and R. Milkman, Gender at Work: The Dynamics of Job Segregation by Sex During World War II (1987).

30. Not even a written affirmative action plan guaranteed that an employer was serious about trying to integrate women into nontraditional work. In *Parker v. Siemens-Allis, Inc.*, for example, the evidence showed that as late as 1980, the company's machine shop remained 95% male, while the electrical department was 85% female. 601 F. Supp. 1377, 1379 (E.D. Ark. 1985). Although the company tried to defend these disparities by arguing that women were not interested in working in the machine shop, the company's own affirmative action plan contained the following statement: "'There are some things about the job that appeal to the females such as: clean working conditions, routine work, which once learned, gives the female the opportunity to plan the family budget, menu and other responsibilities . . .'" *Id.* at 1385 (quoting the company's affirmative action plan).

31. *See, e.g.,* Ste. Marie v. Eastern R.R. Ass'n, 650 F.2d 395, 403 (2d Cir. 1981); EEOC v. Mead Foods, Inc., 466 F. Supp. 1, 3–4 (W.D. Okla. 1977).

32. Davis v. City of Dallas, 483 F. Supp. 54, 61 (N.D. Tex. 1979) (emphasis added).

33. Typically, anecdotal evidence shows that the employer discriminatorily rejected individual women applicants or discriminatorily discouraged others from applying. For this reason, it is sometimes referred to as "victim testimony." For evidence that people who experience discrimination are reluctant to claim the mantle of victimhood, see Bumiller, *Victims in the Shadow of the Law: A Critique of the Model of Legal Protection,* 12 Signs 421 (1987); Crosby, *The Denial of Personal Discrimination,* 27 Am. Behav. Sci. 371 (1984).

34. *See, e.g.,* EEOC v. Sears, Roebuck & Co., 628 F. Supp. 1264, 1324–25 (N.D. Ill. 1986) ("EEOC's total failure to produce any alleged victim of discrimination serves only to confirm the court's conclusion that no reasonable inference of sex discrimination can be drawn from [the] statistical evidence . . ."), *aff'd,* 839 F.2d 302 (7th Cir. 1988); EEOC v. Korn Indus., 17 Fair Empl. Prac. Cas. (BNA) 954, 959 (D.S.C. 1978) ("There has been no showing that any female ever wanted to work for the Hardware Division"), *aff'd on other grounds and remanded,* 662 F.2d 256 (4th Cir. 1981).

35. *See, e.g.,* Kohne v. Imco Container Co., 480 F. Supp. 1015, 1027–28 (W.D. Va. 1979) (acknowledging that "many of the female [employees] prefer the jobs to which they are assigned,' but citing the testimony of other women employees to conclude that women were "interested in the spectrum of traditionally male jobs at the plant"); Ostapowicz v. Johnson Bronze Co., 369 F. Supp. 522, 537, 538 (W.D. Pa. 1973) (acknowledging that the employer had produced "a large amount of testimony that certain women were happy in the plant and thought that there was no discrimination," but relying on the fact that a number of women had not opted out of the class to reject the lack-of-interest argument), *aff'd in part and vacated in part on other grounds,* 541 F.2d 394 (3d Cir. 1976), *cert. denied,* 429 U.S. 1041 (1977).

36. This point can be illustrated through the following example. Suppose the plaintiff's evidence shows that of 100 people hired by the employer, only 5 (5%) were women. By comparison, of the 1000 workers that plaintiffs contend were eligible for hire in the local areas, 400 (40%) were women and 600 (60%) were men. Now suppose the employer proves that of the 400 women plaintiffs contend were eligible for hire, 200 (50%) lacked interest in the work. The employer might contend that women's lack of interest explains their under-representation. But if 50% (300) of the men in the original pool also lacked interest in the

work, the number of eligible male workers would decline from 600 to 300. This would leave a final pool of 500 eligible and interested workers, 200 (40%) of whom are women and 300 (60%) of whom are men. Thus, the proportions of men and women in the final pool would be identical to those in the pool originally proposed by the plaintiffs. The lack-of-interest argument cannot explain why the employer's hirees included only 5 (5%) women, when the pool of eligible and interested workers included 200 (40%) women. To explain this statistical disparity, the employer must show that, whatever the number of workers in the original pool who were interested in the work, only around 5% were women and 95% were men. This would mean that of the original pool, women were 19 times less interested than men in the work.

37. The outcomes of blue-collar and white-collar cases do not vary significantly. Courts rejected the lack-of-interest argument in 59.0% (23 out of 39) of the claims involving blue-collar jobs, and in 53.3% (8 out of 15) of the claims involving white-collar jobs.

38. EEOC v. Mead Foods, Inc., 466 F. Supp. 1, 2 (W.D. Okla. 1977).

39. *See id.* at 4.

40. EEOC v. Service Container Corp., 19 Fair Empl. Prac. Cas. (BNA) 1614, 1616 (W.D. Okla. 1976).

41. Ste. Marie v. Eastern R.R. Ass'n, 650 F.2d 395, 403 (2d Cir. 1981).

42. In these cases, the courts did not require the employers to prove that being male was a bona fide occupational qualification (BFOQ) for the jobs. Under the BFOQ defense, the employer must document that the jobs require certain essential tasks that "all of substantially all women would be unable to perform." Diaz v. Pan Am. World Airways, 442 F.2d 228, 235 (5th Cir. 1969), *cert. denied,* 404 U.S. 950 (1971); *accord,* Dothard v. Rawlinson, 433 U.S. 321, 333 (1977) (citing the *Diaz* formulation approvingly).

43. Logan v. General Fireproofing Co., 6 Fair Empl. Prac. Cas. (BNA) 140, 144 (W.D. N.C. 1972).

44. EEOC v. Mead Foods, Inc., 1, 3 (W.D. Okla. 1977).

45. It is not clear why employers resort to different explanations for sex segregation in the blue-collar and white-collar contexts. Perhaps employers have realized that it would be implausible to attribute sex segregation to women's domestic roles in blue-collar settings, where women with family responsibilities have long labored in jobs that demand as much of their time as the higher-paying jobs done by men. In numerous cases in this study, women were assigned to lower-paying female jobs in factories, even though those jobs were apparently on the same shifts as the higher-paying, male-dominated jobs. *See, e.g.,* Mitchell v. Mid-Continent Spring Co., 583 F.2d 275, 279 (4th Cir. 1978), *cert. denied,* 441 U.S. 922 (1979) (noting that plant supervisor testified that the company permitted male-only machine set-up employees to transfer between the day and night shifts, but refused to permit female-only machine operators to do so, because "'there was a shortage of men. However, females were easier to hire.'"). Conversely, employers may have realized that they could not plausibly defend women's absence from white-collar work with images of physical difference, because white-collar work is light, clean work of the type associated with femininity in the blue-collar context.

46. *See, e.g.,* Gillespie v. Board of Education, 528 F. Supp. 433, 437 (E.D. Ark. 1981), *aff'd on other grounds,* 692 F.2d 529 (8th Cir. 1982) ([M]ales who are pursuing careers in education are often the principal family breadwinners. Women . . ., on the other hand,

have frequently taken teaching jobs to supplement family income and leave when this is no longer necessary . . .")

47. According to the court, "women tend to see themselves as less competitive" than men and are "more interested than men in the social and cooperative aspects of the workplace." EEOC v. Sears, Roebuck & Co., 628 F. Supp. 1264, 1308 (N.D. Ill. 1986), *aff'd*, 839 F.2d 302 (7th Cir. 1988). To support these generalizations, the court cited the testimony of the historian hired by Sears, *see id.* at 1308 n.42, who attributed these alleged attributes to women's historic domestic roles. *See* Offer of Proof Concerning the Testimony of Dr. Rosalind Rosenberg, EEOC v. Sears, Roebuck & Co., 628 F. Supp. 1264 (N.D. Ill. 1986) (No-79-C-4373).

48. Sears' retail testing manual described a commission salesperson as a "special breed of cat" who has a "sharper intellect" and "more powerful personality" than noncommission salesworkers, *Sears*, 628 F. Supp. at 1290, and as someone who is "active," " 'has a lot of drive,' " has " 'considerable physical vigor,' " and " 'likes work which requires physical energy.' " *Id.* at 1300. Sears also administered to sales applicants a test that included such questions as, " 'Do you have a low-pitched voice?,' " " 'Do you swear often?,' " " 'Have you done any hunting?,' " and " 'Have you played on a football team?' " *Id.* at 1300 n.29.

49. That Sears' characterization of the commission sales job varied dramatically from the way the job was defined in an earlier era shows that there is nothing necessary or inevitable about the way Sears characterized it. In the period from 1890 to 1940, when department store managers were eager to attract women to retail sales jobs in the newly expanding service sector, managers defined the essence of "good selling" in stereotypically feminine terms rather than the masculine ones emphasized by Sears. *See* S. Benson, Counter Cultures: Saleswomen, Managers, and Customers in American Department Stores, 1890–1940, at 130–31 (1986).

50. *See, e.g.,* EEOC v. H.S. Camp & Sons, Inc., 542 F. Supp. 411, 446 (M.D. Fla 1982); EEOC v. Mead Foods, Inc., 466 F. Supp. 1, 4 (W.D. Okla. 1977).

51. *Mead,* 466 F. Supp. at 3.

52. EEOC v. Cook Paint & Varnish Co., 24 Fair Empl. Prac. Cas. (BNA) 51, 56 (W.D. Mo. 1980).

53. Ostapowicz v. Johnson Bronze Co., 369 F. Supp. 522, 537 (W.D. Pa. 1973), *aff'd in part and vacated in part on other grounds*, 541 F.2d 394 (3d Cir. 1976), *cert. denied*, 429 U.S. 1041 (1977).

54. *Id.* at 537.

55. This point is similar to the one Joan Scott has made about the equal-versus-difference debate. *See* Scott, *supra* note 7, at 43–47. For an exploration of how the dichotomization of "woman" and "worker" legitimated the sexual division of labor in the nineteenth century, see Scott, The Woman Worker in the Nineteenth Century, in La Storia Della Donne (Duby & Perrot, eds. 1991).

56. *See* Brief for the Equal Employment Opportunity Commission as Appellant at 7, EEOC v. Sears, Roebuck & Co., 839 F.2d 302 (7th Cir. 1988) (Nos. 86-1519 and 86-1621). The EEOC argued that "men and women who are alike with respect to [these background] . . . characteristics would be similar with respect to their interest in commission sales." *Id.* at 38.

57. *See* EEOC v. Sears, Roebuck & Co., 839 F.2d 302, 261–62 (7th Cir. 1988) (Cudahy, J., concurring in part and dissenting in part).

58. *Id.* at 362 (emphasis added).

59. See Bem & Bem, *Does Sex-Biased Advertising 'Aid and Abet' Sex Discrimination?*, 3 J. Applied Soc. Psychology 6 (1973) (finding that whereas only 5% of women expressed interest in telephone "lineman" and "frame-man" jobs when an advertisement described these jobs in sexually-loaded language, 25% expressed interest when the language was more sex-neutral, and 45% expressed interest when the ad was written to appeal to women); C. Cockburn, *supra* note 5, at 181 (arguing that women respond to advertisements describing jobs in masculinized language as "more of a warning than an invitation").

60. *See, e.g.,* Hill v. Western Elec. Co., 12 Fair Empl. Prac. Cas. (BNA) 1175, 1179 (E.D. Va. 1976), *aff'd in part and rev'd in part on other grounds,* 596 F.2d 99 (4th Cir.), *cert. denied,* 444 U.S. 929 (1979) (sex-segregated advertising); Babrocky v. Jewel Food Co., 773 F.2d 857, 867 (7th Cir. 1985) (word-of-mouth recruiting).

61. See, for example, Wilkins v. University of Houston, in which the Fifth Circuit refused to characterize word-of-mouth recruiting as sexually discriminatory, despite the fact that the court had long recognized word-of-mouth recruiting to be racially discriminatory. According to the court, "the obstacle of wide-spread segregation faced by potential black employees . . . is not present for women seeking university faculty positions" . . . [because] women . . . have been educated at the same institutions and by the same professors as their male counterparts." 654 F.2d 388, 400 (5th Cir. 1981), *vacated on other grounds,* 459 U.S. 809 (1982). In the Fifth Circuit's view, the brave new world of sexual equality has arrived on college campuses; female students are as likely as males to be favored and recommended for faculty positions by their (mostly male) professors. For evidence refuting this rosy scenario, see Fiske, *Lessons,* N.Y. Times, Apr. 11, 1990, at B8, col. 1, which reports a recent study finding that, among other disadvantages experienced by female college students, "faculty members consistently take male students and their contributions more seriously than females and their ideas."

62. For a summary of studies showing sex differences in young people's early occupational aspirations and a discussion of the social mechanisms through which their aspirations come to be gendered, see Marini & Brinton, *Sex Typing in Occupational Socialization,* in Sex Segregation in the Workplace, *supra* note 2, at 192.

63. *See* J. Jacobs, *supra* note 2, at 94–97.

64. *See id.* at 97–98, 140–42.

65. *See id.* at 148–49. Jacobs found that other independent variables—including number and ages of children, weeks employed, and hours worked per week— did not substantially alter women's probability of moving between female-dominated and male-dominated occupations. *See id.* at 149–50. Jacobs' findings are consistent with Rosenfeld's, who found that women's likelihood of changing the sex-type of their occupations was independent of their marital status and whether they had interrupted their careers to care for children. *See* Rosenfeld, *Job Changing and Occupational Sex Segregation: Sex and Race Comparisons,* in Sex Segregation in the Workplace, *supra* note 2, at 56, 72–76. Ironically, Rosenfeld found that "[t]he only effect of family responsibility . . . [was] for white *men,*" who were less likely to move from a male-dominated to a female-dominated occupation if they were married. *Id.* at 74 (emphasis in original).

66. *See* Beller, *Occupational Segregation by Sex: Determinants and Changes,* 17 J. Hum. Resources 371, 383 (1982); England, *The Failure of Human Capital to Explain Occupational Sex Segregation,* 17 J. Hum. Resources 358, 167 (1982).

67. *See* Corcoran, Duncan & Ponza, *Work Experience, Job Segregation, and Wages,* in Sex Segregation in the Workplace, *supra* note 2, at 171, 188; England, *supra* note 66, at 368.

68. *See* Beller, *supra* note 67 at 384–85; Daymont & Statham, *Occupational Atypicality: Changes, Causes and Consequences,* in 5 Dual Careers 107 (L. Shaw ed. 1981).

69. Studies have universally found that women do far more child care and other domestic labor than men. *See, e.g.,* S. Berk, The Gender Factory: The Apportionment of Work in American Households (1985); M. Geerken & W. Gove, At Home and At Work: The Family's Allocation of Labor (1983).

70. For example, Jacobs concluded that "marital and family responsibilities simply are not powerful factors in producing mobility from male-dominated into female-dominated occupations." J. Jacobs, *supra* note 2, at 190–91. Similarly, Rosenfeld concluded that "[f]or neither black nor white women was there much support for the idea that extent of family responsibilities influences the chance to move from or to a sex-typical occupation." Rosenfeld, *supra* note 65, at 77.

71. That women with and without primary family responsibilities are almost equally likely to be found in, or to move into, nontraditional occupations may reflect a number of underlying phenomena. First, many nontraditional jobs probably do not pose any greater barriers to family life than do traditionally female jobs. Indeed, as the pay equity movement has emphasized, portraying the jobs men do as inherently more demanding than the jobs women do is part of the very ideological framework that stigmatizes women as marginal workers. Second, to the extent that some nontraditional jobs do make demands that are difficult for primary family caretakers, many women are willing to undertake those demands despite the back-breaking double-burden. Particularly for working-class women, the higher wages for nontraditional jobs enable them to give their children greater opportunities, such as a college education.

72. *See* K. Gerson, Hard Choices: How Women Decide About Work, Career, and Motherhood 53–55, 198 (1985).

73. Gerson's study of a group of women aged 27 through 37 from varying socioeconomic backgrounds confirms this theme of change and development over time. Of the women who reported having early domestic orientations, 67% changed their orientations to nondomestic ones as adults; and of the women who reported nondomestic origins, 63% became domestically-oriented as adults. Furthermore, neither parental expectations nor maternal role models predicted whether the women took domestic or nondomestic paths. Of those whose parents had emphasized the importance of marriage and family, only 47% were domestically oriented as adults; and of those whose parents had stressed education, work and self-sufficiency, only 62% held primarily nondomestic orientations as adults. *See id.* at 55.

74. *See* C. Williams, Gender Differences at Work: Women and Men in Nontraditional Occupations 72–74 (1989).

75. *Id.* at 6.

76. *Id.* at 141.

77. *See* M. Walshok, Blue-Collar Women: Pioneers on the Male Frontier 121 (1981). *See also* K. Deaux & J. Ullman, *supra* note 11, at 74 (reporting that of the 103 women in nontraditional jobs in steel mills, the vast majority had previously been employed in traditionally female jobs); M. Martin, Hard-Hatted Women: Stories of Struggle and Success in the Trades (1988) (revealing that of the 18 women in nontraditional trades who discussed their

employment history, 14 had previously held female-dominated jobs); J. Schroedel, Alone in a Crowd: Women in the Trades Tell Their Stories (1985) (revealing that of the 15 women in nontraditional blue-collar jobs, 20 had previously held female-dominated jobs).

78. M. Walshok, *supra* note 77, at 120.

79. *See id.* at 136, 138, 156.

80. *See id.* at 132. Walshok suggests that the pre-labor market explanation is class biased. Because economically privileged women do not necessarily take paid employment for granted, they may have the luxury of exploring and clarifying their work interests before they enter the labor market. In contrast, working-class women must begin working early in life in whatever jobs they can find. Thus, "employment may be the first step and the primary context in which [their] values and interests become solidified . . . [They] might discover a whole world of unanticipated interests and abilities on the job which then become the impetus for training or education at a later phase in life." *Id.* at 272. Yet, the pre-labor market explanation may also fail to capture the experience of many middle-class women. In case studies of women in medicine and law, Jacobs found that substantial numbers of women entered these professions mid-career, after beginning in female-dominated occupations. This suggests that such women were not raised with atypical sex-role expectations, but rather contested their early socialization and entered male-dominated professions when the opportunity became available. *See* J. Jacobs, *supra* note 2, at 155–64.

81. For an overview of research in this tradition, see P. England & G. Farkas, Households, Employment and Gender: A Social, Economic, and Demographic View (1986).

82. R. Kanter, Men and Women of the Corporation 263 (1977).

83. *Id.* at 252.

84. *See* J. Jacobs, *supra* note 2, at 141–43.

85. The overall level of sex segregation declined during the 1970's because in absolute numbers, more women entered male-dominated occupations than left them. The level of segregation would have declined much more dramatically, however, if there had been less attrition of women from male-dominated occupations. *See id.* at 142–43. Jacobs found that this same pattern of attrition continued into the 1980's. *Id.* at 4.

86. C. Cockburn, *supra* note 5, at 165.

87. See, for example, E. Chinoy, *Automobile Workers and the American Dream* (1955); Dubin, *Industrial Workers' Worlds: A Study of the 'Central Life Interests' of Industrial Workers,* 3 Soc. Probs. 131 (1956); Guest, *Work Careers and Aspirations of Automobile Workers,* 19 Am. Soc. Rev. 155 (1954); Mayer & Goldstein, *Manual Workers as Small Businessmen,* in Blue-Collar World 537 (A. Shostak & W. Gomberg eds. 1964); Pennings, *Work-Value Systems of White-Collar Workers,* 15 Admin. Sci. Q. 397 (1970). For a summary of these and other similar studies, see R. Kanter, *supra* note 82, at 140, 143, 147–48.

88. For a critique of earlier sociological studies for analyzing men's relationship to employment on a "job model" but analyzing women's on a "gender model," see Feldberg & Glenn, *Male and Female: Job Versus Gender Models in the Sociology of Work,* 26 Soc. Probs. 524 (1979).

89. For summaries of research documenting the existence of separate internal career ladders for men and women, see Hartmann, *Internal Labor Markets and Gender: A Case Study of Promotion,* in Gender in the Workplace 59, 59–66 (C. Brown & J. Pechman eds. 1987); Roos and Reskin, *Institutional Factors Contributing to Sex Segregation in the Workplace,* in Sex Segregation in the Workplace, cited above in note 2, at 248–51.

90. *See, e.g.*, Coverman, *Occupational Segmentation and Sex Differences in Earnings*, 5 Res. Soc. Stratification & Mobility 139 (1986); R. Cavendish, Women on the Line 80–97 (1982).

91. R. Kanter, *supra* note 82, at 159 (emphasis in original); *see also* Laws, *Psychological Dimensions of Labor Force Participation of Women*, in Equal Employment Opportunity and the AT&T Case, *supra* note 11, at 125, 141.

92. *See* R. Kanter, *supra* note 82, at 69–99. A growing literature documents various ways in which employers have constructed traditionally female jobs so as to require women to display behaviors that are commonly considered preexisting attributes of "femininity." *See, e.g.*, S. Cohn, The Process of Occupational Sex-Typing: The Feminization of Clerical Labor in Great Britain 91–115 (1985) (showing that British employers saved labor costs by forcing women clericals to quit work when they marry, but legitimated such marriage bars by arguing that women value family commitments more highly than wage work); V. Beechey & T. Perkins, *supra* note 5, at 45–76, 77–101 (showing that employers have built gender into the way they structure hours, achieving flexibility in male jobs by adding overtime to full-time jobs, but doing so in female jobs by constructing them as part-time).

93. *See* R. Kanter, *supra* note 82, at 140–51.

94. *See, e.g.*, M. Martin, *supra* note 77, at 150 ("The company was pushing affirmative action, because it had a class-action suit brought against it by a group of women in the mines in 1973. I was hired four years after the suit was filed. . . ."); *id.* at 71 ("The process of entering the San Francisco Police Department . . . began for me in 1973. That's when community groups got together and filed a suit to open up the job to women and minorities. . . ."); *id.* at 216 ("Like many of the first women in their locals I've met across the country, I started in 1978, when affirmative action guidelines were mandated."); J. Schroedel, *supra* note 77, at 35 ("Some people came around and said we are looking for women to apply . . . [T]hey came around because EEO or somebody was down on them to get more women in the program.").

95. J. Schroedel, *supra* note 77, at 35.

96. M. Walshok, *supra* note 77, at 137–38.

97. J. Schroedel, *supra* note 77, at 77. For discussions of the importance of community-based programs for women in nontraditional employment, see M. Walshok, *supra* note 77, at 167–68; Law, *supra* note 11, at 45–46, 53–55, 72–76.

98. M. Walshok, *supra* note 77, at 140.

99. *Id.* at 142.

100. *Id.* at 147–48.

101. *Id.* at 145. Other studies have reported that women in blue-collar trades value the challenge, freedom, and intrinsic rewards of the job, just as their male co-workers do. *See, e.g.*, K. Deaux & J. Ullman, *supra* note 11, at 131–33.

102. *See* M. Walshok, *supra* note 77, at xix–xx.

103. Although traditional goals and timetables probably provide the best incentive for employers to change the practices and policies that lead to segregation, some lower courts who have held employers liable have declined to impose numerical relief. *See, e.g.*, Catlett v. Missouri Highway & Transp. Comm'n, 828 F.2d 1260, 1268–69 (8th Cir. 1987), *cert. denied*, 485 U.S. 1021 (1988); Jordan v. Wright, 417 F. Supp. 42, 45 (M.D. Ala. 1976). Unfortunately, recent Supreme Court decisions will make it even easier for trial courts who

are so inclined to refuse to grant such relief. *See* United States v. Paradise, 480 U.S. 149, 167 (1987); Local 28, Sheet Metal Workers v. EEOC, 478 U.S. 421, 445 (1986).

104. *See, e.g.*, G. Nielsen, From Sky Girl to Flight Attendant: Women and the Making of a Union 81–103 (1982) (describing how early Title VII decisions helped redefine the flight attendant job in less sexist, more professional terms).

105. *See, e.g.*, EEOC Guidelines on Discrimination Because of Sex, 29 C.F.R. § 1604.11(a) (1989).

106. For women in male-dominated jobs, harassment is apparently less likely to take the form of supervisors' demands for sexual favors and more likely to take the form of sexual taunts and other actions by co-workers that are part of a larger pattern of hostility intended to drive the women away. Foremen and supervisors usually acquiesce in the harassment. *See* Crull, *Searching for the Causes of Sexual Harassment: An Examination of Two Prototypes*, in Hidden Aspects of Women's Work 228, 228–30 (C. Bose, R. Feldberg & N. Sokoloff eds. 1987); Pollack, *Sexual Harassment: Women's Experience vs. Legal Definitions*, 13 Harv. Women's L.J. 35, 37, 50 n.51 (1990).

107. *Id.* at 221–22.

108. For theoretical explanations of how skewed sex ratios lead to harassment, *see* B. Gutek, Sex and the Workplace 129–52 (1985); R. Kanter, *supra* note 828, at 206–42.

109. Some of the earliest surveys documenting the existence of sexual harassment are described in C. MacKinnon, Sexual Harassment of Working Women 26–30 (1978). More recent studies include U.S. Merit System Protection Board, Sexual Harassment in the Federal Workplace: An Update (1988); U.S. Merit System Protection Board, Sexual Harassment in the Federal Workplace: Is it a Problem? (1981); and Gutek, *supra* note 108.

110. M. Walshok, *supra* note 77, at 211.

111. *See, e.g.*, Gutek & Morasch, *supra* note 2, at 67–68 (finding that women in male-dominated occupations and jobs were more likely to report harassment and to have experienced negative consequences from it than women in other work settings); Martin, *Sexual Harassment: The Link Joining Gender Stratification, Sexuality, and Women's Economic Status*, in Women: A Feminist Perspective 57, 61 (J. Freeman 4th ed. 1989)(citing studies showing that, the greater the proportion of men in a work group, the more likely women were to be harassed).

112. *See* O'Farrell & Harlan, *Craftworkers and Clerks: The Effect of Male Co-Worker Hostility on Women's Satisfaction with Nontraditional Jobs*, 29 Soc. Probs. 252, 259 (1982)(finding that half the women in white-collar, female dominated occupations who considered moving into blue-collar, male-dominated occupations expected that they would be subjected to harassment if they did so).

113. *See, e.g.*, Gutek & Morasch, *supra* note 2, at 68 (finding that that 20% of women in nontraditional work quit a job at some point because of sexual harassment, while only 9% of the larger sample did so); Gutek, *supra* note 108, at 119 ("By making insulting comments and touching women sexually, some men may try to 'make life miserable' for women in the [nontraditional jobs], encouraging them to leave. The relatively high turnover rate among women in [these jobs] suggests that this is a successful strategy for force women out").

114. *See, e.g.*, M. Martin, *supra* note 77, at 11; Eisenberg, *Women Hard Hats Speak Out*, Nation, Sept. 18, 1989, at 272-73; Pollack, *supra* note 106, at 4–5 & nn. 6, 7.

115. A recent newspaper article noted, for example, that a growing number of women engineers have become so discouraged by their discriminatory treatment that they are leaving

engineering to pursue alternative careers. Arundel, *Stagflation for Female Engineers*, N.Y. Times, Oct. 1, 1989, at F32. Other studies have documented the disproprotionate attrition of women from law firms, *see, e.g.*, Menkel-Meadow, *Exploring a Research Agenda on the Feminization of the Legal Profession: Theories of Gender and Social Change*, 14 Law & Soc. Inquiry 289, 307 (1989); Weisenhaus, *Still a Long Way to Go for Women, Minorities*, Nat'l L. J., Feb. 8, 1988, at 47, 48, and there is evidence that women leave in part because of discrimination. *See, e.g.*, Liefland, *Career Patterns of Male and Female Lawyers*, 35 Buffalo L. Rev. 601, 609–611 (1986); Quade, *Myth v. Ms.: Why Women Leave the Law*, 13 Barrister 28 (1986).

116. *See* M. Walshok, *supra* note 77, at 188.

117. Eisenberg, *supra* note 114, at 272. For other stories of how women have been subjected to acts by foremen or co-workers that threatened or caused physical harm, see M. Martin, *supra* note 77, at 33–34 ("[The men] didn't want the women to replace them, so they pulled stunts. Someone cut the chain holding up a big motor mount I was welding. It fell down on me and burned my arm to the bone."); *Id.* at 257 (". . . I had to start checking all the parts on my machine because Dick would loosen stuff on it, which could kill you."); J. Schroedel, *supra* note 77, at 256–57 ("The men harassed me a lot . . . I went in the women's room, and I cried, because a man pushed me under a machine. . . . The men admit they think it's a man's job and a woman has no right out there.")

118. For example, one of Atlanta's most prestigious corporate law firms, King & Spaulding, planned to hold a "wet T-shirt" contest featuring its female summer associates, even while the firm faced a sex discrimination lawsuit in the Supreme Court. After complaints, the firm decided to hold a swimsuit competition instead. One of the firm's partner's later told the Wall Street Journal that the "winner" of the competition had been offered a job upon graduation, remarking: "She has the body we'd like to see more of." *See* Burleigh & Goldberg, *Breaking the Silence: Sexual Harassment in Law Firms*, A.B.A J., Aug. 1989, at 46.

119. In one recent case, Lipsett v. University of Puerto Rico, 864 F.2d 881 (1st Cir. 1988), the lone female resident in a general surgery program was forced to endure sexual advances and touching; sexually explicit drawings of her body and other pornography in public meeting rooms; her supervisors' refusal to talk to her, permit her to operate, or assign her other work tasks; discriminatory standards for evaluating her performance; sabotage of her work, including falsification of medical records to make it appear as though she and another female resident had made an error, *id.* at 881, 886–94, and "a constant verbal attack, one which challenged their capacity as women to be surgeons, and questioned the legitimacy of their being in the Program at all," *id.* at 905.

120. Price-Waterhouse v. Hopkins, 109 S.Ct. 1775, 1782 (1989).

121. *See* V. Beechey & T. Perkins, *supra* note 5, at 102-119; C. Williams, *supra* note 74, at 88–130, which show how the cultural constructions of the same job vary depending upon whether men or women do it. For example, one machine tools company that employed only men as crane operators explained that women did not want to drive cranes because "that was hot, heavy, dirty work and women didn't do that sort of work." V. Beechey & T. Perkins, *supra* note 5, at 105. But another such company that employed women defined the job in feminine terms, and suggested that women were actually better crane operators because they had a "sensitive touch" learned through knitting. *Id.* at 106.

122. J. Schroedel, *supra* note 77, at 20–21; *see also* C. Williams, *supra* note 74, at 61 (noting that the Marine Corps segregates basic training because "[r]egardless of whether

training standards are compromised in fact, the sight of women mastering the feats of basic training makes it appear that the training is not rigorous enough").

123. *See* C. Cockburn, *supra* note 5, at 172.

124. *Id.* at 185.

125. *Id.*

126. *Id.* at 186.

127. *Id.* at 101.

128. *Id.* at 188.

129. *Id.* at 176.

130. The contradictions within the men's ideological justifications are exposed as the men's careers unfold. Early in their careers, when they do hands-on machine work, male engineers defined the masculinity of their jobs in terms of a hard/soft dichotomy that defines "hard," physical work as masculine and "soft," intellectual work as feminine. In middle age, however, many of these same engineers must move on to managerial "desk" jobs that they once denigrated as unmanly. *Id.* at 195. They then adopt an intellectual/non-intellectual dichotomy that, ironically, associates masculinity with the intellectual and femininity with the physical. *See id.* at 196–97.

131. *See e.g.,* Collins & Blodgett, *Sexual Harassment: Some See It . . . Some Won't,* 59 Harv. Bus. Rev. 76, 90 (1981)(noting that majority of managers responding to a survey said that women employees should be able to handle on their own whatever sexual harassment they face).

132. Rabidue v. Osceola Refining Co. 805 F.2d 611, 620–21 (6th Cir. 1986), *cert. denied,* 481 U.S. 1041 (1987)(quoting Osceola v. Rabidue, 584 F.Supp. 419, 430 (E.D. Mich. 1984)).

133. For explorations of this concept, see Coombe, *Room for Manoeuver: Towards a Theory of Practice in Critical Legal Studies,* 14 Law & Soc. Inquiry 1 (1989); Schultz, *Room to Maneuver (f)or a Room of One's Own: Practice Theory and Feminist Practice,* 14 Law & Soc. Inquiry 123 (1989).

IV

Critical Practices

16

The Issue of Foundations: Scientized Politics, Politicized Science, and Feminist Critical Practice

Kirstie McClure

And new Philosophy calls all in doubt,
The Element of fire is quite put out;
The sun is lost, and th' earth, and no mans wit
Can well direct him where to looke for it.
And freely men confess that this world's spent,
When in the Planets, and the Firmament
They seeke so many new; they see that this
Is crumbled out againe to his Atomies.
'Tis all in peeces, all cohaerence gone. . . .
                    —John Donne, 1633 *An Anatomie of the World*

In the history of Western political theory, invocations of chaos have repeatedly provided an incitement to order, a provocation for "epic" efforts to reconstitute, to restructure, the order of the world. Disorder unsettles the boundaries of the known and beckons the architectonic impulse of the theorist, a pattern of "challenge and response" that has been held constitutive of the world-creating character of political philosophy.[1] This insistence that the task of political theory is to reconstitute the political order as a whole is one which contemporary feminists have neither simply replicated nor wholly escaped. To the extent that such epic reorderings have been historically associated with revolutionary change, contemporary feminist theorists tend both to echo and to distance themselves from such grand aspirations.[2] There is, to be sure, no paucity of feminist calls for the radical restructuring of both theory and practice, as well as claims to have made various inroads upon the project of transformation. And yet, contrasted to most modern images of revolution, such changes appear diffuse, tentative, multidirectional, even ambiguous or equivocal. If the events of 1789 in France, as Tocqueville claimed, were never "so inevitable" and yet "so completely unforeseen," the feminist revolution of the late twentieth century might be aptly characterized as one never so persistently proclaimed and yet so infinitely deferred.

This is not all to suggest political failure. To the contrary, it may signal the rumbling of a different sort of revolution. Its very diffuseness may partake of a certain shift in the terms of "the political": an insistent inclusion of questions conventionally deemed outside of political concern, a reluctance to narrow the political field to contests for the sovereign power of law and, in some quarters, a certain suspicion of engagement with those struggles at all. While the first half of this century may have witnessed a new political form in the totalitarian state, the closing decades may well herald its inversion: a new political formlessness, various struggles and agitations enacted beneath, across, within, and apart from extant political institutions and structures, unconnected by any overarching organization or ideology. Ernesto Laclau and Chantal Mouffe, for example, speak of the contemporary "politicization of the social," as a new phase in "the democratic revolution," extending from nineteenth-century workers struggles to the contemporary agitations of women, racial and sexual minorities, and other marginal groups. "What has been exploded," they argue, "is the idea and the reality itself of a unique space of constitution of the political. What we are witnessing is a politicization far more radical than any we have known in the past, because it tends to dissolve the distinction between the public and the private—not in terms of the encroachment on the private by a unified public space, but in terms of a proliferation of radically new and different political spaces."[3] For feminist critical practice in these late days, the question of the character of "the political"—and thus necessarily the allied questions of what constitutes political theory, political practice, and their mutual relation—raises the disconcerting dilemma of how to articulate oppositional practices in this seeming hollow between a revolution always already not quite arrived and the uneasy fluidity, apparent fragmentation, and internecine conflict of disparate oppositional agencies.

This broad image of our time suggests the difficulty attending any adjectival specification of contemporary politics. To speak of "feminist politics" in such a context cannot be to point to a single definitive struggle. It is to refer neither to a determinate theory nor to a delimited range of empirical issues or questions of practice. Rather, facing this political formlessness from the inside, as products and producers rather than observers of its dilemma, to speak of feminist politics is to suggest a location of particularly intense contestation in a world in which "the political" is an unsettled terrain. It is to evoke a site not only bounded by the distinction between feminism and its opposition, but fissured by ongoing controversies over the meaning of feminism itself: by debates over goals, strategies, tactics, and agencies; and by debates, further, over the relationship between feminism and other forms of critical and oppositional struggle around the politics of race, class, postcolonial status, sexual identity, able-bodiedness, and doubtless still others yet to be articulated. It is, in short, to suggest that "feminist politics" encompasses not only the critical practices through which feminists define, confront, and engage that which we aspire to change, but includes as well the multitude of critical practices among and between feminists differentially positioned within these controversies and debates. To use a term of relatively recent favor, it is to speak not of *feminism* but of *feminisms;* but it is also to insist that the plural/ism thus inscribed demarcates a site of political difference and contestation rather than a neutral zone of benign diversity.[4] It is also, necessarily, to speak not *about* "feminist politics," as if one's words were somehow outside the dynamics and divisions of their referent, but to speak from within that domain. In such a context to speak at all is to speak politically.

This essay explores the problem of authority in political discourse, more narrowly in feminist politics so understood, and finally, more specifically still, with regard to what Sandra Harding calls "the science question in feminism." In the most general terms, I am concerned with the political stakes at issue in the debates proliferating around what Harding refers to as "feminist empiricism," "feminist standpoint epistemologies," and feminist postmodernism—debates which have increasingly disrupted, modified, and (for some) displaced the conventional typification of liberal. Marxist, socialist, and radical feminist theoretical frames. My purpose here, however, is not simply to recirculate these epistemological divisions, much less to winnow out a range of acceptable or appropriate feminist positions within them, but to consider their relationship to that earlier way of marking divisions within feminism. In so doing, I will suggest that the political problematic attending these controversies quite exceeds their conventional reduction to arguments over which "theory" is most fit to "guide" feminist practice. At issue here, to put the matter broadly, is the question of feminism's relationship to the contemporary configuration of "the political," and more particularly to the political sensibilities, cultural codes, and habitual patterns of inference sedimented within that configuration.

These, I think, are rather more recent and more specific than the epochal category of "modernity" implies. Their general, if uneven, institutionalization into a dominant political culture over the past century constitutes a proximate historical horizon with a number of distinguishing features, among which two, for the purposes of this paper, are perhaps most significant. First, the political substance of this configuration is post–laissez faire. It is marked, in other words, by the late-nineteenth-century assimilation of the realm of "the social" as an object of political care, concern, and instrumental intervention as well as by a concomitant relegation of classical liberal political discourse to the periphery of cultural authority. Second, conjoined with this assimilation of the social, and distinguishing this configuration from traditional political paternalism, is the increasing weight accorded scientific and social scientific knowledge as necessary components of properly political analyses. "Society," in this configuration, is understood not as an organic whole to be tended or sustained, but a complex, dynamic, and ordered system of comprehensible social processes amenable to human direction and manipulation, if not control.

In the United States, arguably since the Progressive era but certainly since the Second World War, this configuration has generated a distinctive political sensibility, one for which "politics" is strongly identified with problem-solving activities within a bounded social system. Here, the privileged form of political knowledge is cast as the diagnosis of social problems, the isolation of their underlying causes, and the recommendation of specific sorts of practical interventions in system dynamics as their appropriate "solution." Within this understanding, what is taken in the last instance to authorize the production of reliable political knowledge is "theory," with paradigmatic status accorded (though not without resistance) to systematic, comprehensive, causally explanatory social scientific theory. Taken together, these broad characteristics distinguish the contemporary configuration of "the political" as what might be called "scientized politics." That is, politics become understood causally and instrumentally, as if from an Archimedean point of sovereign leverage, as the procedures and practices necessary for sustaining, managing, or improving the performance of the social system as a whole. Within this understanding, the power to authorize political action is the prize for which rival theoretical frameworks compete, while political commitment becomes figured as allegiance to one particular theoretical explanation of the social world and loyalty to the policies and practices it validates as politically appropriate.

With this configuration in mind, the present essay offers an account of what seem to me to be the political stakes implicit in the recent emergence of "the science question in feminism." Through a critical reading of Alison Jaggar's *Feminist Politics and Human Nature* and a consideration of Harding's work itself, it explores the problem of authority in feminist discourse both before and after epistemological allegiances became a fashionable way of marking divisions in feminist political theory. In both contexts, the discussion is informed by three broad questions. First, what is it that authorizes the discourse of a feminist? What sorts of things, in other words, render feminist claims to the production of political knowledge appropriate or inappropriate, persuasive or questionable, valid or disputable? Second, how are various responses to this question related to the sorts of things that are taken to authorize political discourse more generally? To put the issue somewhat differently, what, if anything, is the political specificity of feminist theory? Finally, what is the relationship between such strategies of authorization and the dominant contemporary understanding of "the political"? Various sections of the essay foreground different aspects of these questions, but the general point can be briefly summarized: However narrowly it might begin, serious critical attention to the question of what authorizes political discourse opens out onto the broader terrain of what is taken to characterize "the political" in specific historical and cultural locations, and thus extends further into the ways in which any such characterization both generates and sets limits to what will be authorized in turn as properly political theory, appropriate political practice, and their mutual relation. Amidst the contemporary "proliferation of radically new and different political spaces," to avoid such attention may well be to relinquish the possibility of a feminist politics commensurate with a time and place in which "the political" itself is a matter of intense dispute.

I

What is it that authorizes the discourse of a feminist? In the United States as recently as the early 1980s the question was susceptible, if not to an answer, at least to what appeared to be a fairly broad consensus upon what might count as legitimate responses. While feminists in general mounted a severe substantive critique of "politics as usual," then as now feminism was most properly portrayed in the plural. Differences within feminism, however, were typically represented as controversies between competing sources of *theoretical* authority; its divisions most commonly framed in terms of two theoretical traditions—liberal and Marxist—that vied for allegiance within political discourse more generally, and with reference further to radical feminism and socialist feminism as more recent critical alternatives. The typologies of feminist politics offered in Alison Jaggar's *Feminist Politics and Human Nature* as well as *Feminist Frameworks: Alternative Theoretical Accounts of the Relations Between Women and Men,* coedited with Paula Rothenberg, are good examples of this portrayal, though there are, to be sure, important differences between them.[5] Despite such differences, they nonetheless share a common metatheoretical concern: to represent, albeit with a distinctly feminist face, the authority to account for the political condition of the world as a struggle between alternative theoretical frameworks. In this respect, both are sufficiently suggestive of the conventions and concerns informing that portrayal, and of certain difficulties gnawing at its edges, to provide a basis for considering the problem of authority in feminist theory, as well as the understanding of "the political" that such a picture suggests.

Locating an initial conception of "the political" in *Feminist Politics and Human Nature,* and a fairly ecumenical account of the character of the feminist challenge to it, is far from a matter of deep hermeneutics, for the question is addressed in explicit terms. "Politics," Jaggar notes, ". . . is an extremely broad concept that can refer to many aspects of the management or government of a city or state," ranging from "the science or art of government to participation in governmental affairs, to methods or tactics for affecting governmental politics, or to opinions or principles regarding how society should be governed" (169). "Traditionally," she continues, "political life has been contrasted with so-called private life and political economy has been contrasted with domestic or household economy," and thus "excludes much of women's world" (169). Feminist concerns with "the contemporary organization of child bearing, child-rearing, sexuality, and personal maintenance," she argues, have led some feminists to "challenge the traditional conception of politics as male-biased and androcentric," and hence "to claim a new definition of politics that includes the management or government of every aspect of social life" (169). Further, she suggests, "a few feminists even challenge the customary identification of management with government" by distinguishing the former as "a system of social organization" and the latter as "a system of coercion," a move with far reaching implications:

> If politics is defined as the management of a state, and if a state is defined as a set of permanent institutions through which a unified code of behavior is established and enforced within a certain territory, then politics by definition is concerned with coercive authority. Some feminists believe that the good society should have no coercive government, but should be managed through non-coercive forms of organization. The implication of this view is that, while all of contemporary life may be political insofar as it is structured by coercive relationships, eventually politics, with government, should be abolished altogether. (169)

The critical power of feminism, in this view, lies in its politicization of activities traditionally excluded from "the political," and more specifically in its erasure of distinctions between public and private life, between political and domestic economy. Its "new definition of politics" is thus represented as analogous to nineteenth-century politicizations of the realm of production and exchange. Just, for example, as the radical edge of Marx's theory consisted in its authorization of the political character of knowledges, practices, and agencies operative in the processes of industrial production, so might feminism be seen to authorize the political character of knowledges, practices, and agencies operative in what "traditional" accounts of politics relegated to private or domestic life. In effect, just as Marxist theory and practice politicized what was taken to be the factual terrain of previous political economy by recasting it in a fundamentally different way, so does feminist theory and practice politicize what has been taken as the factual terrain of the private or domestic realm by reconstituting it in fundamentally different terms. Or so, in any case, it seems. To sustain this analogy, however, one must accept the infusion of new substantive considerations as a sufficient marker of the difference between feminist and "traditional" accounts; as a sufficient criterion, in other words, for designating a fundamentally new conception of "the political."

What then, on this account, is the political character of feminism? Clearly, and precisely by its inclusion of activities and concerns previously excluded from politics, it is not the same old wine in the same old bottles. But neither does it seem to be a wholly new vintage in a new-modeled container, for these claims to a distinctively feminist political knowledge clearly bear the traces of the nineteenth-century shift of "the political," and in particular its discrediting of the laissez-faire avoidance of "the social." The passages noted above in general; the claim, in particular, that the "new definition of politics" proffered by feminism "includes the management or government of every aspect of social life"; the subsequent modulation of that claim's totalizing gesture—all these can be understood both to recapitulate, in highly condensed form, significant moments in the nineteenth-century reconfiguration of "the political" in its historical assimilation of "the social," and to situate contemporary feminism in relation to two of the major theoretical authorities that presided over that shift.

The sequential references, for example, to conventional distinctions between public and private, political and domestic economy, figure both liberal and Marxist theory as partners in an androcentric tradition, even as the difference attributed to feminist understandings of "the political" both presupposes and extends the historical disruption of laissez-faire constrictions of that domain in which both Marxism and later liberalism were significant participants. In substantive terms, of course, feminist insistence upon the political character of domestic, familial, and sexual practices departs significantly from "traditional" accounts that dismiss such questions as nonpolitical. This politicization, however, is accomplished by discerning the systematic organization of social power in these practices—that is, by revealing a systematic asymmetry of power based on gender—a move that confirms rather than disrupts the "traditional" view of politics as the "management or government" of social relations. Following this, though, the qualification appended to feminist politicization of "every aspect of social life"—that this is not to be conflated with governmental coercion—effects a distance between feminist politics and the intervening history of both Marxist-Leninism and Stalinism, even as it aligns feminism with the more emancipatory elements of Marx's theoretical project. By thus distinguishing management from government, and allying its concerns with the more liberatory elements of prior "traditions," feminism confirms as well the view that the goal of political activity properly understood is to reorganize or restructure the social system as a whole to better serve human purposes. In these various respects, despite the newness predicated of feminist politics, its political character appears to be equivocal; for it suggests both a departure from and a continuity with "the political" as it has come to be understood in the wake of the rise of "the social."

Rather than rush to resolve this apparent tension, we might pause to consider its implications for feminist theorizing in the present, in the midst of a historical and cultural location within which that configuration appears increasingly unsettled. If, for instance, the familiar typology of feminist political theories—liberal, Marxist, radical, and socialist—represents a range of potentially appropriate responses to the question of what authorizes the discourse of a feminist, what does this tension imply for the political character of the knowledge claims generated by these frameworks? Of the practices that they authorize as political? Is there, perhaps, a sense in which that tension inhabits the typology itself? Might it, for example, inflect what is to count *within* feminism as a properly political theory in the first place, and hence considerations of appropriate feminist political practice as well? And what, finally, might that tension imply for the political character of feminism in relation, on the one hand, to nonfeminist accounts of the political world and, on the other, in relation to the subsequent articulations of alternative feminist accounts of that world? While I cannot explore each of these questions in detail here, on the basis of the metatheoretical considerations forwarded in both *Feminist Politics* and *Feminist Frameworks,* a general consideration of their political stakes is nonetheless possible.

The introduction to *Feminist Frameworks,* for example, offers the following characterization of the political and theoretical character of the "alternative theoretical accounts of the relations between women and men" included in the anthology:

> Feminists are people who demonstrate a commitment to improving women's position in society. Feminist frameworks are systems of ideas, conceptual structures that feminists can use in explaining, justifying, and guiding their actions. Typically, a feminist framework is a comprehensive analysis of the nature and causes of women's oppression and a correlated set of proposals for ending it. It is an integrated theory of women's place both in contemporary society and in the new society that feminists are struggling to build. (xii)

Here, the metatheoretical concerns elaborately developed in *Feminist Politics* are articulated in terms accessible to undergraduates, terms that assert what the scholarly work defends at length as the combined normative, empirical, philosophical, practical, and scientific aspects integral to political theory in general. Feminist political theory, on this account, is necessarily normative in its prescriptions for solving the problem of women's oppression. It is empirical and scientific in its comprehensive causal analysis of that oppression; practical in its intent to explain, justify, and guide feminist action in ending that oppression; and philosophical in the systematic character of its ideas. In sum, on this understanding, feminist theory has three intimately related characteristics: a normative commitment to women's emancipation, a scientific commitment to the explanation of women's oppression, and a practical commitment to social transformation.

On this view, the normative concern with the oppression of women sharply distinguishes feminist from nonfeminist perspectives. Any philosophical or scientific theory may address the condition of women in the world, but feminist accounts are distinctive both for naming this condition as oppression and for their practical purpose of ending it. The authority of feminist over nonfeminist accounts, in the first instance, thus resides in a moral or ethical commitment. By virtue of its practical purpose, however, the requisite foundations of feminism include reliable knowledge of the world: its concern with social change mandates a "consideration of the means for travelling from here to there, a strategy for moving from the oppressive present to the liberated future." (*Feminist Politics*, 16) Properly political feminist theory, therefore, is not only intimately related to "such sciences as psychology, economics, political science, sociology, anthropology, and even biology and the various technologies" (17). It also necessitates a synthesis of these domains, a feminist version of the unity of science:

> To know what can be . . . requires considerable information about what is. To know how certain political ideals can be instantiated, for instance, requires information about human motivation, in order to determine the circumstances in which people will cooperate; it requires information about available technology, in order to determine the social possibility and social costs of satisfying certain human desires; and in order to discover workable strategies, it requires information about the motors of social change. (17)

This gesture to the authority of science, however, is a far cry from granting a primacy to facticity. As a late-twentieth-century perspective, feminism too confronts the competition between scientific theories for the authority to account for the world. As Jaggar puts it in *Feminist Politics*, "the more persistent disputes in the human sciences concern not facts, but the interpretation of facts; that is, they concern which theoretical models will best explain or make sense of the facts" (18). Taking the example of motivational psychology, Jaggar states the issue clearly: "Empirical data are required to develop an explanatory model, but a systematic account is not simply derivable from empirical data. On the contrary, what are to count as data is determined by the conceptual framework set up to guide the project of research" (19). Jaggar's own approach to this in *Feminist Politics* is to link the differences between alternative political and scientific frameworks to parallel differences in their respective conceptions of human nature and society, a move that casts philosophy and science as supportive partners in the service of the normative and practical commitments of feminist theory. My concern here, however, is not with the details of that argument but with the political character of this formulation of the nature and tasks of feminist theory and, consequently, with the political character of the knowledge claims that this understanding of theory authorizes. What conception of "the political," for instance, does this understanding of political theory evoke? What, perhaps more broadly, is its relationship to the existing purposes and arrangements of "the political" in our time?

If, to begin with, we take the systematic character of a theory's account of the world and the comprehensiveness of its causal analysis of that world as the hallmarks of theoretical adequacy, we have not only specified what will count as a "good" theory; we have settled as well upon a particular image of that world.[6] We have, for instance, characterized that world as a "system," and we have specified its politically relevant features as things amenable to causal explanation and instrumental manipulation. If we go on to include in our criteria of theoretical adequacy the practicality or effectiveness of a theory's recommendations for changing that world, we have included more than a pragmatic consideration of the relationship between means and ends; we have, in effect, marked out a particular construction of the dimensions, character, and scope not only of what we will take to be our political world, but of our own political agency within it. Put more concretely, if the political world is a structured system, its dynamics driven by a comprehensive network of identifiable causal relations, not only is the political character of action constituted as instrumental interventions in those dynamics but, further, judgments of the practicality of such interventions are rendered necessarily dependent upon systematic causal understandings of those dynamics. In effect, on this account of adequate political theory, the political character of action becomes significantly circular, conditioned at the outset by the very explanations that our systematic theories produce.

Somehow, this hardly seems a fundamentally new sort of political understanding. Of course, to the extent that the existing purposes and arrangements of "the political" are identified with particular institutions, specifiable policies and practices, and identifiable constellations of social power, it is doubtless productive of potentially significant sorts of social change.[7] To precisely this extent, however, it simultaneously confirms the more general, and quite modern, political sensibility that casts "the political" as coextensive with the organization and management of a system of social relations and that, consequently, renders political action importantly dependent upon the production of properly scientific knowledge of that system. In effect, the political character of this view of feminist theory is as equivocal as the previous view of feminist politics, albeit in somewhat different terms. While that earlier equivocality was noted with respect to the late-nineteenth-century reconfiguration of "the political," here it appears in relation rather to the particular dynamics and present expression of that configuration and to the sorts of knowledges conventionally deemed appropriate to the management of its internal processes.

To say that these knowledges must be "properly scientific," however, is not necessarily to imply that politics either is or could be like a well-oiled machine, despite the common metaphoric invocation of "motors of social change." Rather, it is to recall the myriad ways in which political controversies in the present are persistently recast as scientific questions and debates. This observation, of course, is neither new nor surprising. But it does, I think, imply certain consequences for evaluating the adequacy of feminist theories in the terms suggested above, consequences that emerge fairly clearly in Jaggar's discussion of the connections between politics, epistemology and the justification of feminist theories. Particularly significant are the ways in which this construction of theoretical adequacy frames the distinction between feminist and nonfeminist accounts of the social world in rather different terms than it frames theoretical controversies within feminism; a difference, as I shall suggest later, that operates to the detriment of the political character and possibilities of feminist critical practice.

II

Recall, to begin with, that this account of feminist theory demarcates feminist from nonfeminist inquiry by invoking feminists' common normative commitment: feminist analyses seek not simply to explain women's condition, but to understand its systematically oppressive character and to prescribe appropriate means to end it. Beyond this, however, as represented in *Feminist Politics,* "feminists have no characteristic disagreements with nonfeminist theorists about the general desiderata for an adequate political and/ or scientific theory" (354). Like good moral philosophy more generally, an adequate feminist theory will express "values that are morally or politically desirable"; offer "a guide to conduct that is consistent, comprehensive, and practicable"; and it will be "in some sense impartial" (354). And, like good scientific theory more generally, feminist theory at its best should be "self-consistent"; it should be "well-supported by available evidence"; it should be "comprehensive in accounting for all the data"; and it "should be illuminating or have explanatory power" (354). But despite agreement on these broad moral and scientific criteria of adequacy, feminists "differ systematically *not only from non-feminists but also among themsleves* over the interpretation and application of such theoretical desiderata as impartiality, objectivity, evidential confirmation, comprehensiveness or completeness, and explanatory power" (354–55, emphasis added). From this metatheoretical perspective, then, there are *two* sorts of systematic difference at issue: one that differentiates feminist from nonfeminist theoretical accounts and one that distinguishes among and between feminist theories.

The first of these we have already seen, for it is normative commitment that distinguishes between feminist and nonfeminist accounts of the world. Thus if what *unifies* feminists is a common commitment to identifying, explaining, and ending women's oppression, the systematic character of their difference from nonfeminists hinges upon their adopting "interpretations and applications" of these criteria that, as their bottom line, preclude analyses that sustain the systematic or structural privilege of men. The political effect of this is quite important. By this litmus, none of the traditional theories competing for authority within political discourse more generally is capable of offering a politically and morally adequate account of women's place and condition in contemporary societies. Liberalism is disqualified for the "gender neutrality" produced by its continuing attachment to vestiges of positivist or neopositivist constructions of objectivity and impartiality, while traditional Marxism, despite the feminist potential of its internal debates over the meaning of "objectivity," is inadequate because it continues to discount the oppression of women *aṣ women* within "the science of the proletariat."[8] As a consequence, the political task of self-identified feminists working within those traditions necessarily takes the form of internal critique, and their theoretical contributions consist in introducing the problematic of women's systematic subordination into those androcentric frames.

Here, I think, we can begin to characterize the political stakes of this account of feminist theory more precisely, for this normative emphasis generates the dominant form of feminism's relationship to the "scientized politics" of the present. If, for instance, the contemporary configuration of "the political" is taken to be coextensive with the systematic organization and management of social relations, and if the production of political knowledge in this context can be understood as a competition between alternative scientific and social-scientific theories for the authority to account for its internal dynamics, Jaggar's normative litmus takes on a dual function in defining the relationship between feminist and "traditional" accounts of the political world. In a context in which, as Jaggar notes, extreme positivist versions of "objectivity" have been largely rejected (356–58), feminism of any sort is normatively superior to any remaining holdouts for strict "value neutrality." Further, however, and precisely because the same broad criteria of theoretical adequacy are seen as common to feminists and nonfeminists alike, feminist analyses can stake a claim to being better *science* as well. In effect, the normative litmus operates in conjunction with the *general* agreement on good science and good philosophy to validate feminism as a legitimate theoretical contender for the privilege of authorizing political knowledge. Feminist theoretical frameworks are different, perhaps, from their nonfeminist competitors in their interpretation and application of those criteria for adequate theory, but they are nonetheless qualified to vie for the mantle of scientific authority in their explanations of the political world. With respect to the mechanisms of "science as usual," in short, the normative litmus becomes a way of politicizing science without disrupting the *general* privilege accorded scientific explanations in the broader world of "scientized politics."

But if this "politicized science" aptly characterizes the political stakes attending the systematic difference between feminist and nonfeminist theories, it is insufficient to account for the political stakes involved in the claim that feminists "differ systematically among themselves" over the metatheoretical criteria of theoretical adequacy. Bluntly put, since the normative litmus constitutes feminist unity, it cannot account for feminist divisions. The closing chapter of *Feminist Politics* addresses this metatheoretical dilemma, opening with, then elaborating, the following observation:

> There are many ways of being a feminist. Contemporary feminists are united in their opposition to women's oppression, but they differ not only in their views of how to combat that oppression, but even in their conception of what constitutes oppression in contemporary society. (353)

Liberal feminists locate that oppression in "unjust discrimination," traditional Marxists in women's "exclusion from public production"; for radical feminists women's oppression inheres "primarily in the universal male control of women's sexual and procreative capacities"; while socialist feminists focus their analyses through "a revised version of the Marxist theory of alienation" (353). While each of these theoretical frames is distinctively feminist, on this analysis they are nonetheless "ultimately incompatible with each other" (353). The problem here, since feminist political theory is motivated not by an abstract attachment to universal values but by a practical commitment to ending women's oppression, is decidedly political; for these divisions within feminism are represented quite explicitly as mutually exclusive theoretical authorities competing for the privilege of guiding feminist practice. Absent the normative litmus that distinguished feminist from nonfeminist accounts, however, the political character of theoretical adequacy takes a decisively scientistic turn. Within feminism, in other words, this account of feminist theory clearly begins to mirror the "scientized politics" characteristic of political discourse more generally, as questions of explanatory adequacy—consistency, evidential confirmation, comprehensiveness in treatment of available data—become increasingly central. Two examples of this strategy will, I hope, serve to substantiate this claim: the initial consideration of what is omitted as a "distinctive" feminist theory, and the critical commentary on the theoretical adequacy of "radical feminism."

The introductory chapter of *Feminist Politics* provides a clear, concise, and nuanced discussion of the relationship between feminism and political philosophy as well as a brief précis of the work's general approach. It acknowledges numerous difficulties associated with attempts to categorize social theory and, foreseeing possible objections, defends its own "system of categorization." Two important sorts of objections in particular are addressed: first, that the fourfold typology omits some views altogether and, second, that other views are not seen as identifiably separate theories. The omission of both religious and existential feminism, for instance, is justified on three grounds: they are "implausible," they stand "outside the mainstream of feminist theorizing," and they "have little connection with socialist feminism"—here considered the "most plausible" of available feminist theories (10). More indicative, however, of the weight accorded scientific authority in evaluating competing feminist claims to political knowledge are the reasons given for refusing the status of distinctive feminist theory to "black feminism," to the work of "non-black feminists of color," to "anarchist or anarcha-feminism," and to "lesbianfeminism."

Black feminism, for example, "is not treated as a separate theory because black feminists utilize a variety of different theoretical approaches," including liberalism, Marxism, black nationalism, radical feminism, and socialist feminism (11). A focus on "the situation of black women," on this account, brings black feminists under the normative umbrella of generic feminism, but their divided allegiances to multiple theoretical frames preclude consideration of their analyses "as reflective of a single black feminist perspective."[9] While the omission of black feminism arises from its commitments to many different theories, the exclusion of "anarchist or anarcha-feminism" stems from the multiplicity of distinct views gathered under an excessively broad theoretical rubric. Variously informing liberal/libertarian discomfort with the state, Marxist hopes for its ultimate dissolution, and socialist-feminist "critiques of hierarchy and authoritarianism on the left," as well as radical-feminist "attacks on patriarchal power in everyday life" (11), anarchism is, apparently, too anarchistic to constitute a distinctive feminist theory. Once again, a "distinctive" feminist theory is a *unified* feminist theory reflecting a *single* perspective: without a "single conception of human nature and society" there is, properly speaking, no theory (11).

By itself, perhaps, an insistence that proper feminist theory be unified, that it rest clearly upon a "single conception" of human nature or society, is not necessarily indicative of a scientific agenda of theoretical evaluation. In addition, however, this account identifies "comprehensiveness" as a further indicator of theoretical integrity—a criterion that serves to exclude the work of "non-black feminists of color" and "lesbianfeminists" from consideration. Both of these perspectives are described as lacking a "distinctive and comprehensive theory of women's liberation" (11). Work by "feminists of color," for example, is disqualified as a "comprehensive theory" because it remains "mainly at the level of description"; while the practical strategy of separatism provides a basis for including most lesbian analyses under radical feminism (11). Although the latter, comprised of diverse "analyses of women's oppression" and "a variety of visions of women's liberation," is characterized as having had problems framing its "distinctive insights within a comprehensive theoretical framework," its theoretical unity is located in "a conviction that the oppression of women . . . was causally irreducible to the oppression of any other group" (11–12).

This defense of exclusions only intimates the metatheoretical approach that emerges more distinctly as the comparison of feminist theories is elaborated. Even at this early point, however, the shape of what will count as properly political feminist theory is discernible: it is not content with "the level of description"; it is unified and comprehensive; and its comprehensiveness is strongly associated with a concern for causality. This vocabulary begins to suggest the weight of scientific criteria, and hence the possibility of "scientized politics" as a strategy to demarcate divisions among rival feminist theoretical camps; and the political stakes of this strategy are perhaps most clear when these criteria are deployed as a critique of radical feminism. In this context, the political character of this understanding of feminist theoretical adequacy becomes quite *un*equivocal, for the brunt of its criticism is that the latter's inadequacies as a properly scientific theory render it inadequate as a guide for feminist political practice.

There is a persistent theme, for instance, in Jaggar's criticism of radical feminism that sets it apart from her evaluations of liberal feminism, traditional Marxism, and socialist feminism. While discussions of the latter focus on disputes over the "interpretations and applications" of the broad criteria of theoretical adequacy noted earlier, the critique of radical feminism more frequently involves metatheoretical observations on the nature of theory itself—observations that pivot far less on unity and comprehensiveness than upon the centrality of systemic causal explanation as a benchmark of adequate theory. Despite an acknowledgment, for example, of the possibility that different forms of theory might emerge from different theories of knowledge as well as from choices of "phenomena" to be theorized, Jaggar foregrounds conventional scientific emphases on the explanatory tasks of theory and the distinction between explanation and description:

> When social phenomena have to be explained, it is common to think of a theory as postulating certain underlying mechanisms that will provide a causal explanantion of observed patterns of regularity in those phenomena. If one thinks of a theory in this way, it is evident that an adequate theoretical account of any social phenomena presupposes an adequate description of those phenomena: if the phenomena in question are misdescribed, if existing regularities are unrecognized or if regularities are asserted that are unimportant or even non-existent, then the theoretical inquiry will be misdirected. (267–68)

While theory and description cannot be sharply separated, "it is possible to distinguish between theories and descriptions in terms of the levels of reality to which they refer" (268). Descriptions, in this sense, are "theory-laden" insofar as they are necessarily "compatible or incompatible" with theoretical accounts of the "level" to which they refer. Thus while "theories are supposed to explain rather than contradict observations or descriptions, they may imply that certain observations have been misinterpreted or that the supposed data should be redescribed" (268).

In this metatheoretical account of feminist theoretical adequacy, radical feminism is both promising and deeply problematic. On the one hand, radical feminists challenge androcentric descriptions of reality by suggesting, for example, that "what has been called consent must be renamed coercion" and that "supposedly free women are in fact enslaved" (268). In this redescription of reality they "make us see old facts in new ways and . . . perceive regularities where we saw none before" (268). On the other hand, however comprehensive and systematic such redescriptions may be, however unified a conceptual framework they might suggest, and, indeed, despite many radical-feminist disavowals of any intention to be building theories, on this view "they are doing something . . . often thought of as preliminary to theory, namely, they are engaged in description" (268). The difficulty here parallels the ground noted above for omitting the work of women of color: radical feminism never moves beyond the descriptive to a properly theoretical analysis, a dilemma figured symptomatically in the subtitle of the first section of *Feminist Politics* wholly devoted to a critique of radical-feminist politics, "Practice Without Theory."

Radical feminists, Jaggar argues, have exceeded the boundaries of traditional political theory by becoming "increasingly imaginative and nonlinear":[10] they "created new music, new poetry, new drama, and new science fiction"; even their prose writing "became more impassioned, metaphorical, and epigrammatic," using "every available linguistic resource . . .

to jolt the audience out of its accustomed ways of perceiving the world . . ." (287). Through these strategies, radical feminists are acknowledged to have "revealed a different reality," but from the metatheoretical perspective adopted here this falls far short of theoretical adequacy—and the following critical comments bluntly note why:

> What radical feminism has not done is provide an account of the underlying causes of the patriarchal system.
>
> . . . For most radical feminists, it is enough to show what men are like: to show that heroes rape, that bosses rape, that husbands rape, that fathers rape. To reveal these secret atrocities is indeed an achievement, but it is only the first part of ending them.
>
> . . . [P]oetic and impassioned writers such as Daly, Rich, and Griffin . . . demonstrate vividly *how* men enslave women, but they do not provide a theoretical explanation of *why* men do so. (287)

Cognizant of radical-feminist disavowals of traditional theory—and yet committed, as we have seen, to the idea of theory as a singular guide to practice—Jaggar's metatheoretical strategy here undergoes a rhetorical shift. "Theoreticism," she notes, should indeed be disavowed, for it involves abstraction and jargon that render "theoreticians the authoritative source of knowledge" (288). But, she suggests, there is a difference between theoreticism and theory properly understood: while the former may be justly abandoned, the latter provides the only adequate guide to political action. Anger may provoke such action, but "outrage is not necessarily the best guide to the action that should be taken"; indeed, citing the radical-feminist creation of rape-protection centers, Jaggar suggests that the very immediacy of anger opens "the possibility that women might exhaust their energies in tackling symptoms rather than underlying causes" (288–89). Such centers are without doubt important; "[b]ut it is also necessary to discover how to end rape completely." Theoreticism in this context is out of the question, but theory is essential, as the following claims suggest:

> Theory alone will not liberate women. But women's liberation seems equally unlikely to result from simple activism, not grounded in a systematic understanding of women's situation. . . . If the assumptions and implications [of activism] are not reflected on consciously and systematically, that is to say, if they are not part of a theory, then they are likely to be problematic.
>
> . . . [T]he radical feminist analysis goes beyond the conventional appearance of women's equality and even privilege to reveal an underlying

pattern of subordination and degradation. Reality, however, has more than one level. . . . [R]adical feminist analysis still leaves many important questions unanswered. In particular it does not explain the material reasons for men's subjugation of women. The existing radical feminist analysis needs to be supplemented by an account that embraces a deeper level of reality. (289)

Here, finally, there is no ambiguity or equivocation about the relationship between explanation and description, or about the primacy of the former:

[T]he radical feminist analysis provides a redescription of women's reality, a redescription that is not theory-neutral but that is also not theoretically complete or adequate because it does not provide a causal explanation of the reality that it describes. (289)

The deep flaw in radical feminism is thus its failure to go beyond describing "the appearance of women's oppression," its failure to "identify the oppressive forces and their laws of operation" (381). Its insistence that women name their experience has been important, "but it has not recognized explicitly that this experience must be analyzed, explained, and theoretically transcended" (381). In short, while disrupting androcentric views by valuing women's standpoint and experience, it has failed to comprehend that an "adequate expression" of such a standpoint "must be a theoretical and scientific achievement as well as a political and artistic one" (381).

What then authorizes the discourse of a feminist in a world that has jettisoned the illusion that "the facts" speak for themselves? Within this way of marking the division within feminism the broad answer appears now, as it did at the outset, to be "theory"; but it also appears, finally, to be only a particular sort of theory: unified, comprehensive, reflective of a single conception of society or human nature, and devoted to systematic causal explanation. If, as I have suggested, the existing purposes and arrangements of "the political" in our time—however varied their particular local, institutional, and practical expressions—inhere both in the systematic "management and government" of social relations and in the production of the scientific knowledge such management requires, the metatheoretical perspective circulated by *Feminist Politics* clearly affirms this configuration. The entry fee for the privilege of competing with "traditional" political and scientific theories for the authority to produce political knowledge—the price of a feminist "politicized science"—here appears quite unequivocally as an internalization of the "scientized politics" typical of that broader terrain to adjudicate theoretical differences within feminism. What initially seemed a reciprocal and mutually supportive relation between the normative, scientific, and practical characteristics of feminist theory has taken on a different cast; for the scientific commitment to systemic causal explanation, rather than *serving* emancipatory and transformative concerns, has come both to condition them and to determine their limits. By the end, there is a certain irony to Jaggar's own initial characterization of the contribution of scientific knowledge to feminist theory: it provides substance to ideals, it sharpens critiques of oppression, and it helps feminists "avoid idle speculation by setting limits to social and political possibility" (18). One might say, indeed.

III

While the preceding interpretation is doubtless itself open to objection, it nonetheless signals the significance of Sandra Harding's *The Science Question in Feminism* and intimates the political stakes of the epistemological controversies roiling in the wake of that work's provocative recasting of internal divisions within feminist theory. "Science," of course, was not newly a "question," either on the terrain of political discourse more generally or within feminism; but this text has provided a site where these very different critical perspectives could be productively conjoined.[11] The title itself marks both a disquiet at the intersection of feminist theory and the philosophy of science and a broader disturbance amidst the singular faith of a secular world; the first paragraph of its preface aptly flags the unsettling character of this conjuncture:

> Since the 1970s, feminist criticisms of science have evolved from a reformist to a revolutionary position, from analyses that offered the possibility of improving the science we have, to calls for a transformation in the very foundations both of science and of the cultures that accord it value. We began by asking "What is to be done about the situation of women in science?"—the "woman question" in science. Now feminists often pose a different question: "Is it possible to use for emancipatory ends sciences that are apparently so intimately involved in Western, bourgeois, and masculine projects?"—the "science question" in feminism. (9)

Where *Feminist Politics* attempted to invest feminist theory with the privileged status of "better science," *The Science Question* disrupts that privilege by interrogating the epistemological basis and political stakes of scientific authority itself. At the same time, however, and precisely by virtue of this disruption, it also recasts the problem of authority in feminist discourse by explicitly problematizing the presumption of a general scientific consensus on theoretical adequacy to establish the critical limits of a feminist "politicized science."

The political edge of Harding's work might be broadly characterized by noting two specific points at which its metatheoretical agenda significantly differs from that of *Feminist Politics*. Both works can be read as responses to the question of what authorizes the discourse of a feminist, and both pursue their concerns through a typological representation of divisions within feminism. But while *Feminist Politics* accepts the conventional demarcation of theoretical authorities—liberal, Marxist, radical, and socialist feminisms—and attempts to determine which is most capable of scientifically grounding feminism's emancipatory and transformative commitments, *The Science Question* identifies "feminist empiricism," "feminist standpoint epistemologies," and "feminist postmodernism" as distinctive, if interrelated, feminist challenges to the authority of science itself. Thus while *Feminist Politics* renders feminists' normative concern for emancipation and practical commitment to social transformation dependent upon the production of more comprehensive scientific explanations, Harding's critical project interrogates this ground. And in so doing it undermines the feminist version of "politicized science" implicit in the earlier work as well as its attendent complicity with the ordinary operation of "scientized politics" as a strategy for evaluating alternative feminist theories.

Second, and again indicative of a broad commonality, both works adopt a chronological narrative of their respective typologies, presenting each type of feminist theory as a response to difficulties generated by its predecessor. Despite this parallel, however, the two narratives pursue rather different strategic agendas. Consistent with its construction of a normatively feminist "politicized science," for instance, *Feminist Politics* seeks "a sound methodology to provide the basis for a theory and practice that will liberate women" (10); and consistent with its deployment of "scientized politics" to adjudicate differences among various feminist approaches, its purpose is to "prepare the way for a resolution of those differences . . . that can provide a sound basis for future political work and future theoretical development" (13). Its strategic agenda is thus not only to identify the strengths and weaknesses of each theoretical frame, but to *resolve* the question of how feminists should judge between them. By comparison, the strategic agenda of Harding's metatheoretical narrative is far more open-ended, particularly in its distance from the project of authoritatively *prescribing* a "sound basis" for methodological unity.[12] Considering trends in feminist critiques of science, it aims to identify "tensions and conflicts between them, inadequate concepts informing their analyses, unrecognized obstacles to and gaps in their research programs, and extensions that might transform them into even more powerful tools for the construction of emancipatory meanings and practices" (10). While it does not suggest that feminists abandon "attempts to describe, explain, and understand the regularities, underlying causal tendencies, and meanings of the natural and social worlds" or that we disavow "systematic inquiry," it does insist on the possibility of "far-reaching transformations in the cultural meanings and practices of that inquiry" (10). In this respect, again, it recasts the relationship between feminists' normative/emancipatory, practical/transformative, and scientific/explanatory commitments as an open question. In effect, not only does Harding's approach refuse to settle the instabilities or resolve the differences among the feminist approaches that it discusses, but it explicitly links these instabilities and differences to a pervasive contemporary unsettling of scientific authority more generally, as well as of the political and social world to which its knowledge claims are directed.[13]

Taken together, these differences suggest a broader distinction between Harding's and Jaggar's respective metatheoretical projects. In keeping with its avoidance of prescription and with its recasting of the divisions within feminism as epistemological *questions,* the categories of Harding's typology bleed into one another, their common colors partaking in a wider challenge the "social uses" of science in the past century as "the direct generator of economic, political, and social accumulation and control" (16). "Feminist empiricism," "feminist standpoint epistemologies," and "'feminist postmodernism,'" in this context, are complexly interrelated tendencies or trends of feminist inquiry rather than unified and analytically distinct "theories" of knowledge capable of identifying discrete problems and proposing specific solutions. In this sense *The Science Question* is less a displacement of political questions onto epistemological controversies within science than an insistent politicization of the methodical production of scientific knowledge itself, particularly as this has been institutionalized within the contemporary configuration of "the political."

In all these respects *The Science Question* can be read as an essay, a tentative or preliminary exploration, of the possibility of articulating a feminist politics adequate to a historical location in which that understanding of "the political"—as well as the knowledges that have framed its management of social problems—have become widely contested. While *Feminist Politics* suggested that what authorizes the discourse of a feminist is "theory," and what authorizes the best feminist theory is "science," Harding's work calls all such settled assumptions precisely into question. As a consequence, it simultaneously unhinges what that earlier view could confidently pronounce as the regulatory authority of science over feminist political inquiry and hence, finally, of the authority of scientifically adequate feminist political theory to define properly political feminist practice. By insisting that science is a *question,* in other words, Harding interrupts the very mechanism through which *Feminist Politics* guaranteed and controlled the linkage between feminism's normative commitment to emancipation and its practical commitment to social transformation. Absent the unquestioned authority of science—that is, without implicit confidence in unified, comprehensive,

consistent, systematic causal explanation of a presumptively systematic social world—the character of feminist theory, the efficacy of feminist practice, and the nature of their mutual relation becomes itself indeterminate.

From the metatheoretical perspective forwarded by *The Science Question,* what authorizes the feminist production of political knowledge is . . .
well, a diverse range of epistemological commitments, none of which can
claim do so unproblematically, and all of which are inseparable from broader
controversies over the political character of modern science as a cognitive
linchpin within the contemporary purposes and arrangements of "the political." Needless to say, this is hardly comforting. Indeed, to the extent that
feminist political analyses, and feminist political theory more generally, depend upon an initial characterization of women's oppression as a systemic
"problem" to be "solved" by instrumental interventions in the causal dynamics that produce it, so does the political character of feminism necessarily remain equivocal. Harding's own stance in this regard is not to abandon explanation, but rather to acknowledge the political tensions within and
between feminism's epistemological divisions explicitly:[14] she suggests "that
we think of feminist epistemologies as still transitional meditations upon the
substance of feminist claims and practices," and that "we should expect,
and perhaps even cherish" their "ambivalences and contradictions" (141).

Toleration of ambiguity, ambivalence, and contradiction, however, is
a tall order for a culture steeped in the lore of scientific authority, persuaded
of the general systematicity of the world, and habituated to the problem-
solving instrumentality characteristic of the modern image of "the political."
And such latitudinarian tolerance is a taller order still for such academic
corners of that culture as make the study of politics their profession. To be
sure, Harding's epistemological divisions have been widely recirculated. And
yet many of these discussions show a marked tendency to avoid, to trivial-
ize, or, more crudely, to suppress the ambivalences and nuances of the critique of science within which, in Harding's presentation, that typology was
generated. Let me conclude, then, by remarking briefly on how such re-
deployments continue to generate important political stakes in struggles for
authority in feminist discourse.

A moment ago I characterized *The Science Question* as an essay that
invited a rearticulation of feminist politics commensurate with the broader
unsettling of "the political" in our time. It does not follow from this, however, that subsequent deployments of its epistemological categories necessarily sustain this critical and political edge. Indeed, and quite to the contrary, what Harding evokes as subtly intertwined differentiations between
"feminist empiricism," "feminist standpoint epistemologies," and "feminist
postmodernism" are often reconstructed into rigorous and mutually exclusive analytic distinctions—rather as if the complexly blended tonalities and
richly mixed washes of a Helen Frankenthaler canvas were transformed into

the hard-edge linear clarity and primary colors of a Mondrian geometric. Whatever else this might accomplish in the context of particular arguments, it bears witness to persistent habits of reading and categorization easily assimilated by, and often explicitly marshalled into the service of, the metatheoretical strategies of "scientized politics." In a world long accustomed to the routinized competition between political theories to authorize the production of political knowledge, one of the most persistent of these habits is the rapid translation of broad patterns of affinity or difference into figurations of political partisanship. Through such translation, theories become something rather akin to ideal-type personifications of disciplined political parties, complete with loyal and mutually exclusive memberships as well as distinctive platforms, programs, campaign promises, slogans, and the like. As liberals, conservatives, and Marxists are *supposed*—in the modern configuration of "the political"—to be characterized by distinctive political theories, social analyses, programmatic goals and specifiable agencies or methods for achieving them; so have feminist theories been conventionally categorized along the same lines.

As we have seen with Jaggar's *Feminist Politics,* these habits have a decided tendency to recapitulate, even as critiques, the scientized politics of that configuration by taking systematic explanatory social theory as paradigmatic of theory as such. Clearly exemplified by that work's analysis of radical feminism, one way such habits can sustain those purposes and arrangements is by applying the evaluative criteria of systematic social theory to a disparate perspective, taking its neglect of causal explanation as a lack of practical utility, then discounting it as a serious competitor for authorizing the feminist production of properly political knowledge. Similar habits of typification significantly structure many treatments of the modern/postmodern divide, as well as discussions of the juncture between these broader debates and controversies over alternative feminist theories of knowledge. In both contexts, figures of epistemological partisanship are marshalled onto the field as mutually exclusive programmatic unities competing for the authority to guide political practice. Thus what appear more generally as set battles, modernist defenders of the emancipatory promise of the Enlightenment arrayed against the modernicide legions of poststructuralism, find an echo in representations of "feminist empiricism," "feminist standpoint epistemologies," and "feminist postmodernism" as partisan factions competing for the privilege of authorizing feminist politics.

One difficulty, of course, with such broad representations is their tendency to miscategorize the loyalties of the partisans involved.[15] But this is not what I take to be most problematic, for the political dilemma is not the accuracy with which such categories are filled but the conception of theory that drives the construction of these categories in the first place. While the interrogation of science may disrupt the authority of previous explanatory social theories to stipulate the relation between feminism's normative concern for emancipation and practical commitment to social transformation, the habits of "scientized politics" nonetheless linger on. In particular, these feminist epistemological controversies continue to be framed largely as arguments over the capacity of their respective *theories* to produce and sustain—in short, to authorize—connections between feminism's normative, practical, and explanatory commitments. Although the "theory" privileged here is a specific "theory of knowledge" rather than a specific "social theory" as conventionally understood, *theory* is again charged with the task of providing an authoritative foundation for a unified politics capable of effective intervention in the operative dynamics of a social whole.

To say, however, that the habits of "scientized politics" persist in this context is not to say that their substance lingers on as well. It is not, in other words, to claim that such figurations *necessarily* reconfirm the contemporary configuration of "the political" as social administration. Instead, it is to point to two rather different possibilities. On the one hand, it is to note that such figurations of epistemological partisanship *can* confirm that configuration by blithely assuming systematic causal theory to be the paradigm of theory *per se*. Where this *is* the case, they affirm both the modern understanding of "the political" as the systematic management of social relations and the metatheoretical strategy of "scientized politics" to adjudicate between alternative feminist theories.[16] Second, however, it is to suggest that where feminists arguably avoid this possibility the consequent relationship of theory to normative, transformative, explanatory commitments necessarily becomes a central problematic within feminist discourse itself.[17] In short, if theory is not to be held accountable to the dominant criteria of scientific adequacy, both its capacity to authorize the production of feminist political knowledge and its bearing upon feminist political practice become not questions of epistemological allegiance, but sites of political contestation in the broadest sense.

The issue here, however, is not a "choice" between feminist practice unguided by theory and feminist theory unconnected to practice. This polarity itself only reproduces the political difficulty to which *Feminist Politics* finally succumbs: the figuration of atheoretical "description" and "theoreticism" as the bogs and precipices from which properly feminist scientific theory *cum* properly scientific feminist theory must guard the progressive march of feminist practice. Nor is it a question of defining an "alternative theoretical framework" to which feminists should henceforth cleave their politics. Such a definitional displacement of scientific theory, by replicating the theory/practice distinction as it has come to be understood through the scientific model, would simply reinscribe the subservience of practice to theoretical authorization.[18] Instead, the task at hand is to rethink the political character of the desire for comprehensive causal theory as a reflection of the "truth" of the social world—to examine, rather than yield to, the supposition that "theory" is a guarantor of practical imperatives, a fund of justifications for instrumental action, and an authoritative foundation for permissions and prohibitions through which feminist politics might be at once unified and disciplined. It is, in short, to consider critically the embeddedness of that image of theory within the political sensibilities, cultural codes, and patterns of inference characteristic of the dominant contemporary configuration of "the political."

Perhaps, amidst the contemporary proliferation of political sites, we might address the task of criticism by figuring "theory" less as a noun than as a verb. Rather, in other words, than restricting attention to "theories" as intellectual constructs bent on representing the truth of the world, we might attend to "theorizing" as itself an activity—as a contingent and located social practice without the security of foundations, as well as a political practice always and inescapably implicated with power. "Theorizing" in this sense is always contestable, not simply or narrowly in terms of the "truth" of its content or the "accuracy" of its representations, but more broadly in terms of its filiations, disaffiliations, and equivocations with the dominant contemporary understanding of "the political." So understood, "doing theory" might entail a wariness of converting an authoritative "it is" into a latter-day "thou shalt," while theoretical controversies might prove less intent upon adjudicating or settling practices and more concerned with mobilizing meanings. Finally, it might also open consideration of the possibility that what is at stake in these contests is a matter neither of explanatory adequacy nor of political efficacy as conventionally understood, but a matter of breathing room for the articulation of new knowledges, new agencies, and new practices—a matter, in short, of working toward a new configuration of "the political."

NOTES

I am indebted to Bonnie Honig, Leslie Patrick-Stamp, and Kathy Ferguson for their thoughtful criticisms of earlier versions of this essay, and to the editors of the present volume for their assistance in sharpening its argument.

1. Sheldon S. Wolin, *Politics and Vision* (Boston: Little, Brown and Company, 1960), p. 8. See also his *Hobbes and the Epic Tradition of Political Theory* (Los Angeles, Calif.: William Andrews Clark Memorial Library/UCLA, 1970) and "Political Theory as a Vocation," in *Machiavelli and the Nature of Political Thought*, Martin Fleisher, ed. (New York: Atheneum, 1972), pp. 23–75.

2. Marilyn Frye's recent essay, "The Possiblity of Feminist Theory," offers a good example. She suggests that feminists have "undertaken, as we must, to rewrite the world. The

project of feminist theory is to write a new encyclopedia. Its title: *The World, According to Women.*" This project, however, is marked by a different spirit than the Encyclopedia of the *philosophes:* "What we are writing, *The World, According to Women,* has never been anything but an anthology, a collection of tales unified, like any yarn, only by successively overlapping threads held together by friction, not riveted by logic. There is no reason to predict or require that it must forever hold together at all." The essay is published in *Theoretical Perspectives on Sexual Difference,* Deborah L. Rhode, ed. (New Haven: Yale University Press, 1990), pp. 175 and 184, respectively.

3. Ernesto Laclau and Chantal Mouffe, *Hegemony and Socialist Strategy* (London: Verso, 1985), p. 181.

4. I have considered the political meaning of these two terms in a different context in "Difference, Diversity, and the Limits of Toleration," *Political Theory* 18, 3 (August 1990), pp. 361–92.

5. (Totowa, N.J.: Rowman and Allenheld, 1983) and (New York: McGraw-Hill, Inc., 1984), respectively. Differences between the two works, however, invest their similarities with a greater weight than might otherwise be the case. Notwithstanding the distance between them in audience and level of address, and in spite of the substantive differences between their respective typologies, they nonetheless operate within a common understanding of the character of "the political," as well as a common view of the relation between theory and practice that feminist political knowledge should properly serve. Further citations to this work appear in parentheses in the text.

6. The account to follow is considerably indebted to Sheldon Wolin's critique of the "behavioral revolution" in "Political Theory as a Vocation," cited above in note 1.

7. This is not, in other words, to deny that real effects are generated by the adoption of any particular theory over its rivals. For example, significant social consequences follow from state policies authorized by supply-side rather than Keynesian economy theory; and yet both operate within the terms of the dominant understanding of the political. It is this, indeed, that makes it possible to view the practices and policies they differentially authorize as political choices. Neither, however, problematizes the equation of "politics" with state policy regarding the management of the economy.

8. See Alison Jaggar's more detailed accounts of this problem in both liberalism and liberal feminism, pp. 175–203 and 355–58, and in traditional Marxism, pp. 229–44 and 358–64.

9. Alison Jaggar, *Feminist Politics,* p. 11. Needless to say, this is highly problematic. While a normative commitment to ending the oppression of women appears sufficient to distinguish feminist from nonfeminist analyses, a normative commitment by black feminists to ending racial oppression as well seems insufficient to constitute a "unified" black feminist theory. *Feminist Frameworks* makes a gesture toward recognizing this by including a separate section on "Feminism and Women of Color," but there too such perspectives are not granted the status of "theory."

10. *Ibid.,* p. 287. A similar discomfort with more literary modes of expression is evident in Jaggar's initial discussion of radical feminism. Excepting Firestone, for example, their "style of writing is invariably poetic and allusive rather than literal and exact" (p. 95). Similarly, although their conception of women as a class or sex-class is insightful, it tends to appear in "an intuitive and non-theoretical way" (p. 102). Such artistic contributions, Jaggar contends, may be vital, but they are not to be understood as political action. Cultural pro-

ductions, on this account, "can never effect . . . changes in the material base of society.
. . . Patriarchy will not fall to words, spells, or songs" (p. 295).

11. It is not the only such site; but its rewriting of divisions among feminist perspectives as epistemological differences found almost immediate uptake. Donna Haraway also signals this conjuncture, in "Situated Knowledges: The Science Question in Feminism and the Privilege of Partial Perspective," *Feminist Studies*, 14, 3 (Fall 1988), pp. 575–99, and in her political history of primatology, *Primate Visions: Gender, Race, and Nature in the World of Modern Science* (New York: Routledge, 1989) as well as elsewhere.

12. This is not to say that, in this work at least, Harding has abandoned the *aspiration* to such unity. Rather, it is to emphasize that her deference to the axiom of systematicity characteristic of the dominant contemporary understanding of "the political" is evidenced through a strategy of deferral rather than imposition. I am indebted to Kathy Ferguson for her helpful criticism of this portion of my argument.

13. See also Sandra Harding, "The Instability of the Analytic Categories of Feminist Theory," *Signs*, 11 (1986), pp. 645–64; and "Feminism, Science, and the Anti-Enlightenment Critiques," in Linda J. Nicholson, ed., *Feminism/Postmodernism* (New York: Routledge, 1990), pp. 83–106.

14. In a later essay, "Feminism, Science, and the Anti-Enlightenment Critiques" (see previous note), Harding has reiterated this suggestion as a call for a "robust and principled ambivalence," a "self-conscious and theoretically articulated" ambivalence, "a positive program." She urges a recognition that these epistemological and political tensions are not disputes "external" to feminism on which feminists somehow must choose sides, but are themselves "generated . . . [by] . . . tensions and contradictions in the world in which feminists move" (86).

15. See, for example, the interchange in *Signs*, 14, 1 (Autumn 1988), between Daryl McGowan Tress and Jane Flax over the latter's "Postmodernism and Gender Relations in Feminist Theory," *Signs*, 12, 4 (Summer 1987).

16. Although space prohibits its consideration here, a prime example of this is Robert Keohane's recent commentary on the possibility of a feminist international relations theory, "International Relations Theory: Contributions of a Feminist Standpoint," *Millennium: Journal of International Studies*, 18, 2, pp. 245–53.

17. Two examples of such avoidance come to mind, each of which presents a different response to the dilemma of authority I've attempted to sketch. One possibility is to defer the question to the future, as I think is done by Harding's work itself as well as by Nancy Hartsock's recent essay, "Foucault on Power," in *Feminism/Postmodernism*, edited by Linda Nicholson (New York: Routledge, 1990), pp. 157–75. Here, Hartsock emphasizes feminist theory as an *aspiration* rather than an accomplishment, a deferral that arguably distances feminist theory from complicity with the routine practice of scientized politics: if we don't *have* a theory yet, it can hardly be a competitor for scientific authority. Even as an aspiration, however, this model of theory disqualifies attempts to eschew systematic explanation, and especially those characterized by the term "postmodern."

A rather different strategy for avoiding feminist complicity with "scientized politics" entails bringing theory itself to heel, a strategy pursued by historian Karen Offen in "Defining Feminism: A Historical Comparative Approach," *Signs*, 14 (Autumn 1988), pp. 119–57; "Feminism and Sexual Difference in Historical Perspective," in Deborah L. Rhode, ed., *Theoretical Perspectives on Sexual Difference*, pp. 13–20; and "The Use and Abuse of History," a review of Denise Riley's *"Am I That Name?" Feminism and the Category of "Women" in History* (Minneapolis: University of Minnesota Press, 1988) and Joan Landes's *Women and the Public Sphere in the Age of the French Revolution* (Ithaca, N.Y.: Cornell University Press, 1988), *The Women's Review of Books*, VI, 7 (April 1989). Offen foregrounds the normative and practical commitments of feminism in the present by replacing the quest for systematic explanation with that of historical understanding. Dispensing with the goal of comprehensive explanation at the outset, she not only effects a distance between feminism and science but attempts further to render theoretical claims to the production of political knowledge accountable to a different authority entirely: specifically, to the disciplinary authority and expertise of "practitioners of the historical craft."

    18. In this context Harding's aspiration to feminist critique modeled on the "critical social sciences" rather than the strongly empiricist or positivist natural sciences is a step in the right direction. But however useful the implicit distinction betwen "critical" and "uncritical" sciences might be for feminist critiques of natural science, it nonetheless flattens out significant controversies between interpretive approaches over the tasks and political character of social or political theory as well as its relationship to "science." See, for example, Jürgen Habermas, *Theory and Practice* (Boston: Beacon, 1974); Seyla Benhabib, *Critique, Norm, and Utopia* (New York: Columbia University Press, 1986) and "The Generalized and the Concrete Other," in *Feminism as Critique,* edited by Seyla Benhabib and Drucilla Cornell (Minneapolis: University of Minnesota Press, 1987); Marie Fleming, "The Gender of Critical Theory," *Cultural Critique,* 13 (Fall 1990); Charles Taylor, *Philosophy and the Human Sciences: Philosophical Papers 2* (Cambridge: Cambridge University Press, 1985); Michel Foucault, *The Archaeology of Knowledge* (New York: Harper and Row, 1972) and *The Order of Things* (New York: Vintage, 1970); and Jean-François Lyotard, *The Postmodern Condition: A Report on Knowledge* (Minneapolis: University of Minnesota Press, 1984).

17

Feminism, Citizenship and Radical Democratic Politics

Chantal Mouffe

Two topics have recently been the subject of much discussion among Anglo-American feminists: postmodernism and essentialism. Obviously they are related since the so-called "postmoderns" are also presented as the main critics of essentialism, but it is better to distinguish them since some feminists who are sympathetic to postmodernism have lately come to the defense of essentialism.[1] I consider that, in order to clarify the issues that are at stake in that debate, it is necessary to recognize that there is not such a thing as "postmodernism" understood as a coherent theoretical approach and that the frequent assimilation between poststructuralism and postmodernism can only lead to confusion. Which is not to say that we have not been witnessing through the twentieth century a progressive questioning of the dominant form of rationality and of the premises of the modes of thought characteristic of the Enlightenment. But this critique of universalism, humanism, and rationalism has come from many different quarters and it is far from being limited to the authors called "poststructuralists" or "postmodernists." From that point of view, all the innovative currents of this century—Heidegger and the post-Heideggerian philosophical hermeneutics of Gadamer, the later Wittgenstein and the philosophy of language inspired by his work, psychoanalysis and the reading of Freud proposed by Lacan, American pragmatism—all have from diverse standpoints criticized the idea of a universal human nature, of a universal canon of rationality through which that human nature could be known as well as the traditional conception of truth. Therefore, if the term "postmodern" indicates such a critique of Enlightenment's universalism and rationalism, it must be acknowledged that it refers to the main currents of twentieth-century philosophy and there is no reason to single out poststructuralism as a special target. On the other side, if by "postmodernism" one wants to designate only the very specific form that such a critique takes in authors such as Lyotard and Baudrillard, there is absolutely no justification for putting in that category people like Derrida, Lacan, or Foucault, as has generally been the case. Too often a critique of a specific thesis of Lyotard or Baudrillard leads to sweeping conclusions about "the postmoderns" who by then include all the authors loosely connected with poststructuralism. This type of amalgamation is completely unhelpful when not clearly disingenuous.

Once the conflation between postmodernism and poststructuralism has been debunked, the question of essentialism appears in a very different light. Indeed, it is with regard to the critique of essentialism that a convergence can be established among many different currents of thought and similarities found in the work of authors as different as Derrida, Wittgenstein, Heidegger, Dewey, Gadamer, Lacan, Foucault, Freud, and others. This is very important because it means that such a critique takes many different forms and that if we want to scrutinize its relevance for feminist politics we must engage with all its modalities and implications and not quickly dismiss it on the basis of some of its versions.

My aim in this article will be to show the crucial insights that an antiessentialist approach can bring to the elaboration of a feminist politics which is also informed by a radical democratic project. I certainly do not believe that essentialism necessarily entails conservative politics and I am ready to accept that it can be formulated in a progressive way. What I want to argue is that it presents some inescapable shortcomings for the construction of a democratic alternative whose objective is the articulation of the struggles linked to different forms of oppression. I consider that it leads to a view of identity that is at odds with a conception of radical and plural democracy and that it does not allow us to construe the new vision of citizenship that is required by such a politics.

The Question of Identity and Feminism

One common tenet of critics of essentialism has been the abandoning of the category of the subject as a rational transparent entity that could convey a homogeneous meaning on the total field of her conduct by being the source of her action. For instance, psychoanalysis has shown that far from being organized around the transparency of an ego, personality is structured in a number of levels which lie outside of the consciousness and the rationality of the agents. It has therefore undermined the idea of the unified character of the subject. Freud's central claim is that the human mind is necessarily subject to division between two systems of which one is not and cannot be conscious. Expanding the Freudian vision, Lacan has shown the plurality of registers—the Symbolic, the Real, and the Imaginary—which penetrate any identity, and the place of the subject as the place of the lack which—though represented within the structure—is the empty place which at the same time subverts and is the condition of constitution of any identity. The history of the subject is the history of his/her identifications and there is no concealed identity to be rescued beyond the latter. There is thus a double movement. On the one hand, a movement of decentering which prevents the fixation of a set of positions around a preconstituted point. On the other hand, and as a result of this *essential* nonfixity, the opposite movement: the institution of nodal points, partial fixations which limit the flux of the signified under the signifier. But this dialectics at nonfixity/fixation is possible only because fixity is not given beforehand, because no center of subjectivity precedes the subject's identifications.

In the philosophy of language of the later Wittgenstein, we also find a critique of the rationalist conception of the subject that indicates that the latter cannot be the source of linguistic meanings since it is through participation in different language games that the world is disclosed to us. We encounter the same idea in Gadamer's philosophical hermeneutics in the thesis that there is a fundamental unity between thought, language, and the world and that it is within language that the horizon of our present is constituted. A similar critique of the centrality of the subject in modern metaphysics and of its unitary character can be found under several forms in the other authors mentioned earlier. However, my purpose here is not to examine those theories in detail but simply to indicate some basic convergences. I am not overlooking the fact that there are important differences among all those very diverse thinkers. But from the point of view of the argument that I want to make, it is important to grasp the consequences of their common critique of the traditional status of the subject and of its implications for feminism.

It is often said that the deconstruction of essential identities, which is the result of acknowledging the contingency and ambiguity of every identity, renders feminist political action impossible. Many feminists believe that, without seeing women as a coherent identity, we cannot ground the possiblity of a feminist political movement in which women could unite as women in order to formulate and pursue specific feminist aims. Contrary to that view, I will argue that, for those feminists who are committed to a radical democratic politics, the deconstruction of essential identities should be seen as the necessary condition for an adequate understanding of the variety of social relations where the principles of liberty and equality should apply. It is only when we discard the view of the subject as an agent both rational and transparent to itself, and discard as well the supposed unity and homogeneity of the ensemble of its positions, that we are in the position to theorize the multiplicity of relations of subordination. A single individual can be the bearer of this multiplicity and be dominant in one relation while subordinated in another. We can then conceive the social agent as constituted by an ensemble of "subject positions" that can never be totally fixed in a closed system of differences, constructed by a diversity of discourses among which there is no necessary relation, but a constant movement of overdetermination and displacement. The "identity" of such a multiple and contradictory subject is therefore always contingent and precarious, temporarily fixed at the intersection of those subject positions and dependent on specific forms of identification. It is therefore impossible to speak of the social agent as if we were dealing with a unified, homogeneous entity. We have rather to approach it as a plurality, dependent on the various subject positions through which it is constituted within various discursive formations. And to recognize that there is no a priori, necessary relation between the discourses that construct its different subject positions. But, for the reasons pointed out earlier, this plurality does not involve the *coexistence,* one by one, of a plurality of subject positions but rather the constant subversion and overdetermination of one by the others, which make possible the generation of "totalizing effects" within a field characterized by open and indeterminate frontiers.

Such an approach is extremely important to understand feminist as well as other contemporary struggles. Their central characteristic is that an ensemble of subject positions linked through inscription in social relations, hitherto considered as apolitical, have become loci of conflict and antagonism and have led to political mobilization. The proliferation of these new forms of struggle can only be theoretically tackled when one starts with the dialectics and decentering/recentering described earlier.

In *Hegemony and Socialist Strategy,*[2] Ernesto Laclau and I have attempted to draw the consequences of such a theoretical approach for a project of radical and plural democracy. We argued for the need to establish a chain of equivalence among the different democratic struggles so as to create an equivalent articulation between the demands of women, blacks, workers, gays, and others. On this point our perspective differs from other nonessentialist views where the aspect of detotalization and decentering prevails and where the dispersion of subject positions is transformed into an effective separation, as is the case with Lyotard and to some extent with Foucault. For us, the aspect of articulation is crucial. To deny the existence of an a priori, necessary link between subject positions does not mean that there are not constant efforts to establish between them historical, contingent, and variable links. This type of link, which establishes between various positions a contingent, unpredetermined relation is what we designated as "articulation." Even though there is no necessary link between different subject positions, in the field of politics there are always discourses that try to provide an articulation from different standpoints. For that reason every subject position is constituted within an essentially unstable discursive structure since it is submitted to a variety of articulatory practices that constantly subvert and transform it. This is why there is no subject position whose links with others is definitively assured and, therefore, no social identity that would be fully and permanently acquired. This does not mean, however, that we cannot retain notions like "working-class," "men," "women," "blacks," or other signifiers referring to collective subjects. However, once the existence of a common essence has been discarded, their status must be conceived in terms of what Wittgenstein designates as "family resemblances" and their unity must be seen as the result of the partial fixation of identities through the creation of nodal points.

For feminists to accept such an approach has very important consequences for the way we formulate our political struggles. If the category "woman" does not correspond to any unified and unifying essence, the question can no longer be to try to unearth it. The central issues become: how is "woman" constructed as a category within different discourses? how is sexual difference made a pertinent distinction in social relations? and how are relations of subordination constructed through such a distinction? The whole false dilemma of equality versus difference is exploded since we no longer have a homogeneous entity "woman" facing another homogeneous entity "man," but a multiplicity of social relations in which sexual difference is always constructed in very diverse ways and where the struggle against subordination has to be visualized in specific and differential forms. To ask if women should become identical to men in order to be recognized as equal, or if they should assert their difference at the cost of equality, appears meaningless once essential identities are put into question.[3]

Citizenship and Feminist Politics

In consequence, the very question of what a feminist politics should be, has to be posed in completely different terms. So far, most feminists concerned with the contribution that feminism could make to democratic politics have been looking either for the specific demands that could express women's interests or for the specific feminine values that should become the model for democratic politics. Liberal feminists have been fighting for a wide range of new rights for women to make them equal citizens, but without challenging the dominant liberal models of citizenship and politics. Their view has been criticized by other feminists who argue that the present conception of the political is a male one and that women's concerns cannot be accommodated within such a framework. Following Carol Gilligan, they oppose a feminist "ethics of care" to the male and liberal "ethics of justice."

Against liberal individualist values, they defend a set of values based on the experience of women *as* women, that is, their experience of motherhood and care exercised in the private realm of the family. They denounce Liberalism for having constructed modern citizenship as the realm of the public, identified with men, and for having excluded women by relegating them to the private realm. According to this view, feminists should strive for a type of politics that is guided by the specific values of love, care, the recognition of needs, and friendship. One of the clearest attempts to offer an alternative to liberal politics grounded in feminine values is to be found in "Maternal Thinking" and "Social Feminism" principally represented by Sara Ruddick and Jean Bethke Elshtain.[4] Feminist politics, they argue, should privilege the identity of "women as mothers" and the private realm of the family. The family is seen as having moral superiority over the public domain of politics because it constitutes our common humanity. For Elshtain "the family remains the locus of the deepest and most resonant human ties, the most enduring hopes, the most intractable conflicts."[5] She considers that it is in the family that we should look for a new political morality to replace liberal individualism. In women's experience in the private realm as mothers, she says, a new model for the activity of citizenship is to be found. The maternalists want us to abandon the male liberal politics of the public informed by the abstract point of view of justice and the "generalized other" and adopt instead a feminist politics of the private, informed by the virtues of love, intimacy, and concern for the "concrete other" specific to the family.

An excellent critique of such an approach has been provided by Mary Dietz[6] who shows that Elshtain fails to provide a theoretical argument which links maternal thinking and the social practice of mothering to democratic values and democratic politics. Dietz argues that maternal virtues cannot be political because they are connected with and emerge from an activity that is special and distinctive. They are the expression of an unequal relation between mother and child which is also an intimate, exclusive, and particular activity. Democratic citizenship, on the contrary, should be collective, inclusive, and generalized. Since democracy is a condition in which individuals aim at being equals, the mother-child relationship cannot provide an adequate model of citizenship.

Yet a different feminist critique of liberal citizenship is provided by Carole Pateman.[7] It is more sophisticated, but shares some common features with "Maternal Thinking." Pateman's tone bears the traces of radical feminism, for the accent is put, not on the mother/child relation, but on the man/woman antagonism.

Citizenship is, according to Pateman, a patriarchal category: who a "citizen" is, what a citizen does and the arena within which he acts have been constructed in the masculine image. Although women in liberal democracies are now citizens, formal citizenship has been won within a structure of patriarchal power in which women's qualities and tasks are still devalued. Moreover, the call for women's distinctive capacities to be integrated fully into the public world of citizenship faces what she calls the "Wollstonecraft dilemma": to demand equality is to accept the patriarchal conception of citizenship which implies that women must become like men while to insist that women's distinctive attributes, capacities, and activities be given expression and valued as contributing to citizenshp is to demand the impossible because such difference is precisely what patriarchal citizenship exludes.

Pateman sees the solution to this dilemma in the elaboration of a "sexually differentiated" conception of citizenship that would recognize women *as* women, with their bodies and all that they symbolize. For Pateman this entails giving political significance to the capacity that men lack: to create life, which is to say, *motherhood*. She declares that this capacity should be treated with equal political relevance for defining citizenship as what is usually considered the ultimate test of citizenship: a man's willingness to fight and to die for his country. She considers that the traditional patriarchal way of posing an alternative, where either the separation or the sameness of the sexes is valorized, needs to be overcome by a new way of posing the question of women. This can be done through a conception of citizenship that recognizes both the specificity of womanhood and the common humanity of men and women. Such a view "that gives due weight to sexual difference in a context of civil equality, requires the rejection of a unitary (i.e., masculine) conception of the individual, abstracted from our embodied existence and from the patriarchal division between the private and the public."[8] What feminists should aim for is the elaboration of a sexually differentiated conception of individuality and citizenship that would include "women *as* women in a context of civil equality and active citizenship."[9]

Pateman provides many very interesting insights into the patriarchal bias of the social contract theorists and the way in which the liberal individual has been constructed according to the male image. I consider that her own solution, however, is unsatisfactory. Despite all her provisos about the historically constructed aspects of sexual difference, her view still postulates the existence of some kind of essence corresponding to women *as* women. Indeed, her proposal for a differentiated citizenship that recognizes the specificity of womanhood rests on the identification of women *as* women with motherhood. There are for her two basic types of individuality that should be expressed in two different forms of citizenship: men *as* men and women *as* women. The problem according to her is that the category of the "individual," while based on the male model, is presented as the universal form of individuality. Feminists must uncover that false universality by asserting the existence of two sexually differentiated forms of universality; this is the only way to resolve the "Wollstonecraft dilemma" and to break free from the patriarchal alternatives of "othering" and "saming."

I agree with Pateman that the modern category of the individual has been constructed in a manner that postulates a universalist, homogeneous "public" that relegates all particularity and difference to the "private" and that this has very negative consequences for women. I do not believe, however, that the remedy is to replace it by a sexually differentiated, "bi-gendered" conception of the individual and to bring women's so-called specific tasks into the very definition of citizenship. It seems to me that such a solution remains trapped in the very problematic that Pateman wants to challenge. She affirms that the separation between public and private is the founding moment of modern patriarchalism because

> the separation of private and public is the separation of the world of natural subjection, i.e. women, from the world of conventional relations and individuals, i.e. men. The feminine, private world of nature, particularity, differentiation, inequality, emotion, love and ties of blood is set apart from the public, universal—and masculine—realm of convention, civil equality and freedom, reason, consent and contract.[10]

It is for that reason that childbirth and motherhood have been presented as the antithesis of citizenship and that they have become the symbol of everything natural that cannot be part of the "public" but must remain in a separate sphere. By asserting the political value of motherhood, Pateman intends to overcome that distinction and contribute to the deconstruction of the patriarchal conception of citizenship and private and public life. As a result of her essentialism, however, she never deconstructs the very opposition of men/women. This is the reason that she ends up, like the maternalists, proposing an inadequate conception of what should be a democratic politics informed by feminism. This is why she can assert that "the most profound and complex problem for political theory and practice is how the two bodies of humankind and feminine and masculine individuality can be fully incorporated into political life."[11]

My own view is completely different. I want to argue that the limitations of the modern conception of citizenship should be remedied, not by making sexual difference politically relevant to its definition, but by constructing a new conception of citizenship where sexual difference should become effectively nonpertinent. This, of course, requires a conception of the social agent in the way that I have defended earlier, as the articulation of an ensemble of subject positions, corresponding to the multiplicity of social relations in which it is inscribed. This multiplicity is constructed within specific discourses which have no necessary relation but only contingent and precarious forms of articulation. There is no reason why sexual difference should be pertinent in all social relations. To be sure, today many different pratices, discourses and institutions do construct men and women (differentially), and the masculine/feminine distinction exists as a pertinent one in many fields. But this does not imply that it should remain the case, and we can perfectly imagine sexual difference becoming irrelevant in many social relations where it is currently found. This is indeed the objective of many feminist struggles.

I am not arguing in favor of a total disappearance of sexual difference as a pertinent distinction; I am not saying either that equality between men and women requires gender-neutral social relations, and it is clear that, in many cases, to treat men and women equally implies treating them differentially. My thesis is that, in the domain of politics, and as far as citizenship is concerned, sexual difference should not be a pertinent distinction. I am at one with Pateman in criticizing the liberal, male conception of modern citizenship but I believe that what a project of radical and plural democracy needs is not a sexually differentiated model of citizenship in which the specific tasks of both men and women would be valued equally, but a truly different conception of what it is to be a citizen and to act as a member of a democratic political community.

A Radical Democratic Conception of Citizenship

The problems with the liberal conception of citizenship are not limited to those concerning women, and feminists committed to a project of radical and plural democracy should engage with all of them. Liberalism has contributed to the formulation of the notion of universal citizenship, based on the assertion that all individuals are born free and equal, but it has also reduced citizenship to a merely legal status, indicating the rights that the individual holds against the state. The way those rights are exercised is irrelevant as long as their holders do not break the law or interfere with the rights of others. Notions of public-spiritedness, civic activity and political participation in a community of equals are alien to most liberal thinkers. Besides, the public realm of modern citizenship was constructed in a universalistic and rationalistic manner that precluded the recognition of division and antagonism and that relegated to the private all particularity and difference. The distinction public/private, central as it was for the assertion of individual liberty, acted therefore as a powerful principle of exclusion. Through the identification between the private and the domestic, it played indeed an important role in the subordination of women. Recently, several feminists and other critics of liberalism have been looking to the civic republican tradition for a different, more active conception of citizenship that emphasizes the value of political participation and the notion of a common good, prior to and independent of individual desires and interests.

Nevertheless, feminists should be aware of the limitations of such an approach and of the potential dangers that a communitarian type of politics presents for the struggle of many oppressed groups. The communitarian insistence on a substantive notion of the common good and shared moral values is incompatible with the pluralism that is constitutive of modern democracy and that I consider to be necessary to deepen the democratic revolution and accommodate the multiplicity of present democratic demands. The problems with the liberal construction of the public/private distinction would not be solved by discarding it, but only by reformulating it in a more adequate way. Moreover, the centrality of the notion of rights for a modern conception of the citizen should be acknowledged, even though these must be complemented by a more active sense of political participation and of belonging to a political community.[12]

The view of radical and plural democracy that I want to put forward sees citizenship as a form of political identity that consists in the identification with the political principles of modern pluralist democracy, namely, the assertion of liberty and equality for all. It would be a common political identity of persons who might be engaged in many different purposive enterprises and with differing conceptions of the good, but who are bound by their common identification with a given interpretation of a set of ethico-political values. Citizenship is not just one identity among others, as it is in Liberalism, nor is it the dominant identity that overrides all others, as it is in Civic Republicanism. Instead, it is an articulating principle that affects the different subject positions of the social agent while allowing for a plurality of specific allegiances and for the respect of individual liberty. In this view, the public/private distinction is not abandoned, but constructed in a different way. The distinction does not correspond to discrete, separate spheres; every situation is an encounter between "private" and "public" because every enterprise is private while never immune from the public conditions prescribed by the principles of citizenship. Wants, choices and decisions are private because they are the responsibility of each individual, but performances are public because they have to subscribe to the conditions specified by a specific understanding of the ethico-political principles of the regime which provide the "grammar" of the citizen's conduct.[13]

It is important to stress here that if we affirm that the exercise of citizenship consists in identifying with the ethico-political principles of modern democracy, we must also recognize that there can be as many forms of citizenship as there are interpretations of those principles and that a radical democratic interpretation is one among others. A radical democratic interpretation will emphasize the numerous social relations in which situations of domination exist that must be challenged if the principles of liberty and equality are to apply. It indicates the common recognition by the different groups struggling for an extension and radicalization of democracy that they have a common concern. This should lead to the articulation of the democratic demands found in a variety of movements: women, workers, blacks, gays, ecological, as well as other "new social movements." The aim is to construct a "we" as radical democratic citizens, a collective political identity articulated through the principle of democratic *equivalence*. It must be stressed that such a relation of *equivalence* does not eliminate *difference*—that would be simple identity. It is only insofar as democratic differences are opposed to forces or discourses which negate all of them that these differences are substitutible for each other.

The view that I am proposing here is clearly different from the liberal as well as the civic republican one. It is not a gendered conception of citizenship, but neither is it a neutral one. It recognizes that every definition of a "we" implies the delimitation of a "frontier" and the designation of a "them." That definition of a "we" always takes place, then, in a context of diversity and conflict. Contrary to Liberalism, which evacuates the idea of the common good, and Civic Republicanism, which reifies it, a radical democratic approach views the common good as a "vanishing point," something to which we must constantly refer when we are acting as citizens, but that can never be reached. The common good functions, on the one hand, as a "social imaginary": that is, as that for which the very impossibility of achieving full representation gives to it the role of an horizon which is the condition of possibility of any representation within the space that it delimits. On the other hand, it specifies what I have designated, following Wittgenstein, as a "grammar of conduct" that coincides with the allegiance to the constitutive ethico-political principles of modern democracy: liberty and equality for all. Yet, since those principles are open to many competing interpretations, one has to acknowledge that a fully inclusive political community can never be realized. There will always be a "constitutive outside," an exterior to the community that is the very condition of its existence. Once it is accepted that there cannot be a "we" without a "them" and that all forms of consensus are by necessity based on acts of exclusion, the question cannot be any more the creation of a fully inclusive community where antagonism, division, and conflict will have disappeared. Hence, we have to come to terms with the very impossibility of a full realization of democracy.

Such a radical democratic citizenship is obviously at odds with the "sexually differentiated" view of citizenship of Carole Pateman, but also with another feminist attempt to offer an alternative to the liberal view of the citizen: the "group differentiated" conception put forward by Iris Young.[14] Like Pateman, Young argues that modern citizenship has been constructed on a separation between "public" and "private" that presented the public as the realm of homogeneity and universality and relegated difference to the private. But she insists that this exclusion affects not only women but many other groups based on differences of ethnicity, race, age, disabilities, and so forth. For Young, the crucial problem is that the public realm of citizenship was presented as expressing a general will, a point of view that citizens held in common and that transcended their differences. Young argues in favor of a repoliticization of public life that would not require the creation of a public realm in which citizens leave behind their particular group affiliation and needs in order to discuss a presumed general interest or common good. In its place she proposes the creation of a "heterogeneous public" that provides mechanisms for the effective representation and recognition of the distinct voices and perspectives of those constituent groups that are oppressed or disadvantaged. In order to make such a project possible, she looks for a conception of normative reason that does not pretend to be impartial and universal and that does not oppose reason to affectivity and desire. She considers that, despite its limitations, Habermas's communicative ethics can contribute a good deal to its formulation.

Whereas I sympathize with Young's attempt to take account of other forms of oppression than the ones suffered by women, I nevertheless find her solution of "group differentiated citizenship" highly problematic. To begin with, the notion of a group that she identifies with comprehensive identities and ways of life might make sense for groups like Native Americans, but is completely inadequate as a description for many other groups whose demands she wants to take into account like women, the elderly, the differently abled, and others. She has an ultimately essentialist notion of "group," and this accounts for why, in spite of all her disclaimers, her view is not so different from the interest-group pluralism that she criticizes: there are groups with their interests and identities already given, and politics is not about the construction of new identities, but about finding ways to satisfy the demands of the various parts in a way acceptable to all. In fact, one could say that hers is a kind of "Habermasian version of interest group pluralism," according to which groups are not viewed as fighting for egoistic private interests but for justice, and where the emphasis is put on the need for argumentation and publicity. So politics in her work is still conceived as a process of dealing with already-constituted interests and identities while, in the approach that I am defending, the aim of a radical democratic citizenship should be the construction of a common political identity that would create the conditions for the establishment of a new hegemony articulated through new egalitarian social relations, practices and institutions. This cannot be achieved without the transformation of existing subject positions; this is the reason why the model of the rainbow coalition favored by Young can be seen only as a first stage toward the implementation of a radical democratic politics. It might indeed provide many opportunities for a dialogue among different oppressed groups, but for their demands to be construed around the principle of democratic equivalence, new identities need to be created: in their present state many of these demands are antithetical to each other, and their convergence can only result from a political process of hegemonic articulation, and not simply of free and undistorted communication.

Feminist Politics and Radical Democracy

As I indicated at the outset, there has been a great deal of concern among feminists about the possibility of grounding a feminist politics once the existence of women *as* women is put into question. It has been argued that to abandon the idea of a feminine subject with a specific identity and definable interests was to pull the rug from under feminism as politics. According to Kate Soper,

> feminism, like any other politics, has always implied a banding together, a movement based on the solidarity and sisterhood of women, who are linked by perhaps very little else than their *sameness* and "common cause" as women. If this sameness itself is challenged on the ground that there is no "presence" of womanhood, nothing that the term "woman" immediately expresses, and nothing instantiated concretely except particular women in particular situations, then the idea of a political community built around women—the central aspiration of the early feminist movement—collapses.[15]

I consider that Soper here construes an illegitimate opposition between two extreme alternatives: either there is an already given unity of "womanhood" on the basis of some a priori belonging or, if this is denied, no forms of unity and feminist politics can exist. The absence of a female essential identity and of a pregiven unity, however, does not preclude the construction of multiple forms of unity and common action. As the result of the construction of nodal points, partial fixations can take place and precarious forms of identification can be established around the category "women" that provide the basis for a feminist identity and a feminist struggle. We find in Soper a type of misunderstanding of the antiessentialist position that is frequent in feminist writings and that consists in believing that the critique of an essential identity must necessarily lead to the rejection of any concept of identity whatsoever.[16]

In *Gender Trouble*,[17] Judith Butler asks, "What new shape of politics emerges when identity as a common ground no longer constrains the discourse of feminist politics?" My answer is that to visualize feminist politics in that way opens much greater opportunity for a democratic politics that aims at the articulation of the various different struggles against oppression. What emerges is the possibility of a project of radical and plural democracy.

To be adequately formulated, such a project requires discarding the essentialist idea of an identity of women *as* women as well as the attempt to ground a specific and strictly feminist politics. Feminist politics should be understood not as a separate form of politics designed to pursue the interests of women *as* women, but rather as the pursuit of feminist goals and aims within the context of a wider articulation of demands. Those goals and aims should consist in the transformation of all the discourses, practices and social relations where the category "woman" is constructed in a way that implies subordination. Feminism, for me, is the struggle for the equality of women. But this should not be understood as a struggle for realizing the equality of a definable empirical group with a common essence and identity, women, but rather as a struggle against the multiple forms in which the category "woman" is constructed in subordination. However, we must be aware of the fact that those feminist goals can be constructed in many different ways, according to the multiplicity of discourses in which they can be framed: Marxist, liberal, conservative, radical-separatist, radical-democratic, and so on. There are, therefore, by necessity many feminisms and any attempt to find the "true" form of feminist politics should be abandoned. I believe that feminists can contribute to politics a reflection on the conditions for creating an effective equality of women. Such a reflection is bound to be influenced by the existing political and theoretical discourses. Instead of trying to prove that a given form of feminist discourse is the one that corresponds to the "real" essence of womanhood, one should intend to show how it opens better possibilities for an understanding of women's multiple forms of subordination.

My main argument here has been that, for feminists who are committed to a political project whose aim is to struggle against the forms of subordination which exist in many social relations, and not only in those linked to gender, an approach that permits us to understand how the subject is constructed through different discourses and subject positions is certainly more adequate than one that reduces our identity to one single position— be it class, race, or gender. This type of democratic project is also better served by a perspective that allows us to grasp the diversity of ways in which relations of power are constructed and helps us to reveal the forms of exclusion present in all pretensions to universalism and in claims to have found the true essence of rationality. This is why the critique of essentialism and all its different forms: humanism, rationalism, universalism, far from being an obstacle to the formulation of a feminist democratic project is indeed the very condition of its possibility.

NOTES

1. See the issue of the journal *Differences*, 1 (September 1989), entitled "The Essential Difference: Another Look at Essentialism" as well as the recent book by Diana Fuss, *Essentially Speaking* (New York: Routledge, 1989).

2. Ernesto Laclau and Chantal Mouffe, *Hegemony and Socialist Strategy. Towards a Radical Democratic Politics* (London: Verso, 1985).

3. For an interesting critique of the dilemma of equality versus difference which is inspired by a similar *problématique* from the one I am defending here, see Joan W. Scott *Gender and The Politics of History* (New York: Columbia Univ. Press, 1988), Part IV. Among feminists the critique of essentialism was first developed by the journal *m/f* which during its eight years of existence (1978–1986) made an invaluable contribution to feminist theory. I consider that it has not yet been superseded and that the editorials as well as the articles by Parveen Adams still represent the most forceful exposition of the antiessentialist stance. A selection of the best articles from the 12 issues of *m/f* are reprinted in *The Woman In Question*, edited by Parveen Adams and Elisabeth Cowie (Cambridge, Mass.: MIT Press, 1990 and London: Verso, 1990).

4. Sara Ruddick, *Maternal Thinking* (London: Verso, 1989); Jean Bethke Elshtain, *Public Man, Private Woman* (Princeton: Princeton University Press, 1981).

5. Jean Bethke Elshtain, "On 'The Family Crisis,'" *Democracy*, 3, 1 (Winter 1983) p. 138.

6. Mary G. Dietz, "Citizenship with a Feminist Face. The Problem with Maternal Thinking," *Political Theory*, 13, 1 (February 1985).

7. Carole Pateman. *The Sexual Contract* (Stanford: Stanford University Press, 1988), and *The Disorder of Women* (Cambridge: Polity Press, 1989), as well as numerous unpublished papers on which I will also be drawing, especially the following: "Removing Obstacles to Democracy: The Case of Patriarchy"; "Feminism and Participatory Democracy: Some Reflections on Sexual Difference and Citizenship"; "Women's Citizenship: Equality, Difference, Subordination."

8. Carole Pateman, "Feminism and Participatory Democracy," unpublished paper presented to the Meeting of the American Philosophical Association, St. Louis, Missouri, May 1986, p. 24.

9. *Ibid.*, p. 26.

10. Carole Pateman, "Feminism and Participatory Democracy," pp. 7–8.

11. Carole Pateman, *The Disorder of Women*, p. 53.

12. I analyze more in detail the debate between liberals and communitarians in my article "American Liberalism and Its Critics: Rawls, Taylor, Sandel and Walzer," *Praxis International*, 8, 2 (July 1988).

13. The conception of citizenship that I am presenting here is developed more fully in my "Democratic Citizenship and The Political Community," in *Community at Loose Ends*, edited by the Miami Theory Collective (Minneapolis, MN: University of Minnesota Press, 1991).

14. Iris Marion Young, "Impartiality and the Civic Public," in *Feminism as Critique*, edited by Seyla Benhabib and Drucilla Cornell (Minneapolis: University of Minnesota Press, 1987) and "Polity and Group Difference: A Critique of the Ideal of Universal Citizenship," *Ethics*, 99 (January 1989).

15. Kate Soper, "Feminism, Humanism and Postmodernism," *Radical Philosophy*, 55 (Summer 1990), pp. 11–17.

16. We find a similar confusion in Diana Fuss who, as Anna Marie Smith indicates in her review of *Essentially Speaking, Feminist Review*, 38 (Summer 1991), does not realize that the repetition of a sign can take place without an essentialist grounding. It is for that reason that she can affirm that constructionism is essentialist as far as it entails the repetition of the same signifiers across different contexts.

17. Judith Butler, *Gender Trouble. Feminism and the Subversion of Identity* (New York: Routledge, 1990), p. xi.

18

Fighting Bodies, Fighting Words: A Theory and Politics of Rape Prevention

Sharon Marcus

Some recent arguments about the incompatibility of poststructuralist theory and feminist politics designate rape and the raped woman's body as symbols of the real. Mary E. Hawkesworth, in an article entitled "Knowers, Knowing, Known: Feminist Theory and Claims of Truth," defines two tendencies of what she calls "postmodern" thought—a conflation of reality and textuality, and an emphasis on the impossibility of ascertaining the meaning of texts. Toward the end of her essay she states:

> The undesirable consequences of the slide into relativism that results from too facile a conflation of world and text is particularly evident when feminist concerns are taken as a starting point. Rape, domestic violence, and sexual harassment . . . are not fictions or figurations that admit of the free play of signification. The victim's account of these experiences is not simply an arbitrary imposition of a purely fictive meaning on an otherwise meaningless reality. A victim's knowledge of the event may not be exhaustive; . . . But it would be premature to conclude from the incompleteness of the victim's account that all other accounts (the assailant's, defense attorney's, character witnesses' for the defendant) are equally valid or that there are no objective grounds on which to distinguish between truth and falsity in divergent interpretations.[1]

Hawkesworth makes three claims: that rape is real; that to be real means to be fixed, determinate, and transparent to understanding; and that feminist politics must understand rape as one of the real, clear facts of women's lives.

As her argument unfolds it contradicts each of these claims. The subject of the second quoted sentence is "rape"; the subject of the third quoted sentence is "the victim's account of these experiences." This substitution of account for event implies the very inseparability of text and world which Hawkesworth had previously criticized in postmodern thought, and indeed leads her to reverse her characterization of postmodernism: where earlier in the piece postmodernism conflated the fictive and the real, here it problematically separates them because it considers a woman's account of rape "an arbitrary imposition of a purely fictive meaning on an otherwise meaningless reality." The subject of the paragraph shifts again in the fourth quoted sentence, this time to the rape trial, which Hawkesworth insists will adjudicate among competing accounts of the rape; she ends the paragraph with a barrage of legalistic terms—"the standards of evidence, criteria of relevance, paradigms of explanation and norms of truth" which, she holds, one can and must use to determine the truth value of rape accounts. Such a conclusion in fact jettisons feminism's selective political focus on the raped woman, since "standards of evidence" and "norms of truth" derive their prestige from their claims to apply equally to all men and women, all points of view, and all situations. Hawkesworth's argument that the reality of rape must be the "starting point" of feminist politics thus leads her to espouse a supposedly apolitical system of objective judgment. Her climactic assertion that "there are some things that can be known" could be the summing-up of a rapist's defense as easily as that of his prosecution.

Hawkesworth intends to distinguish this empiricist, epistemological view of rape from the textual, postmodern view. Where she insists on rape's reality, she sees postmodernism insisting on rape's indeterminacy as an event, and hence on the impossibility of ascribing blame to a rapist and innocence to a victim.[2] Where she turns to the legal determination of blame, Michel Foucault, a theorist whom she associates with postmodernism, cautions against repressive measures which might stigmatize male sexuality and advocates instead making economic reparation to raped women.[3] Yet ultimately Hawkesworth adopts the same *perspective* on rape that her postmodern opponents do: in the eyes of all these thinkers, rape has always already occurred and women are always either already raped or already rapable. Hawkesworth believes that women can derive power from proving that they have been made powerless and from identifying the perpetrators of this victimization. Postmodernists take issue with the notions of law, action, knowledge, and identity which would enable a woman to label a man her rapist. But for both parties, when they think about rape, they inevitably see a raped woman.

Hawkesworth does not address this fundamental fit between her view of rape and the postmodern one; nor does she rebut the specific content of postmodern analyses of rape. Rather, she asserts the incompatibility of postmodern theories of language and reality with feminist political action against rape. This assertion actually contradicts one of feminism's most powerful contentions about rape—that rape is a question of language, interpretation, and subjectivity. Feminist thinkers have asked: Whose words count in a rape and a rape trial? Whose "no" can never mean "no"? How do rape trials condone men's misinterpretations of women's words? How do rape trials consolidate men's subjective accounts into objective "norms of truth" and deprive women's subjective accounts of cognitive value?[4] Feminists have also insisted on the importance of *naming* rape as violence and of collectively narrating stories of rape.[5] Though some of these theorists might explicitly assert that rape is real, their emphasis on *recounting* rape suggests that in their view actions and experiences cannot be said to exist in politically real and useful ways until they are perceptible and representable. A feminist politics which would fight rape cannot exist without developing a language about rape, nor, I will argue, without understanding rape to be a language. What founds these languages are neither real nor objective criteria, but political decisions to exclude certain interpretations and perspectives and to privilege others.

In this essay I propose that we understand rape as a language and use this insight to imagine women as neither already raped nor inherently rapable. I will argue against the political efficacy of seeing rape as the fixed reality of women's lives, against an identity politics which defines women by our violability, and for a shift of scene from rape and its aftermath to rape situations themselves and to rape *prevention*. Many current theories of rape present rape as an inevitable material fact of life and assume that a rapist's ability to physically overcome his target is the foundation of rape. Susan Brownmiller represents this view when she states in her influential 1975 book, *Against Our Will: Men, Women, and Rape,* that "in terms of human anatomy the possibility of forcible intercourse incontrovertibly exists. This single factor may have been sufficient to have caused the creation of a male ideology of rape. When men discovered that they could rape, they proceeded to do it."[6] Such a view takes violence as a self-explanatory first cause and endows it with an invulnerable and terrifying facticity which stymies our ability to challenge and demystify rape. To treat rape simply as one of what Hawkesworth calls "the realities that circumscribe women's lives" can mean to consider rape as terrifyingly unnameable and unrepresentable, a reality that lies beyond our grasp and which we can only experience as grasping and encircling us.[7] In its efforts to convey the horror and iniquity of rape, such a view often concurs with masculinist culture in its designation of rape as a fate worse than, or tantamount to, death; the apocalyptic tone which it adopts and the metaphysical status which it assigns to rape implies that rape can only be feared or legally repaired, not fought.

Feminist antirape literature, activism, and policy development on rape in the United States during the last two decades have increasingly concentrated on police procedures and legal definitions of rape. This focus can produce a sense of futility: rape itself seems to be taken for granted as an occurrence and only postrape events offer possible occasions for intervention. Although feminist drives to change the legal definition of rape, to increase the penalties for rape and to render the terms of a rape trial less prejudicial to the raped woman have publicized rape's seriousness as a crime, an almost exclusive insistence on equitable reparation and vindication in the courts has limited effectiveness for a politics of rape prevention. Quite literally, the rape has already occurred by the time a case comes to court; a verdict of guilty can in no way avert the rape itself, and no one has proven a direct link between increased penalties and convictions for a crime and a decreased incidence of that crime. The notorious racism and sexism of the United States police and legal systems often compromise the feminist goals of a rape trial. Interracial rape cases constitute a minority of rapes committed and rapes brought to trial, but when the rapist is white, exhibit significantly lower rates of conviction than intraracial rape cases, and much higher rates of conviction when the rapist is Afro-American. In both intra- and interracial rape trials, raped Afra-Americans often do not obtain convictions even in the face of overwhelming evidence of brutalization; raped white women have great difficulty in obtaining convictions against white rapists. In the relatively smaller percentage of cases where they have been raped by Afro-Americans, white women often obtain legal victories at the cost of juries' giving currency to racist prejudices and to patronizing ideologies of female protection. These biases fabricate and scapegoat a rapist of color and implicitly condone the exploitation and rape of women of color.[8] Finally, courtroom trials assert first and foremost their own legitimacy and power to judge events, and only grant power to the vindicated party on the condition that the court's power be acknowledged.

Attempts to stop rape through legal deterrence fundamentally choose to *persuade men* not to rape. They thus assume that men simply have the power to rape and concede this primary power to them, implying that at best men can secondarily be dissuaded from using this power by means of threatened punishment from a masculinized state or legal system. They do not envision strategies which will enable women to sabotage men's power to rape, which will empower women to take the ability to rape completely out of men's hands.

We can avoid these self-defeating pitfalls by regarding rape not as a fact to be accepted or opposed, tried or avenged, but as a process to be analyzed and undermined as it occurs. One way to achieve this is to focus on what actually happens during rape attempts and on differentiating as much as possible among various rape situations in order to develop the fullest range of rape prevention strategies.[9] Another way to refuse to recognize rape as the real fact of our lives is to treat it as a *linguistic* fact: to ask how the violence of rape is enabled by narratives, complexes and institutions which derive their strength not from outright, immutable, unbeatable force but rather from their power to structure our lives as imposing cultural scripts. To understand rape in this way is to understand it as subject to change.

The definition of rape as a linguistic fact can be taken several ways. One common conjunction of rape and language refers to the many images of rape which our culture churns out, representations which often transmit the ideological assumptions and contradictions of rape—women are rapable, women deserve rape/women provoke rape, women want rape, women are ashamed of being raped/women publicly lie about being raped. While these cultural productions can collude in and perpetuate rape in definite and complicated ways, the statement that rape is a linguistic fact should not be taken to mean that such linguistic forms actually rape women.

Another crucial, literal way to understand rape as a linguistic fact is to highlight the presence of speech in rape. Contrary to received wisdom, which imagines rape as a wordless, absolutely impersonal attack, most rapists take verbal initiatives with their targets in addition to deploying physical aggression. Many rapists initially engage their targets in friendly or threatening conversation; many speak a great deal during the rape and demand that the women whom they rape either talk to them or recite particular phrases. Internalized strictures on what can be spoken and on what is unspeakable— which restrict men and women differently—structure rape situations as much as physical inequalities do, particularly when a woman knows a rapist—the most prevalent rape situation.[10] Women's noncombative responses to rapists often derive as much from the self-defeating rules which govern polite, empathetic feminine conversation as they do from explicit physical fear.[11] To prevent rape, women must resist self-defeating notions of polite feminine speech as well as develop physical self-defense tactics.

A "continuum" theory of sexual violence links language and rape in a way that can be taken to mean that representations of rape, obscene remarks, threats and other forms of harassment should be considered equivalent to rape. Such a definition substitutes the remarks and threats which gesture toward a rape for the rape itself, and thus contradicts the very meaning of "continuum," which requires a temporal and logical distinction between the various stages of a rape attempt. In a "continuum" theory which makes one type of action, a verbal threat, immediately substitutable for another type of action, sexual assault, the time and space between these two actions collapse and once again, rape has always already occurred. Such verbal acts should be countered and censured for what they are—initiatives to set up a rape situation. To make them metaphors for rape itself, however, occludes the gap between the threat and the rape—the gap in which women can try to intervene, overpower and deflect the threatened action.[12]

Yet another way to analyze rape as a linguistic fact argues that rape is structured like a language, a language which shapes both the verbal *and* physical interactions of a woman and her would-be assailant. To say that rape is structured like a language can account both for rape's prevalence and its potential prevention. Language is a social structure of meanings which enables people to experience themselves as speaking, acting, and embodied subjects.[13] We can outline the language of rape in the United States along raced and gendered axes. The language of rape seeks to induce in white women an exclusive and erroneous fear of nonwhite men as potential rapists and legitimizes white men's sexual violence against all women as well as their retributive violence against nonwhite men in the name of protecting or avenging white women. At various historical moments this language has intensively designated Afra-Americans as targets of rape attempts—so much so that generations of Afro-Americans have developed definite languages of resistance to rape. Simultaneously or at other times, the language of rape may also address women of color as generic "women." The language of rape solicits women to position ourselves as endangered, violable, and fearful and invites men to position themselves as legitimately violent and entitled to women's sexual services. This language structures physical actions and responses as well as words, and forms, for example, the would-be rapist's feelings of powerfulness and our commonplace sense of paralysis when threatened with rape.

As intractably real as these physical sensations may appear to us, however, they appear so because the language of rape speaks through us, freezing our own sense of force and affecting the would-be rapist's perceptions of our lack of strength. Rapists do not prevail simply because as men they are really, biologically, and unavoidably stronger than women. A rapist follows a social script and enacts conventional, gendered structures of feeling and action which seek to draw the rape target into a dialogue which is skewed against her. A rapist's ability to accost a woman verbally, to demand her attention, and even to attack her physically depends more on how he positions himself relative to her socially than it does on his allegedly superior physical strength. His *belief* that he has more strength than a woman and that he can use it to rape her merits more analysis than the putative fact of that strength, because that belief often produces as an effect the male power that appears to be rape's cause.

I am defining rape as a scripted interaction which takes place in language and can be understood in terms of conventional masculinity and femininity as well as other gender inequalities inscribed before an individual instance of rape. The word "script" should be taken as a metaphor conveying several meanings. To speak of a rape script implies a *narrative* of rape, a series of steps and signals whose typical initial moments we can learn to recognize and whose final outcome we can learn to stave off. The concept of a narrative avoids the problems of the collapsed continuum described earlier, in which rape becomes the inevitable beginning, middle, and end of any interaction. The narrative element of a script leaves room and makes time for revision.[14]

We are used to thinking of language as a tool which we preexist and can manipulate, but both feminist and poststructuralist theories have persuasively contended that we only come to exist through our emergence into a preexistent language, into a social set of meanings which scripts us but does not exhaustively determine our selves. In this sense the term "rape script" also suggests that social structures *inscribe* on men's and women's embodied selves and psyches the misogynist inequalities which enable rape to occur. These generalized inequalities are not simply prescribed by a totalized oppressive language, nor fully inscribed before the rape occurs— rape itself is one of the specific techniques which continually scripts these inequalities anew. Patriarchy does not exist as a monolithic entity separate from human actors and actresses, impervious to any attempts to change it, secure in its role as an immovable first cause of misogynist phenomena such as rape; rather, patriarchy acquires its consistency as an overarching descriptive concept through the aggregation of microstrategies of oppression such as rape. Masculine power and feminine powerlessness neither simply precede nor cause rape; rather, rape is one of culture's many modes of feminizing women. A rapist chooses his target because he recognizes her to be a woman, but a rapist also strives to imprint the gender identity of "feminine victim" on his target. A rape act thus imposes as well as presupposes misogynist inequalities; rape is not only scripted—it also scripts.[15]

To take male violence or female vulnerability as the first and last instances in any explanation of rape is to make the identities of rapist and raped preexist the rape itself. If we eschew this view and consider rape as a scripted interaction in which one person auditions for the role of rapist and strives to maneuver another person into the role of victim, we can see rape as a *process* of sexist gendering which we can attempt to disrupt. Contrary to the principles of criminology and victimology, all rapists do not share fixed characteristics, nor do they attack people who are clearly marked as rape victims. Rape does not happen to preconstituted victims; it momentarily makes victims. The rapist does not simply *have* the power to rape; the social script and the extent to which that script succeeds in soliciting its target's participation help to create the rapist's power. The rape script preexists instances of rape but neither the script nor the rape act results from or creates immutable identities of rapist and raped.

The script should be understood as a framework, a grid of comprehensibility which we might feel impelled to use as a way of organizing and interpreting events and actions. We may be swayed by it even against our own interests—few women can resist utterly all the current modes of feminization—but its legitimacy is never complete, never assured. Each act can perform the rape script's legitimacy or explode it. By defining rape as a scripted performance, we enable a gap between script and actress which can allow us to rewrite the script, perhaps by refusing to take it seriously and treating it as a farce, perhaps by resisting the physical passivity which it directs us to adopt. Ultimately, we must eradicate this social script. In the meantime, we can locally interfere with it by realizing that men elaborate masculine power in relation to imagined feminine powerlessness; since we are solicited to help create this power, we can act to destroy it. This is not to say that women must demonstrate resistance to provide *legal* proof that sexual overtures were undesired. A resistance criterion for defining rape has often been used to absolve rapists by expecting women trained in passivity to be able to display the same levels of aggressivity as men.[16] But clearly it is preferable to have stopped a rape attempt ourselves than to have our raped selves vindicated in court. We should not be required to resist to prove our innocence at some later judicial date, but we should do so to serve our own immediate interests.

Before we can combat the creation of our powerlessness and of the rapist's power, we need a more detailed understanding of the underpinnings of the rape script. The rape script takes its form from what I will call a *gendered grammar of violence,* where grammar means the rules and structure which assign people to positions within a script. Between men of different races, this grammar predicates white men as legitimate subjects of violence between all men and as subjects of legitimate sexual violence against all women; it portrays men of color as ever-threatening subjects of illegitimate violence against white men and illegitimate sexual violence against white women. In an intraracial context, this grammar generically predicates men as legitimate perpetrators of sexual violence against women. I will address the difference between violence between men and sexual violence in greater detail below, but within the category of general violence we should distinguish among "legitimate violence between," "illegitimate violence against," and "legitimate violence against." Legitimate violence *between* men signifies a competitive pact between potential equals which permits venues for violence; in the United States today, this suggests an intraracial configuration of sparring partners. Illegitimate violence *against* implies that the violence is an unjustifiable and unthinkable attack which challenges social inequalities and can thus legitimately be responded to in unthinkable ways such as lynching; dominant U.S. culture tends to label most initiatives by men of color against whites as "illegitimate violence against." Intraracial male violence against women does not challenge social inequalities and hence is commonly thought to be legitimate; women's resistance to this violence is considered unthinkable and often condemned when it occurs. The dominant grammar of rape subsumes intraracial sexual violence under the rubric of gender; it does not activate race as a meaningful factor when a man rapes a woman of the same race. Nor does the dominant grammar of rape actively acknowledge paragrammars of gender which do not foster marking women as objects of violence, just as the dominant grammar of language does not acknowledge paralanguages to be anything more than opaque and ungrammatical "dialects."

The gendered grammar of violence predicates men as the objects of violence and the operators of its tools, and predicates women as the objects of violence and the subjects of fear. This grammar induces men who follow the rules set out for them to recognize their gendered selves in images and narratives of aggression in which they are agents of violence who either initiate violence or respond violently when threatened. A grammatically correct mirror of gender reflects back to men heroic images in which they risk death, brave pain and never suffer violence to be done to them without attempting to pay it back in kind. This mirror reflects back to women images which conflate female victimization and female value; this grammar encourages women to become subjects by imagining ourselves as objects.

Feminist theory has widely acknowledged that when women follow social conventions we recognize and enact our gendered selves as objects of violence. It is by now a feminist truism—but nonetheless still an important feminist truth—that the criteria of feminine beauty and worthy feminine behavior, if enacted without any modification, create a trammeled, passive person. Our culture's various techniques of feminization tend to buttress the rape script, since the femininity they induce "makes a feminine woman the perfect victim of sexual aggression."[17] Studies of rape scenarios enable us to differentiate at least two grammatical positions appointed to and adopted by some women in a rape script, both of which go against women's interest in preventing rape. An interpretive stance of *empathy,* a quality deemed feminine even when detached from female practitioners, prods some women to identify with rapists rather than to defend themselves from rapists' desire to destroy their targets. One author, Frederick Storaska, even advocates empathy as a mode of self-defense, reasoning that men rape to compensate for a lack of self-esteem and love; he thus claims that when women respond lovingly to potential rapists, they no longer feel compelled to rape.[18] Even if we accept this dubious premise for heuristic purposes, we still observe that it places all human agency on the male side: to avert rape, a woman must make a man feel like a full human being, rather than force him to recognize *her* will and humanity. A second, communicative stance of *responsiveness* encourages women not to take the offensive in a dialogue with a would-be rapist but to stay within the limits he sets—she can consent or not consent, acquiesce to his demands or dissuade him from them, but she does not actively interrupt him to shift the terms of discussion.[19]

Though feminist theorists of rape have thoroughly analyzed how women serve as objects of violence, they have focused less consistently on how women become *subjects of fear* and what effect this subjection has on our enactment of rape scripts. (By subjection, I mean a process which does not simply oppress, dominate and destroy women but one which incites us to become subjects by subjecting us to fear.) Various theories have recognized that rape causes fear, but have ignored the other half of the vicious circle— that often rapes succeed as a result of women's fears. In *The Female Fear*, Margaret T. Gordon and Stephanie Riger have argued that the distribution of fear corresponds to the other unequal distributions of privilege in U.S. society.[20] Even though women in fact are neither the sole objects of sexual violence nor the most likely targets of violent crimes, women constitute the majority of fearful subjects; even in situations where men are empirically more likely to suffer from violent crimes, they express less fear than women do, and tend to displace this fear onto a concern for their mothers, sisters, wives, and daughters which usually takes the form of restricting their mobility by means of warning these women not to go out alone or at night.[21]

The grammar of violence assigns women a disadvantageous position in the rape script because it identifies us as objects of violence and because it offers the insidious inducement of a subject position which assigns us an active role vis-à-vis *fear*—a role which is all the more insidious for its apparent agency. Whereas masculine fear triggers the notorious "fight-or-flight" response, feminine fear inspires the familiar sensations of "freezing"—involuntary immobility and silence. Women learn to recognize ourselves as subjects of this fear and thus to identify with a state which does not elaborate our subjectivity but dissolves it. This fear may differ from one rape situation to another. Acquaintance and marital rapes distort the contract of male protection of women and shatter the community of care established between lovers; they may produce an uncanny, dreadful estrangement from familiar expectations. A sudden attack by a stranger may produce shocked, stunned terror. At the broadest level, however, the grammar of violence dictates that feminine fear concentrate the self on the anticipation of pain, the inefficacy of action, and the conviction that the self will be destroyed. Feminine fear precipitates all violence and agency outside of its subject; it thus disables its subject from risking possible pain or death in order to defend herself, since that risk can seem viable only if the subject perceives herself as possessing some violent capacity on which she can draw to try to survive pain or elude injury. Feminine fear also seems to entail a complete identification of a vulnerable, sexualized body with the self; we thus come to equate rape with death, the obliteration of the self, but see no way we can draw on our selves to save that self and stave off rape.

In terms of rape prevention, this grammar of violence and fear also structures what can be called an *instrumental* theory of rape and determines ideas about feminine self-defense. The instrumental theory of rape, propounded by Susan Brownmiller in *Against Our Will,* argues that men rape because their penises possess the objective capacity to be weapons, tools, and instruments of torture.[22] Traditional self-defense advice given to women assumes this quasi-invincibility of the male body and advocates passive avoidance techniques. This counsel cautions against the use of any type of weapon unless the woman can be sure to use it effectively; the implication is that unless one is absolutely certain that one's actions will be effective, one should not attempt to defend one's self at all. When police manuals do mention that one can wield impromptu weapons, they tend to cite flimsy and obsolete accessories such as hatpins, rather than suggest that women carry more serviceable objects. These same manuals often neglect to mention male genitalia when they designate the vulnerable points of a potential rapist's body, thus perpetuating the myth of the unassailably powerful penis. These views enact, in effect, a gendered polarization of the grammar of violence in which the male body can wield weapons, can make itself into a weapon, and benefits from an enforced ignorance concerning its own vulnerability; the female body is predicated by this grammar as universally vulnerable, lacking force, and incompetent to supplement its deficiencies with tools which could vanquish the penis's power by dissimulating it. In a culture which relentlessly urges women to make up for our lacks by accessorizing, we are told that we cannot manage bodily accessories if we manipulate them for purposes of self-defense, and that we will be best served by consenting to be accessories to our own violation. We are taught the following fallacy—that we can best avoid getting hurt by letting someone hurt us. We absorb the following paradox—that rape is death, but that in a rape the only way to avoid death is to accept it. Consenting to the death of rape forms our only possibility of fighting for our lives, but these lives will have been destroyed by the rape. Fear forges the link between these contradictory statements: rape is so terrifying because it is like death, and this totalizing fear disables us from combating the rape.

We can begin to develop a feminist discourse on rape by displacing the emphasis on what the rape script promotes—male violence against women—and putting into place what the rape script stultifies and excludes—women's will, agency, and capacity for violence. One of the few books on rape prevention, Pauline Bart's and Patricia H. O'Brien's remarkable *Stopping Rape: Successful Survival Strategies,* has persuasively disproved the widespread belief that resistance to rape will lead only to injury because it will anger the would-be rapist. The authors deftly point out that "advising women to either comply or risk injury assumes that rape itself does not result in injury." They also show that in their sample, there "was no relationship between the women's use of physical resistance and the rapists' use of additional force over and above the rape attempt," and that passive responses often led to increased violence on the rapist's part.[23] Their surveys of women who prevented rape attempts consistently show that resistance does work, and that often minimal signs of it—an assertive remark, a push, a loud scream, flight—can suffice to block a man from continuing a rape attempt. Many women were able to prevent rape even when the rapist threatened them with a gun or knife. We can translate this finding into the terms of our grammatical framework by saying that the grammar of violence defines rape as an act committed against a subject of fear and not against a subject of violence—not, that is, against someone whom the would-be rapist assumes would attempt to fight back.[24] This assumption forms such an integral part of the rape script that we can say that simply by fighting back, we cease to be grammatically correct feminine subjects and thus become much less legible as rape targets.

In order to understand the difference which fighting back can make, we must distinguish sexualized violence from subject-subject violence. Sexualized violence anticipates and seeks its target's subjection as a subject of fear, defenselessness, and acquiescence to injury. In subject-subject violence, each interlocutor expects and incites violence in the other, whereas in sexualized violence women are excluded from this community of violence.[25] Subject-subject violence underlies intraracial masculine homosocial competition, in which men fight one another with the understanding that they are following the same rules and that one man can expect to receive from another any violence which he metes out to him. Although on one level the men are opponents, on another level they cooperate in their agreement to play the same game.

This gentleman's agreement does not obtain in a rape situation. Bart and O'Brien's analysis shows that unassertive, accommodating strategies which assume a contract situation of "mutual self-interest and good-will" fail to persuade a rapist who in no way identifies with the interests or subjectivity of his target.[26] Flight can work more effectively than rational negotiations since it simply breaks away from a script of polite, empathetic response to a potential aggressor. Verbal self-defense can successfully disrupt the rape script by refusing to concede the rapist's power. Treating the threat as a joke; chiding the rapist; bargaining to move to a different place, to perform only certain acts, or to have the rapist put any weapons he might have aside, are all examples of verbal methods which have in some cases thwarted rape attempts because they assert a woman's agency, not her violability, and a woman's power, rather than her fearful powerlessness. A rapist confronted with a wisecracking, scolding, and bossy woman may lose his grip on his power to rape; a rapist responded to with fear may feel his power consolidated. While we cannot underestimate the power of talking back and talking at the rapist, physical retaliation goes even further to disrupt the grammer of rape. Directed physical action is as significant a criterion of humanity in our culture as words are, and we must develop our capacities for violence in order to disrupt the rape script. Most women feel more able to use verbal strategies than physical ones—but it is precisely this feeling which indicates that the rape script has colonized our minds and bodies, positioning us as vulnerable to rape. Physical action poses the greatest challenge to most women as we think about preventing rape—and because it is our greatest point of resistance, it is the grammatical dictum we could flout to our greatest advantage.[27] The use of physical retaliation undermines the powerlessness which the scenario of violence and fear scripts for us. By talking back and fighting back we place ourselves as subjects who can engage in dialogic violence and respond to aggression in kind; in addition to offering us an opportunity to elude or even overpower an assailant, self-defense undermines a would-be rapist by catapulting him out of his role of omnipotent attacker and surprising him into having to fight someone whom he had marked out as a purely acquiescent victim.

Legislation backs up the objectifying violence of the rape script by not defining rape as an assault, which would fall under the rubric of subject-subject violence against persons, but as a sexual offense. This definition separates sexual parts from the person and views them as objects which have been violated. I have been arguing that to prevent rape, we must resist a would-be rapist's attempt to place us in a sexualized, gendered position of passivity and that instead we fend off the rape by positioning ourselves as if we were in a fight. For definitional purposes, however, rape is clearly neither sex nor simple assault. Rape could best be defined as a sexualized and gendered attack which imposes sexual difference along the lines of violence. Rape engenders a sexualized female body defined as a wound, a body excluded from subject-subject violence, from the ability to engage in a fair fight. Rapists do not beat women at the game of violence, but aim to exclude us from playing it altogether.

We have seen that subject-subject violence presumes a contractual relation between its participants, who engage with one another as equals who agree to disagree. This subject of contractual relations also underwrites the subject of property ownership. In capitalist culture one owns property by virtue of being free to contract with equals to exchange it. Alienability and the power to contract for the transfer of alienable goods form the basis of property in things, in others, and in one's self. A masculine capacity to alienate the self in a risky encounter which involves a contractual exchange of aggression positions men as the subjects of property in themselves. This capacity, combined with a sense of entitlement to women-as-property, positions men as potential rapists in the rape script. Violation entails the invasion and destruction of property; it is the obverse of alienation which demarcates the boundaries of a property and maintains its integrity in the face of circulation. Since women are considered to be property and thus not to own it, it is not possible to enter into contracts with us and thus implausible that we would resist attempts to appropriate us.[28] If what one owns expresses what one is worth and hence what one merits, women seem to own only our violation—hence we are often said to "deserve" rape.

Many feminist theorists have focused on how the infliction of violence against putative female objects is related to the view that women are also considered objects of property. Lorenne Clark and Debra Lewis, in *Rape: The Price of Coercive Sexuality,* have offered a thoughtful analysis of the relationships among rape culture, rape laws, and property laws. They show that the adherents of rape culture see female sexuality as a property which only men can truly own, which women often hoard, which can thus justifiably be wrested from us, and which women themselves merely hold in trust for a lawful owner. Rape thus becomes the theft or violation of one man's property rights by another. Clark and Lewis advocate transforming rape from a crime against a valuable object to a crime which violates a female person's right to contract to exchange her own sexual property. They thus seek to reinforce women's property in themselves and to guarantee women's "right to the exclusive ownership and control of their own bodies."[29]

This move criticizes male property in women but sustains a definition of female sexuality as violable property. The call for female ownership of this property does not displace this injurious definition; it merely erects legal impediments to carrying out naturalized violations. While I have argued that we can prevent rape by positioning ourselves as subjects of violence and objects of fear, to assume property-in-ourselves and that our selves are property will only extend, not challenge, the hold which rape scripts have over women. The rape script strives to put women in the place of objects; property metaphors of rape similarly see female sexuality as a circumscribable thing.[30] The theft metaphor makes rape mirror a simplified model of castration: a single sexual organ identifies the self, that organ is conceived of as an object that can be taken or lost, and such a loss dissolves the self. These castration and theft metaphors reify rape as an irrevocable appropriation of female sexuality.

The rape script describes female bodies as vulnerable, violable, penetrable, and wounded; metaphors of rape as trespass and invasion retain this definition intact. The psychological corollary of this property metaphor characterizes female sexuality as inner space, rape as the invasion of this inner space, and antirape politics as a means to safeguard this inner space from contact with anything external to it. The entire female body comes to be symbolized by the vagina, itself conceived of as a delicate, perhaps inevitably damaged and pained inner space.

Antirape activists have often criticized the false demarcation between an inside and outside of rape in terms of geographical space: rape culture spawns spatial contradictions by warning women not to go outside because of possible rape, but most rapes occur inside women's homes. Denaturalizing this myth unveils the boundary between inside and outside and indicates the irrelevance of this inside/outside distinction for fighting rape: if rape can occur inside, then "inside" is no longer what it is meant to be— sheltering, separate and distinct from an unsafe, external realm. Yet antirape theorists often continue to map external and internal spatial divisions onto the female body by using invasion as a metaphor for rape. This metaphor coheres with the gendered grammar of violence outlined earlier, since positions vis-à-vis violence coincide with spatial coordinates: a subject of violence acts on an object of violence to define her as the boundary between exterior and interior, which he crosses, and as the immobilized space through which he moves.[31] Precisely because the invasion metaphor coheres so strongly with the grammar of sexualized violence, we should question its efficacy in helping women fight rape. The need to define rape and to assert its existence can distract us from plotting its vanishing point. To combat rape, we do not need to insist on the reality of an inside/outside distinction between the female body and the world; this distinction may be one of the rape script's effects, but if so, it is this distinction we must dissolve in order to undo rape.

Neither all women nor all rape survivors represent rape as an invasion of female sexual property. Bart and O'Brien's work has shown that many women represent rape as the extraction of a service and define it "as something done with a penis, not something done to a vagina."[32] My previous claim that rape scripts gender suggests that we view rape not as the invasion of female inner space, but as the forced creation of female sexuality as a violated inner space. The horror of rape is not that it steals something from us but that it makes us into things to be taken. Thus, to demand rights to ourselves as property and to request protection for our vulnerable inner space is not enough. We do not need to defend our "real" bodies from invasion but to rework this elaboration of our bodies altogether. The most deep-rooted upheaval of rape culture would revise the idea of female sexuality as an object, as property, and as an inner space.

Such a revision can and should take multiple directions. One possible alternative to figuring female sexuality as a fixed spatial unit is to imagine sexuality in terms of time and change. The use of past sexual history in rape trials to determine the probability of consent and to invoke claims of right based on past consent (used to defend the rape rights of boyfriends and husbands), demonstrate that rape culture consistently denies female sexuality the ability to change over time. Rather than secure the right to alienate and own a spatialized sexuality, antirape politics can claim women's right to a self that could differ from itself over time without then having to surrender its effective existence as a self. The title of a book on acquaintance rape, "I Never Called It Rape," provides an emblem of this conception of female sexuality. This title expresses a nonunified consciousness for which the act of naming the active desire not to have intercourse does not coincide with the nonconsensual sexual act; it insists that this split self can come to power and knowledge over time. The title conceives of female sexuality not as a discrete object whose violation will always be painfully and instantly apparent, but as an intelligible process whose individual instances can be reinterpreted and renamed over time.

I have argued against understanding rape as the forced entry of a real inner space and for considering it as a form of invagination in which rape scripts the female body as a wounded inner space. We can elude the limits of an empiricist approach by developing a politics of fantasy and representation. Rape exists because our experience and deployment of our bodies is the effect of interpretations, representations, and fantasies which often position us in ways amenable to the realization of the rape script: as paralyzed, as incapable of physical violence, as fearful. New cultural productions and reinscriptions of our bodies and our geographies can help us begin to revise the grammar of violence and to represent ourselves in militant new ways. In the place of a tremulous female body or the female self as an immobilized cavity, we can begin to imagine the female body as subject to change, as a potential object of fear and agent of violence. Conversely, we do not have to imagine the penis as an indestructible weapon which cannot help but rape; we can take the temporality of male sexuality into consideration and bear in mind the fragility of erections and the vulnerability of male genitalia. *Stopping Rape* reports the words of one woman who had been threatened with death unless she cooperated with her rapist: "'If he's going to kill me he'll just have to kill me. I will not let this happen to me. And I grabbed him by his penis, I was trying to break it, and he was beating me all over the head with his fists, I mean, just as hard as he could. I couldn't let go. I was just determined I was going to yank it out of the socket. And then he lost his erection . . . pushed me away and grabbed his coat and ran.'"[33]

I have tried to show that such self-defense is not merely an immediately effective and practical strategy; as female violence and as the refusal to accept the rapist's body as powerfully real and really powerful, this self-defense strikes at the heart of rape culture. Self-defense of course offers no final solution: it will not always be sufficient to ward off rape and it should certainly not be necessary. While the ethical burden to prevent rape does not lie with us but with rapists and a society which upholds them, we will be waiting a very long time if we wait for men to decide not to rape. To construct a society in which we would know no fear, we may first have to frighten rape culture to death.

NOTES

I would like to thank Sylvia Brownrigg, Judith Butler, Jennifer Callahan, Susan Maslan, Mary Poovey, and Joan Scott for their critical readings of earlier drafts of this essay. My thanks also go to all the women and men who have talked about rape with me as well as to the participants in the National Graduate Women's Studies Conference in February 1990 where I presented these ideas.

1. Mary E. Hawkesworth, "Knowers, Knowing, Known: Feminist Theory and Claims of Truth," *Signs: Journal of Women in Culture and Society*, 14, 3 (1989), p. 555.

2. Hawkesworth does not cite specific poststructuralist discussions of rape. For more detailed discussions of the relationship between textural criticism and sexual violence, see Teresa de Lauretis, "The Violence of Rhetoric: Considerations on Representation and Gender," in *Technologies of Gender: Essays on Theory, Film, and Fiction* (Bloomington: Indiana University Press, 1987), pp. 31–50; Frances Ferguson, "Rape and the Rise of the Novel," *Representations*, 20 (Fall 1987), pp. 88–112; and Ellen Rooney, "Criticism and the Subject of Sexual Violence," *Modern Language Notes*, 98, 5 (December 1983).

3. See Monique Plaza, "Our Damages and Their Compensation: Rape: The Will Not to Know of Michel Foucault," *Feminist Issues* (Summer 1981), pp. 25–35. She cites Foucault's statements in *La folie encerclée* (Paris: Seghers/Laffont, 1977).

4. See, for example, Anna Clark, *Women's Silence, Men's Violence: Sexual Assault in England, 1770–1845* (London: Pandora Press, 1987); Lorenne Clark and Debra Lewis, *Rape: The Price of Coercive Sexuality* (Toronto: The Women's Press, 1977); Angela Davis, *Women, Race and Class* (New York: Vintage Books, 1981), esp. "Rape, Racism and the Myth of the Black Rapist," pp. 172–201; Delia Dumaresq, "Rape—Sexuality in the Law," *m/f*, 5 & 6 (1981), pp. 41–59; Sylvia Walby, Alex Hay, and Keith Soothill, "The Social Construction of Rape," *Theory Culture and Society*, 2, 1 (1983), pp. 86–98; Susan Estrich, *Real Rape* (Cambridge: Harvard University Press, 1987); Frances Ferguson, "Rape and the Rise of the Novel"; Susan Griffin, *Rape: The Politics of Consciousness*, Rev. 3rd ed. (San Francisco: Harper and Row, 1986); Liz Kelly, *Surviving Sexual Violence* (Minneapolis: University of Minnesota Press, 1988); Andrea Medea and Kathleen Thompson, *Against Rape* (New York: Farrar, Straus and Giroux, 1974); Ken Plummer, "The Social Uses of Sexuality: Symbolic Interaction, Power and Rape" in *Perspectives on Rape and Sexual Assault*, June Hopkins, ed. (London: Harper & Row, 1984), pp. 37–55; Elizabeth A. Stanko, *Intimate Intrusions: Women's Experience of Male Violence* (London: Routledge & Kegan Paul, 1985).

5. See *I Never Called It Rape: The Ms. Report on Recognizing, Fighting, and Surviving Date and Acquaintance Rape* (New York: Harper and Row, 1988).

6. Susan Brownmiller, *Against Our Will: Men, Women and Rape* (New York: Simon and Schuster, 1975), p. 14.

7. Mary E. Hawkesworth, "Knowers, Knowing, Known," p. 555.

8. Members of other groups such as Hispanics and Native Americans have and still do experience similar inequities; our culture's alacrity to blend sexual and racial oppression

means that any other group in the process of becoming racially stigmatized could find itself enmeshed in these webs of injustice. However, Afro-Americans have historically borne the brunt of symbolizing rapist and raped to the white imagination, and it is for this reason that I refer specifically to Afro- and Afra-Americans as well as to the more generic group "men and women of color." For further discussion of rape and antiblack racism, see Hazel Carby, "'On the Threshold of Woman's Era': Lynching, Empire, and Sexuality in Black Feminist Theory," in *Critical Inquiry*, 12 (Autumn 1985), pp. 262–277; Angela Davis, *Women, Race and Class*; Jacqueline Dowd Hall, "'The Mind That Burns in Each Body': Women, Rape, and Racial Violence," in *Powers of Desire*, edited by Ann Snitow, Christine Stansell, and Sharon Thompson (New York: Monthly Review Press, 1983), pp. 328–49; Rennie Simson, "The Afro-American Female: The Historical Context of the Construction of Sexual Identity," in *Powers of Desire*, pp. 229–35; Deborah Gray White, *Ar'n't I a Woman: Female Slaves in the Plantation South* (New York: W. W. Norton & Co., 1985).

9. See, for example, Pauline Bart and Patricia O'Brien, *Stopping Rape: Successful Survival Strategies* (New York: Pergamon Press, 1985), especially chapter 3, "The Rape Situation," pp. 23–31.

10. See Andrea Medea and Kathleen Thompson, *Against Rape*, p. 25.

11. See Nancy Henley, *Body Politics: Power, Sex, and Nonverbal Communication* (New Jersey: Prentice-Hall, 1977); Robin Lakoff, *Language and Woman's Place* (New York: Octagon Books, 1976), and Sally McConnell-Ginet, Ruth Borker, Nelly Furman, eds., *Women and Language in Literature and Society* (New York: Praeger, 1980).

12. The way in which the continuum theory equates all signs of intended, projected violence with realized, completed violence curiously mirrors myths that women provoke rape (and thus cannot be said to be raped at all). These "provocation" theories interpret all perceptions of female sociability—a smile, a nod, or even saying nothing at all—as signifying sexual consent and as thus obviating the need for further negotiation. Here too, the time and space between acts vanishes and women become always already raped, "seduced," or "seductive." For a demonstration that efforts to keep seduction and rape logically distinct continually fail because seduction and rape alike define female sexuality as passive, see Ellen Rooney, "Criticism and the Subject."

13. For discussions of the relevance of this definition of language to feminist analyses, see Teresa de Lauretis, "Violence of Rhetoric," especially pp. 41–42, and Joan W. Scott, "Deconstructing Equality-Versus-Difference: Or, The Uses of Poststructuralist Theory for Feminism," *Feminist Studies*, 14, 1 (Spring 1988), p. 34.

14. My definition of a script differs from the sociological one posed, for example, by Judith Long Laws and Pepper Schwartz in *Sexual Scripts: The Social Construction of Female Sexuality* (Hinsdale: The Dryden Press, 1977). They write: "By sexual scripts we mean a repertoire of acts and statuses that are recognized by a social group, together with the rules, expectations, and sanctions governing these acts and statuses" (2). This definition focuses on scripts as prefabricated interactions between bearers of fixed roles, rather than as a process which in every instance must strive to reproduce itself and its performers. Although the authors note that the institutionalization of one script entails that "alternative scripts are denigrated or denied," they conceptualize each individual script as secure from implosion and internal contestation (6). I argue that these scripts are self-contradictory and can be challenged from within. One crucial contradiction of the rape script is that it casts women as weak victims yet posits massive amounts of force and violence as necessary to rape us. We can thus draw from the

rape script itself the implication that we may possess more force than the script leads us to think we do.

15. Angela Davis makes a similar point when she argues that rape by slave owners and overseers was the one act which differentiated between slave men and slave women. Rape from without inaugurates sexual difference within a group of men and women otherwise equal, hence otherwise indistinguishable. *Women, Race and Class*, pp. 23–4.

16. See Susan Estrich, *Real Rape*.

17. Susan Griffin, *Rape: The Power of Consciousness*, p. 16.

18. Frederick Storaska, *How to Say No to a Rapist and Survive*, cited in Pauline Bart and Patricia O'Brien, *Stopping Rape, passim*.

19. See Ellen Rooney, *"Criticism and the Subject,"* for a critique of "consent" as a criterion of rape and the ways in which it precludes the theorization of female sexuality.

20. Margaret T. Gordon and Stephanie Riger, *The Female Fear* (New York: Free Press, 1989), p. 118.

21. *Ibid.*, p. 54.

22. See Susan Brownmiller, *Against Our Will*, p. 14.

23. Pauline Bart and Patricia H. O'Brien, *Stopping Rape*, pp. 40–41.

24. See, for example, the Queen's Bench Foundation report on interviews with rapists: when asked why they chose a target, 82.2% said because she was "available" and 71.2% because she was "defenseless"—terms which amount to the same meaning, since "available" here means "available to be raped." *Rape: Prevention and Resistance* (Queen's Bench Foundation: San Francisco, 1976).

25. Teresa de Lauretis follows René Girard in calling this type of subject-subject violence "'violent reciprocity' . . . which is socially held in check [and promoted] by the institution of kinship, ritual, and other forms of mimetic violence (war and sport come immediately to mind)." "Violence of Rhetoric" p. 43.

26. Pauline Bart and Patricia H. O'Brien, *Stopping Rape*, pp. 109–10.

27. Jeffner Allen underlines this point when she criticizes "non-violence as a patriarchal construct" and as a "heterosexual virtue [which] charges women to be 'moral,' virtuously non-violent in the face of the 'political,' the violent male-defined world. The ideology of heterosexual virtue entitles men to terrorize—possess, humiliate, violate, objectify—women and forecloses the possibility of women's active response to men's sexual terrorization." *Lesbian Philosophy: Explorations* (Palo Alto: Institute of Lesbian Studies, 1986), pp. 29, 35.

28. See Maria Mies, *Patriarchy and Accumulation on a World Scale: Women in the International Division of Labor* (London: Zed Books, 1986), p. 169.

29. Lorenne Clark and Debra Lewis, *Rape: The Price of Coercive Sexuality*, p. 166.

30. Clark and Lewis are not the only authors to use the rape metaphor; Pauline Bart and Patricia H. O'Brien compare rape laws to trespassing laws, *Stopping Rape*, p. 21; the *Ms.* report on acquaintance rape compares definitions of rape with those of theft, p. 22, and Susan Estrich makes several analogies between theft and rape, *Real Rape*, pp. 14, 40–41.

31. See Teresa de Lauretis, "Violence of Rhetoric," pp. 43–44.

32. Pauline Bart and Patricia H. O'Brien, *Stopping Rape*, p. 20.

34. *Ibid.*, p. 38.

19

Gender, Power, and Historical Memory: Discourses of Serrano Resistance

Ana María Alonso

The State and Subjectivity: Power, Identity and Historical Memory

Some recent writing on power has been concerned with displacing an essentialist and reified notion of the state and with formulating an alternative, expanded conception of the political.[1] Focusing on the question of how rule is accomplished, much of this work has been influenced by Antonio Gramsci's notion of the state as "political society + civil society, in other words, hegemony protected by the armor of coercion,"[2] by Foucault's stress on power's "capillary form of existence,"[3] and by the feminist notion of the personal as political. Rather than seeing rule as resting on interdictions, the exercise of power is viewed as productive—of meanings, truths, bodies, selves, in short, of forms of doing, knowing, and being. Meaning becomes located in discursive practices produced, contested, and transformed in sociohistorical action rather than in a sui generis scheme of timeless categories.

If hegemony, as Ernesto Laclau and Chantal Mouffe argue, is not "an external relation between preconstituted social agents, but the very process of discursive construction of those agents,"[4] then power is central to the production of social identities. Such a notion of hegemony allows the integration of dimensions of subjectivity such as gender and ethnicity into analyses of domination and subordination. Class is no longer the privileged form of oppression that must overdetermine all other forms. Gender and ethnicity recover their specificity as dimensions of discursively and politically organized subjection which are key to the construction of both the body personal and the body politic.

A concern with history is integral to this approach to power and meaning. Hegemony is produced and reproduced, challenged and renegotiated in social action and action is always historically situated. Moreover, if social action is mediated by a history, it is because the past has a political and discursive significance. Memory, meaning, and power are internally related.[5] Thus, an inquiry into the construction and dissemination of historical memory, itself a central site for the production of effects of power, is critical for an analysis of hegemony.

Ironically, the danger in deploying an expanded concept of the political in which meaning and power are interpenetrated is that dominant forms of control and significance can appear so pervasive as to preclude the possibility of resistance. Yet if we view hegemony in historical and processual terms, then the attempt by dominant groups and classes to impose a "discursive regime"[6] on the whole of society can be seen as subject to contestation and never fully achieved. Struggle becomes possible and spaces for counterdiscourses and for practices of resistance are opened up. As Teresa de Lauretis argues, there is always a "tension of contradiction, multiplicity and heteronomy" between "the (represented) discursive space of the positions made available by hegemonic discourses and the space-off, the elsewhere, of those discourses."[7]

So-called prepolitical discourses of resistance, long dismissed as "lacking an ideology," can be interpreted in a new way once we recognize that rule is not simply effected through the formal apparatus of government and that the voices of protest need not be articulated in a "rational," post-Enlightenment idiom to be "political." Deploying discourses rich in bodily symbols, such forms of resistance often focus on the constitution of subjectivities, disputing and redefining the ways in which power is invested in social identities. Challenging the dominant origin stories which fix, naturalize, and legitimate a hierarchized order of forms of identity and power, such counterdiscourses ground an alternative vision of the body personal and the body politic in an historical memory which disputes official representations of the past.

What I shall do in this paper is ground these theoretical points in an analysis of *serrano* discourses of resistance. The *serranos* or "people of the mountains" are the non-Indian inhabitants of the Sierra Madre of the state of Chihuahua, Mexico. In order to advance projects of territorial conquest and domination of indigenes, particularly the Apache, the state mobilized *serrano* peasants for warfare in the eighteenth and nineteenth centuries. Warfare between colonists and indigenes became construed as a struggle of "civilization" against "barbarism." A reciprocal metaphorization characterized discourses of warfare and production: the goal of both practices was the domestication of a nature whose wildness was construed as a perpetual threat to social order and civility.

To the end of developing a "warrior spirit" among non-Indian peasant men, the state promoted a construction of gender and ethnic honor which predicated masculine reputation, access to land, and membership in a corporate community on valor and performance in warfare against "barbarians." Not only the battlefield but also the agricultural field became a key site for the production of male peasant honor. The conjunction of fighting and farming is what made these men not just life takers but also life givers.

If non-Indian peasant men were construed as "Just Warriors," non-Indian peasant women were considered "Beautiful Souls,"[8] icons of vulnerable innocence and virtue who had to be sheltered and protected by the hardier sex. In this discourse, "civilized" women became symbols of an ethnic and sexual purity purportedly threatened by the "onslaughts of the savages." The female body and its metaphorical extension, the home, became the field of honor for women, a field whose boundaries had to be maintained and guarded by men.

From the late 1850s to 1910, interlinked processes of state formation and capitalist development transformed Mexican society. Though the effects of these processes on frontier society are discernible in the 1860s and 1870s, the incorporation of the periphery into the capitalist world market and its increased integration into the nation-state was limited until the defeat of the Apaches in 1886. The one-time agents of "civilization," the militarized *serrano* peasants, subsequently became redefined by the state as the new barbarians in need of order and mastery. Not only did the corporate land grants and the relative political autonomy of *serrano* communities come under attack, but also these specialists in violence became the object of technologies of order and power designed to "reduce" what was now construed as the wild and socially threatening masculinity of *serrano* men.

Serrano peasants did not passively accept the social dislocations and reversals in status position and class situation engendered by these large-scale transformations. Beginning in the late 1850s but particularly after 1886, they engaged in nonviolent and armed forms of resistance. From 1910 to 1920, the Chihuahuan *sierra* became a key focus of peasant revolutionary activity.[9]

In this paper, I will be concentrating on the discourses of *serrano* peasants from Namiquipa, a community located in the foothills of the Sierra Madre about two hundred miles south of the United States-Mexico border. Though I will largely be dealing with the constructions which oriented both everyday and armed forms of resistance from the 1880s to 1920 and which advanced a critique of capitalism and of the forms of subjectivity which development and state formation implied, I would like to emphasize that much of this vision is still characteristic of Namiquipan peasants today.

Capitalism as the Midas Touch: Honor and Wealth

While in Namiquipa, I often went to visit Doña Aurora,[10] who had been born at the turn of the century and who had lived through the Revolution of 1910 to 1920. Like others of her generation, Doña Aurora had a highly developed historical memory and a great interest in and concern with the past. When we talked about people and events long gone, we often spoke in the present tense. I will continue to do so here.

One day I encouraged Doña Aurora to tell me about the Müllers, the owners of the *Hacienda de Santa Clara* who, from the 1860s on, had repeatedly tried to appropriate thousands of hectares of Namiquipa's corporate land grant. "Were they good or bad people?" I asked. Doña Aurora put away her sewing and lit a cigarette.

> "Well," she said, "I heard that the daughter, Maria Müller, was intimate with her own brother. Imagine! She became pregnant and they locked her up in a jail of water (*carcel de agua*) for a week. When they took her out of there, she was so swollen she never walked again. She was enormous. Everywhere she went, she had to be carried about by servants whom she constantly abused. That's what rich people are like."

All sorts of unusual things happened at Santa Clara. Some of Müller's sheep were born with human faces. One of the most bizarre events, from Doña Aurora's point of view, was the birth of a fetus from the feces of an Indian peon that had been heated and quickened into life by the sun. The *hacendado* sent the cowboys out to find and bring the fetus to the house, where it was kept and where it grew into a baby.

Doña Aurora often commented that "*los ricos*," the rich, had formed illicit sexual unions and had "made a mess of kinship." Her Santa Clara stories are about the disordering of reproduction. Fetuses are born from excrement, babies are conceived through incest. The reproduction of human life is a synecdoche for the reproduction of social life. In the *Hacienda de Santa Clara* reproduction has become disordered and the boundaries that separate and distinguish between the social and the natural, the pure and the impure, the human and the animal, no longer exist.

In these as well as other stories, incest becomes a privileged symbol of an illicit hoarding of substance which underlies the *ricos'* inability to reproduce human and social life in orderly, morally sanctioned ways. For the Namiquipans, the socially and divinely sactioned form of sexual union involves the commingling of divergent bloods. Incest is a transgression of divine law and social morality, associated with the realm of the devil and with infrasocial being. A metaphorical equivalence is established in these narratives between the incestuous hoarding of bodily substance and the capitalist accumulation of wealth. Though wealth had been a sign of honor in Northern society prior to 1886, the social prestige of the dominant classes was dependent on patrimonial forms of redistribution. But after 1886, traditions of beneficence were displaced in the scramble for the spoils of progress. For the Namiquipans, the failure to redistribute wealth, like the failure to commingle blood, became a sign of the dishonor of the rich and of the evil of capitalist accumulation.

But incest is a multivocal symbol. In Doña Aurora's story, Maria Müller's permanent and unnatural bloating is an enduring sign of the rich's violation of other norms and meanings which regulated social personhood and which endowed identities with social value. The Müllers' incestuous union transgressed the values of sexual chastity central to the honor of women and was a breach of the duty to protect the sexual purity of sisters which was key to the honor of men. A sign of evil and infrasocial being, of an illicit hoarding of substance and wealth, of a contravention of the norms and meanings which underwrote gender identities, and of a violation of prescribed duties to kin, incest indexed multiple dimensions of the rich's lack of honor.

The peasants' attribution of incestuous relations to the dominant classes denied the latter the virtue which had previously legitimated their social precedence. Incest was a sign of the power of the rich. But for the *serranos,* this power, like that of the devil, was evil and antisocial.[11] Since the *ricos* were dishonorable, no social respect and esteem was due to them nor could their power have legitimacy.[12] Whereas official discourses construed "the rich" as the creators of order and progress, popular counterdiscourses represented them as the generators of disorder and retrocession. For the peasants of the *sierra,* the *ricos'* lust for gold had led to the chaotic and immoral disruption of the forms and activities through which human and social life were produced and reproduced. The surreal quality of the stories I have discussed expresses the *serranos'* experience of social dislocation, of living in a disordered world where the implicit understandings which configure reality can no longer be taken for granted. Order and reality could only be restored if those who still possessed honor defied the elite and the regime which served its interests.

Honor became the "capital" of the dispossessed. In the words of Placido Chávez, son of one of the Chávez brothers, leaders of the *serrano* rebels of Tomochi who repelled several federal army expeditions before being defeated in 1892:

> My father and my uncles always belonged to the humble class and never disposed of [economic] capital: their only capital—one which was greater and more precious—was their work, their self-esteem and their honor, an honor without flaw or stigma.[13]

Yet after 1886, the *serranos* began to be dispossessed of even this most precious capital. Doña Aurora told me that rich entrepreneurs, many of whom had immigrated to Namiquipa after 1886, seduced and impregnated the virgin daughters of the local peasants. Kinship was really in a disastrous state, she would say angrily. Others told me that prior to the Revolution, landowners and estate administrators cuckolded *hacienda* peons and defiled their brides by exercising the *droit du seigneur* on the wedding night.[14] Located at the gateway between the social and the infrasocial, the female body was construed by the *serranos* as a point of great vulnerability for the honor of both men and women, one which had to be constantly guarded or reputations would be destroyed and society would be plunged into a state of disorder. The rich had disordered human and social reproduction not only by hoarding their own bodily substance, but also by illicitly appropriating that of others.

Recall that in one of Doña Aurora's Santa Clara stories, the fetus which the cowboys were ordered to take to the *hacendado's* house was born from the excrement of an Indian estate worker. Doubly subjected, the Indian peon is the epitome of a tamed and feminized[15] being whose body and activity are the object of others' control and appropriation. This story creates a set of metaphorical equivalencies which link disordered reproduction, the appropriation of workers' bodily substances, and capitalist accumulation.

That the rich reproduced themselves and their wealth by illicitly expropriating the bodily substances of the poor is made quite explicit in a speech given by one *serrano* revolutionary at the beginning of 1911. Speaking to the peons and cowboys at one of the *haciendas* of Luis Terrazas, Chihuahua's biggest landowner and political boss, this revolutionary exclaimed: "We consider it unjust for one sole man to possess all the land. Your patron is the owner of much hoarded/stored[16] wealth, unjustly obtained from the toil and the sweat of so many poor workers."[17] While the subjectivity of peasant women was reinscribed through sexual defilement and rape, that of men was reconstituted through agrarian dispossession and proletarianization. For the *serranos,* depeasantization was as dishonorable as rape. How was agrarian dispossession perceived as both dishonorable and dishonoring? What was the logic which construed the appropriation of surplus value as a loss of the value attached to the social self? It is to these questions that I now turn.

Blood, Gold, and the Rhetoric of Agrarian Grievances

From the 1860s to the 1900s *serrano* peasants from the frontier military colonies of the Guerrero and Galeana districts complained to state functionaries that their corporate rights to land were being contravened.[18] In these *ocursos* or petitions, a frontier construction of agrarian rights in which land is not just a means of production but also a sign of honor and of social personhood continues to be affirmed in the face of a new official rhetoric in which land has become a sign of capital, a commodity whose value is determined by the market.

Serrano petitions for the redressal of agrarian grievances begin with an historical account of the state's establishment of frontier military colonies[19] and recapitulate the compact between the state and the peasant warrior communities. As the descendants of Namiquipa's *originarios* or primordial colonists recall, the settlers were obliged to fight the Apache and to fulfill military obligations to the state as well as to work the land and to make it bear the fruits of their toil. The *serranos* affirm that they have fulfilled their duties and comported themselves as honorable and civilized men, both in the agricultural field and on the battlefield.

These petitions go on to provide a history of the Apache Wars in which the "civilized" settlers' role in the conquest of the "barbaric Indians" is idealized and heroized. Possession of land is construed as an emblem of ethnic and gender honor, acquired in the struggle of "civilization" against "barbarism," an index of men's abilities to domesticate a wild nature. Writing in 1894, the municipal council of Namiquipa affirms that,

> [s]ince the year 1778 and until very recently, the descendants [of the original colonists] and those who actually possess the aforementioned land have defended it . . . against the frequent and tenacious attacks of the barbaric Indians, irrigating with their own blood, as with that of their ancestors, the land which until now they have peacefully possessed.[20]

As the figure of "irrigating the land with blood" indicates, there was a reciprocal metaphorization between warfare and agriculture. Possession of land on which blood has been shed is simultaneously a sign of men's capacities to destroy and to regenerate life. Possession of land is also a sign of community membership and family continuity. The blood on the land is a mediating symbol which links the living to each other and to the dead, and which conjoins place and identity. The land belongs to those who have been born in the *pueblo,* to those whose blood links them to the past generations who struggled to defend the patrimony of the community and of their families.

Honor and the land which is its emblem are won through the sacrifice of blood and not the payment of gold. Writing in 1865, the Galeanenses assert that their land "was to be bought not by gold but by torrents of blood. . . ."[21] As these texts indicate, the rhetoric of agrarian grievance and redressal is rich in bodily symbols and is organized by a contrast between blood and gold.

The signs of blood, of the struggle of the "civilized" against the "savage," and of the "sacrifices" which the compact of conquest entailed are inscribed in the land itself. As the Namiquipans write in 1901,

There still exist, in the contours of this population, signs which indicate the places where our grandfathers, fathers, and brothers succumbed to the knife of the savage, fulfilling the obligations which had been imposed on them.[22]

For the *serranos*, the community has the right to sovereignty over the territory its sons had lost their lives defending. The sacrifice of blood is what has reclaimed the land from the wilderness and redeemed the "civilized" from the "barbaric." The land belongs to those who fought for it, not simply because this was the condition of the compact between state and settlers, but also because by spilling their blood on the land, by inscribing their deaths in the contours of a territory, the peasant warriors and their descendants have transformed it, have inextricably linked it to their bodies and made it their own.

Not just the signs of blood, but also those of the toil of generations, are etched in the land and are the legitimate indexes of its ownership as well as the true measure of its value. As the Namiquipans write in 1908:

We see with deep sorrow that those lands which we justly esteem to be ours, received from our fathers and fecundated with over a century's constant work, are passing into the hands of strangers through a simple petition and the payment of a few pesos.[23]

Represented as the recipient of personal bodily substances, the land is both an object of social activity and its symbol. Embodied in the land—blood, as shed in fighting and as inherited from ancestors—and sweat, as shed in work—are signs of the self, of the continuity of family and community, and of the human activity which has domesticated a wild nature. Notice that there is an analogy here between production and reproduction. With their bodily substances, men irrigate and fecundate both the land and women. As immutably as the conjugal tie conjoins men and women by commingling their blood, the shedding of bodily substances in production and warfare links life and death, destruction and regeneration, place and being, land and personhood, activity and its object. The inscription of the self and of the self's productive activity in the object of work is the privileged sign of possession, not the payment of gold or the procurement of a title.

In these petitions, the *serranos* ask the state for "justice," that is, for the honoring of the frontier compact and the reestablishment of the symbolic ties to the land broken by agrarian dispossession and commoditization. Justice is located in an idealized frontier past which is contrasted to the injustices, humiliations, and disorder of the present. The *serranos* invert the logic of official history: "progress" has not meant social advance but retrocession. Indeed, the peasants of Janos go so far as to say that they were better off in the Colonial period:

Today in 1910, which marks the one-hundredth anniversary of our National Independence, in this *pueblo* we receive a coarser treatment than when there were Viceroys on our soil; just the fact that the aforesaid title [to our lands] was issued in those times, by the Caballero de Crois [*sic*] who ceded the aforementioned ejidos to our ancestors, so that they would come [and populate the region], without mentioning [the payment of] rents, nor the exaction of small or large taxes, indicates the truth of this without any doubt.[24]

Not only the peasants of Janos but also, those of Namiquipa re-present the founding charter of their communities, De Croix's decree of 1778, as constitutive of a utopian society, of a benign, paternalistic social order. Writing in 1908, the Namiquipans locate an ideal of social reproduction in the past: "In the said decree, with paternal care, are fixed all the measures necessary to the formation and conservation of these pueblos. . . ."[25] But it must be remembered that this vision of history is constructed in relation to and inflected by the struggles of the moment. Moreover, though this popular memory delegitimates the official epic of "progress," it reproduces much of an earlier version of history organized by the state which heroized the struggle of "civilization" against "barbarism." Though the effects of power entailed by "progress" are exposed and criticized, those imposed by an earlier state project of "civilization" are rendered invisible.

The frontier logic invoked by the *serranos* to legitimate their claims was no longer effective. All of the petitions for the redressal of agrarian grievances which I have examined here were rejected. By the last decades of the nineteenth century, the transformations and dislocations of order and progress had created an "ideological disjuncture"[26] between the frontier peasants on the one hand, and the dominant classes and the state on the other. Whereas for the state and the elite, land had become a commodity, for the *serranos,* it continued to be a sign of ethnic and gender honor obtained through the work and the warfare that had domesticated the wilderness, a right sanctified by the sacrifice of blood and sweat. The ideology and the interests of the state and the elite were not consistent with a reaffirmation of the rights of a frontier peasantry that had become identified with disorder and retrocession. The relative autonomy of peasant corporate communities had to be undermined and the social life of agrarian *pueblos* had to be regulated by the new technologies of power that would proletarianize and transform the peasant into the docile subject of the epic of progress.

Agrarian dispossession was one of the main grievances which spurred *serrano* resistance. The frontier notion that land belonged to those who fought for it was particularly conducive to armed revolution. On the one hand, the state had broken the tacit reciprocity of the colonial pact and the state's authority had lost its claim to legitimacy. Military obligations had been fulfilled but once the frontier was pacified, the *serranos* were denied the fruits of their blood and the honors which they had earned by fighting. On the other hand, armed resistance was a form of reaffirming the frontier logic of land rights. But it is not just as a material means of production that land is important to peasants. For the *serranos,* land was as necessary to the symbolic reproduction of the community, of the household/family, and of the self as it was to the material reproduction of human and social life. The bodily substances inscribed in the land were multivocal symbols of gender and ethnic honor and of community membership and continuity. Agrarian expropriation entailed a redefinition of subjectivities and a perceived alienation of honor, of the social value accorded to the self. It was construed as an illicit form of appropriation by the rich of the poor's bodily substances and of their very selves. This will become more evident if we examine the contrasting attitudes to working on one's own land for oneself, one's family, and one's community, versus selling one's labor power and hence, one's self, to a master.

Productive Activity and Wage Labor

One day in Namiquipa, we were admiring the *chile* harvest of a friend who was born around 1906. "I have always dedicated myself to my fields/ tasks (*labores*)," he said with pride, "I have never had to work *de raya.*" The expression, "*dedicarse a sus labores*" (to dedicate oneself to one's fields/ tasks), is commonly used to characterize and to refer to productive activity on one's own lands. Here the noun *labores* means both fields and work on one's fields; the same term is used to denote the activity of work and its object. Notice that the verb *dedicar(se)* is reflexive: the self is both the subject and the object of the action. Moreover, the possessive pronoun is used to stress personal control over the land and over the activity of work.

By working on their lands, the peasants of *serrano* towns, such as Namiquipa, not only ensured the material reproduction of household and community but also realized themselves as honorable men. Going to the *labor* is an activity which is key to the production of masculine identity since the socialization of the "natural" self is accomplished though the domestication of nature. A man who is "hardworking" (*muy trabajador*) is a "man of respect" (*hombre de respeto*) who fulfills the obligation to "maintain his family" (*mantener su familia*) entailed by a fully socialized masculinity. Such a man is a good *jefe de familia* (family chief), an honorable patriarch. By contrast, a man who is "lazy" (*flojo*) is a *sinverguenza,* that is, a man without honor who neglects his duties to his family. Such men are commonly held to lead a life of vice (*vida viciosa*), drinking, stealing, and committing petty crimes. Unlike hardworking men, *flojos* are not considered to be either "good members of the community" (*buenos vecinos*) or good husbands and fathers.

Possession of land has always been key to this self-realization through productive activity. The self-mastery which is integral to masculine honor and identity is realized through work on one's own fields. As our friend who claimed never to have worked *de raya* said, "*A mi nadie me manda,*" (nobody bosses me about). A man who works his own land is in control of his productive activity. He decides what, when, and how to plant. Given the limitations of nature, he controls the rhythms of his work.

In contrast to salaried employees who are thought to depend on others for their sustenance, men who work their own land are perceived as maintaining themselves and their families. To call a man a *mantenido* (one who is maintained by others) is to defame him. Indeed, in the late nineteenth and early twentieth century, *mantenido* was used by peasants to insult policemen and other salaried municipal employees.[27] In contrast to the independent producer who is fully male, the *mantenido* is both like a child and like a woman because he relies on others for his sustenance.

Clearly, a man's status and identity as a *jefe de familia,* as an honorable patriarch, is contingent upon his role in production. Power and autonomy are viewed as aspects of masculine identity which can only be realized if a man is his own master, that is, if he controls both his work and its object, the land. The selfmastery which control over one's productive activity and its object implies is critical to men's embodiment of socially valued forms of masculinity. The fields which are willed to descendants are the enduring symbol of a man's honoring of duties to kin and community and of his realization of the patriarchal ideal. In the construction of subjectivity, class situation and gender identity are reciprocally defined.

The possession of land is critical not only to the embodiment of *serrano* ideals of gender but also, to the reproduction of ethnic identity. On the frontier, possession of land and the practice of agriculture became signs which differentiated the "civilized" from the "barbarians." Possession of land was a sign of ethnic honor, an index of the "reason" (*razón*) which allowed nature to be domesticated and socialized, and of the self-mastery which distinguished "civilized" men from subjected Indians who, like the peon in Doña Aurora's story, were dependent beings who were the object of others' control. In the construction of subjectivity, class, gender, and ethnicity were interlinked in complex ways.

In contrast to *dedicarse a sus labores,* which implies self-mastery and control over the process and object of work, *trabajar de raya,* the phrase which continues to be used to designate wage labor, connotes dependence and self-alienation. On *haciendas* which retained their work force through debt peonage, the *raya* was the record kept of the debts owed by workers to the enterprise's store. As such, the *raya* was a symbol of the worker's personal subjection. As the phrase, *trabajar de raya* indicates, wage labor was and still is strongly associated with personal servitude and dependence on another. Other signs of the idiom of wage labor also connote dependence, powerlessness, and emasculation. For example, during the Porfiriato, the verb *enganchar*, to hook, was used to refer to the hiring of workers. The figure recalls the sexual act which is a trope for domination and subjection: those who were hooked were rendered as powerless as women. What the idiom of wage labor implies is that the worker's subordination to the master is predicated precisely on his humiliation as a man.

As the frontier was transformed into the border, capitalist development opened up new jobs in mining, in railroad construction, and on *haciendas*. Labor in the Northern provinces were scarce because the frontier had always been less densely settled and because U.S. enterprises on the other side of the border attracted many Mexican workers.[28] In order to obtain workers, Chihuahuan capitalists had to offer better salaries and conditions; workers in Chihuahua were better paid and treated than those elsewhere in Mexico.[29] Yet, noncapitalist forms of labor retention, such as debt peonage, continued to be deployed. The symbolism of personal servitude coexisted uneasily with a capitalist rationality according to which the worker's labor was freely exchanged for wages.

Different forms of productive activity involve workers in distinct types of social relations and imply diverse forms of subjectivity. Despite the high pay and better conditions enjoyed by Chihuahuan workers, as opposed to those elsewhere in Mexico, for dispossessed peasants from the Guerrero district, proletarianization was a humiliating and dishonoring alternative. Wage labor represented the alienation of the self and the expropriation of personal bodily substances. The symbolism of personal servitude made evident the extent to which *trabajo de raya* abrogated the self-mastery critical to the production of masculine honor. Many *serrano* men were not willing to engage in symbolic practices which undermined their masculinity and threatened their personal autonomy. For example, Cruz Chávez, son of another of the rebel leaders from Tomochi, refused to allow himself to be humiliated and symbolically emasculated by the administrator of one of Luis Terrazas's *haciendas*. Since Chávez would not kiss the hand of the administrator, he was told to find work elsewhere.[30] Not surprisingly, Chávez was later to join the revolutionaries of the municipality of Namiquipa.

The conflict between the values of masculine honor and the servility of wage labor is quite clearly illustrated by a dispute between Gregorio Calzadíaz, a well-to-do tenant of one of the Müller's ranches, and one of his hired hands, Abraham Ontiveros, which occurred in 1907.[31] Calzadíaz ordered Ontiveros to perform first one task and then another. Tired of being bossed about, Ontiveros told Calzadíaz "that he was not a boy to be going from here to there." Calzadíaz replied "that he paid him his money so that he would do what he ordered him to." Ontiveros answered that, "after all, he [Calzadíaz] was not a man," and tried to slap Calzadíaz on the face, but the latter hit him over the head with a goad stick first.

This dispute follows the lineaments of an affair of honor: a challenge to masculinity is issued and evokes a corresponding riposte. Calzadíaz's disrespectful mode of giving orders offends Ontiveros sense of masculine honor because it makes visible the asymmetry in power between master and worker. Moreover, Calzadíaz's remark implies that by buying Ontiveros's labor power, he has also purchased his self and that Ontiveros owes him not just his work, but also his personal subordination. Ontiveros rejects this claim on his self, affirming his honor by that by buying Ontiveros's labor power, he has also purchased his self and that Ontiveros owes him not just his work, but also his personal subordination. Ontiveros rejects this claim on his self, affirming his honor by denying that Calzadíaz has bought the right to dominate and humiliate him: he insists that he is not a boy but a man. He tops this by impugning Calzadíaz's masculinity and by slapping his face, the privileged index of a challenge to honor. Like Cruz Chávez, Ontiveros refuses to accept the symbolic emasculation and the dishonor which the alienation of one's labor power entailed.

Clearly, the frontier ideology of gender honor conflicted with the servile image of the docile worker. To be in someone else's power compromised a man's personal autonomy and self-mastery. Wage labor implied a form of subjectivity which did not permit *serrano* men to embody their ideals of masculine identity. The dependency which wage labor entailed made a man like a child and like a woman. Thus, despite relatively good wages and working conditions, the *serrano* peasants resisted proletarianization.

As A. Strauss observes, "Identities imply not merely personal histories but also social histories . . ."[32] For the peasants of Chihuahua's one-time military colonies, productive activity was not a commodity to be bought and sold but instead, a sign of gender and ethnic honor. The honorable man could not be the docile laborer. A whole history militated against the servile alienation of the self which wage labor entailed. Subaltern forms of social identity, which were the historical product of the frontier struggle between "civilization" and "barbarism," conflicted with the new forms of subjection/subjectivity fostered by processes of state formation and capitalist development. Honor could only be maintained through work on one's own fields. Land was a means of both material and symbolic reproduction, a sign of ethnic and gender honor, of community and family continuity. The vision of honorable productive activity contrasted radically with the servility of wage labor. Whereas to work for oneself, one's family and one's community on one's own lands was a form of self-realization, to labor for wages was a form of self-alienation, emasculation, and humiliation.

The alienation of corporate lands disrupted the peasant economy. Moreover, it threatened the reproduction of the peasant community. Once tenaciously defended against Apache raids, the *pueblo* was now to be defended against the attacks of the agents of order and progress. In addition, depeasantization and the loss of lands had consequences for the production and reproduction of locally valued forms of social identity. Resistance to proletarianization was not just a question of economic insecurity as is commonly argued but also, a question of power and subjectivity. Class situation, status position, and social identity are all implicated in these peasants' attempts to maintain their frontier way of life and to retain control over their labor and the object of their productive activity: the land.

Conclusions

In order to understand resistance, we cannot simply focus on institutional politics but must also pay attention to the politics of everyday life, to the ways in which power is experienced and negotiated outside of formal contexts, to the effects of power on identities and bodies.

Serrano resistance was an attempt to contest the symbolic and material reversals which threatened the reproduction of a whole way of life as well as of locally valued forms of identity rooted in a frontier past. The peasants of the *sierra* had a concept of identity antithetical to that advanced by capitalism, one which stressed the social dimensions of personhood and grounded the value of human beings in honor rather than in wealth.

As the privileged locus of masculine power and feminine virtue, gender was a key site for the reinscription of subjectivities and for the negotiation of honor. The social transformations engendered by capitalism and state formation were understood and experienced as a collective and personal dishonoring which undermined the embodiment of *serrano* ideals of gender. The competition for gender honor is one instance of the everyday negotiation of power. To be dishonored is to be in a liminal state. The actor's everyday status cannot be recovered until honor is avenged. In this sense, nineteenth century *serrano* rebellion and twentieth century revolutionary mobilization can be seen as collective and personal taking of vengeance. Indeed, for the *serrano* Eligio Cisneros the revolution was just that. Recalling the history of abuses which preceded 1910, Cisneros comments:

> For those of us who were witnesses of those brutal acts—those which paved the way—[the revolution] was not a surprise. Maybe those who proceeded in that [brutal] manner, ignored, surely, that each act of cruelty engenders an act of vengeance, by virtue of a natural law.[33]

Armed struggle was not only a form of vengeance but also, the reinstantiation of the founding act of *serrano* communities—land and honor would go to those who defended the family and the *pueblo* against the agents of disorder. Milan Kundera has written that "the struggle . . . against power is the struggle of memory against forgetting."[34] Clearly, *serrano* resistance was oriented by an historical memory which inverted the relationship between past and present advanced by the official logic of progress. But this popular memory was also inflected by earlier state projects of territorial conquest and domination of indigenous groups and its re-presentations rendered invisible multiple effects of power.

Stuart Hall has noted that the study of popular culture has shifted between "two, quite unacceptable, poles: pure 'autonomy' or total incapsulation [*sic*]."[35] Clearly, the popular cannot be treated as if it were a wholly unified and fully achieved domain, capable of constituting memory and meaning in pristine isolation from official constructions and effects of power.[36] But this does not mean that the popular is a fully dependent and determined domain either.[37] Hegemonic discourses are not monolithically installed nor are they automatically reproduced by subaltern groups and classes.[38]

The relationships between popular and official discourses, like those between subaltern and dominant groups and classes, are not fixed but constantly negotiated. Produced on a shifting terrain of control and conflict, popular culture reproduces dominant significations and also transforms and contests them. Instead of oscillating between "pure autonomy" and "total encapsulation," the study of popular culture should attempt to recuperate this dialectic of reproduction and transformation, accommodation and resistance—what Hall calls "the dialectic of cultural struggle" (1981:233).

If popular discourses of resistance cannot be read as allegories of the "politically correct" neither can they be read as "prepolitical," as Hobsbawn (1959) and others have done. By imposing Western political categories on others, these sorts of readings fall short of a full grasp of cultural alterity and of the dialectics of cultural struggle. Moreover, if the point of departure for analysis is an expanded conception of power, such discourses are not "prepolitical" for they contest the inscription of power in identities and bodies.

The body, which Terry Turner has aptly called "the social skin,"[39] is a critical medium for the inscription and naturalization of effects of power. The meanings of the body politic are given a "natural alibi" in the body personal. As Jean Comaroff points out:

> Through modes of socialization (both implicit and explicit) the "person" is constituted in the social image, tuned, in practice, to the . . . system of meanings that lies silently within the objects and conventions of a given world. . . . [O]nce they have taken root in the body, acquired a "natural" alibi, such meanings assume the appearance of transcendent truth. The physical contours of experience thus appear to resonate with the external forms of an "objective" reality.[40]

Alibis imply an "elsewhere." Effects of power and meaning are fixed and rendered immutable through an ontology which situates the "social skin" in the "elsewhere" of a nature outside of society and history, and hence beyond social transformation.[41] What the rich bodily symbolism of peasant discourses of resistance demonstrates is that the "social skin" is a site of political contest and transformation, that there is a somatics of rule and of resistance to rule.

Though *serrano* resistance contested certain forms of subjectivity advanced by state centralization and capitalist development, other effects of power, implemented by an earlier state project of frontier conquest, continued to be construed as "natural" and valorized as "honorable." As a personal and collective avenging of honor, *serrano* resistance reaffirmed locally valued forms of gendered subjectivity which prescribed male control of female sexuality and generativity and which entailed the enclosure of women in the safety of a domestic domain whose entrances and exits were guarded by men.

For Namiquipan men, armed struggle was an opportunity to reactualize themselves as "Just Warriors," as *macho* destroyers but also as patriarchal life-givers, self-sacrificing Christs who redeemed others by offering up their own lives. Just as they had not fought in the campaigns of the Apache Wars, the majority of Namiquipan women did not join or accompany the revolutionary troops as did other Mexican women.[42] This is consistent with cultural constructions of gender and ethnicity as well as with the patriarchal rhetoric of protection. However, this is not to say that women did not support the revolutionary struggle or that they were seen as playing no role. Their role as mothers and wives of fighters was glorified. Indeed, Pedro Rascón y Tena, a Namiquipan revolutionary, deemed the women's "sacrifice" a higher form of heroism than that of the men:

> It is not only on the battlefields—where the strident explosions of the canons resound and where the earth is fecundated with the sweat and the tears and the blood of our brothers who fight and who raise altars to the *Patria*—it is not only there where heroism, that sacred virtue, is exercised; in each humble hut, in each home, there are beings who suffer and who water/irrigate with their tears the bloody altar. The breasts of these beings do not harbor hatreds or bastardly ambitions and it is love which leads them to sacrifice. Women! Here are the martyrs of all the bloody epics of history.

> When he takes his leave, the warrior rends the soul of his mother, fills the heart of his wife or betrothed with bile, and marches to battle—sad and tearful, yes . . . but soon enough, [the warrior] dissipates [his sorrow] with triumph or death. [But] those women, each time they wish to console themselves with the idea that the beloved man for whom they cry

marched to the post that duty assigned him, feel—through and through—
something terrible, something inexplicable, which rebels in their entrails
and seems to kills them.

Sometimes that sentiment triumphs in them and crazed [with it], they ask
who, and with what right, has torn from their arms the beloved being. At
other times, the most frequent, the sentiment of duty triumphs and they
contribute with their tears to the holocaust; but always, their hearts shed
bitter tears.

When the widow contemplates the son who, stammering, asks for his
father, she tells him with pride that he died for the *Patria;* but these words
do not leave her mouth without knotting themselves in her throat and
without moving her heart. It is glory or it is pain which produces these
emotions. Blessed be the Marias who in the valor/value of life cry for
their loves at the foot of the Cross.[43]

In this text, women are sanctified and heroized as icons of the Virgin Mary
who put patriotic duty above maternal instinct and who contribute the lives
of their men to the revolution just as the Virgin contributed Christ's life to
redeem humanity. Women's contribution to the struggle is a source of social
esteem. But the value of their sacrifice is mediated through men's actions.
Their bravery consists in knowing how to let their men kill and die.

I did find the name of one Namiquipan woman—Camila Salais—included on a list of revolutionaries.[44] She was the widow of Rafael Lópes,
the first revolutionary killed in Namiquipa on 20 November 1910. But those
whom I asked about her could not remember her. When speaking to Namiquipan women about their experiences in the revolution and those of their
mothers, sisters, aunts . . . I heard about suffering, hunger, bereavement,
sickness, rape . . . Popular memory is consistent with Pedro Rascón y Tena's
vision of men's and women's roles in the Revolution. Doubtlessly women
served as important conduits of information (today women's "gossip" plays
a key role in local politics). Surely they participated in nonviolent forms of
resistance (as they do today). But these are not the stories I heard, nor are
they the ones told in the archives. The silences of memory are also eloquent.

"The standpoints of the subjugated," as Donna Haraway notes, "are
not 'innocent' positions."[45] As a reaffirmation of patriarchal forms of gendered being, *serrano* insurrection reproduced forms of subjectivity which
perpetuated the oppression of women by men. As Ilene O'Malley comments:

[Forms of domination] emasculated lower-class men, who recovered their
manhood during the revolution by assaulting the socio-economic structures that had oppressed them. They then took their places, at least in
theory, as equals in the post-revolutionary society. As they conceived it,

equal manhood included the prerogatives of the patriarch. That entailed the continued oppression of women as women, although women shared in the improved status of their classes.[46]

Eric Wolf has observed that "ideology not only represents class relations, and not only naturalizes social relationships, but it anchors itself in concepts and symbols of the . . . orectic [sic] pole, in blood and sex and other primordial constructs."[47] In blood and sex, in gender and ethnicity, power finds alibis that are very difficult to expose.[48]

Class, gender and ethnicity were complexly concatenated in *serrano* subjectivities. *Serrano* discourses of resistance attest to the centrality of gender in the inscription of power and powerlessness. My reflections on these discourses indicate that the denaturalization of masculinities is key to a feminist analysis of gender and power.[49] My analysis also confirms that gender is not only the social construction of distinctions between/among femininities and masculinities and of relations between/among women and men, but also a primary site for the production of more general effects of power and meaning.[50] This implies that gender should be as key a category in the analysis of domination and resistance as ethnicity and class have been.[51] What should be at issue is not assimilating one form of oppression to another but instead, uncovering the mutually supporting as well as contradictory relations among them.

NOTES

This essay is based on a more extended and comprehensive analysis presented in Ana María Alonso, "Gender, Ethnicity and the Constitution of Subjects: Accommodation, Resistance and Revolution on the Chihuahuan Frontier," Ph.D. dissertation, (University of Chicago, 1988). An earlier version of this essay was published as "'Progress' as Disorder and Dishonor: Discourses of *Serrano* Resistance" in *Critique of Anthropology*, 8, 1 (1988). I thank the editors of *Critique* and Luna Publishers for giving me permission to publish this revised version here. In writing this essay, I have benefited from the comments of many persons and especially from the suggestions made by Elizabeth Weed, Barbara Babcock, and other participants in the seminar on Gender, Ethnicity, and Race held at the Pembroke Center for Teaching and Research on Women, Brown University (where I was a fellow) during the 1987–1988 academic year, and from the insights of Jean Comaroff and Daniel Nugent. The fieldwork and archival research on which the essay is based were carried out collaboratively with Daniel Nugent from 1983 to 1985 and in July/August 1986. Funding was provided by the Social Science Research Council, the Inter-American Foundation, and the Center for Latin American Studies, University of Chicago. I acknowledge with thanks the guidance and support provided by Friedrich Katz, Raymond T. Smith, and Jean Comaroff who supervised my research. As ever, I am deeply indebted to the people of Namiquipa, Chihuahua and to the many persons in Mexico who made my research possible.

1. E.g., Philip Corrigan and Derek Sayer, *The Great Arch: English State Formation as Cultural Revolution*, (New York and Oxford: Basil Blackwell, 1985); Philip Corrigan, *Social Forms/Human Capacities: Essays in Authority and Difference*, (New York and London: Routledge, 1990); essays in *Feminism and Foucault: Reflections on Resistance*, edited by Irene Daimaond and Lee Quinby, (Boston: Northeastern University Press, 1988); Cynthia Enloe, *Bananas, Beaches and Bases: Making Feminist Sense of International Politics*, (London: Pandora, 1989); Stuart Hall, "On Postmodernism and Articulation: An Interview With Stuart Hall," *Journal of Communication Inquiry*, 10, 2, (1986); Stuart Hall, "The Toad in the Gardern: Thatcherism Among the Theorists," in *Marxism and the Interpretation of Culture*, edited by Cary Nelson and Lawrence Grossberg, (London: MacMillan Education, 1988); Joan W. Scott, *Gender and The Politics of History*, (New York: Columbia University Press, 1988).

2. Antonio Gramsci, *Selections From the Prison Notebooks of Antonio Gramsci*, edited and translated by Quintin Hoare and Geoffrey Nowell Smith, (New York: International Publishers, 1971), p. 263.

3. Michel Foucault, *Power/Knowledge*, (New York: Pantheon, 1980), p. 39.

4. Ernesto Laclau and Chantal Mouffe, "Recasting Marxism: Hegemony and New Political Movements," *Socialist Review*, 12, 6, (1982), p. 100.

5. An internal relationship is one which is constitutive of the elements which are related; cf. Bertell Ollman, *Alienation: Marx's Conception of Man in Capitalist Society*, (Cambridge: Cambridge University Press), pp. 27–42.

6. Michel Foucault, *Power/Knowledge*.

7. Teresa de Lauretis, *Technologies of Gender: Essays on Theory, Film, and Fiction*, (Bloomington: Indiana University Press, 1987), p. 26.

8. See Jean B. Elshtain, *Women and War*, (New York: Basic Books, 1987), for the concepts of the "Just Warrior" and the "Beautiful Soul."

9. The synopsis presented in the preceding paragraphs is based on Ana María Alonso, "Gender, Ethnicity."

10. I have not used her real name.

11. Cf. Michael Taussig, *Shamanism, Colonalism and the Wildman*, (Chicago, University of Chicago Press, 1987).

12. According to J. A. Pitt-Rivers, "Honour and Social Status," in J. G. Peristiany (ed.), *Honour and Shame: The Values of Mediterranean Society*, (London: Weidenfeld & Nicolson, 1965), pp. 72–73, the rebellion of the *campesinos* of Andalusía, Spain also was prompted by a popular vision of the dominant classes' loss of honor: "the term of respect towards a member of the ruling class became extended in *señoritismo* to mean the rule of corruption and social injustice."

13. Placido Chávez Calderón, *La Defensa de Tonuchi*; (Nesro Oray: Editorial Jus, 1964) my translation. I have translated the Spanish *lacra*, a sore or scab which is an index of illness, as "stigma." Whereas to possess honor is to be in a state of social and personal well-being, to lose honor is to bear the signs of sickness.

14. Popular histories also recount this defilement and dishonoring of women. See Alberto Calzadíaz-Barrera, *Víspera de la Revolucíon (Abuelo Cisneros)*, (Mexico City: Editorial Patria, 1969); Teodosio Duarte Morales, *El Rugir del Cañón*, (Ciudad Juárez, Chihuahua, 1968).

15. The hypermasculinization of unconquered "barbaric" Indians and the feminization of subjected Indians is discussed at length in Ana María Alonso, "Gender, Ethnicity." Cf. Michael Taussig, *Shamanism, Colonialism and the Wild Man: A Study in Terror and Healing,* (Chicago: University of Chicago Press, 1987).

16. The Spanish is *riqueza almacenada*. An *almacén* is a storehouse. According to Edwin B. Williams, *The Williams Spanish & English Dictionary*, (New York: Charles Scribner's Sons, 1963), p. 32, the verb *almacenar* means both to store and to hoard. *Riqueza almacenada* evokes an image of crops produced by *hacienda* workers stored for sale as commodities; what workers produce through activity and sweat is appropriated and transformed into *riqueza almacenada* by the patron.

17. Cited in Teodosio Duarte Morales, *Rugir*, my translation.

18. *Archivo de Terrenos Nacionales, Reforma Agraria*, Mexico City, (hereafter *ATN*), 1.24(06) exp. 3, March 17, 1865, peasants of Galeana complain about the alienation of their lands as *baldíos* to Enrique Muller; *ATN* 1.21(06) exp. 516, December 24, 1869 & *ATN* 1.21(06) exp. 520 complaints from peasants of Yepomera and Temósachic whose lands are being sold as *baldíos; ATN* 1.29(06) exp. 48, February 8, 1900, Namiquipans ask that the Müllers respect the boundaries of their Colonial land grant; *ATN* 1.24(06) exp. 23, March 20, 1901, agrarian representative of Namiquipa complains that *foraneos* are acquiring rights in the *comun repartimiento* lands; *ATN,* July 28, 1908, peasants of Namiquipa complain that their lands are being sold under the umbrella of the 1905 Municipal Land Law; 1.29(06) exp. 45, peasants of Cruces complain that their lands are being sold to outsiders as *baldíos;* Janos file, complaints 1908 and May 5, 1910 by Porfirio Talamantes and peasants that land is being sold to strangers under rubric of 1905 Municipal Land Law. Archivo Municipal de Namiquipa, Namiquipa, Chihuahua, Mexico, (hereafter *AMN*) box 1–D May 1, 1894, from municipal council of Namiquipa to Chihuahuan government, complaining about the alienation of the community's lands to the Müllers; *AMN,* March 21, 1895, statement on land question by municipal council. All subsequent quotes from these *ocursos* (petitions) are my translations. Other agrarian complaints can be found in *Archivo del Distrito de Guerrero*, Guerrero City, Chihuahua, Mexico, (hereafter *AMCG*).

19. "Military colony" is used here in an analytic sense and should not be taken to refer only to those settlements expressly designated as "military colonies" by the Mexican state. Janos and Galeana, like Namiquipa and Cruces, were established as military colonies in the Colonial period.

20. *AMN,* box 1–D, May 1, 1894, from municipal council of Namiquipa to Chihuahuan government.

21. *ATN,* 1.24(06) exp. 3, March 17, 1906.

22. *ATN,* 1.24(06) exp. 23, March 20, 1901.

23. *ATN,* July 28, 1908.

24. *ATN,* Janos file, May 5, 1910; the peasants of Janos, Galeana district, protest against the municipal administration's charging of rent for use of ejido land and for use of water, pasture, and timber.

25. *ATN,* July 28, 1908.

26. The concept of an "ideological disjuncture" is taken from Daniel Nugent, "Mexico's Rural Populations and *La Crisis:* Economic Crisis or Legitimation Crisis," *Critique of Anthropology*, 7, 3, (1988).

27. Disputes in which *mantenido* is used to defame a man's honor can be found in Archivo del Juzgado del Municipio de Namiquipa, Namiquipa, Chihuahua, Mexico, (hereafter *AJMN*).

28. Friedrich Katz, *The Secret War in Mexico*, (Chicago: University of Chicago Press, 1981), p. 10.

29. Friedrich Katz, *Secret War*, p. 10; Mark Wasserman, *Capitalists, Caciques and Revolution*, (Chapel Hill: University of North Carolina Press, 1984), pp. 118–120.

30. This story was told to us by his nephew.

31. *AJMN*, May 30, 1907, "Criminal contra Valerio y Abraham Ontiveros por lesiones."

32. A. Strauss, *Mirrors and Masks: The Search for Identity*, (London: Martin Robertson, 1977), p. 764, cited in Philip Abrams, *Historical Sociology*, (Ithaca: Cornell University Press, 1982), p. 230.

33. Eligio Cisneros, cited in Alberto Calzadíaz Barrera, *Víspera*, p. 175, my translation.

34. Milan Kundera, *The Book of Laughter and Forgetting*, (Harmondsworth: Penguin Books, 1981).

35. Stuart Hall, "Notes on Deconstructing 'the Popular,'" in *People's History and Socialist Theory*, edited by Raphael Samuel (London: Routledge and Kegan Paul, 1981), p. 222.

36. Michael Bommes and Patrick Wright, "'Charms of Residence': The Public and the Past," in *Making Histories*, [Centre for Contemporary Cultural Studies] (Minneapolis: University of Minnesota Press, 1982), p. 255.

37. Stuart Hall, "Deconstructing the 'Popular;'" Antonio Gramsci, *Prison Notebooks*, p. 333.

38. Michael Bommes and Patrick Wright, "'Charms of Residence': The Public and the Past," p. 207.

39. Terry Turner, "The Social Skin," in *Not Work Alone*, edited by J. Cherfas and R. Lewin (London: Temple Smith, 1980).

40. Jean Comaroff, "Bodily Reform as Historical Practice: The Semantics of Resistance in Modern South Africa," ms. prepared for *The International Journal of Psychology*, 18, 2, (1983), pp. 4–5.

41. Cf. Roland Barthes, *Mythologies*, (New York: Hill and Wang, 1972), pp. 127–130.

42. Some of the women of Tomochi, however, did participate in the armed defense of their community which was attacked by several federal army contingents in the early 1890s; on this see Placido Chávez Calderón, *La Defensa de Tomochi*, (Mexico City: Editorial Jus, 1964). On women's participation in the Mexican Revolution see Shirlene Ann Soto, "The Mexican Woman: A Study of Her Participation in the Revolution, 1910–1940," PhD dissertation, (University of New Mexico, 1977); Anna Macías, *Against All Odds: The Feminist Movement in Mexico to 1940*, (Westport, CT.: Greenwood Press, 1982); Elizabeth Salas, *Soldaderas in the Mexican Military: Myth and History*, (Austin: University of Texas Press, 1990).

43. Diary of Pedro Rascón y Tena, written during 1910 and 1911, my translation; I thank his relatives in Sonora for letting me consult it.

44. "List of the persons who are in the active service of the Anti-Reelectionist Troops;" *AMCG*, box 76, Namiquipa, May 17, 1911.

45. Donna Haraway, "Situated Knowledges: The Science Question in Feminism and the Privilege of Partial Perspective," *Feminist Studies*, 14, 3, (1988), p. 584.

46. Ilene O'Malley, *The Myth of the Revolution: Hero Cults and the Institutionalization of the Mexican State 1920–1940*, (London: Greenwood Press, 1986), pp. 136–137.

47. Eric Wolf, cited in Ashraf Ghani, "A Conversation With Eric Wolf," *American Ethnologist*, 14, 2, (1987), p. 361.

48. Joan W. Scott, *Gender*, pp. 44–50.

49. Cynthia Enloe, *Bananas*.

50. Joan W. Scott, *Gender*; Teresa de Lauretis, *Technologies*.

51. Joan W. Scott, *Gender*.

20

A Pedagogy for Postcolonial Feminists

Zakia Pathak

I

For ourselves, teaching undergraduate students at Miranda House, a women's college at Delhi University, we may state at the outset that our pedagogical practice is directed at producing from the literary "work" a "text" which engages with our concerns as Indians and women at the present time.[1] While respecting the cultural specificity of the work in the producing culture, we are committed to "making" a politics for it that will enable us to live our lives more critically.[2]

It is being increasingly recognized/resisted that the production of meaning is governed by ideological perspectives, implicit or theorized. "Even the most seemingly intuitive encounter with a literary text is . . . already theory-laden. . . . [T]here is no reading that does not bring to bear a certain context, interpret from a certain angle or set of interests, and thus throw one set of questions into relief while leaving others unasked."[3] We believe that our task as teachers is to create an awareness of these interests and thereby of the subject positions from which they emerge. The first objective of any political program is to work toward an understanding that the contradictions of textual practice are the effect of a multiplicity of subject positions, often perceived as contradictory and impossible to reconcile. Whether we then proceed to make it our responsibility to change the perceptions of interests by bringing to bear other contexts, other angles, is another issue, though in practice we have found that it is difficult to keep the two separate. "We need to see discourse structures in their fullness and power . . . and the way to see one discourse is to see more than one."[4] We have had to be wary

426

in classroom discussion of arousing resistances which might be counter-productive to our project, and so sometimes have to leave open the issue as to whether the subject position temporally privileged in the differential of identity is to be changed or cherished.

This exercise in cognition dramatizes more often than not, not the fractured subjectivity that might be expected given the disturbing impact of modernizing trends upon traditional practices in the culture outside the classroom, but a unified, singularly untroubled subject. This subject is an effect of that "competence" which is acquired by a formal education in reading patterns, structures, codes.[5] Every literary work comes to us with encrustations from the metropolitan university and this form of intertextuality produces its own subject, also sometimes called the "informed" reader, who represents some kind of ideal. The literary perceptions of the reader, when she is Indian, connect only tangentially, if at all, with her understanding of the political and social problems she lives with outside the classroom. This separation between academic litspeak and the lay discourses of the culture,[6] between Academy and World, is tacitly permitted by a practice which historicizes the work in the producing culture but regards historical intervention in its reception as an inexcusable tampering with the truth of the work.

It is of course arguable that this separation between litspeak and culturespeak[7] marks the reception of a literary work in any culture, given the marginalization of literature everywhere, and that it is not peculiar to our situation as a once-colonized people. However that may be, it is surely the case that where First World texts are taught in a Third World university the problem takes on a sharper edge. We seem to assent to the exertion of proprietorial rights of interpretation as expressed through the determination of interpretive paradigms by canonized criticisms—which determine the production of meaning. Our pedagogical politics takes issue with such property rights. In a complex and ongoing process of abrogation and appropriation[8] we bring to the literary work other discursive paradigms which attract our own concerns.

This essay proposes to share our practice in teaching four texts prescribed in the undergraduate syllabus. In the section which follows, Section II, we read the Book of Job and *Murder in the Cathedral*. In our readings of both works we displace the paradigm of religion as revelation; it was the nineteenth century that subjected the Bible to Higher Criticism, eroding its revelatory status and opening up religion to other discourses. In *the Book of Job*, we introduce the discourse of law which interrogates religious discourse. In *Murder in the Cathedral*, we identify an emerging discourse of nationalism, and show how church and state sought to appropriate nationalist rhetoric. These discursive paradigms enable us to move into discussion of the major controversy of the present times, the Mandir Masjid dispute. The Mandir-Masjid dispute centers upon the religious significance of a site in the town of Ayodhya in Uttar Pradesh. Extremist Hindu organisations, the Vishva Hindu Parishad (VHP) and the Bajrang Dal (BD), backed by the Bharatiya Janata Party (BJP), which is a political party, claim that the god Ram was born on the site; that a temple had stood there before it was demolished in the 16th century by the Moghul monarch Babar, who erected a Mosque there. Muslim organisations, the Indian Union Muslim League (IUML) and the Babri Masjid Action Committee (BMAC) deny this. The Hindu organisations have vowed to remove the mosque and reassemble it elsewhere and to build a temple on the site. The Muslim organisations have vowed to defend the mosque. Passions, already running high, became inflamed after the BJP leader Advani took out his *rath yatra* (chariot procession) in mid-1990 which traversed several states and left bloody riots in its wake. Advani was arrested as he crossed into Bihar, the BJP withdrew its support to the minority government of the Janata Dal, under Prime Minister V. P. Singh, and the Government fell. A breakaway section of the JD, the Samajawadi Janata Dal, (GJP) formed the Government but resigned in early 1991. General elections were held in May/June 1991. The BJP made the Ayodhya dispute its central plank for campaigning, calling all Hindus together under the banner of the god Ram. When the results of the elections were announced, they had increased their tally substantially.

In Section III we are led from discourse structures to inscriptions. In two novels, Conrad's *Lord Jim* and Forster's *A Passage to India,* we show how the literary category of genre, far from being a neutral descriptive category, inscribes a reality. Ideological inscription is noted in the female psyche; and the political unconscious, it is suggested, may be gendered.

II

We began our engagement with the Book of Job by considering its status as a theodicy. First, we made the put-togetherness of its structure visible, by examining the process of inclusions and exclusions from the epics, folktales, and poems of wisdom literature. By this means it could accommodate dissenting voices without compromising the theological centrality of Yahweh. Secondly, we showed how the Yahweh figure was an evolving creation of history, from the moody and capricious god who could only be propitiated to the just god of the prophet Amos. Thirdly, we showed how religion constructed history, reading national disasters as visitations of God's wrath over infractions of Mosaic Law. Later, individual histories problematized divine justice; when the law of retribution was extended to individual fates, undeserved suffering could not be explained. Fourthly, we brought in the discourse of law in the contemporary society by pointing to the Sanhedrin, which decided all cases of infraction of the law, including those arising from differing interpretations by the Scribes and Pharisees.

Finally, quoting Hollander in Kermode,[9] we showed how religious texts are constituted by hermeneutical fiats; the Torah was strategically accommodated as the Old Testament while its historical dimension was disparaged and its truths projected as allegories, the true meaning of which could be found only in the Gospels. We concluded by suggesting that the agony of Job was that of a subjectivity fractured by contending discourses of revelation and law, identifying in the text the attendant machinery of proof, argument, intermediary and so on. Job's capitulation to Yahweh could be seen as a submission to the discourse of revelation dominant at that historical moment, against which the discourse of reason was still powerless.

This reading of the Book of Job enabled us to pass on to similar issues involved in the Mandir Masjid dispute: the clash of the two discourses occasioned controversy. The dispute had been referred to a court of law but the Hindu organisations refused to co-operate, claiming that matters of religious faith, that is the birthplace of Ram, could not be adjudicated in a secular court. Muslim organisations produced historical evidence from an impressive array of scholars, in support of their stand (many of these are leftist in orientation; the BJP is rightist). When the SJP Government managed to bring the Hindu organisations to the negotiating table, these produced their own interpretations of history and religious texts to support their stand. The status of historical fact was questioned. The affinity of much of contemporary politics to the situation in the Book of Job as we read it was extended to Yahweh/Ram. Just as the theological insistence on Yahweh as the one Supreme God was politically motivated to unite the people of Israel, weaning them away from allegiance to previous Canaanite gods and so to consolidate them into a nation, so the primacy conferred on the godhood of Ram was targeted, we suggested, to consolidating the Hindu vote in favor of a party which, projecting a Hindu nationalism, hoped to be catapulted into power.

We are aware that in making a politics for the Book of Job we are implicitly positing a form of historical essentialism between two countries divided by centuries of time and worlds of space. It may or may not be the case that we share similar histories; that is for the historians to debate. What is important is that we have arrived at this essentialism, in positing a problematic, in which empirical facts have played a part, and so hope to have avoided the odium attaching to that intuitive essentialism which is an *a priori* concept.[10]

It has been asked of us why in our reading of the Book of Job our feminist identity was not activated. Perhaps a recapitulation of the teaching process during the first term—August/September 1989 and January/February 1991—might go some way in answering that. We had at the start of the course suggested a few topics which might be discussed, among which was the marginal figure of Job's wife and her single utterance: "Curse God and die." Shortly afterward, Mr. Advani's *rath* started rolling and tension escalated. Our reading the text as the conflict of two discourses, religious and legal, unequally empowered, was clearly an immediate response to the contemporary political scene. In other words, the feminist concern was temporally subordinated. It is not that different works foreground different subject positions; but that the subject position privileged in the differential of identity is responsive to the call for political action. If we were to teach the text today, the feminist perspective might well be privileged. Two young women continually hit the media headlines as the greatest crowd-pullers for the BJP. Both are religious persons, having renounced the life of the *qrihasti*, or house holder; Sadhvi Rithambari, by a formal vow, Uma Bharati informally. Both are saffron-clad, the colour of the Hindu religious person. Uma Bharati stood for election and won by a handsome margin. Are these women traditional or modern? They have been seen as daringly different, articulating a new cultural code for women. On the other hand, they have to resort to a conservative one, where a certain moral authority is accorded a public figure who renounces sexuality. Similarly, the large turnout of women in the BJP rallies and marches which, they claim, marks a historical departure and a modernising trend, might be read as conservative, since it was in the cause of religion, as the women saw it. Certainly it was the conservative stereotype of woman, as the repository of sanity and compassion, that was encapsulated in the slogan of the Communist Party of India, (at the other end of the political/ideological spectrum), during its women's rally at Ayodhya; it can be translated thus: "This is the cry of the Indian woman: stop this slaughter!" The wife of Job was doomed to be silenced on two counts: she spoke against her God and against her husband.

Eliot's *Murder in the Cathedral* has traditionally called for a twofold approach. It is the story of a martyrdom and of the baptism of people into faith by the blood of martyrs. It has also been tackled from the biographical angle where the author's eventual personal conversion to Catholicism is read as motivating the play. In our classroom practice these paradigms were displaced so as to recuperate a history read, under the Foucaultian paradigm, as the story of power which circulates in a network. The traditional concept of the freely choosing individual, Thomas of Canterbury, rent by temptations but finally regaining that serene unity which he brings to his decision "out of time," to which his "whole being gives consent," was displaced by a multiply-constituted subjectivity: the royal subject of the King ("O Henry! O my King!") with whom he identifies ("I *was* the King, his arm, his better reason"); the servant of Christ ("No traitor to the king. I am a priest/A Christian saved by the blood of Christ/. . . . My death for his death"); the man of ambition ("The last temptation . . . to do the right deed for the wrong reason"). In this complex power struggle we isolated an emerging rhetoric of nationalism which imaged "England" on grounds of race, religion, and class.

Tempter: King is in France, squabbling in Anjou. . . .
             We are for England. We are in England.
             You and I my Lord, are Normans.
             England is a land for Norman
             Sovereignty. Let the Angevin
             Destroy himself, fighting in Anjou.
             He does not understand us, the English barons.
             We are the people

Third Priest: The Church is stronger for this action.
             Go, weak sad men . . . homeless in earth or heaven.
             Go where the sunset reddens the last grey rock
             Of Brittany, or the Gates of Hercules
             Go venture shipwreck on the sullen coasts
             Where blackamoors make captive Christian men. . . .

Tempter: I am no trifler and no politician . . .
             I am no courtier . . .
             It is we country lords who know the country
             And we who know what the country needs.
             It is our country. We care for the country.
             We are the backbone of the nation.

And against these definitions of the nation, there is that of the oppressed, the women of Canterbury, suffering because of the power struggle between church and state. They construct England in terms of the past conceived as golden:

A rain of blood has blinded my eyes. Where is England?
Where is Kent? Where is Canterbury?
O far far far in the past . . .
It is not we alone, it is not the house, it is not the city that is defiled
But the world that is wholly foul.

The "nation" is always constructed from the perspective of a set of interests. Moving to our contemporary political situation, the extremist Hindu position on the Mandir Mesjid dispute has thrown up the notion of "Hindutva"—concept/ideology/identity/state of being? It is the subject of ongoing debate. It was on the plank of Hindusva that the BJP won its spectacular electoral successes in 1989 and 1991. The attempt to appropriate nationalism which Eliot's play, in our reading, presents led easily to our situation, where Hindutva is projected as co-eval with nationalism. We might have carried forward, from the Book of Job, the paradigm of conflicting discourses in terms of the discourses of law and party politics. How does a party claim to represent the national interest and yet not attract the provisions of the Representation of People's Act (Section 123 (3) and 3(A)) of 1951? In a fascinating article in the *Times of India* of 24 April 1991, Rajdeep Sardesai lists the history of cases filed under this law. In a case before the Bombay High Court, the B.J.P./Shiv Sena (S.S.) lawyers, defending the "inflammatory" election speeches of Sena chief Bal Thackerey, claimed that the judges were using "Western dictionary" definitions of Hinduism and were therefore unable to appreciate the contextual variance in a speech given in the local language and at a public meeting. It appeared to suffer transformation in the discursive situation of "the cold atmosphere" of the judicial chamber. In the Kunte vs. Prabhoo case of 1989, the B.J.P./S.S. alliance had insisted that Hindutva is a geocultural, even nationalistic notion. Justice Bharucha accepted that Hindutva had cultural connotations but ruled that the objective of Mr.Thackerey's speeches was patently and admittedly the protection of the Hindu religion. As for the slogan: *"Garv se kaho hum Hindu hai"* (announce with pride that I am a Hindu)—slogans were among the material facts filed—senior judicial functionaries felt that while in itself the slogan is unobjectionable under the law, if spoken at an election meeting, it can be a corrupt practice inasmuch as a direct relation is being established between the candidate on the podium and the audience. Dr. Prabhoo was disqualified by the High Court. A woman lawyer and social activist, Vasudha Dhagamvar entered the Hindu nationalism controversy from the columns of the *Indian Express* of 25 August 1989. Arguing against the demand to abolish the canopy at India Gate since it is a memory of British colonial rule, she pointed out that nationalism by the time of the Second World War had gripped the *middle classes*. Leaders of the *lower caste* movement in the late nineteenth century—notably Jyotiba Phule—who had suffered at the hands of the Brahmins were on record as saying that they did not want the British to go. It is clear that statements derive their semantic value from the archive in which they are lodged. It is so with the term "nation." We can emerge from Eliot's play to a study of the dissemination of meaning in Indian political history.

III

With *Lord Jim,* we enter into the problematic area of the functioning of genre. Genres are not neutral descriptive categories; they institute a reality and inscribe a subject. The Patusan story has been widely regarded in canonized criticism as a fantasy. But the fantastic is always inserted into a mimed reality against which it defines itself.[11]

A genre may be defined as a mode and a structure.[12] Because fantasy is inserted into a mimed reality, the novel will contain the structural elements of both. The structural markers of realistic narrative are the focalization of the hero, a scrutiny of the psychological motivation of his actions, disambiguation, that is, effacement of all play with being/seeming and the effacement of utterance; this is the "text in a hurry."[13] The narrative is hitched to a megastory which illumines it, creating expectations on the line of least resistance through a text already known. Historical and geographic names are stable semantic entities linking the text to the megatext, itself valorized. Against these criteria, Patusan defines itself as fantasy. Jim is focalized; the conflicting perspectives on his action, so crucial a part of the Patna story, are missing. There is hardly any psychological investigation of his actions ("It came to him . . ."). There are no proper names which provide semantic stability. In one crucial respect, however, the narrative departs from the fantastic mode in that the utterance is almost effaced; the phatic and deictic signals so abundant in the Patna story are minimized here so that Marlow's voice slides imperceptibly into something like omniscience. His framing of Patusan as a fantastic space has magnetized a whole line of critics—cloud-cuckoo land, Edenesque, anti-Paradise, a different time and space, something in a dream.[14] The competent Indian reader, reading off these signals, becomes complicit with the framing of the Orient and its representation as a land of intrigue and unrest, of lecherous rajahs and poisoned coffee, of talismanic rings which command fealty to the white man—finally, with the image of the white man bringing civilization to a benighted people.

Now, the canonized Todorovian theory requires that no poetic or allegorical reading be made since these destroy the fantasy (the moral of the animal fable is held to do this).[15] Todorov also requires that the hesitation of the reader, suspended between two levels of interpretation, natural and supernatural, must be sustained to the end. It seems to us this condition coerces the reader into accepting the Orientalist reading of the Orient as a truthful rendering. It is our contention that this "hestitation" provides a space where a pedagogical politics can begin to operate. To choose to read referentially is to come across natural interpretations which might otherwise pass unnoticed in this dense text, as for instance the fact that Jim was the only man in Patusan who possessed gun powder? To read referentially is to recuperate a recognizable reality where a land is violated by successive streams of invaders, by armed might, or by trade (the Celebes, the Europeans); where religion is exploited for power (Sherif Ali); where the invader initially colludes with a selected native power until he gradually gains supremacy (Jim with Doramin).

The realistic mode has fallen into some disrepute today because of its truth claims. Notwithstanding, we suggest that, so far as the white text is concerned, the privileging of realistic markers yields a recognizable reality which puts us on guard against Orientalist representations. Fantasy is today valorised because it is read as providing an alternative version of reality to which we can aspire and toward which we can work. This is a temporal (historical) construction of the genre which must be accepted if genres are to retain their explicative power. But spatial determinants must also be recognized in the construction of a genre; reading from here, Orientalist fantasy is not so much a subgenre of fantasy as a new function. Subversion and escapism do not exhaust the possibilities; fantasy can also operate to *subserve* a political reality.

As women, we attach a special importance to the figure of Jewel. In most critical accounts, she is invisible; not surprisingly, since most critics leap from Stein to Gentleman Brown. In the shaping of Jewel, the structural markers of fantasy predominate. She has no proper name. She too is focalized; there are no disambiguating, psychologizing perspectives on her actions. There is no play between being and seeming; indeed Marlow's narrative makes her into an icon. She remains in the imagination in a series of fixed poses; always dressed in white, a high childish voice; an arm held aloft holding a torch; standing beside Jim's empty chair issuing commands of war; and finally, her black hair loose, her face stony, only the eyes straining after the shape of a man torn from her side by a dream. Her relations with Jim are romanticized. "They came together like knight and maiden, meeting to exchange vows among haunted ruins." Here Jewel is modeled after the Lady of chivalric romance, mystically conceived and sexually pure. But this figure too has to be inserted into the mimed reality. This exercise prompts the conclusion that the narrative attempts to mystify the realistic markers in order to emasculate their import in the white text.[16] Jewel's father and grandfather were white; among the possibilities which prevented her father from marrying her mother was "merciless convention." In all likelihood, therefore, Jewel is a half-caste and illegitimate. In other words, she is located in the megatext in a history of miscegenation. Now, miscegenation always occurred outside matrimony. Whereas the thrust of this narrative is to present the relationship of Jim and Jewel as if within the matrimonial bond. "Jewel he called her as he might have said Jane, with a peaceful, marital homelike effect." "This was the theory of their marital evening walks." This repression of sexuality within the matrimonial bond constitutes Jewel as the Angel in the House; the iconicity of representation seeps into a stereotype of patriarchal discourse. Jewel is not the Kuchuk Hanem figure of Orientalist discourse, offering a more libertine, less guilt-ridden sex, with the promise of untiring sexuality and of fecundity.[17] Patriarchal and Orientalist discourses are imbricated in the novel; the metaphor of the East as the bride ready to be unveiled by her lord is a recurring motif. Jewel's madness, in a referential reading, would qualify as that anomie which so often afflicted the English person in the colonies, cut off from his own kind.[18] Spilling over to the political story, it constitutes the Orient under white protection as fulfilled and flourishing.

As Schaeffer notes, the logic of inclusion has a radically ambiguous status since genres are temporally constructed. "Genre is always provisional because no immutable criterion decides whether any text belongs to a given genre. . . . This relation of inclusion calls for a decisional aspect irreducible to any definitional determinism."[19] By naming the genre to which Patusan belongs as Orientalist fantasy, we are led to perceive that Jewel is constituted at the intersection of generic traditions which repress female sexuality. This enables us to move toward considering the operation of the patriarchal stereotype in our own culture. It has been so deeply internalized as to be inscribed into the female psyche. Homi Bhabha defines the stereotype as a falsification, not because it is a simplification, but because it is "an arrested, fixated form of representation that in denying the play of difference constitutes a problem in the representation of the subject in social relations."[20] This stereotype is a site of combat in an ongoing debate of tradition versus modernity, where the Indian woman—*Bharat nari*—is constructed as chaste and homeloving, god-fearing, living in and through her husband, even following him into the funeral pyre "voluntarily." In classroom discussion we have learnt not to simplify this ideology as male manipulation or female hypocrisy. There is an excess which cannot be contained in such formulations. At its worst it colludes with patriarchal power in an orgy of submission; at its best it sustains the institution of family, which we still valorize.

Our reading of Forster's *A Passage to India* activated our racial and feminist identities. It would be more accurate to say that our critique of the generic operations of *A Passage to India* was constructed by our subject position as Indian and as a once-colonized people. As such, we read the horror of miscegenation as inscribed in the political unconscious of the Englishman and as structuring the text. But in confronting *A Passage to India* with a recent novel by Deborah Moggach, *Hot Water Man*, which parodies it, our feminist identity provided a source for agency inasmuch as it enabled us to break out of the subject position which constructed the West as other. In the process it also raised the question as to whether the political unconscious is gendered.

The horror of miscegenation is vividly recounted by Ben Shepherd in his account of the case of Peter Lobengula, in the 1920s.[21] Lobengula was the son of the African chief of Matabele, annexed by the British. He was brought to London as a part of a circus troupe, and met and married an Englishwoman, Florence Jewell. The news threw Fleet Street into a frenzy. "Miscegenation has long been regarded as a crime against civilisation" (*The

Spectator). "A stupendous act of folly and physical immorality" (*The Daily Mail*). When approached to perform the marriage service, several members of the clergy refused. The general opinion was that there is something disgusting in the mating of a white girl with a dusky savage. In India too the authorities were alarmed by signs of any intimacy between Englishwomen and Indian men. Lord Curzon refused permission to the Rajah of Puderkottai to proceed to England for the coronation since he suspected that he might marry an Englishwoman. It infuriated Curzon to see the daughter of the Duchess of Roxburgh dancing with the Rajah of Kapurthala at Buckingham court.[22]

Early critical discussion placed Forster in the nineteenth century's general tradition of the *Bildungsroman*. Even when his "mystical atheism" was appreciated, he was classed with the later Victorians like Butler and Meredith. Today in contrast, his work is perceived as belonging to a symbolist aesthetic; his use of symbol and a pervasive disquiet marks him as a modern.[23] It is in the Caves Section of the novel that the realistic mode is arrested and the social comedy turns sharply away from the direction it was headed for; even detective investigation is displaced by a metaphysical quest. We suggest that the horror of miscegenation was too deeply inscribed in the political unconscious to allow exploration in the realistic mode as was possible in Forster's Italian novel, *Where Angels Fear to Tread*.

The manuscript drafts of the novel show that Forster was contemplating two possibilities in the Caves: a physical assault and a mutual embrace. It is conjectured that he abandoned this line of development out of weariness of marriage fiction and the man-woman relation. At the trial, not only does Adela withdraw everything because she cannot be sure of who followed her into the cave, but the question itself suddenly loses interest for her, leaving Forster to pursue his metaphysical quest. "In fiction by women," however, "the female domestic space of the romance is foregrounded as a form of value and power and self fulfilment.[24] Deborah Moggach's *Hot Water Man* suggests what could have happened in the caves. "Through a double process of installation and ironising, parody signals how present representations come from past ones and what ideological consequences derive from both continuity and diffference."[25] The blurb on the dust cover of *Hot Water Man* installs *A Passage to India* unambiguously: *Hot Water Man* must inevitably remind readers of *A Passage to India* as East and West meet once again in confusion." The encounter is updated. India is now postindependence Pakistan, the civil administrator is an executive in a multinational firm represented by the American Duke Hanson as well as the Englishman Donald Hanley. Donald and Christine are married and childless; the emotional relationship is also sterile. Like Adela, Christine is out to discover the real Pakistan, spurning the codes of the compound and haunting the bazaar. There she picks up a relationship with a Pakistani guide. This story climaxes with their visit to Gintho (which the narrator points out is an anagram for Nothing), noted for its cure of infertility. When Christine goes to the hot water springs, the guide stays behind in the guest house and goes to sleep. On her return she rapes him. "And how she had used him. She had confused and inflamed him . . . she . . . was the worst colonialist of them all." She becomes pregnant. The narrative—and the novel—ends on her relieved sobbing when the baby is delivered and she realizes that the color of its skin will not give her away. In the second narrative strand, Donald, who is out to discover his grandfather's military past in all its splendor in India, discovers instead that he had a native mistress by whom he had had a child. Donald sets out to find his half-uncle and to make amends; but when he actually meets the man, he cannot connect. "Close up in the flesh it was impossible to believe that this man was his uncle. Perhaps he did not want to believe it. There was simply no connection" (258). In the third narrative strand, Duke Hanson, whose wife is away in the States, has an affair with a Pakistani woman, educated at an elite school in England, professionally competent and with political connections useful to him. But he will not marry her. "You mean I've been your bit of fun on the side," she ripostes with bitterness when he gives her his feeble reason: "It just won't work." He swears that he meant it, to which she replies with dry anger: "You meant it with an eye on the fucking calendar." In an accusation reminiscent of Fielding's reprimand to Adela ("What have you been doing? Playing a game or studying life or what?"), she raves: "What on earth did you think you were doing? Having a little cross-cultural communication? Getting to know the natives?"

Hot Water Man is metafictional. It is process made visible by a mimesis of process.[26] In recuperating what might have happened in the Caves, it is ironic-parodic in naming the central silence of its progenitor. It exposes the duplicity which at least in part motivates the flight from realistic social comedy into a metaphysical dimension and a symbolist aesthetic: "the contradiction between . . . the ideological project and the literary form which creates an absence at the centre of the text. . . . [T]he text is divided, split."[27]

In a scandalous success of 1921, *The Sheik,* by E. M. Hull, the white heroine is raped by an Arab Sheik and, after several repeat performances in the desert, learns to enjoy it. The concluding chapter reveals him to the heroine, and to the reader, to be the son of an English lord. *Hot Water Man* spurns this duplicity. In moving interracial sex out of the genre of pornography and relocating it on the axis of race, *Hot Water Man* exposes the limits of the liberal ideology which inspired *A Passage to India.*

What is of crucial importance for the pedagogic enterprise is the meaning we produce from the conflictual relation between the two novels. From one perspective, *Hot Water Man* is the discourse of Anglo-India for whom the metropolitan liberal Englishman was the Other.[28] It is a fact of history that the Ilbert Bill, introduced in the nineteenth century to remove the provision that Englishmen in India could not be tried by an Indian judge, ran into violent opposition from the Anglo-Indian community and had to be withdrawn by the British government. From that perspective, *Hot Water Man* in its derision of liberal self-delusion remains within the discourse of Orientalism, at its margins. We must decide if *we* wish to remain within the subject position which is an effect of that discourse. One way of breaking out—in the interests of a less factional perception which would be truer to our more complex relation with the West outside the classroom—which is invested with desire—is to locate *Hot Water Man* in the counterdiscourse to Orientalism. Articulated by a female novelist, within the Western culture, it suggests that the horror of miscegenation is inscribed in the white *male* psyche, and creates a gender affiliation across race.

IV

It will be evident by now that our pedagogical practice is heavily indebted to recent advances in critical theory that have opened up the concepts of author, text, reader, and meaning. In acknowledging this debt, we lay ourselves open to the charge of being neocolonialists, because, in arguing for the validity of a response to English literature shaped by our perceptions of our contemporary political history, we ground these perceptions in European critical theory. This would qualify us as that "comprador intelligentsia" who "mediate[s] trade in cultural commodities of world capitalism at the periphery."[29] By publishing abroad and in India, we may be perceived as selling an India to the West and a West to India. Against this intelligentsia is posited the world of popular culture, unconcerned with the problems of neocolonialism, borrowing freely from the West and refusing otherness: "antinational," asking only for "a simple respect for human suffering."[30] But it is the price we have to pay for engaging in the activity of critique that we should be crucially aware of our multiple subjectivities and how they are determined. We might regret but cannot regain that lost wholeness. Moreover, critique may also advance a claim to being antinational inasmuch as it denotes "reflection on the conditions of possible knowledge and the system of constraints which are humanly produced."[31] As such it addresses a variety of structures of domination anywhere in the world. As Third World readers of First World texts, our opportunities for intervention in political action are limited; it is in order to increase them that our pedagogical practice resists the hegemony of metropolitan critical traditions and contends for the kind of reception of texts we have described in this essay.

But opposition to these traditions is equally to be found within the metropolitan university. Is our debt to critical theory then a case of abrogation without appropriation? "The concern of the Third World critic should properly be to understand the ideological subtext which any critical theory reflects and embodies and the relation this subtext bears to the production of meaning," says a black critic.[32] The ideological subtext of critical theory, as we understand it, is oppositional thinking where structures of domination are perceived to be oppressive. We do not identify such thinking with a composite "Indian" response; we have positioned ourselves in this essay as teachers at the university, as teachers of literature, as women, in fraught relation with other "Indians." To acknowledge this multiplicity of subject positions is not to valorize a fractured subjectivity as we have often been accused of doing. It is certainly to recognize our debt to critical theory while still being moved by an imagined community of selves; and, going on from here, to try and forge a corporate identity for Miranda House; not by evading an identity crisis but by "staging" it.[33] This essay is another attempt toward that objective. And the history of such attempts could be the theme of another essay.

NOTES

The grammatical marker of the first person throughout this essay will take the plural form— we/our/us—since the essay represents a consensual position on pedagogical practice which emerged—and was constantly being refined—in continuing discussion with my colleagues, Saswati Sengupta and Sharmila Purkayastha. *Ave atque vale.* My thanks to Sharada Nair and Lola Chatterji for helpful comments, and to the Nehru Memorial Library for reading facilities. I am grateful to the Academic Foundation, New Delhi for permission to include this article, commissioned by them for their projected publication *Outstory*, ed. Mobua Lahiri et al.

    1. Roland Barthes, *Image/Music/Text* (New York: Hill and Wang, 1977), pp. 155–64.

    2. Tony Bennett, in A. P. Foulkes, *Literature and Propaganda* (London: Methuen, 1983), p. 19.

    3. Gerald Graff, "The Future of Theory in the Teaching of Literature," *The Future of Literary Theory*, Ralph Cohen, ed., (New York: Routledge, 1989), p. 250.

    4. Robert Scholes, *Textual Power* (New Haven: Yale University Press, 1985), p. 144.

    5. Jonathan Culler, "Literary Competence," *Reader Response Criticism*, Jane Tomkins, ed., (Baltimore: Johns Hopkins University Press, 1980), p. 116.

    6. Gerald Graff, "The Future of Theory," pp. 257, 269.

    7. Here culturespeak is to be understood as lay discourse *about* culture.

    8. "Abrogation is a refusal of the categories of the imperial culture, its aesthetic, its illusory standard of normative or "correct" usage, its assumption of a traditional and fixed meaning inscribed in the words. It is a vital moment in the decolonising of the language and the writing of "english," but without the process of appropriation the moment of abrogation may not extend beyond a reversal of the assumptions of privilege, the 'normal' and correct

inscription, all of which can be simply taken over and maintained by the new usage." Bill Ashcroft, Gareth Griffiths and Helen Tiffin, eds. *The Empire Writes Back: Theory and Practice in Post-Colonial Literatures* Routledge, (London, NY 1989) p. 38.

9. Frank Kermode, *The Genesis of Secrecy* (Cambridge, Mass.: Harvard University Press, 1979), p. 18.

10. ". . . the recent revival of essentialism dating from the early 1970s . . . stems from the ideas of Hilary Putnam and Saul Kripke and their insight that the knowledge of essences and of many other necessary truths need not be *a priori*, need not, that is, be intuitively self-evident, and independent of all empirical confirmation or disconfirmation." Peter Crisp, "Essence, Realism and Literature," *English* (Spring 1989), p. 55.

11. Christine Brooke-Rose, *The Rhetoric of the Unreal*, (Cambridge: Cambridge University Press, 1981), p. 234.

12. Fredric Jameson, *The Political Unconscious* (London: Methuen, 1981), pp. 107–10.

13. Philippe Harmon, in Christine Brooke-Rose, *Rhetoric*, pp. 85–94.

14. Frederick Karl, *Readers Guide to Joseph Conrad* (London: Thames and Hudson, 1960); C. B. Cox, *The Modern Imagination* (London: Macmillan, 1986).

15. Christine Brooke-Rose, *Rhetoric*, p. 68.

16. "Faced with the difficulty of telling Jim's story, Marlow does not arouse his audience's expectations; indeed he admits that love stories repeat themselves and are quite banal. Then he starts to talk, *somewhat mysteriously* (italics mine), about a grave, the mother's grave, the mother's background, fate, the fate of distinguished women and eventually the grotesquely deformed tale of Jim's Jewel. Thus he manages to add a touch of originality to a worn out archetypal topic." *York Notes* (Longmans, 1985), p. 37.

17. Edward Said, *Orientalism* (London: Routledge and Kegan Paul, 1978), pp. 6, 186–88, 190.

18. B. J. Moore-Gilbert, *Kipling and Orientalism* (London: Croom Helm, 1986), p. 139–42.

19. Jean-Marie Schaeffer, "Literary Genres and Textual Genericity," in Gerald Graff, *The Future of Literary Theory*, p. 177.

20. Homi Bhabha, "The other question: difference, discrimination, and the discourse of colonialism," in *Literature, Politics and Theory*, Francis Barker, and Peter Hulme, eds. (London: Methuen, 1986), p. 162.

21. Ben Shepherd, "Showbiz Imperialism; The Case of Peter Lobengula," in *Imperialism and Popular Culture*, John Mackenzie, ed. (Manchester: Manchester University Press, 1986) pp. 94–112.

22. Kenneth Ballhatchet, *Race, Sex and Class under the Raj, 1793–1905* (New Delhi: Vikas, 1979), pp. 96–122.

23. Malcolm Bradbury, *Forster, A Collection of Critical Essays* (New Delhi: Prentice Hall, 1979), pp. 1–6.

24. Janet Batsleer, Tony Davies, Rebecca O'Rourke and Chris Weedon, "Gender and Genres: Women's Stories," *Rewriting English: The Cultural Politics of Gender and Class.* (London & N.Y.: Methuen, 1985), p. 95.

25. Linda Hutcheon, *The Politics of Postmodernism* (London: Routledge, 1989), p. 93.

26. Linda Hutcheon, *Narcissistic Narrative* (New York: Methuen, 1984), p. 5.

27. Catherine Belsey, *Critical Practice* (London: Methuen, 1980), p. 107.

28. B. J. Moore-Gilbert, *Kipling and Orientalism* p. 7, 8.

29. Kwame Anthony Appiah, "Is The Post In Postmodern The Post In Post-Colonial?" *Critical Inquiry*, 17, 2 (Winter 1991), p. 348.

30. Kwame Anthony Appiah, "Is the Post?" pp. 349–56.

31. Paul Connerton ed., Introduction, *Critical Sociology* (Harmondsworth: Penguin, 1976), pp. 17, 18.

32. Henry Louis Gates, Jr., "Authority, (White) Power, and the (Black) Critic," in Ralph Cohen, ed., *The Future of Literary Theory*, p. 343.

33. Gerald Graff, "The Future of Theory," p. 267.

V

Postmodern Post-Script

21

The End of Innocence

Jane Flax

And although I sensed that everything going on inside me remained
blurred, inadequate in every sense of the word, I was once more forced
to admire the way in which everything fits together with a sleepwalker's
precision: the desire of most people for a comfortable life, their tendency to believe the speakers on raised platforms and the men in white
coats; the addiction to harmony, and the fear of contradiction of the
many seem to correspond to the arrogance and hunger for power, the
dedication to profit, unscrupulous inquisitiveness, and self-infatuation
of the few. So what was it that didn't add up in this equation?
—Christa Wolf, *Accident: A Day's News*

Part of a Story

In the Spring of 1990 I was invited to discuss an earlier version of this
paper with a group of women who teach in a well-known and successful
women's studies program. I had just spent two days as the only woman at
another conference at the same university, and I was looking forward to a
more friendly and productive exchange. Instead, I was quite surprised by
the atmosphere of tension and hostility that erupted as soon as I entered the
room. The last time I recall experiencing such hostility from a group of
expected allies was in 1967 when conflicts about Black Power and the role
of whites erupted in the civil-rights movement. The intensity of feelings and
the sense that one's integrity, history, identity, and place were at stake re-
minded me of those earlier and equally painful encounters. Other participants in this meeting commented upon the tension, but no one could explain
or alter it.

445

The participants repeated many of the claims that some feminists make about postmodernism.[1] "You cannot be a feminist and a postmodernist," I was told. Postmodernists are a- or even antipolitical. They are relativists; if we take them seriously, any political stance will be impossible to maintain or justify. Feminists must generate and sustain a notion of truth so that we can adjudicate conflicts among competing ideas and legitimate the claims of (some) feminist theorists and activists. Since postmodernists believe there is no truth, conflict will only be resolved through the raw exercise of power (domination). Postmodernists' deconstructions of subjectivity deny or destroy the possibility of active agency in the world. Without a unitary subject with a secure, empirical sense of history and gender, no feminist consciousness and hence no feminist politics is possible. Since postmodernists believe meanings are multiple and indeterminant, if you write clearly and comprehensibly you cannot be a postmodernist. In fact, postmodernists write obscurely on purpose so that no one outside their cult can understand them. One must choose between total acceptance or rejection of their position. Acceptance entails abandoning feminism or annihilating its autonomy and force, subordinating it to a destructive and inhospitable, male-dominated philosophy.

Neither these claims nor the evident emotional investments were illuminated in this particular encounter. But the experience did highlight some of the questions at stake in feminist debates about postmodernism: what are the relations between knowledge, power, and action? What kind(s) of subjectivities can demand and support feminist politics? What are the relationships, actual and potential, between feminist theorizing and the practices of feminist politics? Is the actualization of feminist visions of the future dependent upon the production of better feminist knowledge or theories of knowledge (and in what sense is this so)? What are the statuses of feminist intellectuals, especially those who teach in universities, in relation to each other, to other women and to power of various kinds? What forms the self-consciousness of feminist intellectuals and what motives and desires (including unconscious ones) drive us to make the kinds of claims about our selves and the nature and status of our theorizing? Can feminist theorizing (and women's studies programs) develop best in isolation from nonfeminist modes of thought? Should feminist theorists try to produce new grand theories as inclusive and self-sufficient as Marxism claimed to be?

Dreams of Innocence

Postmodernism is threatening to some feminists because it radically changes the background assumptions and contexts within which debates about such questions are usually conducted. While it is often recognized that white-feminist politics in the West since the 1960s have been deeply rooted in and dependent upon Enlightenment discourses of rights, individualism, and equality, the epistemological legacy that feminists have inherited from these same discourses has only recently been called into question.[2] Postmodernism, especially when combined with certain aspects of psychoanalysis, necessarily destabilizes the (literal and figurative) grounds of feminist theorizing, just as it does many other forms of Western philosophy. If one takes some of its central ideas seriously, even while resisting or rejecting others, postmodernism is bound to induce a profound uneasiness, or threatened identity, especially among white Western intellectuals, whose consciousness and positions are among its primary subjects of critical analysis.

While there are many aspects of the threat that postmodernism poses to the self-understanding of white Western intellectuals, there is one I will emphasize here. Postmodernism calls into question the belief (or hope) that there is some form of innocent knowledge to be had. This hope recurs throughout the history of Western philosophy (including much of feminist theory). While many feminists have been critical of the content of such dreams, many have also been unable to abandon them.[3]

By innocent knowledge I mean the discovery of some sort of truth which can tell us how to act in the world in ways that benefit or are for the (at least ultimate) good of all. Those whose actions are grounded in or informed by such truth will also have *their* innocence guaranteed. They can only do good, not harm to others. They act as the servant of something higher and outside (or more than) themselves, their own desires and the effects of their particular histories or social locations. The discovery of such truth would enable political theorists and philosophers to solve a central philosophic and social problem: how to reconcile knowledge and power (or theory and practice).[4]

A central promise of Enlightenment and Western modernity is that conflicts between knowledge and power can be overcome by grounding claims to and the exercise of authority in reason.[5] Reason both represents and embodies truth. It partakes of universality in two additional ways: it operates identically in each subject and it can grasp laws that are objectively true; that is, are equally knowable and binding on every person. This set of beliefs generates one of the foundational antinomies in Enlightenment thinking— superstition/domination versus knowledge/freedom (emancipation).

Knowledge in this scheme has a curious double character. It can be simultaneously neutral and socially beneficial (powerful). The Enlightenment hope is that utilizing truthful knowledge in the service of legitimate power will assure both freedom and progress. This will occur only if knowledge is grounded in and warranted by a universal reason, not particular "interests." The accumulation of more knowledge (the getting of more truth) results simultaneously in an increase in objectivity (neutrality) and in progress. To the extent that power/authority is grounded in this expanding knowledge it too is progressive, that is, it becomes more rational and ex-pands the freedom and self-actualization of its subjects who naturally con-form their reason to its (and their) laws. Power can be innocently or purely emancipatory; "rational" power can be other than and not productive of new forms of domination. Such power can be neutral (it cannot hurt anyone) and transparent in its exercise and effects. Hence it is not really power at all, especially when it works by/through such neutral mediums as the law.

Obviously this dream rests on a number of wishes. We must assume that the social as well as the physical universe is governed by a uniform, benevolent, and ultimately nonconflictual set of laws. Conforming our be-havior to nonunitary or malevolent laws would generate conflicts and dif-ferences that could not themselves be lawfully resolved. No neutral "deci-sion procedure" would exist that could determine how conflict could be resolved without privileging one position rather than another. Power would lose its innocence without its protective grounding in a universal, neutral good for all. Order would have to be (at least to some extent) imposed rather than dis-covered. Knowledge would be seen as useful for some (persons and effects) and oppressive to others. Actions generated by knowledge would have unpredictable and differential effects.

We must also assume that a homogeneous form of reason exists within all humans and that this reason itself is not determined or affected by other (heterogeneous) factors such as desire or historical experience. Humans must have "privileged access" to the operation of their own reason and be able to understand its intrinsic limits (if there are any). Otherwise the reason that is our lawgiver would itself be contaminated by particularity and contin-gency. This reason could not be a reliable source of knowledge about our selves, a dis-coverer of objective truth, or an authority that a noumenal being ought to obey.

Three of the discourses feminists have attempted to adapt to our own purposes, liberal political theory, Marxism, and empirical social science, express some form of this Enlightenment dream. The coherence and moral force of each theory is dependent upon its grounding in some of these En-lightenment beliefs. Liberal political theorists from John Locke to John Rawls attempt to distinguish legitimate authority from domination by listening for and recording Reason's voice. They claim they are articulating a set of rules or beliefs in Reason's own language. In order to hear Reason's language a rite of purification must be undergone (imagining a "state of nature" or drawing the "veil of ignorance" around oneself)[6] to strip away the merely contingent or historical. The rights or rules that are truly Reason's own and hence bind-ing on all will then re-present themselves. Conformity to these (neutral) laws by the state and its subjects guarantees the rationality, justice, and freedom of both.

Marxists have their own variant of this dream. Their "objective" ground tends to be History rather than Reason, although in their account History itself is ultimately rational, purposive, unitary, law governed, and progressive. In the Marxist view, events in history do not occur randomly; they are connected by and through an underlying, meaningful, and rational structure comprehensible by reason/science. The pregiven purpose of history is the perfection of humans (especially through labor) and the ever-more-complete realization of their capacities and projects. Marxist theory and its articulator (the Party, the working class, the engaged intellectual) have a privileged relation to History.[7] They speak but do not construct its "laws" and legitimate their actions by invoking its name. Since History, like Reason, has an essentially teleological and homogeneous content, we can look forward to its "end." Then all sources of irresolvable conflicts or contradictions will disappear and authority will take the form of the administration of things rather than the domination of persons. Power will be innocent and human actions, in conformity with our highest and most emancipatory potentials.[8]

Empirical social science also inherits, reflects, and is the beneficiary of Enlightenment dreams. Here the relationship between knowledge and power is mediated by science, or at least by a particular understanding of science. Just as Enlightenment philosophers privilege reason as the unique means of access to and voice of the Real, they privilege science as the ideal form of knowledge. Modern philosophy, as exemplified by Kant, began with the task of explaining how scientific knowledge is possible, that is, how physics could develop such accurate and reliable knowledge of the physical world.[9] Until recently, most influential modern philosophers did not attempt to throw into doubt the belief that science does generate such knowledge.

Social scientists also rarely questioned science's relationship to the Real. Their concern was whether such knowledge could be obtained about the social world and if so what methods were most likely to produce such results.[10] They adopted the Enlightenment belief that science is the ideal form of knowledge, the exemplar of the right use of reason and the methodological paradigm for all truth claims. They accepted a story about science created by pre-Kuhnian philosophers in which reason in science takes the form of a "logic of discovery." This logic is universal and binding on all scientific practitioners. It is neutral in the sense that it affects neither the subject/investigator nor the object/data. Science's "successes" (dis-coveries) are due to the adherence to this logic by its practitioners. The "scientific method" enables all those who use it to dis-cover (not construct) the truths of its objects—bits of the Real which exist independent of the scientist and the scientific modes of investigation.[11]

A grounding in science preserves the innocence of the social scientist. Knowledge acquired by the proper methods must reflect the Real (which is also the rational, the benevolent, and the true). Hence knowledge produced by social science can simultaneously (and without contradiction) be neutral, useful, and emancipatory. It can be on the side of good and have no unjustifiable costs. Social scientists' knowledge and power can be innocent of bias, prejudice, or ill effects for anyone. Its innocence is warranted by the (universal) truth/laws in which it is grounded.

The plausibility, coherence, or even intelligibility of these claims obviously depend upon a set of unstated background assumptions. These assumptions include a belief that truth and prejudice are clearly distinguishable and dichotomous categories, that there is a neutral language available to report our discoveries, that the "logic of discovery" operates independent of and without distorting either its subject (user) or object of investigations, that the "scientific" process if self-correcting and self-governing (it will gradually but necessarily eliminate any biases or false knowledge), that the social world is stable, homogeneous, and lawfully structured, and that these laws are good and uncontradictory, that is, work to the equal benefit of all.

We can then assume that there is no fundamental disjunction between the discovery and the administration of social laws. The Real of science has an unchanging and unchangeable existence independent of the knower; it is not merely created or transformed by humans in the process of doing science. Since the scientist speaks with and represents the voice of the Real, "primary" and "applied" social science are merely two facets of the same process—displacing ignorance and prejudice and replacing it with the neutral rule of reason. Action grounded in scientific/expert knowledge is hence an innocent form of power whose operation and effects are as transparent and universally accessible as the scientific enterprise. Expert rule generates neither privilege nor domination in its exercise, rather it results in the good of all.[12]

Twentieth Century Nightmares: The Centers Will Not Hold

The modern Western sense of self-certainty has been undermined by political and intellectual events. The meanings—or even existence—of concepts essential to all forms of Enlightenment metanarrative (reason, history, science, self, knowledge, power, gender, and the inherent superiority of Western culture) have been subjected to increasingly corrosive attacks. The challenges to Western political-economic hegemony and to political and cultural colonialism, the rise of nationalist movements in the Third World, women's movements everywhere, and antiracist struggles have disrupted the order of things.

Western intellectuals' sense of epistemological security has also been disrupted by internal dissent. The "essential contestability" (and the "all too human" contingency) of the constituting notions of Enlightenment metanarratives have been exposed. This creates a crisis of innocence, since these notions then become mere artifacts that humans have created and for whose effects and consequences we alone are responsible. It is difficult for humans to live without secure grounds below and ontological or transcendental guarantees from above.

Although not without ambivalence and partial complicity with the old regime, psychoanalysts, postmodernists, and feminists have contributed to the undermining of the foundations of Western thought. Psychoanalysts call into question the autonomy of reason, the equation of consciousness and mind, and the unity and stability of the self. They emphasize the existence and partial autonomy of an inner world pervaded by desire and fantasy. This inner world has unconscious and uncontrollable effects on other aspects of human subjectivity such as thought. Postmodernists compose more complex and less hopeful stories about the relationships between knowledge, power, history, and subjectivity.[13] Feminist theorists argue that ideas about knowledge are dependent upon and made plausible by the existence of specific sets of social relations, including gender.[14] The epistemological stories philosophers have told tend primarily to be about the experiences, problems, and acts of repression of a stereotypical white, Western, masculine self.

Postmodernists believe philosophy occupies a constituting and legitimating position within metanarratives of Enlightenment that continue to structure Western culture. Hence, the deconstruction of philosophy is a political responsibility and (at least qua philosophers) their most salient and subversive contribution to contemporary Western culture. Western philosophy remains under the spell of the "metaphysics of presence."[15] Most Western philosophers took as their task the construction of a philosophic system in which something Real would and could be re-presented in thought. This Real is an external or universal subject or substance, existing "out there" independent of the knower. The philosopher's desire is to "mirror," register, mimic, or make present the Real. Truth is understood as correspondence to it.

For postmodernists this quest for the Real conceals most Western philosophers' desire, which is to master the world once and for all by enclosing it within an illusory but absolute system they believe re-presents or corresponds to a unitary Being beyond history, particularity, and change. In order to mask his idealizing desire, the philosopher must claim his knowledge is not the product, artifact, or effect of a particular set of historical or discursive practices. It can only be the Real expressing itself directly in our thought.

The philosopher also obscures another aspect of his desire: to claim a special relation and access to the True or Real. The presence of the Real for us depends on him—the clarity of his consciousness, the purity of his intention. Only the philosopher has the capacity for Reason, the love of wisdom (philo-sophia), the grasp of method, or the capacity to construct a logic adequate to the Real. Just as the Real is the ground of Truth, so too the philosopher as the privileged representative of the Real and interrogator of truth claims must play a "foundational" role in all "positive knowledge." Hence, too, the importance of epistemology within modern philosophy. Epistemology serves as the means to purge, clarify, or demarcate the philosopher's consciousness, for himself, for the benefit of other philosophers, and ultimately for humanity as a whole.

Postmodernists attack the "metaphysics of presence" and the Western philosopher's self-understanding in a number of ways. They question the philosophies of mind, truth, language, and the Real that underlie and ground any such transcendental or foundational claims. Postmodernists claim that there is and can be no transcendental mind; on the contrary, what we call mind or reason is only an effect of discourse. There are no immediate or indubitable features of mental life. Sense data, ideas, intentions, or perceptions are already constituted. Such experiences only occur in and reflect a variety of discursively and socially determined practices. The problem of the relation between the "mind" and "things in themselves" becomes infinitely more complex. One cannot even assume that the mind has some universal, transcendental, a priori categories or concepts that always shape experience in the same, even if unknowable, ways. Instead the categories or concepts by and through which we structure experience are themselves historically and culturally variable. "Mind" is no more homogeneous, lawful, and internally consistent in or over time than is History.

Truth for postmodernists is an effect of discourse. Each discourse has its own distinctive set of rules or procedures that govern the production of what is to count as a meaningful or truthful statement. Each discourse or "discursive formation" is simultaneously enabling and limiting. The rules of a discourse enable us to make certain sorts of statements and to make truth claims, but the same rules force us to remain within the system and to make only those statements that conform to these rules. A discourse as a whole cannot be true or false because truth is always contextual and rule dependent. Discourses are local, heterogeneous, and often incommensurable. No discourse-independent or transcendental rules exist that could govern all discourses or a choice between them. Truth claims are in principle "undecidable" outside of or between discourses. This does not mean that there is no truth but rather that truth is discourse dependent. Truth claims can be made by those who accept the rules of a discourse or who are willing to bridge across several. However, there is no trump available which we can rely on to solve all disputes. Prior agreement on rules, not the compelling power of objective truth, makes conflict resolution possible.

Postmodernism is not a form of relativism because relativism only takes on meaning as the partner of its binary opposite—universalism. Relativists assume the lack of an absolute standard is significant: "everything is relative" because there is no one thing to measure all claims by. If the hankering for an absolute universal standard were absent, "relativism" would lose its meaning and force. Instead we would have to pay more attention to the conditions under which conflicting claims can be resolved and those where only political actions, including the use of force, are sufficient. We cannot understand knowledge without tracing the effects of the power relations which simultaneously enable and limit the possibilities of discourse. Even consensus is not completely innocent, since traces of force may be found in the history of any set of rules that attain and maintain binding effects. While force or domination is not required to settle all disputes, discourse alone will not resolve irreconcilable differences.

Postmodernists contest all concepts of language in which it is described as a transparent, passive, or neutral medium. Each of us is born into an ongoing set of language games that we must learn in order to be understood by and to understand others. Since humans are "speaking animals," our personhood is (at least partially) constructed by language. Language speaks us as much as we speak it. Furthermore, the meaning of our experience and our understanding of it cannot be independent of the fact that such experience and thought about it are grasped and expressed in and through language. To the degree that thought depends upon and is articulated (to ourselves and others) in language, thought and the "mind" itself will be socially and historically constituted. No ahistorical or transcendental standpoint exists from and by which the Real can be directly and without construction/ distortion apprehended and reported in or by thought.

In addition, there is no stable, unchanging, and unitary Real against which our thoughts can be tested. Western philosophers create an illusory appearance of unity and stability by reducing the flux and heterogeneity of the human and physical worlds into binary and supposedly natural oppositions. Order is imposed and maintained by displacing chaos into the lesser of each binary pair, for example culture/nature or male/female. The construction of such categories as and through opposition expresses and reveals the philosopher's desire for control and domination. Once these oppositions are seen as fictive, asymmetric, and conditions of possibility for the philosopher's story, then a premise that underlies all variants of the metaphysics of presence can be revealed: to be other, to be different than the defining one is to be inferior and to have no independent character or worth of one's own; for example, "woman" is defined as a deficient man in discourses from Aristotle through Freud. The superior member of the pair maintains his innocence. Unlike the inferior *he* is secure in his independence and natural superiority; he is within but not of the dyad. Like Aristotle's master or husband, his is the active matter, determining and generative within, but never affected *by* his coupling. There is no disorder within him and hence none within Being as such, but there may be disorderly objects requiring the exercise of his mastery. In the Enlightenment self-understanding, this view is an "optimistic," humane and "progressive" one; eventually all difference/ disorder will be brought within the beneficent sovereignty of the One.

The postmodernists regard all such wishes for unity with suspicion. Unity appears as an effect of domination, repression, and the temporary success of rhetorical strategies. All knowledge construction is fictive and non-representational. As a product of the human mind, knowledge has no necessary relation to Truth or the Real. Philosophers create stories about these concepts and about their own activities. Their stories are no more true, foundational, or truth adjudicating than any others. There is no way to test whether one story is closer to the truth than another because there is no transcendental standpoint or mind unenmeshed in its own language and story.

Philosophers and other knowledge constructors should seek instead to generate an infinite "dissemination" of meanings. They should abjure any attempt to construct a closed system in which the other or the "excess" are "pushed to the margins" and made to disappear in the interest of coherence and unity. Their task is to disrupt and subvert rather than (re-)construct totalities or grand theories. Postmodernists must firmly situate themselves as constructs within their own discourses. The imperial, impersonal, Cartesian ego is to be deconstructed and its desires set free to play within and as language. The "view from nowhere" is replaced by admittedly partial and fragmentary multiples of one.[16]

Feminist theorists also pose profound and still inadequately confronted challenges to many understandings of our social life and knowledge. One of the most important contributions has been to reveal and problematize gender relations. Gender has been reconceived as a highly variable and historically contingent set of human practices. Gender relations pervade many aspects of human experience from the constitution of the "inner self" and family life to the so-called public worlds of the state, the economy, and knowledge production. Gender is not a stable thing; it is certainly not a set of anatomical or biological attributes, although the relation of gender to embodiment is an interesting and controversial question among feminist theorists. We cannot even claim that gender is a universal or unitary relation present in all cultures, because it is a category that feminist theorists have constructed to analyze certain relations in our cultures and experiences. The concept must therefore reflect our questions, desires, and needs.

Feminists have successfully engaged in genealogical investigations of the generative power of male dominance within the production of knowledge. We have begun to track the suppression of knowledge of gender and its essential role in the structuring of individual experience, social relations, and knowledge itself. We have also begun to explore the suppression and devaluation of knowledge arising from certain dimensions of women's and men's experiences. The necessary connections between the suppression of certain experiences and forms of knowledge and the persuasiveness and power of the claims Western culture makes about the nature of its knowledge have become more evident.[17]

Feminists insist that masculinity and femininity are effects of gender systems. Feminists' conceptualizations of these categories provide a necessary counterpoint to and basis for criticism of the weaknesses (or absence) of postmodernist positions on gender.[18] Feminists understand masculine and feminine in terms of power and domination, not as positions in language which any subject can assume. Gender relations are interwoven with and reinforce other preexisting and constituting social relations such as race. In all such relations of domination, no subject can simply or voluntarily switch sides. We receive certain privileges or suffer certain injuries depending on our structural positions, no matter what our subjective intent or purposes may be. Men can no more easily resign from masculinity and its effects than I can from being white. Both men and women are marked by gender relations, although in different and unequal ways.

Indeed, from a feminist viewpoint, it appears (at best) quite odd that many postmodernists are unaware of the problems in their approach to gender. While they are emphatic in their claims that the subject is a thoroughly constituted but not a constituting being, writers such as Derrida appear to adopt a voluntaristic (indeed almost free-will) approach to gender identity. If subjectivity is constituted by pregiven categories like masculine or feminine, no individual subject can escape the effects of these categories any more than s/he could speak a private language. Unless the entire discursive field (and each subject's unconscious) is changed, these categories will continue to generate particular forms of subjectivity beyond the control of individuals, no matter how freely the subject believes s/he is playing with them.

The End of Innocence and the Crisis of Representation

Postmodernist deconstructions of representation and the "innocence" of truth and psychoanalytic displacings of reason are profoundly unsettling for feminist intellectuals. Of the three modes of theorizing discussed here, feminist theories are the most overtly and self-consciously political. The action most psychoanalysts seek to effect is an individual therapeutic cure. Postmodernists, especially in the United States, have been primarily concerned with disruptions of discourses whose location in and effects on relations of domination are (at best) highly mediated. Feminist theorists take as their primary object of investigation and intervention the gender systems which continue to generate and reproduce relations of domination. No other movement or mode of thinking has taken as its central commitments the analysis and elimination of their oppressive effects.

However, postmodernist discourses disrupt master narratives of the West and the language games in which terms like freedom, emancipation, or domination take on meaning. Lacking "privileged" insight into the "laws" of history or reason's operations, firmly situated within discrete, contingent but constituting gender, class, race, and geographical locations, no longer serving as the neutral instrument of truth or the articulator of a homogeneous "humanity's" best hopes, what authorizes the intellectual's speech? We become hesitant to speak for or prescribe our good(s) for others. Contemplating Auschwitz or a possible "nuclear winter," we can no longer sustain the illusion or the hope that "true" knowledge is only sought by the virtuous, is a priori generated by the good and when put into practice will only have the beneficial results we intend. It is more difficult to separate normative discourse from potential exercises of power or to conceptualize power entirely innocent of domination.

Despite postmodernist challenges and their own deconstructions of the gender-based relations of power that generate the content and legitimacy of many forms of knowledge, many feminist theorists sustain the Enlightenment hope that it is possible to obtain "better" knowledge and epistemologies. By better, they mean (at minimum) knowledge and epistemologies less contaminated by false beliefs and dominating relations of power. They believe feminist theories are progressive; that is, they are freer from these effects than previous thinking and therefore represent a higher and more adequate stage of knowledge. Many feminists also continue to argue for the necessary relationships between better knowledge and better practices.[19] Without the secure ability to make truth claims, the feminist project of ending gender-based domination is doomed.[20]

One of the most persuasive advocates of such positions, Sandra Harding, argues that epistemologies are partially justificatory schemes. Like moral codes, they challenge the idea of "might makes right" in the domain of knowledge claims. Access to such schemes is especially necessary when unequal power relations exist. It is in the interest of the weak to contest on the ground of truth rather than with force. Feminists also need some defense against and alternatives to traditional discourses about women and about means of obtaining truth, since both of these may be gender biased. We also need decision procedures articulable to other feminists to guide choices in theory, research, and politics. When traditional grounds for knowledge claims are not adequate we need to justify our claims to ourselves and to others. This theory should be accountable to many different women. Difference should be taken into account, both as cultural variation and as domination. We also need decision procedures to guide practice; knowledge can be a resource to help organize strategies against domination. Ultimately Harding seems to think, as do Nancy Hartsock and others, that the success of the feminist projects of creating effective analyses of gender and of ending gender-based domination depends on our ability to make truth claims about the "objective" status or our knowledge and our rights.

I believe these arguments are profoundly mistaken and, to the extent to which they are (unconsciously) intended to maintain the innocence of feminist theories and politics, dangerous. Operating within the Enlightenment metanarrative, these feminist theorists confuse two different claims—that certain kinds of knowledge are generated by gender-based power relations and that correcting for these biases will necessarily produce "better," knowledge that will be purely emancipatory (that is, not generated by and generative of its own relations of noninnocent power). They are not content with constructing discourses which privilege some of those who have previously lacked power (at the necessary expense of others) but wish to claim dis-covery of ways to increase the general sum of human emancipation. These theorists assume that domination and emancipation are a binary pair and that to displace one necessarily creates new space for the other. They conceive disruption of the given as entailing an obligation to create something new. The legitimacy or justification of disruption depends in part on the nature of what is offered in place of the old. They fear what will emerge in disrupted spaces if they are not in feminist control. In order for the new to be secure and effective, it must be located and grounded within a new epistemological scheme. Like other Enlightenment thinkers, they believe innocent, clean knowledge is available somewhere for our dis-covery and use. Although the discovery of new knowledge may be dependent upon disruptions of previously existing power relations, the effects of its social origins are somehow transformed by epistemological means. Epistemology also gives a force to new knowledge (independent of politics) that it would otherwise lack.

These claims reflect the difficulties of abandoning the Enlightenment metanarrative that cannot, despite its promises, deliver us from domination or enable us to construct or exercise knowledge innocently. Harding and others assume (rather than demonstrate) that there are necessary connections between truth, knowledge, emancipation, and justice and that truth and force or domination are necessarily antinomies.

On the contrary, I believe we need to rethink all these concepts, let them float freely, and explore their differences. All epistemological talk is not useless or meaningless, but a radical shift of terrain is necessary. I would like to move the terms of the discussion away from the relations between knowledge and truth to those between knowledge, desire, fantasy, and power of various kinds. Epistemology should be reconceived as genealogy and the study of the social and unconscious relations of the production of knowledge. Philosophers would abandon wishes to adjudicate truth claims and instead would engage in linguistic, historical, political, and psychological inquiries into forms of knowledge construction and conflict within particular discursive formations. Such inquiries would include investigations into the philospher's own desire and place within particular social locations and discourses. We can also analyze what has occurred within different discursive practices and articulate why one set of practices appears to be preferable for certain pragmatic purposes.

Responsibility without Grounds

A belief in the connections between truth and knowledge at this point in Western history seems far more likely to encourage a dangerously blind innocence rather than to prepare the ways for freedom or justice. We should take responsibility for our desire in such cases: what we really want is power in the world, not an innocent truth. The idea that truth is on one's side is a recurrent element in justificatory schemes for the actions of terrorists, fundamentalists, and producers of dangerous technologies. Part of the purpose of claiming truth seems to be to compel agreement with our claim (if it is true, then you as a "rational person" must agree with me and change your beliefs and behavior accordingly). We are often seeking a change in behavior or a win for our side. If so, there may be more effective ways to attain agreement or produce change than to argue about truth. Political action and change require and call upon many human capacities including empathy, anger, and disgust. There is no evidence that appeals to reason, knowledge or truth are uniquely effective or ought to occupy privileged positions in strategies for change. Nor do epistemologies necessarily reassure people that taking risks is worthwhile or convince them that political claims are justified. It is simply not necessarily the case (especially in politics) that appeals to truth move people to action, much less to justice.

Thus Harding confuses the need for justification with the need for power. Arguments can lack force (in the political sense) no matter how well they may be grounded in some epistemological scheme. Furthermore, arguments about knowledge are motivated in part by a wish to maintain an innocence and an innocent form of hope that are actually quite dangerous. Just because false knowledge can be utilized to justify or support domination, it does not follow that true knowledge will diminish it or that the possessor of "less false" knowledge will be free from complicity in the domination of others.

A concern for epistemology can mask the desire to claim a position of innocence in which one person's clarity does not rest on the exclusion of an other's experience. It can also be motivated by an illusory wish to discover a set of neutral rules which guarantee that adherence to them will not result in the distortion or erasure of someone's "truth." Speaking in knowledge's voice or on its behalf, we can avoid taking responsibility for locating our contingent selves as the producers of knowledge and truth claims. Talk of adjudication and justification assumes that neutrality, or at least consensus, is possible. But this in turn presupposes there are no irresolvable differences, that harmony and unity are desirable, and that effective knowledge and political action must rest on a secure, nonconflictual common ground. Consensus is privileged over conflict, rule following over anarchy.

Some negative consequences of these beliefs can be seen in contemporary feminist theory. As some feminists have argued recently, an intensified concern about epistemological issues emerged at the same time as women of color began to critique the writings of white feminists. The unity of categories such as "woman" or "gender" was found to depend upon the exclusion of many of the experiences of women of color (as well as women outside the overdeveloped world, poor women and lesbians).[21] As much if not more than postmodernism, the writings of women of color have compelled white feminists to confront problems of difference and the relations of domination that are the conditions of possibility for the coherence of our own theorizing and category formation. But our guilt and anxieties about racism (and our anger at the "others" for disturbing the initial pleasure and comfort of "sisterhood") also partially account for the discomfort and difficulties we white women have in rethinking differences and the nature of our own theorizing and statuses. Since the projects of postmodernism and women of color overlap here, I wonder whether there is a racial subtext at work that requires more attention. Since directly attacking women of color or voicing our resentment of them (in public) would be politically unthinkable, is it easier and more acceptable for white women to express our discomfort with difference discourses and the politics of knowledge claims by categorically rejecting postmodernism and branding it politically incorrect? Such constituting acts of exclusion or repression can only become evident when the power relations which enable the construction of knowledge claims are explicitly addressed.[22]

Establishing or adjudicating truth claims will not help us achieve a central feminist objective: to destroy all gender-based relations of domination. Claims about domination are claims about *injustice* and cannot be given extra force or justification by reference to Truth. Claims about injustice belong on the terrain of politics and in the realm of persuasive speech, action, and (sometimes) violence. As Machiavelli argues, politics requires a morality and knowledge appropriate to its unique domain. Claims about injustice can operate independently of "truth," or indeed any corresponding counterclaim about a transcendental good or (substantive) justice.[23]

Once we begin to make claims about gender injustice, we have irrevocably entered the realm of politics. We need to learn ways of making claims about and acting upon injustice without transcendental guarantees or illusions of innocence. One of the dangerous consequences of transcendental notions of justice or knowledge is that they release us as discrete persons from full responsibility for our acts. We remain children, waiting, if our own powers fail, for the higher authorities to save us from the consequences of our actions. Such wishes depend on and express our complicity with what Nietzsche calls the "longest lie," the belief that "outside the haphazard and perilous experiments we perform there lies something (God, Science, Knowledge, Rationality, or Truth) which will, if only we perform the correct rituals, step in to save us."[24]

To take responsibility is to firmly situate ourselves within contingent and imperfect contexts, to acknowledge differential privileges of race, gender, geographic location, and sexual identities, and to resist the delusory and dangerous recurrent hope of redemption to a world not of our own making. We need to learn to make claims on our own and others' behalf and to listen to those which differ from ours, knowing that ultimately there is nothing that justifies them beyond each person's own desire and need and the discursive practices in which these are developed, embedded, and legitimated. Each person's well-being is ultimately dependent on the development of discursive communities which foster (among other attributes) an appreciation of and desire for difference, empathy, even indifference in the others. Lacking such feelings, as the Jews in Germany or people of color in the United States (among many others) have discovered, all the laws and culture civilization can offer will not save us. It is far from clear what contributions knowledge or truth can make to the development of such feelings and communities.

At its best, postmodernism invites us to engage in a continual process of dis-illusionment with the grandiose fantasies that have brought us to the brink of annihilation. For this is part of what is missing from Christa Wolf's equation: in different situations, people in the West are on both sides, the few and the many, and it is extremely difficult for us to accept and live such unstable and painful ambivalence. But these junctures are exactly where responsibility beyond innocence looms as a promise and a frightening necessity.

NOTES

1. Perhaps because I am a political theorist and psychotherapist, I read work by authors such as Richard Rorty, Jacques Derrida, Jean-François Lyotard, and Michel Foucault as having a much broader focus than questions about the nature of language and the extent to which it is a constituting force in subjectivity and society. As I see it, their major contribution is to question the institutions and self-consciousness of *modernity* (e.g., post-Enlightenment Western culture). Hence I will use the term postmodernism rather than poststructuralism throughout.

2. Recent attempts to grapple with this legacy include Joan Wallach Scott, "The Sears Case," in her *Gender and the Politics of History* (New York: Columbia University Press,

1988); and *Theoretical Perspectives on Sexual Difference,* edited by Deborah L. Rhode (New Haven: Yale University Press, 1990).

3. Examples of this double position of criticism and hope include Sandra Harding, *The Science Question in Feminism* (Ithaca: Cornell University Press, 1986); Carol Gilligan, *In a Different Voice* (Cambridge: Harvard University Press, 1892); Nancy Hartsock, "The Feminist Standpoint: Developing the Ground for a Specifically Feminist Materialism"; and Catharine MacKinnon, "Feminism, Marxism and the State: Toward Feminist Jurisprudence," both reprinted in *Feminism and Methodology,* edited by Sandra Harding (Bloomington: Indiana University Press, 1987).

4. I have been deeply influenced in the development of this essay by Stuart Hampshire's recent book, *Innocence and Experience* (Cambridge, Mass.: Harvard University Press, 1989).

5. Kant articulates this promise most clearly. See Immanuel Kant, "What is Enlightenment?," reprinted with his *Foundations of the Metaphysics of Morals* (Indianapolis: Bobbs-Merrill, 1959).

6. On the state of nature, see John Locke, *The Second Treatise of Government,* in *John Locke's Two Treatises of Government,* edited by Peter Laslett (New York: Cambridge University Press, 1960). On the veil of ignorance, see John Rawls, *A Theory of Justice* (Cambridge, Mass.: Harvard University Press, 1971), chapter 24.

7. For more extensive critiques of a variety of Marxist theories, see Isaac D. Balbus, *Marxism and Domination* (Princeton: Princeton University Press, 1982); and Hilary Manette Klein, "Marxism, Psychoanalysis, and Mother Nature," *Feminist Studies,* 12, 2 (Summer 1989), pp. 255–78.

8. "The knell of capitalist private property sounds. The expropriators are expropriated . . . capitalist production begets, with the inexorability of a law of Nature, its own negation." Karl Marx, *Capital,* vol. 1 (New York: International Publishers, 1967), p. 763.

9. Immanuel Kant, *Critique of Pure Reason* (Garden City, N.Y.: Doubleday, 1966), especially the introduction.

10. Many social scientists and philosophers of social science continue to write as if they are completely unaware of the implications of recent philosophic developments for their foundational notions. See for example, Alexander Rosenberg, *Philosophy of Social Science* (Boulder, Col.: Westview Press, 1988); or *The Use and Abuse of Social Science,* edited by Frank Heller (London: Sage Publications, 1986). Feminist theories or postmodernism are either not mentioned or are acknowledged and then ignored in many of these texts.

11. Thomas Kuhn, in *The Structure of Scientific Revolutions* (Chicago: University of Chicago Press, 1962), is one of the first to question this set of assumptions. For further reflections, see the essays in *After Philosophy,* edited by Kenneth Baynes, James Bohman, and Thomas McCarthy (Cambridge, Mass.: MIT Press); and *The Institution of Philosophy,* edited by Avner Cohen and Marcelo Dascal (LaSalle, Ill.: Open Court, 1989).

12. David Ricci, *The Tragedy of Political Science* (New Haven: Yale University Press, 1984); and Raymond Seidelman with Edward J. Harphan, *Disenchanted Realists* (Albany, N.Y.: SUNY Press, 1985) discuss the recurrent power of this belief in American politics and political science.

13. Especially Michel Foucault, *Power/Knowledge* (New York: Pantheon, 1980); and his *Politics, Philosophy, Culture* (New York: Routledge, 1988).

14. See the essays in *Gender/Body/Knowledge,* edited by Alison M. Jagger and Susan R. Bordo (New Brunswick: N.J.: Rutgers University Press, 1989); and *Feminist Challenges: Social and Political Theory,* edited by Carole Pateman and Elizabeth Gross (Boston: Northeastern Press, 1986).

15. This phrase is from Jacques Derrida, "Violence and Metaphysics," in his *Writing and Difference* (Chicago: University of Chicago Press, 1978); see also Richard Rorty on "foundational illusions," in his *Philosophy and the Mirror of Nature* (Princeton: Princeton University Press, 1979), especially p. 6.

16. On what a postmodernist philosopher might do, see the essays in Avner Cohen and Marcelo Dascal; Kenneth Baynes *et al.;* Richard Rorty, Chapter 8; Richard Rorty, *Consequences of Pragmatism* (Minneapolis: University of Minnesota Press, 1982); Jacques Derrida, *Positions* (Chicago: University of Chicago Press, 1981); Michel Foucault, *Power/Knowledge;* and Nancy Fraser, *Unruly Practices: Power, Discourse and Gender in Contemporary Social Theory* (Minneapolis: University of Minnesota Press, 1989).

17. The essays in Carole Pateman and Elizabeth Gross; and Alison Jagger and Susan R. Bordo discuss these questions. See also Luce Irigaray, *Speculum of the Other Woman* (Ithaca: Cornell University Press, 1985); Hélène Cixous and Catherine Clément, *The Newly Born Woman* (Minneapolis: University of Minnesota Press, 1986); and the essays in *Feminist Perspectives in Philosophy,* edited by Morwenna Griffiths and Margaret Whitford (Bloomington, Ind.: Indiana University Press, 1988).

18. Cf. Jacques Derrida, *Spurs/Eperons* (Chicago: University of Chicago Press, 1978) and the sympathetic critiques of postmodernist positions by Naomi Schor, "Dreaming Dissymmetry: Barthes, Foucault and Sexual Difference," in *Men in Feminism* edited by Alice Jardine and Paul Smith (New York: Methuen, 1987); Alice A. Jardine, *Gynesis: Configurations of Woman and Modernity* (Ithaca: Cornell University Press, 1985), especially chapter 9; Susan Bordo, "Feminism, Postmodernism and Gender-Skepticism," in Linda J. Nicholson, ed., *Feminism/Postmodernism*; (New York: Routledge, 1990); and Judith Butler, *Gender Trouble: Feminism and the Subversion of Identity* (New York: Routledge, 1990).

19. Such arguments have been made by Sandra Harding, "Feminism, Science, and the Anti-Enlightenment Critiques," and Christine Di Stefano, "Dilemmas of Difference: Feminism, Modernity, and Postmodernism," both in Linda J. Nicholson, ed., *Feminism/Postmodernism*; and by Mary E. Hawkesworth, "Knowers, Knowing, Known: Feminist Theory and the Claims of Truth," in *Feminist Theory in Practice and Process,* edited by Micheline R. Malson, Jean F. O'Barr, Sarah Westphall-Wihl, Mary Wyer. (Chicago: University of Chicago Press, 1989).

20. For strong statements of this position, see Nancy Hartsock, "Foucault on Power: A Theory for Women?," in Linda J. Nicholson, ed., *Feminism/Postmodernism*; and Mary E. Hawkesworth, "Knowers, Knowing, Known." Much of the feminist debate on postmodernism turns on a political question: whether the legitimacy and efficacy of feminist practices and claims require an epistemological justification/grounding. On this debate see Nancy Fraser and Linda J. Nicholson, "Social Criticism without Philosophy: An Encounter between Feminism and Postmodernism," and Seyla Benhabib, "Epistemologies of Postmodernism: A Rejoinder to Jean-François Lyotard," both in Linda J. Nicholson, *Reminism/Postmodernism*; Linda Alcoff, "Cultural Feminism versus Post-Structuralism: The Identity Crisis in Feminist Theory," in Micheline R. Malson, *et al., Feminist Theory*; the essays in *Feminist Studies,* 14, 1 (Spring 1988); Donna Haraway, "Situated Knowledges: The Science Question in Fem-

inism and the Privilege of Partial Perspective," *Feminist Studies,* 14, 3 (Fall 1988), pp. 575–99; Nancy Fraser, *Unruly Practices*; and Kathy E. Ferguson, "Interpretation and Genealogy in Feminism," *Signs,* 16, 2 (Winter 1991), pp. 322–39.

21. Barbara Christian, "The Race for Theory," *Feminist Studies,* 14, 1 (Summer 1988), pp. 67–79; Audre Lorde, *Sister Outsider* (Trumansburg, N.Y.: Crossing Press, 1984); Deborah K. King, "Multiple Jeopardy, Multiple Consciousness: The Context for a Black Feminist Ideology," in Micheline R. Malson *et al., Feminist Theory*; Elizabeth V. Spelman, *Inessential Woman: Problems of Exclusion in Feminist Thought* (Boston: Beacon, 1988); Biddy Martin and Chandra Talpade Mohanty, "Feminist Politics: What's Home Got to Do With It?," in *Feminist Studies/Critical Studies,* edited by Teresa de Lauretis (Bloomington: Indiana University Press, 1986); and Bernice Johnson Reagon, "Coalition Politics: Turning the Century," in *Home Girls: A Black Feminist Anthology,* edited by Barbara Smith (New York: Kitchen Table: Women of Color Press, 1983).

22. As I argue in *Thinking Fragments* (Berkeley: University of California Press, 1990), postmodernism is not above criticism or without flaws. I would not claim that anxieties about race and other differences are the only source of its rejection. I am trying to make sense of part of the emotional vehemence with which some feminists reject these writings, sometimes with only minimal knowledge of them. The intensity of the emotional response is puzzling, especially among people who generally respond to ideas in a much more complex and nuanced manner. On postmodernism, race, and gender see bell hooks, *Yearning* (Boston: South End Press, 1990).

23. See Stuart Hampshire, *Innocence and Experience*; Agnes Heller and Ferenc Feher, *The Postmodernism Political Condition* (New York: Columbia University Press, 1989); and Judith N. Shklar, "Injustice, Injury and Inequality: An Introduction," in *Justice and Equality in the Here and Now,* edited by Frank S. Lucash (Ithaca: Cornell University Press, 1986).

24. Richard Rorty, "Method, Social Science, and Social Hope," in *Consequences of Pragmatism,* p. 208.

22

Feminism and Postmodernism

Linda Singer

The expression "feminism and postmodernism," as it often operates in a contemporary context, makes a proposal, a proposal of conjunction. In the face of the ubiquity of this expression, especially within the discourse of professional scholars, and the intensity that usually accompanies discussion of this subject, I have been tempted to interrogate the nature of the linkage being offered, to think about the conceptual strategic and theoretical function of this "and." What is the nature of the proposal being made? What desires are invested in this formulation? What agendas are enacted in proposing or resisting this conjunction of "isms"? How does one who finds herself in some relationship of both affiliation and distance from these signifiers position herself in order to both pose and respond to these questions?

If one is endeavoring to address this nexus of issues from something like an indigenous perspective—that is, from a position of both acquaintance and sympathy or attraction to a variety of the discourses and practices collected under these umbrella signifiers—it is clear at the outset that none of the questions can be answered in the singular. It is both ironic and paradoxical that the terminology of "feminism" and "postmodernism" works dramatically against the grain of much of the writing, theory, and practice to which they are supposed to refer, since such terminological collection works to occlude, deny, or obscure the very differences, particularities, and specificities upon which feminist and postmodern projects so often insist. The viability and credibility of paradigmatic designators like "feminism" and "postmodernism" depends upon the production and circulation of some system or criteria of linkage, which establishes circuits of inclusion and exclusion. Yet as the indigenous literature of feminism and postmodernism

464

both asserts and symptomatizes, such foundations are entirely phantasmatic, presented only as perpetual absence, as that which can never be adequately articulated or represented. Insofar as both "feminism" and "postmodernism" operate not only as textual designators but also as forms or contexts for social production and exchange, the surplus signification attached to these signifiers is in a perpetual process of formulation and revision. In both contexts, not only is there little agreement amongst practitioners of that which they may in any sense be said to have or enjoy in common, but the terms, apparatus, and scope of these signifiers are very much a matter of open and intense confrontation. Such historical specificities will further complicate the question of articulating the nature of the proposal being made when conjoining "postmodernism" with "feminism." How does one do justice to the diversity of viewpoints, voices, and textual strategies signified by these terms, while also trying to isolate specific sites of conjunction, consensus, or agreement.

The question of justice or doing justice is but one of the issues that arises in the consideration of the proliferation of attempts to find some site of conjunction between postmodernism and feminism. The question of desire is another. What lack is being aimed at in these gestures, what needs are proleptically satiated when such linkage is achieved, even episodically, or ideolectively? What sort of pleasure is written into the text of "feminism and postmodernism," and what sort of pleasure flows from our readings of it?

The erotic underpinnings of the text of "feminism and postmodernism" that I am pursuing are distinguishable from all those particular texts which symptomatize or betray the influence of feminist and postmodern writing. With these latter texts, the relationship between "feminism" and "postmodernism" is one of an informal and often unthematized cross-fertilization, symptomatized by choices of language, register, and textual strategies. But the text of "feminism and postmodernism" asserts/desires a far stronger and more highly articulated connection—a connection with legislative force and authority to establish a sort of intertextual social contract. The force behind this contract is that which aims at writing or inscribing limits discursively, epistemically, and strategically. The outcome projected is some sort of alliance, and recognition of reciprocal indebtedness, that can be represented and practiced systematically for its exponents and the audiences their work addresses.

The desire to legislate or construct some paradigmatic protocol for the linkage of postmodern and feminist theory bespeaks/symptomatizes a desire inherited from a far earlier phase in "the history of theory." The libidinal formation I see at work in this contemporary enterprise has much in common with "the Cartesian complex," that historically specific albeit longstanding desire to unify and consolidate knowledge through a series of methodological prescriptions, and through the establishment of some definitive frame of relevance. Although the object of desire pursued by contemporary theorists is other than what it was for Descartes, whose work pursued an ideal of objectively necessary truth of a kind immune to erosion or dispersal through doubt, the Cartesian impulse toward systematic consolidation through establishment of connections of coherence remains in force. Such impulses toward systematicity are particularly ironic in a contemporary context, however, given the postmodern fixation on the phenomena of endings—the end of metaphysics, history, humanism, art, and the era of the subject, each of which radically forecloses any promise of closure offered by the ideal of systems. In the work of postmodernists like Jean-François Lyotard and Jean Baudrillard, for example, the notion of system modeled (as it was for Descartes) on the orderly relationships inherent in a rational and divinely originated world are displaced by the more episodic and unpredictable connections of network—modeled on information and communication networks which disperse, circulate, and proliferate exchanges in a way that belies any myths of unitary origins, foundations, or essences.

From the standpoint of a range of feminist theories, from both sides of the Atlantic, which have also focused on eroding or undermining the stabilization effects of the systems of nature, essences, and patriarchy, the impulse to establish some privileged relationship with postmodern discourse which is intended to have regulative impact on the conduct of feminist theory and practice is also surprising. Part of the history of feminist theory has been a progressive series of attempts to frame or pursue feminist issues under the regulatory and strategic practices initiated by some other theoretical paradigm. Over the last thirty years, for example, proposals have been made in the direction of Marxism, socialism, phenomenology, psychoanalysis, and semiotics, amongst others. The motives and rationales for these specific conjunctions have varied. But with each successive attempt, there has always emerged, almost in tandem, a discourse of resistance to prescriptions, either on the grounds of the inadequacy of the particular paradigm being proposed, or on the level of resistance to alliance with the project of "grand theory" in general, that is, a critique of the impulse to systematize and consolidate knowledge, and through it, power.

Given both the theoretical and rhetorical privilege given to notions of dispersal and differences, and given both discourses' investments in antiessentialist epistemology, the nature of the impulse which prompts contemporary movements of consolidation and coalition both within and between these paradigmatic enterprises calls for further interrogation of its motives, independently of questions of feasibility or utility. Given the extent to which such movements run counter to the thematic and rhetorical postures assumed by both discourses (in a variety of stylistic and ideolective variations), I think the question of motive or desire must be pursued indirectly, that is, by examining the strategies by which such linkages are made, rather than through an analysis of the substantive reasons and arguments offered in support/defense.

To interrogate desire is already to assume a relationship of transferential ambiguity with the interrogated, and hence to risk being sutured, caught up in the figures and formations from which one also needs to keep some critical interpretive distance. In this case it means I will operate in some unhappy alliance with the totalizing tendencies of the legislative discourse I am working to problematize or dismantle. In order to foreground what I see as three of the dominant strategies for pursuing the linkage of feminism and postmodernism, I will be operating from a somewhat globalizing stance, which will diminish awareness of the specificities of these strategic pursuits, their particularities and differences. That which is resisted returns to the resistor. The text that follows cannot entirely resist its own totalizing tendencies in articulating three ways in which the linkage between feminism and postmodernism is being figured or metaphorized in contemporary writing. But such consolidating effects will only be temporary, destabilized by a conclusion which speaks in the imaginary voice, the voice of the imaginary other, which both situates and problematizes whatever globalizing gestures might already have been set in place.

One strategy employed to link feminism and postmodernism has been a kind of metonymic analysis, in which some particular perspective or set of texts is made to stand in for or represent "feminism" or "postmodernism" writ large. In this case, the offer being made is much like a proposal of marriage—a linkage of individuals marked by proper names in a relationship of exchange of asymmetrical and differentiated obligations and desires. Such conjunctions are often motivated, like marriage proposals, by a situation of perceived need. One attempts to conjoin perspectives because Foucault's analysis of power needs to be informed by more specific attention to the operation of sexual difference, as articulated by feminists like Luce Irigaray or Simone de Beauvoir, or because American feminist theorists like Adrienne Rich or Andrea Dworkin are said to need a theory of split subjectivity like that provided by Lacan. Such atomistic unions occur throughout the literature, and, as good marriages should, continue to produce a variety of hybrid offspring with polymorphous paradigmatic affiliations, the new breed of "hyphenated" feminists and postmodernists.

At this level, therefore, there is evidence of a certain kind of marital conjunction of postmodernism and feminism in the work of all those who have been influenced and interpellated by texts that are placed in these two different camps. In these cases, conjunction is elective, selective, and, therefore, circumscribed in its scope and impact. There is ample evidence of a multifaceted exchange of concepts, problematics, and language in a range of writers and writings, but it is not clear how such particular strategic in-scriptions bear on the question of paradigmatic conjunction. Some marriages work, others don't. Some seductions are reciprocated, others resisted. Any form of elective engagement can also be refused. Argumentatively, one can make a stronger or weaker case for the possibilities and prospects of such elective affiliations depending on one's choice of proper names, on who is brought in to stand for "feminism" or "postmodernism."

Even when such marriages seem to work as sites of production and fertility, such unions have no legislative or regulatory status with respect to other texts and positions which resist acknowledging the legitimacy or de-sirability of such unions of convenience. At best, these marital conjunctions of feminism and postmodernism offer evidence of affiliation in an episodic intertextual mode, but cannot adequately address the question of whether such unions are merely fortuitous, or are in some way paradigmatically bind-ing, necessary, or desirable. Such evidence is also vastly inadequate to the task of trying to persuade a resistor to such unions since such a person has easy access to a range of counterexamples. Divorces, abuses, and cases of incompatibility make regular appearances in our intertextual judicial sys-tems.

For these reasons, the demand or expectation of romantic exclusivity and/or marital fidelity between feminism and postmodernism seems woe-fully misplaced. Furthermore, as in the traditional marriage contract, ex-pectations about purity and fidelity are unequally distributed, in this case weighing more heavily on the developmental course of feminist theory than on postmodernism. Both from within and from outside feminist discourse, there re-emerges with regularity these days a cautionary invective with re-spect to the appropriation of the language concepts and rhetoric—like that of the subject or personal identity—which has been placed in a problema-tized epistemic suspension by postmodern tactics of deconstruction. While such cautionary considerations are not without merit (and many, at least to my mind, are truly compelling), it is both presumptuous and pre-emptive to assume that such considerations must occupy some privileged position with respect to the development of feminist theory in the range and breadth of its concerns and approaches. Any attempt to totalize the theoretical resources of contemporary feminism under the sign of postmodernism seems on the face of it to speak from a distinctly nonpostmodern place, which may help explain why the demand is seldom made in reverse; that postmodernism necessarily take feminist concerns into consideration in developing its the-ory. Insofar as feminism and postmodernism call attention to the way in which discourse is situationally articulated (by conditions of reception, the specificities of the text's addresses, and so forth), any prospect of radical paradigmatic loyalty/affiliation is or should be read as foreclosed. There can be no arranged marriage between feminism and postmodernism. Hence their conjunction might be better thought in other ways.

One alternative formulation of the conjunction of "feminism" and "postmodernism" has been that of a kinship or family resemblance. The relationship is thus like that of siblings who share common genetic origins, and yet also are placed in a differential familial semiotic characterized by division of labor, accompanied by a certain rivalry. Considered in this light, it is possible to construct a narrative of common origins or parentage for feminism and postmodernism in post-Hegelian critical traditions of thought like Marxism, existentialism, and psychoanalysis. They can also be read as the offspring produced by the kind of critical cultural practices that commanded social visibility, especially in France and the United States during the late 1960s. One theme that recurs with variations in each of these critical paradigmatic spheres is an explicit discursive strategy of challenging the terms, conventions, and symbols of hegemonic authority in ways that foreground the explicitly transgressive character of this enterprise.

In conspicuous opposition to canonical philosophy and systematic metaphysics which operate with the assumption that this is the best or most rational of all possible worlds, critical philosophy merges from a recognition of lack, and from the desire to force acknowledgment that things are not as they should be. With this critical enterprise emerges a different set of strategies, protocols, and conventions for theoretical writing. Rather than endeavoring to represent what is or to provide the foundations for that which is known as "common sense," the critical traditions that are crucial to the genesis of both feminist and postmodern discourses pose as conspicuous affronts to and violations of the hegemonic common sense, as it is variously configured. Part of the tradition of critical writing that postmodernism and feminism inherit, albeit in ways that are differentially specified, is a tradition of writing as a form of resistance, writing which works not to confirm cohesion, but rather to disrupt, destabilize, denaturalize.

Part of what can also be said to constitute the family resemblance linking postmodern and feminist theory and practice is their respective ways of resisting and challenging established forms of power by undermining the legitimacy and validity of the mechanisms by which that power is sustained. What allies these particular incursions into the political economy of knowledge is a strategy of disclosing that things are not as they should be by also exposing all the ways in which things are not as we say they are. Both feminist and postmodern writing depends upon relativizing, ironizing, and circumscribing the mechanisms and tactics by which dominant authorities entrench themselves, legitimated by the totalizing voice of what Kierkegaard called "the ethical universal," a voice which speaks from nowhere to everyone, sufficiently disinterested so as to be undifferentiated and globalizing in its effects. Like the critical traditions that preceded them, feminist and postmodern discourse disrupt the project of closure by consensus, by insisting on exposing how differences inscribe themselves, even when they are explicitly refused or denied. The voice of rationality is shown to be riddled with contradictions it cannot exclude.

This insistence on difference, while in some senses allying feminism and postmodernism as discourses challenging the hegemonic dominance of a legislative rationality, also pose serious problems when feminism and postmodernism pursue their connection in other than this postural sense. In other words, those very differences—in emphasis, strategy, and concern—can become bones of contention and sibling rivalry. There is no shorthand way to characterize these differences—nor could such an account be sufficiently totalized so as to do justice to the range of relationships between feminist and postmodernist enterprises. And I, for one, would want to resist what is often offered as a facile distinction between feminism's political engagement and postmodernism's aestheticized self-absorption. That there are sites of serious contention between them is episodically and intertextually overdetermined like any sibling rivalry.

The rivalrous tensions which are characteristic of all familial relationships, also differentially position feminism and postmodern ambivalences about their respective ancestries and origins in the intertextual nexus of relationships that constitute "Western culture." Postmodern discourse can both claim origins in canonical culture (Nietzsche, Heidegger, modernist aesthetics) and therefore also displace the anxiety this arouses by focusing not on origins but on "ends"—the end of history, philosophy, art, and so on. Feminist discourse, by contrast, tends to begin from a relationship of exclusion and exile with respect to these same institutions. This may be why some feminists are drawn to postmodernism's claim that all this is, in some sense, over, ended. But one can also read in this recognition a counter impulse/desire—not to ironize but to retrieve that of which one has been deprived. To speak not in the language of death and ends, but rather to focus on births and beginnings, lost origins, and to do so with more *jouissance* than irony. Feminist discourse, is precisely not a member of the old boys clubs which can tire of their games and call an end to them. Not that feminist discourse can claim to be immune from the effects of this game playing, and its sociosymbolic imaginary. But because so much of that imaginary has produced discernible effects, of the kind that, on many occasions, merits outrage, judgment, indignation—just the kind of tone and frame that postmodern cool works so hard to avoid.

Outrage and irony are two very different sorts of responses affectively and strategically, but they are not mutually exclusive. Neither irony nor political enthusiasm can expect, or be expected to function as the transcendent tonal frame for discourses of resistance. To focus on this difference is not to try to reach some essentialist site of fixed division, nor is it clear that all feminist and postmodern writing could be fairly characterized by this division. The focus in this context is strategic, with respect to the concerns about potential hegemonic paradigmatic domination of one of these discourses by the other, as well as out of concern for understanding the affective and stylistic frame in which many of the sites of contention are drawn. Because outrage and irony are not foundational authorizing grounds, but rather matters of discursive and argumentative strategy that also bespeak differences in the positional nature of these discourses, such focus helps to amplify a sense of kinship relation between them that does not, at least in principle, amount to a relationship of dominance and submission. Outrage and irony are not only not mutually exclusive, but also produce a kinship of effects with respect to the objects so addressed. Both can work as forms of resistance to a dominant hegemonic rationality, and to the forms of knowledge and power they produce. Hence, although the relationship between postmodernism and feminism can be read as a familial relationship of allied resistance, this conjunction enjoys or operates with no regulative or legislative force/authority with respect to the course and development of these particular forms of critical discourse. Rather both feminism and postmodernism problematize the prospects of pre-emptive consensus, as well as interrogating the desires which set this expectation in motion. Though allied both through their choices of targets, and to a lesser degree their sense of common parentage, feminism and postmodernism cannot be expected to develop in some sort of lock-step symmetry with one another, since each emerges from an interpretation and appropriation of origins and historical positions that is specific and nontransferable.

Born of a similar intertextual legacy, feminism and postmodernism have been invested in rather different sets of priorities, and in establishing different kinds of claims. The kinship that exists between feminism and postmodernism neither implies nor inscribes any particular disciplinary agendas or accommodations—except as these are electively explored and exploited in particular and localized modes. The kinship between postmodernism and feminism cannot be formulated as some localizing set of Kantian imperatives—except perhaps by those who seek through oversimplification and reduction to discredit the authority and fecundity of these discourses in their differences.

The kinship metaphor, however, suffers from some of the same limits as that of the marital model. One may post the question of which feminists are kin to which postmodernists. In some cases, these family resemblances will be more readily apparent than in others. And it is clear to anyone engaged in these enterprises that neither feminism nor postmodernism operates as one big happy family. A kinship system establishes linkage marked by a system of proper names and ritualized exchanges. Yet as signifiers of the paradigmatic imperative to resist pre-emptive totalization and condensation, feminism and postmodernism are not really proper names marking individuals linked by pre-established relationships like kinship. Rather postmodernism and feminism operate more like the names given those fictive entities known as corporations, under whose auspices a wide range of enterprises are organized and collected in ways that consolidate and maximize their profitability without assuming any essential relationship between them. This form of strategic conjunction, born of a logic of maximizing utilities, may be a better way of metaphorizing the motives for the conjunctive relationship in which feminism and postmodernism are currently placed. Corporate mergers are not undertaken as romantic projects of desire, nor out of the need for some form of mystical communion. They are strategic unions born of an interest in consolidating competition, diversifying one's assets, or operating from a greater position of strength and viability in the market place.

The advantage of this metaphor over the marital and kinship proposals is that a model of corporate merger assumes, and in fact proceeds from, a recognition of the diversity and division of the function between and amongst the two entities to be merged, without the expectation of some unifying principle or medium of identity or unification, like those which have traditionally been assumed about persons. Furthermore, the nature of the desire is recast from that which might be said to emerge indigenously from the needs or desires of the parties themselves, and instead displaces the motive onto a larger and nonclosable logic of a political economy of production, distribution, and exchange. In its more optimistic formulations, the prospect of a merger between corporations is undertaken as a way of intensifying and enhancing the value of each entity taken separately. More ominously, as recent events have disclosed, such "mergers" can ultimately amount to "takeovers" in which one entity is subsumed and subjected to the demands of the other. It is these dual possibilities that help fuel the debate about the desirability of such conjunctions and anxiety about their possible consequences.

Some of the proposed linkages between postmodernism and feminism emerge from a modification of this corporate metaphor. The hope is that the viability of these enterprises will be enhanced by a pooling of resources—which in this case are mostly conceptual and strategic currencies. But beyond the value emergent from these exchanges, one of postmodernism and feminism's major assets is the audiences and intertextual networks and institutions this work has collected and solidified over the years. Hence we should not be surprised that many writers, journals, and publishers are interested in paradigmatic crossovers—texts that address multiple, already-established spheres of sensibility as one strategy for expanding potential readership. For while the audiences for those overlap—they are also distinct. At this historical moment, feminism and postmodernism seems to be a relatively "hot," marketable duo.

Part of its appeal as a new line of commodity is that "postmodernism" is saturated by the signification of "newness," functioning as a substitutable signifier for that which used to be called "the avant-garde." It is this associative signification and the complex of needs and desires condensed by it that help explain why, at a time when the word "revolutionary" is now more often attached to commodities than mass social movements, feminism and postmodernism are ultimately recuperated in the forms of market logic and rationality they both work to disrupt, if not with the promise of revolutionary transcendence, then at least with critical, outraged, and ironic discourse which displaces and destabilizes that logic and rationality with respect to its own mythologies and master narratives. "Newness" sells, even to consumers already acculturated to anticipate the eternal return of the same, in the form of next year's model.

Some of those waiting poised on the cusp of newness are writers, academics, and cultural critics, even those who claim no longer to have been seduced by belief in the coherence or truth value of such a position. The suspended belief in the novelty of some corporate conjunction between feminism and postmodernism serves a double, albeit also contradictory, purpose. It is that which both sells texts and motivates their censorship. It moves toward proliferative productions, and is used to justify more restriction on the production and distribution of writing and other forms of cultural production. It is a conjunction that is not true or grounded, necessary or verifiable. It is a conjunction made in the name of truth and freedom on the one hand, ignorance as the restrictive deployment of hegemonic force on the other. But for those who are somehow positioned/interpellated explicitly by these paradigmatic signifiers, and the collection and contradictions of historical forces they gather, the proposal of conjunction prompts reflection on that space between and on what it means to take up one's place there. My intuition, and one in which I take a certain amount of pleasure, is that part of the appeal of this conjunction is that it represents some moment of convergence and reciprocal recognition of the need for work which resists a climate where cultural production and pedagogy are being regulated in the interest of buttressing the legitimacy of a progressively more suspect and unjust social order.

For someone like Allan Bloom, feminism and postmodernism are but two of a group of suspects, which must be rounded up and herded out of academic pedagogy and scholarly legitimacy, so that the one great conversation that constitutes the Western cultural tradition can go on undisrupted, and undisturbed. Although feminist and postmodern interventions threaten the fluency and common language of that conversation in different ways, for different reasons, and with differential consequences, I think that the polymorphous fracturing set in play by these writings and practices in their very diversity has been intensive enough in its effects to prompt an explicit mandate for the reimposition of some supposed classical values, and cultural literacy. Figures like William Bennett and E. D. Hirsch who no longer try to conceal the political agenda inscribed with the construction and promulgation of a canonical cultural consensus can be taken as some of the stranger hybrid offspring of this conjunction between feminist and postmodern discourse. The need to reassert the necessity for establishing arbitrary canonical points of cultural reference, assimilation, and interpellation only emerges when the centrality and hegemony of those markers have been seriously challenged or eroded.

Feminist and postmodern theory and practices have done much to reconfigure the Western cultural imaginary in ways that authorize and legitimate the enactment of differences as an explicitly critical enterprise and hence are conjoined, perhaps beyond any elective enterprise of intention or desire, by the enemies they make, and the forms of challenge and resistance they provoke. Both feminism and postmodernism have been subjected in recent years to conservative reductionist critiques, which operate by constructing each as a monolithic dogmatic discourse, opaque to outsiders, organized by arcane rhetoric and rituals from within. This reductionism aims at organizing social outrage and anxiety against these perceived threats, and thus serves many of the same strategic purposes as did the myth of the monolithic communism in the 1950s by providing an impetus for a sentimentalized return to the familiar, the canonical, the classic.

The conjunction of feminism and postmodernism helps sustain for many of us, the prospect of some multipronged, albeit uncoordinated, counterculture—some intertextual network of resistance to those forces which seek to appropriate cultural artifacts as pedagogical instruments of authoritarianism and acculturation to dominance. At a time when even liberal appeals for tolerance seem to go unheeded by those at the NEA and NEH and the education department amongst others, conspicuous gestures of resistance take on added import—whether or not these efforts take the form of some particular substantive agenda or not. That may be why feminism and postmodernism are often conjoined more easily by their opponents than by their practitioners as members of the New Right's hit list—along with other offenders—like racial, ethnic, and gay studies. Their connotative force speaks absent any specific content or rhetoric.

So as I've been thinking about the fates of postmodernism and feminism in their current configurations, I also imagine the Bush-Reagan cultural-power brokers and their hired pens thinking about the same thing and fretting that the stable world of official culture over which they assume regulatory and preservative responsibility is currently being reassembled and rewritten in ways that even the most explicit forms of censorship cannot contain. I imagine their concern in contemplating the conspiracy of forces that is working to displace their cultural icons, and thereby dismantling the hegemonic forms of cultural literacy from which, presumably, much of their power and privilege stems. I envision rooms of cryptographers working to translate these feminist and postmodern texts—in efforts to break these conspiratorial codes. I imagine their frustration as these hieroglyphics clog their binary circuitry.

Those of us who operate in the postmodernist and feminist universes can laugh with Medusa's glee at the thought of feminists and postmodernists locked in some disciplinary long march toward some already specified "great beyond." Not all of us are yet infected by the eliminationist imaginary that seems to dominate the power elite. But in our moments we need also to recognize that our fears of paradigmatic encroachment from another critical strategy are not very well placed and that the major threats to discourses of resistance come from those who seek to still the play of differences with regulative canonical devices. What tends to resist any specifiable resolution of relationship between feminism and postmodernism is that their argument cannot be formulated or expected to take the form of some dogmatic positional/legislative discourse. The thematic and strategic interplay between these paradigms, and their opposition tends to work against any mechanism of unification. The "and" therefore keeps open a site for strategic engagement. The "and" is a place holder, which is to say, it holds a place open, free from being filled substantively or prescriptively. The "and" holds/preserves the differences between and amongst themselves. To try to fix that space by mapping it—setting landmarks, establishing fixed points of conjunction-directionality—is precisely to miss the point of a conjunction which is also always already nothing. Just as problematic as attempting to fix some site of connection would be the attempt definitively to prohibit intercourse between feminism and postmodernism, especially if one takes into account the historical process in which the contours and integrities of both paradigms is constantly being revised, rewritten, reformed. There is little need to organize some form of mass resistance to the conjunction of feminism and postmodernism—since the substantive and juridicial nature of the connection is in itself empty—and exists only as written or deployed or rewritten.

We can recognize the eternal return of our master narratives of control through insight, through freedom which lifts the veil of untruth only, as those prepostmodernists like Nietzsche wrote, at great cost and at great risk. This is complicated by our own multiple investments in forms of knowledge and fictions, and in forms of writing designed for legislation, that finds itself confronted with forms of power immune to legislation. But as makers and readers of stories, we also recognize the possibilities of contradictory interpretation, multiple readings, and effects. So, if the fiction of some conspiratorial connection between feminists and postmodernists engenders anxiety in the hearts and heads of the hegemonically powerful and institutionally entrenched—this might be a story that is worth repeating—at least until such time as such stories are no longer necessary.

Index

Notes on Contributors

Ana María Alonso is assistant professor of Anthropology at the University of Arizona. She has been a Rockefeller Humanist-in-residence at the Southwest Institute for Research on Women at the University of Arizona (1990–1991) and a fellow at the Pembroke Center for Teaching and Research on Women, Brown University (1987–1988). She has published articles on revolutionary mobilization, social memory, gender, and the role of the state in the formation of social subjectivities in Mexico, and on AIDS and sexual practices among U.S. "Hispanics." Currently, she is completing work on her book *En/Gendering Subjects: Domination and Resistance on Mexico's Northern Frontier*.

Judith Butler teaches in the Humanities Center, at the Johns Hopkins University. She is author of *Gender Trouble: Feminism and the Subversion of Identity* (Routledge, 1990).

Rey Chow teaches in the Department of Comparative Literature at the University of Minnesota-Minneapolis. She is the author of *Woman and Chinese Modernity: The Politics of Reading between West and East* (University of Minnesota Press, 1991).

Drucilla L. Cornell is a Professor of Law at the Benjamin N. Cardozo School of Law, Yeshiva University. She is the author of numerous articles on critical theory, feminism, and "postmodern" theories of ethics. With S. Benhabib, she coedited *Feminism as Critique: On the Politics of Gender* (University of Minnesota Press, 1987). She published her first book, *Beyond Accommodation: Ethical Feminism, Deconstruction, and the Law*, with Routledge in 1991. Her second book, *The Philosophy of the Limit*, will be published in 1992, also with Routledge.

Christina Crosby is associate professor of English at Wesleyan University, where she also works with the women's studies program. She is the author of *The Ends of History: Victorians and the Woman Question* (Routledge, 1991), and is working on a study of money and credit.

Jane Flax teaches political theory at Howard University and is a psychotherapist in private practice. Her recent work includes *Thinking Fragments* and essays on Kant, on justice, and on subjectivity.

Donna Haraway's teaching and writing in feminist theory and science studies are addressed to the politics, histories, and cultures of modern science and technology. Teaching in Women's Studies and the History of Consciousness Board at the University of California-Santa Cruz, she is the author of *Crystals, Fabrics, and Fields: Metaphors of Organicism in 20th Century Developmental Biology* (Yale University Press, 1976); *Primate Visions: Gender, Race, and Nature in the World of Modern Science* (Routledge, 1989); and *Simians, Cyborgs, and Women: the Reinvention of Nature* (Free Association Books (London), 1990, and Routledge, 1991).

Mae Gwendolyn Henderson is associate professor in the Departments of African-American Studies and English at the University of Illinois at Chicago. She is author of several articles on black women's literature and coeditor of the five-volume *Antislavery Newspapers and Periodicals: An Annotated Index of Letters, 1817–1871* (G. K. Hall, 1980). Her monograph on black expatriate writers will be published by Oxford University Press. Currently she is developing a black feminist theory of reading.

B. Honig is assistant professor of Government at Harvard University and author of *Negotiating Positions: Politics from the Perspectives of Virtue and Virtù* (forthcoming, Cornell University Press).

Ruth Leys is associate professor in the Humanities Center at the Johns Hopkins University. She is currently completing a book on the history and sexual politics of the multiple personality.

Sharon Marcus is a graduate student in the Humanities Center at the Johns Hopkins University. She is currently working on a dissertation concerning the representation of living space in nineteenth-century French and British novels.

Kirstie McClure teaches at the Johns Hopkins University in the department of Political Science and the Humanities Center. She is currently working on a book, *Postmodernity and the Subject of Rights*, which explores the political limits and possibilities of the language of rights in the postmodern condition.

Chantal Mouffe is a political philosopher attached to the Collège International de Philosophie in Paris. She is the editor of *Gramsci and Marxist Theory* (London; Boston: Routledge and Kegan Paul 1979) and coauthor with Ernesto Laclau of *Hegemony and Socialist Strategy: Towards a Radical Democratic Politics* (Verso, 1985).

Zakia Pathak teaches English in Miranda House at Delhi University. Her research interests include theory and its uses, and the female as subject. She is the author of "Drabble's *Waterfall*: An Appropriation of Eliot's *Mill*," in *Woman/Image/Text: Feminist Readings of Literary Texts,* edited by Lola Chatterjee (Trianka (New Delhi), 1986).

Mary Poovey is the author of *The Proper Lady and the Woman Writer: Ideology as Style in the Works of Mary Wollstonecraft, Mary Shelley, and Jane Austen* (University of Chicago Press, 1984) and *Uneven Developments: The Ideological Work of Gender in Mid-Victorian England* (University of Chicago Press, 1988). She is professor of English at the Johns Hopkins University.

Rajeswari Sunder Rajan teaches English at Miranda House at Delhi University. Her research interests include feminist theory and Third World politics. She is the author of "Male Mentors and the Female Imagination: George Eliot's Intellectual Background" and "Katherine Mansfield and the Question of Women's Writing," in *Woman/Image/Text: Feminist Readings of Literary Texts,* edited by Lola Chatterjee (Trianka (New Delhi), 1986).

Denise Riley lives and works in London. Her work includes *War in the Nursery: Theories of the Child and Mother* (Virago, 1983); *"Am I that Name?" Feminism and the Category of "Women" in History* (MacMillan, 1988) and several collections of poetry including *Dry Air* (Virago, 1985).

Naomi Schor is William H. Wannamaker Professor of Romance Studies and a member of the Graduate Program in Literature at Duke University. She is coeditor, with Elizabeth Weed, of *differences: A Journal of Feminist Cultural Studies*. Her most recent book is *Reading in Detail: Aesthetics of the Feminine* (Methuen, 1987). She is now completing *Idealism and the Novel: Recanonizing George Sand*.

Vicki Schultz is an assistant professor of Law at the University of Wisconsin Law School. Previously, she was a lawyer for the United States Department of Justice, Civil Rights Division, where she brought Title VII cases on behalf of plaintiffs. She has written about feminist legal theory as well as the relationship between law, gender, and work. Her current research examines the law's response to job segregation and to harassment of nontraditionally employed women.

Joan W. Scott is professor of Social Science at the Institute for Advanced Study. She is author, most recently, of *Gender and the Politics of History* (Columbia University Press, 1988).

Linda Singer was an Associate Professor of Philosophy at Miami University before her death in August of 1990. She published widely in feminist theory, popular culture, phenomenology, and aesthetics. She presented "Feminism and Postmodernism" at a session of the Radical Philosophy Association in 1989. She spoke often and with great intellectual provocation at such meetings, and she published a number of important essays including "Power-Pleasure-Bodies" in *differences* (1:1). Her book, *Erotic Welfare: Sexual Theory and Politics in the Age of Epidemic,* will be published by Routledge in 1992.

Gayatri Chakravorty Spivak is Professor of English and Comparative Literature at Columbia University. Her work includes, *In Other Worlds: Essays in Cultural Politics* (N.Y.: Routledge, 1987) and the forthcoming, *Epic and Ethic,* coauthored with B. K. Matilal, and *Outside in the Teaching Machine* (both from Routledge).